pulp

truth & beauty: the story of pulp

mark sturdy

OMNIBUS PRESS

LONDON / NEW YORK / PARIS / SYDNEY / COPENHAGEN / BERLIN / MADRID / TOKYO

Exclusive Distributors:
Music Sales Limited,
8/9 Frith Street,
London W1D 3JB, UK.

Music Sales Corporation,
257 Park Avenue South,
New York, NY 10010, USA.

Macmillan Distribution Services,
53 Park West Drive,
Derrimut, Vic 3030,
Australia.

To the Music Trade only:
Music Sales Limited,
8/9 Frith Street,
London W1D 3JB, UK.

www.omnibuspress.com

Contents

Introduction

On the evening of June 24, 1995, I was sitting in my parents' living room, listening to a live radio broadcast of Pulp playing at Glastonbury. It's almost eight years ago now, but it could have been yesterday.

I'd already been a fan of Pulp for a while. Of course I had – it was 1995, after all, and loving Pulp was mandatory. It was just what you did. The year before, my friend Ian had given me tapes of *Intro* and *His 'N' Hers* and, despite my initial reluctance, I was quickly seduced by Jarvis Cocker's intensely sleazy, intelligent, nasty, funny, poignant lyrics, and the band's intriguingly atmospheric twist on pop music. In the months that followed, things had gradually become more exciting, as Cocker infiltrated his way into mainstream pop consciousness in a way that singers in indie bands simply didn't do: with TV moments like the "I HATE WET WET WET" sign on *Top Of The Pops* and his triumphant performance on *Pop Quiz*, there seemed to be something vaguely heroic about Jarvis' ascent. He was the kind of person you'd always wished was a pop star but never was, and as he rose, seemingly effortlessly, from indie obscurity to legitimate celebrity (somehow without losing any credibility on the way), there was a feeling that this wasn't just someone's career path you were watching: he was doing it on 'our' behalf as well. It's impossible to explain, but at their greatest moments (and there's been a few), Pulp seemed to have the uncanny ability of making us feel as if we were up there with them.

Which brings us to 1995. The middle of a glorious summer, with Pulp, having only very recently become absolutely enormous with 'Common People', doing their biggest concert ever, as last-minute replacement for another group, in front of 100,000 people – all of whom seemed to be going absolutely mental.

Usually when bands play gigs of this size, a retrospective Greatest Hits-type set is to be expected. At this point, Pulp had only had one real hit, so this wasn't an option: instead, amongst the scattering of material from the last couple of albums, we got a load of brand-new, barely heard songs that were presumably going to feature on the next record – amongst them 'Monday Morning', 'Underwear', 'Sorted For E's & Wizz', and one that we later found out was called 'Disco 2000'. And again, rather than the usual confused reaction that new songs get from big audiences, they seemed to be greeted as old favourites: never has the phrase 'instant classic' seemed more appropriate. It was one of those rare times in music that brings you completely into the present: it wasn't something that needed comparing to anything that had gone before, it wasn't something that only became good in retrospect, it wasn't something that made you look forward to what was going to happen next. It was simply *now* – and it didn't make any difference whether you were onstage at Glastonbury, standing in the crowd watching, or listening to the radio on your own in a living room somewhere in North Yorkshire: all you could do was revel in the moment.

Jarvis' chat between the songs simply added to the sense that here and now was the best time and place we could possibly be. "This is a good thing that's happening here, us all in this place," he deadpanned early in the concert (you'll be unsurprised to hear that I've still got the tape). "And do you know what's happening in the outside world?"

"No!" replied the audience.

"And do you care?"

"NO!!!"

"When you go home on Monday morning, you're going to go home to a different world. But we're not thinking about that now because this is Saturday night, and the furthest thing from our minds is Monday morning. But this song is called 'Monday Morning' . . ."

The best moment came a little later on. "All right, this is the last new song we're playing tonight. This is a song about . . . you know if you grow up in a town, and everybody else wears a white shirt when they go out on a Friday night, with short sleeves, and maybe a moustache if you're a bloke, or if you're a girl, stilettos. And when you see them in town, there's a pack of about 10 of them, and they laugh at you because they think that you're the weird one, you know. *[Enormous, prolonged cheer]* And this is about how we are going to have our revenge on them and it's called 'Mis-Shapes'."

"Mis-shapes, mistakes, misfits," the song began, *"raised on a diet of broken biscuits, oh. We don't look the same as you, and we don't do the things you do, but we live round here too oh baby. Mis-shapes, mistakes, misfits – we'd like to go to town but we can't risk it, oh. 'Cos they just want to keep us out, you could end up with a boot in your mouth, just for standing out, oh really. Brothers, sisters, can't you see? The future's owned by you and me. There won't be fighting in the streets – they think they've got us beat but revenge is gonna be so sweet . . ."*

All right. As if things hadn't been triumphant enough already, this seemed to be pretty much sealing it. And then the chorus: *"We're making a move, we're making it now, we're coming out of the sidelines. Just put your hands up, it's a raid. We want your homes, we want your lives, we want the things you won't allow us. We won't use guns, we won't use bombs, we'll use the one thing we've got more of; that's our minds."*

The song continued in the same vein for another couple of verses and choruses, but that was really enough. "That's one thing you can't buy," remarked Jarvis afterwards. "Something up here. You can go to anybody, you can have plastic surgery for your face, but you can't shove anything inside your head that's going to make any difference at all. So: we rule. So there. You and whose army?"

All right. Again, this was the kind of thing that bands simply didn't sing about. The fact that it was happening seemed miraculous: this was a song that essentially expressed feelings of bitterness about being marginalised and ridiculed, and yet it felt celebratory and universal – even if you hadn't specifically been on the receiving end of the kind of small-town violence that the song was inspired by (which I certainly hadn't). It was about something bigger than that. The massive audience response said it all – it wasn't even just about me. It was about *us*. All of us. Whoever that meant.

There was only one way for the concert to end. "If you want something to happen enough, then it actually will happen, OK?" Jarvis told the audience. Massive cheers. "And I believe that. In fact, that's why we're stood on this stage after 15 years – 'cos we wanted it to happen, you know what I mean?" Massive cheers. "So, if a lanky get like me can do it, and us lot, then you can do it too. All right? So on that positive note, this is the last song, we can't play anymore after this. This is . . . 'Common People'."

Wow.

The 24-year-old writing this now isn't quite the same person as the 16-year-old who sat listening to that concert. I can even see, in hindsight, that 'Mis-Shapes' may or may not have said as much as I thought it did about giving me a sense of smug superiority over certain people at school who (probably quite rightly) laughed at my hair or whatever. But that concert was the start of something for me that's still with me to this day.

Pulp became my favourite group. They were great on so many levels. The media attention at the time obviously focused on the Cult of Jarvis, his lyrics, his looks, his personality, his style, which was understandable: he really was extremely good at being a pop star. And much as the man himself may now look back in horror at the Michael Jackson Brits incident and its repercussions, at the time it felt like yet another joyous piece of vindication on the part of real people against the kind of bloated, empty-hearted, corporate showbiz crap that normally passes for pop music. Which was a lot more fun, and considerably less misanthropic, than it sounds.

But the music itself was just as important. *Different Class*, the 1995 album that contained all those amazing new songs we'd first heard at Glastonbury, managed to range from enormous, stomping anthems to sleazily atmospheric monologues to gentle, tender balladeering, whilst still somehow remaining definitively Pulp and unimpeachably pop. And every subsequent Pulp record I've heard since, whether new or old, always seems to add yet another twist.

It quickly became apparent that this was a band with a history to be caught up on. Press around the time of *His 'N' Hers* and *Different Class* often alluded to a "mottled indie past" but tended not to delve much further than that – it seemed that, although Pulp had apparently been going for 15 years or more, for ease of research their history officially went back as far as 1992 and the material collected on the *Intro* album. What about the other stuff then?

As well as following the present-day Pulp, I made a point of trying to unearth some pre-history. With the band's level of fame at the time, of course, it wasn't hard: some of the millions of interviews that Jarvis was doing at the time saw him talking about the band's pre-fame years a bit, and there seemed to be an ever-growing list of back-catalogue stuff appearing in the shops: the Eighties singles compilation *Masters Of The Universe*, the old albums *Freaks* and *Separations*, the ancient début record *It*. All of these were often brilliant, and never less than interesting. But compared to the coverage afforded to the more recent records and the people who'd made them, they still seemed to be relatively shrouded in mystery.

It seemed that there was certainly a lot of Pulp to find out about, but no way of finding out about most of it. Increasingly, if I read a music press article about Pulp (or one of the rash of cheap cash-in biographies that appeared around 1996), the main thing I could find to say about it was often, "That's wrong . . . that's wrong . . . that's wrong . . . and what about this, this and this?" There was only one thing for it – I'd have to write a book myself.

That was 1996; now, in 2003, it's finished. It's taken a long time.

Of course, to say that this book has actually taken seven years to write would be misleading: I haven't been writing about Pulp non-stop from that day to this. Life, as they say, has a habit of intervening. But, as I suspected, there was also a lot of Pulp to write about: almost 25 years of Pulp, in fact, taking in countless incarnations of the band, forgotten songs and bizarre stories, *and* all the stuff they've done since they've been famous.

In the process of researching this book, I've been fortunate enough to be able to draw on the recollections of a great many members, ex-members and associates of the band. Without exception, the people I have interviewed have been extraordinarily helpful, patient, generous, amusing and wise. If this book has any merit at all, then the credit must go to them.

There are, inevitably, a number of people who it hasn't been possible for me to interview. Although Nick Banks very generously gave me several hours of interview time at short notice, a series of attempts over several years to elicit the participation of the other current members of Pulp came to nothing. Jarvis apparently wishes to remain "an enigma", and Pulp's management, perhaps understandably, seem unwilling to involve the rest of the group without his blessing. I should add, however, that he has made no attempt to stop me, allowing various friends and relatives to speak to me and authorising the use of some early photos.

Ex-members of Pulp I would have liked to speak to, but ultimately couldn't, include Mark Swift, who I did manage to track down but who unfortunately had a busy patch at work that coincided with the run-up to my deadline; Tim Allcard and Steven Havenhand, both of whom don't seem to be keen on speaking to the media in general; Magnus Doyle, who was out of the country for much of the period when I was writing the book; and Peter Mansell, Captain Sleep and Antony Genn, all of whom I was unable to contact. Still, there's always the second edition.

Seven years on from the genesis of this book, and plenty of things have changed, both for its author and its subject. However, one constant remains: Pulp are still really very, very good indeed. Being, as you are, the kind of person who reads long, weighty books about them, you'll probably know this already. However, if this book results in more recognition of Pulp's history, or increased appreciation of their body of work, then it will have been worthwhile. And if anyone who reads it finds something in Pulp's story – and, for me at least, there is plenty – that's entertaining, inspiring or intriguing, then it will also have been worthwhile.

So, this is my book about Pulp. I hope you enjoy it.

Mark Sturdy
January 2003

Acknowledgements

Thank you to all the members, ex-members and associates of Pulp I've been fortunate enough to interview: John Avery, Nick Banks, Peter Boam, David Bocking, Suzanne Catty, Saskia Cocker, Nigel Coxon, Murray Fenton, Wayne Furniss, David Hinkler, Simon Hinkler, Julie Hobson, Jonathan Kirk, Martin Lilleker, David Lockwood, Glen Marshall, Ogy McGrath, Paul Mills, John Nicholls, Michael Paramore, Tony Perrin, Jamie Pinchbeck, John Quinn, Nick Robinson, Jim Sellars, Russell Senior, Jon Short, Alan Smyth, Ian Spence, Nick Taylor, Philip Thompson, Garry Wilson. Thanks also to Mark Estdale and Steven Havenhand.

Thank you to Chris Charlesworth, my editor at Omnibus, for his faith, patience and resisting a justified urge to strangle me.

Thank you to Alex Deck from Pulp People for her consistent help and encouragement.

Thank you to Sarah and Emma at Matrix/Wessex, Paul at Axis Studios, Louise at Radio 1, and the nice anonymous lady in Universal Island A&R.

Thank you to Chris Wicks and Zbysiu Rodak for assistance with picture research.

Thank you to all the members of the various Pulp internet discussion groups since 1997, in particular Giles Bosworth, Richard Bradley, Stephen Bray, Sally Burn, Christine Cartier, Ian Clark, Steve Devereux, Julien Dhennin, Scott Frazer, Paul Haswell, Jamil Jivanjee, Rebecca Naylor, Michael Siou, Sarah Wilson.

Thank you to Chris Bailey, Mat Beal, Lisa Bentman and Andy Davis for their help in the early stages of this book.

Thank you to Kelly from Rough Trade, Erin Morris and John Turner for trying.

Thank you to Ginger Video Services (UK) Ltd.

Thank you to Messrs Ferraby, Jewitt, Morris and Weston for being amusing.

Thank you to Howard, Dana, Deano and anyone else who's had the misfortune of having me in their house while I've been writing this book.

Thank you to everyone I've forgotten.

Thank you to Mum, Dad and Elliot.

This book is dedicated to Louisa, without whose support, encouragement and inspiration it wouldn't be here. Thank you.

Chapter 1

"I don't know what a pop star personality is, but I always wanted to be in a group from a really early age and used to pretend that I was. When I was about 12 or 13, at school, there was a gang of about five of us and we were all in a group. I'd say, I'm the singer, he's the drummer, and stuff like that . . . I wouldn't tell them. It just made it seem more interesting when you were walking down the corridor, imagining that we were a group with all the other kids clapping us."

– Jarvis Cocker, 1995

Finding a starting point for the story of Pulp isn't as straightforward as it might seem. The first incarnation of the band assembled at school in 1978, but in a sense that doesn't really mark the true beginning of Pulp: that happened both much later, in the sense that Pulp didn't mutate into something recognisable as the band we now know until well into the Eighties, and much earlier, in the sense that the first Pulp's transition into reality from a schoolboy fantasy in the mind of Jarvis Cocker, the band's vocalist, lyricist and sole surviving original member, happened very gradually. Yet it would be misleading to say that Jarvis and Pulp are therefore one and the same: despite the innumerable line-up changes of the past 25 years, part of the point of Pulp is that it has always been A Group, an enterprise far greater than the input of any one of its members. Even so, Jarvis is the single linking factor between the Pulp we know now and the sundry earlier Pulps from which it sprang and, therefore, there's probably a case for saying that the story of Pulp really begins on September 19, 1963: the date of Jarvis Cocker's birth.

When Jarvis' parents, Mack and Christine, met at a Sheffield University Rag Ball in 1962, they were "about as bohemian as you could be in Sheffield."[1] Mack was a jobbing jazz trombonist and actor, while Christine had hitch-hiked around France before becoming an art student in Sheffield. Things changed abruptly when Christine found herself pregnant with Jarvis, forcing her to give up her studies and settle down. One shotgun wedding later, the couple were living next door to Christine's parents in the unremarkable Sheffield suburb of Intake.

Jarvis' early life, though, was far from impoverished. His father was the son of a magistrate, his mother's parents ran a construction company, and he remembers his maternal grandparents' house, next door to the maternal home in Intake, as being "quite grand, actually. It was the sort of manor house in the area before other houses were built. We lived in what had been the stables or something next door which had an orchard in the back garden."[2] What's more, the family (augmented after two years by a daughter, Saskia) managed holidays in Ibiza and Majorca – a big deal for the mid-Sixties.

At the age of five, Jarvis contracted meningitis. "I'd been to the swimming baths, and remember eating a packet of crisps – the ones that had a clear star on the front – and starting to feel really ill."[3] He very quickly found himself in a local children's hospital for the painful and risky operation: "You had to be in isolation. I was in a whole row of glass-walled rooms. You could see other kids but couldn't talk to them. It was quite strange."[4]

"I've since realised that there was quite a big chance that I might've died. They got all the class I was in at school to write letters – they didn't exactly say, 'Sorry you won't be around much longer,' but they wouldn't have gone to so much trouble if they didn't think I was on my way out. Everyone bought me all these great presents because they thought I was going to die, but they had to burn them all when I left the hospital in case they were contaminated. The only things I was allowed to take home were a couple of cheap, plastic spacemen that could be sterilised in boiling water."[5]

The incident left its mark on Jarvis in two ways: firstly in the revelation that Adults Lie. By the time of the operation, paralysis had begun to set in, necessitating the draining of fluid from his spine with a huge needle. "The doctors told me I had to be brave and that if I didn't make a big noise, then I could see my mum afterwards." He didn't cry, but when he asked to see his mum, "They said, 'No, she's gone home.' That probably had quite an effect on me, knowing that adults lie quite badly. You shouldn't lie about things like that, should you?"[6]

The second legacy was his permanently damaged eyesight, necessitating the wearing of a pair of thick, black-framed NHS glasses. He was already a distinctive-looking child, but the specs made the package complete: "I looked like an ugly girl. [Intake] was a normal Sheffield suburb, a bit rough maybe, but I was the only kid on the block with long hair, which my mum wouldn't cut. Long hair and skinny rib jumpers with really short shorts, as she made her own clothes, so it would look like a jumper dress."[7]

2

And then there was the *Lederhösen*. "My uncle married a German woman, and their relatives used to send me leather shorts – *Lederhösen* – the sort that Austrian goatherds wear, with a picture of a stag on the bib. Mum thought they were really cute. I went to school looking like an extra from *Heidi*, or an alpine shepherd boy. It was mortifying.

"Of course, in a school in the suburbs of Sheffield, this wasn't normal behaviour. I managed to cajole my grandmother into buying me some normal shorts, and I'd change on the way to school. People would generally call me names and think I was odd."[8]

"I never wanted to be different," he adds. "I wanted to be the same. I just wanted to wear shorts that were vaguely near the knee rather than somewhere up here (meaning the top of his thighs)."[9]

To complete the effect, there was the fact that, well, he was called Jarvis Cocker. "That was a cross to bear, although now I think it's all right. I don't know why I was called Jarvis – my mum going to art college, probably, which may explain why my sister's called Saskia: she was Rembrandt's wife."[10]

Though his bizarre appearance meant that he was never going to be in with the in-crowd, Jarvis was reasonably popular with his classmates at Intake Infants School – amongst them Peter Dalton and Mark Swift, both of whom would play an important role in the Pulp story later. Jarvis' sense of humour and attractively quirky personality were sufficient to deflect the worst of potential bullying, as one former schoolfriend remembers:

"He were just tall and weird, weren't he? First time I met him, he'd got these shoes, and they were like Cornish pasties. The stitching had come undone at the top, and he was walking around going, 'Talking shoe, talking shoe.' He was always quite a striking dresser – he'd never quite adhere to the school uniform. His hair was always pretty wild as well. When he was on *Shooting Stars* [a BBC comedy quiz show that Jarvis guested on at the height of his fame] years later, it was just like sitting next to him in class – he wasn't trying hard, he was just being himself."

In and out of school, Jarvis was an imaginative, creative child with an interest in dressing up and make-believe: "My mum made me a cape," he remembers. "I wore some purple tights and a Batman mask. I used to go shopping with my mother dressed as Batman."[11]

And music was already on the scene, as his sister Saskia remembers: "We were brought up in a house with music. I mean, our dad played in a band and used to be in a group with Joe Cocker – they used to call themselves The Cocker Brothers. There were always musicians in our house – me and Jarvis would get up to go to school with bodies laid on the floor, comatose. Music was always around, and both of us were always very interested in it . . . he always sang: he was in school plays, musicals and stuff, and he was in the choir."

The next complication in Jarvis' early life came when he was seven with the sudden departure of his father. By all accounts something of a Billy Liar character, Mack had felt constrained by domesticity and family life, and in 1970 vanished overnight, heading first to London and then, in order to avoid paying alimony, to Sydney. It was several years before his family back in Sheffield, who had assumed he'd committed suicide, heard from him.

In the absence of any financial support from her wayward husband, Christine was forced to give up her artistic aspirations in order to look after Jarvis and Saskia. "She sacrificed her career when father left and went to emptying fruit machines," remarks Jarvis. "I feel bad about that now. Didn't appreciate it at the time."12

Without Mack, and with Christine, Saskia and his grandmother around him, Jarvis was destined to spend his formative years in a predominantly female environment, which he believes had a far greater effect on him than his father's departure in itself: "I think a lot of the reason I found it difficult when I started going out with girls was because I was brought up around so many of them. Through a biological accident, there are lots more females than males in my family and I just thought of them as friends and considered myself to be the same as them. But when you start going out with people, you start to realise that that battle of the sexes thing does exist."13

Even so, he refuses to feel disadvantaged by the fact that he only had one natural parent about during his formative years: "That always gets me – the assumption that, if you've been brought up in a one-parent family, then that's it, you're the product of a broken home, yet another symptom of society's decay. I mean, my mother was very strict. If you wouldn't stand still when you were having your hair brushed, you got the hair brush broken over your head. You know those ones with the white plastic spines? I've had so many of them broken over my head. In the end, she started buying wooden brushes and things got really dangerous."14

In autumn 1975, at the age of 11, Jarvis moved from primary school to the nearby City Comprehensive School. He'd developed into a bright, studious pupil who, in time-honoured fashion, tended to slip into the persona of the class clown to deflect the ridicule that his odd appearance and lack of sportiness and/or trendiness might attract.

"The first thing I remember Jarvis doing was when we were being taught how to play rugby by a sadistic games teacher," recalls former classmate Jim Sellars. "I remember seeing him running up the sideline with the ball, these gangly legs going everywhere, I was laughing so much I just fell

4

over. I remember him as someone who you could look at and be amused – he could amuse you without trying, really."

"My first memories of Jarvis were that he was geeky, but not cool-geeky," remembers Jon Short, who was in the year above Jarvis. "He was tall, and odd-looking, with his wire glasses. He used to wear these Polyveldt shoes and brown trousers, but not in any sort of trendy way."

Even so, a circle of friends who were on a similar wavelength – amongst them Peter Dalton, Mark Swift, Glen Marshall and David Lockwood – meant that Jarvis was no social outsider. "He was obviously popular within that group of people," recalls City School maths teacher Mike Jarvis. "They were a group of very intelligent people who got on. In a comprehensive school like ours, he was going to appeal more to the intelligentsia bit, and there were some very bright people around. There would have been some rougher diamonds who wouldn't have appreciated him, I guess, but I don't specifically remember anything like that."

Before he'd reached his teens, music was looming large in Jarvis' life, and he was already beginning to harbour vague fantasies of pop stardom – fuelled, naturally, by a diet of Saturday morning repeats of *The Monkees*:

"It was probably The Monkees [that crystallised his ambitions], although I know that sounds stupid. The only decent records my mother had at home were Beatles' records. I think my dad took the good ones with him when he left. Anyway, the rest of it was Blood, Sweat & Tears and crap like that. But The Monkees were on telly a lot and I used to fantasise about being a pop star. I was already thinking of the advantages. One of them was that you could pay someone to show episodes of *The Monkees* whenever you wanted."[15]

"I don't know what a pop star personality is," he reflected many years later, "but I always wanted to be in a group from a really early age and used to pretend that I was. When I was about 12 or 13, at school, there was a gang of about five of us and we were all in a group. I'd say, 'I'm the singer, he's the drummer,' and stuff like that . . . I wouldn't tell them. It just made it seem more interesting when you were walking down the corridor, imagining that we were a group and all the kids were clapping us."[16]

"I do see Jarvis as someone who was a celebrity when he wasn't famous," says another schoolfriend, David Lockwood. "He was always an eccentric, larger-than-life kind of person. He always had it in him to become a star, personality-wise if not musically. He never played both sides of an LP – he'd always get bored of things after a few songs."

Christmas 1976 brought Jarvis' pop star fantasies one step closer to reality when, at the age of 13, he became the owner of a musical instrument for the first time. Saskia: "Me mum used to go out with a German diver called Horst Hohenstein, who actually used to dive with Jacques Cousteau, and he gave Jarvis his first guitar, that he still plays now."

"That was exciting," says Jarvis, "because then I could kind of be a bit of a guitar hero in me bedroom. Which is a bit sad really – I would rather have been out on a corner, trying to talk to girls or improve my social skills or play football or something. That would've been healthier I think!"[17]

Hours after school were now being spent by Jarvis trying to perfect riffs on his treasured Hopf semi-acoustic. "My mother used to say it was plinky-plonk," he remembers. "She's say, 'Come down here and have your tea. Stop all that plinky-plonk.'"[18]

Progress was slow, and it quickly became apparent to Jarvis that he wasn't going to emulate his mum's Beatles' records, or the anonymous American sessioners whose jangling The Monkees were miming to, in a reasonable amount of time.

And then?

"Then punk rock happened."[19]

Up until now, Jarvis had been longingly eyeing Led Zeppelin's two-LP behemoth *Physical Graffiti* in the local Virgin Megastore. But as punk swept its way into mainstream culture at the start of 1977, its scorched-earth ethos and thrilling, noisy, elementary music changed everything. "The great thing about punk was you had to decide almost instantly whether you were for it or against it. It was so hardline. I remember listening to local radio, Radio Hallam, and the DJ said, 'Well, you will not be hearing any punk rock on this station. It's terrible.' You just wouldn't hear that now. So I thought it was great."[20]

It's a cliché now, of course, but it's easy to forget that punk's effect on the musical landscape of Britain *circa* 1977 was unique, unrepeatable, revolutionary and incredibly exciting. Just a few months before, one pretty much had a choice between vacuous thirtysomething prog-monsters (Genesis, Yes, Zeppelin) and hermetically sealed disco-pop (Bee Gees, Abba). By the spring of '77, The Sex Pistols (who had caused ructions the previous December with the much-celebrated Bill Grundy TV incident) had just released their second single, 'Pretty Vacant'; The Clash, with The Buzzcocks, Slits and Subway Sect, were tearing up and down the country with their White Riot tour, taking punk out of London and into the provinces for the first time; and elsewhere the likes of The Damned, The Stranglers and many others were making a splash for the first time. Jarvis was 13-and-a-half years old and ripe for the picking.

He began listening to John Peel's Radio 1 show religiously, exposing himself to all of the above and more through 1977. What's more, the anything-goes ethos of punk fashion gave Jarvis a new confidence in his undeniably individual appearance. "Up to then I used to hate the fact that I stuck out. But when I was about 13, it became an advantage not to be the same as everyone else. That's when I started going to jumble sales and buying my own clothes."[21]

He also plucked up the courage to go to his first concert: The Stranglers at Sheffield's Top Rank. Unfortunately, it wasn't a great night. "Believing in the punk spirit of individuality and self-expression I went along in a jumble-sale jacket and a blue tie that my mother had crocheted for me. And all these people in mohicans took the piss and said I was a mod. The irony is that punks used to take the piss out of Teddy boys and that's exactly what they've become: the modern Teds."[22]

It was a disenchanting experience, but it couldn't quite quell the excitement and the sense of new possibilities opened up by punk. What was more inspiring still, as the year drew on, was the emergence of a rash of post-punk bands filtering through Peel and into Jarvis' bedroom that went beyond the minimalistic, blank *attack* of punk, maintaining instead that essential attitude and energy but producing something more interesting and adventurous. By the end of the year, bands like Joy Division, Wire, Magazine, The Swell Maps, Half Japanese and Crime were all using comparatively elementary musical ability not just to make a lot of noise and frighten the grown-ups (although this was always a commendable activity in itself), but create what were arguably great works of Serious Art.

It was after prolonged exposure to these varied examples of what was possible without ten years' tuition at the Prog College Of Music that, one day in November 1978, during an O-level economics class, Jarvis (by then aged 15) and his friend Peter 'Dolly' Dalton (14) decided that they were going to start a band.

"Obviously the message of punk was that you just learn three chords in a week and you're away," says Jarvis. "I thought, 'Yeah, let's have a go at it.' And I persuaded some friends to come to my house on a Friday night when my mum was out, and we started rehearsing."[23]

But before the issue of actually making any music arose, the crucial question of what they were going to call themselves had to be addressed. Jarvis and Peter agreed that Jarvis' original choice, Pulp (after the 1972 film starring Michael Caine), wasn't enough – they needed something with a bit of weight. Someone else in the economics lesson, as it happened, had a copy of the *Financial Times*, which listed the coffee bean Arabicas in its Commodity Index. One slight misspelling later, Arabicus was christened.

"Punk rock gave us the idea that anyone could do it," said Jarvis later, "'cos none of us had any ability."[24] Virtuosity notwithstanding, according to his sister Saskia, Jarvis had always harboured creative leanings that went beyond schoolboy fantasies of pop stardom: "In English, his stories and things were fantastic – he had some read out on radio. He was a very good storyteller. He was never what you'd call a fantastic musician, but he was always very good at writing. So he was always a good singer, and quite proficient as a guitarist, but not kind of outstanding."

Peter Dalton, meanwhile, had known Jarvis since primary school, and would turn out to be one of the most important components of the early Pulp. While, like Jarvis, he was no virtuoso, he was reasonably proficient on keyboards and guitar (and also xylophone and cornet, which he'd played in the school orchestra). What's more, he would quickly become, and remain, Jarvis' main collaborator through a number of important steps in Pulp's movement from schoolboy fantasy to 'proper' band.

The first of these steps took place when the band first convened at Jarvis' gran's house in Intake for their first rehearsal. Jarvis, of course, sang and played guitar; Dolly played guitar and Jarvis' gran's organ ("That was the only thing that was amplified, so you couldn't hear anything else,"[25] Jarvis would later recall), and Dolly's younger brother Ian kept time on the coal scuttle. The first song they learnt to play was, in time-honoured guitar novice style, The Animals' 'House Of The Rising Sun' – its six chords being reasonably easy to master. It was followed up with a Cocker/Dalton original, 'Shakespeare Rock'. Inspired by English Literature lessons on Hamlet, it boasted the lyrics:

I've got a baby only one thing wrong
She quotes Shakespeare all day long
Said 'Baby you're ignoring me'
She said 'To be or not to be'
Shakespeare rock
Shakespeare roll
Shakespeare rock
Shakespeare roll
Said 'Baby you're making me sick'
She said 'Alas, poor Yorick'
Shakespeare rock
Shakespeare roll
Shakespeare rock
Shakespeare roll

Chapter 1

It wasn't Jarvis' first foray into Shakespeare – a little while before, he'd appeared as Sir Andrew Aguecheek in a school production of *Twelfth Night*, as his classmate Julie Hobson recalls: "He was so lanky and giddy-looking that he did a really good performance, but he seemed very nervous, so he probably wasn't as comfortable as he was with being in a band. I think that was the only one he acted in – most years he'd be scene-shifting, like I was."

Arabicus drifted into inactivity after a couple of practices, but by early 1979, Jarvis and Dolly were making a second attempt at forming a band, this time during a private study period at school. The first new recruit was David Lockwood (universally known, because his middle name was Angus, as Fungus) on bass. "Jarvis and Peter had played around and come up with the name Arabicus, but they weren't really doing anything," he remembers. "They just went, 'Do you want to join?' so I said, 'Yeah.' Then our friend Glen Marshall decided that he was going to become the manager, just as a sleazy businessman kind of thing. He took me to the first rehearsal because I didn't know where Jarvis' house was, and because I didn't have a bass I just played the bottom four strings of an acoustic guitar – I didn't, and still don't, have any kind of musical ability, but it didn't matter because nobody could hear me. Like most people, I didn't take it seriously at all – it was just a reason to get together. I mean, I'm willing to believe that all along Jarvis thought it was his goal to become a pop star, but I don't think anyone else did really – it was just a giggle."

"Fungus couldn't play at all," laughs Saskia. "But he was a good person-ality – that seemed the first priority really, that if you've got the right per-sonality you were in, it didn't matter if you could play much. It was just like a big gang really – people'd come in and do a bit and then go off and do something else."

"Fungus was just Fungus," says Glen Marshall. "He was a bit of an oddball really, but he was my best friend at the time. He was very eccen-tric, very clever – we'd got similar interests at that point, and he'd tend to bounce these ideas off us. He had an influence on the Pulp thing through the art side of things – he'd do posters for them. He was a bit like Jarvis in that he could go and do his own thing. He obviously liked the idea of being in a group, but he wasn't dedicated enough to learn the bass or any-thing like that. It was just a fun thing for him, really."

Meanwhile, Glen Marshall's appointment as manager came about, he says, as a result of "being close friends with everyone who was in the group, and knowing I'd got no musical talent myself. Fungus was in a similar place – we were all best friends, and he decided he'd play bass. But he couldn't play it, so he decided to teach himself while he was in the band, and failed miserably. So I thought it would be better to be manager, because then you can't go wrong. The tenuous link, which I think was why everybody accepted it, was that I'd got a hi-fi tape recorder and I taped all the rehearsals. I'd transport this massive tape deck with me, and take it up to Jarvis' house and plonk it down, and I'd be recording everything they did – we just used to leave it on throughout, so you'd get this cross-banter and everything, then a bit of music."

Glen would continue to do non-musical things with the band for the next two years, taping rehearsals, organising the accounts (such as they were), and making Super 8 films of the band. "He wasn't really serious as a manager," says David Lockwood. "He was just playing on the Spinal Tap thing of being the sleazy exploitative character who was pulling the strings behind the scenes. Although he did turn up to all the rehearsals with his tape recorder, which was surprising, 'cos they must have been pretty boring."

Soon after, Jarvis got his way and Arabicus became Arabicus Pulp. "People were having problems saying Arabicus," remembers Fungus, "so Jarv came up with Pulp as a contrast, and then before long it became just Pulp." The next step was to find a drummer, and after letting Saskia have a go for one rehearsal ("It was a bit of a shambles really – there's a very funny tape of me playing the drums with the dog barking outside"), classmate Mark Swift, better known as Dixie, took his place behind the scuttle. "He was one of Jarvis' oldest friends," says Saskia. "They'd known each other right through infant school."

The moniker Dixie, as David Lockwood explains, came about "because he was small, like in Pixie and Dixie and Mr Jinx. Although there was no Pixie or Mr Jinx. In the group, we all had these personae, which were pretty much of our own choosing. Glen was sleazy businesslike Glen, I was wacky unpredictable Dave, Dolly was hunky beefcake Pete . . . I can't remember what Dixie and Jarv were." As for the group's ambitions at the time, "I think maybe as time went on they got more serious in terms of wanting to play to people, but not serious in terms of wanting to play and become successful. Apart from Jarvis, I don't think anyone at that time saw it going beyond the sixth form. It was something that we just did."

With a full line-up in place, practices began in earnest. Gran didn't like the noise, so Dixie, Dolly, Fungus and Jarv, with Glen tagging along with his tape recorder, relocated next door to Jarvis' mum's front room. "She always used to go to the pub on a Friday, so we'd have like three hours on our own to mess about," explains Jarvis. "I did want to be in a group, and I guess people agreed to be in it with me – I guess I was the one who made the mistake of taking it seriously."[26]

The repertoire grew quickly – Peter Dalton came up with a song called 'Queen Poser' ("Just two words we'd read in the *NME* and strung together – not anything meaningful"[27]), and there was another Jarv/Dolly collaboration called 'What You Gonna Do About It'. "That was one of the really early ones," says Philip Thompson, another schoolfriend who would later become a member of the band. "Jarvis and Peter, I think, put it together. It was a real tinny punk-type song, real basic stuff – it was just repeating *'What you gonna do about it'* – *der! der! der!* – *'what you gonna do', der-der-der-der-der, dur-dur-dur-dur-dur, der-der-der-der-der,'* then you'd go back to the chorus."

Fungus remembers a song called 'I've Been Looking At The World Today' which "had a line in about 'Toilet rolls and dead sea scrolls', which I always liked," and another Jarvis composition called 'You Should've Known': "That was one of my favourites," he remembers. "It was all to do with . . . well, I don't know whether you'd call it political, but it was all to do with the idea of somebody just being happy in their own little world, ignoring what's going on outside as the tanks are coming in and knocking down the walls." Astonishingly, he can still remember the lyrics:

Someone died last night
As you polished up your shoes
But you were unaware
'Cos you never watched the news
Too involved in your own existence
To see the world outside
It's all too challenging
You just prefer to hide
You ironed your trousers
As the tanks came rolling in
You felt so safe within your home
And when the walls came down
You should've known
You should've known
You should've known

Fungus' own most notable contribution to the Pulp repertoire, meanwhile, was his 'vocal' on a number called 'Message To The Martians': while Jarvis played the bass line to 'New Dawn Fades' by Joy Division, Fungus would make 'alien noises'. "It was originally just them messing about self-indulgently on their instruments, with me nonsensically jabbering away down a microphone," he remembers. "In the end I was replaced by a synthesiser, which was probably a good move."

"The beat to that was quite infectious," remembers Glen. "It was one that sort of grew on you. There were two hits on the bass drum, then one on the snare, then one, then two – it were a repetitive beat, and you got Jarvis strumming over the top of that. They'd play a fifteen-minute version – it was quite addictive."

'The Condom Song', meanwhile, took things from the ridiculous to, er, the even more ridiculous. Glen Marshall: "At the time, that was quite risqué, to talk about condoms. Nowadays you'd probably qualify for a *Blue Peter* badge or something. It was 'Come on, come on, give me a condom,' and they'd just chant it."

Then there were the cover versions – 'House Of The Rising Sun' was still there, along with The Troggs' 'Wild Thing' ("Actually we could only do the first bit,"[28] remembers Jarvis) and a version of quirky US new-wavers Devo's 'Gut Feeling'. "That was a popular one on their [Devo's] first album," says Glen, "that's quite easy to play. Never did it live, but that was one that sounded good. That was the first concert they went to – we were all into Devo, so we all went to City Hall to see them."

Things were going well – without actually presenting anything to the public, Arabicus Pulp was managing to become a well-known name around City School, finding plenty of ways to create a cult other than by endearing themselves to people with their music. "It was a bit like a club in that sense," remembers Fungus. "By the time they were actually out and playing concerts, they had enough of a fanbase from school for their audience to outnumber the main band quite a lot of the time." The school soon found its corridors covered with small gold "Arabicus Pulp Are Damned Good" stickers, "Friends Of Pulp" T-shirts were made, and there were even plans for a Pulp stage play, written by Jarvis, Fungus and Glen. Fungus: "We knocked it up in an English lesson when we had to be quiet – the teacher wanted to speak to the girls, or something. Glen and Jarvis wrote it, then I changed it all when I typed it. It had bits taken from Monty Python and all sorts – it was about this alien baby which has got these antennae, but for some reason people don't notice . . . anyway, it never got performed."

"I suppose we were sort of Pulp's first groupies," remembers Julie Hobson, another City School cohort. "Me and my friends used to follow them around everywhere. I did snog Jarvis once at a party, in someone's living room. For a long time. I kept getting up, and he kept coming back and fetching me. I finally got away from him, and I was talking to Jamie and people in the other room for most of the night after that. I felt really sorry for him, because he looked really sad after that. It was really embar-rassing to snog Jarvis at school, but he was really nice – he wasn't the type of lad who mauled you or jumped on your bones, or anything. He was really sweet and gentlemanly. Well, he was when I snogged him, but that's all you did when you were 15, snog. I only ever went to Jarvis' house once, at a Christmas party one year. It was a really big house – it belonged to his grandma, and he and his mum and Saskia lived in part of it. I remember being in his mum's bedroom, and she had this half-finished mural on the back of her bed. She was a very artistic-looking sort of person, she always looked very happening."

By summer 1979, despite six months of rehearsals, Arabicus Pulp didn't yet have sufficient expertise, equipment or money to make proper recordings or play live: although Fungus had upgraded from the bottom four strings of an acoustic guitar to a Hofner semi-acoustic bass he'd inherited from his brother, Dixie was still keeping time on the coal scuttle, Peter was without a keyboard and the only form of amplification was Jarvis' mum's record player. Even so, they still wanted to present something to the public, and the solution was a short film called *The 3 Spartans*, made on Glen Marshall's Super 8 camera. It wasn't their first foray into celluloid – a few months earlier, Glen had made a video for 'Shakespeare Rock', featuring Jarvis, Dixie and Fungus sitting in Jarvis' backyard, reading Shakespeare books and then, um, rocking (or jumping about with guitars). There was also something called *The Film Starring Arabicus Pulp* which never progressed beyond the opening titles and a few shots of the group walking up and down Mansfield Road.

The 3 Spartans was conceived one afternoon in Jarvis' living room around August '79. "It was one of those days when we weren't doing anything in particular," says Glen, "and then *The 300 Spartans* came on the telly. It was one of those crap films that you just sit and watch. We watched it through, then we said, 'We'll do a remake.' But there were only three of us, so we called it *The 3 Spartans* – Jarvis, Dolly and Dixie. Fungus was around at that point, but he wasn't involved in the film. He lived out of town, in Killamarsh – Sheffield's since grown so much that it's probably not classed as out of town any more, but at the time it seemed like the back of beyond. So he didn't always get to everything we did, but I think he would have been in there had he lived locally. So I filmed it, and we just had a laugh doing it." Mark Swift was going to play the third Spartan alongside Jarvis and Peter, but his mum wouldn't let him out because he was having his tea. To compensate for the loss, they made use of all the resources at their disposal – i.e. lots of hard hats and garden canes.

The film's cassette soundtrack is sadly long since lost, but the silent footage still survives in the hands of Glen Marshall. Made in Peter Dalton's back garden, it lasts around four minutes, and opens with Jarvis addressing the masses (represented for the film by lots of garden canes with hard hats on them, planted in Mr Dalton's vegetable patch). The next scene features Jarvis and Peter slapping each other repeatedly on the shoulders till they fall over (in a parody of the way everyone greets each other in the original film). This is followed by a fight scene, with the two protagonists hitting each other with garden canes, and then a funeral procession (Jarvis, Peter and a cane with a hard hat on the end, walking past the camera). A brief and baffling shot of someone in a tree, another fight scene, a bizarre advert and the credits roll.

The film was shown in a City School classroom for a week of lunchtimes sometime around autumn 1979, and a combination of novelty value and the band's pseudo-celebrity status around the school meant that *The 3 Spartans* was a runaway success, bringing in enough money from the 10p admission to allow the group to buy their first drum kit – a snare, bass and cymbal donated by Jarvis' mother's boyfriend's dad, who had played in a dance band. Jarvis: "My mum put the name on the front in sticky tape. It cost £10, which I suppose was quite cheap."[29]

Soon after, Arabicus Pulp officially dropped the Arabicus to become, simply, Pulp. Arabicus was a bit of a mouthful and, despite its mundane coffee-bean origins, sounded, well, just a little bit too prog. "It was an unwieldy name," Jarvis has since said, "and we knew it was rubbish, and no one understood the term anyway, so we dropped it after a year. People hated it and it was frequently spelt wrong. We've been billed as Pope and The Pulps before.[30]

"In the end, Pulp has ended up being quite appropriate, in terms of pulp magazines and all that. One dictionary said, 'Cheap mass-produced stuff that is considered to be of no worth in the time it was done.' But often stuff like that comes to sum up the periods it was made in. It's like if you want a picture of 1980, you don't go and listen to a Cabaret Voltaire record, you listen to Sonia or something. Well, she weren't around then, but you know what I mean."[31]

Towards the end of 1979, buoyed by the success of the film, the newly christened Pulp were beginning think to of playing live. Things had moved quickly in the year since the band had started – a little too quickly for reluctant bassist David Lockwood, who was shortly to become the first in a long line of ex-members of Pulp. "I wasn't pushed, I jumped! I left because there was this impending thing that they were going to get serious – well, not serious in the sense that they are now, but serious in the sense of actually playing in front of people. There was no way I wanted to do that, so I just dropped out."

Jarvis' recollection of Fungus' departure was that "he used to play the songs twice as fast as everybody else so he could get to the end quicker and go and have a lie down and something to eat. He couldn't get rid of that competitive spirit – he thought it was like a sport or a race, where the first one to the end was the best. He couldn't really grasp the concept of all playing at the same time."[32]

"It's funny how people remember things differently," says David Lockwood now. "Perhaps I just wanted to get it over with, but I don't remember it that way. I just couldn't play."

The new bassist was another schoolfriend, Philip Thompson (or Pip). "I was in the same class as the others and everything," Pip remembers, "and I think it was during a Geography lesson just after Fungus left that they asked me to join. They knew I was into music, so I just went, 'Oh, I'll have a go at that.' I joined pretty much straight after Fungus left, but I didn't actually play with them till the New Year – I needed to save up my Christmas money so I could buy the bass off Fungus. It was a pretty snazzy bass – a Hofner semi-acoustic. It had the original plastic strings on it . . . Jamie's still got it, the git – I wish I'd not sold it!"

"He were a good lad," says Glen Marshall. "He lived out of town a bit though, so he wasn't really in the mainstream of the group."

With Pip on board, the new improved Pulp made its live début in the hall of City School, one lunchtime around February or March 1980. Glen Marshall: "It took a lot of organisation – I had to go and see the headmaster, to convince him that it was an acceptable thing to do. Then we had to get [maths teacher] Mr Jarvis to record it – that was a big thing at the time, because he had a proper tape machine. They were mainly playing their own songs, although I can't remember what was on the running order. I think they'd got one or two that they thought were half decent at that point."

Schoolfriend Jon Short remembers his role in the rehearsals: "I'd been involved with classical music at school – I was quite experienced from doing a lot of concerts with orchestras, so Mike Jarvis, their maths teacher at the time, said, 'These lads in my class have got this band called Pulp, they're doing a concert at school, and I want you to give them some tips on stage presentation,' which we thought was hilarious. I'd gone home and listened to all my live records – there was *Genesis Live*, I remember that. I went back to school that night and we all got together in the music block – I just quoted all these lines that Peter Gabriel had said. Jarvis was looking at me, just thinking 'What a pillock.' After ten minutes, it just degenerated."

"Because I was so bad," says Pip, "I used to come on and do about three songs – I'd do little cameos as a bad bass-player. 'Message To The

Martians' was one of them, and 'Stepping Stone' was another. After that, as time went on, I got to know the songs, and I ended up doing them all. The bass we had was probably the only decent bit of equipment we'd got. Dolly had a keyboard by this time – he'd saved up from his job in the local supermarket. And he had this real cheapo electric guitar, which I think cost £30 brand new. We'd borrowed a wah-wah pedal for it, and he went mad on that."

Glen Marshall remembers a slightly muted reception: "You had expectations of this pop concert, where everyone would rush to the front of the stage and there'd be a massive throng of people clapping and cheering – but they were playing, and people were just stood down the aisles going, 'What are they doing?' So there was no atmosphere whatsoever. We'd been to the chemistry department to try and create some special effects, magnesium flares and things, but they all failed miserably. In retrospect, it wasn't the right environment because the school hall was quite a vast place to be doing it without a dedicated mass audience."

"It wasn't the best of concerts," says maths teacher Mike Jarvis, "but the kids thoroughly enjoyed it. If someone'll go up and play, kids will enjoy that sort of thing happening. They had their fanbase within their own year anyway, so all the older kids were into it. I recorded it on reel-to-reel, but the only thing I can remember about it was at the start, while they were tuning up, Jarvis saying, 'E chord, bastard!' to Peter. They weren't happy with the concert though, so I didn't keep the tape."

Saskia Cocker's memory of the concert is slightly more forgiving: "They just played one lunchtime, and everybody loved them. It was that school thing, you know – a bit cheesy, but very funny. It was a nice thing at school; they were a good set and everybody just really, really liked them."

Having made their first foray into live performance, it was time for the group to make another film. The follow-up to *The 3 Spartans, Star Trek (With Spaghetti Western Overtones)* was a sci-fi epic based around the curious premise of Star Trek beaming down on to a planet where everybody was in a spaghetti western. Its genesis was a script meeting in Glen Marshall's bedroom: "After we did *The 3 Spartans,*" says Glen, "we decided to do this *Star Trek* production as well. We actually tried to sit down and plan that one. Everyone was into *Star Trek*, so everybody just chipped in ideas. At the time, Jarvis had got a derelict house across his yard, so we had access to that. We had this bar scene where we could go in and do some of the filming.

"The opening shot was Jarvis in a poncho, swinging this *Star Trek* mobile, and somebody tipping a tin of spaghetti hoops over it. We were just making it up as we went along. I think we just filmed it all in one day. We'd had a party the night before, and we got two girls involved: Karen Fletcher, who Dolly was obsessed with at the time, and I was going out with a girl called Deborah Farnell, who was Karen's best friend. But just as we were about to film, Deborah said, 'Do I *have* to be in it?' and I gave in and said no. So Karen was in it, but Deborah wasn't. There was a lad called Kevin Jackson who was the object of ridicule sometimes, and he agreed to be the object of ridicule for the film. Lee Fletcher, Karen's brother was in there – I think Lee wanted to be involved with the group, but he was into the heavy rock scenario, so he didn't really fit in with the thing, with Dolly always being into the latest trend and Jarvis being into the individual sort of thing. I think there were a few who sort of tried to become involved."

Like its predecessor, the one surviving copy of *Star Trek (With Spaghetti Western Overtones)* is in the hands of Glen Marshall, and has lost its soundtrack. The plot is nigh on impossible to decipher, but you'll see Jarvis in a poncho, Ian Dalton and future Pulp bassist Jamie Pinchbeck in *Star Trek* uniforms, Kevin Jackson throwing rocks around on a piece of wasteland, the controls of the SS *Enterprise* represented by an abacus, Dixie hanging from a noose, and more.

"I remember the main technological feat in that was when we got somebody to dematerialise," says Jamie. "We were there one frame, and disappeared the next. We were quite proud of that. It was all pretty amateurish, obviously, but entertaining."

On February 16, 1980, the *Sheffield Star*'s Pop Page announced that local promoter and sometime *Record Mirror* writer Marcus Featherby was planning to release a compilation LP of unsigned South Yorkshire bands called *Bouquet Of Steel*. Anyone who wanted to be on the album was invited to contact Marcus, and Pulp subsequently did. "We took over a tape," says Jarvis, "which was pretty dodgy. He wouldn't have us on the album, but took pity and put us in the brochure – it says something like a cross between Abba and The Fall."[33]

Reportedly, the tape (probably some long-lost collection of home recordings made by Glen Marshall) wasn't the only thing that was dodgy: few people who were on the early Eighties Sheffield band scene speak highly of Marcus Featherby. "I went with them to see him," says Glen. "I remember being sat down in this old house . . . he sort of came across as being a bit shady – it got to the point where I was thinking, 'Hang on, we might get ripped off here.' I think he referred us to some studios that we went to look round – we were going to hire one of those, but never did."

Featherby (not his real name – the *Sheffield Star*'s Martin Lilleker reckons he must have changed his name at least three times and was originally of Irish descent) was a busy figure on the Sheffield scene around the time, with a hand in most of the many promising bands that were emerging there in the late Seventies and early Eighties. "I was just passing through," he said of his arrival in the city in a rare 1981 interview with the *Star*, "but I stopped over for the night because of train problems. I went to the Limit Club on West Street, heard Vice Versa [later known as ABC] and thought, 'This is it!' I've been here ever since."[34]

Amongst the many bands that Featherby involved himself with at one time or another were Artery, Mortuary In Wax and The Stunt Kites, all names from a period often seen as a golden era for Sheffield bands – not that there was ever a unifying sound that could be identified with the city. A typical bill at the Limit *circa* 1980 might veer from spiky proto-goth to synthpop and straight-ahead heavy rock, while in the *Star*, Featherby identified the essence of Sheffield music as lying not in any one musical style but in the "insular, independent, self-supporting" attitude inherent in many of the bands there. All characteristics, it could be said, that Pulp have managed to display in spades over the years.

"Marcus *was* dodgy," alleges the *Star*'s Martin Lilleker, "obviously from the money point of view, plus . . . well, there was always this element of that about him where you'd wonder why he'd devote so much time to these young lads in bands. He managed Danse Society, and the drummer, Paul Gilmartin, was a very good-looking lad, and he always used to play with just shorts on. I can remember standing next to Marcus at the bar, and Marcus saying, 'Ooh, isn't he gorgeous?' and I'm thinking, 'Why are you involved with this band, Marcus?' But he was all right, was Marcus. He did a lot of good things, but he did a lot of bad things – he never paid anybody. He was a bit of an egotist too, he was always full of himself. If only he'd have paid people, done this, that and the other, he would've been like Tony Perrin, who's probably made a fortune – and lost one – through managing The Mission and All About Eve."

Even so, over the next few months, Marcus Featherby was to prove an asset to the fledgling Pulp, taking them under his wing and helping the four inexperienced 15- and 16-year-olds make their first steps on to the local band scene. "We'd go round and see him quite a lot," remembers David Lockwood. "He got them started with the gigs at Rotherham and the Leadmill and supported them quite a lot, even though I'm sure he once said he didn't personally like Pulp." Jarvis would later recall that "although Marcus seemed to be a strange and dodgy character, it worked out well for us. Otherwise, we wouldn't have known how to go about getting concerts because we were too young to get into pubs. We wouldn't have existed without him."[35]

The *Bouquet Of Steel* album emerged in May and, although Pulp weren't among the nine Sheffield bands on the album, their brief mention in the booklet, which served as a rough guide to the then-burgeoning South Yorkshire band scene, served as their first flash of fame. "My first regret after I left the band," muses David Lockwood, "perhaps the only one, actually, was when the *Bouquet Of Steel* compilation came out. Pulp were in the booklet and it said 'Philip Thompson – bass'. If they'd have contacted Marcus a week or so earlier, it would've been my name in print! At that stage Pulp hadn't played anywhere, but they were down on the page before Saxon. I mean, all it said was the four names and a couple of lines, but it was real!"

Featherby had given Pulp a slot which was to be their first public perform-ance, at his *Bouquet Of Steel* festival at the Sheffield Leadmill, so it was a surprise for all concerned when the band suddenly found themselves making their début a month prior to the festival, supporting The Naughtiest Girl Was A Monitor at the Rotherham Arts Centre on July 5, 1980. "Marcus Aardvark, as we used to call him, just phoned Jarvis' mum that morning and said, 'Do you want to support this band? Get yourselves to Rotherham Arts Centre,'" remembers Philip Thompson. "We heard that in the morning, and by the afternoon we were playing. It was just like, 'Ace! We've got a gig! Yay, let's get there!'"

Accordingly, that afternoon saw Jarvis, Dolly, Pip and Dixie, with Glen and Fungus (who was roadieing and doing the lights) in tow, pile into the back of a mobile grocer's van they'd borrowed from one of Jarvis' neigh-bours and make the journey to Rotherham to perform to an audience of around thirty schoolfriends and members of other local bands. "Jarvis started the concert with 'Are you ready to rock, Rotherham?'" remem-bers Pip. "It was real stadium rock stuff. He was always taking the mick out of things like that, even back then. There was one song – I can't remember which – where he'd quite often end up lying on his back, thrashing his legs about. For the encore, we did a version of 'Leavin' Here', which we'd heard on a Motorhead EP, just because it was dead easy to play. We'd reworked it, though, and did it as a reggae tune – trying to bring a bit more to it of what we were about."

The Rotherham concert also saw Philip Thompson's most notable con-tribution to the Pulp repertoire, in the form of a song called 'Disco Baby': "That was my claim to fame," says Pip. "At the time we wrote it, I was listening to Public Image, and that was my weak attempt at doing Jah Wobble. I was just messing about on the bass, and then Jarvis came in and we did a bit more, and then on the afternoon when we were setting up for the Rotherham concert, we decided to put it in – a real two-minute job."

"It went down much better than you'd have thought, actually," remembers Glen Marshall of the concert. "It was quite a reasonable performance. There wasn't a massive crowd or anything, but nothing went disastrously wrong. It was just the naïveté of our situation: when we turned up, Jarvis just had his guitar and his plectrum – we didn't have any amplifiers. We had to borrow everything from this other group, The Naughtiest Girl Was A Monitor – they couldn't believe that we were a band trying to get gigs, and we were pinching all their equipment."

Pip also remembers the slightly aghast response from the headlining band. "It was the time of the electronics scene in Sheffield, and Naughtiest Girl wanted it to be all dark and moody. They were talking to the lighting bloke about all these effects they wanted, and we were sat there with this really, really shitty set of instruments. I just remember them saying, 'Are they fucking taking it serious?'"

After the show, Pulp were offered a gig at Sheffield's Hallamshire Hotel by Bob Eady, from local band The Defective Turtles. "He came up after and offered us a show," Peter Dalton remembers. "I said, 'Why, do you think we're good?' and he said, 'No, I thought you were crap, but I think people will like you.' At least he was being honest."[36]

Nevertheless, it seemed like a not inauspicious début – especially for a concert that had come together in less than 12 hours. "We were there at midnight," remembers Glen, "and we suddenly realised that we had all this equipment we couldn't get home. I had to call me dad to come and fetch us – it was that sort of planning."

Playing live in public was a big step forward for Pulp, but soon after the Rotherham concert they found themselves a drummer short with the departure of Mark Swift. "Dixie was absolutely brilliant at keeping time," says Philip Thompson, "but I'm not quite sure how much he was into it. At the Rotherham concert, we borrowed an electric drumkit – like ours, I think it only had a bass and a snare or something – and I remember him coming away saying, 'Oh, that's easy!'"

"I don't think Dixie was bothered, particularly," reckons one schoolfriend. "He just wasn't that musical." David Lockwood agrees: "Dixie didn't actually like it, I don't think. Like me, he just wasn't keen on performing."

The new drummer was another schoolfriend, Jimmy Sellars. Like the others, he'd known Jarvis through most of school: "I can't actually remember how I got involved with the band. Probably I just happened to be around, and they said, 'Do you want to play?'"

Jimmy was actually more of a pianist than a drummer, but he was still the most accomplished musician so far to have joined Pulp. "He was another one who we weren't too sure about," says Glen Marshall. "He was actually quite professional, which added another dimension when he joined because he could play keyboards quite competently – not brilliant, but Dolly was sort of like, 'That's not the sort of sound we want.' I think what impressed us was when he came in and played 'The Entertainer', that easy riff you can play on the piano that sounds really impressive."

Jimmy's first onstage appearance came within a few weeks of joining, when Pulp played second-from-bottom of the bill at an all-day *Bouquet Of Steel* festival at the newly opened Leadmill club on August 16, 1980. The Leadmill at the time was a far cry from the nationally renowned, multi-million pound concern it has since become. "It was just an old bus garage at that time," remembers Pip. "There was no bar, and no real stage – just this platform. There were bands on all day, and we just happened to be second on. There was hardly anybody there, with it being the middle of the afternoon – it was mostly all these old hippies who'd been involved in getting the Leadmill opened.

"When we came on, we were throwing spice – that was the slang Shef-field word for sweets – into the audience. It ended up with everyone throwing all these oranges and sweets back at us! It was just riotous. One of these guys in the audience had this son who looked like he was three or four years younger than us, and he had this real punky, spiky green hair. He was just going lairy, throwing the stuff back at us. So I think he enjoyed himself.

"We borrowed this tape delay feedback system off Jimmy's brother for 'Message To The Martians', so we could make even more weird noises – that was what that one was about, just making noises. We had a rehearsal at Jimmy's house once, and played 'Message To The Martians' for about 20 minutes. At the end of it, his mum came in and said, 'Ooh, that's really nice, can you play it again?' It was that sort of thing. Years later, I heard *This Is Hardcore* on the radio when it first came out, and the first thing I thought was, 'The strings in that are 'Message To The Martians'!' It couldn't be anything else."

The oft-repeated story that Jimmy Sellars stopped playing 30 seconds into *Stepping Stone* is, apparently, untrue: "If that happened, then I'd have remembered it – I definitely never stopped playing during a song onstage. I just remember desperately trying to keep time on the drums, and being very nervous."

It is true, however, that Philip Thompson caused untold hilarity (and secured his place in Pulp legend) by falling into the audience during 'Stepping Stone'. "It was the first time we knew feedback existed," says Jarvis. "We'd been playing through the record player at home, and could never play that loud because the neighbours would complain. He walked away from the amp, hoping it would stop, and ran out of stage."[37]

In the audience was future Pulp member Peter Boam, then a 16-year-old from Chesterfield who was just beginning to promote band nights in Sheffield pubs and play with his own band, Mortuary In Wax: "It wasn't their best day," he reckons. "They were even more ramshackle than usual. They suddenly had this 2,000-watt PA instead of playing in the school hall with a 30-watt radiogram or whatever. Very quickly, they got a reputation as the crappest band in Sheffield – the absolute crappest band, because they couldn't play. But they were entertaining, so everybody went to see them, even though they were crap. Very ramshackle. Very B-52s influenced, I'd say."

Also present at the Leadmill concert was Russell Senior, a 19-year-old champion of Sheffield music and frontman of a bedroom band called The Bath Bankers – which also gave its name to the fanzine that he produced. *The Bath Banker* would have the distinction of becoming the first publication ever to carry an interview with Jarvis, after Russell met the group backstage following the Leadmill concert. "Pulp were raucous and fun with wit and humour," remembers Russell. "They did a funny version of '(I'm Not Your) Stepping Stone' and the bassist fell offstage during it, which was all highly amusing."[38]

Jarvis and Russell quickly became friends, thanks in no small part to the other reason Jarvis was fast becoming a minor local celebrity: his Saturday job in the local fish market. "He had a very convincing patter for selling fish," remembers Russell with amusement, "with lots of sexual innuendo around it. People would ask, 'Have you got any crabs on you, cock?' and he'd say, 'Ooh missus, the trouble with me,' and scratch himself, or, 'I've got a lovely piece of tail end for your husband, love.' He was one of the best performing fishmongers I'd ever seen.[39] He'd charm all these old ladies into buying more crabs than they needed and things. They loved him: he'd be, like, 'Would you like an extra claw, Mrs Hayworth?' – so the sexual innuendo was there at an early age, really. That was what brought us together. He was a very good fishmonger."[40]

"This was part of my mum's drive for me to make friends," says Jarvis of his first job, which happened to come along around the same time as everybody from school was starting to have lots of groovy parties: "It was quite exciting going along to these parties and trying to snog girls, but of course smelling of fish at parties is not so good. So every night after work I'd scrub my hands with bleach for 20 minutes, but then I'd go out with these pink shiny hands that smell vaguely of fish and bleach. Pretty sad really . . ."[41]

One of Jarvis' experiences in the fish market would soon be documented in the infamous early Pulp classic, 'I Scrubbed The Crabs That Killed Sheffield'. "That was quite a good, intelligent little song," says Glen. "That was typical of Jarvis – taking a song from everyday experiences but putting a different slant on it."

The day after the Leadmill show, Pulp made the first of many, many appearances in the tiny upstairs room at Sheffield's Hallamshire Hotel. The Hallamshire, on West Street, was one of the most popular places for local bands to play, and over the next couple of years would practically become Pulp's home venue. "The Hallamshire was quite a good place to play," remembers Glen Marshall. "Whereas the school hall were like a vast cavern with nobody moving, the Hallamshire had everyone packed in, stood on seats at the back, and everybody had had a few drinks – at least you'd got an atmosphere. I think that's why those shows were the most successful early ventures into live performance."

Equipment was still lacking at first. "We just used to turn up without any gear," says Jim Sellars, "and say, 'Can we borrow yours?' After they'd set up, we'd just get on stage and start using their instruments. We just assumed that that was what you did. This guy was saying, 'No way, you're not using my drums,' and we were going, 'Well we can't go on then, 'cos we haven't got any.' He must have let me in the end, because I remember bashing the shit out of them – all the drums were knackered! I'd smashed the sticks, and ended up cutting my finger on the snare or something and splashing blood all over them as well . . ."

"For the first couple of concerts at the Hallamshire," says Pip, "I remember we'd go on the bus with all the instruments, which was a little bit bizarre. You could get the 95 from Jarvis' house, it cost 2½p, and it'd drop you off more or less just outside the Hallamshire. Because I didn't have a case for it, I'd keep the bass in a binbag, and we carried the drums around in this battered old suitcase. Everybody used to be fairly shocked when we'd turn up with all this stuff, because most of the bands we supported must have been 25, if not older – they'd been through work and everything, and took it dead serious. Then these young kids would turn up with no equipment, but ideas about what they wanted to do – and we'd get on and do it.

"The sound wasn't punkish, exactly. It was quite a hollow, tinny,

Devo-y sound . . . a bit like The Regents – not many people will have heard of them now, but they had this one hit with '7 Teen'. I don't think all that much has changed, except Jarvis getting better musicians around him, and being able to afford better production. I think a lot of people thought that, if [he had] not become as big as he has, then he was definitely going to become something in music. A lot of people got friendly with him because they thought he was going to make it. When we first started, everyone was trying to do this dark electronic stuff, and then there were all these funk bands, with 15 people on stage, and then there was this rock-y, new wave scene. But all through that, Pulp were always different, always themselves, and I think that's why so many people latched on to them in Sheffield.

"You could tell then that Jarvis was decent at writing songs, and he was gradually learning at that. He could play guitar, but you wouldn't have said he was a musician really. Jarvis' mum used to have to put up with a lot, though – we used to kick her and her friends out into the kitchen so we could practise in the living room. I think she deserves a mention for her part in our development!

"We went down quite well with most of the audiences. When we started doing the Hallamshire gigs, it was mainly people from school who'd come and see us, but fairly quickly, a lot of people from the Poly or the University suddenly picked up – the art school types. A lot of people from other bands would come along to see us as well . . . Sheffield music at that time was all serious electronics, and I think they were amazed that we had the cheek, they were just going, 'What the hell are they doing?' Right from when we started, there was always a really good atmosphere when we played. I noticed that more after I left. I think the main reason most of us were doing it – me and Dixie, and Jamie and Jimmy as well – was that it was a laugh. You know – you were in a band! And you enjoyed yourself."

Jimmy Sellars: "We always went down well, I think, because we were entertaining – people laughed. Jarvis was always the main focus – if anything, it might have been musically crap, but it was visually entertaining. It was the time when we were in the sixth form, 16 or 17, and people were starting to go out for the first time – go downtown, get into drinking, watching bands, stuff like that. People always enjoyed seeing us, even if it was just for a laugh."

Jarvis was developing his skills as a songwriter, but, as Glen Marshall points out, "I don't think anybody paid much attention to what he'd written. It was just whether it produced a decent sound, and I think people were surprised when it did. Jarvis' vocal chords at the time weren't as hot as they are now, and he tended to have the microphone pressed right up against his lips, so you couldn't always make out exactly what he was saying. But he always had that style of talking within the song, and he'd always got that sort of storyline involved in the way he'd put the song together. He always used to jump around like he does now, but not so much on stage."

"When something was going badly, or at least Jarvis thought it was," remembers Fungus, "he'd go into his writhing-around-on-the-floor thing. Because he was tall and thin but wore old, baggy clothes, he'd look very strange when he'd stick his legs up in the air like he was in electric shock or something. That generally got the audience back on his side."

While the vast majority of the songwriting was now shouldered by Jarvis, Peter Dalton's role was still a central one in early Pulp. "He was as into it as Jarvis," reckons Glen Marshall. "It was them two, really, that were the mainstay of the group. Everybody else had offered something, but those two were dedicated." He'd developed an appealingly squiggly synth style, and was responsible for a lot of the bizarre musical and visual ideas that characterised Pulp *circa* 1980/81. "Dolly was always very faddish, very into the latest trends," remembers Philip Thompson. "I remember one day, he turned up and said, '*A cappella!* We've all got to go out and buy microphones!' We were like, 'Get real!' He was always coming up with ideas like that."

"He was actually a very talented musician," says Peter Boam. "He added something unique that made Pulp very different – I mean, musically they were always on the brink of being shambolic, but they somehow managed to transcend that."

Their next show, at Peter Boam's Ritblat Tube night at the Royal Hotel (which also saw Mark Swift return to the drumstool when Jimmy Sellars injured his hand and was relegated to singing harmony vocals with Jarvis on a song called 'You're Too Cruel' – "Not that I can sing for toffee, but there you go") was reviewed in the local *NMX* fanzine by Martin X-Russian: "*. . . their music seems to be a mixed bag of all things modern, as if they listen to the John Peel show every night in an endless quest for influences. They look so young you think they ought to be too busy studying for their O-levels to be messing about with these damned pop groups, but I understand one of them works in the fish market. Anyway, they don't appear to have seen enough of life to be obsessed with doom and despair, instead covering more superficial subjects such as 'Message From The Martians' and 'Disco Baby'. Despite comparatively elementary musical ability and a slight togetherness problem they're a fun band and definitely one to watch in the future.*"[42]

It was in pursuit of a solution to that "slight togetherness problem" mentioned in the *NMX* review that, shortly after the concert at the Royal,

Philip Thompson was asked to leave Pulp. "I turned up at Jarvis' one day for a practice," he remembers, "and they said, 'We've had a meeting, and we've decided we need somebody who can play the bass a bit better.' Basically they were saying I was shit, which was fair enough because looking back I was, but I was a bit upset at the time because I'd been enjoying it. I was offered the job of Artistic Director or something, and I thought, 'Fuck off! I don't want to ponce around, I want to play in the band!' We stayed mates, but I was a bit narked about it at the time. It was sort of a progression – Jamie was slightly better than me, and then it got into people like Simon Hinkler who were more musical."

Pulp now consisted of Jarvis, Dolly, Jimmy Sellars and new bassist Jamie Pinchbeck. "His dad had a car like a tank," remembers Jim. "It was this big estate car, and you could get all four of us and the drumkit in the back."

Musically, Jamie was a notch or so above Pip or Fungus, having previously played in a City School heavy rock band called Satan, "although we never played anywhere – we just practised at home for a while. I never learned to read music or anything – it was just a matter of picking up a guitar and practising."

He also made occasional contributions to the songwriting, as David Lockwood recalls: "Jamie was the first one other than Jarvis and Peter to try and write something else, which was a song called 'Devil Doll'. It did get played I think, but other than that I don't think it ever went much further than Jamie's imagination!" He would have slightly better luck with a song called '(What's Wrong With) My Girl', which would become an occasional fixture in Pulp's live set. "I think he loved the adulation he got," says Fungus, "and to be up on stage at the Hallamshire or wherever with everybody shouting, 'Jamie One-String!' Even though it was kind of mocking, he was still up there doing something, outside of the character that he normally was. It was escapism, really."

"I wouldn't say Jamie was in with the trendy element of life at that time," says Glen Marshall. "He was quite mainstream – into heavy rock and everything. The thing about Jamie was that he was dedicated – he actually did learn how to play the bass."

The new line-up's first appearance was at the George IV pub – a concert which also saw Pulp's stage presentation take on a new dimension. "We had a big sheet up at the back with 'PULP' written across it, and loads of lights and stuff on the stage," remembers Jim Sellars. "It was just to make it look more interesting and grab people's attention a bit more."

Over the coming months, the stage presentation would become increasingly elaborate. Jarvis: "One of my favourite groups was Devo, and they used to wear boiler suits and stuff like that, so we came up with the idea that we could do the same kind of thing. We got some curtain material from school and got me sister to make it into clothes for us. That only lasted a couple of concerts though, because it looked stupid. Looking back, I can see how people had trouble taking us seriously, I really can."[43]

The concert was followed up by a return to the hall of City School for two concerts to raise money for the school to buy a new computer. "Everybody had to pay to get in," says Julie Hobson, "and some of us were standing on the door for them. I just remember Jarvis and his mates on the stage being silly. It ended up with Swifty and loads of kids from our year and above pogoing in the middle of the hall, just going really crazy, and all the little kids standing round watching them, thinking 'My God'."

The start of 1981 saw Pulp competing (at 24 hours' notice) in a *Sheffield Star* talent contest at the YMCA, "which was a bit of a laugh," said Jarvis, even though they didn't win. "People in the audience slag and you get grannies going [. . .] The bloke said 'like the attack, like the attack'. The judges were a panel of Sunday school teachers." Also competing was an even younger Sheffield band, Vector 7-7 from Frecheville High School, whose members included future Pulpsters Wayne Furniss and David Hinkler.

"Visually, Pulp were an oddball bunch," remembers David. "There was Jarvis with his National Health glasses and, well, just the way he was. Then there was Jamie, who almost had a dandelion fluffball hairstyle – he was just a big ball of blond hair. He had a really strange way of playing the bass – he'd pluck the strings upwards, really rapidly. And Pete Dalton was jumping about all over the place, very active and over-the-top. As well as guitar and synthesiser, he'd be moving around and hitting bits of percussion: he was never in the same place twice.

"The sound wasn't too good because obviously the guitars and amplifiers weren't very good, plus, like us, they were only 16 or 17, so the musicianship wasn't great. But you could tell that behind all that was an excellent songwriter, and they sounded very, very promising." Sadly, Pulp still came away from the contest empty-handed, other than the helpful advice from the judges that they needed to be "a bit tighter".

A return to the Hallamshire followed, witnessed by local musician Nick Robinson (then with The Comsat Angels, and later a member of Dig Vis Drill, who would one day tour with Pulp): "In those days, I used to check out the opposition, as we saw them then, and I saw a mention of Pulp in the *Sheffield Star*, so I thought I'd go down and have a look. I can't remember much about the concert; just that I really enjoyed them. They had this really quirky sound, and lots of people were jumping about. They had a complete lack of interest in being musicians – they weren't showing off or anything like that. It was more image than music, really – they were into wacky clothes, standing in a line. Jarvis wasn't out at the front particularly, but he seemed to be attracting some attention – he had some kind of presence, even then."

Glen Marshall: "Jarvis always perpetuated the same odd movements, the same mannerisms and eccentricities – just at a more advanced level as time's gone on. He was always very clever, but very individualistic. He was very popular, very much a part of our group, but in some senses he was a one-off as well, and nobody could replicate anything he did or imitate him – he was always doing his own thing. When he was part of something, he was also his own man, sort of thing. He's quite good at being able to bring himself into the team and take himself back out, isn't he?"

"He always seemed special," reckons Jamie Pinchbeck. "It's hard to say why – maybe just the way he looked, but he always had talent. He was quite a popular person at school, not really too insecure in any way. He dealt with hecklers quite well – he always had the wit to cope with that sort of thing. He was always good at talking to the audience, although not to the extent he is now, obviously."

Pulp's gradual climb up the Sheffield band pecking order continued apace with their first slot as headline band in their own right – at a Wimpy burger restaurant on the Fargate shopping precinct. "Our payment for the night was something off the menu," remembers Jim Sellars. "I remember I wasn't bothered about having anything to eat, and Saskia said, 'Can I have your cheeseburger then?' so I said fair enough."

The support band were Pulp's City School cohorts Crude, featuring Jon Short on bass. "Pulp had been going for a couple of years," he remembers, "and then we'd done this Crude band, which was really just a laugh. It was blue to start off with, but we'd had to stop when we started doing gigs: we changed all the lyrics so that 'Premature Ejaculation' became 'Video Invasion', and 'Blond Pubes' became 'Want You'. Anyway, our first-ever gig was at this Wimpy Bar on Fargate, supporting Pulp, and they well and truly humiliated us because they were very good."

The double-bill was successful enough for the two bands to make a follow-up appearance a couple of weeks later, at the community centre just down the road from the school. Jon Short again: "We'd had this singer called Lloyd, who was a really great frontman – he used to model himself on David Coverdale, and he was brilliant at throwing the microphone stand around, but he was tone deaf. So we decided to get rid of him, and Ricky did the singing at this concert at Stradbroke. Ricky was just one of those people that everybody loved at school, so we did the first set and went down a storm. As it happened, all of Shep's gang came in, all the people who'd left the year before, and they thought we were great, had a real good laugh. And then Pulp came on, and for some reason, probably because everyone was a bit too drunk, people started messing around. The crucial moment came when this lad Watto started plonking away on a piano that was on the floor, next to the stage. It degenerated into anarchy, and Jarvis just walked off. We were all having a laugh about it, thinking, 'Oh yeah, we've blown 'em off stage,' and then we went downstairs and Jarvis was crying. You realised then, I suppose, that he was the only one who was taking it seriously."

To top it all, that same night Jimmy Sellars announced that he was leaving Pulp . . . to join Crude. "There wasn't any bad feeling," says Jim now. "It was just that I was in a few bands at the time, and it was too much – I had to go over to one or the other." It must've been something of a blow for Jarvis, but any despondency must have been short-lived: within a month, Pulp had acquired a new drummer in the form of 15-year-old Wayne Furniss. Wayne (known as 'Foetus' thanks to his diminutive presence) had been Vector 7-7's guitarist, but he'd been taking percussion lessons at school and spotted the "Pulp need drummer" advert in the local Virgin Megastore. He approached Jarvis at a concert by then-fancied local goth combo New Model Soldier at the Hallamshire, got the job on the spot, and within a couple of weeks was onstage with Pulp at the Hallamshire.

With this new addition, the 'classic' early Pulp line-up was complete. The quartet of Jarvis, Dolly, Jamie and Wayne would remain together for the rest of Pulp 1's natural lifespan, as the band continued to grow in popularity, make their first recordings and take their first tentative steps outside Sheffield. "As time went on," says David Lockwood, "they gradually got more musical and less schoolboy-ish as better people came in. I don't know whether that was Jarvis' goal, or whether he just wanted to keep it moving. I think perhaps it was more important to him for it to continue than for it to get better as such."

Gigs came thick and fast through spring and summer 1981, helped no doubt by some of Jarvis' amusing publicity stunts. He and Wayne earned the grand sum of 24½p each from busking on Fargate one afternoon, and then there was the Pulp rock festival in Jarvis' backyard on Mansfield Road ("Just like Glastonbury, only with about 12 people," says Wayne). The crowning glory, however, came on June 3, when Jarvis Cocker, Wayne Furniss and Jamie Pinchbeck were arrested for flyposting in the name of the Rock Against Flyposters campaign. Peter Boam: "At the time, there was loads of punk bands and new wave bands in and around

Sheffield, and everyone was flyposting. The *Sheffield Star* came out saying, 'We're going to have an anti-flyposting campaign!' So Jarvis did Rock Against Flyposting, which he flyposted all over Sheffield!"

Pulp's increasing confidence after a year of gigging is evidenced by the fact that, by that summer, they felt ready to make some professional recordings. The Naughtiest Girl Was A Monitor had recommended local eccentric Ken Patten's home studio, so after much saving up and scraping-together of money, on August 7, 1981 Pulp's first demo was cut. Patten was an ex-employee of Radio Sheffield and champion of local music whose semi-detached council house doubled, Joe Meek-style, as a recording studio. Jarvis: "He was about 55 and had a studio set up in his house – you recorded in his bedroom and he had closed-circuit television to see you weren't messing around. And because his wife didn't like the noise, you had to use this Symmons kit – not a real kit, just these plastic pads.

"He claimed to have invented the Vocoder some time in 1950. He said, 'You've heard 'Mr. Blue Sky'? How much do you think they cost?' So I said, 'I dunno, about £2000.' 'Well, I've made one – fifty pence.' He claimed to have got throat mikes used in World War II bomber planes, that worked on vibration. You could plug it into a synth and then, if you opened your mouth, you'd get the Vocoder effect. The 50p was for a toilet roll leading to a mike because it was very quiet!"[44]

"It was strange in that it was in a semi-detached house in Handsworth," remembers Wayne. "I remember getting a headache at one point, and his wife gave me some smelling salts. I'll never touch *them* again. I played the drums upstairs and he had his little mixing desk in a back room somewhere. I couldn't really drum properly on this plastic kit he had, but at the time I thought it turned out all right. I wouldn't mind hearing it again, actually."

Sadly, no copies of the demo in its entirety are known to survive – only one track, 'What Do You Say?' survives, thanks to its inclusion on the following year's *Your Secret's Safe With Us* compilation album. Described by Jarvis in a local fanzine of the time as being about "waking up and finding you haven't got the same face you went to bed with – very existentialist"[45]. 'What Do You Say?' is a tuneful, uptempo, minor-key number, held together by Jamie's nimble, ska-influenced bassline. On first examination, the neatly rhyming lyrics – *"Woke up in the morning/ Raised my head still yawning/ But I was in for a surprise"* – are pure English homework cuteness, but lines like *"And so I rest my case/ I don't want another's face"* suggest that there's possibly something deeper going on.

'Please Don't Worry', meanwhile, was probably the closest that the early Pulp had to a theme song – it made its live début sometime around the end of 1980, and would remain a more-or-less constant feature of the set for the next three years. The lyrics – *"A true blue experience is what you need now/ You need to know when and you need to know how/ Ambiguous wording clouds the issue once more/ You'll never know what it was that you saw"* – are clearly about something but it's not quite clear what, and the loveable chorus and Dolly's typically wibbly synthesiser hook make the whole thing impossible to dislike.

'Wishful Thinking' was similarly one of the longest-lived of Jarvis' early songwriting efforts, and (uniquely amongst the early tunes) managed to make it on to Pulp's début album *It* two years later. The Pulp 1 version had a harder, more guitar-based arrangement, and actually carries the song more successfully than the softer, more acoustic cut that appears on the album. "It's another one that kind of embarrasses me," said Jarvis years later, "because it's a very direct love song – I remember who it's about, and it just gets me. But it's all right."[46]

The final track on the demo, 'Turkey Mambo Momma', was another quirky, uptempo, slightly Devo-esque number. Jarvis jabbers on semi-comprehensibly about being trapped on a South Sea island by a woman with voodoo powers, Dolly toots away on his cornet, and a good time is had by all. Like everything else on the demo, it's also a demonstration of how far the songwriting had developed in the year-and-a-half since 'Shakespeare Rock'. As one early member of the group remembers, "The first few songs were quite basic, but by around '81 we had some quite good stuff, I thought. We were big anti-rock: the Bunnymen were influences, and Devo, Wire, XTC. We never consciously decided our style, it just evolved."

Sounding quite a lot smoother than live recordings from the same period, Pulp's earliest studio recordings still stand up today – the songs on the Patten demo show the Pulp of 1981 to have already developed a sound of their own, with all the individual band members showing themselves to be competent and distinctive on their instruments, gelling together to make a sound that recalls (amongst others) XTC, The Specials and The Cure's first album. While Jarvis' voice sounds thinner and perhaps less assured than it would 18 months later when *It* was recorded, it's still likeable enough, and more than capable of holding a tune. Jamie: "It turned out quite well – I remember we thought it was brilliant at the time. It was just something we wanted to do to give to people to try and get gigs, and maybe attract labels."

While Pulp braced themselves for the slew of offers they would surely receive in the wake of the many copies of the demo they sent out to various record companies, gigging continued in Sheffield. The audience of one show at The Mill is remembered by Wayne as including "these two big blokes saying we were shit all night – then they came up and asked us how you got a gig in Sheffield, and they turned out to be The Mau-Maus, who were quite big on the punk scene at that time." And then there was a night at the George IV at which "Jarvis got upset and threw himself under a table and cried because he was fed up with people watching him jump around rather than listen to the music. He actually said, 'We'll not bring any instruments next week, I'll just come along and throw myself around a bit.'"

Some rather more encouraging feedback came from *NMX* fanzine in a review of a September 22 appearance at the Hallamshire: *"Pulp look about five years older than when I saw them a year ago and they're much better, great in fact. They remind me of Big In Japan (remember Big In Japan? If anyone's got a copy of their EP they want to part with let me know), The Dole, I'm So Hollow, Cult Figures, Soft Boys and a million garage punk/pop bands with a touch of Sixties weirdness in their hearts and guitars. The singer wins my nomination for any snappy dresser of the month award going, psychedelically tasteless in faded pink trousers, pukey green shirt, suede jacket, glasses and dorky non-hairdo, and they deserve credit for trying to stir interest among usually apathetic audiences. After all, when a group stick something like a cross between a dunce's cap and a multicolour cardboard KKK mask over their heads one tends to sit up and ask why? Not to mention the dancers, two girls in black, complete with veils, who would undoubt-edly be in the Human League now if they'd been down the Crazy Daizy on the right night. The dramatic impression was spoiled somewhat when one of them fell off the stage and I never did discover why they were carrying toilet rolls (unless they were just nicking them from the pub), but it all contributed to the sense of occasion."*[47]

That night was the first time the band employed Jarvis' sister Saskia and her friend Mandy Hill as dancers. They dressed in black (complete with veils) and draped the band in toilet paper (a gimmick that would serve Pulp well – see the cover of *Freaks*). "They were there to add some flair to the occasion," says Glen. "The initial thing was that everyone stood still and played their guitars – there was no life to it. So one of the ideas was that Saskia would come on and add a bit of glamour to it."

On this particular night, the effect was slightly spoilt when Saskia tripped over the drums and broke the only light they had on stage: "That was really embarrassing. I was drunk – I'd had half a lager and half a cider, then half a lager again, and I fell off stage!"

The cardboard hat gimmick, inspired by Jarvis' favourite group Devo, had the four members of the band standing in a line with their multicol-oured conical headgear spelling out the word "PULP". To complete the image, the band had been cultivating the regulation Pulp hairstyle: "Peter started to grow his hair like Jarvis'," remembers Julie Hobson. "Sort of short at the back, with a silly bit at the front. They all started to have this mop – Jamie's was natural, but Jarvis started to grow his bigger and shaggier, and Peter grew this bit over his eyes. Both of them dyed their hair orange as well."

It was an exciting time for the group – in a very short time, Pulp had moved from a half-serious Friday night hobby to a fully legitimate pop group that was beginning to attract some deserved acclaim and recognition. Not bad for a band whose eldest member had only just turned 18. The only way was up . . .

Chapter 2

On Saturday, October 10, 1981, John Peel played a Radio One Roadshow at Sheffield Polytechnic. Jarvis and Jamie went along and, after much plucking-up of courage, found Peel afterwards and gave him a copy of the Ken Patten tape. "It was 50p to get in," Jarvis would tell Peel in an interview 14 years later. "I gave you the first demo tape we'd ever done, and you said you'd listen to it in the car on the way home and I thought, 'Mmm, I wonder about that.' And then about a week and a half later, I got a phone call at me mum's house from your producer saying that you wanted us to come and do a session, so we were very excited."[48]

The Peel session was, of course, the most significant thing to happen to the early Pulp. By autumn 1981, they'd just about reached the stage where they could draw a respectable audience as headlining band in one of Sheffield's smaller pub venues. Appearing on national radio – and not just national radio, but on British radio's most-listened to and most respected alternative music programme – was a massive leap forward.

Exactly four weeks after the Sheffield roadshow, on Saturday November 7, Jarvis, Peter, Jamie and Wayne piled excitedly into the back of a hired van and began the journey to the BBC's Maida Vale studios in London. The band's meagre equipment was augmented for the occasion by, amongst other odds and ends, the school xylophone and a bass amp borrowed from classmate Jon Short, who came along for the ride. "I said, 'I'll lend you the amp if I can come,' so me and my mate Lee Fletcher went down – Lee was the number one Jarvis fan back then. Anyway, we set off at about four in the morning in this really grotty Transit van that we'd hired for the day. It took about five hours to get down. We parked at Maida Vale, and the hire driver put this note on the windscreen that said 'Broke down' so nobody would arrest him."

The session was produced by Dale Griffin, formerly drummer with Seventies glamsters Mott The Hoople, whose musicianly credentials were a long way from Pulp's poppier, anti-rock, anti-virtuoso approach. "I think he kind of thought ... well, we *were* just a bunch of daft kids,"[49] remembers Jarvis. Jamie also recalls there being a feeling that band and producer might not be on quite the same wavelength: "When he first came in, and he had long hair and cowboy boots, we were wondering whether he'd be the right person for us. Saying that, though, it turned out well in the end."

Indeed, Griffin may well have been exactly the right person to nurse Pulp through the 12-hour recording session, reconciling their youthful energy and enthusiasm with a more serious, professional approach to actually getting something on to tape. Jon Short: "Although they'd done the Ken Patten stuff, they were quite naïve in terms of using a studio, and it was Dale Griffin's job to produce it. In 12 hours, I think he did a remarkable job."

The tracks chosen for the session reflect the fact that Pulp were perhaps most comfortable with the songs they'd already recorded with Ken Patten a few months previously: 'Turkey Mambo Momma', 'Please Don't Worry' and 'Wishful Thinking' all make a reappearance. 'Please Don't Worry' was embellished for the occasion with a homemade syndrum (built by someone in Wayne's class), eliciting a nonplussed reaction from Griffin: "That was the main bit where he had this look of disgust on his face," remembers Jarvis. "You know how you used to get these things in *Practical Electronics* where it'd teach you how to build your own syndrum? It was made out of an old electronic calculator with one of these pressure-sensitive burglar alarm mats that you have under the carpet. We were in this posh studio and there's the drummer sat there hitting this mat with a calculator attached to it, and this stupid *Pzzzzzzz!* noise coming out of it. I think he just thought, 'Mmm, I'd like this to finish soon so I can go home.'"[50]

The fourth track was a newly written number called 'Refuse To Be Blind', and was the cause of some embarrassment for Jarvis when he played the track in 1995: "I suppose it's because I'm the singer . . . it just sounds like I'm trying too hard. It's a bit like when you find a bit of poetry you wrote when you were 17 and you try to say everything about the world in three sentences. It always seems a bit too much. The main thing that makes me cringe is that we didn't know how to finish the song, and we were looking at all the bits of exciting machinery in the studio that we'd never seen before – 'Oh, what does that one do?' The bloke started turning the knob, and the voice started going [daft sci-fi voice] 'Re-fuuse to be blii-ind'. It sounded like a Dalek, and we thought that was really good, so we made him do that, even though he didn't really want to. We went back up to Sheffield in the van thinking that was really fantastic."[51]

Despite Jarvis' lack of fondness for the track today, the band held 'Refuse To Be Blind' in high regard at the time – with its tempo changes, squelchy synth noises and long instrumental section, it was certainly the most musically impressive thing that Pulp had so far attempted. "I always liked that one – it stuck around for a while," remembers Jamie. "As songs dropped out of the set and got replaced by other ones, that was one that was there for the rest of the time that I was in the band. When we recorded it, I remember putting two bass lines on, and the producer going, 'What do you want to do that for?' But we left them both on, and it turned out quite well in the end."

"I always thought that was a bit of a classic," confesses future manager Tony Perrin, "and I was sad that that one got dropped when they went in to do the album, although I suppose it wouldn't have fit in too well. It's a shame that the first record that they made couldn't have been an extension of where they were at that time. Obviously they were on to something, then the group kind of split up. If that group had stayed together for another 8 months and made an album, I think it would have been a fairer starting point for the group than the *It* album."

The recording and mixing of the session drew to a close around midnight, and Pulp made their way back to Sheffield in the Transit. "We were really tired on the journey back," remembers Jon, "and most of us fell asleep. I remember waking up and seeing a motorway sign for Mansfield, then looking across at the driver and seeing him fast asleep on the steering wheel. It was like slow motion – next thing, we hit the cat's eyes on the hard shoulder and it made a really loud noise, which woke up the driver, and he wrenched the steering wheel so we were back on the road . . . I'd like to say that I woke him up myself and saved Pulp's lives, but I wasn't quite quick enough."

The session was broadcast on Peel's show a week and a half later, and gave a lot of people their first taste of Pulp. Local musician Murray Fenton's reaction was probably typical of most of those who heard the session at the time: "I didn't know what to make of them, to be honest. I mean they weren't really my cup of tea, but to their credit – and it's still to their credit to this day – they were one-offs, even then. Everything they've done through all their time together, in one form or another, has always been quite off the beaten track. Anyway, my first impression of them was that they were just odd. I mean, I wasn't exactly a stranger to odd music, but . . . they were odd in that they looked odd while the music was quite accessible, and ramshackle as well. It's really hard to describe, especially 15 years later."

For some of those who had followed Pulp in Sheffield before the session, however, it came as a mild disappointment: "It seemed like a very bland representation of songs that I knew quite well," says David Hinkler, who had been acquainted with Pulp since the Leadmill concert a year and a half earlier. "Compared to how they sounded live, they lost a lot of action – they were a very visual band at the time as well."

It's probably true that the session failed to capture entirely the magic of Pulp live, but it's probably also true that no studio recording could quite convey the "carnival of lunacy" (as *Melody Maker*'s Frank Worrell would put it in Pulp's first music press feature a couple of months later) that was the essence of the band. Whatever, the session still more than stands up today – four tracks of taut, upbeat, likeable pop.

All this, though, is really beside the point. What mattered at the time was that Pulp – four Sheffield schoolkids aged between 16 and 18 – *had done a Peel session*. That fact alone transformed the group's position in the Sheffield scene almost overnight. Very quickly, they went from odd fanzine articles and sporadic gigs on the Sheffield pub circuit, occasionally headlining at smaller venues like the Hallamshire and the George IV, to support slots with big local names like Artery and The Danse Society; headlining slots at the Limit; an appearance as the only Sheffield group on a compilation album of northern bands; out-of-town gigs; and even pieces in the national music press (and, of course, on the front of the *Sheffield Star* – "they wanted to take pictures of us in school uniform and 'stage gear' – you know, before and after," remembers Jarvis, "but we refused to do that"[52]). Requests from Pulp's burgeoning fanbase, both at school and on the wider Sheffield scene, would also mean that the session would be repeated twice over the next three months – making it the first Peel session in the programme's history to be broadcast three times in such a short period. David Hinkler: "Surrounding the Peel session, Pulp were very much the band to watch – they got a lot of attention. Just the idea of being asked to do it, regardless of how it turned out, did them a lot of good."

"They caught people on the hop, really," says Murray Fenton. "There was a bit of a splash about it in the local paper and stuff – everybody was like, 'God, who are these people?' Nobody had really heard of them beyond regional Sheffield gigs. And obviously it snowballed for them after that."

David Lockwood: "I thought it was pretty amazing when, after I left, they were getting such serious recognition, like the Peel Session. It was never my dream though – apart from all the early Pulp gigs I went along to, the only concert I've ever been to was Queen at Wembley."

The session also had a personal significance for Jarvis: "That was my main piece of armoury in my case to my mother to say that I didn't want to go to university. I had a place to go and do English at Liverpool University, but I really wanted to do the band. We'd been on national radio, so I thought, 'Ooh, yes, I could be a child star.' So she allowed me to defer my place and stay in Sheffield to do the band. Unfortunately, nobody else's parents were that liberal . . ."[53]

Days after the first broadcast of the Peel Session, Pulp were asked by Statik Records' Nigel Burnham to contribute to *Your Secret's Safe With Us*, a double-LP compilation of unsigned bands from Yorkshire, Lancashire and Teeside. Impressively, Pulp (who contributed the Ken Patten demo of 'What Do You Say?' because there wasn't time to do any new recordings) were the only Sheffield band included on the LP – overtaking many of the far more established groups they'd supported in the preceding 18 months.

Unfortunately, on its release in February 1982, the album itself (a successor to the far more successful *Hicks From The Sticks* collection from a couple of years earlier) turned out to be something of a damp squib. Despite some national music press coverage and the inclusion of some bands which had reasonable followings at the time (amongst them Doncaster's I Scream Brothers, The Chameleons, who would attract a moderate indie cult following through the '80s, and Indians In Moscow, whose Rob Mitchell would cross paths with Pulp much later), it failed to make the independent Top 30. "It was good to be asked," concludes Jarvis, "but Statik certainly showed no interest in us after it was released."[54]

Even so, Pulp's contribution to the album stands up very well among the proliferation of Joy Division and Japan copyists – they're one of the few bands there who have a sound that is unmistakably their own, rather than making futile attempts to make an impression by slavishly trying to emulate the trends of the time.

A more satisfying, if perhaps more modest, career step came on January 16, 1982, when Pulp played their first out-of-Sheffield gig at Bath University, supporting Sheffield synth-goth outfit New Model Soldier. Appearing in front of an audience of 1,500 students who'd never heard of them was quite a step up from playing in front of dozens, or at most a couple of hundred, at the Hallamshire or George IV. "They were quite into us too," remembers Peter Dalton. "It was our best response to date."[55]

The concert was organised by the university's New Wave Society – or more specifically, second-year Management Studies student Russell Senior. "After New Model Soldier's set, it ended in a riot because the bouncer got punched after all these punks arrived who didn't take kindly to all this racket. I was nearly expelled as a result – I was called into the bursar's office to account for my behaviour in organising this gig! My rough opinion on the live Pulp of that time was a likeable shambles, but not to be regarded seriously like, say, New Model Soldier who did 'Anorexic Beauty' and other dark and disturbing classics. I'd say that they were actually more of an influence when I joined Pulp than the early Pulp were. Jarvis at that time had undeniable charisma but was very much acting the clown, which tended to dilute it a bit for me."

A tape survives of Pulp's set from that night, providing a rare document of the early Pulp live experience. The show opens with a noisy guitar instrumental appropriately titled 'Thrash', and includes spiky, good-spirited renditions of most of the Ken Patten/Peel tracks ('Please Don't Worry' seems to get an especially good reception), plus versions of some songs, such as 'Teen Angst' and 'How Could You?', that would be included on the band's second demo tape, recorded a few months later. There's also a number called 'Zhivago', introduced by Jarvis as "that rare thing in modern music, a Russian love song". Driven along by an appropriately jerky, Eastern-sounding bassline, thudding, syncopated drums and some nicely dissonant guitar, it manages to bring about images of lost love amongst frozen wastes quite nicely while Jarvis sings about *"Days out in the snow"* that *"seem so long ago – love warmed the icy blast, but now those days are past . . ."* The encore, after a hysterical announcement from Russell (acting as MC for the evening), is the splendidly daft 1980 song, 'I Scrubbed The Crabs That Killed Sheffield'.

Apart from the rough edges, the main difference between studio Pulp and live Pulp *circa* 1981/82 is the atmosphere that comes through on the live recordings. It feels unmistakably like a real *group* playing together, four personalities bouncing off each other with all the energy, ambition and, at times, totally misplaced self-confidence that can only come from being 17 or 18, in a band and playing the biggest gig you've ever done. They can verge from super-earnest to super-daft within seconds, and take the audience with them. Musically, Dolly's wobbly Moog synth (made more wobbly still by copious use of the pitch-bend wheel) is much more prominent than on the studio recordings, complimenting the eccentricity of Jarvis' vocals and stage presence. Wayne's drumming embellishes rather than drives, peppering the proceedings with lots of *Hawaii Five-O* style rolls. And Jamie, while perhaps the least technically proficient of the four, is also the one who gels the whole thing together – his distinctive walking bass lines are usually pretty simple, but they also bring some much-needed solidity to the enterprise, playing a role not unlike the one that Candida Doyle would play years later. Subsequent incarnations of Pulp may have been more sophisticated musically, but recordings such as this show that the early Eighties model was still a great band, worthy in its way to stand alongside anything that came after.

A fortnight after the Bath concert, Pulp made their first appearance in the UK music press – a one-page feature in *Melody Maker* written by Frank Worrall, with photos taken by Marcus Featherby. Worrall seems quite taken with the group, pronouncing the Peel session to be "deliciously innocent pop" and finding himself "unable to resist" 'What Do You Say?', adding that "Pulp proved to be a most bizarre visual proposition. Fronted by Jarvis, the tallest teenager I've ever shook hands with, they flocked round me like curious vultures eyeing up a prey. I'm haunted by splashes of wild colour, off-beat clothes and hair and an underlying purity which just doesn't seem to fit."

Jarvis and Peter do most of the talking, discussing Pulp's artistic aims (Peter: "We'd like to see pop getting back to an innocent, trashy, disposable medium, which allows more time for humour and cuts down on the gloom." Jarvis: "But just because we've got a sense of humour doesn't mean that we want to be seen as some kind of 'joke' band"), the subject matter of Jarvis' songs ("I just don't want to write about kicking the Russians out of Poland. I'd rather that be said from a political platform than having somebody on a music stage say it. We're simply not interested in either sloganeering or coming on all pretentious and illegitimately boastful . . . At bottom, I suppose I write what you'd call love songs. It's universal, probably the main emotion in life. So if I can say something politic about love everyone can at least relate to it"), and the Pulp live experience (Jarvis: "We see ourselves very much as a challenging live group. I know it sounds like a real cliché but we'd really like people to move away from their preconceptions. We find it amusing to get up on a stage six inches above everyone else. They're expecting something abnormal from us, so we just try to make them see that they shouldn't do. They're as important as us; together we can have a real fun party but if they won't play we find it difficult to motivate ourselves"). Overall, the group comes across as ambitious, intelligent, self-aware and, despite Jarvis' protestations to the contrary, ever so slightly naïve and overconfident. Jarvis' closing comments on Pulp's future just about say it all: "I'm wary of signing to a big company and then releasing a single. I think it's better for credibility to release a single on an independent first, then you can build from a good base, with people looking at you with that important initial respect. We just want to get on to *Top Of The Pops* as soon as we can. Wacky surrealist comedians, that's us. You've got to laugh or we'll cry."

A week after the interview went to press, Jarvis found himself at least momentarily brought down to earth at a concert at Sheffield Polytechnic's Totley site, supporting New Model Soldier. Many years later, Jarvis was shown a photo from the concert during an *NME* interview. "I remember this gig actually," he commented. "It was at the Poly and it was a really bad concert. I was terribly depressed afterwards, 'cos there was this girl I really fancied at school and this was the first time I managed to persuade her to come and see us live. Then we didn't play very well and I blew it."

Murray Fenton was at the party, thrown by Russell Senior, that both bands went to after the show: "I was there with [New Model Soldier mainman] Dave Kurley – Russell used to have these do's, and I went along thinking, 'Yeah, it'll be a decent piss-up,' and there were all these canapes, with everybody just sat around talking. There were like seven or eight people there, and I was thinking, 'Well, everybody must be coming later.' And then Jarvis and Steve Genn turned up – Pulp had been playing this Sheffield Poly site in the middle of nowhere, and it'd turned out it was some sort of lecturers' do. I remember them coming back saying, 'Fucking hell, we thought there'd be students there, and we've been playing to all these idiots.'"

Setbacks aside, the several Giant Leaps Forward that Pulp had recently made meant that the band's confidence and ambition (both artistic and career-minded) were both at new highs – as evidenced by the recruitment in mid-February of a fifth member, ex-Vector 7-7 member David Hinkler (known to all as Henry after *Happy Days* actor Henry Winkler), on guitar, trombone and keyboards. "I think the catalyst in getting me into the band was that Jarvis wanted the trombone, to make things sound a bit different. He knew me as a pub acquaintance, and obviously he knew I'd been in a band with Wayne. The first thing I did when I joined was to play guitar, which I'm a complete buffoon on, but I tried to edge myself out of that and into keyboards. I think Jarvis wanted his songs to be fully represented on stage – there were bits missing because there weren't enough people to play the parts that he'd written.

"At first, I just played on some songs – guitar and a bit of trombone, to fill the sound out. Not long after I joined, though, I said to Jarvis that if I could get into playing keyboards that'd be great, and we started having a keyboard set up at either side of the stage: there was a synthesiser and one of those Yamaha portable things, which had some wacky sounds in it that Jarvis wanted to utilise."

The five-piece Pulp's first live appearance was at the Marples, support-ing then-fancied goth band The Danse Society. In the audience was Tony Perrin, a one-time acolyte of Marcus Featherby who was now managing Artery and flyposting around Sheffield for major record labels: "I didn't really think much of the music, to be honest – it seemed secondary to Jarvis' personality, that was what grabbed me. Jarvis back then was exactly the same person as he is today – I don't think he's changed fundamentally that much, other than becoming a lot more worldly. Soon afterwards, I heard the Peel session, and that was the first time I realised they actually had any songs. I asked them if they wanted to support Artery at the Marples later the same week, and that was kind of how I came to know the band." Within a few months, Perrin would become Pulp's manager.

Artery themselves were amongst the most respected bands in Sheffield at the time. "They were like gods at the time, almost," remembers Michael Paramore, vocalist with contemporaneous local bands Heroes Of The Beach and In A Belljar. "They were just brilliant, they had a whole musical career without going outside Sheffield. They got on the cover of the *NME* and a centre spread sort of thing. They were just amazing, brilliant live, never recreated it on records or any sessions, but live they were just unbelievable. You just never quite knew whether they were going to kill themselves or not. There was one occasion when, I think it was [guitarist] Mick Fidler just disappeared on the window ledge at the Marples – the venue is about four or five floors up and he just went out of the window and came back sort of a few windows further along.

"They were always fighting on stage, him and Gouldthorpe. They'd just kind of lose it with each other and start fighting. You never quite knew what was going to happen. There was always somebody balancing on the top of a stack of speakers and stuff. It was one of those things where you went and it was always a very tense gig. Jarvis was always there as well – you just got to see certain people in the audience down the front."

John Quinn, who later crossed paths with Pulp more than once as the *Sheffield Star's* Pop Page editor, also saw Pulp around this time: "A couple of friends had seen Pulp at the Marples on the Monday and had come back raving about them, so me and another friend went to see them on the Thursday. They were all dressed in outfits made from curtain material, which I think they'd stolen from the school library. Very bright, visually. Jarvis was jumping about a little bit, and saying a lot of strange things between the songs. They were pretty entertaining actually, especially Jarvis. Jarvis' sister and a couple of other girls were throwing toilet rolls into the crowd so that they were unravelling, and at one point somebody got a wet toilet roll and threw it back, and it hit Jarvis in the face, which was quite funny. He got quite a lot of that – he stood out, obviously, and he set himself up to be ridiculed a bit. I think he was trying to be a serious artist, but because of the way he looked it was pretty difficult for him. He had a really sticky-up haircut at the time, which people in the crowd were laughing at – like Terry Hall out of the Fun Boy Three, only taller. He just looked completely absurd – he looked good, but he looked bad at the same time.

"They had some quite nice songs, I remember. They did a couple of songs from the Peel session, but I can't remember which. Wayne was about two years younger than the rest – he looked about two feet tall at the time."

The Marples concert was reviewed by *Sounds'* Pete Scott who, while noting Pulp's "wilfully eccentric . . . fairground/carnival feel" and reckoning them to be "an initially enjoyable but ultimately unfulfilling experience", surprisingly didn't find anything to say about the typically bizarre visuals the audience was treated to that night. "We had curtain fabric draped all over the stage," remembers David Hinkler, "and there were a lot of lights involved – as well as ones that shone down on to the stage, we'd have standard lamps and daft things like that. We all wore these glittery blouse things as well. That concert went down really well, actually."

It was around this time that the band started to display more sophisticated ambitions that would eventually lead to the smoother, quieter sound of the *It* album. Excellent new songs like 'Red Letter Day', the moody, synth-based 'You Go First' or the manic, twitchy ska of 'You've Got A Face' (all preserved on a surviving live recording from the period) all display a maturity and originality that was some distance ahead of the scratchy garage pop of the Peel session. "Once I got in there," remembers David, "it started to change towards a more keyboard-based sound, less up tempo. The songs were getting better all the time as well – Jarvis was already a good songwriter, but he was getting better and better."

Concerts kept coming through February and March, including headline slots at Sheffield's Limit club and the Hallamshire, and even an appearance in London (at The Moonlight Club, supporting the long-forgotten A Crown Of Thorns). By spring 1982, however, A-levels were approaching, resulting in a scaling-down of Pulp activities while Jarvis, Jamie and Dolly concentrated on studying (Henry and Wayne, being two years younger than the others, also had their O-levels to worry about). All three had won good university places and, in spite of the excitement of the past few months, it was no certainty that anyone other than Jarvis (who had already decided to defer his place at Liverpool University for a year) was going to stick around Sheffield to continue with Pulp after that summer.

"It was exciting," says Glen Marshall of Pulp's modest steps toward stardom in late 1981 and early 1982, "but everybody knew that all this could finish as soon as school finished. It was in the back of everyone's mind – 'it's good while it lasts but it could all end', sort of thing. You were never sure whether Jarvis would dare to go mainstream, or whether he'd become more like a few other groups round Sheffield who were kind of famous for having cult status – Cabaret Voltaire, Artery, ClockDVA. You didn't know whether Pulp were going to become the cult thing in the Sheffield area and get more and more eccentric. I mean, John Peel wasn't exactly mainstream, and a lot of the groups that he had on subsequently vanished into obscurity. But they had started to become a name that was recognised around Sheffield. They were unique, but there were a lot of groups trying to get themselves well known."

By spring, there was an air of disenchantment amongst everyone in the band. The increased exposure that Pulp had received in the preceding months was failing to consolidate into anything that looked like a career – some initial interest from Armageddon Records had come to nothing, and Statik, who had released *Your Secret's Safe With Us*, were more interested in furthering the career of The Chameleons. "The attention they were getting after the Peel session was all very exciting," says Saskia, "and I think university places were put off because of it. But of course it wasn't to be."

Wavering morale and academic commitments notwithstanding, Pulp managed a couple of concerts during April (one at the Limit, and another at a party for the British Association of Young Scientists at Sorby Hall – "That was a nightmare," remembers Wayne. "I've never seen so many pairs of spectacles"), and also recorded a new demo tape, this time at Rotherham's Kaley Studios.

"The studio was almost like an old office, just down a run-down street in Rotherham," remembers David. "The surroundings were a bit depressing, to be honest. Emotive was the word – nobody was quite sure what was going to come of the band. It looked like it was winding down because Jamie and Peter were going to have to leave soon."

Kaley was one step up from Ken Patten (they were allowed to use their own drumkit!), but still hardly Abbey Road. The session was produced by Simon Hinkler, David's brother and keyboardist with Artery.

"I guess I was just asked if I'd do it," says Simon. "I used to do all the production stuff for Artery, in fact I produced quite a few Sheffield bands in the early Eighties, especially people I liked. At that time, none of the guys in Pulp had much idea how to approach the studio. It was only an 8-track, so I had to do the usual organising of what goes where, microphone placing and stuff, plus coaxing the best performances out of everyone on the day. The engineer thought it was unusual when I asked him to patch in some reverb. Then he had to dig out some crappy old spring-reverb unit which was all he had. As was always the case in those days, money was tight and we were against the clock, so it was all very rushed."

Nonetheless, the band persevered and committed the requisite four tracks to tape – two established live favourites ('How Could You Leave

Me?' and 'Why Live?') and two relative newies ('Teen Angst' and 'Barefoot In The Park'). "It sounded quite good," says David. "The equipment and technology in low-budget studios wasn't really up to much at the time, so it was a bit bland, but the songs were good enough to carry it through."

Indeed, the results of the session show a considerable progression from the Peel session of five months before. 'Barefoot In The Park' is a candyfloss-light slice of power pop – *"Alternative reality/ Reject responsibility/ We're walking barefoot in the park/ They lock the gates when it gets dark,"* sings Jarvis over yet another of Dolly's seemingly inexhaustible supply of wobbly keyboard riffs. Equally upbeat is the melodic, danceable synth-pop of 'Teen Angst', with giddy, jumbled lyrics about girls and parties over a pseudo-Specials ska bassline. 'Why Live?', meanwhile, was the oldest song on the demo, and also the most guitar-based. The lyrics are teenage misery taken to an extreme, beginning with *"To moan and whine about my life is my prerogative/ Pessimistic overviews are all I have to give"* before getting depressing. Meanwhile, David's jangly, almost Spanish-sounding guitar and Peter's xylophone build up a suitably mournful atmosphere. Finally, 'How Could You Leave Me?' (or 'How Could You?' as it was usually known) was another long-standing live staple. It's also the only Pulp song that wouldn't sound too out of place in a late-night jazz club – Jamie's convincingly sleazy bassline and Wayne's appropriately swishy, swingbeat drumming provide the backbone of the tune, while Peter contributes some slightly inept bluesy guitar and Jarvis quavers over the top about Betrayal, Loneliness and Things. Henry adds some vibraphone-toned keyboard flourishes and Simon Hinkler chips in with a rather fine piano solo.

On all the tracks, Dolly's synthesiser is much more to the fore, and David's presence on keyboards and guitar fills the sound out noticeably. Jarvis also seems to have progressed as a lyricist, leaving behind the lightweight jollity of 'Turkey Mambo Momma' and 'Please Don't Worry' in favour of more tangible subject matter. While the demo is still nowhere near as entertaining as the band's live shows, it nevertheless stands up well as what turned out to be Pulp Mark I's final statement.

At the time, though, the band's enthusiasm for the recording was slightly muted – Jamie Pinchbeck even claims not to remember the session at all. David: "I don't even know what was done with that demo, because I don't recall anything coming of it at all. They were all really good songs, though, and it's a shame that nobody can get hold of it any more. I remember Jarvis wasn't happy with it, but then he tends to be a bit ashamed of a lot of the early stuff, which I don't think he should be – even if some of the lyrics are a little bit schoolboy-ish, the songs are an example of how, even at that age, he was a brilliant songwriter."

If the demo was intended as a final attempt to give the first incarnation of Pulp a push into the big time, it was in vain: although practices continued through May and June, more concerts did not follow – the band finally fell apart after the end of Jarvis', Peter's and Jamie's A-level exams. Dolly's father, who was the headmaster of a local primary school, saw a better future for his son than messing around with these ridiculous pop groups, and Jamie Pinchbeck had also made the decision to go to Manchester University to do a degree in Civil Engineering.

"We thought the Peel session was brilliant," remembers Jamie, "but the disappointment came afterwards, when we got a few music press features, but the band didn't take off. When Jarvis decided that he was going to take a year out and not go to university, I seriously thought about it, but because we'd not really got very far in two years I decided against it. There was never any bad feeling – I saw Jarvis once or twice afterwards, and went to a couple of Pulp concerts after I left, but we lost touch after a while. I'm very happy for Pulp's success though, and I admire Jarvis for sticking it out for so long."

Peter Dalton's enforced departure was a heavy blow, both to Pulp and to Dalton himself: he'd started the band with Jarvis four years previously and, by some accounts, was no less serious about the band. "I think he toyed with the idea of not going to university," says Glen Marshall, "but he came under severe family pressure because his dad was the headmaster of a school . . . but to be fair, they did support him by letting him buy the synthesiser." (Incidentally, Jarvis' oft-told story of how, when Peter told his dad that he wanted to stay with the band, he picked up his dinner and threw it at him is a complete invention.)

David Hinkler: "In the unlikely event that Pulp got a record deal or something, then I think Peter and Jamie were going to stay in the band, but it was a bit early to be aiming that high. They knew that when that month came around of that year, they'd have to leave, and I suppose that was evident in their attitude towards the band, because I don't think they ever took it half as seriously as Jarvis did. There were plenty of emotive periods when there was a feeling of, 'Are we actually going anywhere?' and I think that Jarvis was a bit disappointed that they didn't want to give it another year. They were always good friends, though, and Jarvis put that first, and thought, 'Well, if they've got to go, they've got to go.' This is no reflection on what I think of Peter and Jamie, but I think it was best for the band that they did go in that they were replaced by people who had more to offer musically."

On the other hand, other associates of the band hold the view that the end of Pulp Mark I marked the passing of Pulp as a group in the true sense of the word: Jamie and Dolly may have been replaceable as musicians, but what couldn't be replaced was the sense of Pulp being a close-knit collective where each individual member was an important part of the whole. This feeling of being a 'proper band' was something Pulp would not rediscover for a long time.

Despite losing Peter and Jamie, Jarvis now looks back on this period as "a really magical time. I remember thinking that this was it, that it was music all the way for me from then on. So I decided I wasn't going to university. I was going to stay in Sheffield and carry on with the group."[56]

Chapter 3

When Peter Dalton and Jamie Pinchbeck went, it was clear that the Pulp that had started in 1978 was gone. This left Jarvis in something of a dilemma – he'd already committed to taking a year out from university to continue the group, but in Jamie and (especially) Peter he'd lost the two people who had formed the core of what Pulp had been. As a result, the summer of 1982 would see him dabble in various things before making any serious attempt to work with a version of Pulp again. "I don't think he went into any big depression or anything," says his friend Jim Sellars. "He just needed a bit of time to assess things and decide what he wanted to do."

Yet in another sense, at the time the uncertainty of what was going to happen next didn't seem to matter – at the age of 18, with A-levels over and school out forever, he was enjoying his first taste of freedom. "That time was wonderful," remembers Saskia. "Everyone was such good friends – we'd go off on day trips together and everything. And all the music was great, and it's never been like it since – where you could go out every night of the week and see a band, and everyone was there. Everyone was a misfit, but it was OK because we were all together. There were so many good bands – Dig Vis Drill, Comsat Angels, Treehouse, New Model Soldier . . . There was the music, but then there was the way of life around it as well. It was lovely."

"It's like that song 'Looking For Life'," says Tony Perrin. "He was broadening his horizons, becoming a person." The mood of that summer was reflected in Heroes Of The Beach, a shambolic, short-lived band that Jarvis and Dolly guested with for a one-off concert at the Hallamshire in August.

Heroes Of The Beach had existed a couple of years earlier as a sixth-form band, and had now been reformed by original members David Bocking (sax) and Mick Shaw (guitar), with the line-up completed by a host of schoolfriends and Sheffield band scene characters: Tim Allcard and original singer Michael Paramore played tin-can percussion; Greg Thompson sang; Jarvis contributed guitar and occasional vocals; Dolly, keyboards and cornet; Steve Genn, bass; and Nick Taylor, formerly of another Sheffield band called A Major European Group, played drums.

"Heroes Of The Beach was open to anyone else who wanted to be in it, really," says Bocking. "It was a band that I'd formed with a friend of mine called Mick Shaw, and we met Jarvis quite often at the Hallamshire. He joined Heroes Of The Beach really, I think, as a change, something to do. Anyway, for two concerts, he played guitar, and he sang 'Evel Knievel', which was a song he wrote with Dolly, an anthemic tribute to the famous motorcycle stuntman – it was a classic of its period. I've a feeling we may have been without a singer at that point, and Jarvis certainly sang one or two of the songs."

Nick Taylor: "We had a song that we called 'Psycho Killer' because it had a bassline similar to the Talking Heads song. We did one that had like a rockabilly beat that we called 'Stray Cat Strut', and a Pulp song, 'Refuse To Be Blind', and two songs, 'Nylon Strands' and 'Incubus', that myself and Mag [Magnus Doyle] had done before in a band called Blimp."

The band's repertoire also included the old Pulp song 'Mr. Morality'; another Jarvis/Dolly original, the title of which is lost in the mists of time, about Alphabetti Spaghetti which lifted its hook from a Crosse & Blackwell advert; and a pair of mime acts, to Gang Of Four's 'I Love A Man In Uniform' and 'Come On Eileen' by Dexy's Midnight Runners. "We were light-hearted to the extreme," says Steve Genn, and one suspects he's not lying.

The concert was promoted with a publicity stunt from Dolly, Jarvis, Steve Genn, Nick Taylor and Greg Thompson, who were pictured eating their breakfast on Fargate and got into the *Sheffield Star* for their troubles, eating cornflakes in their pyjamas. "That first concert they did got a fair bit of attention," remembers Murray Fenton. "They got airtime on local radio, on the news. There was quite a little buzz about how it was going to be a lot of fun, and it was. They were really ramshackle, but it was a good laugh."

The non-serious nature of Heroes Of The Beach probably reflects the fact that at this stage, Jarvis really wasn't sure where he was going to go next – even to the point of looking outside music altogether. Around the time of the Heroes concert, word reached Sheffield that the newly launched Channel 4 was auditioning presenters for a new alternative music programme, to be called *The Tube*. Jarvis went along for an audition. "That was very exciting," remembers Saskia. "Me and my mum and my cousin Hannah all went – it was in Birmingham. They actually accepted him; they wanted him not to be one of the presenters in the studio, but to go round and see bands, do things for them at various venues. They said that was what they wanted him to do, but then they decided that they weren't going to do that. So all that fell away, which was another disappointment."

Pulp finally regrouped some time around the beginning of August, due at least in part to the proddings of Tony Perrin, Artery's manager who had decided he wanted to work with Pulp. "There were debates going on between me and Jarvis at the time," says Tony, "as to whether he should take his place at Liverpool University or defer it for a year and give music a crack. Obviously it must have been what he wanted to do, because I wouldn't have been able to persuade him, but I nudged him in the direction of music. I was flyposting for major record companies around Sheffield at the time, and I had a little bit of spare cash, so I managed to scrape together about £500 or £600. I went to Jarvis and said, 'Look, I've got this bit of money, you've got some songs, why don't we just go in and make an album's worth of music and I'll try and get it released. And Jarvis was up for that, but unfortunately he didn't have a band.

"So my first port of call was to turn to Simon Hinkler, who'd produced some of the demos they'd done before, so he was kind of in the chair as their producer, and he was the only person I knew with enough musical ability to put something together. Then we just scouted around and picked up musicians from friends and people that Jarvis knew and people that Simon knew."

"I was going out with Saskia then," says Simon, "and spent a lot of time at their house. Consequently I'd hang out with Jarvis and work on song ideas with him. It felt like I was just helping out as a friend at first, but I became so involved with arranging and writing parts for the songs that after a while I officially joined Pulp, although I was still in Artery."

Although Wayne and Henry (both a couple of years younger than Jarvis, Jamie and Dolly) were still around, it was Simon Hinkler who would be Jarvis' main collaborator in the new Pulp. In contrast to the 1978–82 model's punkish, anti-musicianship approach, he was a skilled multi-instrumentalist: as well as acting as Pulp's full-time bass-player, producer and arranger, he would also contribute guitar, keyboards and percussion to recordings over the next year.

Since 1980, Simon had been keyboardist, and latterly guitarist, with Artery, one of the most respected bands in Sheffield at the time, but, according to his brother David, "he was just disillusioned by the fact that Artery had lost their way, with members leaving and what have you, and felt he needed another theme to get in on."

"It was very exciting when he joined Pulp," says Saskia, "because he'd been in Artery, and they were fantastic – really well liked in Sheffield. Even when David joined, it was exciting to have the brother of someone from Artery in the group. But Simon just really liked what they did, and musically he was very good. He was better than they'd ever had – suddenly they had someone who knew what he was doing. I think he contributed quite a lot, and gave the group a very different sound."

With Simon on board, things progressed quickly and, after barely a month together, Jarvis, Simon, David and Wayne were ready to make their first recordings as the new Pulp. Tony Perrin paid for three hours in Sheffield's Input Studio one Sunday evening, resulting in a four-song demo tape, entitled *Spice*. Simon's production, arranging and playing on the session ensured that it sounded much more glossy and professional than the old Pulp, while the songs themselves are evidence that Jarvis was trying to move away from the giddy, trashy style of his older songs to something that at least aspired to be a little more serious.

"Being without a proper band, Jarvis was trying a new direction," says Simon. "He had a great way of coming up with song ideas, where he'd sit down with a guitar and find a riff or chord progression, then kind of mumble and mutter gibberish with the occasional word or phrase thrown in. It was really funny when he was round my place one day and I played him a chord progression I'd just made up. He started singing *'mumble hum la la la lighthouse mumble la la.'* I started laughing and said, 'What? *Lighthouse?!*' "

Of the songs demoed at Input, 'Sickly Grin' was the track perhaps most reminiscent of the old Pulp – indeed, Peter Dalton makes a cameo appearance playing cornet alongside Henry's trombone. *"It seems the present style to wear a toothy smile – no matter how events may go, to never let emotions show. Being happy's fine, but not all the time . . ."* It was probably deliberate that the song's rather earnest lyrics are set to perhaps the most relentlessly jolly Pulp tune ever and, although it was deemed too poppy for inclusion on the album Pulp would shortly start work on, Jarvis nonetheless held it in sufficiently high esteem to include it as an extra track on a limited edition Pulp rarities EP many years later.

'Taking The Plunge', later retitled 'Sink Or Swim' and described by Jarvis as being "about standing on the threshold of life," is a charming, self-consciously naïve number that does indeed capture all of Jarvis' uncertainty and confusion as, at the age of 18, he found himself suddenly making the jump from tender schooldays into adult life: *"I see it's time for me to take the plunge instead of sitting round and watching everyone . . . Decisions now affect my future days, but are they right or wrong – well who on earth can say? Well it's my turn to see what I can see. I may be frightened, but would anyone not be?"* The music is just as polite and likeable, richly melodic with a laid-back, almost jazzy feel and an instrumental passage (with a keyboard solo *and* a trombone solo) worthy of any daytime chat show.

One of the last songs rehearsed while Dolly and Jamie were still in the band, 'The Heat Of The Day' was, as David Hinkler recalls, "very guitar-orientated – almost rock, and much more uptempo than the *It* stuff." It's also one of the only recorded songs (along with 'Looking For Life') that capture the jangly, guitar-'n'-organ sound that Pulp momentarily toyed with in autumn 1982. Rhythm guitars clatter along in a manner vaguely reminiscent of The Velvet Underground's 'What Goes On', insistent drums are to the fore, and the whole thing is by far the closest Pulp came to rocking out in the early Eighties.

"We were both into the VU," says Simon. "On those earliest songs I collaborated on, there were a few which still hung onto the old Pulp sound, which was quite VU-ish – let's just say Sixties-ish. But the writing moved away from that for the album, or rather, those type of songs didn't make it onto the album in the end."

The final track on the demo, 'Boats And Trains', was the winsome mandolin-based ditty that was later included on *It*, and was the only thing on the demo tape that foreshadowed the gentle, acoustic direction that the band would shortly take. It's clear that at this point, technical accomplishment aside, Pulp Mark 2 was still in its formative stages – the four songs on the demo could have been the work of at least three different bands. While the tenderness of 'Boats And Trains' and 'Taking The Plunge' held the blueprint, more or less, for what Pulp would soon become, the light-weight pop of 'Sickly Grin' harked back to the old Pulp and 'The Heat Of The Day' pointed towards something else altogether.

The main thing that can be gleaned from listening to these songs is that the collaboration between Jarvis and Simon produced something very different to what Pulp had been for the past four years. The ramshackle, eccentric feel was gone and, while Jarvis' melodic songwriting had always been there, it was now that it began to take centre stage.

As it turned out, Simon Hinkler's arrival wasn't the end of Pulp's personnel upheavals. Wayne Furniss had played on only two tracks on the *Spice* demo, contributing bass to 'Boats And Trains' and guitar to 'The Heat Of The Day'. The drums on the session were played by Artery's Garry Wilson. "I think Simon might have had some problems with my style of drumming," reckons Wayne. "After that, I wasn't quite as involved – I played guitar with them live once, and I'd do little bits on recordings, but it wasn't the same as before. I think being pushed out is perhaps putting it a bit too strongly, but there were other people coming in who were playing a greater part."

Simon Hinkler: "I don't remember exactly what happened with Wayne switching instruments, but I think we were just trying to find the balance that worked best. I mean, for live shows I ended up playing bass, and I think that was just because it needed doing. I was still in Artery at the time, and there was always a feeling, from me more than anyone else, of my position in Pulp being sort of temporary, or even secondary to Artery."

Wayne's initial replacement on drums was Peter Boam, who had first seen Pulp at the Leadmill concert in 1980. "I first met Jarvis not long after that," he recalls. "I can't remember where, but I'd got in with all that lot – Pulp and the guys who were playing in Vector 7-7, David and Wayne, and Dean. I was organising gigs at the time – I was only 17 or something, I wasn't even allowed to get drinks. I used to run a gig at The Royal in Sheffield, called The Ritblat Tube – quite a big venue. Then there was a smaller one called the George IV that I used to run as well, which was also known as the Wedge Club. I was in with all the local musicians because everyone wanted to know me, because everyone wanted a gig.

"I was in some shitty band called Mortuary In Wax. It was called that because I'd been in a previous band who'd wanted to change their name, but they didn't know what to change it to. So I just got a dictionary and got 'mortuary' and 'wax'. OK, put an 'in' in there. But nobody realised that there was a band from Manchester called Nightmares In Wax at the time.

"Anyway, I was doing that, and when I was 16 I had my record out through Marcus Featherby, which was called 'The Face', on Pax Records. It sounds like 16 Holes did it, but I did that, and at the same time Simon was in Artery, who were stuck on Aardvark, which was also Marcus Featherby. And so Simon and I knew each other as nodding acquaintances.

"How I came to join Pulp was that there was a slack night at the Hallamshire, and I said, 'Let's just do a jamming gig.' At the time, jamming gigs were in – people'd show up with guitars or whatever they wanted to bring, and they'd got a gig. It doesn't matter if it's any good or not, because rehearsal rooms are expensive, pubs are cheap and you could have a drink.

"Anyway, Jarvis and Simon showed up at this gig. There was no drummer, so I ended up on drums, and they must have come to some idea over that night, because they came up to me afterwards and said, 'Would you like to join the band?' I was in two minds because I didn't want to take anything too seriously. I didn't know anything about the machinations of the band, with people going off to university. I also didn't realise that I was about to join a band that was managed by Tony Perrin, who I never liked, or that he was going to put up the money to do an album. I knew Pulp as this great, garagey schoolboy band, and that was the band that I wanted to join really. I was told Wayne wanted to move to guitar – he'd been guitarist in Vector 7-7, and I think that was his main instrument. He's definitely a better drummer than I'll ever be!"

"Pete used to have unusually long curly hair for those days," remembers Simon Hinkler, "and he wore a dress for one gig and looked remarkably like a pre-pubescent girl. He was kind of crazy, and a misfit like the rest of us."

Between Peter's joining at the end of August and starting work on *It* late in November, there would be very little visible Pulp activity – apart from one concert in October, nothing would be heard from them until the new year. One of the reasons for this is that, for the academic year 1982/83, Simon Hinkler was spending most of his weeks at piano-training college in Newark, some 45 miles outside Sheffield. "I used to just come back to Sheffield on the weekends and cram it all – plus going out at night. If there was a gig or something to do during the week, I'd come back for it. I remember an Artery gig in Nottingham where I just met the rest of the band at the venue and went back to Newark after."

Tony Perrin: "The band, insofar as it was a band, wasn't really a solid unit. They weren't really in a situation where they could jump in the back of a van and just run down to the Hallamshire and do a gig. They didn't have a rehearsal room – they were still practising in Jarvis' mum's garage, and I guess it was impractical for them to do that. Plus Simon had his own commitments with Artery, who were reasonably busy at the time, so playing live didn't seem to be something that they needed to do at that time. The priority was to get the songs together for the album."

The first fruits of this getting-together of songs were heard on October 24, 1982 at Pulp's first concert in six months, at the Crucible Studio Theatre, supporting the Artery offshoot Treehouse. A Pulp sound was showcased that night that was a long way from both the earlier ramshackle synth-pop version of the group, and the softer, acoustic sound that would emerge on *It*. Old songs like 'Please Don't Worry' and 'How Could You Leave Me?' were still around, but on new material like 'Coming Alive' (later retitled 'Looking For Life'), 'My Lighthouse', 'I Wave You Goodbye' and 'Blue Girls', Wayne's and Jarvis' jangly guitars were to the fore, and David was concentrating on a Sixties organ sound. Apart from 'Looking For Life', none of the material that Pulp later released represents the way they sounded at this point – 'My Lighthouse', in its original form, had a different chorus melody and a much more jangly, guitar-based feel, while the original full band arrangement of 'Blue Girls' was considerably louder and more uptempo than the subsequent album version. Of the two unrecorded numbers played that night, 'I Wave You Goodbye' was a slightly Stranglers-ish, organ-based number with a tasteful roaming bass-line, while 'Mr. Morality' was a lightweight, wacky number that dated back to the old Pulp.

In the audience was former bassist Philip Thompson. "I remember talking to Peter Boam beforehand – we were chatting away about stage presentation and things, and next thing he was up on stage with a pinafore dress and his hair back in a bunch, which I thought was magnificent. There was a bit of a strange reaction from the crowd though – a lot of 'Fookin' poof!' type stuff. There were all sorts of people turning up. I was sat next to this short, fat balding bloke with a beard, thinking, 'What are you doing here?', and then I turned round and it was John Peel with his wife!"

The band line-up on the night was Jarvis on vocals, Wayne Furniss on guitar, David Hinkler on keyboards, Simon Hinkler on bass and Peter Boam on drums. "They'd brought me in as a drummer for the Crucible concert," remembers Peter, "which was the biggest joke in the world. Afterwards, I said to Simon, or Simon said to me, I can't remember which, that we ought to get someone else in to play on the album. Which was a good move, because I'm just not a drummer."

As a result, shortly after the concert, Peter Boam moved from drums to guitar, displacing Wayne Furniss for the second time in two months. Quite understandably, Wayne was less than happy about this, and Peter's move to guitar was very shortly followed by Wayne's departure from Pulp. Peter Boam: "He'd been replaced on drums, then replaced on guitar, and I think he felt he was being pushed out. I felt terrible about it, because it was me who kept replacing him on everything! Everybody felt quite bad when he left – that's why Jarvis invited him back later to play on a track on the album. It was never anything personal – I'd known him for years before Pulp, and he was a good bloke."

"Things were changing," says Wayne Furniss now. "It wasn't Dolly and Jamie leaving so much as the other people who were coming in. It was six of one and half a dozen of the other, really – if I hadn't have left I'd have been pushed out anyway. There wasn't any animosity, though – bearing in mind that my life was changing as well, I think things had run their course."

"After he was replaced on drums," says Wayne's friend David Hinkler, "he wasn't really doing much, and I can remember him telling me he wanted to move on. He'd gone from being The Drummer to just an extra on the scene, and he felt that his talents would be better appreciated elsewhere."

November saw Jarvis himself taking a break from Pulp, attaching himself to a band called In A Belljar – an undeniably peculiar Sheffield music/performance art collective featuring Tim Allcard, Mark Tillbrook, Michael Paramore and his sister Julie. Jarvis already knew Michael via his previous group, Heroes Of The Beach, the original version of which had been part of the same scene of young Sheffield bands as the old Pulp.

"I left Heroes Of The Beach," remembers Michael, "and met up with Tim Allcard, and we formed a band called In A Belljar and started playing loads of gigs – we played two or three a week sometimes, and that's where I really got to know Jarvis – he used to come to our gigs and it was just after he'd split up with the original version of Pulp and he actually asked to join our band.

"We didn't have any sort of conventional instruments – we just used to sing and make noises with various things like tin cans. We'd get big tin cans and just sort of arrange them all so that they were in a row. We used to have this order of what we played on certain songs – we weren't that good musically but we'd arrange the tin cans in order so that we could actually hit them and then the melody was there. We'd play anything that'd make a sound, and we had those little transducers that you'd attach to things – like little microphones, and you'd get really nice sounds out of anything, really. It was quite a noisy sort of sound, there was a lot of screaming and wailing over the top. I used to do vocals, which was quite funny – I used to sing and Jarvis would play a tin can, which was a bit of a misuse of resources . . . really it was just rubbish, it should've been the other way round!

"Tim used to write some of the lyrics and I used to write some of the lyrics, and every so often Tim would read a poem out, and we'd kind of make noises in the background. Or we'd sing almost like kids' type songs, just all of us singing – not harmonies, but that kind of idea, and then Fun Boy Three came along and made a success of it, and that was that!

"I think Jarvis just joined because he thought we were quite nice people. I think he thought we'd be decent mates rather than anything other than that. So he just asked to join. When all your mates go off to university, it can be a bit daunting if you're left on your own I suppose. I don't really know why he joined but it was all right, it was a good laugh. We'd just sort of go and play in the street, it didn't really bother us where we played. We didn't have any kind of musical plans other than just making a noise, whereas Jarvis always had probably a bit more musical ambition than we did."

Nonetheless, the band were soon playing quite frequently around Sheffield – normally at the Hallamshire Hotel, where the promoter, one Nick

Banks, would tend to book them as support band at every opportunity. "They were my favourites. Tim had his poetry and they'd string washing lines across the stage – you couldn't really see, you might be able to see the top of someone's head, and all the equipment was homemade: they'd have a wooden microphone stand, tin cans, and they'd be smacking bits of wood together for a snare sound, that kind of thing. They'd have Tim and Michael's poetry and Jarvis would be doing music with a battered acoustic or something. There was 'Lots And Lots Of Yachts', 'Stephen And His Leather Jacket', which I believe was about Stephen Singleton, brother of whatsit Singleton out of ABC – always a bit of a mousy little kid who always had this leather jacket on. Always went out with very ugly girls – he used to think you could get them easier, and they'd be more grateful. He was no oil painting himself. He was with a new one every week."

Murray Fenton: "In A Belljar used to have washing lines across the stage and play amongst all this washing, and they just used to hit things and stuff. That was like a direct mixture of performance art and being a band – I wouldn't say it was music; it was peculiar to say the least."

Meanwhile, Jarvis and Simon were working out exactly what sort of album Pulp were going to be making when they went into the studio at the end of November. Simon: "Jarvis and I had talked extensively about the album before we even started it, and one of the things we were certain about was that we both hated those big drum sounds, which were so common in the Eighties. We were both into, among other things, early Leonard Cohen, and liked the way the production and arrangements left plenty of room for the song. The nature of the collection of songs we'd got suggested that kind of production. Also, *Hunky Dory* by David Bowie is just about my favourite album of all time, and I know Jarv liked it too. Saskia played it a lot. Jarvis was a collector of old vinyl, and I know he was a fan of John Barry – as I am. Also, there was a little-known French band he played a lot that I think might have been called Antenna – they were good, and certainly an influence on the quieter sound.

"I think that the main reason was Jarvis' reaction against the noisy ramshackle earlier Pulp – wanting to move on, try something different. It seems to me that there were a few things around at the time that were more laid-back in the wake of punk, new wave, post-punk. Things like Everything But The Girl and Sade were charting. Without actually wanting to be anything like those two examples, I think it was kind of a relief to chill down a bit after several years of frantic music. Even Artery went more acoustic around the same time. Another way of looking at it is that the Sheffield scene of the late Seventies and early Eighties was very off-the-wall and experimental, but after a few years of that, some people tried a more mature approach."

The new, mature Pulp finally began work on their début album when Jarvis, Simon, Peter and David entered Sheffield's Victoria Studios on November 27, 1982. Jarvis remembers Victoria as being "quite dangerously bad . . . the main thing I remember about it was the bloke had this one mike that he was totally proud of. He used to go, 'That's Cliff Richard's mike, that.' I said, 'What are you on about?' And he said, 'Cliff Richard's done loads of vocals on that mike. Fucking great.' And he insisted on using it on everything. Whenever you were recording a bit of guitar or something, he'd get Cliff Richard's microphone out. So, basically the whole album was done on Cliff Richard's mike."[57]

"It was an awful place, really bad," remembers David. "It was in the middle of an old, run-down industrial set-up in one of the less salubrious areas of Sheffield. Very depressing place."

Tony Perrin: "Dreadful as it was, I think it was probably the best studio in Sheffield at the time. Sheffield didn't exactly have the choice of studio facilities that it's got these days. I remember lugging that bloody piano up three flights of stairs. I remember hanging around in the freezing cold waiting for the guy to turn up with the keys. I remember the guy who owned the studio was a pain in the arse, going on about Cliff Richard's microphone that was his pride and joy. I don't remember much else about that place, apart from it being cold and miserable. We just kind of drifted in and tried things out as much as we could on what was a ridiculously small budget."

The first problem that had to be tackled was who was going to drum on the album. Wayne was now out of the group (although he did reappear to play some guitar on 'My Lighthouse'), and Peter's drumming, while adequate for the Crucible concert a few months earlier, was agreed by all concerned not to be good enough for the record. As a result, Simon decided to call again on his sometime Artery bandmate Garry Wilson. "I was working as a doorman at the Lyceum at the time," remembers Garry, "and I'd kipped there one Friday night. The next morning, after spending the night in this haunted theatre, I saw Simon, who said, 'Come round to Victoria Studios and do some drumming for the Pulp album.' So I went along, he told me what he wanted for each song, I put all my parts down that day, and that were it."

With Garry on drums and Simon leading the band, most of the album's basic tracks were put down on the first day of the sessions, with the rest of the two-week recording time mostly dedicated to overdubbing, refining and mixing. "We were trying to get that Leonard

Cohen feel of musicians playing together," says David, "so quite a lot of it was done live in the studio, putting basic tracks down and then layering them up. We found it quite difficult to do because the studio only had two rooms, which were adjacent to each other – there was no corridor between the mixing room and the room where we were playing, so there was no soundbreak."

Apart from Jarvis on vocals, Simon on bass and Garry on drums, very little was certain about who played what on the album. If one track had Peter on acoustic guitar, David on keyboards and Wayne making a guest reappearance on electric guitar, the next might have Jarvis on guitar, David on trombone and Simon doubling up on bass and piano. "It was the most all-over-the-place set-up I've ever come across," says David. "There was no set pattern as to who played what. What Jarvis had done was to enrol a list of musicians that he knew could play various instruments fairly well, but he'd also enrolled, in Simon, Peter and myself, three very competitive people who played the same instruments and wanted to get as much of themselves as possible on to all of the tracks. There was a bit of disharmony, I think, between Simon and Peter – they both had their own style, which they were both good at. That competition aspect spread to me a bit because everybody wanted to get in on the keyboards."

Peter Boam remembers the situation slightly differently: "It was sharing tasks more than anything else. We'd go, 'Oh, I don't fancy doing that bit, you can play that bit better, why don't you do that bit?' 'OK, I'll do that bit and you do this bit.' For example, on 'Wishful Thinking' I played the main piano track, but at the same time Simon was there, playing that motif at the top end of the piano because he could play it better than I could. That was the way it worked – if somebody could play something better than somebody else, then they'd do it, which I think was perfectly reasonable. I mean, Jarvis played very little guitar on the album because, while he's great in other ways, he ain't the world's best guitar player."

However, regardless of who played what, the musical direction came very definitely from Jarvis and Simon, with the others' input being largely restricted to adding parts as and when required – an arrangement that was a source of particular frustration to Peter Boam, who, prior to the sessions, had spent some time helping Jarvis arrange some songs for the album: "Simon wasn't available, so because I played piano and guitar and knew how to arrange things, Jarvis phoned me up and said, 'Look, we've got to get this album together 'cos we're meant to be recording it next week, why don't you come round and arrange some stuff?' So I'd arrange it and we'd do a tape of it. When we went into the studio though, Simon would show up and, because Tony Perrin was always there, I would tend to get knocked back because as far as he was concerned Simon was the boss-man. For certain sections of that album, I did a lot of work that never saw the light of day. That was the main reason I didn't like Tony."

Simon Hinkler: "If there's one thing that doesn't work in a band it's mixing by committee. The fact is that the *It* album was all about recording the ideas that Jarvis and I had worked on that summer. I still have a cassette of the two of us sitting in his mom's living room with a couple of guitars working out all sorts of bass lines, guitar, and overdub parts for that album. The way we recorded it was the way we'd planned it. I reckon it was pretty frustrating for Pete because he really wanted more input, but Jarvis and I had such a clear idea of where we were going that any third opinion would have just complicated things. Having said that, Pete made a major difference to 'Blue Girls'. That song was originally going to be a guitar based track, but he suggested doing it on the piano and did a great performance, which ended up as the main featured instrument."

Later on in the sessions, Jarvis and Simon decided to beautify the tracks with some breathy female backing vocals, courtesy of Jarvis' sister Saskia and a schoolfriend called Jill Taylor. "After most of the stuff had been done," remembers Saskia, "Jarvis asked me whether I'd like to do some singing with Jill, so we came into Victoria for a day or two. What a place. It was interesting, but God! There was a rowing boat in the kitchen – that was where you sat and ate, and there was a rowing boat there. There wasn't any heating either, so it was absolutely freezing cold. But to me, and to everybody, it was very exciting. That was the first time I'd ever been in a recording studio."

"Saskia and Jill actually make a major contribution to the overall mood and sound of the record," says Simon. "Saskia was quite nervous, which sometimes comes through, but in a really, really good way. I think they both did great."

The final additions were some clarinet and flute flourishes on 'Wishful Thinking', 'Blue Girls' and 'Love Love', courtesy of Barry Thompson, father of Heroes Of The Beach's Greg. David Hinkler: "He looked exactly as you'd expect someone called Barry Thompson to look – he looked just like Barry Norman! He knew the clarinet and flute inside out. He'd played with the Syd Lawrence Orchestra, and he was quite different to the rest of us, with him being an older bloke."

"Barry Thompson was a pro," remembers Simon. "First he did the parts that we had planned for him, then some other stuff as an ad-lib take, such as the flute in 'Blue Girls'."

"That was a surprise," remembers Peter. "I had a day off, and when I came back in there were all these clarinets and flutes all over everything, and I have to say I don't think it really worked – it would have been a decent enough record left as it was. But that was typical of Jarvis at the time – he'd do anything just to make it sound different. Plus, we had to be in and out of that studio fucking quick, so it was a bit of a make do and mend job."

Towards the end of the sessions at Victoria, the shortcomings of the studio were beginning to take their toll. "Because the studio was so shit," says Peter, "what got in to people's minds was 'This just isn't working.' We'd be trying to get something out of something, but God, we'd get some airborne noise from some factory across the road, and that'd affect the 16-track. Or something's coming through the desk from taxis, you know. All this crazy stuff's going on and what it was doing, rather than making us perform, was to hold us back – we were worrying about the next thing that was gonna go wrong. The plan had been that we were going to do the whole thing at Victoria, mixing and everything. But after one night's mixing, I think me, Jarvis and Simon all said, 'We can't fucking work here any longer.' And then Perrin was panicking a bit, because it was cheap. I've heard that it was all he could afford at the time, but if that's the case then we should have waited."

After the end of the sessions, there was another break while the particulars of the album's release were organised, and Jarvis amused himself by playing at another Heroes Of The Beach reunion concert, this time a daytime show at the Leadmill on New Year's Eve, 1982.

"It was a sort of kids' event," remembers David Bocking. "It was mainly people who normally came to see us and Jarvis, I suppose. Steve jumped off the stage at one point and started walking around on his hands, but I think the story about him exposing himself* could be a bit apocryphal. We did a mime to 'Come On Eileen' which I don't think was particularly appreciated."

The band's repertoire was largely the same as the August show at the Hallamshire, with the added attraction of a cover of 'Cars In Motion' by Artery, on which Simon Hinkler himself joined in on guitar. "Jarvis and I were both in awe when we played that onstage with Simon," remembers Michael. "We both knew all the words – I think we probably knew

---

* Mark Webber's 'History of Pulp' article in Issue 2 of the Pulp fanclub magazine *Disco-Very,* published in 1995, tells us that Heroes Of The Beach "wound up doing a concert for children and parents which ended in uproar when Steve Genn pulled his trousers down".

the words to every Artery song, they were that big in our lives at the time."

Ogy McGrath, later the singer in Dig Vis Drill, was in the audience for the concert: "It was before the place even had a licence. We were approached in the street by Tim Allcard, who we knew from In A Belljar, and he was just going, 'Come to this gig, it's free.' So we went in, and Jarvis was up there doing solo stuff with Steve Genn playing bass. Steve kept telling Jarvis off 'cos he was out of tune and Jarvis was going, 'Stop it, stop it,' and this pissed Scottish guy was going to beat Jarvis up because he thought he was crap. He handled it OK, though. He was doing a song that went *'Eeeeeeee-eeeeeee-vel Knievel, yes I'm Eeeeeeee-eeeeeee-vel Knievel'* ad *nauseam*, to which the Scottish guy objected."

"It was a lunchtime gig, around Christmas," recalls John Quinn. "Julie was just hitting things, playing a tambourine or something, and Tim was doing his terrible poems about yachts."

Martin Lilleker just remembers, "Tim, blowing some sort of horn, something that made a hell of a bloody noise, and then shouting some fairly obscene poetry at the audience. I think this might have been the one where he had one half of his hair cut short, and the opposite half of his beard shaved. But what the rest of the gig was like is gone."

"They did a thing where the first 20 people in got a free Mars bar," remembers Murray Fenton. "I went, and it was just full – there were hippies and skinheads and punks, every kind of thing. They were chucking boiled sweets out from the stage, and there were all these little kiddies there who were allowed in because it was an all-day type thing. And these kids started chucking them back, and it just got more and more – they started chucking oranges out, and I remember one of these skinheads threw this orange from the back of the Leadmill, and it just whizzed past Jarvis' glasses. Steve Genn used to walk on his hands, that were his little party piece, and he'd got my friend's bass round his neck while he was doing it. God knows how he did that. I think that concert was lost on the people who were there, though, as is the wont of most of these festival-type things.

"I've still got some memorabilia from those gigs – they'd bought a load of those tacky posters, paintings of tiger's heads, stuff like that, and just got a biro and wrote 'HEROES OF THE BEACH' on the back of them. That was their merchandise. The gigs were chaotic – there was no order to them, and I don't think there was meant to be. They were meant to be amateurish, but it was a laugh."

Meanwhile, back in Pulpland, it was apparent that the band did have something that could have passed for a finished record, but at only five tracks ('My Lighthouse', 'Wishful Thinking', 'Blue Girls', 'Love Love', 'In Many Ways'), it was more of an EP than a mini-album.* Tony Perrin: "Basically I'd run out of money to finish the record, so I played the tapes to Tony K from Red Rhino, who I already had a relationship with through doing stuff with Artery, and asked if he wanted to chip in a bit of money to finish the record and put it out. He liked the tracks, so I basically said we needed another £500 to go down to Southern and record another track, so he stumped up the money for that."

Tony Kostrzeva (generally shortened to Tony K for obvious reasons) had set up Red Rhino as a record shop in York in 1977, and the business had subesquently grown into a distribution company, and then a record label that put out releases by bands like Hula, Red Lorry Yellow Lorry and Skeletal Family. The distribution company had handled Artery's releases, and as a result Tony Perrin approached Tony K with a view to releasing the Pulp album on the label. "I can remember hearing the music," says Tony K, "and going, 'Oh this is good, I do like this,' and 'Lighthouse' I think was an outstanding piece of music, I really liked it, but as far as individuals goes, there wasn't anything of any great depth. As far as characters go, nobody made an impression – Jarvis certainly didn't. All there was was the music, which I was into that I wanted to bring out."

As a result, in January, Jarvis and Simon, with Garry Wilson, Saskia Cocker, Jill Taylor and Jon Short (a schoolfriend roped in to play some cello on the session) in tow, spent a day in London's Southern Studios, finishing off what became the first Pulp album, *It*. Thanks to Red Rhino's handy cash injection, Southern was a slightly more upmarket choice than Victoria, allowing the record to be polished off to the satisfaction of all concerned without the frustrations that blighted the main sessions. 'My Lighthouse' and 'Blue Girls' were remixed, with Jarvis recording a new vocal for the latter, and 'Joking Aside' was recorded as an extra track to fill

---

* The album sessions at Victoria Studio also yielded two songs that never surfaced on vinyl. A run-through of the live perennial 'Please Don't Worry' was laid down for possible release as a non-LP début single, but scrapped in favour of 'My Lighthouse'. 'Sink Or Swim' (which had already been recorded for the *Spice* demo under its original title 'Taking The Plunge') was abandoned before it could be mixed.

Simon: "'Please Don't Worry' was an old song, and out of step with the newer stuff. 'Sink Or Swim' seemed too lounge singer-ish for the mood of the album – and is not that good a song anyway."

"I think it was a mini-album because Jarvis might have been a bit unsure about how good some of the songs were that he had going at the time," reckons David. "What he really did was get seven songs that he'd be happy putting down on vinyl. Also, 'Please Don't Worry' and 'Sink Or Swim' had been knocking around for quite a few months, so I think he didn't want to have old stuff hanging about."

out the album. Garry Wilson: "I drove them all down to London because I was the only one who could drive. I hadn't got a clue what the song sounded like, so Simon got an acoustic guitar and said, 'It sounds something like this, can you think of any drumming to do with it?' Within the space of about 15 seconds, it were like 'Yeah! I do,' and I did it in one take. I spent the rest of the day hanging round the studio, then I drove everybody back, got about two hours' sleep, then I had to drive back down to Heathrow Airport because we were off to Italy the next day to go on tour with Artery. So that whole day was like, *Je suis un rock star* – yes!"

Finally, with 'Boats And Trains' grafted on to the album from an earlier session, the album was ready for consumption. Red Rhino's Tony K then presented Pulp with the choice of either setting up their own label imprint or releasing the album on Red Rhino. The decision was made to go with Red Rhino, and *It* was finally released on April 18, 1983 to almost total indifference from the record-buying public.

"In a lot of ways I couldn't get anybody that interested in it," remembers Tony K. "A lot of people said it was too lightweight, and nobody particularly thought much of it. At the time, indie rock had sort of moved on to goth, there was a lot of good metal around, reggae was massive, and you had lots of jangly indie pop, and sadly Pulp were bracketed in that. I thought that was sad, and wrong, because there's a quality in the songs but it just got bracketed, which still happens in many genres. It got written off as a bit of whimsical, limp-wristed indie pop stuff, and people just never gave it the time of day. You needed to give it a proper listening-to to realise that it was good accessible music, and there was something going on in the songs."

The album did receive one supportive and considered review from Dave McCulloch in *Sounds*, awarding it 4 out of 5 and commenting, "A brave attempt to make this year's cult album, *It* finally fails because it puts style above content", but the *NME* didn't even acknowledge the record's existence, and *Melody Maker*'s Steve Cross mercilessly tore into it, reckoning it to be "gooey to the gills, an aural description of the word emetic, and akin to shoving your face into a giant strawberry cake . . . It really doesn't bear up at all for the outside listener, although I've no doubt all involved are sincere and believe in it."

Tony K: "It's really difficult to move it forward when you go to talk to somebody in the press or a radio station, or in retail, the head buyer at HMV or Virgin, and obviously you need their support to get stock everywhere, and you'll point to one review and they'll point to the other! Stuff like that doesn't help you; if anybody's clued up, you can't just hoodwink them. In some ways the band didn't help themselves; live they were a bit lacklustre. There was no presence. Jarvis now, if you believe the media, has the presence, but at the time that certainly wasn't there, either as a performer or being able to work the media or the press as a personality. I believed in the songs and the writing ability, but there wasn't a lot else."

"Looking at the two completely different reactions it got from *Sounds* and *Melody Maker*," reflects David Hinkler, "for somebody to give it four out of five and somebody else to give it virtually zero, it's hard to glean anything at all. It was one of those albums where the only people who really got it were the people who actually played on it. It's all right trying to have different ideas on an album, but if people don't understand why you're doing it, they won't latch on to it."

Tony Perrin was responsible for the abstract green sleeve artwork, accurately likened by *Melody Maker* to a smear of jam on a football field. "I don't know what it was meant to be – I was just sat at my kitchen table in my flat up in Sheffield with my pots of paints and a sheet of paper, messing about and trying to come up with stuff. I took it up to Jarvis' house and he went, 'Oh yeah, I really like that.' Prior to that, before we settled on the *It* title, we went through lots of other ideas, and one of the early suggestions was to call the album *Poppy*. I remember doing a watercolour of these bright, vivid splashes that could loosely be called poppies, and taking it up to Jarvis. I remember his mum saying, 'Oh, that's really nice, why don't you do pictures like that, Jarvis?', which I think put him off that idea at a stroke."

The record itself is unmistakably juvenilia in terms of the music released under the Pulp name after 1983, but no less interesting for that – indeed, despite the flaws (and there are many, ranging from the occasionally rather overcooked arrangements, to Jarvis' songwriting, which is clearly the work of a developing, rather than fully formed, talent) it's a rounded, coherent set of songs that stands up quite well as a work on its own, regardless of what came after.

The chiming lead track 'My Lighthouse', reckoned by Jarvis to be the best song on *It*, was chosen for release as a début single, making it to the shops a month after the album. The song had gone through a lot of changes on its way to being recorded, as Wayne Furniss remembers: "It was much more of a jangly, guitar-based, sort of thing when we first played it at the Crucible a few months before. When the record came out, I was surprised that it had such a different sound."

Peter Boam: "The middle bit, the *'You and I in our high tower'* bit, that originally was totally different. It had totally different chords, totally different melody – it was a rewritten song. That was what it was like: we were always working on the hoof. I had a bit of homework for that one too –

Simon said it needed some backing vocals, so I went home and worked them out, and came in and did them with Jarvis, Saskia and Jill the next day. I'm actually proud of that, because I think it transformed the song: originally, instead of going up in the chorus, with that soaring feel, it kind of went down. It didn't really work before."

While Jarvis has said that 'My Lighthouse' was inspired by the then-popular arthouse film *Diva* ("There's a bloke living in a lighthouse, which looked cool"[58]), Peter recalls the song's inception being slightly more down-to-earth: "The way I remember it, Simon and Jarvis were at a loose end one day, and Jarvis went, 'I want to write a song, but I don't know what to write it about,' and Simon went, 'Oh I don't know, write it about a lighthouse.'"

'Wishful Thinking', the quintessential adolescent unrequited love song, was written in 1981 by a 17-year-old Jarvis and was by far the oldest song to make it on to the LP. "That was my favourite song on the album," says Peter. "Probably because it was the most complete. I don't like the flute on the end, but I must say that that wasn't my idea! Garry played the drums with timpani sticks – the ones with big round balls on the end, rather than normal drumsticks. That really worked, 'cos it helped to get that big, Phil Spector-y sound."

Like the unreleased 'Taking The Plunge' before it, 'Joking Aside' is one of the songs that says most about Jarvis' state of mind *circa* 1982/83 – there's a very palpable awareness of his own naïveté as he finds himself moving from the realm of adolescent dreaming into the real world, along with a sense of uncertainty that he's doing anything like the right thing: *"Viewed from outside these pursuits I'd not tried seemed possessed of a certain allure, but now they're no longer a source of mystery my faith in them's more unsure. Now the time to play is over, time to dispose of the lies, time to show what's really on my mind . . ."* Lyrical territory that would be revisited, albeit with considerably more vitriol, twelve years later in 'Monday Morning'.

"'Joking Aside' turned out really well," remembers Simon Hinkler. "I remember Jill and Saskia having all sorts of fun going for that *bierkeller* vibe in the instrumental, which still makes me smile every time I hear it. Jon Short was a good find – someone who could play cello who wasn't a square."

Jarvis had roped in his old schoolfriend Jon Short to add the song's distinctive cello part: "I think Jarvis and Simon had decided they wanted some sort of country and western fiddle thing – something that I've never to this day heard done on a cello, but never mind! I did it in one take, which wasn't that good – it's on the record, so you can hear all the mistakes and bum notes for yourself. What surprised me was that Jarvis and Simon seemed to really like it: I was going, 'Are you sure you don't want me to do it again?' but they were like, 'No, that's great, fantastic!' What impressed me, though, was how quickly Simon worked in the studio. He played just about everything on that track himself, and he put it all down in the space of an afternoon."

The fact that Jarvis and Simon were the only members of Pulp to appear on 'Joking Aside' (recorded a month after the rest of the album at London's Southern Studios) was something that David Hinkler – destined to be the junior partner in Pulp in status as well as age – felt slightly uncomfortable about. "Although I like the song, that was an example of how Simon was trying to step in and co-run the whole thing with Jarvis – the basic track was just him and Jarvis, plus Garry Wilson. I didn't know anything about it until they came back from Southern and they'd decided it was going to be a part of the album."

Peter Boam was less concerned about his non-involvement in the recording of the track. "I'd co-arranged it beforehand with Jarvis and Simon, which was a first. Normally it'd be Jarvis and Simon, or Jarvis and me, who'd come up with something and present it to the rest of the band, but this time we all three did it together. I didn't go down to the session at Southern though, which I'm glad about in a way. There are a few things that I'd have disagreed about."

'Boats And Trains' was also grafted on to the album from outside of the main sessions, being culled from August 1982's *Spice* demo tape. Possibly more by accident than design, it turned out to be very close to the sound of the main *It* sessions at Victoria, so Jarvis, Simon and Tony Perrin decided to put it on the end of side one to fill out the album. "That had a sort of Venice, gondolier type of vibe, with the mandolin," says David Hinkler. "I liked that one a lot. At the same time though, it's an example of what I wasn't happy with about the sound of the album – there was no percussion, and the bass was that far back in the mix it was almost non-existent."

Of all the songs on the album, 'Blue Girls' went through the most changes between its original form and the way in which it finally appeared. "The first take, which was subsequently wiped, was a full band recording," remembers Peter. "We're talking four-in-a-bar, quite loud and fast, and I was absolutely sure it didn't work. So I went home that night after the session, played it on the piano, and said, 'What do you think of this?' They said, 'Oh, we'll give it a try,' and it ended up my piano version on there. What's on the album is the first time I played it in the studio, just a run-through really. It was never intended to be on the record."

During the final album session at Southern in January, Jarvis and Simon took advantage of the extra studio time to smooth off some of the rough edges. The piano track was treated with a heavy reverb effect ("to cover up all my mistakes," as Peter says), and Jarvis re-recorded his vocal. "When we first put it down at Victoria, he couldn't quite reach down to some of the notes," remembers Peter, "so at Southern, they varispeeded the tape – made it a bit higher so he could sing it, then slowed it down again."

The result was one of the tracks from *It* that you love or loathe – according to taste, it's either an example of the album's poncey ballad tendencies at their worst (David: "It was far too soft – there was so much reverb on the piano, it might as well have been three blocks away! I've always felt that 'Blue Girls' would have been better with drums and bass behind it."), or one of the most quietly sublime songs that the early Pulp recorded.

Moving from the sublime to the ridiculous, the astonishing 'Love Love', a brave stab at Forties American jazz, was another love-or-loathe number. "I don't know if it's a pisstake or what," says the *Sheffield Star's* Martin Lilleker, "but it's just a classic pop song, isn't it? You can imagine Bacharach or someone doing it."

David agrees: "The sound of the album never did a lot for me, apart from 'Love Love', which had the heaviest bass drum I've heard in my life! We wanted to get a traditional jazz band sound on there, get the trombone in. I actually wrote that part in a couple of hours, out on the balcony at Victoria while they were putting everything else down. Considering I was only 17, 18 at the time, and I've never been brilliant on the trombone, the traditional jazz feel came across a lot better than I thought it would."

The final track was 'In Many Ways', a soft, acoustic number (with a melody slightly recycled from 'Barefoot In The Park') that ends the album on a suitably wistful note. "For that one, we thought it'd be nice to have us all playing guitar together," says Peter. "There was me, Jarvis, and Simon – he played bongos, but overdubbed a guitar later. For some reason David wasn't on it, but he was supposed to be there too."

The album was followed a fortnight later by the release of 'My Light-house' as a single, slightly remixed at Southern by Simon and Jarvis in the vain hope of grabbing the attention of reviewers and radio programmers. "On the single," notes Jarvis, "the drums and backing vocals are slightly louder, because the idea on the album was to have the drums as quiet as possible. We were definitely anti-rock at that point."[59]

The B-side was 'Looking For Life', a jangly rocker from the Victoria sessions that had originally been titled 'Looking For Love'. David: "One practice, quite early on, Simon said something like, 'Nah, you can't call it that, it sounds too poofy.' So Jarvis changed it to 'Coming Alive', and eventually it became 'Looking For Life'. When we recorded it, we knew it was going to be the B-side of the first single, and therefore just about the first time we were going to be heard on record, so everyone was trying to get as much of themselves on it as possible. We were recording it more or less live in the studio, and while I was putting my bit down on the organ, all of a sudden bloody Peter's stood next to me playing alongside me at the other end of the keyboard!"

"I also did a backing vocal," remembers Peter, "that was rightly buried! No, I can't remember what I was singing. Jarvis went, 'Sounds like bloody Gene Pitney' – one of the most exacting pieces of criticism I've ever had."

Whatever its flaws, *It* deserved to sell more than the 300 copies that it in fact managed. "I was disappointed when it wasn't successful, obviously," says Tony Perrin. "I didn't expect it to set the world alight, but I thought it might have at least dented the nation's consciousness, which of course it didn't do."

Saskia: "If you don't have those expectations then you shouldn't be doing it – I mean, everybody does. So we were disappointed, but people liked it in Sheffield and round about. Everyone was really proud of it at the time. I just remember that suddenly these songs were produced that sounded really professional, and there were all these people on it who could really, really play. It was amazing, really. Listening to it now, it makes you cringe, but at the time everybody was so pleased – it was like a very posh record. To say Jarvis was so young at that time, there were some very, very good songs, even though he'd absolutely hate them now."

Simon Hinkler was less surprised by the album's lack of success. "By that time, I didn't have any expectations for any band I was in ever going anywhere. Doing good music was the motive. I'd been repeatedly disappointed after releasing Artery records, and thought that the record buying public had no taste. Only buying what was on Radio One and *Top Of The Pops*. If I'd thought the album was ever going to actually sell I would have asked for more writing credit than just the 'My Lighthouse' one I got."

David puts *It*'s lack of commercial success down to its idiosyncratic (for 1983) sound. "I didn't have a problem with any of the parts – it's just that the sound of it did nothing for me. Regardless of the fact that Simon and Jarvis wanted it to sound different, it was too laid-back. With it not being a very drum-orientated album, it was too thin, in some areas, to carry it. If the drums had been brought up a bit on some of those tracks, I'm sure that it would have transformed them. As it was, though, it was just an oddball mix of tunes."

Garry Wilson is more sympathetic to the soft, understated sound of the album: "I thought it was good – I still listen to 'Joking Aside' now and again. I remember somebody at the time saying the drums weren't loud enough, but I think that was part and parcel of that kind of sound."

Tony: "At the time, I was happy with the way it turned out. We didn't really have anything to hold it up against and say, 'Well, it should have been this or that,' and much as Jarvis has disowned it since, it basically was his record. I just provided Jarvis with the opportunity to record some music and put some songs out. But looking at it today, I think it only really stands up as a document of where the group were at at that time – or where Jarvis was at at that time, because there wasn't really a group."

"I was glad in some ways to have a record out," says Peter Boam, "but I think the album was too much of a compromise – I wanted a sound that was a bit more hard, whereas Simon is quite conservative. If Jarvis had taken more of a guitar, bass, drums approach maybe with the girly backing vocals and stuff added on top to take some of the corners off, rather than trying to make this very sophisticated album for no money in a shit studio, then it would have been a more honest record. Maybe at the time Jarvis didn't want to be as honest as he is now – I mean, you've got to remember that it was the Eighties, and *everyone* was pretending to be something they weren't. But the main problem was that we didn't have enough time. We didn't know the songs well enough, hadn't gigged enough, and things just hadn't gelled. Saying that though, there are certain parts on *It* that I really like."

Simon Hinkler: "I have to say that I'm really fond of this album. I know Jarvis looks back on it as being a naïve period in his young life, but everything on there is good, and represents how things were for us at that time. I genuinely have fond memories of that period as being one of a really lovely circle of people. It was something that meant a lot to me, and to Jarvis too. To me it was a wonderful time, and I'm glad we saw the project through and have this record to remember those days by."

The album came as a surprise to many of Pulp's Sheffield audience, who still knew the group as a wacky, ramshackle school band. "Those of us who'd go and see them at the Hallamshire were quite surprised by how it sounded," says photographer David Bocking, who had played with Jarvis in Heroes Of The Beach earlier in 1982. "It was a lot more pleasant and acoustic and laid-back, but people did like it, even though it did sound a bit young in some ways."

"Pulp were quite well regarded," remembers John Avery of Hula. "Especially as they were so young. It seems strange to say it now, but Pulp were seen back then as the young, up-and-coming band. Elsewhere on the Sheffield band scene, it was starting to go a bit dark – the industrial thing was just starting up. Cabaret Voltaire had been around for a while, and their influence was starting to have an impact, as was the darker stuff from the early Human League. A lot of bands were hanging up their acoustic guitars and getting tape machines out, but Pulp seemed to be going the other way!"

John Quinn: "They never really got that smooth live – they tended to be a bit ramshackle, really. It sold very few copies – there were people who would go and see Pulp live because they were always entertaining, but didn't bother with the record. At that time, they were always a better live proposition than a recorded band."

One confirmed fan of the album was Clive Solomon, who two years later would sign Pulp to his newly formed label, Fire Records: "I loved the *It* album for what it was, but oddly enough it kind of fitted in with a lot of the acoustic, indie stuff at the time, which Dave McCulloch at *Sounds* gave a tag, although I forget what it was. Things like Felt, Aztec Camera, even Pale Fountains and a lot of the stuff that Mike Alway was signing to either Cherry Red or El. There were a lot of bands who were indie, but also had a very stripped-down, acoustic approach. I suppose it was the indie equivalent of soft rock, or something."

It is fascinating now in that it provides a musical and lyrical document of the young Jarvis – before he was hit by the influence of the artistic catalyst that was Russell Senior, sex-war relationships, acid house, fame, fortune or London. But it's also worth much more than that – at times, the album manages to combine emotional intensity with a kind of naïve charm in a way that was and is very rare. And even though it might as well come from another universe compared to any collection of Pulp songs released since, it does have one thing in common with everything Pulp have done since in that it is truly unique.

Even so, it's understandable that even as early as 1985, Jarvis was already feeling pangs of embarrassment toward his firstborn. "It was dead sincere at the time," he told *NMX* fanzine. "I'm not trying to make excuses, it makes me sad more than anything else because I seem very naïve and innocent about things, which I don't feel that I am now. It was hankering after something which I didn't have any experience of and when you get to actually have what you've been crying for for a long time sometimes you find that you don't want it and chuck it in the bin."[60]

"In my naïve days," he said many years later, "I thought that you were going to get a girlfriend and then it was all going to be all right. And then you find out that it's not going to be all right."[61]

Chapter 4

By the time *It* was released in April 1983, the new Pulp had already spent several months attempting to re-establish itself on the Sheffield live circuit. After the chopping and changing of the *It* sessions, the line-up had finally stabilised at the start of the year around a core of Jarvis (vocals/ guitar), Simon Hinkler (bass), Peter Boam (guitar), David Hinkler (keyboards/ guitar/trombone). The drumming position was taken up by new recruits Tim Allcard and Michael Paramore, from In A Belljar.

"Jarvis had played in our band," remembers Paramore, "and then he just sort of said that Garry from Artery wasn't gonna play and they needed a drummer. They were playing a gig at the University, I think it was a benefit concert or something like that, so me and Tim sort of went along to practise in Jarvis' outbuilding. It was like a two-man drummer kind of thing – we just learnt the beats. We got a little tape that we had to practise for a few days, and we played about three or four more concerts after that."

Tim and Michael's main contribution to Pulp came from the wilfully odd, performance art-influenced stance of In A Belljar. "They made strange instruments," recalls Peter Boam, "stuff made out of different household objects. They made their own mike stands out of wood, things like that, and they probably brought some of that over to Pulp."

As well as contributing shared percussion to Pulp, Tim made his presence felt by reciting poems between songs. "He was just there for the image, really, with his hair and his strange clothes," reckons David Hinkler. "He was a really top bloke, actually. I think maybe to buy his pass on to the stage, he might have hit bits of percussion, and there was a bit of poetry going on between the songs as well – I remember one that went *'Lots of yachts, lots and lots of yachts. Yachts. Lots and lots of yachts'*, and it just went on like that."

Saskia: "There was 'Lots And Lots Of Yachts', and another one called 'The Blind Can See', which went 'There's us that are blind, can't you see?' Very funny. And then it just progressed; he'd just come on for a few songs and do a few little bits and bobs – tinkling about with a few bells or something, or a couple of sticks."

Simon and David, meanwhile, were both now dividing their energies between Pulp and Artery: Simon had left the group before Christmas, but had rejoined with David in January to tour the group's new album *One Afternoon In A Hot Air Balloon*. They'd already completed a tour of Italy, and were gigging fairly frequently through most of 1983 – more frequently, in fact, than Pulp. "Artery took priority," says Simon. "They were more 'senior' and much more of a serious band then. [Artery vocalist] Mark Gouldthorpe's position was, as long as me and Dave working with Pulp didn't interfere with Artery, then he was OK with it. I don't remember any specific instance of it being an issue with anyone in either Pulp or Artery, but then, I don't remember anyone getting on my case with either band really – I guess because I was a key player in both."

The new six-piece Pulp, meanwhile, had started gigging in January with appearances at Sheffield University, and a dimly remembered event at a wine bar in Chesterfield that constituted an attempt on behalf of the organisers to get into the Guinness Book of Records for the longest non-stop cabaret. By the time of a Leadmill gig with New Model Soldier in February, however, cracks were starting to appear.

Peter Boam: "We didn't play all that well, plus there weren't very many people there, and because we were supporting New Model Soldier, there were all these goths in the audience who just didn't get it. Jarvis had a bit of a fit afterwards because it hadn't gone like he'd wanted it to – he was going, 'It's no good, it's not going anywhere,' and we all had to talk him round and convince him it was all right."

"It had lost some of the wacky stage act that would go about with Pete and Jamie," says David. "That was when people started to perhaps not get it. Before, it was obvious what was going on – it was a display backed up by some good songs. But when they went, the good songs were still there, with a more half-hearted attempt at looking a bit weird and wacky on stage."

For Jarvis, the strain of keeping Pulp going after the passing of the original, school-based, Dolly/Jamie/Wayne band was beginning to show. It wasn't that there was anything particularly wrong with the new Pulp – the new sound was there, the songs were there, the musicians (despite the rather volatile line-up) were there – but somehow it just wasn't the same. The old Pulp had achieved so much in such an exceedingly short time that the experience of leaving school, signing on and starting again from scratch with a new band and no ready-made fanbase (many of the old Pulp fans having headed off to university like Dolly and Jamie) was bound to be quite a comedown.

It was perhaps partly for this reason that Jarvis started inviting an ever-wider group of friends and acquaintances to join Pulp on stage at gigs in roles of varying musical importance. As well as the core band and Tim and Michael, concerts from March 1983 onwards would feature the likes of Saskia and Jill Taylor providing backing vocals (with Saskia also singing lead vocals on a never-released song called 'When You Cry, I Cry', and playing flute on another called 'Stay'); Jarvis' cousin Hannah on triangle and backing vocals at a couple of gigs; and (at one concert at the Crucible) Steve Genn doing . . . stuff.

"That was Jarvis at the time – he was introducing anyone into the band who played an unusual instrument," says Peter Boam. "Instead of saying, 'Right, we're a five-piece,' there were more and more people joining and it was getting diluted."

Pulp was becoming an increasingly nebulous entity, but there was one important new recruit at this stage: 18-year-old drummer Magnus Doyle, formerly of a host of local bands including Blimp, A Major European Group and Midnight Choir. Magnus was a highly skilled, intuitive drummer who managed to bring some much-needed solidity to the Pulp rhythm section. "It was great when he came in," remembers Peter Boam. "I didn't know he was joining, he just turned up one day. He was a good fella at the time. I knew his dad Ken, actually – he was a theatre director who once directed a play of mine."

Doyle's distinctive personality and appearance also brought something unique to Pulp. "He was a really, really lovely person," remembers Saskia. "I was at college with him. He was very, very quiet, very gentle. He was another oddity – everybody was a bit strange who came in, bit of a misfit really. But we were all together, so it was all right. He was a great person."

Simon Hinkler: "He was awesome. Actually I met Candida [Magnus' older sister] before Magnus – it was probably a year or two before I was in Pulp. She briefly went out with Neil McKenzie from Artery, then for a short time after that I used to hang out with Candida – not as a girlfriend really, we'd go for walks and stuff, I just enjoyed being with her. I guess I first met Magnus at their parents' house in Woodseats. Magnus was shaving some kid's hair – it was probably Manners [Peter Mansell]. They were both pretty young then. Magnus was a brilliant drummer – kind of reminded me of Keith Moon. He was very quiet, and also very mysterious. He got stranger and stranger as he got older. I can honestly say that I always admired Magnus and liked him a lot. There was something about him . . . not sure how to describe it . . . as if he knew a secret about existence that nobody else did."

David Hinkler: "When I knew him, he was an absolutely brilliant drummer, very talented, but very quiet. He used to do really weird things to himself – the last thing a bloke would ever want to do would be to have no hair on top and long hair down the sides, but he shaved his head so that he looked as if he'd gone bald. He was mad, but in an understated way – he didn't go round doing stupid things and causing trouble or anything like that."

"His hair was always ridiculous," says David Bocking, "and that was part of the point of Magnus, really. That's how he wanted things to be. He was quiet to speak to, fairly normal and sensible. He didn't have much to say for himself, although I would imagine there were occasions when he would behave differently. In a way, he was fairly typical of the people who were around – he wanted to make a statement in a small way, and he built up his character to being a very strange-looking person who played drums."

"He was one of the quietest people I've ever met," reflects Tony Perrin. "Certainly one of the strangest people I've ever met, but absolutely lovely with it. And he was an absolutely phenomenal drummer. He was a real Keith Moon character – he's one of those drummers who become part of the kit, or the kit becomes part of them. There's no gap."

Nick Robinson simply remembers Magnus as a "thoroughly wonderful guy. We used to go back to his flat and score dope. Totally, utterly strange young man, but completely in control of himself – he'd got his image, and he was totally at ease with that."

Fluctuating personnel and uncertainty about the group's direction aside, the songs, Jarvis' personality and a musically competent core band meant that the 1983 model Pulp still guaranteed a decent evening's entertainment. "We were actually quite good," says Peter Boam. "That was what Pulp was all about really, being a good live band. The sound I was after, and I think Simon was after as well, was quite raw, but lush at the same time. I'm not sure what Jarvis was after though – he's good at saying what he doesn't want, but he's not always articulate about saying what he does want, so you end up barking up a lot of wrong trees!"

"We tried to get it close to the sound of the album," says Simon Hinkler. "When I sound checked, I didn't close-mike the drums, but just used a couple of overheads to catch more of a general kit sound, then put a bunch of reverb on them, which is a pretty unusual thing to do. There was no piano though – in those days you just couldn't get a real piano sound without using a real piano. Bummer of a problem – made it particularly difficult with Artery touring *Hot Air Balloon*, which is all piano."

"We didn't actually play that many songs from the album after we recorded it," reckons Peter Boam. "'My Lighthouse' we used to do, and

'Joking Aside' with the girlies doing their '*la la la*' bit. We played 'Boats And Trains' once or twice, a slightly more upfront-sounding version, with drums, and we did 'Love Love' sometimes, just as a knockabout fun thing. There'd be some earlier stuff – we always used to do 'Please Don't Worry', and open with 'Heat Of The Day' and finish with 'How Could You Leave Me?' Because Jarvis would gab away for ages between songs, we could get away with doing about seven songs in 45 minutes."

On April 3, Pulp played one of the more visually elaborate concerts of the period at the Crucible Studio Theatre. "It was very much back to the stage show we had before," says David Hinkler. "We had lots of lights, and bits of curtain all over the place, and we covered the stage in paper fish."

Peter: "There were thirteen people on stage. All over the balconies and everything. There were people banging tambourines, playing flutes, girlies singing, all sorts of things. Mad."

John Quinn, later of the *Sheffield Star*'s Pop Page, was in the audience. "Peter Boam stood out in that line-up because he had really long hair, like a rocker or something, when all the others were in all these jumble sale clothes. He looked like he'd just left Black Sabbath or something. They were very different to when I first saw them [in February '82]. They'd tried to go a bit more middle-of-the-road, and had a much, much mellower sound. They seemed to go down pretty well, though."

One good show, however, wasn't enough to give Pulp a career, and after the release of *It* the same month the gigs started drying up. The group's one projected London show, supporting the re-formed Artery at Brixton Fridge on May 2, fell through due to bad planning. "I blew that one out," confesses Peter Boam. "Only time I've not shown up for a gig. Nobody was rehearsing, Simon would be off for three weeks, then he'd show up the night before and say, 'Let's do a gig!' I was rehearsing that night for a play I was going to be in the next week and I just said, 'Look, you can't bloody well call me up at 10 o'clock and say we've got a gig.' It was just crazy.

"What made it difficult was that nobody was around at the same time. It was mad – things would be arranged at one minute to midnight, you know. You'd never know when anything was happening. I'd have to travel by train from Chesterfield, which is 12 miles out of Sheffield, and after a while I just started to get pissed off with the whole thing."

A couple of weeks later, Pulp were supposed to play the Marples in Sheffield, but the concert was cancelled when the PA blew up. "God, I remember that," says Peter. "Tony was throwing a tantrum, Simon was trying to act the level-headed pro, and Jarvis was sulking in a corner some-where. Hilarious."

Frustration with the band's inertia led to Jarvis, Peter, Tim Allcard and some forgotten others forming a one-off band called the Jarvis Cocker Explosion Experience for a gig in the Hallamshire in late May. Simon Hinkler was in the audience. "Now *that* was a significant foreshadowing of things to come much later. Jarvis was tongue-in-cheek playing the super-star, and his performance was a lot like the act for which he later became famous around 'Disco 2000'. Actually, I even remember a song from then, called 'The Jarvis Blues', which was really funny."

Peter Boam: "The reason we did it was that Simon was off on his piano tuning course again. Jarvis just said, 'Look, we've got to get out and do something,' so we got together without Simon and called it something else – when Simon was there it was Pulp, and when he wasn't it wasn't. I think we'd done about two or three rehearsals round at Jarvis' mam's house, then we did the gig. We were all pissed. That was the only time 'There Was . . .' got played live. We never did 'Everybody's Problem', thank God."

Ah, 'Everybody's Problem'. Despite the less-than-spectacular sales that *It* and 'My Lighthouse' had achieved, Red Rhino's Tony K had sufficient faith in Pulp to put up the funds for another single. "The whole motiva-tion behind 'Everybody's Problem' was to put something out that could start a fire and provoke some interest," says Tony Perrin. "We'd put out what we thought at the time was a reasonably good album that had made no impact whatsoever, so we thought we'd go all out to do something that'd get people's attention. Failed miserably."

The sessions took place over a weekend in early June (forcing the can-cellation of yet another gig at the Marples), at Southern Studios in London. "Because of the quality of the studio," says David, "it was des-tined to be nothing like anything off *It*. The drums were upfront, and the guitar was quite heavy. There was a lot of disharmony when it was being recorded because everyone was trying to get their own parts up in the mix, saying, 'I can't hear me doing this.' I remember our Simon saying we had to quit this committee-room mixing sort of thing, so everyone else was told to get out of the mixing room while Simon and Jarvis finished mixing it."

The song itself was a ridiculously upbeat, jolly number in the tradition of the likes of 'Please Don't Worry', 'Sickly Grin' and 'Barefoot In The Park' – only more so. Jarvis cringes about his half-hearted attempt at writing a poppy, commercial hit single to this day: "Tony Perrin, in his infinite wisdom, decided that Wham! were a good group, and said, 'You could write commercial songs like Wham!, Jarvis.' 'Everybody's Problem' was the result. As soon as I'd written it, I realised I'd made a grave error."[62]

"The idea was to do some catchy pop song," remembers Peter, "so Jarvis came out with this track, and it was terrible. I mean, Jarvis isn't bloody George Michael and neither am I."

Much as the memory of 'Everybody's Problem' may make Jarvis and Peter shudder, it's not without its merits – if the fact that it's by Pulp is ignored, or even if it isn't, it's a perfectly likeable piece of throwaway fluff. "I always liked 'Everybody's Problem' for what it was," says David, "regardless of who was on it or whatever. If that single had got any decent amount of airplay, it would have sold. Before Pulp were known at all, I told a girlfriend of mine I'd been in a band, and she said, 'Oh, play me something.' So I dropped some records off at her house, one of which was 'Everybody's Problem', and she told me that she and her friend had been dancing to it all afternoon. Anytime I put it on at home, anyone who listens to it says it's really, really great.

"I know it's lightweight, but people need that, don't they? You can't sit glued to your woofer and tweeter all the time trying to work out what's going on. Lightweight stuff's got a place."

Musically, Magnus' drumming gives the track a much harder feel than anything from the album, and David's 'brass section' beefs up the sound thanks to some studio jiggery-pokery: "That was just me on the trombone," he remembers. "I played three parts, then the engineer speeded two up so that it sounded like a trumpet."

Jarvis has claimed that he was unhappy with the song to the point of refusing to sing properly at the session, thus messing up the lyrics on the finished single. David remembers the situation slightly differently: "There was a lot of debate over how Jarvis should sing it. He could either do it in a lower octave or take it completely up into the next octave, and sing it high all the way through. After a while, Jarvis got so fed up with the situation that he just left the rough version on, with him starting low, and going up an octave for the last verse." The only noticeable bit where Jarvis actually fluffs the lyrics is at the beginning of the second verse, which, rather than going *"Choose what you belieblem [sic], but I'm not everyone,"* should go *"It's everybody's problem, but I'm not everyone"*. Even so, it's a less-than-sparkling performance.

Simon Hinkler: "'Everybody's Problem' was not a good song at all, made all the worse by Jarvis' throwaway vocal. I guess Tony was looking to break the band as a pop act, and that song was Jarvis' attempt at writing a hit – which he didn't need to do, because his usual songwriting was good enough, or potentially good enough, without forcing it. As a band we just did our best on the track, but Jarvis decided he didn't want to do this, and sabotaged it when he came to do the vocal, and just left a lacklustre guide vocal on there. Which is daft really, because it's just shooting yourself in the foot. If he didn't want to do that song as a single he should have just said so – after all, he wrote the bloody thing."

The B-side, 'There Was . . .', was a different story altogether: a very gentle number, universally agreed by all who were involved to be the best thing produced by Pulp in that period. Simon Hinkler: "That song definitely captured the sound that was, at least, in my mind for the band. It's beautiful."

"That track's got a really good atmosphere to it," says David Hinkler. "I played that part on the Fender Rhodes [electric piano] in the control room. I was fed up with Simon and Jarvis not wanting drums or bass on anything, so I kept sneaking in bass notes on the Fender while nobody was looking. Fender Rhodes bass can sometimes rumble out quite a lot and it was sending the levels funny on the studio meters. It just filled the room with bass when you hit 'em. But everyone was really, really pleased with that track. There was actually some talk of putting it on the A-side, but we didn't think there'd be much market for it."

Peter agrees: "That track was the nearest we got to how we felt the *It* album, and the band we were afterwards, should've been – my favourite thing that we recorded, definitely. That was the first time the three of us – me, Simon and Jarvis – had worked really well on something together. It was a really nice moment in the studio when, after everything that had gone before, me and Simon were sat playing the same guitar riff at the same time – we'd never done that before, ever. Seeing as it turned out to be the last thing we recorded together, I think that was a good note to end on."

It was the A-side that mattered though and, whether you love it or hate it, 'Everybody's Problem' was a long way away from what anyone wanted Pulp to be. "I thought it was crap even then," says Tony Perrin, "but I've since been landed with the blame for its inception. The thing is, it was such a big deal in those days even to scrape together the money to make a recording that it never entered your head at the end of it to think, 'Well that's crap, let's not put it out.' Obviously in this day and age, with more experience and funds, you'd never do that. You'd make a recording like that and go, 'Well that's not us, let's bin it.' But back then, that wasn't the case."

The sleeve artwork was by Michael Paramore. "I remember doing quite a few different covers for it. I was really into stained glass at the time – that sounds a bit horrible, but in the way I was painting, that sort of style. I did quite a few pictures and they all had Jarvis in them, and Jarvis hated that – he didn't want a picture of him on the cover, so it was this dodgy lino print at the last minute."

The rear sleeve photo, meanwhile, was the cause of yet more rancour within the band. "I remember seeing the record for the first time," says David Hinkler, "and wondering why none of us got any credit on the sleeve – there was just a photo of Jarvis, Saskia and Tim on the back. It started to make you wonder whether it was a money thing, whereby if it does make something then Jarvis would be the only one to get anything for it."

"I don't know why that was to be honest," says Saskia. "Maybe it was just because the three of us looked the most interesting people out of the lot."

"Whether Jarvis knew that the band were going to split up or not I don't know," says Michael Paramore, "but Tim was pretty cool, so I think Jarvis wanted him on the cover, and then he put his sister on the cover 'cos she was his sister and it was just the image he wanted to put over."

Simon Hinkler: "It was Tony's idea for an image. No wonder the band fell apart."

Maybe Tony Perrin had convinced Jarvis that he, Tim and Saskia were the ones best suited to the cover of *Smash Hits*. Even so, the fact that the rest of the band to this day doesn't know what the real story is says something about the cohesion of Pulp as a unit *circa* 1983.

In any event, concerns over which Pulpsters were going to bask in popstar status when it came turned out to be largely academic when 'Everybody's Problem' sank without a trace. *Sounds*, in the only national press coverage the single received, was cruel but fair:

> "... *unmemorable lightweight fey drivel. I'll bet they're fresh-faced young boys, cloned from the wide-eyed and innocent likes of the Lotus Eaters. Their skulls deserve to be crushed like eggshells.*"[63]

A local fanzine was a little more sparing:

> "*Play the B-side first – 'There Was' for this is the essence of Pulp. A haunting gaelic quality surrounds the captured breath of the singer's love song. Return to the A-side for jangling percussion and jolly trumpets on a runaway display of jumbled affections. If you like this kind of lucid sound, the album 'Pulp' [sic] will complete the picture.*"[64]

"I thought it was a cracking single, actually," confesses Martin Lilleker. "I remember saying a number of times that I'd eat my hat if it wasn't a hit, knowing full well that I hadn't got a hat. I can't see why Jarvis would say he was being coerced into doing it by Tony Perrin when he'd been doing that sort of thing anyway, unless he was being coerced all the way through. Jarvis disowns everything though, doesn't he? People who knew Pulp before they became famous loved all those records, but Jarvis won't have anything to do with them now."

Perhaps the most remarkable thing about 'Everybody's Problem' was Jarvis' appearance on the rear-sleeve photo. His hair had grown out from the unkempt nest of a couple of years before, to a quite spectacularly unkempt bouffant nest that would have rivalled The Cure's Robert Smith. The effect was completed by – what else? – a carefully sculpted narrow strip of beard, running down from his ears, joining under his chin, and then creeping up to his lower lip. "The funny thing about it," remembers Jarvis, "was I grew it, and I didn't really know why, and I used to get the piss taken out of me at the fish market where I was working at the time for having it. And then I found my dad's old Student Union card from when he was exactly the same age as me at this time, and he had the exact same beard, and I'd never known that he had that beard.[65] It scared me because I thought I was going to do the same as him, get married and then leave."[66]

Later in June, Pulp finally managed their first gig in two months, at the Marples. The show received a lukewarm review from the usually support-ive Martin Lilleker in the *Sheffield Star*:

> *"Stranger and stranger . . . why were half the musicians hidden behind a screen, I ask myself. Fact is Pulp have probably got some of the best and most commercial songs going. But like the mystery of the disappearing musicians, there is something missing in the execution of the songs. They vary from the laid-back to the jolly, the infectious to the moving. But Pulp still have the amateurish streak that once bracketed them with The Fall. This concert was enjoyable but not quite fulfilling. Next time . . ."[67]*

"That was for contractual reasons," says David Hinkler of the screen. "Because me and our Simon were in Artery as well, people weren't allowed to know that we were in Pulp. Stupid really, considering that Artery were doing practically nothing around that time."

Murray Fenton: "My impression was that the sound was sort of starting to phase over to the basis of the early Fire stuff. It had sort of gone from ramshackle pop to that really dreamy stuff, and then I sort of thought they moved out a bit."

The same night marked Jarvis' first encounter with Ogy McGrath, singer with a new Sheffield band called Dig Vis Drill. "Pulp came to a lot of our early gigs, around '83," remembers Ogy, "and because there'd only be about 20 people there, they'd stand out. We reciprocated after a bit – they approached us in the bar and said, 'We're Pulp, come to our gig at the Marples.' It said something like 'Two bands and a disco' on the poster and it was a pound, which was extortionate in those days – you know, just after decimalisation. I complained to Jarvis about it. I said, 'Hey, where's the fucking disco, man? It's just a tape recorder,' and he went, 'It's what we call a disco. It's playing music loud, that's what discos do.' So that was our first conversation."

Over the next three years, Dig Vis Drill would become one of Pulp's closest allies in the Sheffield band scene, both musically and socially. "Me and Jarv always had good fun," says Ogy. "He used to come to our gigs even when he didn't have to. He'd roadie for us and stuff, and I'd take him to gay clubs and shit. It was funny, around '86 we had this gig in this gay club in Liverpool, and Jarvis just came along for something to do, and he was recognised – that was the first place someone had known him and made a fuss over him, I think."

For the rest of June, the whole of July and most of August, there would be no Pulp concerts at all. The group still existed, but Jarvis, who had real-ised by now that his year out of university wasn't going to bring stardom, was spending more time playing tin cans at gigs with In A Belljar. He also performed with Michael Paramore as Breadcake, playing a gig at the Hallamshire in June, in total darkness. "It was supposed to sound like The Velvet Underground," says Michael, "but I'm not sure how. We just wrote two songs the day before we performed, that basically consisted of a reel-to-reel tape that Jarvis had put Pulp songs on, playing backwards, and there was a really tacky Casio playing over the top and someone just shouted over the top."

On the same bill was Fish, another ad hoc group formed by Tim Allcard, Nick Taylor and Magnus Doyle. "That was percussion and vocal," says Nick. "Tim did vocal and used an air raid siren on one track. Mag and myself did a song that was just percussion and drums, and we just played a bit of drums and then it sort of stopped and then there was this conversation that was based on, when our mate David was in a pub near the practice room which was on Willey Street. He went in the pub and started getting some stick off this bloke who was in the pub 'cos he'd got a lurcher dog. This bloke reckoned it was underfed, and he was saying, no, it was meant to be like that, and the bloke was saying, 'If you come in the pub again with your dog in that state I'm gonna give you some fist.' Mag was doing the side conversation that was this bloke in the pub, or it might have been the other way round, and he was the bloke with the dog and I was the bloke in the pub. Anyway, those sort of things were quite common at that time in the Hallamshire."

Around the same time, Jarvis played another one-off gig at the Hallamshire with Steve Genn as Repressive Minority. They had a song about cockroaches called 'Wiggle Your Antennae'. "Jarvis always seemed to want to keep moving on to the next project," remembers Simon Hinkler, "so before long he started being less enthused about *It*. It was those side projects that eventually drew him away from the band, but I was no different – I think we'd done our thing together and both wanted to move on. I'd started writing new songs for Artery – which was great, because for the first time, I was the main musical force, and got to do everything my own way – something I was ready for after only collaborating."

The next Pulp gig was on Tuesday, August 30, 1983, headlining at the Marples. "Looking back," says David, "that concert was probably the best we did, musically. 'The Heat Of The Day' was the first song in the set, and I remember playing the keyboard and looking up at our Simon on bass, and thinking, 'Yeah, this is going to be a good show.'

"But towards the end, Jarvis really had a go at the audience in a big way. We'd come back for an encore and got lukewarm clapping or something, and Jarvis said, 'Well, I suppose that went over everybody's heads, seeing as most of you are students,' or something like that. And really, the room just went dead, completely. It was a real 'if looks could kill' sort of thing. It might have been because it was coming around to college time again, and Jarvis still wasn't where he wanted to be. He'd started to get very apathetic and annoyed with the situation. But it wasn't a very clever thing to say, considering it had been a good show, and there might have been a few dozen people in the audience who'd not heard Pulp before, and might have come back and seen us again, bought the record or whatever – but he turned them against the band totally."

As it turned out, it didn't particularly matter: within a couple of weeks of the concert, Pulp had split up. "The future," Jarvis later noted, "was cancelled due to lack of interest."[68]

Chapter 5

Russell Senior was born in Firth Park, Sheffield in 1961, the son of a steel-worker. "When I was young," he says, "the family moved to Gleadless, a boring suburb where nothing ever happened. The first big musical excite-ment in my life was glam rock around the age of 12. I guess that no one ever really looks like a proper pop star to me unless they wear lots of eye-liner, preferably glittery. My mother had a boutique, so I did quite well for velvet tank tops, brummie bags, flares and star sweaters. She'd also stopped cutting my hair in junior school, which got me confused for a girl on many occasions, but gave me a head start in the mid-Seventies when rebellion consisted of having long hair and listening to heavy metal bands such as Hawkwind, Led Zeppelin and Black Sabbath.

"On *Top Of The Pops* once, the announcer said, 'We don't have Hawkwind in the studio, but here's some live footage from one of their "gigs".' So there they were, with Liquid Len's lights flowing all around them, long-haired Lemmy, semi-naked Stacia flailing her arms in some bizarre space ritual and the audience freaking out to this soaring wall of sound. And I thought, 'That's what I want to do when I grow up!'"

Around 1976, Senior bought a guitar and formed his first band, Isengard, which he describes as "sort of psychedelic heavy metal. The name was from *Lord Of The Rings*; I think the subject matter of songs was largely sci-fi. When I was 16 came punk rock, the most exciting thing in the world. I fell out with my best friends because they didn't like it. So I went to the school disco with new punk friends, pogoed, got picked on by townies and got banned from that. On one occasion at school, a teacher picked me up by the hair, presumably for wearing a black mesh bag over my head. There was a club called The Improvision. On one week there'd be Motorhead, and the next The Vibrators – I loved it all, apart from getting chased through abandoned car parks by teddy-boys or townies or whoever took a dislike to people wearing safety pins. This affected what I was playing; I took on board the punk notion that long guitar solos are for hippies, and also 'Pretty Vacant' is a lot easier to play than 'Stairway To Heaven'.

"My next band was called The Bath Bankers, derived somehow from the line, *'Wanna destroy bastard wankers,'* from the Pistols' 'Anarchy In The UK', which I believe was banned and changed to the more airplay friendly *'Wanna destroy passers-by'*. The next big influence was The Fall, who were edgy, dangerous, exciting – and very northern in a way only northern people could understand, working men's clubs, grime, desperation, sleaze. I think there were early fragments of songs that got used later in Pulp – certainly the song 'Fairground', which resurfaced on *Freaks*, was pretty fleshed out. The only public appearances were non-events in front of non-audiences.

"There was also a little collaboration with my sister Rachel, called Rachel Tension And The Disruptives. The best thing about this band was the name, although we did do an early version of the song 'Maureen'. Then there was a punk band, which I sang in, with a psychobilly edge, called The Nightmares. I think this was the last band before Pulp and again there were fragments that later found their way into the early Pulp live set such as 'Back In LA'.

"I think all of Pulp had a similar sense of 1977 being a cultural year zero, a revolution to which we all subscribed. The other thing we would probably all subscribe to would be that whilst Sheffield might be an ugly northern town which didn't get fresh basil until 1997, from the late Seventies and into the early Eighties it was one of the most musically inspiring places in the world."

In September 1983, shortly after completing a Business Administration degree at Bath University, Russell Senior joined Pulp.

When Russell joined, it was just in time to see the *It* incarnation of Pulp disintegrate. The process began when Simon Hinkler, who had musically nursed Jarvis through the past 13 months, finally left the group. "It just happened," says Hinkler now. "My head was in a different place, so was Jarv's. I did loads of magic mushrooms in those days, and my life frequently changed course on a whim."

"Things were starting to happen in a way with Artery around then," says his brother David, "and I think he wanted to get back into that. There was a general feeling that things with Pulp weren't going anywhere, and nobody was really sure what was going to happen after 'Everybody's Problem' didn't do anything."

"All I know is that Simon went very, very quickly," says Peter Boam. "I just turned up to a rehearsal and he'd gone. Still don't know why to this day. I think Jarvis had decided he was going to move the furniture a bit – David and I were invited to this rehearsal, Simon was gone, and Russell was there."

As well as his Business Administration degree, Russell had returned to Sheffield with a surrealist play called *The Fruits Of Passion*, a battered Rosetti electric guitar, and a handful of songs he'd written for his old bands The Nightmares and The Bath Bankers, and a headful of ideas. "I'd quite liked the original Pulp," says Russell, "but hated the album. It had nice tunes, but that didn't seem enough somehow – there was no edge to it, and it just didn't have any kind of emotional power. I knew Jarvis felt the same way, so I approached him and said, 'Look, I know you're not happy with the way the band's going, and I think I can help you put it right.'"

Jarvis agreed. "We'd made this gentle, polite LP," he says, "so I thought, 'Fuck off, let's go to the other extreme.'"[69]

The new, hardline, Russell-influenced approach wasn't entirely successful at first: new songs like 'Silence', 'Back In LA' and 'Maureen' (the latter two of which were old Nightmares songs with new lyrics added by Jarvis) were undeniably a long way from the melodic lushness of *It*, but still didn't seem to show much promise for a new Pulp. "It wasn't really Pulp in the sense of what came before or what came after," says Russell. "At that point, the band as such didn't exist – it was just an unsuccessful attempt at making some music. We tried for two pretty bad rehearsals, and gave up."

You only need to compare lyrics and musical approach of the likes of 'There Was . . .' with the initial Cocker/Senior compositions to see that this period found Jarvis at something of a crossroads, both personally and musically. He'd just turned 20 and, after what could be seen as an unsuccessful year out trying to keep alive the remnants of a band that had to all intents and purposes ended a year previously when his schoolfriends had left to go to university, was now faced with the very real option of surrendering to normality, closing the door on his teenage dabblings, and belatedly following his friends to university

"I think Jarvis went to pieces a bit after Simon went," says Peter Boam, "and also he'd had his first shag around that time, which kind of messed him up . . . Musically, he needs a rudder, someone who can mix his palette for him, and when Simon left I was ready to get in there and take over that role." In view of which, it perhaps seems surprising that within a few days of Simon's departure, Peter was gone as well.

David Hinkler: "Peter leaving so soon after Simon was surprising. Pete tended to be miffed by the fact that he didn't get any credit for what he did – he did have some good musical input and some good ideas, but Jarvis and Simon often wouldn't take them on board. Because he and our Simon had always been competing over who played what and how and where, it seemed strange that after one of them had left, the other would go as well. It was like, 'You've got what you want now!'"

However, Jarvis had other ideas about who was going to provide the musical direction in the post-Simon Pulp. "Very quickly," says Peter Boam, "it became very apparent that Russell was driving it – the new stuff just seemed to be riffs rather than songs, and it wasn't that we didn't like it, but all of a sudden it was a different band. So I left – I think after one rehearsal with him. When Simon was in the group, a lot of the time I couldn't get my way because he was always Jarvis' main collaborator. When he left, I was ready to step in and start to organise things, but Russell got in before me. There wasn't any animosity or anything; we were all still friends, but I just didn't go to the practices any more."

David Hinkler stayed for a couple more rehearsals after Peter's departure, but was similarly unconvinced by the new direction: "Russell basically just got noise out of his guitar. One string, naïve, nothing compared to what I was used to. I just thought, 'Why has Jarvis let two competent musicians go and got this idiot in?' Nothing personal against Russell, but I just reckoned he couldn't play. Anybody who had a guitar that didn't have all six strings on it wasn't someone I wanted to work with."

David was also having trouble getting to grips with the famous Pulp Farfisa organ that Tony Perrin had purchased second-hand for the 'Everybody's Problem' sessions. "I just didn't like that instrument at all, so that put me off a bit as well. I tried for two rehearsals in Jarvis' garage, but there was just nothing coming."

The loss of David, Simon and Peter was swiftly followed by that of Tony Perrin's managerial services. "There was no big argument or anything," Perrin says now. "Things just seemed to have drifted to an end. I could appreciate that Jarvis wasn't happy with *It*, but I wasn't really confident of where they appeared to be going. We were going in different directions and I couldn't do anything for him."

In the space of a fortnight, Pulp had seen the departure of three key members and a manager, and the initial attempt to relaunch the band with Russell seemed to be going nowhere artistically. As a result, a dispirited Jarvis decided to give up on the band that had shaped the previous five years of his life, and take up his place at Liverpool University that he had deferred a year earlier.

Well, almost. Despite the seemingly fatal loss of the musical core of the old Pulp and the fact that he was supposed to be leaving Sheffield for Liverpool in a matter of weeks, Jarvis, Magnus, Russell and Tim Allcard had a last-ditch practice in the vain hope that the embers would somehow pick up. Astonishingly enough, they did: the signs that something worthwhile might come of this unlikely collaboration between Jarvis the wannabe-child-star-turned-easy-listening-vocalist, Russell the hardline noise-fixated conceptualist, and two arty Sheffield oddballs ("I think Magnus and Tim spent a lot of time trying to out-weird each other," remarks Peter Boam) were promising enough to prompt Jarvis to defer his university place for another year and stay in Sheffield.*

"I'm sure Russell had a big influence in the change of direction," says David Bocking, a Sheffield photographer who had followed the various incarnations of Pulp since their early days playing the Hallamshire. "He was quite a champion of strange music and noise. Quite how that worked with Jarvis, I don't know. I can imagine Jarvis trying to adapt Russell's approach to Pulp's approach and coming out with what came out, rather than laying down the law and saying, 'We'll play like this.'"

Tony Perrin is more emphatic: "Russell was the catalyst in Pulp becoming a band. Without him, Jarvis would just have drifted off and become a tragic waste. The whole time around *It* was a bit of a non-period really; I don't even think it was Pulp. Pulp existed when they were a school band, and they existed after Russell got his teeth stuck into it, but the period in the middle was Jarvis' solo career – or his first one anyway. It was Jarvis' little scene, before he'd decided what Pulp was going to be. There was no identity, people were drifting in and out in this void that existed after the *It* album. I remember seeing the flyers for these offshoot projects, and thinking, 'What the fuck's Jarvis up to?' They were just one-off gigs with a couple of days' rehearsal in Jarvis' garage, I think. They were all a symptom of when Jarvis was disenchanted with the *It* period, and kind of casting around for ideas and that spark of inspiration that was going to tell him where to go – which Russell provided. The catalyst in what happened thereafter, really, was when Russell came on the scene – that was when they started focusing on a direction and an identity."

Lack of direction and identity certainly wasn't a problem when, his initial plan of producing it with the Crucible Youth Theatre having fallen through, Russell decided to employ the largely idle remnants of Pulp to present his "Dadaist piece of agit-prop", *The Fruits Of Passion*, to the public. For the project, Russell, Jarvis, Magnus and Tim dubbed themselves The

---

* It should be noted that at this point there was no 'Pulp' as such: when Russell, Tim, Magnus and Jarvis first began working together, their main interest was theatre – primarily the production of Russell's play *The Fruits Of Passion*. Although some of the music they provided for the play would later become part of Pulp's repertoire, there would be no actual band until January 1984.

Wicker Players (named after the somewhat insalubrious area of Sheffield that housed the disused silk factory where *It* was recorded, In A Belljar practised, and of which Tim was the caretaker), roping in a couple of friends, Steven Faben and Ellie Ford, to act in the play, and Magnus' flatmate Peter 'Manners' Mansell to help out behind the scenes.

Dig Vis Drill vocalist Ogy McGrath was also asked to appear in the play, "but I'd written a play at the time called *Friendship House*, and after Russell read that I think he kind of went off the idea of me being in it! *The Fruits Of Passion* had characters like First Authoritarian and Second Authoritarian, and I wasn't sure which authoritarian to play. Russell goes, 'There's no difference.' 'But I need to get into my character, do you want me to be low authoritarian, high authoritarian or what?' Great sense of humour, Russell. One day they'll find it and give it him back. I liked him back then though – I think I was the only one in Sheffield who did, so I was ahead of my time in that sense . . ."

The *raison d'être* of the play, which ran for four performances at various venues in Sheffield during December 1983, was the provocation of its audiences. "It was kind of Zurich 1919 revolutionary, very much inspired by Dada," says Russell. "The idea was that people would either walk out in disgust or stay to the end and think it was really cool, and the people who'd stay would be the people who we'd start the socialist revolution with."

The action was interspersed with musical interludes from Jarvis, Russell and Magnus. If abrasive performances of new compositions like 'Maureen', 'Back In LA' and 'Fairground' didn't send audiences packing, the narrative (such as it was) of the play hopefully would: "The stage directions were something like, 'Put vacuum cleaner on stage. Switch it on. Leave it on until audience becomes restless,'" remembers Jarvis with amusement. "The climactic scene was me eating a plate of fake shit at a job interview. I remember the last performance we did, at the Crucible, it looked really real. I looked at Russell and he had this look in his eyes, and I thought, 'I hope you aren't testing me out here.' It turned out he'd employed a new recipe, which I think was peanut butter and chocolate. But it looked very realistic."[70]

"*The Fruits Of Passion* was good actually," remembers Michael Paramore. "I don't know what it'd be like now, you'd probably look at it now and think it was complete crap, but at the time I thought it was quite good. I suppose it was a bit clichéd, like anything you do when you're quite young I suppose, but it had a certain sort of quality to it. It did have a sort of 'war' kind of feel to it in the sense that it was definitely the fascist element and the socialist element – Russell was kind of Socialist Worker, or that movement at the time that was a bit more extreme than Socialist Worker . . . So it did have all those elements to it, but it kind of had arty elements that made it all right rather than just completely . . . twattish!"

But while there is no doubt that the play, as Jarvis says, "crystallised the attitude of the group"[71] at the time, it's not entirely surprising that it wasn't always appreciated by its Sheffield pub audiences. More often than not, performances would degenerate into riots – most famously at a Hallamshire gig, advertised in the *Sheffield Star* as a *Wicker Players Christmas Panto*, which failed to impress locals hoping for *Aladdin* or *Jack And The Beanstalk*. "I just remember them doing something really weird," says Garry Wilson. "The audience were going, 'What the fucking hell's this?' It reminded me of when I went to see Wire in Halifax: they walked on stage, and they had an orange each. They stood in a line and just lifted the oranges above their heads. They did that for 20 minutes while everyone was going, 'Come on yer bastards! Play that song wot we know. Cost me three quid to get in here!'"

After *The Fruits Of Passion* had completed its run, Russell developed many of the same ideas in a series of performance art 'Cabarets' that he organised at the Hallamshire towards the end of 1983. The events were closely related to what The Wicker Players had been attempting with *The Fruits Of Passion*, and included many of the same participants. "They were special events," says Michael Paramore, "probably more worthy than most of the Pulp gigs around that time. Magnus was the star of those: at one event he ate baked beans till he was sick; another he just sat on stage naked, wanking himself off. I remember one time I was on the door and handing out little raffle tickets. You'd win a place in heaven or something. It was, I suppose, like arty crap, but it was quite funny at the time. People'd win a razor blade or a box of matches or something.

"That was around when In A Belljar and all that sort of thing were going on," remembers Murray Fenton. "Sheffield was very arty then. Just about everybody seemed to think that Art played a big part in what they were doing. I think that's where a lot of that stuff stemmed from. I remember that performance art thing in the gig room at the Hallamshire . . . vomit-eating, Magnus having sex with oranges and what have you. That was taking it to extremes. Everyone was just going, 'He's just shagged that orange!' Unbelievable. That was a bit insane."

The most promising signs of a creative future for Jarvis and Russell, though, came from their musical collaboration for *The Fruits Of Passion*. Russell characterises the play, and this period in general, as "very intense. After getting about half the people walking out of this thing and the other half thinking it was really cool, we decided to continue things and make a bit of music."

Russell Senior: "It was obvious that there was some kind of dynamic between me, Jarvis, Magnus and Tim. We decided that we'd form a band and, because it's difficult to get 30 people to come and see a new group at the Hallamshire, we decided that we may as well call it Pulp because it was a name that was known – even though this was really year zero for what happened in the coming years, and what Pulp are doing now."

The initial *Fruits Of Passion*-era band line-up of Jarvis (vocals/guitar), Russell (guitar/violin/vocals), Tim (poetry recital/hunting horn/percussion/keyboards) and Magnus (drums/occasional keyboards) was completed by Magnus' 16-year-old flatmate Pete Mansell on bass. Pete, more commonly known as Manners, had his first practice with Pulp at the inevitable Mansfield Road garage. "It was tiny, and full of all this shit amplification," he remembers. "The first time I went there was for an audition, and Jarvis was holding this little microphone against a cymbal. Russell was playing his Rosetti guitar with a bow. I thought, 'Bloody hell! This is nothing like *It*.' I thought I'd be playing 'My Lighthouse' and all those catchy songs."[72]

Thanks to The Wicker Players' musical experiments of the last few months, the new Pulp already had the beginnings of a repertoire, and so wasted no time recording a new demo tape at Victoria Studio, which by now was under new management and renamed Vibrasound. "We sent it out to every record label," remembers Russell, "with a very pompous, 'You can't ignore this!' type letter. I've still got all the rejection slips somewhere."

It's not surprising that the demo met with such indifference: while the quality of the material is undeniable, the four songs on the tape could easily be the work of at least three different bands, none of which was working in a musical style that was even vaguely bankable back in the age of Linn drum machines, mullets and glossy Trevor Horn production-line pop. 'Coy Mistress' alone could probably qualify as one of the oddest pieces of music ever produced. Less than two minutes long, it features Russell declaiming heavily bastardised lines from that perennial A-level English favourite, Andrew Marvell's 'To His Coy Mistress' ("If we had but world enough and time/ Then this coyness, mistress, would be no crime . . ."). Jarvis provides a gentle keyboard backdrop, punctuated alternately with random xylophone tinkles and the sound of drums apparently being thrown down stairs.

Then there was a two-chord thrash called 'Maureen', based on an earlier Senior composition that he'd played with his previous bands The Nightmares and Rachel Tension And The Disruptives. Jarvis elaborated on Russell's original lyrics, telling the delightfully macabre story of a man who gets a sexual thrill out of being run over by the eponymous character. *"My blood upon the tarmac/ I tore the dress from your back,"* indeed.

If that wasn't enough to send any sensible A&R man packing, there was always 'Little Girl (With Blue Eyes)' – a brilliant, edgy ballad that would eventually serve the band well (uniquely, it was still an occasional part of Pulp's live set 10 years later) but was clearly a little too gauche, lyrically speaking, to be seen as a viable hit single. Perhaps more than any of their other early compositions together, the song's darkly poetic lyric shows Russell's influence on Jarvis' writing: "If I hadn't been there, 'Little Girl' would have been so soppy as to be unlistenable," says Russell. "My typical tactic was to tell Jarvis, 'Stop being so bloody soft.' " In such company, the warped Sixties balladeering of 'I Want You' (*"Now we come to the end of it all, see it squirming almost dead/ No, you can't leave it to die there in pain, you've got to stamp upon its head"*) practically counts as easy listening.

Nevertheless, the demo clearly demonstrates what set this version of Pulp apart from the various bands that had carried the name previously. Like all mid-Eighties Pulp, there's a certain intensity and a tension that is hard to pin down, but impossible to ignore. Perhaps the most palpable evidence is in the lyrics: it's hard to imagine the tender 18-year-old Jarvis behind the whimsy of 'My Lighthouse' and 'Boats And Trains' singing a line as unflinching as *"There's a hole in your heart and one between your legs"* or writing a song with as direct a title as 'I Want You'.

If the new Pulp had succeeded in establishing a powerful, immediately impressive (if none too commercial) musical identity, re-establishing themselves on the Sheffield band scene would prove slightly more difficult. A lack of places to play (the Hallamshire had temporarily lost its music licence, while the Marples' stage area had been converted into a snooker room) meant that there would be no Pulp 3 concert in Sheffield until April 1984.

"It wasn't at all easy to make your mark in Sheffield at that time," remembers John Avery of Pulp's former Red Rhino labelmates Hula. "It was the time when a lot of bands who'd been doing interesting, progressive stuff were disintegrating and splitting up. It was frustrating because you'd be very well known within Sheffield, but just about unheard of outside the city. In The Nursery were just starting up though, and Chakk and Dig Vis Drill – all of whom were very noisy and powerful, although Chakk changed a lot once they got signed. Unfortunately, the industrial stuff didn't really leave a lot of space for quirky guitar-based stuff like Pulp."

"The Sheffield scene was going downhill a bit by '84," agrees Murray Fenton, who by now was playing in the latest incarnation of Artery.

"There were quite a lot of pop bands around – poppy funk music was coming into the mainstream, and people were picking up on that. There was the industrial thing as well – Hula and Chakk, with the advent of FON as a label and a shop. Hula were actually quite good – I saw them when we [Artery] played in Amsterdam, and they had all this film stuff going off. Then there was Treebound Story, who were quite Smiths-y, jangly guitar pop, and Dig Vis Drill, who were . . . one of a kind, really. Very entertaining band. And there was Criminal Sex from Chesterfield, Steve Genn's band Mr. Morality, and Hole In The Wall, who turned into The Happening Men, which then became The Longpigs. And The Ya-Yas, who were brilliant. Really genuine, plucked straight out of the Sixties . . . fantastic. But on the whole, the scene was dying down a bit."

As with the failure of the demo to enrapture A&R men, it seemed that Pulp's wilful individuality was their Achilles' heel as well as their strongest point. The songs that were in the band's repertoire at the time (many of which would see the light of day in the next couple of years on the *Freaks* album and various singles) are easy to make sense of and appreciate in hindsight, but what were audiences supposed to make of skewed Sixties-esque ballads alongside thrashy, trashy rockabilly numbers and wildcards like 'Coy Mistress', at a time when the *Zeitgeist* was defied by Paul Young, Sade and 'Karma Chameleon'? The question would blight Pulp's career for a long time to come.

The new line-up made its live début at the incongruous location of Brunel University Rugby Club, London, on Tuesday, February 7, 1984. "We'd been booked by a friend who then called it off," remembers Jarvis. "We pretended we didn't know. In the interim, they booked a rugby songs band, Ivor Biggun and the Hefty Cocks or something, but they didn't turn up. But the audience were basically the rugby club. We used to start the concerts with this factory siren – we had five minutes of this flipping siren going off [which blew all the fuses in the building, so Pulp couldn't start playing for 20 minutes]. Tim was doing his poems, and people were singing 'You're a wanker'. Somebody did a moony at me, so I kicked him up the arse. The MC tried to stop the concert so I wrestled him to the ground. Then all these rugby players jumped on the stage. I slid out from under them and ran into the dressing room, and we barricaded ourselves in."[73]

"I was only 16," says Pete Mansell. "We turned up and played all these depressing songs off *Freaks* . . . there was a full-scale riot. Someone threw a fifty-pence piece at my bass and took a huge chunk out of it. It was the only money I ever made from the group."[74]

Russell: "Truth and beauty stayed in that night."[75]

For the follow-up concert, at the Cosmo Club in Leeds, Pulp were provided with accommodation and equipment by a band whose climb towards mainstream acceptance would be almost as long and tortuous as their own: Chumbawamba.

"I remember Pulp coming to our very, very small and very knackered PA system, which comprised two speakers and an amp with four channels," remembers the band's Dunstan. "They all stood around the house and garden as though they were in an Ingmar Bergman film. They were all very nice and polite and just a little bit strange. I liked them – they were weird, like us but in a totally different way. More art school than political, but definitely outsiders."

Chumbawamba's Boff remembers "eccentric English clothes all round – less of the polyester and more the colonial in India. Pulp were what we always thought the quintessentially English art school band would be like: foppish, good-humoured, interesting and polite. Loved 'em though."

The concert itself was almost as harrowing an experience for the band as the Rugby Club the previous month. "Cosmo's," remembers Russell, "was basically a brothel. When the MC introduced us, he was going 'and for the gentlemen in the audience, there's plenty of girls there up on the balcony who'll be delighted to meet you' and all that. Tim was doing his poems between songs, one of which was called 'Virgins And Whores', and was pretty blatantly about prostitution. All these gangster types in the audience started making gun shapes with their hands and pretending to shoot us."

When Pulp finally got around to playing on home turf again, at a Sheffield Library Theatre concert with Dig Vis Drill on April 6, they must have been relieved to be slightly better received. "They seemed special, even back then," says Dig Vis Drill keyboardist John Nicholls. "At that gig, I can remember my wife saying, 'I can't see your lot making it, but Pulp's got something about them.'"

Martin Lilleker was in the audience, giving him his first opportunity to compare the new Pulp with the old. "I don't know what Jarvis was into at that time, but there was a definite change of mood. I think the basic song-writing has always been the same, essentially, but the frivolity side of it wasn't there anymore – they'd done a lot of daft songs previously. The band lost its humour for a while – I think Russell used to make them work a bit. They weren't quite as chaotic as the early gigs: they'd obviously rehearsed a bit, and you knew who was going to be the drummer, bassist, guitarist, fiddle-player, whatever. They suddenly became a band again, for the first time, really, since they started out.

"Manners was a very distinctive bass-player, and a very distinctive-looking bloke. He was a star. But the main difference with this line-up would have been Russell and his fiddle-playing, which has always been a source of amazement to me – I thought he was great, making it work so well in that context. I don't think Pulp would ever have got anywhere without Russell, to be perfectly honest. His sensible, serious side got them through, and he was able to work around Jarvis as well."

"The songs were a bit darker," agrees John Quinn, "but Jarvis was still saying the same ridiculous things. I've heard the stories about fights on stage and things like that, but I never saw any of that in Sheffield. The music seemed to be moving towards, not goth, but something darker than they'd been doing before."

"I started listening to them again from that point," says Nick Robinson. "It was obviously very different to how they'd been when I first heard them in '81. I think Jarvis basically just followed his nose – I don't think he ever did anything in a contrived sense. He probably tried to be different, and I think the free flow of people in and out of the band obviously had an effect. He put the songs together to suit the people who were around at the time, I think. He never really went on about his influences, but I'm sure he must have had one or two torch singers from the Sixties that he really liked, 'cos he always had that kind of dramatic, low-pitched delivery to a lot of his songs, which not many people did at that time.

"Russell was obviously an influence – he was a complete David Byrne fan, and everything about him, not just the way he looked, was totally David Byrne, except for the scratty violin of course. I remember his girl-friend had a soft spot for me, and Russell didn't like this. We'd tend to get invited to the same parties then stare frostily at each other all night. He was very good at that."

Russell's appearance on the scene had certainly made an impact: he wasn't averse to rubbing people up the wrong way, but there was no denying that the man had presence. Michael Paramore: "Russell was always very, very serious, and even though he was sort of a revolutionary socialist, you always had the idea that he was maybe a bit of a closet fascist! I don't mean that in a bad way, but he had more of the look of a dictator than a revolutionary socialist. He had that cross between the bloke out of Sparks and Adolf Hitler look, even then. Always reading very serious books, and if you caught a conversation between him and David Kurley, you wouldn't know what half the words meant. The other half you'd never even come across. You never quite knew how to take him: he was either very intelligent or trying very, very hard. But he was very serious.

"I dunno, you just couldn't work him out. For one you got the impression he was from quite a good family – not rich, but anyone whose dad wasn't a postman was rich at the time. And you just got the impression that he was a bit out of place. He was *so* intense – you'd just go to a nightclub and you'd be talking about various things to certain people and you'd be talking to Russell about some sort of design for a backdrop for something he was putting on, you know, and he always seemed to have lots of plans for things. And he seemed to get things done – I mean, these cabaret things were absolutely brilliant."

Simon Hinkler, why by now was dividing his time between his solo project with Mark Gouldthorpe as Flight Commander, working as an engineer at Input Studios and playing in yet another incarnation of Artery, had also been keeping tabs on the new Pulp. "I saw some of those performance pieces. They kind of set the tone for what Pulp was becoming – an 'art band'. After I'd left, I still often saw the band at Jarvis' house because I was still going out with Saskia, and they'd rehearse there a few times a week. My initial impressions of what they were doing was that some of the songs were great and others were crap. At first I thought Russell had influenced Jarvis down the wrong road, as their sound became very trashy, but I soon came to realise this line-up was a very special incarnation of Pulp. The best one ever in my opinion.

"Russell was one of the people who was generally around at the time. You'd see him on Fargate, at gigs, at the pub and at parties. He looked like the keyboard player from Sparks – I'd be amazed if I'm the only person who's said that. It was absolutely no surprise that he played the part of Josef K in the Kafka play *The Trial*. It took me a long time to like Russell, because I found him excessively and unnecessarily confrontational. Something I just got used to in the end."

The band that supported Pulp at the Library Theatre concert, Dig Vis Drill, was one of the most respected new bands in Sheffield at the time, and would quickly become Pulp's closest peers, spiritually if not musically. "I think Pulp had found out that we had a PA," says vocalist Ogy McGrath, "so Russell phoned us up and asked if they could do a gig with us at the Library Theatre, just as the Miners' Strike was kicking off. We got into all that, 'cos we were all working-class miners, and Pulp were from the art school kind of side. So we thought if we got together, they could get some of our political credibility and we could pick up all the young art students, heh heh!

"So we started doing gigs together, and there was a bit of a mutual respect thing. We had lots of songs where I'd ad lib forever, and Jarvis really took a shine to all that. He kept coming to our gigs to see if I did it the same or did it different. Something he's incorporated into his act somewhat. I even used to have a pair of knickers in me top pocket which I'd pull out and use as a handkerchief. Never had an 'I HATE WET WET WET' sign inside my jacket, though. I went to a posh school, so it said, 'I HATE H_2O H_2O H_2O'."

"Dig Vis Drill were quite well thought of in a way," says David Bocking. "They knew that they weren't commercial, and Ogy was very keen on saying that no one else was worth bothering with. He played quite a careful media game at that point. Some of his tracks were quite remarkable in many ways – they were very noisy, and he was quite a good lyricist."

"They had a drum machine, keyboards and two singers, and I suppose they were a bit like a punk hip-hop band or something," remembers another local music fan, Ian Spence. "Very aggressive, very in-yer-face, and they had very good songs – even though the twelve songs they had when they started were the twelve songs they had when they finished five years later! Instead of writing more, they just got longer – they started doing 20-minute epic versions of things like 'Spell Survival'. I used to be good mates with them until Ogy took umbrage when I said something about his stage presentation – he threw his drink over me and he hasn't talked to me since!"

If Pulp and Dig Vis Drill were chalk and cheese musically, they did share a certain radicalism of approach, influenced at least in part by the politics of the mid-Eighties. The Thatcher Tory government was in full swing, and its ruthless monetarist policies and adversarial anti-union stance had a devastating effect on both the economy and psyche of many northern cities, not least Sheffield, whose steel industry (previously one of the city's main employers, of course) was in steep and irreversible decline. Such matters had little direct effect on the lives of anyone in Pulp – no matter how many steel factories were available to work in, they'd still have been on the dole playing in bands – but the social conditions and politics of the time undoubtedly had an effect on the music they were creating and the attitudes they were adopting.

"It'd be hard for any band in Sheffield at that time not to be influenced by Thatcher's Britain and dole culture," says Nick Robinson. "A lot of the miners' troubles were at Orgreave, which is part of Sheffield – that was the place where all the shots came from of policemen on horses, whacking people on the head, and it's a 10-minute bus ride from the centre of Sheffield. There's a place called Keanes where they had a strike for about seven years – they had a picket line outside this factory where they were burning logs and asking for contributions. Extraordinary. Sheffield, being a steel city, was suffering the brunt of the politics of the time – factories closing down left, right and centre, so the whole town was fairly belittled, I think. The north/south divide was fairly clearly marked – it started above Nottingham! I think all the northern cities were well aware that there were lots of bastards down south apparently living the high life while we were paying for it with unemployment. And I think that influenced the musical stance of Dig Vis Drill, Pulp and a lot of bands that were around – there was a bit of a fuck-you attitude about it, perhaps making us want to push things a bit more in whatever direction we were going than we would normally have gone. Dig Vis Drill certainly were influenced by the political situation at the time. Ogy's lyrics were fairly venomous – he used to tackle religion and cancer and politics absolutely head-on. That was part of the appeal of Dig Vis Drill, but part of the limitation as well in that we managed to upset an awful lot of people! Had there been roses and no north/south divide, there probably wouldn't have been as much passion in the music, whatever direction it was going in."

By the middle of 1984, Jarvis had been out of school and living on the dole in Sheffield for two years – a lifestyle that, in various ways, would play a major part in the shaping of not just Jarvis, but Pulp's whole ethos.

"In Sheffield, in the early Eighties, anybody who wanted to do something vaguely creative, or just pretend they wanted to do something vaguely creative but really wanted to doss, would just go straight on the dole after school . . . Everyone used to dole-stroll on Fargate, which was the pedestrian precinct. It could take you a whole afternoon to walk the length of a street that's only 100 yards long, because you might bump into other dole-strollers, or you could just sit down on a bench and watch people walk past, or maybe go and have a cup of tea somewhere, or watch the girl hairdressers coming out of the salon at the top of the road and decide whether you fancied them or not, or just sit next to the fountain. It was good – or at least on a sunny day it was good. In winter it was only for the hardcore.[76]

"Because it was so bereft of anything organised to do, you had to make your own entertainment. So you'd invent an adventure – you'd go through this kind of walk through the sewers of Sheffield, basically."[77]

Russell Senior: "I think Sheffield's a big part of what made Pulp. And I'm very glad that we're thought of as kind of, you know, the team. I think we are the most Sheffield band, and I don't think any other Sheffield bands have the essence of the thing. Sheffield in many ways is an ugly place. The Sheffield thing is, there's an understatement to it. When somebody from

Manchester walks into a room, they're confident, they strut around, you feel a little bit threatened by 'em. And Sheffield people come in, and they kind of doff their cap a bit. But they do have a searing wit. Lovely people, it's just an ugly city."[78]

Jarvis' home life at the time, meanwhile, was also relatively hassle-free. He'd just moved into a flat with Tim Allcard and Michael Paramore in the legendary disused factory on Sheldon Row, just off The Wicker, a large, wide street toward the edge of the city centre. The Wicker had once been the heart of industrial Sheffield, and later the focal point of the city's tourist trade (wicker baskets and figures were a local craft, hence the name) but by the Eighties it was a rather seedy, run-down area of town. In itself, the fact that Jarvis was able to live in the factory rent-free was an indication of Sheffield's industrial decline: the company that owned the place had simply realised that it was more viable for them to rent it out as practice rooms and suchlike (with Tim Allcard as caretaker) than to keep it running as a factory.

Michael Paramore: "It was a very big flat, and very ramshackle. It was converted into a flat, but only insofar as there was a sink and a bathroom. I suppose it wasn't really that much different to living in a squat except you got your electricity, a decent bathroom and so on. The rooms were very big, all the walls were painted on, people would come round and paint on the walls, draw on the walls, so it always had the feel of a squat kind of thing, but then Tim had fixed a boat on the wall for his bed on the top of the ceiling. So it was quite an interesting place to live."

The building was a centre of (in)activity for the dole-strolling, arty, stoned counter-culture that existed in Sheffield at the time. Jarvis' flat was situated between a boxing club and a Boys' Brigade hall; elsewhere in the building was Vibrasound Studio, a band rehearsal space, the karate rooms where the *Sudan Gerri* tracks had been recorded, a street theatre company, a model railway enthusiast's train setup and two table tennis clubs (for reasons obscure, there was a bitter feud between the two factions of ping-pong enthusiasts, to the extent that they would defacate in front of each other's doors).

"Pretty soon," says Jarvis, "the place became a centre for all the freaks, misfits and drop-outs of Sheffield. There were all these travelling, crusty, vegan, circus types everywhere as well, with names like Tarquin, and they were all into stone circles and smoking joints and stuff. They were all minted and it was all, 'Yeah, man,' and 'absolutely terrible, yah' and they all seemed to be jugglers.

"Trouble was, they decided to start up this wholefood co-operative thing – 'Yeah, man, we'll cut out the middle man' – which eventually brought loads of rats into the building. Rats were shitting in the muesli and pulses, but they still kept flogging it to people! You know: 'Get free rat shit with your mung beans' or whatever."[79]

"Jarvis had the attic as such," remembers Paramore, "it was the highest room in the flat and it had lots of beams coming down to the floor. Whereas we were all hanging around town or doing something, he used to sleep 12 hours at least a day – he'd only really get up for band practices, gigs, to go to a club or jumble sales. Mainly jumble sales, actually! He used to just go to jumble sales all the time and come back with carrier bags of stuff like really strange lamps, funny objects that he'd seen and bought, clothes and whatever. His room was the messiest room I've ever seen, piled high with this brilliant stuff, all from jumble sales, with just a tiny path from the door that winded through to his bed.

"The flat on The Wicker was a brilliant place to live, more so at the beginning. Tim's like one of these very social people – you'd come downstairs some mornings and there would be loads of people just asleep all over the place. I used to be painting in my room a lot of the time and there would always be someone new to talk to; no one lived nearby, and the views were just wasteland and the Park Hill flats. It started getting a bit much after a while; too many weirdoes. It was a place a bit like the house in *Fight Club*, and eventually it got filled with just as many nutters!"

Soon after the Library Theatre concert, Tim Allcard left Pulp. The departure of Tim, who Russell in particular credits with a central role in the creation of the modern-day Pulp, has never fully been explained. His non-musicianship, which didn't stretch much further than homemade percussion, strange noises conjured from the hunting horn and the occasional two-finger keyboard part, was probably a factor – what he contributed to Pulp was more apparent in the wilfully odd, performance art-influenced stance that would remain with them throughout the mid-Eighties.

"With In A Belljar," says Tim's friend Michael Paramore, "it was the strangeness element that I think they probably liked. And Tim I suppose really had it in the way he looked. He just added something . . . peculiar, he just made them different to everybody else because nobody else was doing that kind of thing. When they played, they just wouldn't be another band that played 10 songs and went off stage. But he was always a bit of an add-on – not in a bad way, but he was just somebody who was kind of handy to have to add on to the band, he just gave them an extra edge. It wasn't so much that he was in the band – it was much more informal with

Tim in that he just came on and did something. It wasn't like, when Russell left the band it was a big thing. It was just like, Tim kind of did something, and sometimes he didn't, and eventually he didn't anymore."

As well as his musical limitations, Tim's between-songs poetry was reportedly less-than-rapturously received. "His poems were probably wasted on a Sheffield audience," notes David Bocking dryly. "I think he came across as a bit of an academic, who was trying to do something a bit different when people perhaps wanted to see something that was closer to pop music."

Tim's replacement on keyboards was Magnus' sister, Candida Doyle. Typically for a Pulp member, she'd never been in a proper band before: "Well, me and my friends used to pretend. It was only me who could play but we'd all plan what we were going to play and make up names for ourselves but we never did anything ever. I had been playing the piano since I was about six, there was always one in the house . . . I'd liked Pulp for a few years before I joined, then Mag and Pete said I could play piano, so I went along for a practice with Jarvis and Russell and seemed to do OK."[80]

"I can remember seeing her in a pub," says Russell of his first meeting with Candida, "and funnily enough I thought she was really old, because everybody says how young she looks. I thought she was a really sophisticated woman, like you get in Woody Allen films. Anyway, she came in and she's got her own style, which we sort of called 'rinky-dink' because it was fairground, fairy-tale, kind of stuff."[81]

After a shaky start ("I played really quietly at first in case they thought I was crap,"[82] she told *Select* in 1995), Candida's inimitable technique, simultaneously delicate and crude, quickly became a defining characteristic of the Pulp sound. "I don't think she was the catalyst that Russell was," says Tony Perrin, "but I think there's something about her and her personality that goes with that sound, that kind of plasticky vibe that the band always had. I mean, it was to do with the equipment that historically they'd inherited,* but it just fit in with the way she was and is."

Candida's first assignment as a member of Pulp, on May 8, 1984, was the recording of a new, 11-song demo tape. Rather than going into Vibrasound or Input, the band called on the expertise of Dig Vis Drill's John Nicholls to make the tape. John was the owner of a Teac 4-track portastudio, and had the technical ability to make reasonable-sounding recordings without the expense of using a professional studio.

The session took place in The Wicker Karate Rooms, in yet another part of the factory building where Tim Allcard lived. "It was all very low-tech stuff," remembers John. "We communicated by semaphore – there were these flags that had been used for something in karate, and I'd sit in the control room and hold one up whenever I wanted them to start or stop or whatever. It essentially went straight on to four-track. The instrumental backing tracks all went down live, with Jarvis kind of leading the band, conducting them or whatever. He'd be singing at the same time so they knew where they were in the song, but not closely miked, and then he'd overdub his vocals afterwards. If you listen carefully to the tape, there's certain parts where you can hear him singing it slightly differently in the background."

"Everyone respected John, including Jarvis," says Ogy McGrath. "John was a bit older than all of us and he knew everything about electronics, which no one knew in those days. He could fix everything. After we'd played live with Pulp and Jarvis got to see how good John was at things and found out that he had a 4-track, he wanted him to record Pulp. John in those days recorded lots of bands and stuff – never got paid for any of it, I think they might have given him a tenner or something.

"I remember it was when the England football team were touring South America, and that day was the day when they played Brazil and John Barnes scored that great goal. He was only about 19 then, and he dribbled five players and put it in. While Pulp were recording the demo, I was hanging around really drunk – I did a lot of that in those days – and I went, 'Oh no, I've got to watch the football! I can't stay here and listen to you guys.' They went, 'Football! Yer wot?' 'I've got to go man, England are playing Brazil!' And I missed the John Barnes goal because of those guys."

The tape that resulted was an *audio vérité* document of Pulp at their darkest and most extreme, yet with enough mordant garage-pop touches to ensure it remained a highly enjoyable collection of music. About half of the songs – amongst them 'Don't You Know?', 'Anorexic Beauty', 'The Will To Power' and 'Little Girl (With Blue Eyes)' – would later surface on official releases and, while similar in structure and content to the later recordings, generally have a far more raucous sound here, thanks in large part to Jarvis' jangly guitar and Magnus' bin-lid drumming. Candida's toytown organ and synth also seem more prominent on certain tracks, notably 'Don't You Know?' and 'Little Girl'.

The rest of the tape is made up of songs that never surfaced on vinyl, and arguably deserved to. The remarkable 'Take You Back' was a live favourite at the time – a chilling, intense song, based around a five-note keyboard riff, moving from possibly the original Atmospheric Pulp

---

[*] For a long time, Candida's sonic arsenal would be limited to the Farfisa and Casio that had been mainstays of the band's equipment since the beginning of the Eighties.

Monologue (a mysterious, allegorical tale about dank valleys, childhood memories and a journey *"back to somewhere that never existed"*) to a snarling *"la-la-la"* refrain.

'Srpski Jeb' (pronounced, roughly, "serpski yeb") saw Russell taking lead vocals, and is quite possibly one of the silliest Pulp songs ever. Its one line, *"Village maiden gathering mushrooms, down by woodland lakes and brooks, she don't want no Soviet sex, all she wants is Srpski Jeb – hoi!"* is repeated lots of times at varying levels of speed and loudness while the band plonk along in a convincingly Eastern European manner that demands the slapping of thighs. "Very silly song," muses Russell. "Apparently the phrase translates literally as 'Serbian fuck', but I didn't know that – it came from when I was travelling around Europe as a youngster. It was just a Russian aphorism for rough sex."

'Cousins' is another menacing, atmospheric, deceptively low-key piece in the same vein as 'Take You Back', with Jarvis' voice slowly developing from a gentle, foreboding croon into an anguished yelp. The lyrics include such phrases as *"Sick of the sight of every object touched before, possessed, depressed, I shouldn't have to call you, I've got the key to your door"*, *"I'll smile at your father who is sleeping on his feet, waiting for an accident"*, *"It's all too clear, it's all too fair, you fell in love with something that isn't there"*, *"You can't escape the blood and shit, you can't escape you're stuck with it – then again, it might just die away. Die away. Diiiiiieeeeee,"* and, while it's not quite clear what the whole thing's about the overall effect is impressive and slightly unnerving.

Another version of 'Maureen' is also included, closer to the garage-punk spirit of the song than the version laid down at Vibrasound a few months earlier. "I've always liked that track," says John Nicholls. "The way the chorus is down but the verse is up, whereas most songs are the other way round. I remember Jarvis saying he wanted it doing really garagey and grungey, 'cos that was how it sounded when they first rehearsed it in the garage or whatever."

And then there was 'Silence'. Written at Russell's first rehearsal with Pulp in September 1983, 'Silence' is Jarvis' most hated Pulp track of all time, and possibly the starkest, most extreme piece of music the group ever produced. Musically, it's also the most minimalistic: the only accompaniment to Jarvis' tortured vocal (which resembles nothing so much as a Gregorian chant) is Magnus repeatedly playing the same two organ chords and Russell conjuring some strange noises out of Tim Allcard's hunting horn. Although it was the only recording from *Sudan Gerri* to surface on vinyl (on the B-side of the 'Master Of The Universe' single three years later), by the time Fire Records released the mid-Eighties Pulp compilation *Masters Of The Universe* in 1994, Jarvis found 'Silence' too close to the bone, too embarrassing, or maybe just too plain *bad* to allow it to be included on the album. "Oh, it's so depressing," he told *Record Collector* then. "A two-note keyboard drone, someone playing one of those hunting horns you have on the living room wall and me alternately talking and screaming this story about a love affair that doesn't work out. I banned it from going on the Fire compilation because it's terrible – I couldn't live with it being out."[83]

Overall, though, the 11 tracks on the demo – which was given the title *Sudan Gerri* as a reference to the karate move *Chudan Gerri* – have stood the test of time thanks to the strength of the material and the band's uncompromising stance. Even so, back in 1984, the tape was unlikely to get Pulp within a million miles of a recording deal with any sensible money-minded record label. "It was good insofar as they were forging their own identity," says Tony Perrin, "but I just felt that it was too radical, too extreme to really offer much hope of leading anywhere. It was like that line in 'Little Girl' – it was a really pleasant song, but with a nasty twist in it that you just knew was just going to defeat the object of record-ing it and putting it out in the first place. They had too strong a streak of perversity to get anywhere at that point. But it was a few months after that that I saw them at the B-Hive and thought, 'Fuck – there's something really good here.'"

One person who was impressed by the demo was Clive Solomon, who, with the former *Sounds* journalist Johnny Waller, was in the process of starting a label called Fire Records Of London. Waller had been impressed by *It* and went to see Pulp at the Heywire Club in London in May 1984. Although he went out for a pizza and therefore missed most of the gig, Russell subsequently sent him a copy of *Sudan Gerri*, thus beginning a lengthy courtship with the label.

"We'd only been going for a short while at that point," says Solomon. "We'd just put out our first couple of records. It was just a small independ-ent label like many others at the time – as small as they get, I suppose. It was part of the second generation of tiny indie labels – those that missed the punk thing which spawned the original indie labels. We were inspired, I suppose, by labels like Beggars and Rough Trade, the original generation which made it possible for everyone else to press up a few thousand copies of a record.

"Johnny had played me *It*, which I thought was wonderfully good, and based on that we started talking to them. The next stuff I heard from them after *It* was musically very, very different from that album, but then my taste is pretty goddam wide anyway. I like the *It* album because I like a lot of soft rock, and I liked the next stuff because it was, pardon the pun, a bit more freaked-out. The pop sensibilities were still there, but it was definitely more ramshackle, more twisted – I suppose blacker and bleaker. I counted myself a fan by that time anyway, and I'd heard a band that was certainly capable of producing tracks that went across a very wide musical spectrum. I sometimes think I'm alone, but in terms of topline melodies and stuff, Jarvis wrote as good tunes then as some of the stuff he's been acknowledged for more recently. I seemed to really like everything that I heard by them."

June 1984 brought the new Pulp's first publicly available release with the inclusion of the January Vibrasound demos of 'Coy Mistress' and 'I Want You' on a local cassette compilation called *Company Classics No. 3*, which has since become one of the rarest Pulp-related artefacts.

The *Company Classics* series of tapes was put together by Ian Spence, who was a student in Sheffield at the time. "A friend of mine had this label, Company Records, which he'd done a single on, and we just thought it'd be a good idea to do a compilation to promote Sheffield bands. So we did the first one, which was mostly just people we knew, got through a couple of hundred copies of that, and then people started sending us tapes. So we decided to do a second one, which sold about 300, and the third one, which Pulp sent us some stuff for. They were having problems with record labels at the time, so we just thought it was nice of them to give us some of their tracks. It was strange because the third one had more successful bands on it – people like Pulp, who'd already had records out – so we thought that would be the big one, but it sold much less. I've still got a big box of it somewhere. Obviously they didn't have any friends! Of the bands on that tape, we thought Pulp, Dig Vis Drill and The Gallery were the ones who might be successful.

"We got plenty of support from people like Martin Lilleker from the *Star*, and Sheffield University, who let us put on concerts to promote the tapes. The way Pulp sounded live then was pretty representative of what came out on the records – I think it was a few years before Russell managed to get a guitar he could keep in tune though! They always made an effort to look different – they'd decorate the stage, and Russell would be doing his David Byrne impression, and Jarvis was always just Jarvis. He was always very entertaining – but it was always a group, never 'Jarvis plus backing band'."

After a quiet period, Sheffield's local band scene was starting to pick up again. Nick Robinson: "There was quite a lot of activity at that time. There was a lot of synthesised stuff, but there was also a lot of stuff like Pulp and the Diggies who were into producing something a bit more organic. But the only band I'd pigeonhole Pulp with was Artery, because they were really quirky. There was a bit of a loss of direction in the mid-Eighties though – The Human League and ABC had been the frontrunners earlier on, but after that we didn't produce anyone really successful until Pulp and Babybird hit it big. If there aren't any reasonably big bands around, you don't get agents and labels coming out to see you – you have to get out of Sheffield to get recognised."

"Although we got kind of stereotyped with that cold industrial stuff," says Ogy McGrath, "Dig Vis Drill was kind of different to that. Although we used synths and things we were a bit more fun, different kind of attitude. I think they all wanted to make money, whereas we were doing miners' benefits and stuff, trying to do other things. They were all right, but they didn't seem to have a sense of humour, they always took it really serious. Even though Pulp sounded totally different to us, they were in the same sort of scene as us because we'd mix together. Everybody thought Pulp were wacky – wacky was the key word. Wacky wacky wacky. That word will haunt Jarvis."

"As well as all the electronica, there was a lot of poppy stuff," says John Nicholls, "and then you had your wacky Pulps and your crazy, noisy Midnight Choirs. There wasn't really a dominant musical trend between different bands at that time. Pulp were always well respected – they always had a lot of people coming to their gigs. Whether that was because of the music or the wackiness or what, I don't know."

"Sheffield's never had a scene really," reckons Ogy. "It's never had a big record company like other cities. Manchester had Factory, Newcastle had Kitchenware, Glasgow had Postcard, but we never had that really, and that was what we all needed. And it was the only major city that never had a TV station based in it. Every other city had a TV station, and we had to go to fucking Leeds and this and that, and I hated Leeds because of that. I put on Quentin Crisp in Sheffield City Hall once, and I had to take the guy to Leeds to be interviewed for local television! This is a 90-year-old guy we're talking about, and they're going, 'Sheffield? Nah, can't get anything up there mate.'"

For the rest of 1984, Pulp were gigging quite regularly around Sheffield, including one memorable night at the B-Hive on West Street in July that provides a useful insight into the developing relationships and tensions in the new line-up. "For the encore," remembers Michael Paramore, "they did a version of 'Hurry Up Harry' with Manners singing, and Russell stormed off – he was absolutely appalled by it.

"It did really seem like Russell was very, very serious, because Magnus and Manners really liked having a good time, and he didn't appreciate that a lot of the time. Especially with Manners, more than anything – like that occasion, the 'Hurry Up Harry' thing, I mean it's probably not the coolest song to play, especially given the time, when it didn't even have the novelty value of being 20 years old, but it kind of made the gig – everyone there thought it was hilarious, this serious band playing this trashy pop song, but Russell just couldn't see it. I think that would probably happen quite a lot, because I think Russell was in the band for different reasons than Magnus and Manners."

But the fact that Magnus and Pete were the exact opposite of the precious artistic stance that Jarvis and Russell tended to adopt sometimes worked for the band as well as against it. "Whilst Jarvis and I were disappearing up our own backsides," reflected Russell 14 years later, "Candida and Magnus and Pete provided an unpretentious side to it. The Doors said, 'Break on through to the other side,' and I'm sure Jarvis and I were very keen on doing that, but Magnus *was* on the other side. He was totally mad. He would wreck his drumkit, but he'd wreck it during the quiet songs. If he had a couple of beers, his drumkit would be demolished by the end of the first song. I just took it in turns which of them to hate the most, really."[84]

"No way would Pulp be famous now if me and Magnus were in the group," says Pete Mansell. "Jarvis and Russell would be quite straight, and be serious and want it to really work, but me and Magnus didn't care. So they should really have got rid of us far earlier![85]

"I never got anything out of Pulp – not even a free beer, so Mag and I started nicking things and getting out of it. We were young, we were into having a laugh."[86]

"I liked Manners, he was great fun," says Ogy McGrath. "He was the rough boy – the only working-class boy in the band, the only football fan. They all hated football in those days, and we all loved it – thought it was poetry and art before it was fashionable. Now they all like it . . ."

"Why he was there I don't know," says John Nicholls. "He just didn't fit in – in a way it was part of the quirkiness, in that they were all dressed down, and there he was in his T-shirt and whatnot, and his pseudo-Fall image."

The interpersonal tensions did add a certain something to the intensity of this model of Pulp, as Jarvis told an interviewer for the *Sheffield City Press* around the time: "We don't hang around with each other; we don't like each other much. There is a certain tension – I don't like it when everyone gets comfortable."[87]

"Most people have fights with the audience, we have fights with each other,"[88] added Russell.

Even so, although Manners and Magnus were a frequent source of frustration to Jarvis and Russell, the antagonism wasn't entirely one-sided. "I can be a bit of a dictator sometimes," Jarvis admitted in another interview. "I surprise myself because I can be a bit obnoxious. I think because it means a lot to me, I can be a bit of a twat sometimes. In concerts I stop songs halfway through. I know it's not a good thing to do, but I can't help myself. I'm going to have to go and see my analyst."[89]

By the end of 1984, despite an ever-improving live act and an increasing local following for the remodelled Pulp, the record companies still weren't coming knocking. As a result, the band decided to take matters a little further into their own hands and, late that year, put together a ready-made single and video to present to record companies. In theory, the labels would be more attracted to a complete, ready-to-release package because the cash outlay on their part would be minimal – it had worked with Red Rhino and *It*, and the hope was that the new Pulp would be able to pull off a similar deal.

The band therefore took their equipment, a tape recorder and Tim Allcard (to start and stop the tape) to one of the table tennis rooms in the Sheldon Row factory building on November 11 to lay down new versions of 'Maureen', 'Anorexic Beauty' and 'Simultaneous', along with a new song, 'Mark Of The Devil', and an early rocker called 'Back In LA'. 'Maureen' was planned as the lead track, and a cheap video was made soon after the session with the help of someone from Sheffield Art College.

The plan didn't quite pan out as intended: the tape never made it to vinyl, but it did manage to drum up some renewed interest from Fire Records, who would sign Pulp in mid-1985. Clive Solomon, however, casts doubt on whether there was ever any suggestion that Fire might release the demo itself: "The discussions about which tracks they were going to release as singles were going to be discussions about tracks they'd recorded for Fire, rather than material that they'd recorded before they signed with us." In the event, 'Anorexic Beauty', 'Simultaneous' and 'Mark Of The Devil' would eventually be rerecorded (in technically better, but arguably less exciting, form) for various Fire releases, while 'Maureen' and 'Back In LA' never emerged on vinyl at all.

It may have been equal parts accident (Castle Table Tennis Rooms was no Abbey Road and Tim was no Bob Clearmountain) and design that the tracks from the *Ping Pong Jerry* session, even by the standards of mid-Eighties Pulp recordings, have a decidedly low-fi air about them. 'Anorexic Beauty', 'Simultaneous' and 'Maureen' are shredded more viciously than any versions before or after, 'Mark Of The Devil' has a dark atmosphere only hinted at on the rather polite reading that later emerged on the 'Dogs Are Everywhere' EP, and 'Back In LA' is simply filthy. Outside of the studio, Pulp may have been smoothing out some of their more extreme, unpalatable aspects, but *Ping Pong Jerry* was their *White Light/White Heat*.

On December 29, 1984, Pulp played the Leadmill in Sheffield. The show was recorded, and the resultant bootleg tape offers a fascinating glimpse into the sound and soul of 1984 Pulp. On this particular night, Jarvis was short on chirpy between-song banter: he spent the first half of the set complaining about the PA feeding back, and eventually walked off stage and (in Russell's words) "threatened to twat the sound mixer" while the rest of the band filled the time with a brief, improvised instrumental.

Despite confrontations such as this, Pulp's aggressive, avant-garde tendencies had by this time been tempered somewhat. Concerts were now preceded not by a factory siren but by a thumping, bass-driven instrumental called 'Hydroelectric Dam' (one of Russell's "tone poems"), while the rest of the set was split between relatively lush, albeit dark, pop songs ('The Mark Of The Devil', 'They Suffocate At Night'), noisy, abrasive experimental pieces ('Repressive Forkout', 'Take You Back') and sparser, funereal ballads ('Life Must Be So Wonderful', 'There's No Emotion'). Considering that this concert took place 18 months before the recording of *Freaks*, the songs that would subsequently appear on record are surprisingly close to the recorded versions. Yet there's an intensity and an inspiration to some of the performances that was becoming more elusive by the time this version of Pulp made it to the studio: songs that require a sympathetic ear to be enjoyed in their official form, such as 'They Suffocate At Night', are riveting here.

Amongst the better-known songs, the set included a few numbers that were never recorded or released. 'Snow' was a keyboard-drenched melodrama, a sort of 'Lonely This Christmas' rewritten by Nick Cave, that would have fitted seamlessly into side one of *Separations*. "Great song," remembers Russell. "There wasn't any particular reason for not recording or releasing it. It was too long to be a single, and also it was a bit of a Christmas song, so it didn't really fit in at any other time of the year. We just never seemed to get round to it."

The other song played that night that was never recorded was called 'Repressive Forkout'. Mining the same seam of advanced scariness as The Birthday Party, it features Jarvis shouting things like *"I respect her/ I reject her/ I refuse her/ with no warning"* to a backing not dissimilar to 'Tunnel', driven by a buzzsaw guitar riff and Candida's horror-film church organ.

"We never really finished it," says Russell. "Manners came up with the title – because it was a loud, trashy punk thing, it made sense to give it a mock UK Subs, Sham 69 sort of title – you know, 'Repressive forkout, maaan!'"

Pulp's repertoire may have been getting increasingly varied musically, but lyrically the songs all seemed to share one characteristic: they were incredibly miserable. Jarvis had never been a bubblegum artist, but the unrequited love songs and adolescent uncertainty of *It* was one thing – a seemingly endless stream of desperate ballads lamenting hopelessly failing relationships, paranoid rants like 'Simultaneous' and 'Take You Back' and foreboding warnings that The Mark Of The Devil (whatever that might be) was on your back was quite another. Was Jarvis all right?

"He *seemed* all right," laughs Michael Paramore. "I think it was a combination of a lot of things at the time. Part of it was stuff other people were doing at the time, probably listening to Leonard Cohen a lot. A lot of other bands were playing similar sort of stuff, less jolly music I suppose. I don't know, I didn't ever really think he was particularly down, but there's always potential when somebody's sleeping all day in a room jam-packed full of stuff that they're hoarding – but I never particularly picked it up from him. He always seemed OK.

"You go through phases when you're in bands, your first band's always a bit jollier than the one after. With my bands, Heroes Of The Beach was a bit more of a pop band than In A Belljar, which was a bit more serious. I think Russell as well probably contributed to that – he was always interesting to talk to, but always a bit more serious than Jarvis or other people."

By the start of 1985, Fire Records was showing serious interest in signing Pulp. Clive Solomon had already offered them a publishing deal with the label's publishing arm Twist & Shout, and when it transpired that Pulp had been dropped by Red Rhino, discussions began about signing them to Fire.

"If I'm right," says Ogy McGrath, "what Pulp did was get an appointment to go down and see them, and said, 'Can we just go in the room for five minutes before you come in?', and they set it up like they'd have it on stage – they turned it into a Pulp office, with all these little lights and toilet roll and paper fish and things all over, put all the posters up and then turned on the 'Maureen' video for them to listen to, and that got them the deal. That's what they told me anyway!"

To help finalise the terms of the contract, Pulp brought in Tony Perrin to negotiate with Clive Solomon. Tony, who had been busy for most of 1984 touring as bassist with Artery, had renewed contact with Pulp at a concert at the B-Hive in Sheffield before Christmas. "It was the first time I'd seen Pulp in a very long time. I remember just being startled by how they'd gone from this kind of vague collective that didn't seem to have any focus or identity, to being this thing that, whether you liked it or not, you couldn't deny that it had a very strong sense of its own identity. And that was the chemistry between Russell and Jarvis. I remember sitting in a pub with Russell, and he was basically saying, 'That *It* album's crap and it's your fault', and I was saying, 'Well, I think that's unfair, and I really love the album, and I really love Jarvis, and I really love what you're doing now.' He basically said, 'Oh, I didn't realise you felt like that, why don't you get back involved?' And I almost did get back involved, but I can't really remember why that didn't come to pass."

Nonetheless, Tony did keep a tangential involvement with Pulp whilst the Fire deal was being worked out. "The thing had come up with Fire," says Tony, "and Jarvis wanted to do the deal because it seemed to be the only way to get any more records released. Although I don't particularly want to take the blame for the Fire recording contract, I only had a little bit more experience than Jarvis with record contracts, and there was no money for lawyers or what have you. So I basically did what I could to get a better deal with Fire."

"I think there was a fair amount of courtship," agrees Clive Solomon, "discussing terms and everything – it took Tony a while before he felt comfortable, and Pulp felt comfortable, with the deal."

Even so, despite the problems that Pulp were to have with Fire in the coming years, the mood at the time was one of optimism, as John Quinn recalls: "As far as Pulp were concerned, they were pleased to be able to record, to actually have a contract. I don't recall any pressure around the time."

"They seemed happy to be getting involved at the time," says Clive Solomon. "I've no reason to assume otherwise, at least. They'd phone us up, send us nice notes through the post, that sort of thing. Of course they subsequently became unhappy, so you do go back and try and analyse what their feelings were at the time, but all I can say is that the relationship seemed to be perfectly normal.

"I think at the time, the band wanted to be fairly ramshackle – I remember Johnny [Waller] and I used to say, 'You've got some great pop songs here, you could play 'em a bit straighter.' As I recall, I think they very much didn't want to do that. I think it's true that some of the songs on the records would have lent themselves to being produced with more polish, and I think we had a great pop band on our hands, but we also felt that in addition to being a great pop band, they were a very strange, bizarre and wonderful group and we sort of let them do what they wanted to do, really. I don't think they fitted in with anyone or anything – they were quite out there on their own, extremely unique, and I've always enjoyed things that were different. That was one of the reasons why I chose to work with the band. I don't think they would have got signed in a million years by a commercially orientated company that wanted to produce commercial music for the mainstream. I mean, I don't think there was the remotest possibility of that – major taste was quite conservative, which was why groups that were doing something more interesting had to seek more specialist outlets.

"I think I'm probably a fan first and a record company second, which might account for a lot of why we signed the band in the first place. First and foremost, I was a massive, massive fan. On Fire at the time, we had Pulp and The Blue Aeroplanes, and I used to say, 'Well, people don't seem to have that much time for what we do,' but I thought we were working with two bands that completely defied the musical standards of the time in terms of indiedom, never mind the mainstream – they were completely out there, doing stuff that was like nothing else that was around. It was difficult to get people interested in those bands – while they were doing stuff that maybe now doesn't seem so radically different, at the time they were regarded as pretty fucking strange bands."

Meanwhile, after a period of stark, stripped-down stage presentation, the Pulp live experience was moving back towards the bizarre visual spectacle it had been a few years before – albeit with a more deadpan, surreal slant as opposed to the wackiness of the Dolly era. Typically this would involve wrapping everything in sight (walls, drum riser, amps, PA) in tin foil, or draping the stage with mile upon mile of toilet roll, *à la* the sleeve of *Freaks*.

Russell: "It looked fantastic. You'd play in it, and of course you can't move about and it all breaks and wraps around you as you're doing it, and it was wonderful. I think a band sharing the bill with us would probably have thought we were a weird religious sect."[90]

"By taking your own stage set," explains Jarvis, "even if it was only tin foil or something, it was saying, 'Right, well tonight it's not just the same as any other night. It's our night.' But looking back I can see how people had difficulty taking us seriously. I really can."[91]

"Through the Eighties," says David Bocking, "Jarvis was graduating towards the way he performs now. He would have his angular wrist movements and all that sort of stuff, but I think that his clothes sense was more governed at that time by the fact that it was easier to buy bizarre stuff from Oxfam. In a way, it was convenient that he could do that and make a fashion statement as well. I can remember once seeing him after he'd been down to Sheffield market, which he was a great patron of, and he'd got some Seventies greeting cards in purple and lime green which he was really pleased with."

On July 10, 1985, Pulp finalised their recording deal with Fire Records. A year later, the date would be immortalised in the lyrics to 'Tunnel'. "At the time I paid no attention to the date I had chosen for my entrance into the tunnel," wrote Jarvis in his unused sleeve notes for the *Masters Of The Universe* compilation a decade later. "I presumed I had simply picked it out of thin air. It wasn't until I was looking through some old papers that I realised the date's significance – amongst the papers was a copy of our first contract with Fire Records. It was dated – you guessed it – the 10th of July 1985. Had my unconscious mind been trying to tell me something, I wonder? Hmmmmm."[92]

Chapter 6

In the first nine months of 1985, Pulp had managed to play precisely four gigs, all of them in the Sheffield area. For a band about to release what was essentially its début single (the Red Rhino releases could hardly be said to be by the same band that had now signed to Fire), Pulp was underexposed to the point of being virtually invisible to anyone outside South Yorkshire. This changed when, in September 1985, the band embarked on its first-ever national tour – a sort of 'Best of Sheffield' package, co-headlined with Dig Vis Drill, with Mr. Morality footing the bill. Henry Normal (now a scriptwriter for the likes of Steve Coogan and Caroline Aherne, then a mildly popular local poet/stand-up comic) compered, and Simon Hinkler drove the van – as well as filling in on drums for Magnus, who spent most of August and September travelling in India.

"I guess I had the time to spare," says Simon. "I really enjoyed that tour. Being with them as a group of people was a happy and fun experience. As I've said before, they were the proper Pulp at this time. A bunch of misfits that belonged together."

The concept, dubbed The Outrage Tour, was Ogy McGrath's. "During the miners' strike," says Ogy, "I started thinking about forming some sort of co-operative entertainment thing, and Russell liked the idea. So we got what we felt was the best of Sheffield, and presented that to all the universities and towns around the country. They all thought it was some kind of joke – three bands and a poet for 50 quid! But we were all so desperate to get out of Sheffield and do gigs – I don't think Pulp had played outside of Sheffield much at all, and they used to look at us and say, 'How do you get gigs out in London?' Well, there's another phone over there!"

"Ogy had this gung-ho attitude towards self-promotion," says Nick Robinson, who by now had become Dig Vis Drill's guitarist. "He would ring round any venue he could get a number for and say, 'We will play anywhere in England at 24 hours notice, with three bands for 50 quid.' And that's how we got the work – often hundreds of miles away, down in Brighton or somewhere. It would have worked out quite well for us, had the label we were signed to not folded while our first single, 'Cranking Up

Religion', was going up the indie charts ... We tended to play to good crowds though, none of them were really empty."

The third band on the bill, Mr. Morality, was a new Sheffield band formed by Jarvis' longtime friend and one-time Heroes Of The Beach colleague, Steve Genn. (Steve had also briefly been a member of Pulp – he appeared onstage with them for precisely one concert, at the Crucible in 1983. "He wasn't really doing anything," remembers Peter Boam. "Just being a twat, I think.") As well as Steve's presence, there were other Pulp connections: 'Mr. Morality' was the title of an old song of Jarvis' that both Pulp and Heroes Of The Beach played around 1982, and the band's keyboardist was none other than David Hinkler. "They were very influenced by early Pulp initially," remembers Murray Fenton. "Steve'll not thank me for saying that though!"

Mr. Morality's music – remembered by Nick Robinson as "kind of powerpop, strumalong, 12-string guitar stuff, a bit like The Housemartins I suppose" – was a different creature again to the contrasting varieties of sonic radicalism offered by Dig Vis Drill and Pulp, but they did share a certain confrontational attitude – thanks in the main to Steve Genn's famously mouthy onstage demeanour. "If you knew Steve then you saw the band," reckons Ian Spence, "you'd be a bit surprised by how polite they were. Steve was a charismatic performer, a really gobby frontman, but after the initial interest they got with Outrage they never really did anything."

Ogy McGrath perhaps sums it up best. "For me, on The Outrage Tour, Steve Genn was the star. And he's probably the one who'll never make it 'cos he's so talented!

"I always used to criticise retro bands – even in those days, guitar stuff like Treebound Story was retro to me, 'cos we were using synths and computers and stuff. And because of that, people couldn't understand why I'd have Pulp with me, but I thought that Pulp were kind of putting pop on its head as well, in their own way.

"Basically I wanted to destroy everything that anyone ever held precious. And everything we take for granted, I wanted to question. The other thing about me being a little ugly git and wanting to get laid, that was only about 70% of it, I think. But the rest – I wanted to take on the world. I had a kind of Jimmy Cagney, Woody Allen, Johnny Rotten fixation. Basically I was taking the piss out of everybody. The reason why we never made it was that I hated the audience. I hate the idea of anyone coming to see you. I hate the idea of paying to go and see anybody. I always complained when Pulp wanted to put the price up to £2.50 or whatever – no one's paying £2.50 to see us, I want a quid, that's enough! I always wanted a socialist paradise, heh heh, like an idiot! Sad and disillusioned I was in those days. We did all these benefits – Rock against Royalty, Rock against God, Rock against Licensing Laws, Rock against Pop. When I first set off, I realised that the hardest thing in the world is to make people love you, but the easiest thing is to make them hate you, and you'll still sell records. That was my philosophy, really."

Pulp and Dig Vis Drill took it in turns to headline alternate gigs. "Pulp were a bit more well known than us," says Ogy, "but we used to have a bit more publicity than them 'cos I used to say stupid things all the time, do publicity stunts and all that. So that helped us as well.

"We always knew it was an advert for ourselves, we used to put a little stall up where we could sell our own little tapes, posters, badges, all that kind of stuff, and we could make money back that way. And that was where the miners' strike and the steelworkers' strike came in, 'cos we'd do benefits for that, give money towards them. We even started selling Spam! That went down well actually, we got rid of the Spam easy – it was the Pulp records that took time to shift . . . At that time, Pulp were smaller than a cult, but just a bit bigger than a rash. A few people knew them and us, and sometimes we'd go to places where no one'd know us at all. But that was the idea – we thought it was like an adventure. You know, what else were we going to do with our money? Go to nightclubs and take drugs – we did all that anyway, but we'd also go to towns and spend money on doing gigs. Yeah, it was kind of a team, and it was good fun – Outrage was fantastic in those days, it was really creative.

"We all had different ambitions though, you could tell straight away. I was the egomaniac, but deep down I wasn't at all. And Pulp were really quiet and polite, but deep down they were the egomaniacs. They were the professionals, with the discipline and all that stuff. I was gonna be famous, but I never really wanted it in the end, whereas Jarvis was quiet about it, but he wanted it – he really, really wanted it. He wanted to be as big as Elvis. On that Outrage tour, they were all fucking egomaniacs, and everyone thought I was the guy, but it wasn't really like that – Jarvis wanted to be as big as Elvis, Simon Hinkler wanted to be as big as Jimmy Page, Henry Normal wanted to be as big as Woody Allen . . . and me, I just wanted to shag Sue Lawley."

"We all got on well, by and large," says Nick Robinson. "Luckily everyone saw through Ogy, because people who didn't know him thought what an obnoxious mouthy bastard he was, but people who knew him knew he was basically a pussycat. Our backing singer Phil didn't get on well with Russell – there were several incidents, culminating in that scrap in the back of the van. I don't know why that was really – Phil was a bit sensitive because he was basically like the other guy in Frankie Goes To Hollywood, the one who doesn't do very much. So I think he felt he had to justify himself, sometimes physically. And Russell could be quite petulant, and he liked making sarky comments which Phil didn't really understand, but assumed they were rude and took the nark with him!"

Ogy: "Russell helped Pulp in those days because even though a lot of people criticised him, I think he was the key. When they all drifted apart, he kept them together – little things like the business side of things. And tagging up with me was a good move on their part as well, because I'd do a lot of the donkey stuff – not that I didn't want to, I mean it helped me as well. Because I used to say, 'If you make it, I'll help you' – you know, scratch back stuff. And I'm still waiting for my back – it's itchy, it really is itchy. I've got a rash all down the side. It must be off them."

The tour kicked off with a launch concert at the Leadmill on September 22. "Pulp came on and danced for us on stage," remembers Nick Robinson. "They had these silly tragedy masks on – I've got a great picture with Jarvis and Russell pulling these extraordinary poses."

The next day, the tour proper began in Bath. Ogy McGrath: "The first gig on the tour was Bath Moles, and there was a big deal about it because they were supposed to go on last, and we were supposed to go on at 9. But the guy came up to me and said, 'No, you go on at 10,' or something, and I didn't bother to tell them, and Russell started crying really, heh heh. Anyway, we did this gig and they were terrible and we went down fantastic. And they wouldn't talk to me afterwards! I couldn't believe it."

"Musically Pulp would vary completely," reckons Nick Robinson. "One night they'd be stunning, and the next they'd be a bit of a shambles. The thing that held it together for me was Candi's keyboards. She didn't have too many chords to her – she'd just get two fingers three foot apart, bang them up and down, but she got it right *every* night. Didn't take any risks or improvise or anything, and it gave it that kind of foundation. And Jarvis never really had a bad night, for me – he just went for it. The rhythm section wasn't quite so driving as it is these days, so everything tended to have that kind of melancholy air. Magnus was more a musical drummer, I think, than Nick. I remember on the tour, Russell would come out now and again with various sharp comments directed at various members of the band, which used to strike me as ironic because when you heard them play, you'd think he was the one who didn't practise very often!"

"One of John Nicholls' biggest joys in life was Candida's keyboards," says Ogy McGrath. "Every single time she set up, he couldn't stop laughing. He'd get into such a state during the soundcheck, and people who didn't know him didn't know what he was laughing at. He couldn't believe that little Casio thing she used to have, going 'di-di-di, doo-doo-doo'. I think Jarvis just wanted a girl in the band, you know, like The Velvet Underground, 'cos it was cool. But that was John's biggest joy – he'd laugh at Candida's keyboards for 20 minutes, then go back to whatever he was doing before."

The spirit of healthy competition between Pulp and Dig Vis Drill continued at the next stop, at the Thekla in Bristol – a venue on a boat that was owned by none other than the late Viv Stanshall. "We were using computers," remembers Ogy, "which in those days was a really unique, dangerous thing to do. Our computer blew up that night and I went crazy, but Pulp got a fantastic review. After that, they were talking to me again! And after that, we did another gig, and they did better than us 'cos we were still trying to get our computer together, and Russell just came to me and said '2-1, 2-1, 2-1!' I couldn't believe these art school guys were laying this crock of shit on me! Anyway, after we got Russell out of the Avon and dried him out, we talked."

By the time of a Darlington show at the start of October, Magnus had returned to England and to Pulp. He probably wished he'd stayed in India when, whilst enthusiastically thrashing his kit, his swivel drum stool unswivelled and he sat down rather heavily on the exposed point. The concert became more entertaining still when, as John Nicholls remembers, "during Pulp's last number – I can't remember which, but it was probably 'Maureen', they were banging along that much, an amplifier bounced off and smashed the plug through which all their gear was powered. Result: they finished the song acoustically. I still have a picture in my mind of Jarvis, microphone in one hand, drumstick in the other, banging a drum and singing . . ."

Pulp's late '85 touring schedule came to a premature halt in the middle of November when, after presumably drinking quite a lot at a party at Russell's first-floor Housing Association flat (above Sven Books, a sex shop on Sheffield's Division Street), Jarvis decided to impress a girl called Adrienne with his Spiderman impression. In theory, he was going to climb out of a window, along the outside of the building, and come in through the next window.

"I said, 'Do you want to see something quite interesting?' and she begged me not to do it but I was in the mood. It was just senseless bravado, which is quite out of character. I realised that I didn't have the strength to do it, or climb back in, so I had to count to three and let go."[93]

Jarvis fell 20 feet, sustaining a broken wrist and ankle and a fractured pelvis. "I was in poor spirits," he allows, "but I wasn't trying to kill myself. I was just arsing around. But the first thing I thought was that I could have died and it wouldn't have been noble or dramatic, it would have just been pathetic – me hanging there by my fingers saying, 'I can't get back in.' At least in a film, there would have been drums or exciting string music or something."[94]

Jarvis spent the next six weeks in Sheffield's Royal Hallamshire Hospital. Characteristically, Ogy McGrath soon exploited the comedy potential of the incident: "'Cos in 'Little Girl (With Blue Eyes)' it went *'Chalklines round your little hands'*, we went outside where he fell, and I lay on the pavement like a contorted, twisted body. And my mate Phil chalkmarked round my body and put 'JARVIS WOZ ERE' all over it and stuff. I don't think they found it funny. We went to the hospital and he was unconscious and they wouldn't let us see him, and at the time Lionel Ritchie was at number one with that song 'Hello', with that video where the blind girl's a sculptress, and he loves her but he can't tell her that because she's blind, and she carves this bust of him, and then she realised it was him who she loved. So I left Jarvis this note to read when he woke up. It said, 'I've got some good news and some bad news. The bad news is you'll never walk again. The good news is Lionel Ritchie wants you for his new video.'"

Three days after Jarvis fell out of the window, the 'Little Girl With Blue Eyes (And Other Pieces)' EP was released. Pulp's first Fire Records release, and their first vinyl appearance in two years, had been recorded in June at Input Studios, with Simon Hinkler producing.

Simon: "Pulp had, by this time, tried 'self-recording' in warehouse type spaces, but with 'Little Girl' being a single, they wanted better production quality. I think I coaxed them individually and collectively to give tighter performances than they'd probably have settled for on their own – in those days they were particularly sloppy. Producing Pulp back then was like treading a fine line between a stylised production and a bad quality production; between brilliant and crap. I knew what kind of sound Jarvis was looking for, and I would try to get as close to it as I could without everything becoming too mushy and swimming in reverb. I think the 'Little Girl' sessions are typical of that. You can hear the songs are very reverby, as Jarvis wanted. He would sit next to me at the mixing desk and ask me to put more reverb on this, and more reverb on that, and say things like 'make the guitar sound more woolly,' and the overall sound slowly started to suffer. But hopefully I did enough with instrument and vocal placement and EQ to make sure all the instruments could be heard – plus, I secretly kept backing off the reverb when he wasn't looking."

The title track had already been the subject of some dispute with Fire – the band had wanted to release the 1984 *Ping Pong Jerry* session as an EP with 'Maureen' as the lead track, but their label had other ideas. "We argued with Fire for ages about what was going to be the first single," says Russell. "We wanted 'Maureen' but they insisted on 'Little Girl', which wasn't really representative of what we were doing at the time. A few months later there was a bit of a rockabilly revival and they decided that they did want to put 'Maureen' out after all, but of course we'd moved on by then!"

Clive Solomon's recollection is slightly different: "I wouldn't like to say it wasn't the case in case I'm wrong, but I genuinely don't remember 'Maureen' being suggested as a single. 'Little Girl' was more our choice than the band's, though – that was the one that we were in favour of. We definitely felt that that was the obvious track that would get lots of press interest. Like a lot of record companies, we would tend to exercise a view with regard to the A-side because you've got to feel that you've got a track that you can get press interest in or whatever. The choice of other tracks, I'd leave to the band themselves. 'Little Girl' was a great little pop song – I mean, all right, it had the production values of an indie label and a band who I don't think were really interested in making polished pop music at the time, but I think it is a wonderful song and it was material like that that made me want to work with them."

Rancour aside, the end result was a fine record which drew plenty of favourable music press comment thanks to the restrained grandeur of the title track, given extra sheen thanks to Candida's use of John Nicholls' Crumar string synth (the Farfisa had broken down) and Magnus' delicate, understated drumming – not to mention a killer vocal from Jarvis. The critical acclaim, however, was overshadowed by the controversy over the lyrics in the chorus – most famously on Sheffield station Radio Hallam, where DJ Richard Tandy faded it out at 1am, spluttering, "Well, I never expected to hear anything like that from Pulp!"

"There seems to be an attitude in pop music," reflected Jarvis in a fanzine interview a little while later, "that anything is acceptable as long as it's never put directly: it's all right to say *'Let's make love tonight baby, I wanna feel your body'* but not *'There's a hole in your heart and one between your legs'*. I wasn't too surprised."[95]

Russell: "I was very surprised, seeing as we'd been playing that song live and on local radio for years and nobody had even passed comment on it."[96]

As for the rest of the EP, the brooding, schizophrenic, severe 'Simultaneous' was one of Pulp's less successful 'weird' tracks. The intention seems to be 'dark and unnerving', but the actual effect veers more toward being slightly boring. Better was 'Blue Glow', a dark, brooding song which gave evidence of Jarvis' taste for voyeuristic lyrical settings and his growing talent for building up a convincing emotional landscape from minute verbal nuances: *"So late looking up at your window as it bathes me in your blue midnight glow / I wonder why you're not sleeping, and I wonder if you could know. Tonight, make it tonight . . ."*

Meanwhile, Russell made full use of the luxury of having a 16-track studio to play with by overdubbing no less than three violin parts, resulting in a powerful, dramatic, classical-tinged screechy racket. "I don't think Russell's the greatest violin player in the history of music," says Tony Perrin, "but in the early days, he really was bad. I remember Simon suggesting that he should take some lessons, but he was adamant – his big concern was that if he did that then he'd get too good. He was always into experimentation and radical approaches to things – not just musical, as well."

Russell also provided one of the EP's most striking moments with his intensely delivered, deadpan monologue 'The Will To Power'. A survivor from the repertoire of his earlier band The Bath Bankers, the song attracted a certain amount of alarm (and the occasional roar of approval from the "small but vociferous" skinhead contingent in Pulp's live audiences) for its apparent fascist associations and harking back to the spirit of 1933. It hardly needs to be pointed out that Russell – a one-time member of the Revolutionary Communist Party, supporter of the miners' strike and admirer of Arthur Scargill and Michael Foot – was no Nazi, but he was still called on more than a few times to explain exactly what the song *was* about:

"Are we Nazi stormtroopers? Well, they had nice uniforms . . . no, of course not. The song was written in 1983 when we were living in a real SDP kind of environment, where no one had any opinions on anything. I wanted people to take sides, to get off the fence. I'd been reading about Germany at that time and the class conflict. I liked that atmosphere but obviously not from the point of view of being a Nazi. A lot of left-wing statements are too wishy-washy, too nice. I like the sharpness of the Mosleyite addresses. They were on the wrong side but they were better organised.[97]

"To be honest, I wasn't too surprised at the Nazi flak we got. It is in fact a real commie anthem, dedicated to Arthur Scargill and Nelson Mandela and the IRA. The reasons it got Nazi flak are: firstly, it mentions 1933, the year Hitler came to power. Secondly, the title is also a book of Nietzsche writings compiled by the Nazis and taken out of context to try and prove their race theories. Thirdly, I look very similar to Adolf Hitler. On a couple of occasions I've had to dash out of my local when yobbos started shouting 'Zieg Heil!' and taking the piss."

John Quinn: "Knowing Russell looked like Hitler anyway, I thought he was taking the piss, basically. I can't remember there ever being skinheads at Pulp concerts – I don't know whether that's something somebody's made up."

Sadly, although the single attracted plenty of decent reviews, and a fair amount of extra press thanks to the lyrical controversies over 'Little Girl' and 'The Will To Power', a mixture of factors, mainly Fire's lack of promotional clout and the group's inability to promote the record with Jarvis in hospital (a number of concerts had to be cancelled, including an important Fire showcase with Blue Aeroplanes at the Fulham Greyhound), meant that it sold very poorly.

"Pulp were disappointed," Johnny Waller told Martin Aston, "but they weren't naïve yokels. They didn't think they would sign to Fire and make millions. Everyone was thinking more of good reviews and radio play on John Peel and Kid Jensen."[98]

The good reviews were present and correct, but Pulp's records seldom, if ever, turned up on Peel's playlist, which was just about the only place they had any chance of getting a look-in. This must have been especially frustrating and incomprehensible to Jarvis, for whom the big ego boost of Pulp's first Peel session in 1981 had given him the confidence to stay with the band in the first place. "I think we might have got a little bit of radio support from Janice Long when she was doing the *Evening Session*," says Clive Solomon, "but I don't remember Peel ever playing Pulp, and it always struck me that Peel ought to have been a fan, because I think what Pulp were doing was weird enough and different enough to have expected Peel to play them. Maybe there was still too much of a melodic content. But I do remember thinking, 'Why doesn't Peel go for this band?', 'cos I would have expected it."

"This is kind of embarrassing for me," Peel admitted in 1995, "but the next time I really became aware of Pulp again [after the 1981 session] was in 1992 when I saw them supporting The Fall in Cambridge. I came away thinking that was a really good show, and that we must have had loads of sessions from them over the years. So I went to look in Ken Garner's book, and at that stage there was just the one. They must have thought, 'Well, he picks us up, toys with us, plays with us, has his way with us, and abandons us. It's one of those things where if someone had said to us, 'It's been a long time since you had Pulp,' we'd have said, 'Actually it is, let's get 'em in.' As it was, it was something like 12 years . . ."[99]

A lesser problem was the fact that, although they were still respected, and occasionally adored, by Sheffield audiences, Pulp no longer had the benefit of the buzz that had surrounded them four years earlier when they made their initial splash with the Peel session. "With us having been around for so long," Jarvis told the *Star* at the time, "people made up their minds having seen us in 1983. They're not aware that we have changed a lot."[100]

The difficulty, in short, was attracting fans beyond the reliable but relatively small enclave of those who already knew. "They were popular amongst the people who went to see them," says David Bocking. "They weren't popular in the sense that they are now in Sheffield. I wouldn't want to say that they were the most popular of the local indie bands; I couldn't quite say who was, to be honest. They weren't bringing thousands, or even very many hundreds, to every gig that they did. But they were known to be interesting, and to be a worthwhile group. A lot of people thought they were going to go on, eventually, to do great things. It took long enough, but most of us are very glad that they did."

To some, it was beginning to look as if Pulp had missed the turning – as Garry Wilson says, "It was like, 'Come on, you've been going three years now – either pack it in or change your name.' I mean, how many bands do you know who've been around 14 years and suddenly made it big?"

"I've never had commercial expectations for most things that I've ever done," says Clive Solomon. "I do it because I like the band and I like the music. I mean, back in those days, no one played music on indie labels apart from John Peel and whoever was doing the *Evening Session* at that time. You were never going to get more play than that. I mean, this was the days when majors were majors and indies were indies, and you didn't have majors pretending to be indies. There was a massive divide. There was never any question of things on our level breaking through into the mainstream. I mean, even the indie bands that *were* massively big back then didn't have chart success, let alone the obscure end of indie. So I don't think it would have made any difference whether or not the song got banned because of the lyrics – if anything, that worked in its favour because it got more press attention."

Rightly or wrongly, Pulp blamed their label for the single's failure to set the world alight. "I remember there was a lot of contempt for Fire at the time," says Nick Robinson. "I remember Jarvis slagging them off when we were touring, not giving them the push they wanted. They definitely weren't happy."

However, Tony Perrin is not alone in his assertion that "what surprised me through that period was that Fire were continuing to put records out, to be honest. I think it was to their credit that they persevered with them, albeit on a bit of an ad hoc basis."

Jarvis was discharged from the hospital just before Christmas '85, and spent most of January 1986 in a rather rickety-looking antique wheelchair – including, famously, a string of five concerts that had been booked before the accident. "It was quite easy doing gigs in it actually," he says, "'cos I didn't have to do any of that jumping around business. But people used to think I was taking the piss 'cos I always used to walk off stage at the end. The trouble wasn't that I couldn't walk – I just couldn't stay on my feet for long periods of time."[101]

A typical press reaction was that of *Sounds'* Roger Holland who, in his review of the Hammersmith show, implied that Jarvis' wheelchair was a gimmick akin to Morrissey's hearing aid (a mistake Jarvis insisted was corrected in the following issue). "A lot of people thought the wheelchair was just part of the stage act," says John Quinn. "I don't think there were ever any adverse reactions though – people would just say, 'Oh look, there's that stupid Jarvis in a wheelchair.' He got up at the end and walked across the stage. He didn't go very far, but it looked pretty good."

"It was wonderful," says Nick Robinson. "Just like Val Doonican, sat there strumming away on his battered old semi-acoustic on a stage festooned with toilet roll . . ."

"I said to Jarvis, 'You didn't believe me when you joined Outrage and I said I'd put you on the stage and you could show your crutch off,'" says Ogy. "But he hated me 'cos I kept nicking his wheelchair. I wanted to go round Hammersmith and check out what it'd be like to be a disabled person, and he was going crazy 'cos I'd gone off with his wheelchair."

Jarvis' use of the wheelchair on stage, and especially getting up and walking off at the end, is an early example of what was becoming a typical Pulp trait – taking advantage of what was potentially a crippling limitation. "Jarvis isn't stupid," says David Bocking. "He knew that it'd have an impact going on stage in a wheelchair, so it all worked to generate a bit of publicity for them." Even so, Jarvis wasn't willing to go quite as far as Russell, who printed up posters for a gig at the Limit featuring him lying on a hospital bed with lots of tubes coming out of him, but couldn't quite persuade him into going onstage with a trolley and drip.

Unfortunately, Pulp's stint as part of The Outrage tour came to a second, and final, end later in January – after a fight between Russell and Dig Vis Drill's Phil Maverick. "Russell and my backing singer Phil never got on," says Ogy, "and one night while we were loading up the van to go down to this gig in London, Phil just cracked and started attacking him. Beat him up. I couldn't believe he'd done it, and Russell was laying it on, going, 'I can't play tonight, the gig's off.' I bollocked Phil, and we had to go to hospital and get Russell looked at, and we're waiting round and it's snowing outside. There's nothing wrong with him of course, and when we finally got out, we're going, 'C'mon, we've got to go to this gig,' and Russell wanted to sit in the front of the van. 'Get in back, we're going!', 'If I can't sit in the front, I'm not going.' And he fucked off, ran down the street and we chased him with the car. We finally got him, let him sit in the front, and went and did the gig.

"After the gig there was a mix-up about the money, which was something we'd never had before, and Phil went for him again. I was just pissed up with some women or something, and Jarvis comes up to me and goes, 'Ogy, can you keep your backing vocalist under control?' I said, 'Yeah, what's the matter with him?' He said, 'He's just attacked Russell again.' So I had to go and sort all that out.

"And Pulp wanted to leave Outrage, but they wanted half the gigs for the rest of the tour, and they wanted us to just drop out of the other gigs. I said, 'No, we'll do the gigs, we'll be professional about this, we can shake hands, it was all a misunderstanding.' But they said I had to get rid of the backing vocalist or Outrage was over, which I thought was great because we were doing miners' benefits and stuff for redundant steelworkers, and they wanted to make my backing vocalist redundant!

"Pulp owed me 30 quid when they left. Never got that back either. Anyway, we carried on and got Midnight Choir to fill in instead of Pulp. Which was a bad move."

"Apart from Phil and Russell, there was never a big falling-out or anything," says Nick Robinson. "I think Ogy just tried to keep things on the boil by getting anyone in who'd do it – first Midnight Choir, and then The Screaming Trees. Outrage didn't go on for that much longer anyway – in the end we all got pissed off with all that travelling and no bloody money, and the logistics of trying to get three bands together in the back of a van."

At the beginning of February 1986, just over a month after leaving hospital, Jarvis confounded medical science and dispensed with his wheelchair. "When they took the plaster off me legs," he recalls, "the doctor said, 'You do realise, don't you, that the bones in your foot are very fragile? We've tried to put them back in place, but it's impossible to do properly, so you'll always have pain there. And in the end you'll be in so much pain that we'll have to fuse your foot to your ankle. Then you'll never be able to move your foot again.'"[102] The occasional twinge notwithstanding, Jarvis has been fine ever since.

The profound effect his accident had on him, however, would remain with him for years to come: "It made me decide to live in the present and not the future, and gave me time to think about things. It made me realise I didn't have a guardian angel looking after me.[103]

"I thought I was sorted out to be a pop star. I had this very romanticised view of life; I'd never have to bother with shopping or anything practical. Even as a kid I never learnt to ride a bike. I thought I could live on this aesthetic level, head in the clouds. Then I fell out of the window.

"It did me good. Before then I used to get up in the afternoon and avoid the obstacles of the mundane everyday. I'd done nothing except live in the future. I saw myself like a rocket on the launch pad waiting to take off, but it went on indefinitely. I was stuck in a ward with a lot of old blokes who'd worked down the pit and talking to them made me alter my viewpoint. There's nothing like spending six weeks just lying flat on your back to help you take stock.[104]

"In the hospital, I had a lot of time to think. And there was a miner in the bed next to me who'd been in an accident. He was a right nice bloke. The only contact I had with miners before was during the strike. I wanted to support it, but I always remember I was sat outside this pub and these striking miners came by and took the piss out of me because they thought I looked an idiot. Well, I did look an idiot at the time actually. So it was like, I support you in theory but you probably want to cave my head in. Of course, it was just four blokes, not the entire mining community. And I was guilty of generalisation and almost despising my own background. But meeting that bloke in the hospital encouraged me to think I'd been looking in the wrong direction for inspiration. I'd been in Pulp since I'd left school. I'd had this attitude of ignoring day-to-day things, I was hiding from life really, thinking I didn't have to deal with it because I'd become famous soon. I turned round the other way after that. I tried to get into the tiniest details of life, trying to scrutinise everything – I started to write lyrics that way too."[105]

Something else Jarvis had discovered while in hospital was the minutiae-packed short stories of Tom Wolfe, which would prove to be another major influence. "He made stuff I might have dismissed as crap seem exciting – stories about stock-car racing or surfers. It was a revelation. Reality wasn't this grey lump of concrete after all. It's been my personal thing ever since to try and do that – to be specific.[106]

"I was in hospital with quite a strange mix of people and I found out the things that are most pleasurable are small, ordinary things. I read Tom

Wolfe's *The Electric Kool-Aid Acid Test*, which is about subjects like custom cars and surfers in California. Those things didn't interest me particularly, but there's something about the way he gets inside people and takes liberties, I guess, with expressing their thoughts. He's especially good on physical detail and what people are wearing. That set me on a different track with my writing. It's maybe been the biggest influence on my career. I'd always been disappointed with the disparity between what I felt I'd been promised by watching TV and listening to songs as I was growing up and what things were actually like when you experienced them. Generally, entertainment presents things in an idealised, romanticised way. It became my mission, if you like, to try to present things as I think they are rather than as what they're supposed to be."[107]

Some of Jarvis' new, grounded outlook can be detected on Pulp's next release, the 'Dogs Are Everywhere' EP, recorded in February and released by Fire in May. The lyrics to the lead track, written in hospital while recovering from the window incident, were inspired by Magnus and Manners' antics at a gig in Chesterfield the year before: "Magnus and Pete were always pissing about and getting stoned," says Jarvis. "Myself and Russell were very puritanical and thought that was terrible. They'd have these mates hanging around, which got on my nerves. That night, they nicked bottles of beer from behind the bar, and we got into loads of trouble. That's what 'Dogs Are Everywhere' is about – people who display a doggish attitude."[108]

More generally, the song reflects Jarvis' general despair at the way his life appeared to be going, and what he was seeing around him. "It's about dogs in society, male and female," explained Jarvis at the time. "As far as I can work out, man is far nearer to dog than ape. The way they shit on your carpet, that sort of thing. Sometimes you feel like a dog, it's like low-mindedness, brute instinct over higher values. It's a bit of a dilemma. You get the nobility of lions but dogs are stuck with walking down the pavements being dirty. There's no more pathetic sight in the world than a faithful dog."[109] The music, meanwhile, shows just how far the band had progressed since the start of Pulp III. The simple, uncluttered melody, decorated by Russell's delicate slide guitar and reinforced by the kind of one-finger Farfisa backing that was fast becoming Candida's trademark, complimented the lyrics perfectly and ensured that the song hit home more directly and immediately than any Pulp single yet.

'The Mark Of The Devil', meanwhile, was reckoned by Jarvis to be the best song Pulp had at the time and, despite a thin-sounding production and rather polite, over-hasty performance, it's still apparent that as a song it catches the mid-Eighties Pulp at the height of their powers. Propelled by a disco drumbeat (prophetically, a part that Jarvis came up with in one of the band's swap-instruments writing sessions) and Russell's gleeful Eastern European violin scraping, and featuring some deliciously dark lyrics *(". . . and your past is just a bedroom full of implements of cruelty")*, it's a powerful sign of what was to come.

'97 Lovers' provided a change of pace and, according to Jarvis, "was the first time I got some good lyrics out. One bit was about my auntie – in her bedroom, she had a picture of Roger Moore above the bed, with this short towel and dressing gown. I always thought, 'God, I bet it's weird when they're in bed having it off underneath that picture. My uncle must know she's probably thinking it's Roger whilst he's doing it to her.'"[110] As well as Jarvis' ever more observant and pertinent lyrics ("Just take a walk round town and you soon lose count of the deformities," he wryly remarked on the sleeve), the song is another impressive sign of the band's musical progression. Russell's ever more prominent woozy violin combined with the Farfisa and Magnus' kettledrums (another trademark from around this time) to produce a perversely jovial funeral waltz that perfectly complemented the blacker-than-pitch humour of the lyrics.

'Aborigine' was something else again – a powerful, hypnotic one-note drone (titled because of the didgeridoo-like noise at the beginning of the track, courtesy of Russell scraping a violin bow across the bottom string of Pete's bass) that slowly develops into a manic thrash. The story that Jarvis relates over the top is, on the surface, about a fictitious "bloke who's always kidding himself that his life's about to start and become exciting, but ends up wasting his life and becoming very fat,"[111] but it doesn't take too great a leap of the imagination to realise that Jarvis was looking a little closer to home for inspiration. The song seems to be about the disturbing realisation, in the wake of Jarvis' then-recent near-death experience, that excitement and glamour may not be just around the corner after all, and that the only thing that lies ahead might be a lifetime on the dole in Sheffield.

"It wasn't conscious," says Jarvis, "but something lodged in the back of me head, that it was all right because eventually life was going to take on some meaning or something. But then you get this horrible dawning realisation in the middle of the night that maybe it won't. Maybe this is it: that you're going to be looking into this saucepan of reconstituted dried food for the rest of your life, or getting up at two o'clock every afternoon, and that's it. You could just go all through your life on supplementary benefit and then, just at the end, get a pension and that's it. And it was a scary thing when I realised that that could happen unless I did anything about it."

The EP closed with 'Goodnight', described by Jarvis as "a concept piece that sounded like falling asleep. I had to spoil it by having some nightmare part on the end, though."[112] And he does, progressing from a gorgeous, hypnotic, sleepy build-up to a snarling finale assuring the listener that *"you will never wake again"*. Nonetheless, the track is still far from a disaster – very atmospheric, very paranoid, very (that word again) *dark*.

Taken as a whole, the EP is a remarkably diverse and original collection of music, reflecting the broadness of the band's repertoire around that time. "Each song Pulp had could've led off in a different direction," reckons Nick Robinson. "There wasn't an overall song style to them – Jarvis was, and still is, quite experimental with his structures and what have you. He never got into a clichéd rut."

"Even when they were writing obvious, pleasing pop melodies," says Clive Solomon, "I don't think they ever just left it at that – there would always be other elements, whether it was a macabre lyric in 'Little Girl' or whatever. There was an edginess, a tension in their music, even in some of the outright pop songs. That was an element that had always been there, all the little twists."

When it came to releasing the record, Pulp had initially wanted 'The Mark Of The Devil' as the A-side, but, acting on advice from Fire, ultimately decided that 'Dogs Are Everywhere' should be the lead track instead. Clive Solomon: "We felt that 'Dogs' would be a bit easier to take – although I love 'Mark Of The Devil', it was a bit of an oddball kind of track that people might have found more difficult to get a hold of."

Fire's judgement actually paid off in that the EP garnered some of Pulp's best reviews yet – including Single Of The Week, no less, in *Melody Maker*. Jarvis must have been especially cheered by the reviewer's comment that "Once you've heard Pulp you'll never need The Smiths again." Morrissey and co (who released their first single a few weeks after *It* came out) were then at the height of their popularity, enjoying a level of commercial success that was otherwise unheard of amongst dour northern indie bands in the mid-Eighties.

"Yes, I was jealous of *him*, because they were from the north and in a faintly similar vein to us, compared to everything else around," says Jarvis. "But I resented anyone who was successful."[113]

Favourable press notwithstanding, *Death, Desperation, Doom And Dogs* (to give the EP the title it was almost saddled with) sold a miserable 300 copies – even fewer than 'Little Girl'. Despite their increased press profile and vastly more advanced music, it seemed that Pulp were no more popular in terms of sales than they were in 1983.

"Coming after 'Little Girl'," says Martin Lilleker, "it was a move from a lovely song to a dark song. I think they were wilful around that time. I don't know whether it was something to do with the relationship with Fire, but I'm sure that if they wanted they could have put out singles that would've got played on the radio more than they did, and would've done something, and perhaps Pulp would've done something themselves in a big way earlier than they did."

To promote the record, Pulp undertook a rather scattered mini-tour in late April and early May, playing dates in Sheffield, London, Hull and Chesterfield. The tour was the first assignment for a new member of Pulp's entourage: new sound engineer/driver Jonathan Kirk. "I was in a band called Mr President – we were going to get signed up by Warner Brothers, and at the end of the day they decided to sign up Strawberry Switchblade instead – two good-looking women, four adolescent youths, no contest really! So what happened was, our lead singer and songwriter decided that he wanted to make money via a different route, and decided to call it a day. So that left me at a loose end, and I decided I'd set up my own business as a road manager for bands. I got a Business Enterprise grant and bought an old bus, and one of the first things I did was to be Pulp's driver for this string of gigs. When we got to the first one, outside the venue Jarvis said, 'Don't suppose you fancy doing our sound tonight do you?' and I said all right. It was the first time I'd done it, and I just took to it – it's one of the only things I've ever done that I've not had to work at. People were coming up to me after the gigs saying they were really impressed with the sound I'd got, and that was the start of being almost like the sixth member of the band for the next few years."

The Sheffield concert, at the Limit, was notable for another bizarre variant on the band's striking stage presentation: across the stage there was a washing line, from which Jarvis hung various objects in plastic bags (bunches of flowers, severed hands from shop dummies, that sort of thing). "For each song," he explains, "rather than just introduce it, I'd pick up an item and hang it on the washing line"[114]

In the audience was Steve Mackey, 20-year-old bassist with the Stooges-influenced Sheffield combo, Trolley Dog Shag. "I'd seen them about three times," he remembers. "I liked them. They seemed quite self-contained though, quite aloof and I was in really noisy bands, garage bands, and Pulp were like an art band. It didn't seem very welcoming.

"In the middle of 'Mark Of The Devil', Jarvis had thrown his hand in the air and his glasses had come off and went behind him and he was on his hands and knees looking for them, but he couldn't find them and the rest of the band were playing because they didn't know what was going on. It lasted about fifteen minutes and he was crawling around the stage and I thought it was just a show at first, but it wasn't – they'd gone in the hole of the bass drum and the song just fizzled out. That was the first strange thing that I saw."[115]

He met Jarvis and Russell for the first time at an Australian-themed party in Russell's flat. "I had some boxer shorts on with an Australian connection and Jarvis had a pair of rollerskates on with two big springs on the bottom. It was one of those nights.[116]

"I knew Jarvis a bit because me and a friend of mine, Ian (we were in a band together) used to get stoned every Friday night and we'd try and find Jarvis. We were only about twenty and he used to tell us stories – him and Russell used to have this vast collection of stories, so we used to go down really dazed and find them and make them tell us stories about anything and we'd sit there laughing our heads off. Not at them, but they knew lots of really stupid things. That's how I got to know them. At the time Jarvis seemed a lot more mature than us. He seemed like an old man in a young man's body – and not that young either."[117]

The Chesterfield dates on the 'tour' (one of which saw Magnus finish '97 Lovers' lying flat on his back after the kettledrum gradually tipped over on to him during the song) were organised by another young fan, 15-year-old Mark Webber, who had met the band at a concert in his home town in January. "I was doing a fanzine called *Cosmic Pig*," he remembers. "I went and did an interview with them even though I'd only heard one of their songs, and they were just the weirdest bunch of people I'd ever, ever met. I did the interview and stayed and watched the concert, and it was like nothing I'd ever seen. It was great, not at all what they're like now – they used to be quite arty and avant-garde."

Mark (or Zig as he was generally known at the time, allegedly because of a David Bowie obsession) kept in touch with the band "because they lived nearby, and used to play a lot around Sheffield." He soon became a regular at gigs, and began to get acquainted with their eccentricities: "When me and my friends used to go shopping in Sheffield, we used to go round to Russell's house. In his room he had a big frieze of photographs of industry in Eastern Europe, and a display of cigarette boxes from Russia stuck on his wall. Every time we went round he used to make a different flavour of tea for us and we had to guess what flavour it was, and he always used to pretend that it was something weirder than what it was. That was kind of how I got to know them."

On May 15, Pulp headlined the Rock Garden in London, débuting two new songs amongst the by-now familiar material. 'Tomorrow' was an intense, noisy number based around kettledrum, violin, and lots of shouting from Jarvis. According to Russell, "it didn't stay in the set for very long because we realised very quickly that it was fucking awful . . ."

The other new addition to the repertoire, 'Down By The River', was a different story altogether, described by Jarvis at the time as being about how "you may reject something, and then perhaps about six months later you might think, I wish I hadn't done that.' And then you go back to the place where you threw it away, and it's not there anymore."[118] The lyrics – likening a dead love affair to a drowned corpse – are essentially as dark as any Pulp song from this period, but are easier to take thanks to the rather lighter, poetic touch that Jarvis was beginning to develop – and the swaying, waltz-like backing, with some excellent two-finger Farfisa underpinning the melody. The strength of the song was such that, while it didn't really fit in with the records Pulp were making *circa* 1986, it lasted long enough to make it on to *Separations* three years later.

The London concert garnered two wildly appreciative reviews in the national music press. *Melody Maker*'s Martin Aston declared Pulp "a brilliant new pop group, another desperate hope for pop 1986 to stay free of its conventions," while in *Sounds*, John Wilde was enthusiastic almost to the point of incoherence:

> "Of all Lou's lost sheep, these are the oddballest of the lot, some show-off shambling electric busk through a Peter Pan world of scatty, scrappy charm. Often harrowing, they nevertheless give this greatly soothing impression that their rasping, barbed energies are more and less than words. [. . .] Pulp are a mouthful of eyeballs scraped against your insides and it's here that the comedy bulges. They were the best band in the otherworld tonight."

The Velvet Underground comparison invoked in Wilde's review was a not uncommon one at the time, and it's easy to see why: here was another dark, edgy, arty sort of band with weird stage decorations, pitting a fairly traditional pop vocalist/songwriter with an ear for brilliant melodies and moments of surprising tenderness against a violin-wielding avant-garde conceptualist who appeared keen to steer the band down the nearest available abyss at the earliest opportunity (oh, and there was a girl in the band). But were the Velvets a direct influence? Apparently not: Russell remarked in an interview at the time that "we weren't really pissed off [about accusations of Velvets copyism] because we knew that comparison was so inaccurate. We're more influenced by groups like The Fall, really, and if people had picked that up, it might have worried us."[119]

"I'd never actually heard the Velvets at that point," says Russell now, "so when people were comparing us to them we didn't really know what they meant. We heard them later on though, and then it was like, 'Oh great, a kindred spirit!' "

132

Around this time, the band were performing various other songs that never made it to vinyl amongst the more familiar material. 'Nights Of Suburbia' is perhaps the best known, having been immortalised in a live recording from 1985's Dolebusters festival. Vastly different to its similarly titled 1992 companion piece, the song is built around a noisy, angular, steamrollering guitar riff, while Jarvis seems to be revisiting some '97 Lovers'-type scenarios, albeit in a more desperate, up-close and personal way – audible lyrics include *"And we danced, and we danced and the virgins became whores"*, *"It's just one more fish and chip supper away"* and a reference to *"piles of stinking crimplene"*.

'Breaking Down At My Door' is in a similar musical vein to 'Nights Of Suburbia', although more monotonous: the backing seems to stay mostly on one note, while Jarvis yells *"Breakin' up breakin' up breakin' up breakin' up!"* for a chorus. The only surviving recording is again on a live tape, and one suspects that it was a one-off outing. "Improvisation on a fragment was not unusual," says Russell. "Sometimes something happens, sometimes it doesn't."

More impressive was 'Didn't Feel A Thing', a superb song based around a jerky, syncopated bassline, punctuated by some violin that suggests the flight of a particularly deranged bumblebee. "It's a shame that one never got fleshed out," says Russell. "It was one of my favourites from that time – sort of Eastern European punk." Introduced at one concert as being "a song about how hard I am", the song seems to be Jarvis' semi-ironic stab at beating the alpha males that he despairs of in 'Dogs Are Everywhere' at their own game: *"I fell from a very high building, and I didn't feel a thing, no I didn't feel a thing – and I'm telling you all it was nothing, no I didn't feel a thing . . ."* Later, physical invincibility is replaced by emotional invulnerability: *"Don't worry, I've taken precautions – I stopped it before it could start. They're rubber and ribbed for protection, and they fit like a glove round my heart."*

Pulp may have been getting considerable press attention whenever they played in London (which would happen perhaps three times a year), but this had a downside: the stark contrast it made with the level of impact they made anywhere else they might have played – ie, practically none. "It was impossible to get the press and A&R men up to Sheffield," says Ian Spence, who was encountering similar difficulties at the time with his band The Screaming Trees (no relation to the Seattle grunge combo of the same name). "They just weren't interested. So you had to go and play London if you wanted to get noticed. And it was only easy to get gigs in London if you'd pay the venues money – which meant you'd have very little chance of getting any return."

The situation for Pulp was a frustrating and dispiriting one: for two-and-a-half years, the Cocker/Senior/Doyle/Mansell/Doyle line-up had been working steadily in an attempt to build some sort of career, and had reached a point where they were having limited amounts of success – the records were successful critically if not commercially, there was a sizeable local fanbase and a modest London one, and reviews, if sporadic, were reliably favourable and occasionally ecstatic. But without the promotional push of a large and/or influential record label behind them, and without the national profile to attract press and public to the band beyond the appreciative pocket that was already there, Pulp had hit something of a glass ceiling.

The result was that for the rest of 1986, Pulp would be playing steadily fewer gigs while the mood in the band soured – but not before they'd completed their first album for Fire, *Freaks (Ten Stories About Power, Claustrophobia, Suffocation And Holding Hands)*.

The sessions took place at Input in June, with Fire providing a budget not dissimilar to what Tony Perrin had scraped together for *It* – however, £600, which paid for a fortnight in Victoria, was only worth a week at Input. In the absence of Simon Hinkler (touring the world and making lots of money with The Mission), Jonathan Kirk found himself behind the desk instead.

"It was very intense," remembers Kirk of the sessions. "That was the main thing – there was so much to do in that week, and they all really wanted to get it done, it was quite an intense experience getting through it. To save time, I even ended up playing some bits – I think I played timpani on 'Tunnel'. At the end, what we really needed was another two or three days to mix it, but for that we needed more money from Fire – which of course wasn't forthcoming. But despite the conditions of making it, and even though its sound was a bit flat compared to the live shows, I think it's a great record, with some really nice touches. I was proud to have my name on it."

The record opens in suitably bizarre, foreboding fashion with 'Fairground', sung by Russell and salvaged from his Bath Bankers repertoire. Russell begins the song pitching himself somewhere between the ringmaster of a Victorian freakshow and a horrified onlooker, his ominous announcement that *"Sometimes nature makes mistakes"* giving way to a gallery of misfits and oddities, accompanied by manic laughter from Jarvis, apparently relishing his role as the unnerving bloke who stands stock-still in the middle of the waltzer. *"Ha ha ha ha ha ha ha ha"* indeed.

'I Want You' is next, steering us back on to safer ground. Arguably one of the best songs of this period, and marred only slightly here by a rather out-of-tune violin, it's about as close as Pulp *circa* 1986 got to a conventional love song – that is, if you can call Jarvis' lamenting of a love affair where *"I'll break you because I lose myself inside you / I'll make you fit in the space that I provide you / And I'll take you, yes I'll take you just to push you far away"* either conventional or a love song.

"I tried to get Elaine Paige to record 'I Want You'," says Ogy McGrath. "I met her agent through Quentin Crisp, and I was going, 'You've got to cut this song by Pulp!' and they weren't bothered. I bet she'd bite my hand off now. *'You can't leave it to die there in pain, you've got to stamp upon its head'* – there's stuff like that in *Evita*."

'Being Followed Home', a swirling, paranoid number in a similar lyrical vein to 'Goodnight', provides a return to the fear and loathing of 'Fairground', albeit with a lyrical setting that is less surreal nightmare than nightmarish reality. The powerfully atmospheric music, perfectly complementing the panicky, frightened feel of the lyrics, came from what Russell describes as "one of our weird little brainstorming sessions where we'd turn the lights out and say, 'Right, let's create a certain mood.' Like, let's imagine we're in a small seaside town and it's a pursuit, someone's hiding . . . get a certain atmosphere but not be so weird that it wasn't pop music."[120]

'Master Of The Universe', like 'Mark Of The Devil' before it, is an example of a brilliant song let down by a so-so recording. Live, it was one of the most popular songs in Pulp's set – a storming, intense monster of a tune powered by some of Magnus' most inspired drumming. "That was a brilliant song," says Kirk. "Seeing Magnus play it live was an emotional experience – the way it would just build and build, going up towards that climax at the end, and then there'd be those three hits on the bass drum and it'd just cut out. The crowd went crazy every time they played it, without fail." On vinyl, though, it falls rather flat – not least because Russell's throttling, jerky guitar part (arguably the key to the whole song), is all but lost in the mix.

'Master' is still interesting, however, for the early signs of Pulp's next musical direction. The combination of disco (Jarvis wrote the song in hospital using one of the preset rhythms on his Gran's Yamaha Portasound keyboard) and Eastern European (the insistent, plinky-plunk, oom-pah beat) influences would become all the more pronounced over the next couple of years.

Side one closes with one of the highpoints of the album, and perhaps of Pulp's career – the sublimely depressing 'Life Must Be So Wonderful'. It's a sad, brilliant song of guilt and despair, building gradually from a gentle, wistful ballad to an anguished climax. *"Your life must be so wonderful, your visions die and fall,"* laments Jarvis desperately at the song's end, before resignedly adding that *"in the end, nothing ends — just grows fainter and farther away".* Torment and disillusion can seldom have sounded so beautiful.

'There's No Emotion' explores similar territory, but while 'Life Must Be So Wonderful' is a straightforward emotional outpouring, the mood is lightened here (albeit only to reveal still more darkness) by a kind of self-mocking irony. Jarvis described it as being about "being in possession of a heart which suddenly dies on you, but you carry on living,"[121] and as he sings in his best country-ballad voice about his soul that dried away and holding hands "that hold you forever" (remember the album's subtitle), it's not inconceivable that he's, in part at least, poking fun at his endless desperate misery.

Co-written by Russell and his friend David Kurley (and originally performed by Kurley's early Eighties bands Rapid Eye Movements and New Model Soldier), 'Anorexic Beauty' is a song about being simultaneously attracted and repelled by a girl who's starving herself to death. It's dedicated to fallen Seventies child star Lena Zavaroni. "Presumably, this is Pulp's idea of a fun track,"[122] noted *Sounds* dryly. Bizarrely, it was, and the jerky, stop-start punky thrash of 'Anorexic Beauty' is a welcome piece of light relief amongst the tragi-balladry and horrorshow narratives of the rest of the album.

'The Never Ending Story' uses the same unlikely combination of instruments as '97 Lovers' (Farfisa, violin, kettledrum) to vastly different effect – while the aforementioned is a genial funeral waltz, here we have a manic, jerky, heavily Eastern European-influenced number with Russell's name written all over it. Lyrically, it is also one of the most explicit references to the crumbling relationship that supplied the subject matter for most of Pulp's mid-Eighties material. "I was in the middle of the first proper relationship I'd had," says Jarvis. "I'd gone into this terrible depression of finding out what relationships were really like, but not knowing how to deal with it – you go out with someone for six months and spend another 18 trying to split up. All in all, I was not a happy person."[123]

Similar lyrical subject matter is explored by 'Don't You Know?', incongruously set to the most upbeat and poppy tune on the album, featuring what *Record Mirror* described as "the best three piano notes ever played"[124] and an equally pretty solo from Candida. Jarvis seems to be taking a more jovial look at a doomed relationship, even managing to sneak in possibly the earliest recorded example of Sleazy Cocker Innuendo – *"I don't need your excuses, how you tired of trying to stay on top. So just lie back and enjoy it and save your tears for when the kissing stops."*

Finally, we had the epic 'They Suffocate At Night', a "sublime, blackly humorous ballad" (Clive Solomon's words), decorated by some nicely plinky acoustic plucking that lends it a mildly exotic feel, not a million miles away from The Cure *circa* 'The Caterpillar'. One can't help but feel that the song slightly overreaches itself though – it aims at 'genial, doomladen, jolly, ironic' but ends up with just a hint of 'plodding, stuffy, tuneless'.

Musically, the album doesn't have the scope of the 'Little Girl' and 'Dogs Are Everywhere' EPs; extended, experimental pieces such as 'Aborigine' or 'The Will To Power' are notable by their absence. "*Freaks* didn't seem to do a great deal – it seemed to be lacking somewhere," reckons David Bocking. "'Little Girl (With Blue Eyes)' and 'Dogs Are Everywhere' seemed a lot closer to what they should be doing, in many ways." On the other hand, the fact that the album consists largely of more 'traditional' songs does make it an easier record to enjoy – and although many of the songs date back to 1984 and the early days of Pulp III, the choice of poppier, more accessible material does point towards the direction that Pulp would take over the next few years.

Jonathan Kirk: "I don't know whether it's something that happens to every group, but even in terms of my own development with Mr President, we were extremely experimental to start off with, and then we as a group started becoming more commercial, and it's quite interesting because I think as songsmiths, you begin to understand the structure and function of chords, and how they work better. It's like a tool, and I think to start off with Pulp were perhaps not very good at playing their instruments, but obviously had a lot of experimental stuff. By the time I saw them they were getting there in terms of understanding their instruments and what they could do, and the songs Jarvis wrote on guitar, the ballads, were really starting to shine through. In terms of quality in the chord changes, the structure of the song, I don't know whether it's a natural progression for a group to go through, that suddenly they're coming up with stuff that makes you go, 'God, a really, good classic ballad.' 'Dogs Are Everywhere', it's just like, wow – what a song. You write a song about dogs and put some beautiful chords behind it, and it works so well, and I think that, for me, was very much Jarvis developing his songwriting ability.

"It was wonderful to hear the mixture of Jarvis and Russell when I was around; you'd have the experimental ones and you'd have the strong ballads, but I think it's the ballads that carried it through and I think that's why they had such an ardent following."

"It had some great little pop songs," says Clive Solomon of *Freaks*, "and its quota of angsty, broody pieces, and some tracks which rather wonderfully straddled both. I thought it was a great record."

To the band, though, while *Freaks* was by no means anything to be ashamed of, the album was a source of frustration and disappointment. How were they supposed to record the culmination of two-and-a-half years' artistic endeavour in a week? "I think there are some good songs on it," says Jarvis, "but it also irritates me because the songs could've been done a lot better if we'd had a bit more time to do them."[125] Pulp and Kirk had made the best record they could, but one week to record and mix 12 tracks (including the B-sides 'Tunnel' and 'Manon') meant that *Freaks* was only almost a masterpiece.

The actual recordings and performances on the record are, for the most part, perfectly sound – the problem is with the mix. There wasn't enough time to produce a satisfactory final mix in the initial time they'd been allotted, so the plan was that Pulp would come back to Input when they'd persuaded Fire to front enough money to book more studio time, and remix the tracks. However, when they returned to the studio in September, it transpired that the owners had wiped the master tapes to use for another recording.

"A heavy metal guitar solo had been recorded over part of it," remembers Russell. "Jarvis was distraught because he'd been persuaded reluctantly to do the 'roll up, roll up' vocal overdub on 'Fairground', slept on it, hated it, but couldn't change it. We weren't taken very seriously by studios in those days – if you run a recording studio, rule number one is 'Do not wipe your artist's master tapes.'"

As a result, the band were forced to release the initial mix they'd completed in June. This is a great shame, because a remix could well have transformed some of the tracks – some excellent guitar, violin and keyboard parts are buried, while the drums and vocals, generally mixed toward the front, tend to be rather overbearing. Matters aren't helped by the fact that the mastering of the album was also botched – the top end is cut off, and the bass slightly distorted.*

Even so, *Freaks* has stood the test of time – fans who discovered Pulp after they found fame and then went back and discovered the band's earlier output often vote *Freaks* a favourite – a testament to the strength of the songs and the intense artistic vision that united the band at the time.

Jarvis, however, pulls no lyrical punches about how much fun life wasn't back then. "He was quite angry," says Saskia, "and quite down.

---

* Compare the 12″ single release of 'They Suffocate at Night' – the same recording and mix but mastered by someone else – with the album version to get the idea. The single version seems to bring out lots of subtle nuances, in Jarvis' voice especially, that are barely detectable on the album version.

Yes, I think he was a bit pissed off around that time. You know, when you've been at it a long time, you perhaps feel a bit despondent about things."

If Jarvis was the voice of Pulp, the rest of the band (all living on the dole in Sheffield, all doing something that they believed was worthwhile and interesting while the rest of the world steadfastly ignored them) were feeling a similar kind of desperation which contributed to the mood of the album. "I don't listen to *Freaks*," says Russell. "It's not a comfortable record to listen to, but it moved some people. There was probably something wrong with the people it moved – it probably filled a gap in some very twisted lives – but that was probably a reflection of how we were. I mean, I think to be a good artist, you have to be maladjusted. If you're a well-adjusted person, you don't need to do it."[126]

The album's title was a pretty fair reflection of the way Pulp were viewed, both musically and socially, *circa* 1986. "There was a time when Pulp were regarded as a bunch of freaks," says Mark Webber, "and people did go to see the freakshow."[127]

Life in the factory on Sheldon Row was no longer the bohemian barrel of laughs that it had been when Jarvis had moved in a few years earlier. "It kind of went sour in a way. We were becoming marginalised because we were kind of an invisible group of people who just subsisted on the dole. Lots of people freaked out because they'd taken too many drugs or whatever. The trouble is, if you go off-road, you haven't got a map or anything to guide you, and people can end up getting lost."[128]

It had already proven too much for Jarvis' flatmate Michael Paramore, who moved out of the building around this time. "Some of the people who were going down there were a bit too hanger-on-y. I had a few things nicked from my room and stuff so I thought I'd get out. There were people that we used to call 'crazies' – that sounds a bit dated now, but there were real nutters. But not in the way you'd think of a nutter these days. After a while, I think it was one of those places where you could only stay for so long, and then unless you really were mad, it got a bit too much."

Jarvis: "I had one mate – it was sad, really, what happened to him. One night he was in this nightclub in Sheffield and he got glassed by this bloke who'd been just let out of prison that day. He used to like dressing up, *Clockwork Orange* style. He was wearing this white boiler suit and this townie just took exception to it. My mate just went really weird after that. First of all, he developed a military fixation. He used to do landscape painting, but he started adding things to these paintings he'd done, like aeroplanes with people jumping out of them in parachutes. There was another bloke who was going to build a helicopter. He reckoned if he gathered enough bits from army-surplus stores, it would be possible. There was also the bloke with the monk's outfit and a pet rat that used to shit everywhere. He died of a heroin overdose."[129] The latter character's final overdose, reportedly, was preceded by a brutal police beating that came about as a result of his hobby: grave-robbing from Sheffield's Victorian cemeteries.

The wider experience of the Sheffield dole culture that centred around Fargate was no better. "It was quite interesting for a bit," says Jarvis, "but when the YTS came along it cut off all the young blood and that made it a bit sadder, because then you had this block of people just getting older, still having these crazy schemes of what they were going to do, but going no further.[130]

"Sheffield is like any other town. You see people who used to be in bands walking around. And they have a very haunted look. It's very hard to go back to working in a bread shop when you've had that life."[131]

"Fargate was the place where all the unemployed bohos used to hang out," explains Russell. "When we first started out, there was all the heroes of the local scene, but unfortunately a few years later you'd tend to pass them with a bottle of cider in a brown paper bag, and your childhood heroes are old winos."[132]

Jarvis: "I'd find myself walking round the centre of town at Christmas and you'd see office parties, you know, people walking round with silly string hanging off them. I thought, 'God, I'll probably never ever go to an office party.' I mean, it'd strike me with dread now, but at the time it seemed bad to be excluded and be a freak."[133]

In August 1986, with the *Freaks* album in limbo (Input Studios claim they were still waiting for Fire to pay for the studio time before they would release the tapes), Food Records released the various artists compilation *Imminent 4*. It included the Pulp song 'Manon', an outtake from the previous year's 'Little Girl' sessions with a very definite Gallic influence: "I'd got a Serge Gainsbourg album," explains Jarvis, "which had a track called 'Manon'. It's not the same tune but, being naïve, I thought Manon was a man's name. In the end, I found out it was a woman's name! Again, I spoil it by speaking in French towards the end, which is embarrassing."[134] Despite Jarvis' pidgin Gainsbourg, the song does have an undeniable macabre power, thanks in no small part to Russell's sparing but highly effective pizzicato violin.

In the context of *Imminent 4* (one in Food's series of compilations of tracks by 'emerging' indie bands), though, the song probably says as much as needs to be said about Pulp's lack of success in the mid Eighties. Most of the rest of the album is tuneful, jangly C86 indie fare: there's

Bogshed and The Brilliant Corners, both of whom were reasonably well known in their day, and McCarthy featuring Tim and Laetitia who went on to form Stereolab. And then there's Pulp, singing a low-key, near-monotone dirge featuring lyrics, some of which are in French, about a bloke who keeps his dead girlfriend's corpse in his house. Pulp weren't just nowhere near the mainstream in 1986: even when held up next to what was then considered 'alternative' music, Pulp may as well have been from a different planet.

With still nary a sign of a release date for *Freaks* in sight, on October 24, 1986, Pulp spent an evening making a promotional video for 'They Suffocate At Night', which they and Fire had chosen as a teaser single for the album. Even though the band hadn't gigged since July and there was a creeping sense of apathy, the video is evidence that even during lean periods, artistic ambition was still festering in the band.

"It was made by someone who claimed to have done the lighting for *Chariots Of Fire*," says Jarvis of the video, "which impressed us a great deal at the time. In typical Fire fashion we could only afford one roll of film, so he had to keep winding the film backwards and forwards for different bits of the song. I constructed the set in an abandoned warehouse across the road from the factory I was living in at the time. I converted an inspection pit into a kind of sunken bedroom and then filled about 200 freezer bags full of coloured liquid for another bit of the set elsewhere. For some reason, there was a horse skeleton in the building, so that ended up in the film too. Saskia and Steve Genn played two lovers and we kind of watched. I remember being quite pleased with it at the time. The filming went on till about 4 o'clock in the morning and at the end of it the band split up. What a great evening."[135]

The drunken antics of Pete Mansell and Magnus Doyle had often been a source of irritation to Jarvis and, in particular, Russell. After three years of near-constant tension, it was time for something to give. At the end of the video's filming, strained relationships finally reached breaking point: as Jarvis recalls, "Russell was extremely disciplinarian, I was quite puritanical, but Pete and Mag just messed around. It got to a head and everybody had a fight. It wasn't worth the aggro any more."[136]

No one was actually sacked on the night, but soon afterwards, it was decided that Magnus and Pete should leave the band. "I remember saying to Jarvis either they go or I go shortly after that night," says Russell. "What probably happened was that we agreed to have a talk and give them another chance, but things didn't change much – persistent lateness, missing practices, terrible defending."

"Russell was quite different then," says Candida. He'd be really cross when we'd turn up late for practices and that we wouldn't really put as much into it as he and Jarvis did, although they never particularly demanded us to. But that's where the clashes came."[137]

Russell: "It was my fault really, with hindsight. Now I wouldn't be so judgemental about them having a laugh because I'm probably more like that myself now, but back then, the band was like the air we breathed and I was trying to run things like a well-oiled military machine. The video shoot was costing several hundreds of pounds, and it was late, and wet, and they were pissed, and pissing about, so they got the boot."[138]

The Jarvis-Russell-Manners-Magnus-Candida Pulp did manage one more concert: an Oxfam benefit supporting The Railway Children at the Leadmill on November 8. The concert was treated as something of an end-of-era statement, as a piece in that day's *Sheffield Star* (ostensibly written by music editor Dom Roshkrow but clearly straight from the mouth of Cocker) testifies: "Sheffield's best-loved fruitcakes Pulp bring an era to an end tonight when they play their present set for the last time. After tonight they are taking an amazing new direction and so keep an eye out for them on *Saturday Superstore*."[139]

The old Pulp may have been on the way out, but Jarvis and Russell showed no signs of wanting to stop – indeed, they apparently saw the departure of Pete and Magnus as a clean break and an opportunity to move on from the intense miserablism of *Freaks*. Tracks like 'Mark Of The Devil' and 'Master Of The Universe' provided the signposts for where Pulp wanted to go next: "I'd decided disco was the thing to go for," explains Jarvis, "because I was sick of that over-the-top emotional business. Giorgio Moroder didn't have any emotion: it was robot music. I was intrigued with the idea of that beat and style but with something emotional over the top."[140]

The idea stemmed from Jarvis' hospital stay at the start of the year, when he asked his mum to bring in his grandma's Yamaha Portasound keyboard to entertain himself with during his convalescence. As well as using it to write 'Dogs Are Everywhere' and 'Master Of The Universe' while in hospital, it provided the seed of the inspiration for Pulp's new Eurodisco sound: "Because it made music without any feeling at all, because it was a machine, something about it appealed, so that was the turning point, and I started doing more disco things. So I nicked her keyboard. I've still got it actually. I think she gave up after a few days anyway, so I don't think she missed it too much."[141]

Aside from Jarvis' new-found disco-pop infatuation, the other major influence in the new Pulp sound came from Russell's interest in East European folk music. An element of this had been present for as long as Russell had been in the band – see the Slavic plinky-plonk of 'Srpski Jeb', or the Romany fiddling of 'Mark Of The Devil' – but it was only at the end of 1986 and the first few months of 1987, in new songs such as 'Rattlesnake', 'Separations' and 'My First Wife', that it came to the fore. Eastern European disco folk, then. As Russell remarked at the time, "You can dance to our music, but it's easier if you're a Cossack."[142]

After the Leadmill concert, Magnus Doyle finally, definitely left Pulp. "We were sat around in Jarvis' mum's kitchen having a cup of tea," remembers Manners. "We all had our own mugs. Candida's was a Wonderwoman one. Mag said, "Should we split up?" I was taken aback. He was ready to go off travelling in Portugal."[143]

"I think perhaps as time had gone on Magnus had lost interest a bit," says Jonathan Kirk. "He was in tune with Pulp, and he was definitely into it at first, but eventually it reached the point where he had other things that he wanted to do, other sides of himself that he wanted to find. He knew that Pulp could go on without him if he left, so he decided he was going off travelling."

Candida: "He was always wild, but he was a brilliant drummer. He could have had such a career but he wasn't interested, even after Pulp. He got right into the hallucinogenic drug scene, and he was always someone who'd have to take loads more than anyone else. He just didn't fit into Sheffield after that."[144]

Magnus' replacement was Nick Banks, casual Pulp acquaintance and one-time promoter at the Hallamshire. He'd played drums with a range of local bands, starting with Fatal Noise with three Rotherham school friends in 1979 – "We just played punk rock music as only 14-year-olds can." Then there was synthpop combo Phono Industria, followed by God with Paul and Miggs from New Model Soldier. "We gigged around a bit and did the *Star* talent contest which they had every year. They said, 'You can't enter it with a name like that.' You what? This is ridiculous! 'No, no, if you want to enter you'll have to change your name.' But this thing was a good chance to play at the Top Rank, so we changed the name for these things to Red. We did it with Phono Industria as well. We thought we were going to win, but we were pipped to the post by a heavy metal band called Pansa Division, who clocked on every time they went on stage, which was obviously a bit of a gimmick that pushed it over the edge."

Next came The Vicious Circles and One Stop The World, the latter of whom may or may not have appeared in an early episode of *Brookside* (allegedly playing on a TV in the background because one of the band knew someone on the film crew), and Jass. "The main person in that was a guy called Dave Thompson," remembers Nick. "I suppose it was sort of linked to One Stop The World, which was in the early/mid-Eighties industrial vein. Jass was all instrumentals, and there was some odd bits of sampled tape coming in now and again. Russell played a few times, doing a bit of his squawky violin. It was various kinds of jamming – a bit similar to the David Byrne and Brian Eno record, you could see an evolution from that, or a step back from that! But they did actually put one record out – I sort of fell out with Dave Thompson after a bit, and soon after that a record came out called 'Theme' on Wax Trax Records, an American label. I remember when I got a copy, I listened thinking, 'Oh, I might play on this' – it might have been the tiniest, tiniest little minuscule detail if there was anything discernible that I would have put on it. There might have been one millisecond of me on it!"

He'd first encountered Jarvis during an early Eighties stint as promoter at the Hallamshire. "That was back when I was in Phono Industria. Dave Kurley, who was singer in New Model Soldier, was doing it, and said, 'I don't want to do this anymore, I'm fed up with it,' so I said, "We'll do it, as a group." The others did a bit, and eventually I took it over. I had my little book at home by the phone, and only once did we have double bookings. Triumph of organisation. I was doing that for about two years. Yeah, I was only about 16 or 17. I used to sit at the top of the stairs with my table – I met quite a lot of people. It was the first time I met Jarvis, really, doing that. Tim Allcard always used to come and sit at the top of the stairs and not pay his 50p, which I always thought was a bit bad, but I didn't want to say, 'Oi, bugger off,' because he looked a bit strange and I think he used to smoke waccy baccy a lot, and I didn't really know what to do with him.

"I think I first saw Pulp in '83, when they played at the Crucible at Stars On Sundae – there was a lot of people on the stage, fish on strings, people up on the gantry, with Saskia and a couple of others doing backing vocals and things. I remember seeing the *It* sort of line-up in the Marples as well, a bit after, and then they disappeared for a little bit and then came back with Russell and Magnus and I used to go and see them quite a lot – obviously with doing the door at the Hallamshire. I knew Jarvis a bit, and Russell used to come and stand next to me in the Limit for 30 seconds and go, 'All right?' Oh, all right Russ, how you doing? – oh, he's gone. And then he'd be standing next to somebody the other side of the room for 30 seconds.

"And I saw this advert in the Leadmill, 'Pulp looking for drummer' sort of thing, and I thought, 'Oh, I know Jarv a bit, that sounds like the ad for me.' So I saw Jarvis somewhere, think it might've been the Leadmill actually, and said I'd seen the advert, and can I have a go. 'Yeah, all right.' So when are you practising? 'Oh, come up on Sunday to the garage at Intake.' He told me where to go and all that and I said, 'All right, I'll bring me snare drum.'"

At Nick's first practice with the group, the main issue was not whether he was any good, but how they were going to get rid of the English bull terrier that had followed Jarvis home. "I turned up, knocked on the door of his grandmother's house, and he peers out the window – 'Come in!' Opens the door, 'Quick, get in!', shuts the door, and there's this mad dog running round the house. And there's his other dog, Bonzo, running round the other half of the house going equally mental. He's going, 'We've got a bit of a problem here 'cos this dog has followed me home and I can't get rid of it.' And obviously Bonzo's going mental and we need to get rid of it. So I go, 'Fair enough, we'll take it out and try and lose it on the street.' So we're walking round Intake for an hour, this dog following us, going, 'Quick, he's sniffing that lamppost, leg it!' We'd leg it off round the corner and it'd always find us. So eventually we went to the police station, Manor Top, and it was just one of these telephone things. Eventually we grabbed the dog, put it over into someone's drive that had got quite a big fence over it, and legged it off, and the dog was there with its head over the fence whimpering . . . So we legged it back to Jarv's house. What happened to the others I'm not sure – either they'd gone or not turned up, so we thought, 'Oh well, never mind, we'll have another rehearsal on Wednesday or next Sunday,' whatever it was, I can't remember."

"During the course of walking around," says Jarvis, "we talked and got on well, so we thought we'd have him. We'd never heard him play the drums and certainly wouldn't have if we had."[145]

Pete Mansell stayed around for a little longer, but before long had followed Magnus out of Pulp. "I had a couple of practices with a new drummer, Nick Banks," he remembers, "but I left soon after. I was glad to be out of it, to tell the truth."[146]

Jonathan Kirk: "I think it was basically because Jarvis and Russell were very critical of his behaviour, and the fact that he couldn't be relied upon, which was his undoing really. It's like, 'Why don't you just call it a day?' you know."

Before long, Candida was gone too – she could hardly stay in the band while her brother and boyfriend left amid varying degrees of rancour, and besides, she had her doubts about the new Eurodisco direction. Pulp III was very much over.

The band continued, of course, and Candida would later return, but the departure of Magnus and Manners marked the passing of something: there'd never be another Pulp quite like *this* again. Even though members leaving was hardly a new thing for Pulp, this wasn't simply the departure of another drummer or bassist: it was the end of an unrepeatable collaboration between five disparate (and occasionally desperate) individuals. Doyle and Mansell may have had little to do with the words to the songs or the chord changes behind them, but that wasn't the point: what was being lost was something intangible – a strangeness and an intensity that could never be recreated.

"What did happen after that," remembers Russell, "was that we missed them and tried to persuade them to come back, but only Candida would. Whether it was for the best or not I'm not sure. For me Pulp became viscerally exciting and important the first time Jarvis, Candida, Magnus, Manners and myself were in the garage together. I think it set the tone for what was to come. The line-ups before had been too jokey, the line-up that produced *It* had been too poncey, and Jarvis and myself's tentative collaborations had been too arty. As Peter Mansell said, 'You need the yob element.'"

A year later, at the end of 1987, Jarvis wrote a short piece for the sleeve notes of *The Great Fire Of London*, a Fire Records sampler LP that included 'Little Girl (With Blue Eyes)'. He has since said that it sums up his feelings about the era that created that song, and its end:

> *"Well, it's funny to think of it now but at one time it was everything. I mean he never thought of anything else, not one little thing. So, of course, it couldn't stand the strain and it eventually broke. Obvious, you might say; but sometimes you don't think straight; y'know, sometimes you're just plain stupid. Anyway it's over now and it all seems like some kind of dream; did you ever think you could live off love for the rest of your life? Go and get a job mate, get your head out of the clouds, get back in line. Yes we're back from our trip to the moon and in circulation again. Come on, let's go for a business lunch, let's have an office party. Come on then. Yes, I must dash, there's such a lot to be done and I've got to do it. Kiss goodbye to the past with a smile. That's the way babe. Now we can watch the dogs devouring little girls with blue eyes and not feel bad about it. Bye."*

Pulp in 1998, left to right: Candida Doyle, Nick Banks, Jarvis Cocker, Mark Webber and Steve Mackey.
(*Camera Press*)

Jarvis, aged 7, in 1970, hamming it up in a Sheffield photo booth.
This image subsequently appeared on a Pulp calendar in 1997.

ARABICUS PULP
ARE
DAMNED GOOD

Well, they would be one day. A sticker sold by the group at City school, circa 1979.

Total Funds left = £6·70

Funds to be contributed towards
purchase of £30 Drumkit.

D·A· LOCKWOOD PAID £1
to PULP FUND TOWARDS
PRUMKIT

D·A·L HAS PAID £3·40

J·B·L· HAS PAID £3·40

G·M· HAS PAID £2·00

TOTAL FUNDS = £15·65
(Inclusive of K Briggs
15p film admittance
charge)

M·S· HAS PAID £10·00
G·M HAS PAID £1·40
TO MAKE £3·40

TOTAL FUNDS = £26·90
(Exclusive of K Briggs
15p film admittance
charge)

−30p
to remain
in PULP
FUNDS

Four pages from Pulp's accounts book, circa 1979, indicating, amongst other things, that a drumkit was virtually beyond their means and that the public presentation of their film, *The Film Starring Arabicus Pulp,* raised £27.60p.
(*Courtesy Glen Matshall*)

20p to D.A.L FOR TRANSPORT

TOTAL PULP FUNDS = 10p

FILM SNOWING + 10p above
= £27·60 in PULP FUND
(50p paid for Photo film
30p " " 1 Photo)

P. Dalton owes £3·40 to George (Drumkit)
" 60p to M.G.R. (Photos)

P. Dalton has paid above

TOTAL PULP FUNDS £15·59

(£7·80 PAID FOR CYMBALS
99 " " TAPE (STICKY)
89 " " SNOW
89 " " SNOW
55 " " Joss STICKS
£11·12

+ MONEY FOR CARDS = £26·71
PAID TO PAY + DOLLY 30p
TO PAY + DIXI 30p
PAID + PJP 30p
= £27·61

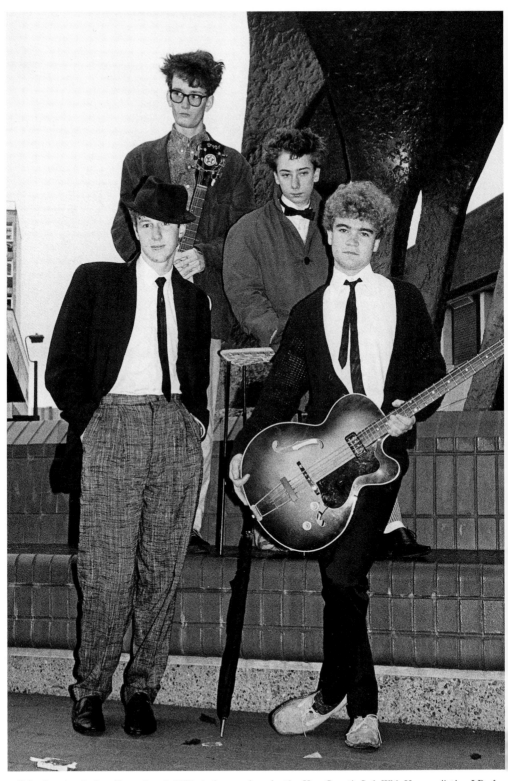

Pulp photographed on December 6, 1981, during sessions for the *Your Secret's Safe With Us* compilation LP of Sheffield bands, left to right: Pete Dalton, Jarvis, Wayne Furniss and Jamie Pinchbeck. (*Chris Wicks*)

Pulp in Jarvis' front room, January 7, 1982, as they appeared in their first UK music press feature - a one-page piece in *Melody Maker* written by Frank Worrall, with photos taken by Marcus Featherby. Clockwise from top: Wayne Furniss, Jarvis, Jamie Pinchbeck and Pete Dalton.

August 1982: the publicity stunt for the Heroes Of The Beach concert wherein (left to right) Steve Genn, Nick Taylor, Greg Thompson and Jarvis were pictured eating their breakfast on Sheffield's Fargate, munching cornflakes in their pyjamas. "That first concert they did get a fair bit of attention," remembers Murray Fenton. "They got airtime on local radio, on the news. There was quite a little buzz about how it was going to be a lot of fun, and it was. They were really ramshackle, but it was a good laugh." (*Nick Taylor*)

Jarvis, Peter Dalton and David Bocking backstage at the Heroes Of The Beach concert at the Shefield Leadmill on New Year's Eve, 1982, collecting sweets to throw into the crowd. (*Nick Taylor*)

Jarvis, his sister Saskia and David Hinkler on stage at The Marples, Sheffield, in the summer of 1983. (*David Bocking*)

Tim Allcard and Michael Paramore from the Sheffield band In A Belljar, contemporaries of Pulp, pictured at the Heroes Of The Beach concert. (*Nick Taylor*)

Wayne Furniss, David Hinkler and Simon Hinkler, October 1982. (*Sheffield Star*)

Jarvis on stage in Sheffield. March, 1983. (*Zbysiu Rodak/SIN*)

Chapter 7

The new Pulp's first live appearance was in November 1986, at the Hull Adelphi. It was only a matter of weeks since the old Pulp's farewell at the Leadmill, but Pulp's new direction was already in place. "When I first played," says Nick, "the only song I think we played from *Freaks* was 'They Suffocate At Night', 'cos I remember the first time I played it I cocked it up. Which became a theme. We were playing that because it was going to be a single, but we must've only played it a couple of times, because then we started playing the new stuff almost exclusively – 'cos Jarvis had his Yamaha Portasound, his grandma's keyboard, and we almost straight away started playing new stuff – you know, new line-up, new stuff, why bother learning the other stuff, which obviously they'd been playing for two years or more? So it was all *Separations* stuff, and also stuff that never got out, like 'Rattlesnake' and 'Death Comes To Town'."

Candida had temporarily returned to the fold for the Hull concert, but by the time of the band's next appearance, at a Fire showcase at the 100 Club in London on December 4, 1986, the band consisted of Jarvis, Russell and Nick, plus a mysterious individual called Captain Sleep on keyboards and new bassist Steven Havenhand, formerly vocalist with sometime Pulp support group Lay Of The Land.

"Lay Of The Land was Rob Mitchell and Steve Beckett's band," recalls Ian Spence. "They'd been looking for a singer after Steven Havenhand left and found this very tall bloke, and suddenly decided they were going to be Curiosity Killed The Cat. They tried very hard to be a proper pop band. They were very heavily Pulp-influenced, with Rob playing the viola. Curiosity Killed The Cat with viola!"[*]

David Bocking: "I didn't know him very well. He was very quiet and reserved – to call Magnus quiet was ludicrous if you compared him to Steven. I don't recall ever having seen him smile, although that's probably

---

[*] Viola/trumpet player Rob Mitchell and drummer Steve Beckett (formerly with punk combo The Sixguns) would, of course, later go on to found Warp Records, which would one day sign Pulp to its Gift subsidiary.

entirely untrue. He was keen on playing in other bands before Pulp, he wore a suit . . . er . . . I think Lay Of The Land were known for producing quite melodic, guitar-based songs."

"He was just one of these enigmatic figures from the Limit," remembers Nick. "He was very thin, he always kind of wore suits, very smart, had a bit of quiffy hair – not Smiths' style, but that kind of early, mid-Eighties sort of thing. He was very kind of – you wouldn't say effeminate, but someone who was not in the laddish culture, which in the Eighties everyone was kicking against. You never heard him speak and he always had a fag in his hand, very delicate, you know. He'd played in this group called Lay Of The Land – I think I might have seen them once at the University or something. I think he might have been going out with Russell's sister at the time. I think they had a very stormy relationship. This was when Russell was living in Rockingham Court, just off Division Street, and I think Steve Havenhand may have been living there at the same time, or he was going out with Russell's sister who was living there at the same time. Something like that."

Captain Sleep was an altogether shadier individual, remembered only dimly by those who were there – to this day, no one knows his real name. "He was really small, kind of like semi-bald," remembers Jonathan Kirk. "He arrived on the scene, quite unsettled, very intense . . . He had that kind of air of fear and loathing about him. You really weren't sure if anybody was home. And if they were home, you weren't quite sure what was going to happen next. Almost like a human Spit The Dog type character, quite tense and fidgety."

Nick: "I've no idea where he came from at all. He was very, very sleepy. We went down in the van to play this 100 Club thing and he was asleep in the van all the way down, played the gig sat on the edge of the stage, then all the way back he was just spark out in the van. He was Captain Sleep. I mean, you get to know somebody by talking to them, don't you, and he was never awake."

The new line-up wasn't quite brimming with promise, then, but the 100 Club concert was by all accounts an impressive comeback, receiving excellent reviews in *NME* and *Sounds*, the latter publication's Roy Wilkinson noting that:

> *"Determinedly low-key in appearance and sound, they're now mining a lugubrious Eastern European musical vein. It's a Balkan beat without the comic overtones of 3 Mustaphas 3 and you could well imagine them breaking into the 'Harry Lime Theme' if they owned a zither and it wasn't a little too cheerful. Cocker's awkward yet mannered Scott Walkerish voice and his*

baiting of the audience, combined with Russell Senior's morosely busy violin, set an intensely melancholic mood which recalls any low-life tableau from Weimar, Germany onwards."

It was, of course, at this convenient point, just as Pulp had moved on from *Freaks*, that a single from the album finally made it into the shops. Fire released 'They Suffocate At Night' on December 15 in 12″ and 7″ formats, the latter of which contained humorously bad edited versions (of the you-can-practically-hear-them-pressing-pause variety) of the A- and B-sides. "You wouldn't believe the publicity stunts I dreamt up for 'They Suffocate At Night'," says Ogy McGrath. "At this orphanage . . . Jarvis didn't go for it though. 'We're not giving plastic bags to orphans,' he said."

The B-side, 'Tunnel', is a noisy, harrowing primal scream of a track, allegorising the loss of direction Jarvis felt his life was suffering *circa* 1986. *"I saw the entrance and went in,"* the sleeve notes read. *"I had nothing else to do; I was bored. That was 15 weeks ago and guess what? I'm lost, it's so bleeding dark in here, that's the problem. But I'm not alone − oh no, there must be hundreds, perhaps thousands, down here with me. We all mill around and bump into each other in the darkness. And the stench of a thousand unwashed bodies hangs in a thick damp fog . . . I walk for at least eight hours every day but I've still never seen even the slightest glimmer of light that would tell me that I was nearing the end of the tunnel. Most of the others are content to just walk on the spot and hum to themselves, but I still make the effort. Hoping that one morning I will wake up in the sun with the sky blue above me. And to be clean again. But I know I'll never be clean again."*

The music is loud, discordant, near-industrial, and of course as far away from either Eurodisco or Eastern European folk as you could conceivably get. "It was one-take improvised brilliance," remembers Russell. "I can remember playing it and coming back into the control room going, 'Did you get that! Did you get that!' The muse was with us then."

The single didn't attract nearly as much press attention as 'Little Girl' or 'Dogs', and didn't sell as well either. "Probably because it was too good a record," says Clive Solomon. "I just thought it was an utterly sublime song. It was an adventurous choice for a single release − I'd like to think it was a joint choice, the band were well into it. I thought that was a great, great song which had a wonderful melodic development to it − I thought it was classic Pulp slow ballad material. It had great artistry as a song, wonderfully atmospheric, and it still had a great hookline in there as well.

"It was a bit deeper as a song, quite a long track too, and maybe it wasn't as immediately accessible as your average 3-minute pop song. Some people really liked it though – we got it played on Radio 1 once or twice on the Saturday afternoon show, which was one of the few programmes outside of Peel and the *Evening Session* that played a small quota of indie stuff. I remember the show's producer Phil Ross ringing me up to tell me how wonderful he thought it was, which was music to my ears. It was more sophisticated, and it's always more difficult to get arrested with a slow song – it's just not obvious C86 chiming indie guitar pop; it was completely out there, like a slow lament, a 'Bitter Sweet Symphony' for its time. To get away with putting out a brooding lament like that you've got to be a big band. I don't think it's the most obvious pop tune in the world, but I thought it had a wonderful richness and atmosphere to it, and a sadness as well. That, to me, is a great song. But there's so much great stuff that gets produced that gets completely ignored because it doesn't exactly fit in with the time."

Although Pulp had made some steps toward establishing a new line-up and sound, at the start of 1987 Jarvis was still looking to see whether there were any other directions in which he could go. He'd already done a solo concert with Captain Sleep at Sheffield Polytechnic performing some "daft disco songs" he'd written on the Portasound keyboard, and he was now taking tentative steps toward forming a new band with ex-Pulp keyboardist David Hinkler and his former Vector 7-7 colleague Steve Naylor. "He asked me to write some songs with him," remembers David. "We did two or three evenings in a Sheffield rehearsal room, trying to put songs together. Jarvis would come along with his guitar and say, 'This is my song for today,' and I'd quite happily play along with it. The only thing that stopped it from working was that, while I've got the ultimate respect for Steve Naylor as a songwriter and musician, he wanted to get in on the act and his input and Jarvis' input were just so totally different, so nothing ever got past a few verses. If Jarvis and me had been on our own together, we might actually have done something. It was just unfortunate that Steve was around, and there was no harmony between his and Jarvis' ideas of what a good song should be."

Jarvis' attempts to form a new group having failed, it was time to get back to Pulp. Captain Sleep had already departed ("he couldn't keep awake for more than two hours," remembers Jarvis, "so we got rid of him because he was depressing"[147]), so the band was once more in the market for a keyboard player. Presumably missing Candida's feminine touch, they specifically advertised for a female keyboardist.

Candida: "I thought, 'Bastards, that's a bit nasty.' But they must have rung me up a bit later and asked me back, as I went along for a practice.

Pete was going to rejoin as well but Magnus wouldn't go along, though we tried convincing him. Actually, he did turn up once but Nick was there, drumming, which made a weird atmosphere. But I'm glad I went back."[148]

"I don't know why Candida stuck it so long," says Russell, "but I'm glad she has. If she ever left, a certain part of the soul of the band would go too. For one, she's a woman, which stops us getting too crude about things, and in her own way, she's quite hardline and strong, with a certain style about her, like a girl/woman."[149]

With the line-up finally stable, Jarvis, Russell, Nick, Steven and Candida settled into rehearsing what was, with a few exceptions, an all-new set of material – the lyrical content of which reflects the fact that, while things had been changing for Pulp musically, they were also changing for Jarvis personally. The toll of five years on the dole in Sheffield failing to sell records, not to mention the realisations he'd come to in the wake of the window incident, had combined to force a slightly more realistic view of the likelihood of imminent stardom. The frustrations of seemingly endless commercial obscurity were certainly beginning to show: "It's about time we made the charts," he told a local Sheffield fanzine in spring 1987. "We've paid our dues . . . You're shouting at the top of your voice and you want people to listen to you."[150]

A more profound change in attitude was evident in the same interview when he remarked that "if nothing happens after this new record comes out, I might get fed up and want to try something else. Is that mercenary? You've got to feel that you're moving forward, progressing. I'd do something completely different to prove I wasn't a one-track mind man. Music is all right but it's not everything is it? People shouldn't get too obsessed with it, there's a lot more interesting things . . . like the countryside."[151]

Much of what Jarvis was feeling at this time is encapsulated in a song he wrote around the same period, 'Love Is Blind', which staggers, like anyone's life, between high drama and high farce: *Instead of walking around with eyes glued to the sky, I'll turn them down to the ground/ Oh and I used to think that maybe one day I'd find the love of my life, but it's so far away that I don't know why/ but I want it all tonight . . . We kissed and laid on the bed, and waited for the ceiling to fall in, but it never did. In the morning it was all still there, the spilled milk and dog turds, in that grey ashtray morning light.* Even the song's title reflected Jarvis' realisation, in the wake of his accident, that there was ". . . no magical thread running through life. It's all random. But once you realise that, it's quite good."[152]

On March 3, Pulp finally got around to playing their first concert of 1987, and their first Sheffield appearance since November, when they played at the Limit Club. Jarvis began the concert by announcing that, "This is the new Pulp", and only a handful of the old Pulp's songs were played, with the rest of the set made up of the new Slavic/Eurodisco material, probably including the likes of 'Death Comes To Town', 'Don't You Want Me Anymore?', 'Separations', 'Rattlesnake' and 'Going Back To Find Her'. The show was reviewed in the *NME* and local magazine *Blitz*, who between them commented on the radical new direction, the tin-foil-decorated stage, Steven Havenhand remaining seated throughout the gig in deference to a broken ankle, and Jarvis' ridiculous taste in jumpers.

As John Quinn recalls, the sound of the new Pulp didn't immediately represent a total break with the old one. "The shift in direction wasn't too abrupt. They couldn't move on that quickly because of the way things were going, with *Freaks* not coming out. They didn't suddenly turn disco – it was a gradual thing."

"I couldn't really get my head round that whole Eastern European period," says Murray Fenton. "I remember seeing them a couple of times and thinking something was going a bit wayward. But they pulled it back in before long."

East European stylings aside, there was a more fundamental musical dif-ference between Pulp *circa Freaks* and the '87 model. With the new songs, the band had developed a far more affirmative, direct style of writing and playing – thanks in part to Nick Banks' drumming style, and in part to Jarvis' incorporation of the infamous Yamaha Portasound into the Pulp musical arsenal.

"Magnus' and my styles are quite different," says Nick. "He's very . . . not jazz but, certainly looser: he'll tit around with the toms quite a bit. Whereas I'm, 'Piss off with all that stuff, let's get down to the nitty gritty' – you know, a more direct sort of style. So that I suppose fitted in very easily with, I wouldn't say our disco direction, but it was a lot more solid. Because when you've got the actual bones of having to play to a Yamaha Portasound, it's very difficult and you can't do anything too flowery, because you'll piss around for a second and you'll come back nowhere near where the Portasound is. There was no technology for having head-phones and click tracks and all this kind of stuff that you use these days: the Yamaha was on a table over there and there was a little light that flashed on the first beat of the bar, and we'd play, and it'd get pretty loud, so the first thing you can't hear is the little 'chh-chh-chh' on the Portasound. So as soon as you can't hear that, you've got to watch for this little light, and if you're on the beat when the light goes, you're in time. If you're not, you're out of time. So it's pretty much impossible to keep in time with it.

"The Portasound was there from the start in quite a few of the songs. It was on 'Separations', and on 'Countdown' and 'Death Comes To Town' – they were songs where it would have started with that and then it would have been sidelined and put away because it was so difficult to deal with. So a lot of songs were written on there so you get a more direct style."

The songwriting process, meanwhile, was becoming more inclusive, and less centred around just Jarvis or just Russell. Nick again: "At the start, Jarvis would say, 'Right, well I've got this thing,' we'd kind of play it, and as people developed their parts, it becomes part of the song. You just keep playing things and your particular bit may change slightly, or someone might suggest, 'Why don't we have a change here?' and you'd have to think, 'Well, what can we change it to?' Or they might come in with the first draft of the song and by the time it gets to the stage when it's played live, you've worked on it that many times that everyone will bring a little bit to it.

"It's always a case of a loose start or a loose idea of something, and it's just a case of people will jam and play it, and you might stop after a bit and go, 'That bit when you went *ner-ner-ner-ee-ner-er-er* was quite good,' and you'd try and go back and remember what you played and try and recreate that again, and generally something else would come up from that. It's kind of an evolutionary thing. I think that's, to a greater or lesser extent, how it's been ever since."

Later in March, Fire released 'Master Of The Universe' as a 12″ single. Following the relative flop of 'They Suffocate At Night', it had been decided to release another single in an attempt to drum up some interest in the forthcoming album. Unfortunately, the choice of A-side – a popular live number which somehow seemed to lose something in the translation to vinyl – meant that 'Master' did no better.

Clive Solomon: "I personally find the song quite hamfisted, but it came out as a single because the band wanted it out – I have a letter from them on file saying, 'Well we've listened to you with regard to choice of previous singles', and they were absolutely insistent, as I recall, that 'Master Of The Universe' was put out. I mean, I think it has some merit in a kind of schlock-metal kind of way, but it wasn't our favourite dimension of Pulp. I never really saw it as disco so much as Pulp just wanting to rock out a bit. A typical Johnny Waller quote would be, 'Well we'll put it out, but don't blame us if everyone says it's fucking awful!' Our only concern was that the A-side would be something that journalists would be into. Sometimes Pulp would listen to us, sometimes they wouldn't . . ."

Solomon's comments are backed up by a letter Jarvis sent him at the time: "We took a tape of the song down to The Limit and got a general thumbs-up from DJs and clientele alike. So there you have it. I'm afraid we're fairly immovable on this one, lads, and I think you should respect our judgement. After all, I think the 'Dogs Are Everywhere' EP would have done a lot better had 'Mark Of The Devil' been the title track as we suggested at the time. Anyway, let us know what you think so we can get things moving."[153]

Because of a lack of new recordings, the B-sides were outtakes from 1984 and 1985. 'Manon' was billed as being a 'New Version', but was in fact almost indistinguishable from the version released on the *Imminent 4* LP the previous year; and the infamous 'Silence' was pulled from the May 1984 *Sudan Gerri* demo.

With regard to the latter, the question of how or why one of Pulp's most unpalatable, amateur-dramatic tracks made it on to vinyl while several lost classics ('Maureen', 'Take You Back', 'Srpski Jeb') remained in the vaults, remains unanswered. Possibly the track's inclusion represented a final two-finger salute from the old, confrontational Pulp – the brief sleeve notes suggest that the EP was intended to be taken as some sort of end-of-era statement prior to the unveiling of Pulp IV. Or possibly, by March 1987, nine months after the A-side had been recorded and four months after the band that recorded it had split up, Jarvis and Russell were past caring what else went on the EP. "Pulp had their own agenda on a lot of things," says Clive Solomon, "and it was definitely them that chose the track listing, not us!"

'Master Of The Universe' received hardly any reviews, and sold poorly, even by mid-Eighties Pulp standards. Regardless of who or what was to blame, the commercial failure of the single was the final nail in the coffin of Pulp's relationship with Fire. "I never saw 'Master Of The Universe' in a shop," claims Jarvis. "I never even got sent a copy, so it was obvious that the relationship between us and Fire wasn't great."[154]

"Labels have lots of problems with distribution unless they've got loads of money," says John Avery, whose band Hula were having similar problems with Red Rhino at the time. "It can be a huge deal to a band – to the label it's just one band, 'We didn't get that record in the shops, what a shame, never mind, let's get the next one out,' but to the band it means you've just wasted a year."

'Master Of The Universe' was followed at long last, on Monday, May 11, 1987, by the *Freaks* album. In the 11 months since it had been recorded, half of the band that had played on the album had left, most of the songs were now no longer in the live set and, while Pulp were supportive of it in the round of promotional interviews, they presumably felt uneasy about talking about a year-old album containing songs they no longer played and had little to do with their current line-up or style.

Given the circumstances of its release, it is perhaps unsurprising that the release of *Freaks* marked the end of Pulp's initial association with Fire Records. "I'd like to have gone on working with them," says Clive Solomon, "but our deal was at an end, and I vaguely recall hearing that they were talking to FON Records. I mean, we're a small label and I certainly wouldn't hold it against a band for looking elsewhere."

The split with Fire wasn't the only partnership in Jarvis' life that ended around this time: it was also at roughly this point that he finally moved out of The Wicker factory building. His new home was a flat above a butcher's shop, shared, in time-honoured Odd Couple fashion, with Russell Senior. Like his previous home, it soon became a storage facility for Jarvis' increasingly large collection of bric-a-brac.

"The thing about Jarvis is that he tends to go to jumble sales and buy a load of useless old clutter," says Russell. "The mantelpiece would be covered with little pottery mice and those birds that dip into glasses. At first I had this hardline policy – I'd bung stuff into a carrier bag and stick it under his bed. But he just wouldn't stop getting stuff. How many people do you know who own five full-length mirrors? And moving house with him's a nightmare. He'll remember the elephant's foot umbrella stand but forget the cooker.

"Also, I don't rate him as a chef. Jarvis brought his girlfriend round for dinner once. He bought this chicken, which was black. And he's saying, 'Are chickens generally this colour raw?' And I'm like, 'Well no, Jarvis, they're more generally pink.' Anyway we sat down to eat and Jarvis brought in these potatoes and lettuce. So we're waiting for the rest of the food to arrive. But it never came. That was it.

"I say all this with the greatest affection. I ought to have known better, really. I'm a fastidious person. I like to keep things tidy. And Jarvis is just the opposite."[155]

"I suppose I do have a lot of stuff," admits Jarvis. "But I was on the dole and there was nothing to do during the day. To satisfy my hunter-gatherer instincts I would go round to jumble sales and collect stuff. I've never really been a person to live with, just you and one other person. It puts too much strain on the relationship. So the time I lived with Russell probably wasn't so great. It was also really cold. It was above a butcher's shop. And my bed was above the butcher's fridge, which made it even worse.

"I can't remember turning up with a black chicken. It's true that Russell would turn up to rehearsals with a list of domestic chores. But I could never concentrate on that kind of domestic thing. It used to depress me. I'd think, God, I want to be a famous person in a band. I shouldn't have to deal with things like pots and Hoovers.

"I did find things out about people by living with them. Russell's got a fondness for walking about without many clothes on. That can be a bit unsettling early in the morning."[156]

Later in May, Jarvis and Russell were interviewed by Nick Reynolds on his BBC Radio Sheffield show, *The Hard Stuff.* Tapes of the interview show the 1987-model Jarvis sounding remarkably similar to the modern-day version – all the self-deprecating humour and peculiar nuances were already in place. Somehow, though, he also seems remarkably *out* of place in the yuppie climate of 1987: the image that springs to mind on listening to the interview is of a sales rep listening to the radio in his red Sierra driving round the outskirts of Sheffield, going, 'What's this bloody plonker on about?' and putting on a Phil Collins tape instead.

"He just looked out-of-place *anywhere*," says Nick Robinson. "Even at parties he'd come in and his fashion sense just was not acceptable to most people in those days. He had the most amazing purple suits and this huge watch – I remember him coming up to me like a little child going, 'Look at this watch!' and showing me this horrible great thing that Bet Lynch might have worn. But he was happy in that, and he was confident with that, and that was why I've got so much time for him – because he stuck to his guns and he didn't allow himself to be side-tracked by critical comments."

The Pulp live experience was also developing into something of a spectacle. A concert at the Limit around the time was described as a "multi-media cosmic tangerine experience"[157] by Russell on Radio Sheffield, with the ever-striking stage decoration reaching new heights courtesy of two acquaintances of the group, remembered only as Penny and Karen. "They were kind of like conceptual/performance artists," recalls Nick. "They did preparation and blowing things on stage. We did one concert – it wasn't us, it was their performance, it might have been the Leadmill, where they were kind of in a white backdrop and a white floor, and we were kind of shoved into one corner, I think I was just playing the kettledrums, we were playing this strange music that we'd written just for them, and they ended up writhing around naked covered in flour. There was a lot of that kind of thing going on. You wouldn't get that nowadays."

Their contribution to the Pulp show was tame by comparison,

consisting, alongside the requisite tin foil, of bubbles, glowing orange globes, slides projection and cine film of motor racing. Writing about the Limit concert in local magazine *Cut*, David Bocking commented on the more positive, less introspective feel to the new material, remarking that Pulp "still look and sound like no one else in the world." His review concluded, "Pulp used to be interesting. Now they're wicked."[158]

Another Pulp gig from this period, at the Barracuda in Nottingham that July, is partially preserved for posterity thanks to the release of two tracks on Mark Webber's *Oozing Through The Ozone Layer* compilation tape later in 1987. The recordings show that the band had developed almost beyond recognition since *Freaks* – both in terms of a more accessible, albeit still stubbornly individual, sound (thanks in large part to the more upfront, assertive rhythm section) and Jarvis' considerably more nonchalant, less demonstrative stage presence. "Right, then," he announced at the start of the concert, "we're Pulp, we've got a handful of songs to sing you. There's somebody just told me there's only a handful of you out there tonight, but who cares, eh? We're going to have a good time together. All right?" Picking a fight with the soundman or storming off stage, as he was wont to do a year or two previously, seemed to be the furthest things from his mind.

'Don't You Want Me Anymore?' appeared, sounding reasonably close to the way it did when recorded for *Separations* two years later, albeit a little more overwrought and heavy-handed. Even so, the spaghetti western high drama (dare we say camp?) of the song is clear enough evidence that Jarvis had moved on from the super-earnest lamenting of dead and dying relationships that characterised much of his writing during the middle years of the Eighties.

'My First Wife', meanwhile, is a remarkable song. Showcasing the same kind of frantic, (polka) dotty two-beat drumming first spotted on 'Master Of The Universe' (not to mention a bone-rattlin' snare drum solo), it gives a pretty clear demonstration of Pulp's brief flirtation with Eastern European folk music. Russell's insistent, spidery minor-key guitar part insinuates its way around the melody line, while Jarvis' intense, wound-up vocal tells a story not of wallowing in romantic misery *à la Freaks*, but (perhaps appropriately) attempting to move on and work out what to do next: *"The day is gone, the night is long, I won't think of love, I won't think of love . . . Don't ask me how I feel, I'm trying not to feel, I won't think of love. And soon this night will end, and I can live again, no I won't think of love, I won't think of love."* It could be said to be the first of many Pulp songs to deal with the subject of trying to escape the rut of a doomed-relationship and Live On.

Astonishingly, this superb song was dropped from the band's set shortly after the Nottingham concert. "That was a very brief outing," says Nick. "It kind of withered on the vine."

Also in July, with the problematic Fire years behind them (or so they thought), Pulp entered a studio for the first time in over a year to record what was to be the new line-up's first single for FON Records of Sheffield. "We knew we didn't want to record for Fire any more," says Jarvis. "Instead, we got involved with FON. We were working more strongly on our Eurodisco sound."[159]

The FON ('Fuck Off Nazis') organisation had been formed by Dave Taylor and ex-*NME* writer Amrik Rai, management team for Sheffield industrial combo Chakk. When Chakk signed to MCA, Taylor and Rai were able to invest the sizeable advance they received into building a state-of-the-art recording studio and expand their management activities.

Ian Spence: "FON was all based around Chakk, who did a single which Richard Kirk from The Cabs produced. That got them on *The Tube* and it was a big indie hit at the time. They managed to get something like £650,000 from MCA Records for a record deal, which Dave and Amrik, their management team, spent on FON Studios. Amrik was a bit of a chancer – he used to buy all the review copies off the *NME* and sell them in FON Records, his shop in Sheffield! So they got a load of money off MCA, invested it in the studio, and in the long term it paid off. But I think it was a bit of a loss leader for MCA, because I don't think Chakk's records ever made that money back. So I think Dave Taylor and Amrik Rai did better out of the band than Jake and the rest of them."

FON the label had already had some success with Age of Chance, who had recently scored a minor hit with a version of Prince's *Kiss*, and the plan with Pulp (and with other bands they worked with, including Treebound Story, Dig Vis Drill and Sedition) was to give them free studio time to record two tracks to a high standard, and then either release the recordings on FON or attempt to license them out to a major label.

At first, both Pulp and FON were enthusiastic: "Dave Taylor's spent more on pizzas for us than Fire ever spent on our promotion,"[160] Russell claimed at the time, his tongue firmly in his cheek. Taylor, for his part, reckoned Pulp to be "a really special band. I mean they've been going for five years and hardly sold a record. They should have a higher profile, because they deserve it."[161]

As a studio, FON must have been a dream come true after years of poking around in the occasionally functional likes of Input and Victoria. Built in 1985 in the space that had once housed The Wicker Karate

Rooms, equipped with a state-of-the-art digital 24-track set-up and staffed with excellent in-house engineers, it was without a doubt the best studio in Sheffield – before long, it was attracting the likes of The Fall, Erasure, James and David Bowie. At last, Pulp had the opportunity to make a record that sounded more or less as they wanted it to!

The sessions were produced by Alan Smyth, a local musician and sound engineer who had handled Pulp's live sound numerous times. "I was just in on the thing because I knew Pulp well and I'd started working at FON Studios as a guest engineer type person. It was a nice studio – it had an Amek Angela desk, good monitors – it was a proper studio. One of the first ones I'd worked in. It had a relaxing room, a kitchenette, and the main studio, so people could slope off to different places. I can't remember if that session was the one with the mice – someone went to make some toast and there was a mouse eating crumbs in the toaster. And every so often the studio door would be open and something would move past – you'd just look round and see a tail disappearing."

The projected A-side of the single was 'Don't You Want Me Anymore?', by far one of the most obvious pop songs Pulp had attempted since the early Eighties. But while the unformed adolescent Jarvis of *It* and before had lurched forgivably between naïve earnestness and schoolboy silliness, here was an archly camp, albeit still pretty gloomy, slice of high drama pitched somewhere between Marc Almond and Gene Pitney. (Jarvis seemingly wasn't the only one thinking along those lines – Almond and Pitney themselves would shortly unite and top the charts with a remake of Gene's tearjerking Sixties cheesefest 'Something's Got A Hold Of My Heart'.)

The other song recorded was 'Rattlesnake', an early Pulp IV number described in live reviews by *Sounds* as "a mad Cossack stomp dominated by frenzied violin", and by *Melody Maker* as "a dotty polka-and-balalaikas shuffle that conveniently disinters *Rasputin* now that Bjork reckons we can shimmy to Boney M again."

Musically, 'Rattlensake' could almost be seen as the exact halfway point between *Freaks* and *Separations* – opening with grandiose, shivering strings and acoustic guitars, it soon drops into one of Russell's trademark gypsy fiddling extravaganzas, *à la* 'Mark Of The Devil' or 'Separations'. Yet the most obvious influence on the song would seem to be Scott Walker, whose legendarily influential solo work Jarvis had just discovered at the time. "People said, 'You'd like Scott Walker,'" he told *Record Collector* in 1994, "but all I'd heard sounded like Tom Jones. It wasn't till 1987 that I understood his genius.[162] I had the flu and somebody did me a tape of Scott Walker to listen to while I was ill. And I put it on and it was all this stuff from his solo albums rather than The Walker Brothers, and I thought that maybe I was having a fever because I couldn't believe how good it was. I liked the way the backing was very lush and orchestral and then the words were often about watching the telly."[163] 'Rattlesnake' certainly bears the mark of Scott – as well as Jarvis' tormented crooning, the introduction to the song bears a striking similarity to 'The Seventh Seal' from *Scott 4*.

Lyrically, it seems to cover similar territory to 'The Never Ending Story', only with a more accessible, less heavy-handed approach. Essentially, Jarvis seems to be singing about a massively regrettable shag: "*I just went back on my promise, one I kept through countless ages / All I did was hold her hand / The world split into two tonight . . . Thought that I could live without it, tried but it just came back stronger / Just one touch and it's all over / I must have it all tonight / And this time it could be forever / It might only last an hour / Turn my head to see her face and / I must give my life tonight . . .*"

"'Rattlesnake' was a good tune," says Alan Smyth. "You can hear the similarity between that and 'Down By The River'. It's in that vein, a bit more uptempo than that, it's got that kind of melodramatic feel which I love, and I know they did at that time."

Both songs benefited from the use of a small string section – the recording of which presented Alan Smyth with some slight difficulties. "It was four cellists, and that would've been great but one of them couldn't play! It was a good session, but I think in the end I just had to face Jarvis and say, 'Look Jarv, you know, three of them are great but one of them isn't.' We did everything to try and mask the fact that he was spoiling it, but in the end we said, 'Look – sorry. You can't play on this, it's just not happening.' It was just like those Les Dawson moments. So we had to be a bit harsh on that particular session to him, and obviously the man was not pleased.

"They were just friends of Jarvis' I think. I mean, it sounded great – they were just doing tremolo stuff, making the sound shimmer, but the out-of-tune one was just *too* out-of-tune to let go. The session was fairly fast as I remember, so when you're engineering it's really intense. Lots of people and lots of different instruments. It was quite full-bore for me, I don't really remember that much about it."

Jarvis reckoned the tracks that resulted from the FON sessions were by far Pulp's best recordings yet. All that needed to be done now was to get them released . . .

Despite Pulp's continuing artistic successes of 1987, the band's career curve was continuing to slump. As summer turned to autumn, there was no sign of a release date for the FON single, live audiences were continuing to decline in size, and gigs became ever more infrequent. It seemed as if things were going in reverse – the band's time on Fire was hardly a pop dream come true, but at least they'd been getting records out.

The lack of new releases meant that it was difficult to truly gauge what level of popularity Pulp really had at this time. "There was certainly the hangover from people who remembered 'Little Girl' and stuff like that," reckons Nick Banks. "In the first six months, we must have played the Hull Adelphi three or maybe four times. The first time we played it was absolutely rammed – it was like, 'This is fantastic.' The second time we played there was like 25 people there. What do you do? Are you doing something wrong, had you just struck a lucky night?

"I remember when we went down to play the Clarendon at Hammersmith, sod all people there, you'd be on the dole, stick a fiver in for petrol or whatever, you get back to Sheffield at seven in the morning or whatever . . . but you have a laugh doing it. So it didn't really matter too much, it wasn't a case of ripping our hair out because we weren't playing to anyone and spending half our money on it – we were having a laugh doing it, having an adventure, so it didn't matter. We were enjoying the music we were playing. I can still see Russell in the front of the Transit, we'd be unloading at seven in the morning, and you'd go, 'Russ, could you help us?' And he'd pretend not to hear!

"I just joined my favourite group. And to do that, that was kind of the be-all and end-all. Have a laugh, see how it goes. You can't do better than join your favourite group, can you? So that was it, basically. If it went nowhere, you'd always be able to say, I did what I could. If nothing happened and it all petered out in 1989, which was very possible, at least you could say, you know, I had that experience."

For Jarvis, though, after almost a decade of failing to become a pop star, it was becoming ever more apparent that something had to change. "It was completely doing my head in," he said later. "If I didn't get out of Sheffield sharpish I was going to end up as a sad character who used to be in a band."[164] As a result, autumn 1987 saw him enrolling on a part-time film foundation course at Sheffield Polytechnic, with a view to getting on to a degree course at the prestigious St Martin's School of Art in London. As for Pulp . . .

"Pulp were kind of at the same stage as us," remembers Nick Robinson of Dig Vis Drill, who were encountering similar problems at the time. "We sort of fell apart, and I kind of hoped they'd keep going. And they kind of were, but you tend to put that kind of band in a pigeonhole – you know, they've had their chance, and they're just going to tick on and fall apart unless they do something radical. And they never really did anything radical, I don't think – just kept at it. They gradually honed their style, and certainly their looks, and I think the main thing was that Jarvis' style eventually came into fashion. When the Scott Walker look and the sort of cheesy lift music sound really came in, they were the masters of that 'cos they'd been working on it for so long!"

By this time, Russell and Jarvis had moved out of their shared flat, Russell having decided he'd had enough ("things were just sinking into squalor"[165]). Jarvis' new home was the spare room in a house that Nick Banks shared with some friends:

"Jarvis turned up with this Transit van crammed with rubbish . . . a cardboard house . . . a little doll made out of plastic fruit. So I started helping out with all these bags and boxes. Then this car pulls up and Jarvis goes, 'Oh it's me driving lesson.' He gets in and the car hops off like a kangaroo. We had to cart all the stuff by ourselves. At first we managed to keep the living room fairly bare, but every so often you'd find a fluffy gonk on the table and you'd think, 'Now whose might this be?'"[166]

"The thing I found most distasteful about Nick," says Jarvis, "was his tea. He's one of those people who just shows the cup the teabag. It always used to make me feel ill seeing him drink a pint-sized mug of this milky water."[167]

Things may have been grim for Pulp career-wise at the time, but that didn't mean it was time to give up. Five months after the initial FON sessions that yielded 'Don't You Want Me Anymore?' and 'Rattlesnake', Pulp returned to the studio in December 1987 to cut a new song called 'Death Comes To Town' in the hope that, as by far the most commercial and contemporary-sounding track they had ever put down, it would be the single that broke the band.

The result was certainly one of Pulp's must accomplished efforts yet: if the unprecedented poppiness of 'Don't You Want Me Anymore?' wasn't enough of an advert for the new Pulp, 'Death Comes To Town' was no less than a full-blown stomping disco classic. Built around a plinky, almost reggae-like Yamaha Portasound beat and pumping bassline, and embellished with some superb swooping violin work and synthetic strings courtesy of Candida's newly acquired Korg Delta, it's not only unusually robust-sounding for mid-Eighties Pulp, but also an undeniably superb pop song. Even further away from *Freaks'* bedsit angst than the rest of Pulp's 1987 output, it revisits the sinister, quietly threatening lyrical scenarios of 'Mark Of The Devil' and '97 Lovers', seemingly casting Jarvis in the role of the grim reaper whilst posing as what could almost pass for a deceptively heart-rending, love song: *"What did I tell you – there was no need to be afraid. You've got such a beautiful body, oh you'll make such a beautiful body . . . The sun that shines through the window in the morning, and the wind that blows the blossom through the trees, and those girls who cross their legs, they'll all stop dead when I can come to town."* Unlikely but darkly brilliant stuff.

Produced at the same time was 'Death Goes To The Disco', a 12″ remix of '. . . Town', featuring 'Radio Ga Ga' handclaps, twice as long as the original with half as many lyrics, with lots of extremely daft echoey bossa nova percussion. Hardly a 'house mix' (as it was described at the time), but an astonishing departure for Pulp at that point. If this wouldn't do the trick and establish Pulp at the heart of British pop, then nothing would . . .

Shortly after 'Death Comes To Town' was recorded, Steven Havenhand ceased to be Pulp's bass player. Problems had arisen during the recording session, as Alan Smyth recalls: "He was very quiet, and not very good. I just remember bits of quiet where he just sat there, being *very* quiet and not really doing much for a long time. I think Jarvis re-did the bass that evening."

Jarvis: "Steven was a good songwriter [for Lay Of The Land, not Pulp] but he was the shyest person I've ever met. Plus, you couldn't hear him play the bass – he was so gentle with the strings, like he didn't want to disturb! He wouldn't loosen up so, in the end, he left."[168]

"We'd played quite a few concerts," says Nick, "the feedback you'd get from the audience was always like, 'Oh, it was great but we couldn't hear the bass.' And if we'd rehearse, say, without Steven Havenhand, Jarvis would play the bass a lot of the time, and his style was very much harder, whereas Steven would just tickle the strings, hardly get any sound out of them, like he thought he'd break his finger. So it just wasn't right because he just wasn't giving the welly that it needed – when it goes loud it's got to go loud, and from one to two isn't very good, it wants to be from one to 10. So he was just deemed not suitable after a while."

Not that Havenhand's extremely quiet playing had been a problem for Jonathan Kirk, who still had the job of handling the band's live sound: "I could increase it on the desk, which is easier than having a loud bass on stage and trying to compete with it. From that viewpoint great, but at the end of the day he was quite undynamic – he just did his job. He wasn't bringing much to Pulp, and he wasn't getting much out of it, and Jarvis and Russell were like, 'He's OK, but there's nothing about him' – especially when they'd had somebody like Manners, when it would be like, 'Is he going to turn up to the practice or not? If he does turn up, will he be out of his head? If we do a gig, will he be sober by the time we go on stage?' At least there was an element of the rock'n'roll kind of thing. He was a lad, but he was an interesting, lovable one."

Pulp's fourth new member in a year was Steve Genn's younger brother, Antony. "He was about 15 or 16, just a young lad," remembers John Quinn. "His brother Steve was a friend of Jarvis and Steve Mackey, and was basically the local loudmouth – you could hear him a mile off. Very talkative, very extrovert, and his brother was basically the same."

Nick: "Genn was drafted in. Couldn't play to start with, had no particular idea, but as is in the Genn character, they can get where water can't. So he was a good fun chap, started to play the bass in his erratic way, and he learnt very quickly."

The beginning of 1988 saw Jarvis once again working outside of Pulp – this time in the studio with Hula's John Avery on a demo of a song called '200% And Bloody Thirsty'.

"'200% And Bloody Thirsty' was a show by the Forced Entertainment theatre group," explains Avery, "who I'd been working with since 1982. I'd done music for some of their shows, and we thought it'd be a nice idea to have a song in one of the shows. Most of what I'd done in the past was background music, and we thought it'd be nice to do something that was a bit more up-front. So we had this idea to write a song and I said, 'Look, I'm not a lyricist.' Tim Etchell, who was one of the main people in Forced Entertainment, and I both really liked what we'd heard of Pulp, and I think we'd seen them quite recently.

"Anyway, I wrote some music, and Jarvis came into the studio – I was still with Hula at the time, so I was using their studio. It was where Ponds Forge leisure centre is now – they built their swimming baths on top of our rehearsal rooms! Anyway, he had some lyrics that he'd written previously, and he just made them work. It was just him and myself in the studio, he knew what he wanted to do, and he came in and did it. It was quite strange for me because he was really on top of what he was doing. I was under the impression that Pulp weren't really doing much, so it was surprising to see Jarvis working so creatively.

"It was a very simple song – we used the instruments which I was favouring at the time, which would be piano, bass, quite acoustic-sounding stuff. Very raw version. The intention wasn't actually to have Jarvis singing it – he wrote the lyrics and did the demo with the intention of having the performers in the play singing it. The demo's probably rather unflattering . . . We then had a few rehearsals with the performers trying to do the melody and Jarvis' lyrics justice.

"It was never actually used in the Forced Entertainment show – although the title '200% And Bloody Thirsty' remained, the show they eventually did was completely different. They postponed the tour and the entire soundtrack was shelved. I did see Pulp play it at the Leadmill a few months later though, which I was quite flattered about."

On January 16, 1988, the *Sheffield Star* Pop Page carried a piece on Pulp, their first in a while, trumpeting the news that the new single, 'Death Comes To Town', was to be released in February, just as soon as Jarvis had done the sleeve. "I'd just started doing the Pop Page for the *Star*," says John Quinn, "when they gave me a tape of 'Death Comes To Town' and did an interview. It sounded really good, but it just never came out. I think what happened was that FON had had a minor hit with a band called Age of Chance, who'd done a version of *Kiss*, the Prince song, and after that they were expecting to have a lot more success. After they signed Pulp up, they had enough money to record the thing, but not to put it out. When I was interviewing them, they were saying, 'Oh, it'll be out in a couple of weeks,' but it never actually happened."

"They fucked quite a few bands around," reckons Ogy McGrath. "The same thing that they did to Pulp also happened to us, and Treebound Story and a band called Sedition. Graham from Sedition ended up running the Leadmill."

The non-appearance of the FON single was a major knock to Pulp's career: the tracks represented everything they had worked on in the 12 months since relaunching after Magnus and Pete's departure. They were, as far as Jarvis was concerned, by far the band's best recordings yet – they were certainly the most commercial and musically accessible – and their emergence at the time would almost certainly have meant a resurgence of interest in Pulp. It might even have meant the breakthrough into the indie consciousness happening in 1988, instead of in 1991 with the release of 'My Legendary Girlfriend'.

"We always thought we were going to put records out with FON," says Nick, "but because Dave Taylor pissed about so long, it was just kind of 'Dave, you keep saying you love the group. You keep saying FON's doing so good, we've got number one singles flying around. Dave, let's get some fucking records sorted out.' 'Oh, I'm just so busy, we'll do it in a bit!' And it just never happened. People had this conspiracy theory that he was trying to keep all the Sheffield groups busy so that no one else could have them. He didn't have the resources or the time – 'cos he was so busy with Age of Chance and Chakk and stuff – to actually get releases sorted out and get 'em physically signed. So we thought, is he trying to keep everyone on the verge – give 'em some studio time, keep them on the verge of signing them, dangling the carrot, 'We're gonna get round to it, we're gonna get your record out', you know? And we put up with that for ages because we knew that Jarv didn't want to have anything to do with Fire. So it was a case of, if FON aren't going to sign us, who is?"

There was still the occasional glimmer to suggest that it wasn't all over quite yet. When, despite a lack of new records and dwindling audiences even back up north (roughly 12 people witnessed Pulp in Chesterfield the same month), Pulp made their first London appearance in over a year at the Camden Falcon in February 1988 they received two rave reviews in the national music press. "Pulp are rock burlesque, devious pop, folk horror, fairground fun," hyperventilated *Sounds*'s Neil Perry. "They are glamorous tack, cheap but deep, and in this dingy pub backroom Pulp glowed darkly with their own peculiar class . . . Pulp are the most unlikely sex machine you'll ever hear. Theirs is an innocent seduction, and beneath it all is a wry smile."

Bob Stanley (later a member of St Etienne and chum of Jarvis') writing in *NME*, was almost as supportive. While allowing that at times Pulp's "sense of theatre gets the better of them," he noted the way in which "Jarvis lurches and leaps like Freddie Garrity with contact lenses . . . In Jarvis' book, love is a never ending David Lynch film – songs like 'Going Back To Find Her' are as black as pitch. Pulp want to be as horribly compelling as a circus freak show. Taking 'Yellow River', 'The Devil Went Down To Georgia' and Leonard Cohen as their inspiration, they come across like an amateur dramatic society hamming up deliberately to upset the vicar."

Overall, it seemed that while Pulp '88 had retained much of the darkness and severity of the previous model, it was leavened by a more palpable sense of humour and irony, not to mention signs of a pop consciousness reported missing presumed dead since 1983, and even (more unprecedented still) sexiness – something which startled Tony Perrin, who caught up with Pulp at a concert around this time:

"I hadn't seen anything of Jarvis for a number of years, and then suddenly he went into this kind of sex god persona, and he was absolutely stunning, and pulled it off. I couldn't believe the transition he'd gone through from this awkward gangly kid to this self-assured, consummate performer. It was a revelation – I mean, Jarvis was the antithesis of sex. I remember when he got his first girlfriend, I had the same sense of shock."

Part of the transformation can be put down to the fact that Jarvis had, for the first time, put his glasses away and invested in contact lenses. Nick: "That will have made a difference because, as we've seen before, if you lose your glasses on stage, should they fall in the bass drum, it can cause a lot of problems. So he went for contact lenses, which I think in a weird way was one of the many catalysts that changed Pulp from being worthy but underachieving to starting on the upward plane. Just a simple thing like getting contact lenses. Because he can be more like himself onstage rather than not wanting to throw his head around because he doesn't want to lose his glasses. And then the haircut changed, he lost the Eighties mop, and it started to look like the Pulp that became known."

The idea of Jarvis as even vaguely sexy is one that was and is met with a mixture of amusement and shock by those who knew him in his pre-fame years. "The phenomenon of Jarvis the celebrity and sex symbol, as opposed to Jarvis the lanky get with halitosis and underarm sweat that women avoid?" muses Russell. "I've shared a bed with Jarvis more than most people other than his girlfriends, and he never seemed terribly attractive to me . . . He wears brown pyjamas and horrible things like that. The first person I ever heard of who fancied Jarvis was my Auntie Val. He reminded her of her first husband in the Seventies with sort of flared trousers and things like that. But he did start to cultivate it. Which was, I think, good for him really."[169]

Pulp's status became yet more precarious in July 1988 when Antony Genn announced that he was leaving the group. Like Magnus Doyle before him, he was very much a part of the hallucinogenic drug scene in Sheffield, and his precarious mental state at the time (Rob Mitchell recalls him opining that "acid is the only reality"[170]) can only have been exacerbated by the fact that he had joined the infamous Nine O'Clock Service, the religious cult that was sweeping Sheffield at the time and subsequently became the subject of the 'Rave Vicar' sex scandal which broke in August 1995.

Steve Mackey: "The acid fucked Antony's life up and he started owing lots of money to different places. Then an envelope came through the door containing £760, which was curiously the exact amount of money he needed to pay off his bills, followed by a visit from these twelve Christians later that night, who sat around and talked through his problems, and said they could help if he came into the church. That's how they used to work. He left after three years, saying it was fucking weird, and 'you wouldn't believe what's going on there'. We thought he was being a bit fucked-up so when it came out in the news, lots of people were doing lots of apologising to him."[171]

"It was getting very pervasive with people our sort of age in Sheffield," says Nick. "You'd see them around – all the girls had their hair in a black bob. Antony was going, 'Aww, just come up and see it, you don't have to bother with owt religious, just come up, it's a good laugh.' You're not getting me like that! And we knew his head was kind of done in through too much acid, he was only 16, and then all these people were being very

very friendly toward him. That's how they work – you're at an emotional low ebb and they go in and everyone's your friend, and they go, 'Come down, we've got loads of great friendly people!' And then it's like, 'You've got to do as we say now because you're in our cult.' I think probably the God Squad said that Pulp were evil because they weren't in the God Squad – 'You can't hang around with those kids anymore.' He's never been one of the most reliable people around, so it kind of wasn't really working out and when he kind of went we said, 'Fair enough.'"

"Quite a few people who went to the same pubs and stuff like that actually ended up joining it," says John Quinn. "It was weird – I remember him raving about it at the time, saying, 'It's brilliant, you should come down.' I was, like, 'I don't think so, Antony.' This was the guy who had appeared naked on stage a few months before, and suddenly turned religious."

Ogy McGrath: "Anton was a great, bright guy before he got fucked up in all that shit. I used to nag him all the time about it, him and Kirky and people like that. I was an atheist a-go-go, and all that stuff used to drive me crazy."

For Jarvis, losing Antony to the Nine O'Clock Service was the last straw after six years of life sliding steadily downhill. There had been no new records in two years, the FON single was refusing to happen, the band seemed incapable of lasting much more than half a year without losing a member, and despite the strong new direction, the band's popularity was at an all-time low, with live audiences sometimes in single figures. Luckily, having completed his foundation course at the Poly, he'd been accepted for a degree course at St Martin's School of Art, and had made the decision to get out of Sheffield and head south.

"I had to realise I'd taken a wrong turn. You know when you're in a car and you take a wrong turn, you don't like to admit it, do you? You think if you keep going you'll come right again. But you don't, do you? I'd spent the best part of a decade in bed and in an unsuccessful band. I was forced to admit I'd been wasting my time. But I was lucky enough to get into St Martin's, so I was off. I just imagined the group would cease to exist."[172]

Antony Genn did stay with the band for one final concert in August 1988 – a planned multimedia farewell extravaganza at the Leadmill known as *The Day That Never Happened*. Low morale notwithstanding, it seems Pulp's artistic ambition at least was still alive and well: the so-called 'concept concert' featured their most elaborate stage presentation yet. Jarvis charitably describes it as "a fiasco".

Mark Webber and his friend Gregory Kurcewicz helped out with the stage decorations. "There were the usual films, slides and tin-foil," wrote Mark in *Disco-Very*, "along with a few trees (sprayed white), dry ice (home-made and very poor – it barely spilled over the saucer it was in), smells (Russell had made some charcoal incense, but of course the Leadmill is a big place so it didn't carry too well), video projection (but the projector broke so we had to make do with a television on the stage), and the most sensitive moment was to be a snowfall during a slow ballad . . . that ended up in a total farce with people running round the stage carrying big hairdryer things."[173]

Nick: "They were trying to get this dry ice blowing around, like you see on *Top Of The Pops*, with a couple of chunks of carbon dioxide. It was absolutely ridiculous. The idea was great – if you had 10,000 quid you could make this look fucking great, but you had ten quid, if that, and some daft kids from Chesterfield trying to sort it out. Great enthusiasm, but the theatre of it all was starting to take over in a way.

"One of the reasons I thought it was a farce was that we were all setting up, and I went, 'Antony, tune your bass.' And he went, 'Yeah yeah, I'll get round to it.' He was fannying around with something ridiculously unimportant. Antony, tune your bass. 'Yeah, yeah.' I'll do it then. And I had no idea whatsoever. So I tuned it, and it must've been nowhere near, and he's on stage and I could see him going, *'It's out of tune!!'* Oh, for fuck's sake . . . He had to have coloured stickers on the neck of the guitar to know where to go, it was that level of incompetence. Too busy fannying around with something else to get it in tune, and that set the whole ball rolling for that evening."

"I remember saying to Richard, Nick's brother, that it was the worst Pulp concert I'd ever seen," says John Quinn. "It just seemed to be a mess. It was a wash-out, basically. I can't remember the actual details – just that it was awful."

"There was that period with Pulp when they really went to town on their shows," says John Avery. "You'd go out to see them and it'd be a whole experience. They'd make a big effort to make their shows special events, and I thought that was great. It was really admirable, but I suppose there's only so much you can do when you've not got much money."

"It was good because no one else was doing it," says Nick, "but a bit after that World Of Twist started, and they had the stage all done up. The *NME* picked up on them and started going, 'World Of Twist, these are great,' you know, and then we started getting reviews and they were going, 'Oh, they're a bit like World Of Twist this Pulp,' and we were like *gaaaarrrrrggggghhh!*"

The Day That Never Happened wasn't definitely Pulp's final concert – but with no bass player, no record deal, a shrinking fanbase and a singer who was about to move to London, to assume that the band had any sort of future at all would have been wildly optimistic.

Jarvis left Sheffield to begin his course at St Martin's in September, and it seemed for a while that the group would cease to be. Russell stayed in Sheffield with his long-term partner Vicky, who was soon to give birth to the couple's first daughter, and concentrated on his antique glass business and designing his board game, The Housing Ladder. Candida soon moved to Manchester with Pete Mansell and began work in a toyshop. Nick variously worked as a design technology teacher, a wreath-maker, and lived on the dole, moving between London and Sheffield.

"When Jarvis kind of buggered off to London, we thought that was it," says Nick Robinson. "In hindsight, he was probably really, really pissed off [about the lack of success], but at the time they just seemed to go on forever and never really get anywhere. They kept pumping out singles at fairly regular intervals, never really getting much more than a bit of critical acclaim. They weren't even going up the ladder slowly – they were staying on the same rung. And then, lo and behold, they jumped to the top."

"As far as I was aware they were finishing," agrees John Nicholls. "He was going to London to do his film course, and I just presumed that was it. But it wasn't long after that that, bang, they were back with a new line-up."

Chapter 8

Not much happened on the Pulp front for the first few months following Jarvis' relocation to London. Adjusting to his new surroundings was more of a challenge than he'd anticipated – Sheffield to London was a big jump after a lifetime living in the former. "I'd heard about St Martin's, read about it in books, and thought, 'This is going to be the glamour I've been looking for, there in the capital city; it will occur.' Of course it didn't."[174]

"It would have been easier to stay in Sheffield – I knew lots of people and felt I had the measure of the place, and then you come to London. In Sheffield, everyone congregates in the centre of town at weekends, which of course they don't do in London, so I'd do sad things like ending up walking around Piccadilly Circus on a Saturday night, wondering where everybody was, but of course it's all tourists. It takes a bit of time to learn these things, and the fact you have to be quite organised about your social life, and meeting people at a certain time and a certain place, because there were only ever two pubs in Sheffield that people went to. You'd walk around London for two months expecting to bump into someone and never did."[175]

Returning to academia was also something to adjust to – especially as St Martin's was hardly comparable to any of Jarvis' previous educational experiences. "The system they seemed to employ at St Martins was a kind of right-on Noah's Ark system where they took two of each – sexuality, race, geographical persuasion. So me and a guy from Liverpool got put on as a couple of token northerners, kind of thing. Every minority group was represented in this class of 20 people. And that was probably the best thing they did, 'cos you were then in with a load of people who were completely outside the experience that you'd come from."[176]

After spending six years struggling with Pulp with success or failure dictated by factors that were largely out of his control, Jarvis' relocation to London could be seen as a move towards taking his life back into his own hands. "It was my decision to move down to London. You know, I decided to go on with education when I wanted to, when I actually wanted to do it. I was really glad that I did that rather than, you know, I guess people usually do it because it's the next thing you do after you finish at school. I always hated that – 'have your fun now, knuckle down now.' I say have the fun now, have the fun now."[177]

Distractions were numerous, but as with the last time Jarvis came close to packing things in and moving on to something else, after the failure of *It*, no matter how much the rational side of his head was telling him to cut his losses and do something else, he couldn't quite bring himself to give up on Pulp. During his first term he'd been working on a video for 'Death Goes To The Disco' using footage filmed at *The Day That Never Happened* concert, and hawking the previous year's FON tapes around in hope of finding a label willing to sign Pulp up for a one-single deal. And while the band itself had been dormant when he'd moved down to London, it wasn't long before Pulp began to show signs of life – thanks in no small part to the appearance on the scene of Steve Mackey.

Steve had already been in London for a year, studying film production at Goldsmiths College. "We'd done a gig at the London Falcon," remembers Nick, "and Steve was one of the ones in the audience, clapping and whooping at the front, really getting into it. It was shortly after that that Antony gave up the ghost and we lost him to the clutches of the Nine O'Clock Service, and I remember saying to Jarvis when he was down in London, 'Why don't you get in touch with Steve Mackey about playing?' because he'd played in Trolley Dog Shag. He said, 'Oh, that's a good idea,' so I think when he got down there he got in touch with Steve."

"I said 'yeah' just like that," says Steve. "I knew Pulp hadn't been successful but, coming from Sheffield, you knew that they were real and genuine. They were a legend there – 1,000 people would go to see them."[178]

"When I moved down to London to do my film course," says Jarvis, "I thought, 'Well, there's more chance of the group staying together if we have another member who's also in London.' It was useful, really, because Steve's social skills are a lot better than mine."[179]

He also had somewhere to live. The house Jarvis was supposed to be living in on moving to London had fallen through, and he'd found himself "confronted with the horror of Elephant And Castle because I ended up living there through some unhappy quirk of fate."[180] Meanwhile, Steve had discovered an empty flat on the floor above the one where he was squatting in Camberwell . . .

"I said I'd sell him my squat for £150," remembers Mackey, "the reason being it was a really torrid block, with kids shooting up on the stairs, so I'd paid for one of those metal doors to be put on which meant no one could break in. So Jarvis and his friend Martin moved in and we moved upstairs, because the view from there faced the whole of London as opposed to just Brixton. I felt bad about asking for money but my flatmate, who was a merchant banker who earned about £40,000 a year, was quite hard-nosed."[181]

As fate would have it, shortly after Steve joined Pulp, the band were contacted by sometime Fire employee Robin Gibson, who was by this time on the staff of *Sounds*, with an offer of playing the *Sounds* Christmas party at Camden indie-toilet institution Dingwalls. "That was good because it felt like we were getting into the journalistic scene of things," remembers Nick.

The concert itself, supporting Creation noiseniks The Membranes, was no triumph – Jarvis himself remembers it as "pretty dismal". Yet Pulp still managed to make an impression, as David Hinkler, who was in the audience, remembers:

"They just sounded really tatty, and just weren't together at all. I was quite astonished that they got the invite. But what shone through was Jarvis' songs and his quirkiness – I think that was what people warmed to, rather than the actual music."

Tony Perrin was also there. "It just amazed me that (a) they existed, and (b) they'd been invited to play the *Sounds* Christmas party. I was just really impressed."

What was most important about the concert was that after several months of living dangerously, it confirmed – to the band themselves as much as anyone – that Pulp was still a going concern.

The start of 1989 saw Jarvis and his flatmate Martin Wallace evicted from their Camberwell squat. "We weren't aggressive enough to argue about it," remembers Jarvis, "so we went over to this tower block in Mile End that had a few spare places. It was only supposed to be a temporary measure, but we ended up spending nine months there which, without any question, were the worst nine months of my entire life.

"I was convinced that a murder had been carried out there because there was all this mail for one person, and because, all the time I lived there, the kitchen sink was blocked. It became an obsession to try and get it unblocked. And there was all this horrible stinky pink mushy stuff, together with this hydrochloric acid-type drain cleaner, and I started thinking that maybe the person living there before had killed his wife and then tried to dissolve her remains down the sink.

"It was horrible, because the bathroom sink was also broken, so I had to wash in a washing-up bowl and I had to do all the washing up in the bath.

That was what really summed things up for me: I was having a bath one day, lying low in the bath, as you do, and I suddenly saw this tomato skin floating on the surface of the water. I thought, 'This is not how I want to live.' " [182]

If nothing else, life in Mile End at least provided Jarvis with material. "People go on about the East End, where everyone's friendly and you don't have to lock your door, but they were the most unfriendly people I've come across in my entire life. Like, you always got served last in the shop if they knew you weren't from around there. I never really got to know anybody who lived there – it's not like *Eastenders* at all.

"There was this pub up the road that we never used to go in where they used to play pool and it was, like, Winner Stays On. Anyway, one night, this kid beat one of the regulars, who went off in a bit of a huff. Come closing time, we saw this bloke who lost the game of pool coming down the road with a shotgun. And this kid of about 17 ran over to warn his mate, and as he did, the bloke with the gun shot and killed him. So, I was thinking of going in the pub the next night, plonking my 50p on the pool table and saying, 'Winner stays alive!' " [183]

Considerably more edifying was Pulp's next live appearance – at the Leadmill in February. "They were fucking brilliant," recalls an early member of Pulp who was in the audience. "Really excellent." Since the *Sounds* concert, the live act had improved in leaps and bounds, both musically and visually. *The Day That Never Happened* debacle had led to the decision to ease off on the over-elaborate am-dram stage presentation, but there was still no limit to the band's resources when it came to ensuring that a Pulp concert was still an Event.

"As the audience were coming in," remembers Jonathan Kirk, "they all got given a bingo card, and Jarvis started the concert by doing the call-out. The thing was, the cards were done in a way that everyone would win at the same time, so Jarvis was calling out the numbers and they were all crossing them off, and when he got to the last one, the whole room shouted *'House!'* – and they dropped straight into 'This House Is Condemned'."

'This House Is Condemned' – a stab at producing a Pulpish slant on the acid house movement of the mid-late Eighties – was something of a bizarre departure for the band, and had actually been a part of the live set for several months, predating Jarvis' departure from Sheffield. However, before long it took on a new significance: to be precise, on May 20, 1989, when Jarvis and Steve travelled from Sheffield to London to go to a rave for the first time.

The trip was a result of Steve's influence. "I was then living with

Barbara Ellen, an *NME* journalist, and we'd started going to Phuture, which was the first Balearic club. My role in Pulp then was the modern-iser, as I was really into acid and house music, and while Jarvis converted me to Scott Walker and Serge Gainsbourg, I got Jarvis into house. So we'd all go to raves like Sunrise and Biology, every weekend, and take drugs, as everyone did, and we became obsessed with technology. We really thought our lives were changing, and the whole world around us. As out-siders, the community atmosphere was quite a special thing."[184]

"We got a coach down to London," remembers Jarvis of that first rave experience, "and everyone seemed to know each other, apart from us knobheads at the back. I remember being surprised that everyone started getting friendly after an hour or so – obviously they'd all dropped their E's at the right time. It was one of those moments.

"We stood in this massive queue, but no one was getting arsey, they were enjoying queuing! We decided to take our drugs before we got in. As we got to the front of the queue, the pills kicked in. We walked into this massive hangar full of people. There was a big wheel going out the back, I'd never seen anything like it before, never experienced anything like it before. It was a revelatory experience. To be honest, it was never that good again."[185]

Going to raves was an eye-opener – especially after years of grim club-bing experiences in the Limit and the Leadmill. Of course, the drugs helped. "I'd had E before, but not in that environment. That place, it seemed perfect, but after six months I got too ill from going every weekend. But I thought that the friendliness at the raves would last. In Sheffield, if you didn't get off with someone, you'd hammer someone out of frustration. This seemed different. I always hoped the feeling would keep going, last past the weekend."[186]

Steve: "It was the end of the Eighties, a really bad time for us as nothing good had happened. We couldn't believe The Smiths were successful because Morrissey's got such an awful voice and just repeated the same thing over and over, *ad nauseam*, and then all this music came along which sounded like the music from the future, like *Star Trek*. You'd go to these raves and it was like a spaceship had landed! Lights were flashing, there were sexy girls, the music was like Kraftwerk . . . it was like the future and you were part of it, and for a while it was like a little secret. Then record companies got involved and it went commercial, but there was a moment when the songs and the movement were bigger than everything else. We used to be gobsmacked . . . you'd go home every day and put on things like Derrick May's 'Strings Of Life' and 'Someday' by C.C. Rodgers, so many great songs."[187]

It's hard to imagine now, but this was a time before dance music culture had become even remotely mainstream – the opening of Ministry of Sound was several months in the future, and acid house raves were new, strange and still very much an underground phenomenon. "I liked the cloak-and-dagger aspect of the raves as much as the music," says Jarvis. He remembers a particularly bizarre event that took place "under the M25, in a tunnel that was built for badgers and deer, so they didn't get twatted by cars. All the sound equipment was at one entrance and it went 400 yards back. I remember thinking that the further I moved back from the music, the further I went back in time. When I saw people right at the back I thought they were Neanderthals! Very strange . . . but it was November too, and that didn't help. It was too cold for warehouses."[188]

Rave culture also gave Jarvis a chance to develop a new slant on his ever-creative choice of wardrobe. "My look for raving was these blue shorts which were very wide and made my legs look really thin, like two pieces of cotton. I matched that with a cotton anorak from a jumble sale – I had the look of a Girl Guide leader. At one do, I put my hair in bunches with these see-through teddy-bear bobbles with baubles on. I didn't wear underwear in those days and the button fly on the shorts tended to come undone. I remember once I looked down after dancing for an hour and seeing my cock was out waving around in the air. I might have started wearing pants after that. There were no uniforms, girls in evening wear or people brushing their teeth, that was fucking mad. People would go out on a limb to do each others' heads in. It was a game, it was fun, I thought it was great."[189]

Meanwhile, by spring 1989, Pulp's future was again starting to look precarious. There was still no sign of any record company interest in the now almost two-year-old FON tapes, and matters weren't helped by the fact that there had been no new Pulp releases in the shops since 1987. "At the time," says Jarvis, "I thought that unless we actually did a record the band wouldn't carry on."[190] But without money or a label, what could be done? Pulp's saviours (to use the term loosely) came in the most unlikely of forms: Fire Records.

Fire's Dave Bedford, who had taken over Johnny Waller's A&R duties, had been at the Dingwalls concert at Christmas, and the label had been hovering in the background in the ensuing months. "He said, 'Why don't we do something?'" remembers Jarvis. "I thought, 'No chance,' but nobody else was interested and so, to my eternal regret, we talked to Fire again. We just wanted a one-off single but they wanted an album deal."[191] They were also offering Pulp a budget of £10,000 for their next album. In

Dave Bedford's words, "Fire had more money, new technology was cheaper, so it transpired that Pulp could make the record they wanted to make."[192]

Despite the attractive offer, Pulp were still reluctant. The opportunity to make another record – and with a proper budget – was irresistible, but no one had forgotten the frustrations and disappointments of Pulp's last spell on Fire. They desperately wanted to release some music, find some connection with the public at large and escape the cycle of diminishing returns that had characterised the past few years. But did they want it badly enough to sign a five-album deal with a record company that was unlikely to offer them what they needed?

It was a near-impossible question to answer, so a plan was hatched that, in theory, would allow Pulp to have their cake and eat it. "Fire were putting the money up for this album," says Nick, "and we were doing it at FON. We had this idea that we could hopefully play Fire and FON off against each other. This studio which was up and coming as *the* studio in Britain – you know, you walk in the door and it's got all these knobs and little flashing lights and stuff, and we thought, 'Well, if Fire put some money up for this record, without us actually signing anything to say that it's got to come out on Fire, we can get this record made,' and then we'd have a really good record that we could take to other people and go 'Quick, sign us before these buggers do!'"

In July, after Jarvis' and Steve's college term had ended, with Fire blissfully unaware of the plot, Pulp spent a day in Priority Studios in Sheffield demoing six of the newer songs in the band's set in preparation for the album sessions. As it was three years since the band had made a record (not including the unreleased FON single, which was now destined to remain so), they'd accumulated quite a backlog of material that was ready to record – 12 songs, in fact, from which nine were picked to comprise what was to become the third Pulp album, *Separations*.*

The sessions for the album took place over a three-week period at FON in August, with Alan Smyth producing. "I'd done sessions with them before, and live engineering – they knew what I could do and those sessions before had turned out to their satisfaction, so they asked. They gave me a remit, which was, 'Can you make us sound like a cross between

---

* In addition, early in the sessions, the band attempted a version of a song called 'Going Back To Find Her', but opted not to include it on the album. "From what I remember it was very similar to 'Down By The River'," says Nick, "a sort of down-tempo, acousticy sort of song, and you don't want too many of them, do you? You want a bit of variety, so it was like, 'This one or that one? That one.'"

Barry White and Pet Shop Boys?' I'll never forget that because halfway through the sessions, a guy called Dave Palfreman [sometime drummer with Sedition, Treebound Story and The Cocteau Twins] walked in and he just stood there and said, 'Bloody hell, this sounds a bit like a cross between Barry White and Pet Shop Boys!' I thought, 'Winner! I've done my job,' there then."

Jarvis summarises the album as "a mixture of some old songs, rearranged quite radically in some senses to try and embrace modern technology, except we didn't know how to operate it, so it all came out sounding a bit weird."

"We ran into problems straight away," says Alan Smyth. "I don't know if Nick'd thank me for this, but they'd asked me to do Pet Shop Boys meets Barry White, both of which are highly accurate playing, and Nick Banks . . . isn't, or wasn't at the time. We tried to do these things with MIDI going on and keyboards with him drumming along to it and it just wasn't happening, it just sounded a mess. I said to Jarvis, 'It's just not going to work 'cos he's not accurate enough.' For things like 'Down By The River' it's absolutely fine, and 'Don't You Want Me Anymore?', that's going to be fine because it's more of a live feel, there isn't much MIDI stuff happening. But in the others, it just wouldn't work. So I had a drum machine at the time and I brought it down and said, 'Nick, here's the drum machine, here's the book on how to use it,' and I showed him how to use it and I just said, 'Just program your drums into this for these certain songs,' for things like 'Legendary Girlfriend'. And all credit to the guy, he didn't freak out, he did it. So that was the first problem, but we got over that in about the first three days."

"I was a bit miffed, at the start," admits Nick. "But being able to hear the end product, I knew that getting it to sound like that playing the drums properly would take a lot of time, a lot of work and a lot of money, and we didn't have those three things. So I was like, whatever it takes to get this record sounding good. We knew that time and budget weren't endless, so we were really trying to get the best-sounding record in the cheapest way – although it still cost £10,000, which compared to *Freaks* is a vast increase. And we knew in FON we had a state-of-the-art studio and we wanted to make the most of it, and pissing around with drums and things would take a hell of a long time. So we thought, well, if we do a more automated treatment, that frees up more time to spend on the instrumentation, trying to get some strings and things on stuff. I remember getting very frustrated sitting in this very small room in FON with a drum machine, trying to replicate what I played on it. I'd never done much like that before, so basically I'm playing it manually into a tape recorder, listening, and replicating it on the drum machine. The number of times I had to get up, shut the door and go off for a walk!

"So a lot of the time it was very frustrating, but once I'd done that, and then could build that into songs, you could hear you were getting a professional-sounding track. Pulp were getting a song recorded properly for the first time. It was great – you know it was like, 'Come on, this is havin' it now!'"

The next problem came with the attempt to incorporate the Yamaha Portasound into the tracks. "They wanted to use those little Yamaha keyboards," remembers Alan Smyth, "which don't have any MIDI outputs. Samplers in those days weren't like they are now, so we had to sample one chord, that'd be a sample, and the next chord, that'd be a sample. And there were echo units and you had to sort of trigger them. If you put the keyboard down on a table, the speed changed, so it'd be slightly different to what it was before. So you couldn't do it that way, that was the next load of problems, but we got through that one. I can't remember what sampler it was, it was something really crap.

"We used Atari STs for the MIDI, linked up to multitrack tape recorders with strange boxes. It took us a long time, but once we got those things down, putting the stuff on top was fast. What actually happened was that on every track we'd end up with 24 tracks of audio, full. So it was a complete mess. I was left alone at that point and it was like, 'Right, sort it out.' So I would make decisions about what was happening in what verse, and what was happening here, and build up the thing like that. And then the next day Jarv and probably Steve would say, 'Yeah we love that bit, we're not so happy with this bit, let's change that round,' and we'd do it that way. I've got really good memories of it – there was a lot of laughter. But essentially I was just intensely busy a lot of the time. It was three weeks but it was full-bore, 16, 17, 18 hours a day. Some days near the end, I just didn't leave."

The album began with the overblown melodrama of 'Love Is Blind', which opened with some spectacularly deranged yelping from Jarvis. "What I always loved about working with Jarvis," says Alan Smyth, "is his ability to be free, really free, and just make noises and silly things, and just do things which other people don't do. On 'Love Is Blind' there's a fair few of those that he was going to take out. It starts with that drumming, and the idea was just to build it up. He wanted it to sound angry I think, and we got the deep throated organ on one of the verses, a Leslie thing I think, sort of full, overdriven, to get the drive of it. I just remember thinking that the song really worked. I was really into the melodrama of the songs and I was trying to get as much dynamic in them as possible so that they went up, then right down, then back up again and exploded. I can't remember what the drum sound at the start is but it's something slowed right down. It just sounded really nice, sort of like a big metal sheet, so we thought that sounded great."

"When we recorded it," remembers Nick, "it was, like, there's only one place for it – first song on the album. Which doesn't often happen, but it was good to play it. It was one of the ones where I was most involved, with quite a drum emphasis, using the kettledrums. I remember Jarvis in the garage saying, 'This one needs a real tubthumping kind of sound,' then you've kind of got to interpret what he's saying, do various things, and with one of them he'll go, 'Yeah, that's what I was thinking of.' I always thought Blur had nicked that one for 'Sunday Sunday'!"

Next was an embellished remake of 'Don't You Want Me Anymore?' – the only song originally recorded for the 1987 sessions to make it on to the album. Alan Smyth: "Again it was about the drama of it, for me. I tried to make the music part of it emotional and just let the song breathe and work. It is different to the original demo, but not much – the other one starts *'dum-du dum, dum-du dum'*, whereas on this one there's a bit where it goes *'oh'* right at the beginning before it starts – it was just one of those things where he said, 'Take it out,' and I said, 'No, it's great – leave it in.' It's just a much better recording in that the bass player when we did it the first time was different and not as good. Steve pushes it forward a bit more, gives it a bit more life."

"I'm not sure if that was a bit of a hangover on the *Freaks* era," says Nick, "one that had started being formulated before. It was one that we played a lot in that late Eighties, early Nineties era."

With *Separations* being far more of a keyboard-based album than any records Pulp had made previously, it's perhaps surprising that Candida had little input into the overall sound. "I really like Candida," says Alan Smyth. "She's lovely, we get on really well. She's just happy to play what she's required to – Jarvis will say, 'Can you do this?' and she does it, and 'Maybe a bit more like that,' and she'll do that. Jarvis played a lot on things like 'This House Is Condemned'. 'Love Is Blind', I played some of the keyboards on that and Jarvis played some of the organs, very deep organs. To be honest a lot of it was I'll play this, you play that, how about this. 'Don't You Want Me Anymore?', that string line at the beginning, I wrote that bit. That was just the way it worked. If someone came up with a good idea, and it was to everyone's approval, then it was in. Which is kind of how most albums work, really."

'She's Dead' is a typical slowed-down Pulp weepie that also shows how the band had developed from the *Freaks* era. The lugubrious melodic style is still there, but the use of layers of gorgeous keyboard sounds results in a far less overbearing effect. "You can certainly see the move on from 'They Suffocate At Night' to that," says Nick. "Obviously not a very exciting subject, you know, so we were trying to bring a bit of a dynamic thing to it."

The violin-soaked high drama of the title track follows, with perhaps one of the more extreme examples of the up-and-down dynamic structures typical of the album: from Russell's monumental screechy violin build-up, the song drops down to the definitive daft Portasound toytown rhythm. Not that Jarvis was in the mood for anything remotely jovial lyrically, of course – 'Separations' is a tale where the naïve belief that you can walk away from a relationship and a town and start life afresh somewhere new turns to loneliness and regret, and the drinks won't do a thing for you but revive some stupid memory – where the wind catches your words and the moon swallows them whole. Heavy stuff.

"In 'Separations'," says Alan Smyth, "Russell's violin playing when he'd got it right, it was like, '*Oh*, that is going to work, it's really good' – the scary, sort of frightening feeling. I like the washes of the cymbals – Nick was playing drums on that one and near the end he was hitting the cymbals with a stick to make them sort of swell like the sea. I said let's get one of those beater things just so you can get that real swwooooo sound. It's just little things like that that I remember."

'Down By The River' is the oldest song on the album, dating back to spring 1986. The gothic fairground feel of the song in its original form is replaced here with a dense, atmospheric feel that makes it one of the highpoints of the album. Candida supplies her inimitable backing vocals – "In fact she was really shy about that," remembers Alan Smyth. "Really, really shy – it took a lot of confidence boosting. That was one of the few when they were all in the room to play it at the same time, as I remember. We separated the sounds out as best we could, and then overdubbed it and repaired the mistakes."

The album splits neatly into two halves – while side one sounds like a logical progression from the old Pulp, albeit with a much more grandiose, upbeat feel, side two encapsulates Jarvis' and Steve's acid house-inspired electronic fixation. "I think acid house probably made a lot of people in bands re-evaluate what they were doing," says Jarvis. "I think that rock music had become very complacent – it thought it had a divine right to exist when it doesn't, it's got to remain interesting to retain people's interest. Acid house made me think, 'Do I still want to be in a band and if I do what do I want to do?' It was a bit of a prod, a little bit of a kick up the arse."[193]

Of course, the second half of *Separations* also reflected Pulp's desire to make disco music that you could *really* dance to, rather than music you could start dancing to, then have to stop or trip up thanks to sudden tempo changes, as with the band's previous nods in this direction. Alan Smyth: "With Jarvis and Steve being into the acid thing and I'd had the Barry White and Pet Shop Boys thing, I think they wanted the accuracy of the MIDI stuff. I remember when they'd been playing acoustic guitars I did an awful lot of muting on certain bits on the desk – I'd have groups of mutes set up so I could quickly silence any sort of background noise after they'd played the bits. There was a lot of button-pushing during the final mixes. But it was to add to the suspense really, 'cos if you have that background noise, it makes it more real. But that again, some of the other bits when everything comes in and there's a lot of live stuff happening it all seemed to work to make it exciting."

'Countdown' was given its original title, 'Death III', by virtue of being Pulp's third stab at a disco-style song, after 'Death Comes To Town' and 'Death II'.* It was also the most recently written song on the album, and the only one cooked up since Jarvis' move to London (the rest all being relics of Pulp's increasingly lean Sheffield years between 1986 and 1988). In it, Jarvis, the 18-year-old star of City School turned failing 20-something pop singer seems to be addressing his dwindling audience, attempting to convince us – and probably himself – that it's not time to write him off just yet: *"It's OK, you don't have to care . . . you owe nothing to me and if I messed it up baby, that's all up to me/ And if you go, then I won't follow, no/ So many times I've been thinking maybe I should/ No I'm gonna stay, I'm going to make my way/ I'm gonna get on through babe, I'm gonna make it all some day."*

"'Countdown' was about waiting for your life to take off," elaborates Jarvis, "and then realising maybe the countdown's never going to stop, you'll never reach zero – and in the meantime, the rocket's getting rusty and if it gets to zero, it wouldn't take off anyway."[194]

'My Legendary Girlfriend', the epic seven-minute centrepiece of the album, is a tremendous piece of music. It transfers Pulp's always-apparent skill for creating an atmosphere by expertly blending whispered monologues and striking musical dynamics from dark tales of weirdness on the streets of Sheffield to a far more accessible angst-stricken hymn to lust.

The song itself dates back to late 1987. "That was about my girlfriend that I'd had in Sheffield," explains Jarvis. "See, I've never liked to mix business with pleasure. I've always kept my private life separate from

---

* It's also the only song on the album not to feature Russell – the descending string sound at the start of each line comes from a 'found' cello sample.

music. So I've always gone out with girls who aren't interested in music, so people always asked me about my legendary girlfriend, because they'd never seen me with her."[195]

Live, the song was a lengthy, intense and semi-improvised *tour de force*, and quite tremendous in its own way, but Pulp had by now learnt that attempting to replicate a song's live strengths by simply going into the studio and playing it in *exactly the same way* was unlikely to produce a satisfactory result. Thus 'My Legendary Girlfriend', while it shared the same basic structure and content as its live counterpart, was produced in a vastly different way – sampled, programmed, edited and re-edited, the result managed to fulfil the Barry White-meets-Pet Shop Boys remit and the requirements of acid house modernity, while provoking many more comparisons. Foremost amongst these were the sleazy, wah-wah guitar-driven, semi-spoken funk of Isaac Hayes, and the Moroderised synth-driven disco of Donna Summer *circa* 'I Feel Love'. More importantly, at the same time it's also vastly different to all of these – a unique, truly original piece of pop music.

Alan Smyth: "It was very much one of the more programmed tracks. I think it gets more live as it goes on, but there's an awful lot of programming on it. We were using E-Magic Creator, which doesn't work like Cubase, where it's linear and you can see it happening – you used to drop down a list. Sometimes you weren't quite sure what was playing then. I was trying to remember where we got the strings from because they're quite nice. The bass, guitar and piano are all played, but we spent a lot of time trying to get it so it was fairly accurate. When they played it live it sounded like this but a bit looser, and I remember them wanting it to be precise. Which is why I did the thing with Nick, you know."

"'My Legendary Girlfriend' was always a set-finishing kind of thing," remembers Nick. "Used to go on a long time. We'd really get into that. When we started that it was always called 'Barry White Beat'. It had that stomping sort of sound, which I suppose that finished version of it is quite a lot gentler in a way – it's got that kind of atmospheric quality to it that I don't think it quite had in the live version. The live version was more like, 'Let's get going and let's keep on going till it stops,' you know. That sort of tension, certainly in the first half of it – then, balls out, let's rock.

"I never really thought of it at the time as a sexy song. He would mumble and kind of whisper nearly all the time in rehearsal because he never had the words. He'd mumble the tune and there'd be little snatches of lyric ideas, but the lyrics are always done at the last minute, like homework on the bus. The way it worked on the record was quite surprising, the way he came out with that tense, atmospheric sort of thing."

Alan Smyth: "At the start, you can hear this 'eeeoooowww', that was Jarvis, swinging a mike round his head in the other room with the amp turned up really loud. It was really hot and there was no air conditioning in that studio. Also there was still some metalworks underneath that used some kind of fucking heating device, and it used to get so hot. So he had his shirt off, swinging that mike round his head. But we softened it down, so it wasn't your kind of rock standard feedback – it just had this nice ambient touch."

Part of what makes the track stand out is Russell's use of wah-wah guitar, which has since been revived by so many acts it's become a cliché, but at the time was barely touched by indie acts and seen as a forgotten relic of the long-gone (and unrevived) disco age. "What you do with Russell," says Alan Smyth, "is you record him for the whole track, and then we would grab the bits we wanted with the sampler and move them to where they really worked. Because his style is . . . I don't know what you'd call it, actually. He's actually a fairly useless player, but at the same time he comes out with moments of absolute brilliance. He'll do a bit and it sounds *fantastic* – but it's in the wrong place. So me and Jarv would sit through, and we all disagreed on the bits, we'd say, 'Let's try that there,' and we'd just move them around and of course they worked as soon as you put them there – when you got them in place it was really like, 'Oh yes, that's brilliant.' 'Cos he's quite brilliant, the way he plays, but there were times when he just couldn't repeat it – he'd just hit it in a certain way. And he liked his old guitars that were cheap and nasty – like the Rosetti, which was a bugger to tune . . . it was full of stuff like that, making the album. Which actually made it far more interesting than a lot of other stuff I've ever done."

'Death II' revisits some of the same lyrical territory as the unreleased 'My First Wife', but in far snappier, more compact form. It's also a far more straightforward piece of songwriting than either 'My Legendary Girlfriend' or 'Countdown' – but no less programmed.

Alan Smyth: "'Death II' has that breakdown in the middle with the sort of ticketty box – that's one of the reasons why it sounds more automated – they did actually use these things on stage but they were playing live to them, and live you can get away with it and it just sort of goes on all the way through. Candida would be playing just the Casio I think so that did all those things, but on the recording the Casio was just part of the texture and the other instruments were put on top.

"One of the verses is virtually me playing everything. It's not something to boast about, I was trying different things and I played it back to them and they said, 'Ooh, we like that,' so it stayed, that was the end of it. The keyboard at the beginning is again that little Yamaha thing, through distortion and through something else I put it through, and I played it to them and they really liked the sound of it, probably because it was quite acid-y. But it was then gated quite hard – we stopped it at certain parts to create little gaps in it. It was actually very hard that, it doesn't sound like it would be, but it meant that I had to sit there going 'diddle-iddle-id', mute, 'diddle-iddle-id', un-mute. It sounds like a piece of piss today, but then it wasn't a piece of piss because of where the sound was coming from. It was coming from something that went 'doodle-iddle-iddle-iddle-iddle', up and down, and we had to put all the breaks in it. It was a really twee sound, and we sat there and discussed it and said, well, how about this, and how about that, and got the sound.

"It was actually a labour of love more than just sticking notes in MIDI things – there was very little MIDI action at all apart from the drums. I think even the 'bowm, bowm bowm' on 'Countdown' was played live."

If the preceding three tracks were a departure for Pulp, 'This House Is Condemned' was nothing short of astonishing – a full-blown attempt at creating an actual acid house track. You've got to take it in its chronological context," says Nick. "1989, house music was coming up, it was the new thing, and we were going out to these rave type do's, getting off our faces, and everyone had to have a stab at it in those days."

Not that the finished result sounded anything like acid house at all. Steve admits that "we were trying to find out about MIDI and didn't know what we were doing. We couldn't handle the technology, which was pretty sad."[196] Still, it's an impressive piece in its own right.

"That was totally automated," says Alan Smyth. "It was all MIDI stuff, and because it was quite early in the days of that, not many of us knew much about it, so we sort of struggled through. You'd sample a bass drum or get a drum machine and find the sound you wanted, then get it in the right place. Jarvis and Steve were in charge of the music. Russell's on it, but again we picked him up and moved him about lots. I've got a feeling it is a Russell song, but I've got a feeling that it didn't sound anything like that when it started! It came from Russell and we built it up around him."

"There's a telephone going off on that – that's an error," notes Nick. "Someone had left the telephone in the studio and it started ringing, and he just kept on. We played it back, heard the telephone and went, 'Sounds all right, that.' One of those accidents."

Steve Mackey had joined Pulp only nine months before, but he was making his presence felt – he'd managed to build up his part to the point at which, while most of the songs on the album had been written before he joined, he was one of the key players in their arrangement and production.

"He's quite a pushy character, in the nicest sense of the word, and quite forceful," reckons Alan Smyth. "He was definitely forcing his opinions, particularly about 'This House' and the sounds on stuff like that – not so much on the others, but definitely on the clubby, if you can call it clubby, type stuff. He was definitely fairly instrumental. But a lot of it is to do with humour, in a subtle way. On that one in particular, it was like, 'Well how about four bass drums there, and chuck that at it as well and see what that's like,' and if it made us smile then it got put in. It wasn't mathematical, it wasn't ever like that, any of the album. The mixes in those days were pushing faders, chinagraph pencils all over the mixing desk, and remembering to press the reverb button on channel 17 at that point in the song, and if you didn't you had to go back to the beginning. So you'd map your way through the song with different coloured pencils. It was a lot of time and effort, but at the end it was brilliant, I was really pleased with it."

With the recording complete, the final mixes were worked on in spare weekends over the next few months, whenever Jarvis and Steve could get to Sheffield. Alan Smyth: "They were in charge of the overall sound, and I was, so it was between us three. Jarvis would have the final say, Steve would put his tuppence worth in, and I'd do the same. We'd have these, not arguments, but discussions that would be quite involved, because to be honest making LPs is a serious business, and if you really think you're right you should stand up for it, which is what I'm like, and what they're like. I actually used an automated mixing desk for about eight channels of the sounds on most of these things – that could remember volumes and positions that made mixing a little bit easier. It's still definitely one of my favourites of their albums. To be honest I think of it as their first major album in that they had a lot more time, so that's why we took a lot of time, and perhaps it went a bit too far down the MIDI route, I don't know. But I'm still pleased and proud of it as a bit of work. The songs I love."

The album was completed in January 1990, and Sheffield DJs Parrot and Winston were put to work to produce remixes of 'This House Is Condemned' ("That, originally, was going to be the version that was on the album," says Alan Smyth, "but it was decided not. I've heard that no one liked it after a week or two!"). For a moment, it looked like everything was in place – record finished to everyone's satisfaction, line-up problems resolved, album ready to go. Was this the beginning of the new age? Er, no.

The whole of 1990 passed without any sign of a new Pulp record.

The plan of using the finished album as bait for other labels to swipe them from Fire's clutches hadn't quite panned out as intended – as Nick remembers, the band "couldn't get arrested. We'd send them out and the rejection letters would pile up." As a result, Pulp were in something of a tight spot: if they weren't going to return to Fire, and no one else would have them, who was going to pay for the £10,000 album they'd just recorded?

For Russell Senior, who had steered the band through six years of financial struggle and now had a family to support, it was the worst possible scenario, and came very close to being the final straw. "He was getting really worried," remembers Nick, "because if Fire have shelled out this £10,000 and we're saying we're not gonna have anything to do with that, they're gonna sue us for the cost that they've given FON to record this thing. It really was the lowest point because Russell was on the verge of saying, 'I've had enough, I don't want anything more to do with Pulp.' It was, 'I don't want to sign back with Fire' . . . [but] . . . no one else was going to sign us. He couldn't really see the future.

"So, it was the low-point, and basically we talked him round by saying, 'We've got this great set of music, it'd be a shame not to get it out.' You know, we might as well sign to Fire otherwise it'll be the end of it all. Then he came round, and we decided that we'd no other things on the table, and the only thing to do was to re-sign back with Fire. A group doesn't really exist unless it's getting records out, and we thought, 'There's no other offers.'"

So the band plumped for plan B, re-signed to Fire, chose 'My Legendary Girlfriend' as a first single from the album . . . and the wait began.

Russell: "You're eight months pregnant and somebody says it's due in a month. You know, when you've been working on an album, and to be told, 'Oh, next month . . . next month,' and this is like years, you know? And it eventually comes out. It was horrible."[197]

Meanwhile, there were no Pulp concerts till the end of the year. What was the point with no record to promote? With no money, two members in London and one in Manchester, it wasn't really logistically or financially feasible for them to continue gigging. "The nearest we ever came to splitting up was during the time I was at college," says Jarvis. "Because we were still waiting for the LP to come out, there didn't seem to be much point in writing new songs. Maybe we'd rehearse every three months or something. Crocodiles can slow their heartbeat to three times a minute if they're conserving energy, and that's kind of like what we were doing. But we weren't actually dead, we just looked like we were."[198]

Still, waiting interminably for your record to come out whilst doing a degree at a prestigious art college in London was, at least, preferable to doing the same thing on the dole in Sheffield. He'd escaped Mile End and returned to a squat in the more bearable Camberwell and, while the initial thrill of acid house had worn off, dance music had found an important and occasionally lucrative part in his life: thanks to his film course and old Sheffield connections, during 1990 he and Steve made videos for Nightmares On Wax and Sweet Exorcist, both acts on Rob Mitchell and Steve Beckett's fast-rising Warp label.

Pulp problems notwithstanding, Jarvis was already finding the Nineties a more comfortable place to live in than the trial that had been the Eighties. "The Eighties was a terrible time for lots of people, not just Pulp," he said in 1995. "If I'm in a bad mood, I really resent the Eighties. It should have been an important time, an era of exploration. I wanted it to be exciting because I was born in the Sixties and you look at the old films and it seems really good, all them parties. Now, suddenly it's your time and everything's gone matt black and grey and people are saying, 'Right, you've had yer fun, that's enough permissiveness, back to Victorian values.' Obviously, it's all a lot better now but then I won't get my twenties back. I want a refund."[199]

"The Eighties were generally a decade when a lot of people got excluded," he elaborated on another occasion. "It was basically an 'I'm all right, just look after yourself and fuck everybody else' kind of message that was coming through, so anything of any real worth was coming from the underground. Everybody had to dig themselves into the fall-out shelter and wait until the Eighties were over, and we're only getting past that now."[200]

Pulp were about to come up for air.

Chapter 9

"I always thought that if more people got to hear the music, it would give a greater indicator of whether it was what people wanted," says Nick Banks. "Outside quite a small band of Sheffield people, only people who delved into the dark recesses of indie music in the Eighties had ever heard of Pulp. So it was, 'Let's get people to hear this music and they can make their own mind up.' And when we'd made things like *Separations*, it was like, we've got something to really go for here. Listening to things like 'Little Girl', and *It*, which I thought was fantastic, I thought this is criminal that this music isn't getting to a wider audience. Because even if yourself and 100 other people think this is a fantastic record, because it's only that small amount of people that have ever heard it, then if it gets to a wider audience then 100,000 people could really like it."

By December 1990, Pulp's period in limbo was finally coming to an end. Fire was gearing up to release 'My Legendary Girlfriend' as a single, and the band played their first concert in almost two years, supporting World Of Twist at the Leadmill – something that rankled because of the amount of press attention World Of Twist had been getting, thanks in part, allegedly, to ideas they'd picked up from watching Pulp.

Nick: "We didn't want to play that concert because World Of Twist had stolen all our ideas, they were crap, and they'd completely taken this Pulp version four thing, and they'd got this great press hype, and all of us were saying, *'They've nicked our time!'* But then we thought, 'Well, we'll do this concert because it's another opportunity to get in front of people. If they're people who are into what's the new thing, we've got to get in there as well.' You can't just stick your head in the sand and go, 'We're not having owt to do with them, they've nicked all our ideas.' You know, you'd still be playing at the bloody Hallamshire. So we did that, year zero again. But then it was different."

After such a long time away from Sheffield, it was an unusual situation to be in: a band had been such a familiar sight in the city for most of the Eighties, and were now barely even returning heroes. "It was frighten-ing looking out into the audience," said Jarvis soon afterwards. "I hardly

189

recognised anybody and there were all these youngsters, mere children. I thought they would boo us off or something. There was certainly a bit of potential for disaster, a bit of a Spinal Tap situation. But they seemed to like us."[201]

Mark Webber: "They did one concert at the Leadmill and they'd got all these new songs like 'Legendary Girlfriend', 'Death II', and they were doing this sort of disco thing and people seemed to really like it, which I think was quite a novelty for them."[202]

So Pulp had managed to get to the stage of establishing their continued presence, and even got a reaction from an audience that suggested that there might just be a niche for them out there. Yet in the cold light of day, it was a very modest achievement: they'd managed to get to this stage plenty of times before – remember the *Sounds* Christmas party? – with nothing to follow it up.

This time, the follow-up came.

That Pulp's next concert, at the Leadmill on 16 March 1991, was filmed for broadcast by Granada TV as part of their *New Sessions* series suggested that something was afoot. The release of 'My Legendary Girlfriend' two days later confirmed it, thanks to a rave review from *NME*'s Stuart Maconie:

> *"Hold the front page! Stop the presses! This is what I thought working for the* NME *would be like. At the fag end of a very ordinary singles column, we grudgingly sling on one last disc . . . and it is fantastic! Do you hear me, you drop-outs! Fantastic! A throbbing ferment of nightclub soul and teen opera. World Of Twist play the theme from* Shaft *with Cathal Coughlan on vocals. Mysterious and grand. Maybe we could have done without the rude noises, but let's not carp. Steve Lamacq tells me that this is the worst song in their set. Which means that Pulp are the greatest rock'n'roll band in the world. I think."*[203]

"Somehow the *NME* picked up on it," remembers Jarvis, "and gave it Single Of The Week. That really was a turning point, basically, because, to our surprise, people started showing interest in us – we got requests to play again. And it was weird because when we were playing in Sheffield before we were like the daft kids playing to a bunch of adults, and somehow in the three-year interim, we went out and started playing and suddenly we were the adults playing to a bunch of daft kids!"[204]

Slightly less pleasing was the *Melody Maker*'s reaction to the single:

"The first 30 seconds of this single are very very steamy indeed . . . and then the damn fool spoils it all by opening his mouth another centimetre or two, and singing. Worse – singing like Bryan Ferry was today's news, instead of World Of Twist."[205]

Not *again*. "I can remember us being described in a number of papers as pale imitators of World Of Twist," says Russell, "which galled a lot because they used to come and see our shows, then went and did it in a rather burlesque way without the soul and intensity that we had. And we watched them zoom past us – you know, it made us angry. We were angry people – we were wound up, we were really bloomin' wired. But I think that's what made us good in a way."[206]

'My Legendary Girlfriend' may have been a bona fide Great Leap Forward – it sold over 1,500 copies, propelling Pulp into the lower reaches of the indie chart for the first time – but any sense that it was going to be a short, quick road to superstardom from hereon in was shortlived. The single was far easier to get a handle on than any slab of Pulp vinyl to date (thanks in part, ironically, to the reference point provided by World Of Twist), and was heard by many, many more people, but that didn't mean that Pulp actually *fit in* or anything. The musical agenda in 1991 was dominated by the shoegazing likes of Chapterhouse, Ride and Slowdive, whose non-existent stage presence, indecipherable lyrics and interminable feedback-drenched guitar noodling was about as far away from the Pulp ethos as was imaginable. Elsewhere, the remnants of the Madchester/ baggy explosion of a couple of years before were still around and, while bands like the Roses and the Mondays shared certain things with Pulp – a tenuous connection with rave culture, roots in northern grimness and an underlying aim of making brash, danceable pop music with colour and humour – the pilled-up, gonzoid likes of Shaun and Bez were a long way away from Jarvis' dry, dour presence and Pulp's more serious, grandiose musical vision.

Jarvis: "The only scene people were writing about was shoegazing, which was a very dismal, crap scene. Chapterhouse, Slowdive – we stuck out like a sore thumb basically because we were trying to put a show on. Instead of looking at our feet, we were looking into people's eyes."[207]

Russell: "People were very happy to hide behind their fringes and their guitars and mumble and all that, and we didn't hide behind that, 'Oh, you've sold out if you get in the charts.' We were the first people that I know of in that kind of scene to say, 'Look, we're failures, we're not selling records. And we believe in what we're doing and if we don't sell records, it means nothing because we've got something to say, and if people aren't listening to it, what's the bloody point?' It's musical masturbation if you just do it in your bedroom."[208]

Steve: "Come and see us and laugh at us, yeah. But it's certainly more interesting than four blokes in jeans and T-shirts stood on the stage. 'Cos that was a prevailing mood in those times – there was shoegazing, and then grunge – quite miserable times, I thought."[209]

On the upside, Pulp were getting more live work than ever before – in April and May, they played five London gigs, as many as they'd done in the preceding five years. With three members now living in London, Nick having by now joined Jarvis and Steve in Camberwell, concerts in the capital were logistically easier, and the band was far more accessible to the music press, which was just beginning to pay attention.

"I remember trying to get gigs at The Venue," says Nick, "I was dealing with them, and the only thing you had to send off was the video of 'My Legendary Girlfriend', and I'd ring up, and we might have got a concert out of that. 'Cos I was trying to be the one to try and push concerts, get things moving, keep the ball rolling.

"When 'My Legendary Girlfriend' got single of the week in *NME*, a spark seemed to go off with the journalists, and you genuinely felt at the time that there was more interest rather than it just peaking and then going back down to no one giving a toss. You got to a kind of peak and it didn't drop down, people were going, 'What's happening next?'"

"It wasn't like we were suddenly up there – we're talking about a one degree incline. But you kept hearing things in the *NME*, and you knew before that if there was something in the *NME* it'd be years before the next mention. But this was, not every week, but every now and again, something else'd get mentioned."

Nick was sharing Steve's squat and teaching Design Technology at the nearby Burntwood Comprehensive School for Girls. "It was a 14th floor squat in Camberwell, at a place called Crossmount House. I think it's been featured in a few episodes of *The Bill*. It was quite orderly, though. We didn't have any dogs on strings. I can imagine living with other band members could be a problem with certain groups. But we were never the kind of outfit where people would suddenly bring out acoustic guitars and singing 'Cwm-by-a' at 5am."[210]

While the music press was starting to paying attention, the public was following suit, with more and more coming to the gigs. And while the London appearances were a good sign of the general upward direction in which things were moving, Nick singles out a show that took place at the end of May in the provincial northern backwater of Halifax as an important turning point. "People going mental for the first time," he remembers. "Actual kids going mental, not just indie types with their notebooks watching because they'd seen a review – kids actually dancing and the PA falling down 'cos kids were going mental. We were coming off stage going, 'What was all that about? *What was all that about?!*' It really did feel like another step had been taken – people, generally kids, getting into the music and having a good time. Amazing."

The fact that Pulp were getting some national attention was just as well: although they were still a hugely popular local legend in Sheffield, the city was simply no longer taken seriously by the music business. "There was a time in Sheffield when the bands were just dire," remembers Ian Spence. "Lots of not-very-good guitar bands. But Pulp were different because you couldn't categorise them as a generic indie band. During the closed season, while the students were away, the Leadmill did a series of gigs to promote Sheffield bands. It was a series of five Sundays through the summer. My band This Machine Kills, which used a lot of synthesisers and drum machines with Pixies-esque guitar, used to get put on with Pulp because us and Pulp were the only bands that didn't fit into the category of standard rocky guitar bands.

"If you were in Sheffield, it was very hard to get any kind of industry attention, or get the music papers up. The record company would tend to be plugged into the Sheffield music mafia, which tended to revolve around the Leadmill and FON. I remember my band once were trying to get some people to come up from London – the Leadmill had organised a big bash for this crap guitar band that they'd got heavily involved in promoting whose name escapes me. Steve Lamacq from the *NME* had come up to see them, and you couldn't persuade him to come and see another band in Sheffield. Even though we'd had a couple of very good live reviews in the *Melody Maker* and *NME*, we couldn't get any record companies to come and see us. I think one came to see us once, and that was it. Dave Gilmour from Island Records, who subsequently went on to sign Pulp, came to see us once, and he was the only A&R man who took any interest in Sheffield.

"When Pulp first came back, they didn't have anywhere to practise, so we let them use our rehearsal rooms. There was a bit of paper in there that said 'Pulp love This Machine Kills', written by either Jarvis or Russell."

Pulp's live set was improving constantly, now opening with an atmospheric, semi-improvised monologue called 'Space' that generally featured the spectacle of Jarvis playing a Stylophone with the instrument behind his head, Jimi Hendrix-style. New songs like 'Live On', 'Babies' and 'She's A

Lady' were gradually sneaking in alongside the now-vintage *Separations* numbers, and the outlandish stage presentation was making a comeback – only this time, rather than multimedia performance art weirdness, we got gilt picture frames with second-hand shoes glued to them and painted gold, and silver footballs hanging from the ceiling. And why not?

"We went to Stonebridge Park Industrial Estate," remembers Nick, "because we'd found this place where those little shops that sell shitty 99 pence footballs got them from. Don't go to the shops, go where *they* get them from, and get them half-price! So we had these great big bags of silver balls, outside my mum's pottery warehouse where we rehearsed at Catcliffe, and outside venues, spraying them all silver – again spending more time on chuffing stage decorations than rehearsing. We were under-rehearsed because we were spending all the time making fucking mobiles out of old footballs!"

Even so, the mini-tour netted Pulp two more excellent live reviews, the London Subterania gig prompting *NME*'s Steve Lamacq to describe the experience as " . . . very grand, but edgy and earnest with it. Pulp are top entertainment, with lots lurking beneath."[211] Meanwhile, a triumphant homecoming gig at the Leadmill on May 25 was raved over by *Melody Maker*'s Ann Scanlon:

> ". . . *With a cool bassist, manic drummer, aloof organist and a guitar/violin player who looks a bit like the demented one in Sparks, Pulp are in a world of their own, a world that's been made all the more surreal by two enormous silver mobiles at the sides of the stage. On top of all this, of course, is Jarvis Cocker. Long, lean and dressed in jeans and a minute nylon sweater, he's a true star. Star as in classic entertainer, as in Barry White, Tom Jones and all those other gits who eventually make their way to Vegas. He's also a great songwriter who, at a time when most pop bands seem so illiterate that you sometimes wonder if you're ever gonna hear a memorable line again, is reeling off songs as structured as 'Separations' or as satirical as 'Love Is Blind'* . . ."[212]

What was significant about these reviews, and the other coverage that Pulp were receiving at the time, was that, unlike the occasional indulgent pat on the head that the press had afforded them in the Eighties, they were coming thick and fast from people whose opinions *mattered*. In 1991, if journalists like Steve Lamacq, Ann Scanlon, Stuart Maconie and Chris Roberts thought you were cool, then you were pretty much cool. The impossible had happened – Pulp were starting to win the approval of the indie taste-making establishment.

To say things were going well would be an understatement. In six months, Pulp had gone from a marginal, almost nominal existence to looking like they could be contenders for almost the first time ever. The fan base was growing, the press gave a toss, 'My Legendary Girlfriend' had been an unprecedented success, 'Countdown' had been remixed for the next single, *Separations* was lined up for release later in the year, and then, at the end of May . . .

And then, at the end of May, Rough Trade, Fire Records' distributors, went into liquidation.

Fuck.

The collapse of the company meant that Fire lost close to £100,000, nearly killing the label off. The 'Countdown' single was merely delayed for a couple of months because the release had been more or less ready to go prior to the crash, but other planned Fire releases, *Separations* included, were forestalled indefinitely. "When Rough Trade went under," says Dave Bedford, "I know the band were fairly gutted. We all were. For six months, we couldn't do anything."[213]

"It was kind of like limbo land," says Nick, "because we'd signed back to Fire and it was like, record's done – right. Let's get it out then. We've signed back to them, forget the past, let's get on with it. And then we were hit by another chain of disastrous events. To us, it was all [Fire] not wanting to put it out. It was like, artwork's got lost, you're gonna have to do all that again, get working on that. Rough Trade, who distributed all Fire's stuff, that all went tits up so there was no point putting records out with no one to get it out to the shops. It would be, that nightmare's sorted, let's get the record out, and there were several of these things, and you just couldn't believe that this was all happening to one label and one band. It just seemed to happen to the Fire-Pulp relationship. You were thinking, well, so-and-so's putting records out, other record companies are surviving, Fire's putting records out somehow, they just didn't seem to be interested in getting this Pulp record out. And we were like, we've spent a lot of time and effort getting this record sounding as good as we possibly could, and it was done, '89, this is top stuff, you know. 'Death Comes To Town' was a fantastic single, and if it had come out when it was recorded, life could've been skewed by a good three or four years. It's an absolute lost classic."

'Countdown' made its way into the shops in August. The lead track had been reworked at FON in May, with a slew of new overdubs added, to the point at which very little of the 1989 original remained – Russell's wah-wah guitar is all over the track, more than compensating for the fact that he wasn't even on the album version, and the synths pump along in a far more comfortable, dance-friendly way – as does Jarvis' new vocal, as dextrous and precise as the original was awkward and heavy-handed.

On the B-side, meanwhile, was Pulp's first-ever foray into electronic disco, 'Death Goes To The Disco' from 1987. As with the 'Master Of The Universe' single, the band seemed to be treating the release as an end-of-era statement – the new songs that were making their way into the live set were moving in a lighter, more organic direction than the disco angst of *Separations*. Kiss goodbye to the past with a smile . . .

The 'Countdown' single was well received, and its more conventional structure meant that it might even have been the first Pulp disco record to actually get played in discos. Yet, while sales were comparable to 'My Legendary Girlfriend', there wasn't the same sense of *WOW!* – rather than advancing Pulp's career any further, it didn't do much more than establish the fact that they hadn't gone away. Still, a little consolation never hurt.

Nick: "You can imagine someone in a nightclub or after a concert putting 'Countdown' on and kids enjoying it. Whereas with 'My Legendary Girlfriend', it's great to grab the attention of journalists, something you might put on when you get home. But here's a record you can bang on that might get people moving. So it could be seen as being up there and getting more attention."

By this time, Simon Hinkler had re-entered the Pulp circle: he was back in Sheffield after five years' service with The Mission, and, as well as busying himself working on the second Flight Commander album, he'd been handling Pulp's live sound. "My girlfriend was Suzanne Catty, a Canadian who used to work for Phonogram [The Mission's record company]. I took her to see Pulp at the Leadmill and she fell in love with them, and offered to be their manager – which she soon became."

Catty had heard Pulp's records through Simon, and was intrigued enough to want to travel up from London, where she was by now working for Hollywood Records, to see Pulp. "It's funny because I tried to see Pulp several times and something always came up – I even got food poisoning on my way to one of their gigs in Sheffield. I finally saw them at the Leadmill, and Simon was bugging me to manage Pulp or get them a deal or *something*! And all I could think of as I watched them play was the marquee at a stadium with 'PULP' in huge letters and the band on a stadium stage with all the toys . . . they just had all the magic. I loved the music already but seeing them live just blew me away. When I went into the office on Monday I tried to convince the Managing Director we should sign them and deal with Fire to get them out of the contract but . . . I left Hollywood a few months later and started managing Pulp pretty shortly thereafter."

196

The fact that Pulp had always proved unattractive to the mainstream music business thanks to their stubborn, square-peg-in-round-hole individuality was no deterrent to Catty's enthusiasm: "I had worked with Pere Ubu and Was Not Was, two of my all-time fave bands, so I knew that the quirky can be a hard sell, but when I saw Pulp I knew that I could get them to the top. I just knew absolutely, positively, the way you do sometimes. And I really wanted to see them at the top, in stadiums, on TV, getting rich. Pulp had *it*, Jarvis has *it* – that magical star quality. Live on stage with all their home-made decorations and stuff . . . magic, sheer magic."

Nick: "She was this Canadian – don't call her American! – go-getter, ball-breaker, person who knew people in the record industry. She came to see us, and she was really, really over-the-top. And for us, who'd had Russell with his A4 clipboard, I was thinking, 'This is what we need – someone who knows the people down in London, who can see the vision from an outside point of view.' Whereas he might be more interested in making sure that all the monitors have got the right tinfoil on, she was going, 'Come on, I can see you playing to 10,000 people a night!'

"So basically she got involved as our manager. And she started firing off letters and getting people in London who were proper music business to know about Pulp, some of whom had heard the name, some of whom had no idea about us. She got the people like Nigel Coxon and Dave Gilmour [of Island Records] up from London to see Pulp. Certainly Dave Gilmour came to see us a lot of times, and he was really like, 'These are fantastic!' after every concert, you know."

While Island Records were beginning to sniff around the group, in September 1991 Pulp found themselves making their return, at long last, to the BBC. Since the heady days of that first Peel session back in 1981, Pulp's radio airplay had been virtually non-existent, but the press attention and live activity that had been happening since the release of 'My Legendary Girlfriend' meant that the nation's alternative radio programmers were slowly beginning to pay attention. It wasn't quite time for a return to the bosom of Peel, though – instead, the band had been asked to play a live session for the slightly less celebrated *Hit The North* show on Radio 5.

In those days before its remodelling as a news/sport station, Radio 5 was fulfilling an ill-defined 'youth' remit, the crowning glory (or one redeeming feature) of which was *Hit The North*, a superb alternative music show broadcast live from Manchester and presented by Mark Radcliffe, who went on to front a near-identical (and now legendary) programme on Radio 1 for the middle years of the Nineties. For the programme, the band ran through excellent renditions of 'Space', 'Death II', 'Live On', 'Countdown' and 'My Legendary Girlfriend',* but the real highlight was the interview segment with Jarvis, reacting with horror when Radcliffe reminded him that Pulp had been going 12 years – "You don't have to tell everybody that, you've got me feeling like a clapped-out old get down here" – and characterising Sheffield as being "a bit like a skip, because it's just full of rubbish – but personally I quite like looking through skips because you can find some good stuff there sometimes."214

Another milestone came in October when Pulp were asked to play their first-ever overseas concerts: two gigs in France as part of an annual festival run by French music magazine *Les Inrockuptibles*. The dates were with Blur and Lush, and the Paris concert was broadcast live to the whole of France. "Going to France was utterly, utterly amazing," says Nick. "I'm not quite sure how it all came about, but we were so, so excited. Playing a concert outside the UK, we were, like, *Yes!* We were still in a Transit van, but this time with windows and seats. We were playing with Blur and Lush – you know, proper rigs and all this kind of stuff. And we turned up on the first day in this Transit with all this shitty equipment piled in the back, and started fannying around with all these silver balls on fishing wire. They'd got all this swanky equipment, they're just like, '*What's fucking going on here?!*' Ten minutes before you're going onstage, you're holding each other up on stepladders fixing these things on the ceiling, the audience is all there going, 'What's going on here?' you know. But they seemed to really like it, all the reviews were good. I think we were doing 'She's A Lady' quite a lot then, because we had the double Stylophone."

Anyone who was concerned that Pulp's charms might not translate to a non-English audience needn't have worried: with the help of Jarvis' highly suspect schoolboy French ("Il chanson s'appelle '*Ma Petite-Amis Legendaire*'"), Pulp won the audiences over, hung out with the stars (Steve was apparently the recipient of a round of drinks bought by Steve and Gillian from New Order), and returned, triumphant, to England to be greeted by a rave review of the Paris show in the *NME*. "They're thoroughly entertaining," wrote Gina Morris. "People are dancing, or crying with laughter, others stare in bewilderment at the weedy Englishman and his wayward French accent. If anything, this festival proves to be Pulp's most difficult examination yet: touring with two cool, established indie bands and in front of an audience distanced by a different language. But Pulp don't even see the hurdles – Jarvis' pidgin French and Elvis moves

---

* During the soundcheck for the session, an amazing live version of 'My Legendary Girlfriend' was recorded, and later released as a limited edition 7″ single on Bob Stanley's Caf label.

transform him into a hero. By the end of the evening the French love him. VIVA PULP!"[215]

As Steve recalls, it was an event that raised Pulp's game another notch: "I can remember thinking when we got to France for the first time, if nothing else I've been in a band that has toured around Europe or I've experienced what being in a band is supposed to be about."[216]

The band's next concert, at Subterrania in London, was no less of a triumph. "To hell with careful qualification," wrote Sharon O'Connell in *Melody Maker* afterwards. "Pulp are magic and Jarvis Cocker is a star."[217] Graham Lineham, writing for the fledgling *Select*, meanwhile, practically exploded with praise:

> *". . . We have a bass player in a turtleneck sweater and a haircut that has* no rightful place in this world. *We have a guitarist, Russell Senior, who looks like all The Velvet Underground crossed with David Byrne. But floating above all this is the religious experience that is frontman Jarvis Cocker.*
>
> *Jarvis wears clothes so unfashionable his body seems to be revolting against them. His jacket looks like a sheep turned inside out. His jeans travel so far up his back they form a relief map of the lower part of his body (hubba!). He dances with the same graceless beauty that Nicholas Cage displayed in* Wild At Heart *– all karate kicks and handchops. And he's forever* pointing at something.
>
> *Visually, Pulp are so fascinating that it's a shock when your mind returns to the music. They are The Fall in Las Vegas with the added bonus that Jarvis, unlike Mark E Smith, can form whole sentences. 'Space' features Jarvis on stylophone, sounding suspiciously like My Bloody Valentine. 'Separations' opens with some* Fiddler On The Roof *style grief from Russell's violin and then switches, without warning, to Candida Doyle's playschool synth which, in technological terms, seems one step up from the stylophone.*
>
> *At a time when you'd require more than Vicks Vapo-Rub to keep up with the current bpm rate, Pulp are a flaming spaceship returning to a time when dancing wasn't just exercise with cigarettes. They are such a good time you might just die watching them.*
>
> *And Jarvis Cocker, in case you missed the clues, is God."*[218]

And it wasn't simply a case of the press finally starting to catch on to Pulp (although the ball that had started rolling with 'My Legendary Girlfriend' meant that this was definitely a factor) – Pulp were undeniably getting better. Thanks in part to Dave Bedford (the one Fire employee the band had a good relationship with) getting them a booking agent for the first time, and in part to Suzanne Catty's enthusiastic hustling, they played more gigs in 1991 than any year before, and as a result the band was tighter than ever. And Jarvis' onstage presence, which in the past had wavered between charismatic genius and apologetic self-deprecation, had begun to develop over the course of the year into something mighty. A definite change in attitude had taken place, exemplified by Jarvis' death-defying rise to the occasion in France.

"One thing that would infuriate me about him," says Russell, "was that he's always been a brilliant performer but he used to undermine it by taking the piss out of himself. He'd work up the audience and then be self-effacing and say, 'We are crap.' If there was a little sound problem, he'd go over to the sound engineer and threaten to smack him, and other ridiculous little absurd theatrics that didn't look dark and intense but kind of stupid. [In mid-1991] . . . things had built up but then fizzled out a bit, and we were still playing depressingly sad gigs to seventy people in London, and we were just shooting ourselves in the foot with that attitude.

"I almost had this argument with Jarvis, being pissed off with him for not being a proper pop star, and it seemed like the group would split up at that time. And then, for some reason, it started feeling pretty good, pretty much overnight. He stopped doing the 'I am a crap, speccy git', and seriously tried to be a proper pop star, and sexy, rather than a parody of a proper pop star. I think he knew that we couldn't just carry on in our own little underground way, held together with a rubber band, so he started taking it seriously."[219]

1991 had been Pulp's best year yet. For the first time in a long, long while they actually looked like contenders again – a fact that hadn't escaped Island Records A&R man Nigel Coxon. Coxon, a former employee of Island Music (the label's publishing arm, where he'd had a hand in signing Lush, Carter USM and Massive Attack), had recently moved to Island Records and already added the likes of PJ Harvey and The Cranberries to the label's roster. He'd first encountered Pulp earlier in 1991. "I'd seen them play a couple of shows and I had those two singles. So I was aware of them and I was sort of keeping tags on them, but another scout called Dave Gilmour had seen them play in Sheffield and said, 'You should check them out again, they were great.' So that's when I got to see them again.

"I just thought Jarvis was an amazing performer, really, and blew me away. They seemed to get a little roll going in '91 on to '92. The first couple of times I saw them were in really strange environments like a student sit-in, and some weird pub somewhere, but the Sheffield shows, they were capable of selling out the Leadmill, obviously being local heroes. So the first time I saw them do that kind of show it was just like, Jarvis was amazing, plus they had some great songs – I think they'd just written 'Babies' then."

Island were tentatively interested, but not quite ready to snap Pulp up yet. The band were left in a frustrating position - Fire Records may have got 'My Legendary Girlfriend' and 'Countdown' into the shops, but as far as Pulp were concerned they weren't providing the push that they needed and deserved – and there was still no sign of *Separations*. The way things were going, Pulp had no intention of making another record for Fire, but with no one else willing to sign them, they were still stuck on the launchpad.

"The relationship with Fire was back to – well, even sourer than before," says Nick. "We didn't want to sign with them anyway but we didn't see any alternative. But it was taking so long for *Separations* to come out, by the time it came out we weren't on speaking terms whatsoever. So we knew that we had to get away from them. Suzanne Catty said that obviously they are incompetent idiots, or sinister madmen, or a bit of both."

One minor hitch prevented them from walking away from Fire – they were only one album into a five-album deal. However, Catty believed the band had definite grounds for divorce: "Russell had wooed me to manage Pulp in part because he thought that I could help them out of Fire Records; they also knew that the contract was bad. I think I remember they told me they had made the deal under 'duress' to pay the FON studio bill. So I got some legal advice and really Fire had breached the contract by not supplying accountings so we notified them that we wanted to leave.

"You can imagine what Clive was like. There was a PR guy named Dave at Fire that the band really liked and I know they thought he would help them, but of course he was really loyal to Fire not Pulp. Anyway, after we notified them, Fire did actually come forth with some financial statements within the terms of the contract, and their view, of course, was that Pulp could not leave and that they hadn't breached. But as we all know, a contract isn't worth the paper it's written on in many cases and the band certainly did not have legal advice before they signed, so we felt pretty confident in our position. Plus something had to move and Pulp were stagnating, so I put the fire under Fire."

Enter Gift Records. "We were friends with the people who ran Warp Records in Sheffield," explains Jarvis, "and they were wanting to start a bit of an indie label off, called Gift. Because we knew 'em and that, they said, 'Well, why don't we release some things by you?'"[220]

Warp was run by Rob Mitchell and Steve Beckett, who had first crossed paths with Pulp half a decade earlier when playing in Lay Of The Land. More recently, Jarvis and Steve had worked on videos for various Warp artists. "They were in a situation where they couldn't go forward with the deal that they had with Fire," Mitchell told Radio 1 in 1998, "and Island Records were hovering around in the background but weren't quite ready to commit for them, and we really loved the new songs they were doing and wanted to put some of their records out. So we ended up putting out three singles. There was a sense at that time that the band were very close to breaking point. They were in a deal they didn't want to be in, they knew what they wanted to be doing, they had all their dreams and aspirations in front of them, but there was just this block between where they were and where they needed to be. And you could sense that if too many other things went wrong, it felt like they would give up."[221]

Warp/Gift was the ideal vehicle for Pulp to take their first steps away from Fire in that, while it was an established label with a proven track record, it was still a relatively small independent. "With Fire," explains Catty, "we were playing hard ball. We'd thrown down the gauntlet and knew they were not going to do anything if we released a record on an indie label, only if it was a major label, otherwise they figured it would just help sell the back catalogue. Sheffield is a small town musically so FON, Warp, Pulp were all family and everyone believed in Pulp and they also believed in me so the Warp single was truly a Gift."

Conveniently, it transpired around the same time that Island, through Nigel Coxon, were willing to finance the recording of some new demos. "It's quite traditional if you're a record company and you're interested," explains Coxon, "to demo some songs if you've seen them, just to be able to live with them." The band could therefore kill two birds with one stone – they could record four songs as a demo tape, then use the same recordings as the basis of the Gift single.

The session took place at FON over three days at the end of January 1992, with Simon Hinkler producing. "That session was difficult," remembers Simon. "A lot of time got wasted, because there was too much of a committee putting in their conflicting opinions of how it should sound. My friend and often Pulp sound man, Mike Timm was there to help me out with the SSL mixing desk and drum sound. He wanted everything close-miked; Jarvis wanted everything distance miked; I wanted a combination of the two. We were against the clock and wasted a whole day fucking about with the drum sound alone.

"The band hadn't done any pre-production rehearsals so they spent a lot of time experimenting with overdubs. Russell had problems playing the violin part properly, and it ended up being sampled and flown in – which also took far too long. So it ended up being a rushed compromise, and consequently not great."

The recording sessions may have been a source of frustration, but the music that resulted still bears testament to the strength of the new material that had been slowly seeping into the band's set during 1991. 'O.U. (Gone, Gone)', which the band had chosen as the single's lead track, was the clearest possible evidence of how the band had changed since *Separations*: with its gloriously cheesy ascending chord sequence (recycled from '97 Lovers' and reckoned by the band to sound like the theme music to an Open University programme – hence the song's title), insistent one-note bassline and deranged Stylophone stabbing, it was as daft and exuberant as the old songs were severe and glum. The likes of 'Countdown' and 'Death Comes To Town' might have been pop songs, and pretty good ones at that, but next to this they were virtually funeral dirges.

"I can never remember any deliberate policy of 'We've had enough of all that dour rubbish,'" says Nick, "but there was a kind of thing of trying to write pop songs. But it's very difficult to write a pop song that isn't kind of cheesy – so much easier to write a song that's down in the dumps. Especially with the idiots in the group, scraping on violins. Very, very difficult. So I suppose in a way I'm contradicting myself; there could have been a conscious decision to try and write more accessible music, 'cos I suppose we'd have a bit of success [with poppier material]. It did take place over a long period of time – it wasn't like we woke up one morning and decided to write a pop song. But after things that'd had a great reaction, like that Halifax thing, we thought that if we can write more songs to get the kids doing *that*, it's going to be better and it's going to be more fun to do."

'Space', meanwhile, was another Atmospheric Pulp Monologue in the tradition of 'Goodnight' and 'My Legendary Girlfriend' – indeed, it had been a part of the live set as early as 1988. To a backdrop of otherworldly 'Telstar'-style sound effects, Jarvis intones a piece that seems to combine his lifelong obsession with outer space and his experience of, and eventual disillusionment with, the Acid House phenomenon – both of which, for Jarvis, represented a blurring between fantasy and reality that ended in sad, sobering lessons.

"I think space is something that a lot of people our age are fascinated with," he told *Volume* magazine at the time. "I'm not a sci-fi buff, don't get me wrong. It's just that I remember when I was young watching the first man on the moon. We were allowed to stay up late. And at the same time there were all these Space Annuals and *Star Trek* on the telly. I suppose it all blurred together, so you weren't sure what was real and what was fantasy. The people at NASA were saying that by 1984 or something, we'd all be living on different planets or whirring around in Space Stations, and we believed them completely. There didn't seem to be any reason why we wouldn't.

"I suppose I realised that it was all a fantasy when I was 22. I didn't have any money and there wasn't much coming in from the band so I was selling off all my belongings. I distinctly remember tromping around Sheffield with a yellow portable washing machine, trying to sell it to get the money for some food. It was pissing down and I thought to myself, 'Jarvis, you were supposed to be living in space by now.' It was pretty obvious by then that it wasn't going to happen. You have to stop living your life for the future."[222]

The song seems to reflect on the feeling that, with rave culture, there was a momentary, real, unexpected sense of lift-off: *"Tonight, travelling at the speed of thought, we're going to escape to the stars. It doesn't matter if the lifts are out of order or the car won't start, we're rising up above the city over forests and fields, rivers and lakes into the clouds and high above us the whole universe is shining a welcome."* But after the honeymoon wears off, the drugged-up, loved-up brave new world is an ultimately hollow experience – *"Oh the stars are bright, but they don't give out any heat. The planets are lumps of rock floating in a vacuum. Yeah, space is cold when you're on your own"* – so he decides to come down and be Jarvis Cocker: *"Now I know space is OK, but I'd rather get my . . . kicks . . . down . . . below . . . come on . . . oh yeah . . . Get Down!"* The clunking, Stylophone'n'2-note guitar rock-out, funky in that peculiarly Sheffield sort of way, that comes next is irresistible.

Also recorded during the FON session, and earmarked as possible A-sides for future singles (it wasn't certain at the time when the band would be able to afford to go into the studio again), were run-throughs of two more new live favourites: 'Live On' and an early attempt at 'Babies'. "I always thought 'Babies' should have been the A-side," says Simon Hinkler. "It's so obviously *the* single from that session, whereas 'O.U.' was probably the worst of the bunch. Jarvis enjoyed being difficult about such things."

'Live On', meanwhile, was destined to be another of those pesky Great Lost Pulp Songs. A staple of the live set through 1991 and 1992 (and the occasional cause of much audience hysteria therein), while not quite of the order of pop jewels like 'O.U.' or 'Babies', it's an undeniably terrific song. "That was always going to be the Big Single," reflects Russell. "We were saving it until we had enough money to record it properly, and then it was going to be the huge number one hit. But somehow it never seemed to fit, and eventually it got superseded."

Musically, the song provides a direct link between *Separations* and the New Pulp: built round a thumping disco beat, a three-chord Farfisa riff and loads of wah-wah guitar, it's a progression from the disco dramas of 'Death II' and 'Countdown', but with a fuller, poppier, more direct feel. The lyrics are a more straightforward, personal portrait of the struggle to move on from a dead relationship, albeit more recognisable and less heavy-handed than the older songs, with a truly classic opening line: *"I woke up in the morning, I was still alive/ The mirror says I'm fifty-five years old/ But if I don't look that way, I'm gonna do OK/ I'm gonna last another day without your love."* Before long, the song explodes into a huge, desperate chorus: *"Oh but I dreamt of you last night, and the world split into two/ I tried to play some stupid records but they're all singing about you/ I can't live on never knowing where my soul is going when I die/ I can't last another day without your love . . ."*

Sadly, the rather weedy-sounding rendition of the 'Live On' that was laid down at FON wasn't quite the sensation that the song was live. "We never felt we could capture its strength as a rumbustious live song," says Nick. "Never seemed very exciting. It was very exciting to play, the audience seemed to get excited, but on record it never seemed to get very exciting. So it just never made that transition, that's just what happens sometimes."

Disappointments aside, with 'O.U.' and 'Space' picked for the single and Gift ready to release it, things were looking good. The only obstacle to overcome now was the rather weak production on 'O.U.' – in common with the other tracks from the FON session, it was a serviceable enough run-through of the song, certainly livelier and more natural-sounding than the robotised *Separations* tracks, but just lacking that special *something* that marked the difference between, on one hand, a good recording of a good band playing a good song, and on the other, a great pop record.

The solution was to give the track to an external producer to remix it. The man for the job, it was decided, was Ed Buller: the ex-Psychedelic Fur keyboardist had begun to make his name as a producer with his work on Spiritualized's *Laser Guided Melodies* album, and had recently been working in the studio with Suede, another group of hotly tipped glam-poppers who were shortly to release their first single. "I'd heard his production on the Spiritualized LP," says Jarvis, "and he sounded able to work with keyboards, rather than concentrating on guitars. We were very impressed – he transformed the song."[223]

"Simon Hinkler had started 'O.U.'," says Nick, "and it kind of went all right, but the end product wasn't as exciting as we wanted it; no kind of life to it. I suppose because *Separations* did have more of an electronic, perfect kind of form to it, you had to kind of keep up the standards, and 'cos we'd been playing concerts where people had been physically moving, which is a good thing, you wanted to try and keep that going, so a record had to be exciting. Simon Hinkler was in a successful group, been in lots of recording studios, and he was your mate, but he wasn't a dedicated producer like Ed Buller was. So it went down to London, he did this remix, he didn't do a great deal to it, but he got it sounding more exciting."

Determined to make a splash with Pulp's first post-Fire single, Suzanne Catty and Gift enlisted the help of an independent radio plugger, Scott Piering, and the PR firm Savage & Best, whom the band had met through their friendship with Lush, and in the early months of 1992 were successfully engineering a wave of hype and anticipation for Suede.

"John Best [of Savage & Best] was one of the first of the people that are still there now to actually come on board," says Nick. "They were kind of doing it in a sort of 'Love the group, want to work with you, I'll do your press for free', as they knew that we'd employ their services when the proper record company had come on board."

"Like everyone else in the industry," says John Best, "when I was working as a journalist, I'd made a snap assessment of Pulp in 1986, and thought they were all right. Miki [Lush vocalist and John's girlfriend at the time] had played with them and Blur in France, and came back saying Pulp were brilliant, and had come on a long way. When we met, I found them more accommodating with people than most other bands, with humility and hunger. After being unsuccessful for that long, you can't hold that many airs and graces. They were happy for the attention."[224]

By this time, the band's internal chemistry was beginning to change – surely thanks in part that the line-up had now been stable for a whole three years, and the sense of Pulp as a unit was therefore stronger than it had been for a long time. "Russell was still quite at the fore," remembers Ian Spence, "but I think his influence waned a bit in the Nineties compared to what it had been before. But he did do a lot of the organising – for a long time, it was always Russell's and Jarvis' band, and the others would seem to be a bit replaceable.

"At first when they came back, things didn't seem to be going too well for them, but then they started to get some good press. And they got a lot of help from the Leadmill – Graham got them a lot of quite high-profile gigs. I remember Jonny Thatcher from the *NME* wanted to do an 'On' piece for them, but they were too old! So sometimes that history made it a bit difficult for them, but when they did that series of singles on Gift, that was the biggest factor in moving them forward, the fact that they financed those singles for them and got them a bit of national attention. They tried to do the same for people like the Various Vegetables, but the records weren't strong enough. But that was the point, for me, when Pulp seemed to have a bit more control over their sound."

As if to emphasise the beginning of a new era, the sleeve artwork for the 'O.U.' single, designed by Jarvis' old Sheffield friend Martyn Broadhead, depicted the old purple and white Pulp logo as used on the 'Countdown' sleeve being progressively obscured by the title 'O.U.' in marvellously garish Seventies-esque orange – the turning over of yet another new leaf. The countdown had begun. Again . . .

Chapter 10

By the spring of 1992, the indie landscape in Britain was far more amenable to Pulp than it had been a year previously. Shoegazing and baggy were being supplanted by a wave of young bands that shared a brighter, poppier aesthetic, often with a slight retro-Seventies edge in one way or another. It wasn't really a movement as such – the similarities between the likes of Cud, St Etienne, Lush, Suede and Pulp were vastly outnumbered by their differences. However, the common threads that the bands shared, along with the fact that some of them tended to rub shoulders in the same Camden boozers and occasionally be spotted at the same gigs and parties, was enough for the music press to lump them together into a 'scene', initially under the banner Lion Pop, and subsequently, Crimplenism.

Stuart Maconie summed up the phenomenon in *Select* a year and a half later: "Pulp and their ilk represented elegantly light refreshment from the staple stodge diet of American grease-monkeys and the embarrassing fag-end of 'baggy'. It came to be called Crimplenism. A kind of movement (although many of the bands had not so much as shared a crème de menthe and eggnog) which emphasised fun, the shared British experience, cool, a weird, second-hand glamour. And Pulp's music, still tiptoeing daintily along the line that separates dark, crazy things from brash and shiny chart pop, exemplified it, even if it was a myth. Pulp were unashamedly closer in spirit to Neil Young the Manchester City footballer and *Space 1999* than Neil Young the free-world rocker and *Wayne's World*."[225]

"It was the start of various journalists desperately trying to stick us in with other groups," says Nick. "There was this Crimplene Scene, Lion Pop, Lion Rock kind of thing. They always like to stick groups in together, stick them in a pigeonhole, and we just didn't really take much notice – it was like, 'Crimplene? We never wear crimplene, it's rubbish!' It was always a myth that Jarvis just wears man-made fibres – he doesn't, unless it's desperately necessary.

"So we didn't feel we were moving towards what people liked, but in hindsight, it feels like people were moving toward what we were offering. It was good because we didn't feel so much out on a limb. It was stoking the ashes, getting some oxygen underneath it. We never really took much heed of it, but it was helpful not to kind of go, 'Oh, we want nothing to do with this, it's disgraceful!', but just keep quiet about it and carry on with our less lonely furrow."

The fact that Pulp were beginning to be seen as part of something, rather than the perennial underachieving outsiders they'd always been, is reflected in the fact that, several weeks before 'O.U.' made it to the shops, it had already been Single Of The Week in *Melody Maker* – alongside Suede's début, 'The Drowners'.

> *"This is colossal. And already I'm torn between these two inspirational records. Oh hell, be unfaithful to both of them simultaneously. Move to a love nest on the sea-front and see them on alternate evenings. And have Thursdays off to get your hair done.*
>
> *'O.U.' (Oh you? Open University?) is three minutes of staggering poptasm. Sharing a similar disdain for the age as Suede (which, of course, makes it feverishly modern), its prime difference is that it is out of control. Jarvis Cocker's love-life brims, it seems, with the elation that comes with phenomenal doubt, pain and failure. 'Cherish and be damned' is Pulp's implicit motto, while Suede are more the 'Damn and be cherished' types.*
>
> *Everything is post-austerity space-race melodrama with an orchestra of organs. Your whole wardrobe flashes before you – embarrassing corduroys, hats and satin tabards – as the night, we are told, is ending. 'He wanted her undressed/ He said he loved her/ She tried to look impressed'. Suddenly, we have lift-off into the outer universe of desire. Turn it up loud enough and the climbing chord sequence will induce the sort of nervous laughter you get on a big dipper. It's a giddy world here and Pulp have captured it in all its radiophonic (in)fidelity in jaw-dropping luv-o-rama.*
>
> *Again, I say you can stuff kitsch, you can bury glamour in a pit. Give me life. Real life in all its heart-stretching, sweat-drenched, love-sick splendour and swirl. These records have it even if they like to disguise the fact.*
>
> *Pulp have been at this kind of thing for ages and their hard times show through and help make this record important and desperate to be heard. As all great pop records should be. Let's hope this is the one that finally gets the message across to the rest of the universe, eh Jarvis?"*[226]

The acclaim was unanimous. *Vox* reckoned the record to be "Irritating, hilarious, inspiring, camp … That godawful synth riff! That nerve-shattering violin noise! Those ace lyrics! A Pulp record is like going to the dentist: you squirm and protest but you know it's good for you in the long run."[227] *NME* opined that, "The glam-shackle Pulp make you think of spaceships and tower blocks and trains. Marvellous."[228] Even *Smash Hits* got in on the act, awarding the single three out of five and commenting on the "cheesy organ, 'attractive' frontman Jarvis Cocker's demented vocals, and the sound of someone falling into a pond playing the synth are the main features of the latest release from this deranged Sheffield group who're heralding the return of The Horrible Jersey in Pop. It'll never be a hit in a million years, but that doesn't seem the point."[229]

That last sentence was unfortunately, if perhaps unsurprisingly, an accurate chart prediction. It's also true, however, that that wasn't really the point. Suzanne Catty: "'O.U.' was a tool, a way to get media to the gigs which otherwise wouldn't even get reviewed. I had been plugging the record companies for months, had met with nearly every A&R department, and we were starting to get a turnout of industry people to gigs, more than just the talent scouts – the heads of A&R were now showing up so we had a major vibe happening. However, critical acclaim means nothing after so many years without other success, so 'O.U.' was designed to give us some airtime, get gigs mentioned, get gigs reviewed, see if Radio One would play it – they did – and give Pulp presence in the market. It was never about charting or selling lots; it was about focusing attention and starting the final stages of the plan."

And it worked. As Nick says, "Just getting into *Smash Hits* gives a good indication of the way things were moving."

So does the fact that, when the band launched the single by releasing hundreds of helium-filled Pulp balloons from Devonshire Green in Sheffield (each balloon had a ticket attached, promising a prize for the one returned from furthest away), the press bothered to come and watch them. Nick again: "We had a big feature in the *NME*; they had the photographs of us doing the balloon launch. So it was like, we are now doing things for real – people are now coming up from London with a photographer and covering some stupid kids letting off balloons on Devonshire Green. Unheard-of."

The single was promoted by Pulp's first-ever proper tour, a 10-date jaunt at the end of May that saw Mark Webber promoted from occasional helper-out, hanger-on and number one fan to the lofty position of Tour Manager. "I don't know how this occurred," says Jarvis, "because he's not the most forthright of people, and the idea of him going up to a bloke who ran a club and demanding money is quite amusing to me now."[230]

Mark: "After being in big businesses, [Suzanne Catty] had all these ideas about how things should be and it started with her saying that they needed a tour manager. They decided that it should be me as Russell and I used to take the money after the concerts and deal it all out. So, I was tour manager, and I didn't know anything about it at all – I made it up as I went along! But, what I did know, after going around and interviewing all these bands for my fanzines, was that tour managers were generally bastards, so I tried the opposite approach and was really nice to everyone – and it worked out well! I once made one girl cry though, because she wouldn't move our drumkit, but that was the only time!"²³¹

The increased visibility that the tour gave Pulp was boosted by major features in *NME* and *Melody Maker*, both of which seemed to be more in tune with the band than previous pieces, emphasising less on the alleged wacky novelty angle of the band and more on the Jarvis Phenomenon – significantly, Jarvis was now being presented as the main group spokes-person, rather than doing interviews together with the rest of the group. "Pulp are the most gratifying project we've ever worked on," says John Best, "because journalists never gave a shit at first . . . We felt that early interviews and pictures involving all of them had only cluttered their image, with garbled chatter about crimplene and spangles and chopper bikes and out-of-sync Seventies nostalgia coming through. People thought Jarvis was a comedian and taking the piss but knowing him personally, we knew there was a lot more going on than such surface fripperies. Lyrically, he had great conviction so it was very frustrating to talk to the *NME* and hear them described as Seventies revivalists like Denim, like they were kitsch. Jarvis had a kernel of something more heartfelt."²³²

The band's repertoire was, by this time, moving on from the now-ancient *Separations* material: a handful of songs from the album remained in the set, but were being superseded by the likes of 'Razzmatazz', 'Your Sister's Clothes' (a wonderfully vicious sequel to 'Babies') and 'The Boss'. 'She's A Lady' was a reliable set opener, 'O.U.' a fitting climax, and 'Babies' a predictable highlight.

Shortly before the tour, the band had recorded a new set of demos, this time at Island Records' Fallout Shelter studio, beneath their Chiswick head office. By this time, both Island Records and their music publishing arm were seriously interested in Pulp. "We had offers from three publishing companies including Island," says Suzanne Catty, "and I knew that if I could get both Island Music and Records it meant I could leverage a better deal – which I did. So Island were interested fairly early on, and Nigel and Toby from Publishing really helped support the band to the record label. Warners were also very interested, and Warner Chappell Publishing, but I knew Island would 'get' the band better than Warners ever would, especially in America. I thought a lot about America in working the deals: it is the big market to break and, while you can do very well around the world, there's nothing like breaking the US market for success and earnings. Besides, Pulp said they really wanted to break the US and I knew we could – no question.

"The tracks for the demo were written in a very short period of time just before the recording started. They delayed and delayed and delayed, then Jarvis and Candida wrote about five songs in one weekend. Both Island and myself had been freaking out that they wouldn't have the material together since they kept procrastinating about the writing. Remember that Pulp must have been nervous too – this was the time to put up or shut up. After all those years of no success, here they were in a major label studio with real record deals on the table, and they definitely were feeling the pressure. But they came through in the 11th hour, and the songs were very Pulp and would give us something to go on with."

Amongst material that would later emerge on various singles and albums over the next couple of years, the session included a couple of songs that never emerged. 'The Boss', so-called because the band reckoned it sounded like Bruce Springsteen (it doesn't), was a hyperactive slice of synth-pop, replete with stabbing, squelching keyboards and an archetypal Pulp-*circa*-'92 chorus: *"Ma ma ma ma ma ma ma ma ma ma ma ma ma ma ma let it go."* Lyrically it's a song of jealousy, voyeurism and failure to move on from a long-past relationship – *"I could never do anything else, so what am I gonna do with myself? I saw him kiss you in the afternoon 'cos I was next door in a double room. I was listening through the wall as he laid you down. I don't know what you did but I heard the sound – oh is he younger? Does he make you laugh?"* – set to incongruously poppy, upbeat music.

"We were just experimenting around that thing of writing 'up' songs," says Nick, "songs that people could get into, rather than slow ballads. Full-on, you know, really fast and aggressive. I listened to it a few months ago, dug some old tapes out – for fuck's sake! Couldn't stand it."

'The Boss' remained part of the live set through to the end of 1992, unlike 'Watching Nicky', which was written for the demo, recorded, and then dropped immediately after. More downbeat and subdued than most Pulp songs of the era, it was apparently based around the same musical seed as 'Babies', but has a gentler, more Sixties-tinged melody. Lyrically, it covers one of Jarvis' recurrent themes: the young girl whose aspirations and dreams are ground down by mundane reality: *"Watching Nicky turn from a girl to a wife is like watching all the life drain out of Nicky. 17 last June, 34 this May – what else can I say about you, Nicky? Oh no, she's not painting any more, spends the evenings locked indoors – something's just not going right for Nicky. Her mother said she'd mind the kid, but when it came, she never did and now you're not smiling anymore, oh Nicky."*

The fact that Pulp could now afford to throw songs away is evidence that, after four years of playing essentially the same set, the creative songwriting juices were beginning to flow again. Nick: "The songs on

Separations were written, and played, and recorded, and then there was the long wait for them to be released. It was like, 'Why write more songs when you're waiting for all this stuff to come out?' It's kind of like a stop on the top of a bottle – let's not bother writing any songs. But it had taken so long, we had to do something, so stuff did start to get written. But, again, probably more in the vein of, 'Let's try and write more uplifting music, albeit in an unconscious, slowly evolving way.'

"It was always going to change to some extent. Steve always puts his opinion forward. I think Russell's input was kind of slowing regarding creating music; obviously the Eastern European style had been eclipsed, and we'd moved on to this more poppy vein. Which Russell was very keen on, but obviously it was much more difficult to do; doing cod Eastern European stuff – easy, classic pop song – difficult. We were all contributing in various ways. There might be sessions where we'd be in the rehearsal room and would say, 'We're going to write a song and we all need to think of ourselves as being deep in the forest, and say, "Right, Steve, you're going to be a bear in the forest, and Candida, you will be the crunchy leaves on the forest floor," ' et cetera, and we'd all have to then make a piece of music by trying to musicalise our characters, our situation, and this might start a jam for twenty minutes, or it could develop. Invariably it'd make a hell of a noise, but every now and again you'd get something nice out of it. And we still did up to the last album, do these sessions where you'd bring a scenario and have to musicalise it, like amateur or school drama kind of things.

"But creatively, the mix does change. Steve coming in was the final brick of the five for this certain amount of time – Pulp was a solid line-up again. We'd had the high turnover of people playing bass, and now it was much more solid."

And what about *Separations* itself? The deterioration of the relationship with Fire, and the label's knowledge that Pulp had decided to go elsewhere, had meant that, for the first half of 1992, Fire had decided to put the album on hold and see what transpired. In the interviews surrounding 'O.U.' the band suggested that the album was probably now not going to emerge. The recordings were three years old, the songs were five years old – it had been delayed so long that it was now an irrelevancy. As Russell said, "It's not exactly crap but seeing as it was made about three years ago it's a bit dated; it's still wearing flares."[233]

It was, of course, at this point that Fire decided to release *Separations* . . . on the same day as 'O.U.'. "You knew full well," says Nick, "that it was not a strange coincidence."

Suzanne Catty: "Fire may have been rotten but they were not

completely stupid. They wanted to capitalise on all my work and the band's new found status as hipper-than-hip. We even did brown T-shirts . . . it took me three months to find someone who sold brown T-shirts! How cool is that."

When the band got wind of the label's plans to put the album out in direct competition to their new single, a meeting was arranged between the two sides, and Fire agreed to delay the album's release for a couple of weeks. Fortunately, Pulp had the ear of the music press by this point, and managed to communicate to the world at large that Fire's press release trumpeting a "brand new album . . . following their recent 'O.U.' single . . . recorded a year ago"[234] wasn't all it seemed. As a result, while the reviews were overwhelmingly favourable, it was made clear to the world at large that this LP was made by a band only distantly related to the one that had just won a new crowd of fans with 'O.U.'. As *NME*'s Andrew Collins wrote, "snaffle up this record merely as an *hors d'oeuvre* served on a dishonest plate."[235]

Much as Pulp publicly dismissed the album as ancient history, the fact that it still got decent reviews as a three-year-old release must have been a painful reminder of the time that had been wasted. "I remember a few people had advance tapes of the album years before it came out," says Ian Spence. "They were saying how exciting that record was going to be, and of course after waiting all that time for it to come out, it wasn't that exciting anymore. I remember Russell bemoaning the fact that wah-wah guitar had become fashionable in the period between him stuffing loads of it on the record and the record coming out . . . I do think they were getting a bit peeved with Fire."

The *Separations* debacle effectively put an end to Pulp's relationship with Fire Records, resulting in a lengthy, painful divorce that would take another year to be resolved. Nigel Coxon, meanwhile, had managed to persuade his superiors at Island that Pulp were worth pursuing, and Suzanne Catty had negotiated a publishing deal with Island Music, with a recording deal to follow. The band signed the publishing deal in July 1992 in the back garden of Island's London offices.

Nick: "It was like, 'Come on, let's do it, its our time.' We made them do us a big cheque like a pools winner with the money on it. Lovely sunny day, out on the lawn, champagne and all the bigwigs and the big cheque and all this and it felt like after all these years we were now in a position to kind of start proving that we were what some people want – people are going to start hearing Pulp's music for once and they can make their own mind up about it."

Predictably, it wasn't plain sailing from hereon in. On the eve of the sessions for 'Babies', Pulp's planned first Island release, the band sacked Suzanne Catty. Her energy, enthusiasm and commitment had been a massive tonic to the band, but the relationship – especially between her and Russell – had deteriorated rapidly.

"Russell only kind of lived round the corner from her at that time," remembers Nick, "and at first he was very into Suzanne helping the band out and moving it in the right direction. But it didn't take very long for him to become very anti-Suzanne. It was this thing of a Sheffield group having its own identity, and this kind of ass-kicking, ball-breaking North American comes in and goes, 'We're gonna kick their fucking asses!' and all this kind of thing, we were like, 'Uhh? Uh! We don't do things like that!' And it was good in a way because 'We don't do things like that' doesn't get you anywhere, but it did rub Russell up the wrong way reasonably quickly. But some of us were like, 'She's doing things for us, getting us interest, let's stick with it for a bit,' you know.

"It came to a head when she was wanting to actually sign a proper management contract, become our bona fide manager and get a 20 per cent cut or whatever. And Russell was dead against it, she was like coming round his house every day for three hours in the afternoon, ranting and raving at him about, 'You should be doing this, you should be doing that.' He said it was driving him up the wall. He didn't need it, you know – if you'd said it to Jon Bon Jovi, he'd understand. If you said it to Russ . . . it's a bit different."

Simon Hinkler, as Suzanne Catty's boyfriend, was in the unenviable position of seeing and hearing the dispute escalate. "It was awful. I'd be upstairs in my studio, and I'd hear these shouting matches going on downstairs. It was never my fight, I was just there to witness it; I just stayed as far away from it as possible. I was caught between a rock and a hard place because on one side was Pulp, who I'd known and loved and worked with for ten years, and on the other was my girlfriend."

Nick: "It ended up being some kind of money thing that meant we'd got to get rid of her. Island couldn't physically give us the money to pay for the single to be recorded because then Fire could sue them for inducing us off their label. It was all a very, very difficult time, so we had to pay for these recordings ourselves so that legally, everything was on the straight and narrow, and when we could cut the ties with Fire, they couldn't come back to sue us again.

"So Suzanne Catty was putting the money up for this recording and saying, 'If you don't sign my contract, I won't put the money up and this song will never get recorded.' So this final ultimatum was like, 'Right, no way – we're not signing a management contract.' So we're going to be held to ransom again, effectively, by another person in the record industry, just over this five grand to get this 'Babies' recording done. So in the end, Jarvis kindly gave the job to Steve to say, 'You're sacked'! So Steve, being the harder one, said, 'You're sacked', she went off in a huff, and Jarvis had to borrow some money off his grandma to get the recording paid for."

"I had been working all weekend," remembers Catty, "and was going to take Candida and Nick and Russell to London on Monday to Island for the recording. Russell came over with Zig and said they were going to go down to London Sunday night instead, and Russell and I had a row about the financial records which he was refusing to cough up. I was supposed to see the accountant Monday while the band were in the studio so it was a big issue. Anyway he left and the next morning I drove down with Candida, Nick and Simon Hinkler. When we arrived at the studio, Russell and Steve pulled me into a side room and basically said, 'You're fired.' No discussion, no 'We have some issues,' or nothing. Just 'Bye' – or rather, 'Fuck off' is how it felt. Worse was they stood there and said it was a band decision but neither Candida nor Nick had known anything about it before I did because we'd been together in the car for nearly three hours that morning and they certainly didn't know. Perhaps one of Pulp's lowest moments.

"It's always been interesting to me that one of the things I told Pulp from the beginning is that one of the key ingredients to success is to have loyalty. That I believed they should have a team of support, manager, lawyer, accountant, agent, record company people . . . and that they work with the team and build a relationship and stay loyal."

The final twist came shortly after Catty had gone, when Pulp and Island convened to review the band's legal situation. It transpired that Island hadn't been told that Pulp were still signed to Fire, and Pulp hadn't been told that Island hadn't been told that Pulp were still signed to Fire. Therefore, to cash the advance cheque they'd just received from Island Publishing would be a direct breach of contract with Fire's publishing arm Twist & Shout Music, and the contract they'd just signed wasn't worth the paper it was written on. Stalemate again.

"Suzanne Catty really kept us in the dark," says Steve Mackey. "We're now very literate in all aspects of the music business but, back then, we just wanted to release a record, and she told us we could free ourselves without much hassle. She had that Canadian/American, 'They won't fuck with me' attitude, and she was so wrong."[236]

Catty's legacy was mixed to say the least. On one hand, there was a highly convoluted legal situation involving three record labels and a

£5,000 debt to Jarvis' grandmother. On the other, there was a band that had been dragged, kicking and screaming, out of part-time hobby status and into another league. After a decade of scraping by, it was arguably thanks to her that Pulp now had a career for the first time. As Russell says, "She was the first person ever to say, 'I can make you stars, and by Christmas.' She's probably my most mortal enemy on earth now but you have to give her the credit for saying it."[237]

The recording sessions went ahead as planned, with 'Babies' and 'Sheffield Sex City' being recorded by Ed Buller over a week-long session at the Island Fallout Shelter, and the B-side then being completed at Protocol Studios the next month. With a brilliant no-budget video made at St Martin's with the help of Martin Wallace and an iconic sleeve design from The Designer's Republic, it was by far the most complete package ever to have surrounded a Pulp record.

The only issue that remained was how the single was going to be released. As long as the band were still technically signed to the Fire, they couldn't sign to anyone else – least of all a behemoth such as Island, which Clive Solomon would be able to profitably sue. And while they'd got away with releasing 'O.U.' by working with a small label like Gift on an *ad-hoc* basis, Rob Mitchell and Steve Beckett didn't have the money to keep Pulp on their own. Therefore, a plan was hatched.

Nick: "Dave Gilmour and Nigel Coxon said, 'Yep, we want to sign Pulp,' but the relationship with Fire meant that it was very difficult to go from one to the other. We hadn't really left Fire by this point, we just said, 'We're not having anything more to do with you.' They still had our names on binding contracts and stuff, so it was a bit of a gamble, but we said to the chaps from Warp, 'Can we use Gift as a smokescreen to get records out by Island.' We'd still be in contract to Fire. So basically Island paid Gift to put our records out, and Gift got us so that their new indie label got a good start."

Although it was a result of a series of unfortunate circumstances, the arrangement actually worked out well for Pulp – remaining, nominally, on a small independent label allowed them to build steadily on the credibility and acclaim they'd been picking up over the previous 18 months without any of the accusations of hype that Suede had attracted with their first releases on Sony-funded Nude Records. Having Island's money behind the releases, meanwhile, meant that Pulp could make records on a reasonable budget, giving them the time and space to develop and adjust to the possibilities of decent studios and proper promotion.

"My view on major record companies," says Nigel Coxon, "is that I still think that they struggle to develop things right at the nurturing stage, and also I did have a problem with my head of A&R at the time, who wasn't a particular fan. So we kind of contrived to use Warp, Gift being a subsidiary of Warp, to start the ball rolling. So I gave Pulp a small development deal, which funded the next two releases; it was roughly 10 grand a single, which financed the recording, the artwork and a couple of really cheap videos. As much as anything, I needed to do it that way round because (a) I thought it was the appropriate way to let a band like that develop – they had outside press and promotions and it was very much outside the record company, but with the record company involved, and (b) so that it could evolve to such a stage that I didn't then have any problem with going to my superiors and going, 'Right, let's do a fully fledged album contract.' "

In the countdown to the single's October release date, Pulp knew that the immediate future was bright, but their business situation was starting to weigh heavily. Nick: "It was like, 'So – here we are, we're just coming up the slope, you've sacked your manager, you've borrowed five grand off your grandma, you hate your record company, you want to sign to another record company that you can't sign to, your records are being put out by a tenuous third party that has no contract or anything with you' . . . It's messy, innit?

"It must've been about this time that we started to look around for another, proper manager to deal with our terrible, terrible affairs. I remember going to see one guy, I think he was Spiritualized's manager. Big bloke, bald head, very shiny brown shoes. We gave him the story, he'd heard of Pulp, liked the group, and he was like, 'I'd love to be able to help you, but I really, really can't get involved with this horrendous, sticky, horrible mess.' Very sensible of him.

"So John Best introduced Jarvis to various managers, he went to see loads of people, and they were all, like, 'How did you get into this situation?!' But if you've been in a failing band for 15 years, you do kind of get into situations. Anyway, John Best put us in touch with Geoff Travis. I remember him saying, 'Yes, you're in a shit situation, I'm not surprised no one wants to touch you with a bargepole . . . but I do. I love the group, I don't mind getting into a sticky situation, I'll take it on board.' And it was like, great! Someone who seems genuinely nice, with such a great track record of being involved in great projects, so it was, 'Right, let's get things moving.' "

Geoff Travis was the founder of Rough Trade Records, one of the most respected and influential independent record labels of the post-punk era.

The label was best known for giving the world The Smiths, but had also released records by a huge number of acclaimed alternative acts from the end of the Seventies through the Eighties, amongst them Cabaret Voltaire, The Fall, TV Personalities, Subway Sect, The Pop Group and innumerable others.

By 1992, although still primarily a label, Rough Trade was beginning to move into management, Travis having got involved with The Cranberries the previous year. "Jarvis came into the office," he remembers, "and sat down, and talked for about two or three hours, telling me his tale of woe. It intrigued me enough to say to Jeanette, 'Let's go and see them play.' They were kind of a cross between The Rolling Stones, Roxy Music and Manfred Mann. Every single song they played in their set seemed like a classic single to me. It was a really exciting mixture of all the best virtues of Sixties pop but in a totally fresh way. They just seemed a very classy English band to me."[238]

"We saw them play in Brighton* the first time," remembers Jeanette Lee, who would end up taking day-to-day responsibility for Pulp's career, "and we couldn't believe how good they were."[239]

Jarvis: "I had a very jaundiced view of the music business until I met Geoff Travis. Him and Jeanette and the people at Rough Trade convinced me that there were some actual human beings still working in the music business, rather than reptiles."[240]

Geoff Travis' principal task was the unenviable one of getting Pulp into the position where they were free from the Fire contract and available to be signed to Island. Oh dear. "It was a total nightmare," he remembers, "because we agreed to take them on, and then the full extent of their legal situation began to dawn on us. So the first year, really, was just a legal nightmare, trying to get them into a situation where they were free and able to continue to do what they did well."[241]

Nick: "The whole mess, he'd got to sort out. He'd got to get us away from Clive Solomon, 'cos he could just have gone, 'Right, I want a million quid,' or whatever, and make sure that Island were still gonna sign us, 'cos at any point they could have just gone, 'Oh, I'm fed up with all this bollocks, sod you.' But they didn't, thankfully. So he had to get Clive Solomon out of the way, and also at the same time, make sure the records are getting put together, keeping the people in Gift happy, although they were all right because they were old Sheffield pals. Just getting it all hammered out – which took a lot of doing."

---

* Probably Sussex University, October 7, 1992.

On a more uncomplicatedly marvellous note, the 'Babies' single was released on October 5, 1992. It was, quite simply, a heroically brilliant record. Ed Buller's production had fleshed the song out from January's weedy FON prototype into something that was in a different league altogether. From the brilliantly naïve guitar plucking of the intro to the '*Yeah yeah yeah yeah yeah yeah yeah*' climax and just about every point in between (although special mention must be given to the ridiculous one-note squelchy synth bit between the verses and Jarvis' immortal '*I only went with her 'cos she looks like you – my God!*' pay-off), practically every second of the song contains another Great Pop Moment.

'Babies' had its origins in a rehearsal jam the previous year. Nick: "I wrote that song, I'll have you know. And don't let anyone tell you different. We were rehearsing in my mother's pottery warehouse at Catcliffe – we rehearsed there for quite a long time, must be from about '88, stuff was stored there till about '95 really. There'd be kids outside shouting, going, 'Yer fucking rubbish!' and we'd go, 'I've got the microphone, I'm louder than you.'

"The others had gone to make a cup of tea, so I was just playing Jarv's guitar. He came back and said, 'What's that?' Dunno! No idea what these chords are. He said, 'Oh, show us,' and I showed him, and we were just like jamming around these two chords. Ten minutes later, there you are. There's the song."

The two chords developed into a jangly indie guitar pastiche called 'Nicky's Song'. "It had Jarvis singing to Nick rather like Elvis sings to the hound dog on *The Ed Sullivan Show*," says Russell. "He used to run around the rehearsal room and grope Nick's breasts during it." On another occasion, he told Radio 1 that "I didn't like 'Babies' much. The guitar riff, '*der-der-dee-doo, der-der-der, dum-dum-der*', that I did on it, the moment I did it I thought, 'That is so bloomin' corny, I'm going to have to come up with something a lot better than that!' "[242]

In its final form, though, the song was irresistible, thanks in no small part to Jarvis' completely ace lyrics. Funny, driven, camp, cheeky and yet at the same time somehow totally serious, after a decade of trying he'd finally hit upon the secret formula of being entertaining without resorting to wackiness, and emotional without being overwrought. And '*Oh I want to take you home/ I want to give you children/ You might be my girlfriend/ Yeah yeah yeah yeah yeah yeah yeah*' is simply as good a chorus as any pop song will ever have.

The story – about, as we all know, hiding in the girl you fancy's sister's wardrobe to watch her having sex – surely couldn't have the slightest grain of truth in it. Well, actually . . . "It was about these two girls who all the boys at school seemed to fancy, and there were always lots of stories, probably most of them made up, of what they were up to. I remember once I was waiting to go into maths class and through the glass panel on the door I could see one of these girls laid on a desk with a boy on top of her. I could just see his legs and her legs over the desk and it looked like something pretty rude was going on. But I actually did once fall asleep in a hotel's walk-in wardrobe. I crawled into it one night, put a pillow down and fell asleep, and when my mother saw I wasn't in my bed she alerted the whole hotel staff and got them to search. For the rest of the holiday, every time a member of the hotel staff saw me, they'd laugh their heads off."[243]

The next track on the EP, 'Styloroc (Nites Of Suburbia)', was based on a fizzy instrumental recorded for the Island demo in May. "I tried to sing along with it," explains Jarvis, "but it sounded like Whitesnake, so I recycled some lyrics from an old song that never got recorded, 'Nights Of Suburbia', and recited them over the top of this stylophone music."[244] In fact, the lyrics weren't from the song itself (a live staple *circa* 1985/6), but from a piece that Jarvis wrote to accompany its inclusion on the *See You Later Agitator* compilation tape in 1987. Yet it fitted in perfectly with the territory that Pulp *circa* 1992 were exploring – a vignette of suburban sleaze, the kind of mixture of drabness and weirdness that Jarvis would have you believe was "happening soon at a cul-de-sac near you."[245]

And then there was 'Sheffield Sex City'. The song was described on the sleeve as "the morning after 'My Legendary Girlfriend'. Trying to get things done but ending up on a tour of the fleshpots of Sheffield in a T-reg Chevette", which about sums it up. "That probably started out with us pissing about, trying to do some jazz funk or something like that," says Nick. "We have these daft sessions where we go, 'Right, let's do a jazz funk song.' And something will come out and we'll end up rolling round laughing. Sometime stuff'll come out and the tape recorder will get switched on, you know."

'Sheffield Sex City' is a truly amazing eight-and-a-half minute *tour de force*, possibly dripping with clammy, obsessive urban filth and frustration, and packed with the kind of telling, minute detail that its predecessor only hinted at: *"The sun rose from behind the gasometers at 6.30 am, crept through the gap in your curtains and caressed your bare feet poking from beneath the floral sheets. I watched him flaking bits of varnish from your nails trying to work his way up under the sheets. Jesus, even the sun's on heat today, the whole city getting stiff in the building heat . . ."* and on and on and on. By the time Jarvis finally gets his girl – on a hilltop overlooking the city at 4 am – you've been dragged around a million shop doorways, puddles of rain, crumbling concrete bus shelters, central reservations and the rest, and you're as fever-ishly exhausted and elated as he (presumably) is. The fact that it was very hot when he wrote the words probably helped.

"I wrote 'Sheffield Sex City' on the first day of summer when it was really hot and everybody had sex on their mind," explains Jarvis. "You've been used to being wrapped up and suddenly you've got this day when you don't have to wear as much and everybody's hormones seem to go absolutely crazy. I wrote the song lying in Hyde Park. I had just met this girl and was thinking about her. I wrote all the words in one go on the first day of summer, it just flooded out. It was either that or go rub myself against a tree, and I didn't want to get myself arrested."[246]

The fact that Jarvis was getting location-specific was significant: if he still lived there, it would have been impossible for him to write about Sheffield in such a way. Years spent hanging round Fargate or staring down on the Sheffield streets through bus windows had filled Jarvis' head with minutiae regarding the foibles of his home town and the people who lived there, but as long as he lived there, there was no way for him to process the data with any real sense of perspective. "In my naïveté," he reflected later, "I thought the whole world was like Sheffield. When I found myself in a different environment, I thought, 'I'd better write all this stuff down before I forget it, 'cos I'm not living like that any more.' People in London don't go round saying, 'Ah, that's ace, that,' and 'I fingered her at t'busstop – awright?' Things that seemed too obvious to write about before weren't any more."[247]

Nick: "Obviously the words came out of moving away from Sheffield, being able to see things from a different perspective, you know. When you move to London, which I did around the same time, your northern-ness gets cranked up a few notches – kind of kicking against these southern ponces swanning around. You start going, 'Eee, I'm from up north, me.' You're looking back on Sheffield and people are thinking, 'Oh, you come from Sheffield, that horrible dour northern city,' and you go, 'No it's not. It's really sexy.'"

Jarvis' new-found lyrical obsession with sex was as much of a develop-ment as his discovery of the wealth of material that Sheffield had provided him with. Of course, there'd already been 'My Legendary Girlfriend', and live reviewers had been occasionally remarking on the hints of sexiness in Pulp since 1988, but 1992 was the year Jarvis the disco sex god went into overdrive. The reaction to 'My Legendary Girlfriend' the previous year had proved an inspiration: "By 1991, what struck me was how sexless pop music had become. I thought I could see a gap in the market. I mean sex is constantly on people's minds, isn't it, but in pop it gets written about in such a stupid or nebulous way, even though it rules people's lives. It's either the Prince approach of doing it all night long or it's like that TV series *The Good Sex Guide*, which was enough to make anyone celibate. Let's consult the manual: I've done me 20 minutes of foreplay; now I can achieve penetration."[248]

"The idea of Jarvis being a sex symbol was utterly, utterly hilarious," says Nick, "'cos *Smash Hits* were starting to pick up on Pulp and starting to go on about sexy Jarvis, and people were just in *fits* of laughter. You know, this spaz who could fall over the pattern in the carpet, who was a scruff and he's not washed his hair in six weeks – and he's sexy? You're fucking kidding! If you look at Pulp in 1986 and then in 1992, and say, 'This man is a sex symbol,' you'd say, 'Go and get yourself examined.' But I suppose for him there was a 'I've never had anyone say this about me; I will accentuate it' angle. I don't know."

Given the momentum that Pulp had built up with previous releases and the sheer quality of the EP, it's not entirely shocking that 'Babies' was well received. *Melody Maker* gave it Single Of The Week; *NME* described it as "sad, seedy, splendid" . . . and *Smash Hits* awarded it Best New Single!

> "*What a fantastic, imaginative and wonderful record! This is a most amusing autobiographical story, about a schoolboy hiding in a wardrobe and watching his girlfriend's older sister getting frisky with her boyfriend. All this and a swinging bassline, groovy guitars and an emotive vocal delivery that could make a grown gladiator cry at 40 paces. 'I wanna give you children. And you might be my girlfriend.' Ahh . . . Pulp could well become the band of all our tomorrows. A most joyful noise hath been created.*"[249]

The single crept up the indie charts through October, helped along its way by a screening of the video on ITV's *Chart Show* and another nationwide tour. In lieu of a Sheffield date, a coach trip was organised down to London for a show at the ULU, resulting in a venue packed out with both hometown devotees and new-found fans. Meanwhile, 'Babies' was on its way to notching up a 16-week stint on the indie chart.

Mark Webber had also been busy – as well as his role as tour manager, he'd started playing with Pulp onstage as an extra pair of hands when needed (contributing stylophone on 'O.U.' and organ on newie 'Pink Glove'), and was now running the band's newly created fan club, Pulp People. Russell had set it up in July, and by October over 100 people had joined – all of whom got regular mailshots detailing the band's activities; a press cuttings scrapbook and a copy of the band's self-produced magazine, *Disco-Very*, which between them told you all you needed to know about the band's long, tortuous and hitherto obscure history; and occasional giveaways such as a square of fabric cut from one of Jarvis' suits (yep, one piece for each member), the clapperboard used in the 'Babies' video and Jarvis' old stylophone (which had been supplanted by an enormous two-stylus model that you could play chords on).

"It was good," says Nick, "because obviously he was a long-term fan and he started doing some helping out, on *The Day That Never Happened* concert and things like that. And he was enthusiastic and seemed able, so he started tour managing. And then in the rehearsal room, Jarvis would be playing instruments and singing at the same time, and it's always a trade off – you can do one well but both badly. He'd concentrate on playing the guitar or something and the singing would get forgotten a bit. So a lot of songs like 'O.U.', 'She's A Lady', things like that, rather than Jarvis having to disappear and play the Stylophone at the same time, which was kind of defeating the object of having this interesting new sound, we said to Mark, or Zig as he almost totally was at the time, 'Can you come along and help out play those bits?' He could play a bit of guitar and stuff like that, so it just seemed the expedient way of doing things – freeing Jarvis up to arse around on stage.

"That obviously grew: as more songs would come along, there'd be a bit more to do – it'd just be a very gradual process of assimilation, and once it starts happening he ends up becoming indispensable. And Jarvis would be saying, 'I've been playing guitar on this,' and he can play guitar and sing, but he can't play guitar, sing and dance around. So it was like, 'Mark will you do this bit of guitar?', right fair enough, and he gradually got more and more involved."

November saw another trip to France, this time to play an hour-long live set for the France Inter radio station's *Black Session* programme, including a version of The Four Seasons' 'The Night' which Pulp took over so completely it's hard not to see it as one of their own songs. They finally returned to Sheffield the following month for the third annual Pulp Christmas concert, at the Lower Refectory, complete with DJing from St Etienne's Bob and Pete; followed by yet another show in France to celebrate the opening of Rough Trade's Paris shop.

The year ended with a triumphant show at the Powerhaus in Islington, for London club Smashed's Christmas party. Some of the audience had obviously done their homework: toward the end of the night, the air was thick with requests for 'My Lighthouse' and 'Maureen'. Instead, they were treated with an under-rehearsed, somewhat inebriated rendition of Greg Lake's 'I Believe In Father Christmas'. Jarvis barely made it to the end of the song, but somehow the sense that Pulp could do no wrong still prevailed.

For Pulp People's Christmas newsletter, Jarvis shared his highpoints of
1992:

*"Finsbury Park . . . BBC coffee at Maida Vale . . . Dancing during a
thunderstorm at a motorway services somewhere on the outskirts of Birmingham . . . Entertaining and thought provoking letters to make long van
journeys pass quicker . . . My first ever glimpse of Scotland . . . Pink panther
stickers in a café on the North Yorkshire moors . . . Zen and the art of Star
Maintenance . . . How many people can you think of with surnames beginning with B? . . . Conversations with Russian exiles in coffee bars . . .
Pouring a bottle of ice cold mineral water over myself in Cardiff and getting
the best sexual thrill I've had in ages (try it with a friend sometime) . . . A
live broadcast to the whole of France on a wet Parisian evening . . . ULU
. . . Powercuts in Brighton . . . Walking sticks in Leicester . . . The Chart
Show in Bristol . . . I owe these experiences to you and that's why I love you
– and I don't care who knows it. Have a marvellous Christmas and Nu Year.*

*PS You were Pulp in 1992 but you've got to be even more Pulp in 1993.
(You owe it to yourself.)"*

Chapter 11

1993 began with the mixed blessing of another big, rapturously received French show, at the Nantes Olympic, with Suede. The latter band's foppish, Seventies-tinged image and rousing indie-glam sound had led to them being linked by journalists to the same so-called Crimplene Scene that Pulp had been attached to – indeed they'd supported Pulp at the Camden Underworld a year before. Now, with both bands' two singles down the line, Suede had grazed the Top 20 and appeared on *Top Of The Pops* – and Pulp were supporting them.

"Suede were another group that supported us in the early days," remembers Nick. "And they sort of overtook us very rapidly – 'See you later chaps.' Another one where we were kind of spitting feathers going *'Another one!* What . . . but . . . *What does he look like?!'* Another one that's pulled the rug from under you and zoomed off into the distance."

On a happier note, Pulp's third single on Gift Records was released on February 15. The A-side was 'Razzmatazz'. Both musically and lyrically, the song represented something of a change of tone from 'O.U.' and 'Babies': the hormones were still there, but in place of the innocent (well, OK, almost innocent) exuberance of its predecessors, the song has a desperate, grim melodrama, returning in some ways to the glumness of the *Separations* era. In three-and-a-half minutes, the song manages to be as ambitious as 'My Legendary Girlfriend', as desperate as 'Countdown', yet as enjoyable as 'Babies'. This time around, Pulp had managed to combine that kind of emotional high drama with proper pop thrills – and instantly recognisable characters and situations.

"It's the most bitter song we've ever done," Jarvis told *Melody Maker* at the time. "But however harsh I am about the people in 'Razzmatazz', I'm not writing from above their level. I've got a lot of experience of being as sad as them, if not more so."[250]

"That was another one that was played quite a lot," remembers Nick. "Another one of these instances where another bit of new technology, well not even new technology, but different technology we'd picked up was used and some songs came out of it. Jarv brought in this old Korg

Trident synthesiser for Candida to play, and the sound of it was the beginning of the song – similar to 'O.U.', with Jarv using the stylophone. A new bit of equipment brought in was often the catalyst to write new songs.

"So we had this Korg Trident, and in the studio it was recorded, and mixed, and it's just not exciting enough. It's just not. We'd done it with Ed Buller and decided that wasn't sufficient, we thought that the drums weren't beefy enough, so we went and re-recorded them with Phil Vinall, who went on to do stuff with the Auteurs and Gene. We went off to a place in Hoxton and re-recorded the drums, and it was all far more exciting."*

The B-side, 'Inside Susan: A Story In Three Parts', was another first: a suite of three songs linked together to tell a story. "You follow this character from early adolescence through to early thirties and married to an architect somewhere in South London,"[251] explains Jarvis. "I was quite pleased when we did that because it's something different. I hate concept albums, but it was quite interesting to have a theme that ran through three songs and told a bit of a story."[252]

The first song, 'Stacks', is a stomping piece of synth-pop. Mark Webber makes his first on-record appearance (playing the stylophone solo), and Jarvis' lyrics perfectly capture the mix of giddiness and poignancy that occasionally characterises early adolescence – special mention must be given to the immortal couplet *"Did you stay over at his place?/ Did you do it? Was he ace?"*

'Inside Susan' itself was another lengthy monologue, less intense and more thoughtful than 'Sheffield Sex City', but no less atmospheric, with yet more of Jarvis' perfectly observed minutiae – *"Her friends will be in the yard with their arms folded on their chests, pushing up their breasts to try and make them look bigger whilst the boys will be too busy playing football to notice. The bus is waiting on the high street when it suddenly begins to rain torrentially and it sounds like someone has emptied about a million packets of dried peas on to the roof of the bus . . ."* Elsewhere in the story, scenes from Jarvis' own youth appear: Caroline Lee is a real person, Jarvis was the tall boy in glasses she

---

* The single also represented the end of an era for Pulp: shortly after the recording, in January 1993, the band's van was burgled and the Korg Delta synth and Russell's orange Rosetti guitar (a staple part of the Pulp sound since 1983) were stolen, never to be seen again. Subsequently, the unimaginable happened and Russell got a Fender Stratocaster . . . "Some idiot nicked Russell's Rosetti guitar," remembers Nick, "one of the worst guitars ever made, and this was one not in very good condition, so what anyone would ever want to do with it, I don't know. Steve got his white Fender bass nicked. By the time we'd got the Island cheque, it was like, 'Pass me the skip, a lot of this stuff's going in it.' Apart from the keyboard stuff, which was quite unique."

used to pretend to be married to, and the German exchange students really did end up jumping out of the bedroom window.

"I think the reason I started writing about it was that I thought I might be in danger of forgetting what it was like," he remarked in 1994. "Also, I like the resilience of youth: people are always packing each other when they're young – you'd be going out with someone and one day they'd say, 'I'm packing yuh, yuh're a right slag,' and nobody would think anything of it, whereas if you said that to someone now, you'd be in the divorce courts, getting sued. I liked the fact that everybody was so insensitive to each other, and quite abusive a lot of the time. It is a sign of immaturity, I'm sure."[253]

The trilogy concludes with the gorgeous '59 Lyndhurst Grove' – not that the trad-Pulp prettiness of the tune took anything away from the quiet viciousness of Jarvis' dissection of suburban middle-class half-life. *"There's a picture by his first wife on the wall, stripped floorboards in the kitchen and the hall . . . He's an architect and such a lovely guy, and he'll stay with you until the day you die. And he'll give you everything you could desire – oh well almost everything; everything that he can buy . . ."*

"'59 Lyndhurst Grove' was inspired by a party I'd been to the week before," he explains. "We were thrown out by an architect but I got my own back by writing a song about the event. It was a really crap right-on party – there were children there. You don't take your children to a party in my book. I sent a copy of the CD to 59 Lyndhurst Grove, the lady of the house, because she was in a bad situation, married to this prick, but she never wrote back."[254]

Being Pulp's most ambitious release so far, 'Razzmatazz' had to have a similarly ambitious video. Rather than simply intercutting a straightforward mimed performance with simple action scenes, as had been the case with 'Countdown' and 'Babies', Jarvis and Martin Wallace decided to take the show on the road. "We were due to be playing a couple of concerts in France," wrote Jarvis in *Disco-Very*, "and so I came up with the bright idea of 'wouldn't it be great if we could shoot the video in the Moulin Rouge in Paris?' Imagine my surprise when they agreed to the idea; the owner even offered to let us use his pet crocodiles! Imagine my even greater surprise when we arrived in Paris to find they had changed their minds.

"Luckily for us, we were staying in one of Jacques Brel's old haunts – the extremely seedy Ideal Hotel in Montmartre – and in a Cliff Richard-like flash of inspiration we decided, 'Let's do the video right here.' We smuggled all the camera equipment into the hotel and shot over the course of one day. Then in the evening we went out, just around the corner on to

La Pigalle (Paris' red light district) and amused the passers-by by shooting some lip-sync out on the streets.

"We arrived back in England still needing some more material, and so gained access to the Sunset Strip strip club on Dean Street at 7 am one Monday morning. We arrived there to find the caretaker asleep on the illuminated stage of the club! We had precisely four hours to film in before the paying punters would be knocking on the door expecting 'An Erotic Xmas Revue – with the emphasis on the X!' We got done just in time.

"The interior domestic shots were filmed in Jane Oliver's flat in Camden. On the day we filmed she'd been out all night so it was easy to get the frayed, slightly numb performance we were after."[255]

The result was worth the traumas – the video perfectly compliments the mixture of seedy glamour and desperation evoked in the lyrics. It also, finally, gave Pulp a visual presence that lived up to their records: the group, and Jarvis in particular, actually looked like pop stars rather than people trying to be pop stars.

If 'O.U.' and 'Babies' had been well received, this time the press went overboard with praise. The lyrical concerns might have been a little too adult for *Smash Hits* this time, but *Melody Maker* gave it their third Single Of The Week in a row, while *NME* reckoned it to be, "Glorious in all its life-affirming, all-encompassing enormity without being void of real substance. Pop irony in full effect. Sick without being smutty; pure without being puerile, Jarvis Cocker takes us through another strange tale of weird sex and pre-pubescent deviance, this time with overtones of malevolent incest and family intimidation. Better than 'Babies' and twice as scary."

And it wasn't just the press that were paying attention – thanks in part to the valiant plugging of Scott Piering, who had gone to the extreme of cropping his hair and having the Pulp's name shaved into the back of his head, in February and March the band made an unprecedented string of TV appearances, including MTV's *120 Minutes*, ITV's *The Beat*, Irish show *JMTV Rocks The Garden* and Yorkshire Television's *The Warehouse*. There was also a second session for Radio 5's *Hit The North*, and a return, at long last, to John Peel to perform three superb new songs: 'You're A Nightmare', 'Pink Glove' and 'Acrylic Afternoons'.

In the midst of all this, the band managed to fit in another 10-date tour, this time a jaunt around the country's student unions supporting St Etienne. "That was one of the first things we were able to do," says Geoff Travis, "and that was almost the first coherent tour that they'd ever done. That was another reason why they hadn't been successful – nobody had ever seen them."[256]

On the eve of the tour, Pulp found themselves unexpectedly moving another rung up the rock'n'roll ladder when their van broke down. "We had no money whatsoever, so any savings we could make had to be done. But we knew we couldn't really do this tour, two weeks up and down the country, with a Transit van sat on amps. You know, it's just horrible. So through someone who knew someone who knew someone, we'd got like a Transit van but it had got a proper compartment for the instruments, and a proper compartment to actually sit on. He had cut up a van he'd kind of converted himself, so it was still pretty ropey, but it was cheap. But when we'd all sort of got ourselves gathered together to meet for this homemade bus, it didn't show up for hours and hours. So Mike Timm, who was doing the sound, goes off to try and sort it out. It turned out this van had died, and we eventually saw it and the seats were hardly bolted in and it was like, 'How are we going to spend three weeks in that?' Not very nice.

"So we said, 'Well, if we don't get this van we're going to miss the first concert and it's not going to be a very good start.' So basically we said, 'Right, someone'll have to nip off to Stardays,' which is a company just outside Sheffield which does, you know, right up to huge trucks, hire stuff. And we were kind of waiting in this garage, and Mike Timm comes round the corner in this beautiful brand new Mercedes, with proper nice coach seats and tables between them. And we were just like, '*Yeeessssss!*' 'Cos you know it was just so horrible in Transit vans sat on amps and this was like, 'This is luxury, this is fantastic.' Got Led Zeppelin on, and it was like this is what its about. We were jumping for joy in the car park."

"I think the St Etienne fans really liked us having Pulp on tour," says vocalist Sarah Cracknell. "Talking about it like that now seems really weird because they're so much more famous than we are, but at the time nobody really knew who they were, and I think St Etienne fans loved them – they went down really well."[257]

The tour garnered yet more favourable reviews, many of which, it has to be said, noted that Pulp upstaged the headlining act by some distance – for example *Melody Maker*'s remark that, "If Pulp could be aurally likened to *Last Tango In Paris*, then Saint Etienne are more like *Take Me High*, that crap film Cliff Richard made in 1973."[258]

"It was our first time supporting anyone on a tour," says Nick, "and it was so exciting. We weren't staying in fancy places at all, but it was that case of seeing another group all the time and seeing how they do things – how they did things well and how they didn't do things very well. Saint Etienne are a great group, but we never thought they particularly cut it very well on the live front. They were using a lot of tapes and all this kind of thing, and we were sort of like, 'This is all very well and good, but where's the bollocks to it?'

"It was good 'cos in a tour you're in a kind of a bubble, and all the two tour parties really got on with one another. They'd watch our show almost every night, we'd watch theirs. It was like, 'This is what it's all about, this is fantastic.' It was kind of what you'd longed and hoped it would be. 'Cos you hear about tours, 'Oh, it's such drudgery, it's terrible.' But it was a great laugh."

Better still was to come in April when Radio 1 chose Sheffield as the venue for its first ever Sound City festival. After taking *NME* on a guided tour of the city, bringing the delights of Fargate, Division Street, FON, The Wicker and the Washington pub to the masses, they played an ecstatically received live set at the Leadmill. Much as they may have finally escaped the tag of being merely a 'Sheffield band', they were still local heroes – only more so.

The St Etienne tour was Pulp's third substantial tour in the space of a year. With ever-increasing live work, plus significant amounts of time spent writing and recording, being in Pulp was starting to look like a full-time occupation. Of course, the proceeds from gigs in front of three-figure audiences and Top 80 hit singles weren't going to allow anyone in the band to sign off quite yet, but it was most definitely time to give up the day job. Nick: "By '91, '92, Pulp was taking up quite a bit of time, so it was good not to have a 9-to-5 job. I came back to Sheffield, did a bit of supply teaching on and off, but nothing too much. People had bits that they did here and there: Russell had his antiques business, he'd do some selling, but he could still have quite a bit of time Pulping, you know. So everyone cleared their 9–5 jobs, kind of clearing their desks for this time that we knew was imminent, when this fat Island cheque was gonna land and we were all going to get wages and be Pulp."

Pulp's place in the *Zeitgeist* consolidated further when the April 1993 issue of *Select* ran a major article on the wave of new British bands who were on the rise after the previous year's American grunge invasion. The Crimplene Scene had evolved into something that people were just beginning to call Britpop – a handful of groups that shared a distinctly Seventies-influenced, glam-poppy edge, and yet looked like they could be serious commercial contenders with a broader appeal than the usual couple of thousand John Peel listeners who frequented toilet circuit gigs up and down the country. Suede were on the front of the magazine – they'd already made it, having just released their début album and cracked the Top 10 with 'Animal Nitrate' – but Pulp, St Etienne, The Auteurs and

Denim were heavily featured. Pulp's momentum had now been building solidly for two years, and the mainstream was starting to meet them halfway – there was no stopping them now.

"Suddenly," commented *Melody Maker*'s Simon Price in an interview around the same time, "it looks as though it's all been worth it. Pulp's name is being dropped everywhere. The lift-off has begun."

"It's probably a combination of the mood of the times changing," remarked Jarvis, "and us getting better. It's quite an ironic thing, but as soon as I packed it in and went to college, within six months people started to like us. Maybe sometimes you can try a bit too hard."[259]

The following month, Pulp went into the studio to record a track for a tribute album to the cult French artist, Michel Polnareff. "I'm not really sure how it came about," says Nick. "At this time the French had really kind of picked up Pulp and were running with it a lot faster than the English press – we were doing all right in England, we weren't complaining, but the French were like, 'This band is *fantastique!*' So we were getting loads of French support in their French way, and I think Jarvis had mentioned in interviews he liked Michel Polnareff's stuff, and someone was doing a compilation, so we did a track for it."

Pulp's contribution was a fizzy, frantic version of Polnareff's '*Le Roi Des Fourmis*', complete with Jarvis singing a phonetic transcription of the original French lyrics (he'd originally tried an English version, but that made the title 'The King Of The Ants' and generally didn't make much sense). The session, which also included demos of two new songs, 'Lipgloss' and the long-forgotten 'You're Not Blind', was recorded at Axis Studios in Sheffield with producer Stephen Street.

Nick: "It was interesting 'cos we were looking round for other producers. We'd done Ed Buller and it was like all right, but we thought it wasn't the be all and end all. So we worked with Stephen Street. He came up to the rehearsal room which was above my mother's pottery shop in Catcliffe, so we were all crowded into this tiny little space. One of the cleanest men you'll ever see – he could go down a coal mine in a white suit and come out looking sparkling. Really nice bloke. It was good 'cos he came to the rehearsal and he listened.

"I thought he was good, Stephen Street. I would have given him as my choice to go on and do the *His'n'Hers* stuff which was kind of imminent. We were working out who was going to do that. But I don't think Jarvis liked his producing 'cos he thought he was too nice, everything was too nice, all too clean. You could kind of hear everything. Which I think's great, but he thought it was a bit too nice, so he didn't feel that was the way forward. But it was a great experiment."

Due to various record company wranglings, unusually not involving Pulp, the Polnareff album remained unreleased until 1999. "Another one of those things where you don't envisage it coming out five years later," says Nick. "It was French time. It was all like, 'Yes we can do this,' and then, 'We'll get it done eventually.' At first everyone's committed to it and 'Yes it's going to be great,' and then something takes over and it comes out five years later."

When asked, at the end of 1993, how he'd felt at the start of the year, Russell Senior's answer was "that I'd misspent my youth in a crap retro band when I could've had a proper job." And how long did he feel that way? "Until July, when we sold out and signed to a major label and I entered heaven."[260]

By July 1993, the legal problems with Fire had finally been resolved. Pulp had agreed to the label's demand of a series of 'points' on the next four albums, and the band were at last free to sign to Island. It's perhaps unnecessary to add that there was champagne.

The first Island release, in October, was *Intro*, a collection of the three Gift singles. The records had only been available sporadically – and in the UK only – so the album provided a convenient starting point for the benefit of the band's ever growing legion of new-found fans.

Considering it's a collection of songs recorded over the space of a year with the use of a full variety of producers and studios, *Intro* works remarkably well, both as a concise introduction to the Pulp aesthetic and as an album in itself – indeed, barring the presence of a couple of songs that were perhaps B-side material ('Space', 'Styloroc') and the absence of a couple of key songs from that period ('Live On', 'She's A Lady'), it's probably a pretty close approximation of the album that, given the chance, Pulp would have made in 1992.

"It was never really meant to be an album," says Jarvis, "but I think it hangs together reasonably. It's got quite an up-and-down quality, because some of the tracks were done with Ed Buller and some were done with ourselves. We're not exactly the Phil Spectors of Sheffield when it comes to producing, so some of it's slightly raggy, but it's got good spirit."[261]

Press acclaim was unanimous – they'd loved the singles, so how could it not be? "While Suede sing about the infinite possibilities of the next life," wrote Peter Paphides in *Melody Maker*, "of surmounting this drizzly everyday torpor, this *is* the next life for Jarvis. On the wrong side of 30 with 12 wayward years in pop behind him, his group have reached an arresting, fantastic climax. And Jarvis, as this mid-price update suggests, has become possibly Britain's grubbiest, greatest sex goon since Quentin Crisp."[262]

The compilation sold well, and provided an ideal prelude to 'Lipgloss', Pulp's first Island single, which followed in November. The song, which had been recorded in July at London's Britannia Row Studios, was in some ways a repeat of the 'Razzmatazz' formula – biting lyrics about a fucked-up woman set to a rousing glitterball tune. "The title," explained Jarvis, "came from a story I heard about an anorexic girl who used to eat only lipgloss. And the rest of the song – about a girl who has her self-confidence bashed down by a bad relationship – is based on someone I know. I think it's important to express these stories so that victims know they're not the only ones suffering."[263]

Musically, 'Lipgloss' is unsurprisingly glossier than any of the Gift singles, an enticing broth of a million twiddly synths and niggling, insistent guitars. Things do go slightly awry when the thrilling, accusatory attack of the verse leads into a chorus that's perhaps a little over-poppy considering the grimness of the subject matter – Jarvis's overexcited yelp of *"He changed his mind last Monday/ So you've got to leave by Sunday/ Yeah"* could be said to be bordering on self-parody. Even so, it's still a single the likes of which most bands would kill for, and one that was fully deserving of the now-obligatory press hurrahs it got.

Elsewhere on the single, the gorgeous 'You're A Nightmare', taken from February's Peel session, was an unexpected return to the balladeering of the *Freaks* era, with an added twist of understated, self-deprecating wit: *"It stopped sometime in May, while you were still away/ Was I in bed, or on a bus? Doing something pathetically ridiculous."* And then there was 'Deep Fried In Kelvin' – nine minutes and 49 seconds of thoroughly nasty genius that provided the perfect antidote to anyone who thought Jarvis might be guilty of romanticising Sheffield's grimy, insalubrious aspects in 'Sheffield Sex City' and 'Inside Susan'. Musically it's a pretty unexciting one-chord jam, but the sheer malevolence of the lyrics, painting a doubtless deservedly grim picture of Sheffield's Kelvin Flats (*"where pigeons go to die"*) makes it riveting: *"Oh children of the future, conceived in the toilets of Meadowhall, to be raised on cheap corn snacks and garage food. Rolling empty tin cans down the stairs – don't you love that sound? Like the thoughts of a bad social worker, rattling round his head, trying to remember what he learned at training college . . ."* It's impossible, really, to quote a line without wanting to quote the whole thing.

Admirably, when signing to Island, Pulp insisted that they retained the services of Scott Piering and Savage & Best, rather than having all the press and plugging done in-house as the label wanted. The result was daytime radio play for the first time ever, a storming live appearance on Channel 4's flagship youth programme *The Word*, a session for Radio 1's Mark

Radcliffe show – and number 50 in the charts. The *proper* charts. All right, so it wasn't quite world domination, but it confirmed what the impressively expensive-looking 'Lipgloss' video suggested: Pulp were now undeniably a proper, successful pop group with great looking hair.

The inevitable British-tour-with-a-handful-of-French-dates-thrown-in followed, including quite a few places they'd played on the St Etienne tour. This time, however, Pulp were filling venues on their own – a situation that was no doubt helped by the fact that, for the first time, they'd been getting respectable amounts of daytime airplay on Radio 1. "It was gradually dawning," says Nick, "that the key to getting a hit record was getting yourself played on daytime national radio, and that meant Radio 1. If you're not played on Radio 1, it ain't going to get played on Hallam FM. Also, getting played on Radio 1 means the press will write about it more, and you get lots more concerts, and people are physically at concerts who are enjoying it.

"By now, we'd play a concert and where it used to be a semi-circle, with dead space in the middle, by now it was people would immediately be right up to the front of the stage. That was another kind of great divide from the time when it might have been good but no one really knows about it, to people knowing they're on to a good thing. I don't know when that change had happened but it had happened, and it was a great feeling. We knew that 'Razzmatazz' didn't get any radio play apart from probably some obscure Peel/Steve Lamacq type thing, but with 'Lipgloss' we knew that you could see it was growing all the time, a bit of radio play and its coming in at 55 or whatever. Just that feeling, it was a very, very exciting feeling – yeah, you're on the radio, you know?"

For the French trip, the band were accompanied by *Melody Maker*'s David Bennun. The resultant piece included a truly immortal story about a night on the streets of Lille with Russell. Having announced that he was "going in search of sleaze", he persuaded the journalist and three members of the road crew to explore what was behind the bolted steel doors of the sprinkling of clubs near the band's hotel.

"With bated breath," wrote Bennun, "we stood outside as Russell boldly faced the first door of dissolution and, briefly doffing his Venusian sunglasses, knocked. The grill shuttled back. Red-rimmed eyes peered at the outlandish sight of Russell in full Pulp regalia. '*Bonsoir, monsieur*,' Russell began. 'With respect, I am a famous English pop star, and I would like to enter your club for free with my friends. Is this possible – *oui ou non?*' The door swung open. Inside, our pupils dilated upon a scene to alarm the Marquis De Sade. A tiny, dimly lit and sedate bar, populated by a few paunchy representatives of the bourgeoisie, led on to an even tinier dancefloor, where my former geography teacher (or reasonable facsimile thereof) and his lady wife were cutting a rug to the hypnotic, sensuous pulse of Simple Minds' 'Don't You Forget About Me'. Three '*Hey hey hey*'s were more than we could stand. We left."

Attempts to enter the next club faltered after Russell's brave attempts to convince the bouncer that he was Bono from U2; the next place they got into saw him bolt for the door after being propositioned by an Algerian in leather trousers.

The following day, Russell reflected that "we have picked up all this 'Prophets of sex and sleaze' business. Which is obviously nonsense, because we're none of us intensely perverted."

"What," interjected Nick, "about you knocking on the doors of sex clubs last night?"

"I think we're all a bit fascinated by it," countered Russell. "I think we're all peering through the door. But I'm not wanting to be hit with an iron bar for fun."[264]

Pulp were about to become legendary.

Chapter 12

From winter 1993 to spring 1994, little was heard of Pulp while they were holed up in Britannia Row with Ed Buller, completing what was to become their début album for Island, *His'n'Hers*. After recording a fresh set of demos in September, the sessions proper had begun in October, and recommenced in December after the *Lipgloss* Tour. "I'd pop into the studio quite a bit," remembers Nigel Coxon. "It was very good, very buoyant. Up until post-*Different Class* it was just an increasingly buoyant atmosphere really. It was kind of everything Jarvis had ever wanted at that moment in his life, and it was suddenly starting to happen. And he was getting that celebrity, pop-star thing that he wanted, and I think that musically they'd just hit an incredible roll, they just were making great single after great single.

"It was very much about Jarvis – and Steve I always thought he was quite influential, even though initially he might not have been massively musically influential, I always felt they were kind of the driving force. I mean, everyone was pretty weird, they were all individual kind of people in their own way, but most of the communication I would have with the band historically would be with Jarvis and Steve, talking about stuff generally, music and things."

The album – appropriately enough for a record whose primary theme was relationships of one sort or another – was completed on Valentine's Day 1994. Its release was preceded in March by another single – the magnificent 'Do You Remember The First Time?'

More so than perhaps any Pulp song before, 'Do You Remember The First Time?' is simply a fantastic pop song. It throbs, it sighs, it sizzles, it swells, it explodes into an absolutely enormous chorus. Sonically weightier than previous efforts, it rocks as well as popping: from the moment that first shimmering chord gives way to the queasy, big dipper-like rising guitar line, it's an instant classic. And the lyrical theme – of losing your virginity, and the contrast between the naïve innocence of early relationships versus the jaded attitudes into which one can fall in later life – is so inspired it's hard to believe it hadn't already been done to death.

"It's certainly quite a bitter song," remarked Jarvis. "It got me thinking about the first time I had sex, and how when you're older you get quite blasé about it. Sex should be an intense and special thing. It's ridiculous how older people can get themselves involved in relationships where all there is is sex; quite sad really."[265]

If anything, the B-side, 'Street Lites', was even better – as lo-fi as the A-side was glossily impressive, but brilliant with it. As with 'You're A Nightmare', it harks back in some ways to the old Pulp, the sound of a band scratching away in a dingy Sheffield rehearsal room with their antique organs and violins, while Jarvis mumbles his darkly obsessive tales over the top. Lyrical passages such as *"Pull the night-time tight around us and we can keep each other warm whilst cars drive by, en route to dried-up dinners and strip-lit kitchens that smell of gas and potato peelings. What you gonna do if you go home and he's not there? It wouldn't be the same if you didn't know it was wrong, oh touch me. And then go whilst I can still taste you, oh yeah leave me. And I'm walking off in the rain somehow . . ."* are simply stunning in the atmosphere they create.

With 'The Babysitter' (the fourth instalment in the Susan saga) completing the package, 'Do You Remember The First Time?' penetrated the chart at number 33. Pulp were top 40 virgins no longer.

When it came to promoting the single, as well as the usual video (an excellent piece of work in itself, with a rather touching air of nostalgia about it as the happy young Seventies couples cavorted on sofas and in shopping trolleys), the band celebrated their new-found status as a generously funded major label act by making a short film, also called *Do You Remember The First Time?*, in which various celebrities – amongst them Terry Hall, Jo Brand, Vivien Stanshall and Justine Frishmann – discussed their first sexual experiences, with Jarvis' own story as a linking thread.

"I have to admit," says Jarvis, "that our ideas were heavily influenced by *Downside Up* which was made by the British film-maker Tony Hill – sorry Tony. Steve phoned up all our interviewees and Martin Wallace and I converted the ping-pong room at Britannia Row Studios into a makeshift studio. The interviews were fitted in whenever people had a spare hour or so, so it was a case of putting down the guitars for a few minutes, talking to a guest and then going back in to record again."[266]

The result was a surprisingly candid, touching and highly amusing 30 minutes. "We tried to make an accessible film," Steve told *Melody Maker* at the time. "The tone of it's light, watchable, funny. We've discouraged the tabloids – there are enough quotes to bury everyone on it, taken out of context, so we've been quite careful there."

"As it stands," added Jarvis, "anyone could watch it, even people who might find our music distasteful. I'm not obsessed with sex, don't get me wrong. It's just that so often it gets written about in an idealised way or a *Carry On* nudge-nudge way. Then again, I don't think it would be so great if it was more open, like I imagine Norway to be, where they discuss it over the breakfast table."[267]

Both the film and video were premièred at the Institute of Contemporary Arts in London in March. "Much to my relief," says Jarvis, "the whole event was a success. I discovered later that someone had actually lost their virginity that very night, a few hours after the screening."[268]

His'n'Hers was released on April 11, 1994. Twelve years, eight months and four days after Jarvis had first stepped through the door of Ken Patten's home studio, Pulp had finally made their 'proper' début album. "It was just a great big sigh of relief really," says Jarvis, "because for the first time ever in our long tortuous history we had enough time and money to do a record as we wanted it. It was really good because, having waited so long for that kind of opportunity, we weren't going to mess it up."[269]

The album opens with the raucous glam-slam of 'Joyriders' – inspired, unsurprisingly, by real-life events. "It happened one day when we'd finished practising," says Jarvis. "I went out in my car and it ran out of petrol, and through a chain of circumstances I ended up surrounded by these kids who'd nicked a Ford Sierra, and one of them said, 'I'll get your car started.' So I ended up in the pouring rain, sat inside this car with these kids who had rave music on really loud, and for some reason eating chocolate limes. I've never really understood that. So I was sharing a chocolate lime, with the guys, in the back of the car, and it was just one of those situations where you can't quite believe you've got into it, and you're thinking, 'This is a dangerous situation, something bad could happen,' so you just have to kind of bluff your way through it. I always think if people sense that you are scared, then I think that gives them a thrill, and then they'll take advantage of that. So I just kind of said things that didn't make sense so they'd think that I was a bit strange, and think twice about doing something to me."[270]

'Lipgloss' is followed by 'Acrylic Afternoons', another twitchy, excitable ode to suburban sex, this time more of a straightforward celebration than 'Sheffield Sex City', but with more of that fantastic imagery. The pure abandon with which Jarvis throws himself into lines like *"Net curtains blowing slightly in the breeze, lemonade light filtering through the trees, it's so soft and it's warm, just another cup of tea . . ."* tempts you to think that no other lyricist has ever been quite so adept at bringing pictures to your head.

"Jarvis is a master of lyrics, I would say," muses Russell. "Jarvis is a really annoying person to work with and to live with. You can send him to go and get your heart pacemaker from the hospital, and he'll forget it, but he'll remember that you've got a little Subbuteo man from Coventry missing, and he'll see one in a jumble sale and get it and bring it you back. I mean, that's Jarvis. The small details is what he does, and I think that comes across in his lyrics. He's just got a knack for doing the most appropriate thing, and I think the music and the lyrics are just a very well-tailored suit."[271]

"At the start of 'Acrylic Afternoons'," says Jarvis, "there's some atmospheric incidental music. Originally, this consisted of this piece known as 'The Tunes Of Evil', a random unsettling noise conjured up out of an old analogue synth. As soon as we'd committed it to tape, strange things started happening in the studio. The mixing desk blew up, the multi-track for 'Joyriders' disintegrated and we had to piece it back together by clever jiggery-pokery. Ed Buller developed strange pains in his back and generally, the vibe went bad. So we had to destroy this music, but the engineer erased the wrong track. Obviously, 'The Tunes Of Evil' didn't want to die.[272] It started off as a bit of a joke, but then even Ed Buller and the engineer believed it was evil and we all agreed that we couldn't put it on the record because it would doom it to failure. It's put me off using synthesisers a bit – I think we might go acoustic from now on."[273] Indeed, towards the end of March, Pulp did just that, recording *Unplugged*-style sessions for GLR radio and MTV's *Most Wanted*.

Next on the album is 'Have You Seen Her Lately?', one of the only songs on the record that suggests it might possibly have been made by the same band that wrote 'I Want You' or 'She's Dead'. It's probably the definitive Pulp ballad: a majestic yet moving piece that puts aside the lyrical minutiae and vicious asides to simply become a moving plea for someone to escape a destructive relationship before it devours them.

Along with 'Lipgloss', 'Have You Seen Her Lately?' is also one of the songs that deals most explicitly with the theme that, according to Jarvis, is at the heart of the album: coupledom and what it can do to you. "Yeah, it's mostly about how, if you get into a relationship, you subjugate parts of your personality. It's that thing where two people start wearing matching clothes, their personalities start to merge, they know exactly what each other's thinking, and they haven't a whole personality of their own anymore. They've just got half of someone else's. If that relationship breaks down, you're suddenly an incomplete person."[274]

Side one closes with the oldest song on the album, 'She's A Lady'. Anyone who had heard it live since its début in 1991 would probably have been surprised by the lack, on the album, of one of the song's main distinguishing features: Russell's frequently remarkable violin part. "I fell out with Ed Buller over that," says Russell. "I was putting my violin on, it was fine, and he sent me home for a week to practise it! In the end, he left it off completely, and, while the anodyne disco version that's on the album is fair enough, I don't think it's got the same emotional rush that someone who'd been to a concert at that time and heard us play the song live would get."

'Happy Endings' is an enormous ballad that teeters precariously on the edge of schlock, but just about manages to be brilliant. Jarvis: "I'm pleased that it turned out well because it was one of those songs that, if not done correctly, could've been really cheesy. It'd been written for quite a long time but we never really played it live because I just knew that it had to be done in a certain way. If you did it totally straight, then it would just seem a bit too like you should get your lighter going and start swaying. It's about that romantic wish that things would turn out right in the end, and so I wanted it to be balancing on a tightrope between being terribly tragic and being kind of pathetic, and I think it manages to do that. You kind of want life and things to have a happy ending, and although you know at the back of your mind that life isn't like a film and it's probably quite unlikely that you're gonna get one, you still would like it – you kind of cling on to that romantic notion that it's going to happen one day."[275]

'Pink Glove' returns to the formula of bitter and twisted sex-obsessed lyrics set to a thumping disco beat. "This," said Jarvis, "is a song about one of those situations where you have to wear something to keep someone else happy . . . It's a trade-off between what you want for yourself and what you're prepared to do to keep them happy and why they liked you in the first place. I've never been in a situation like that, I just write about them."[276] Yes, Jarvis, of course you do.

'Someone Like The Moon' provides a return to sobriety as, over an eerie synth-violin-timpani combination (echoes of '97 Lovers'), Jarvis uses a story of a woman shattered by the end of a relationship to once more explore the disparity between the notions of romance and relationships we get from songs and films, and real life. "I've always had a bee in my bonnet about being sold an illusion by songs and TV. When I got older and started to have relationships and stuff, and found that life doesn't necessarily have a gripping plot, I felt that I'd been conned in some way, so it was always a thing from early on to try and write about what those things really were like, rather than the way they were presented in songs and stuff. You know, people do live life at just as extreme an emotional pitch in a place such as Sheffield, which has got a lot of faults, but people do fall in love and live and die in those places, and I couldn't see that anyone was representing that, and I thought it's just as dramatic as it happening in Beverly Hills or something."[277]

The album closes with perhaps Jarvis' greatest lyrical achievement to date – the gorgeous, moving, childhood's-end snapshot of 'David's Last Summer'. "I'm quite pleased with the lyrics of that one," he said four years later, "because it's quite a good evocation of the kind of summers I had at school – you know, if somebody's parents have gone away, and everybody'd pile round to their house on the Saturday and the party would start while it was still light, and there'd be people copping off with each other and spewing up because they'd had too much cider. It's quite a good, accurate picture of a summer in Sheffield when I was at school."[278]

"That was something that I wanted to do for a long time," he added on another occasion. "There's always that feeling when the sun comes out and you think, 'Oh yeah, I'm gonna have one of those summers, I'll be out all day in the fields climbing trees and stuff,' and you know very well that you're not going to do that, because you have to do real things, don't you? I suppose it's the sap rising. I wanted to write a song that attempted to conjure up that feeling of those summers that probably never happened, but you wish they did."[279]

His'n'Hers was the record that finally, once and for all, legitimised Pulp. It wasn't a record that might have been a classic if they'd had the money to record it properly, or one that might have done well if it had come out at the right time rather than three years late, or one that made sense if you'd seen them live a few times, or one that would have topped the charts in an ideal world but was ignored in the real one. At last, it wasn't a lost classic – it was a Classic. It entered the album chart at number 9. Pulp were . . . successful.

This time, it wasn't just the *Melody Maker* and the *NME* that were championing Pulp – respectable glossy publications such as *Q* and even the dad-rock bible *Mojo* loved the album too. And more respectably still, *The Observer*'s Nicola Barker was one of the first in a long string of broadsheet supplement journalists to profile Jarvis in a way that suggested they really, really fancied him.

The inevitable tour followed, kicking off at Glasgow for that year's Radio 1 Sound City event. In a twist of fate, Pulp had been booked, a couple of weeks before Kurt Cobain's suicide, as a last-minute replacement for Hole. The result was a small, confused, angry Glaswegian grunge element in the audience, which Jarvis, possibly slightly the worse for drink, was in no mood to appease. "I'm sorry if you expected me to have blonde hair and a short dress, because Hole aren't playing this evening. I think maybe Kurt Cobain is tidying his room and Courtney is trying to stop him taking drugs while he does it. It's a hard life being in a band. Getting up at 11 in the morning. It's terrible, that's why people turn to drugs." Cue noisy, unimpressed catcalls, and a furious version of 'Lipgloss' from the band. Later on, someone yells something that seems to raise the question of Jarvis' orientation. "That's it, I'm a poof. I don't care who knows it. Let's all be secure in our own sexual persuasions, eh? It doesn't really matter, does it? I mean, I'm not bothered. You could be making love to whatever species of animal, person or whatever. You ought to learn to be a human being." Massive cheering. By the end of the concert, Pulp seem to have won most of the mob over, with Jarvis' final enquiry as to whether they'd all enjoyed themselves being met with a resounding cheer. Even so, he can't resist a parting shot – "I hope you've met some people who you're going to have conversations with later on, because it should be a social education." Quite right too.

While the tour zipped around the UK and France, Island capitalised on the album's success with another single. Pulp had initially wanted 'Pink Glove' as the A-side, and Ed Buller had prepared a remix of the track, but Island pressed for a reissue of 'Babies'. Some wrangling later, the group agreed, with the stipulation that the original version, not the recent remix, be used on an EP alongside some new material to give the fans value for money.

The result, the *Sisters EP*, was a package that was pretty much impossible to fault. Wrapped in a splendid pop-art airbrush sleeve from *Clockwork Orange* artist Philip Castle, 'Babies' was kept company by the three songs that were completed during the *His'n'Hers* sessions but didn't make the grade for the LP. 'Your Sister's Clothes', originally called 'Glass' because Mark Webber thought it sounded like the American minimalist composer Philip, was an oblique lyrical sequel to 'Babies' – the finer points of the plot are hard to make out, but it seems that the younger sister is getting her own back by getting it on with her elder sister's boyfriend. Meanwhile, the music stomps and burbles away appropriately, with some especially fine violin. "For that one," remembers Nick, "Russ discovered this thing in the studio called varispeed where if they played the tape really slow, he could go *'ding, ding, ding, ding, ding, ding, ding, ding'* and when you played it back it'd be like, *'dingdingdingdingdingdingdingding!'* and it was actually like he was a competent musician. He was loving that."

Next is the soaring, poignant 'Seconds', a song in which Jarvis advances his theory that sometimes flawed, downtrodden people can have a lot more about them than those who have it all – a theme he'd return to a little later on in a certain other song. The issue in 'Seconds', as *Melody Maker*'s Chris Roberts pointed out, is whether second best is something people settle for, or whether it's something they're lucky to get.

Jarvis: "In Sheffield it sometimes seemed the life of my contemporaries was like a marathon – who'd give up first. People'd get picked off one by one, and were falling by the wayside. There got to be less and less people who were still trying to do something, and who kept 'refusing' to settle for second best. Then later you think: oh, but I might end up with fifth best. Also, there's the idea of 'second-hand' people, who've been through the mill a bit. It sounds a very silly analogy, but it's like reconditioned tyres, remoulds. You have to get remoulded before you go back out on the road. I don't think that's a negative or sad thing at all. I think it's quite interesting, third or fourth time around."[280] And still it feels like morning . . .

Lastly, there was 'His'n'Hers', a gleeful demolition of middle-class domestic coupledom, with a generous helping of shagging thrown in for good measure. *'Shove it in sideways'*? Nice.

The single was Pulp's biggest hit yet, entering the charts at number 17, meaning that – *yes!* – at long last, Jarvis got to fulfil his lifelong ambition and appear on *Top Of The Pops*. Pulp had already been cheated of one appearance – 'Do You Remember The First Time?' nearly made it, but the programme's makers decided they'd have shortlived New Wave of New Wave-ers S★M★A★S★H instead – but this time it was for real. *Yeah yeah yeah yeah yeah yeah yeah* indeed.

Nick: "I suppose when you start out being in a group, you never think, 'One day I will be on *Top Of The Pops*, because you never know if it's going to happen or not. You've no idea, so when it does happen, it's, like, *wow!* We had our taste of *Top Of The Pops*, and from that moment on you can honestly call yourself a pop star."[281]

Of course, Jarvis wasn't going to let this momentous occasion pass without incident. Pulling a pair of bright pink spotted knickers out of his pocket during the middle eight and tossing them into the audience is always a good move, but the moment of glory came when he opened his jacket at the song's climax to reveal the words "I HATE WET WET WET" on the inside – a cheeky comment on the insipid fake soulsters whose homogenised version of The Troggs' 'Love Is All Around' had just begun a mind-numbing three-month spell at the top of the charts. Totally unnecessary and thoroughly childish? Yes. Exactly the kind of thing we all dream of doing, and live in hope that, failing that, someone'll come along to do it for us? Er, yes.

Nick: "Wet Wet Wet had been at number one with that chuffing song for God knows how long. It was so boring – who's buying this bloody thing? It was our way of saying, 'Look, stop it.' "[282]

"I always hated Wet Wet Wet," Jarvis told *Melody Maker* soon afterwards. "Even when 'Wishing I Was Lucky' came out, I thought they were one of the worst pop groups in the world. It's Marti Pellow's smirk, I suppose. But you see, I found out that *Top Of The Pops* was going to go out live, and I thought if I didn't do something to surprise the powers that be, even if it meant we were banned from the show for all time, I'd never forgive myself. They all thought it was quite funny, actually."[283]

Steve: "When Jarvis did anything like that, they were never things planned as far as I know, so it seemed funny at the time. Because it was funny."[284]

Better still was to come the following month when Jarvis made an equally legendary appearance on BBC1's Saturday teatime schedule-filler, *Pop Quiz*. The series was, as the title suggested, essentially an extremely ordinary music trivia quiz, presented by a pre-*Millionaire* Chris Tarrant and generally featuring some pretty banal C-list celebrity panellists. The show was tailor-made for Jarvis to shine like a diamond on a dungheap, and he didn't disappoint. As *Select* magazine wrote afterwards,

> *"With much fringe-flicking and audience saluting, Jarvis, Des'ree and Chesney Hawkes fought it out against Marcella Detroit, Toby Jepson of Little Angels and Patric, ex of formation-dancing fetishists Worlds Apart.*
>
> *Introduced by Chris as 'a mixture of Scott Walker, Morrissey and Quentin Crisp', Jarvis displayed an unrivalled knowledge of Hot Chocolate in the lyric round. 'Yes that is sheer poetry by Errol Brown, it is of course* It Started With A Kiss.*' He helped out Chesney who was having difficulty naming two members of Suede: 'Er, Brett Anderson and Bernard something, er, Bernard Burtman?'*
>
> *Confidence boosted by full marks on the individual round for his answers to tough questions on fellow Sheffield sizzlers The Human League, he proceeded to take over the final quick-fire round to make sure his team romped home."*[285]

Jarvis' team – or, more accurately, Jarvis – won 47 to 34 and, in a funny sort of way, things were never quite the same again. "I was completely pissed," he admitted later. "I felt I'd struck a blow. Those kinds of things are important to me. I was sick of people letting you down, being crap and boring on shows like that. If you think, this person is from a group that is my kind of thing, not a cheese-master like they usually have on, then you want them to do well."[286]

The thought occurred, and not for the last time, that we'd just got the kind of pop star we'd always wanted.

The metamorphosis of Jarvis from Minor Indie Celebrity to All-Encompassing Pop Messiah continued over the summer with a string of festival appearances. T in the Park, Glastonbury and Reading, all of which were televised, demonstrated that Pulp's music was now, without a doubt, big enough to communicate itself to thousands on an open-air stage in the middle of the afternoon – as was Jarvis' personality. His between-song chat had acquired a kind of deadpan mock-*gravitas*: not many people could say things like "It's easy to get lost here, so if you want to get your bearings, you are at Glastonbury, we're Pulp and we're going to play some songs" sound so incredibly *weighty*, yet somehow funny at the same time. Pronouncements like "You can't be anything but what you are – and that's not a life sentence, it's a fact" (at Reading, just after playing a new song called 'Common People') should, by rights, make you want to smack him for being so pompous, but instead they manage to be Godlike.

Meanwhile, Fire Records were ensuring that there was no danger of Pulp's back catalogue getting lost in the rush toward the glorious pop future: they'd already reissued *Freaks* on CD, and in summer 1994 followed it up with *Masters Of The Universe*, a useful compilation of the *Little Girl* and *Dogs* EPs, plus the two singles from *Freaks* and their attendant B-sides. Jarvis agreed to write sleeve notes for the release on the understandable condition that 'Silence' was omitted, only to see his contribution replaced, upon the album's release, with a piece written by Clive Solomon.

"I don't know why," he remarked, "because it doesn't say anything completely derogatory about Fire."[287] Perhaps not, but maybe it wasn't the wisest move to include the 'Tunnel' story (from the rear sleeve of 'They Suffocate At Night') in its entirety, followed somewhat unfairly by comments drawing attention to the fact that the date he chose in the song for the day his life lost direction was the same date Pulp signed to Fire Records. Also, perhaps Clive Solomon wasn't overly keen on allowing Jarvis to air his view that Pulp's first period on Fire coincided with "the most depressing period in my life", and that the songs were "recorded in Sheffield in crappy little studios for hardly any money"[288] – not on the back of one of his own releases, anyway.

"I thought they were very cynical," says Solomon, "and rightly or wrongly, I took offence at the very negative inferences about Fire. Basically, it was a bit much. He can express his opinion at any time – but here, he had the chance to be constructive."[289]

The row meant that Jarvis refused to help Fire with their reissue of *It*, which appeared in October. The album had already been re-released earlier in the year by Cherry Red Records, who had bought the Red

Rhino back catalogue from Tony K after the label's collapse in 1988. However, it transpired that the *It* album had never been Red Rhino's to sell, having always been owned by Pulp and Tony Perrin.

"I called Cherry Red," says Perrin, "and said, 'Do you realise that I own the rights to the recordings, and you can't do that.' They basically said, 'Well we bought it in good faith, we paid Tony K good money for it, so we're putting it out.' At first I contacted Geoff Travis at Rough Trade, but I don't think he wanted to get involved, didn't think it was worth it, so I spoke to Nigel Coxon, and I think they took the view that there was so much Pulp back catalogue stuff out there that it wasn't really worth *them* getting involved and blocking it, so the last port of call was to turn to Clive Solomon. He reckoned he also had some claim to the rights, so I had to throw my hat in with him because he was the only one who had any interest in stopping Cherry Red selling the record. So he got it blocked, got the records recalled, remastered the album and reissued it on Fire." Just to complicate things further, the Cherry Red CD had also included the tracks from the 'Everybody's Problem' single, which then had to be omitted from the Fire CD at the last minute when it transpired that Red Rhino *had* owned those two songs, and therefore that the rights now rested with Cherry Red. As a result, barring the odd release on obscure Cherry Red sampler compilations, 'Everybody's Problem' and 'There Was' remain unavailable to this day.

Tedious legal shenanigans aside, the Pulp machine was continuing to march forward. A new Peel session was recorded at the start of September, featuring three fresh songs, 'Underwear', 'Common People' and 'Pencil Skirt', that had been premièred at the summer's festival appearances. Even better, later the same month, Pulp found themselves up for the prestigious Mercury Music Prize, *His'n'Hers* having been nominated as one of the albums of the year. At the prize-giving ceremony at London's Savoy Hotel, a representative from each of the ten finalists was invited in turn to say a few words before the winner was announced. Pulp stepped up to the podium and – yes – it was time for another Jarvis Moment.

"Music is my first love," he announced to the gathered masses, who chuckled in recognition of the first line from John Miles' kitsch Seventies epic 'Music'. "And it will be my last," he added, to further amusement, before going on to give a word-perfect rendition of the entire song. Sadly, it wasn't quite enough to win the judging panel over – *His'n'Hers* lost out by a single measly vote to the horror that was M People and their opus of homogenised soul-pop tack that was *Elegant Slumming*. Ouch.

Magnanimity was not on the agenda. "We booed," said Jarvis. "We needed the money.[290] They're absolutely terrible . . . the thing I hate about them the most is that you get the feeling that they really think there's some kind of 'quality' in what they do, when really it's just complete blandness. I love disco music and that, but I like stuff like Whigfield, where it's just a pop song and it's not trying to be anything else. I mean, M-People must be really ashamed of the fact that they play disco music. They must be, just because they feel the need to aspire to this idea of 'quality'. I saw that woman with the pineapple on her head go past, and I just looked in the opposite direction. Later, I was particularly violent towards a fruit bowl."[291]

More happily, the following day Pulp embarked on their first-ever American tour: a fortnight of dates as support to Blur. The coupling was significant: Blur had, earlier in the year, been the first major success of what was now being described (much to the horror of the main protagonists) as the 'Britpop explosion'. With the art-school pop of their *Parklife* album and singles like 'Girls & Boys' and 'To The End', they'd gone beyond the approval of the music press and the indie cognoscenti to legitimately huge success, teen adulation, cover of *Smash Hits* and all.

It was a long time since an alternative act had broken through into the mainstream with such force, and Blur's success – and that of Oasis, who, having denied from the outset that they were an indie band, had scored a string of huge hits in 1994 – suggested that there was something in the air. Strong premonitions that Pulp would be next over the top were reinforced on their return from America, when, again with Blur, they played two huge shows at Aston Villa Leisure Centre and Alexandra Palace.

One would have expected the predominantly teenaged and female crowd to be there essentially for Blur, and therefore largely indifferent to Pulp's charms – after all, Blur were massive, and Pulp's biggest single so far had peaked at number 17. Yet, at both gigs, 'Joyriders', 'Do You Remember The First Time?' and 'Babies' all met with delighted yelps of recognition, and the room exploded.

"There are mutterings of 'Shouldn't they all be in school or something?', but this was always more Pop Concert than Indie Gig," wrote the *Melody Maker* reviewer afterwards. "Pulp, only lately getting used to cheers, are greeted tonight with screams, proper screams, that ring like tinnitus throughout their set . . . They'd used a backdrop slide reading 'Applause' earlier on; the fitting cue card at the end might have read 'Untrammelled hysteria of a sort more commonly associated with North Korean state funerals.'"[292]

Reassuringly, there didn't seem to be any danger of Jarvis blanding out in the face of new-found mass acceptance: if anything, it seemed he had more to say. "You cannot buy credibility," he informed the audience at Aston Villa. "You cannot go and live in a shit area and expect it to rub off on you and make you be cool. People who live in those places don't wanna live there."

"Don't go for the safe option," he added later on. "If safe's here and dangerous is there, then you walk the tightrope between those two things. And you take the risk of people maybe laughing at you or thinking you're doing something stupid, and it's dangerous because you may fall off the tightrope, but at least you're trying to do something interesting. All right?"

After another French mini-tour in October, Pulp spent the rest of the year back behind closed doors, working on new material for the next record, playing occasional shows – such as when they were asked to play at the Ministry of Sound launch party for Quentin Tarantino's *Pulp Fiction*. Jarvis had already written an appreciation of the film for *Melody Maker*, and it could be said that Tarantino's work shared a certain something with that of Pulp: both took a familiar form – violent American films or short English pop songs, take your pick – and added a new twist by littering them with popular culture references.

"I thought *Pulp Fiction* was great," said Jarvis. "I never went to see *Reservoir Dogs* for ages after it came out, because I don't really like violence in films. It's sort of like heavy metal guitars. You can use it in a really cheap, sensationalist way, or else a bit more intelligently. But I don't think Quentin Tarantino's films are about violence anyway. They're about talking. He gets accused of just making films about other films, old pop records, crap Seventies TV shows and stuff, but sadly, people's heads are full of that stuff, and it's just lying if you have lots of dialogue and nobody ever alludes to that stuff. You go into a pub and it's all people ever talk about."[293]

A couple of days later, Jarvis' one-man invasion of the previously barren land of mainstream media continued when he appeared as a guest presenter on *Top Of The Pops*. "Like meeting Geoff Travis, and *Pop Quiz*, presenting *Top Of The Pops* felt like a turning point for me. Take That were number one with 'Sure', so I said at the end that 'Take That *are* Top of the Pops,' which [producer] Ric Blaxill liked, and he made everybody else say it afterwards. I know Jimmy Saville probably did it first but I revived it. But don't get me wrong, I'm not forging a career here. I'm not that bothered. I just do something if it's worth doing – or if it's paid well enough."[294]

1994 ended gloriously with two more landmark concerts. First there was the Prince's Trust Gala Concert at the enormous Docklands Arena, where Pulp played 'Babies' and a new tune called 'We Can Dance Again' on the same bill as East 17 and (yikes) Phil Collins. Then, on December 18, came *Pulp At Christmas*: a special concert at the Theatre Royal in London that finally managed to nail that sense of glitzy showbiz *event* that Pulp had been struggling to achieve since 1988's *Day That Never Happened*. The venue, as *NME*'s Rupert Howe noted, helped.

> *"Even while you ascend the soft-carpeted stairs to the stalls (under the lofty sneers of the assembled ushers, who view the assembled feather boas, glitter jackets and charity shop cocktail wear with a look of half-suppressed distaste), there's a sense of occasion that rarely lifts the spirits when traipsing into the Academy in Brixton.*
>
> *And when the house lights dim and the fire curtain goes up to reveal a huge white staircase ascending to the heavens and a twinkling backdrop of fairy-light stars, it really seems like showtime. Not that Jarvis does anything as obvious as mincing slowly down the stairs for his entrance. Instead he darts on from the side of the stage, launches into 'Love Is Blind' and starts a few of his angular* Generation Game-*style dance moves.*
>
> *More than ever he's got the chance to play in the spotlight and, naturally, takes full advantage. The Alan Partridge-meets-*Saturday Night Fever-*era-Travolta look (cream slacks, navy blazer, white tasselled scarf) is well up to Royal Variety Performance standards. If ever her Maj calls, no doubt Jarvis will be there."*[295]

As well as the requisite *Intro* and *His'n'Hers* numbers, the set included, for the first time in many years, 'Love Is Blind', 'Death Comes To Town' and 'I Want You' – which Jarvis explained to the audience came from 1989, 1987 and 1984 respectively. Surely he wasn't making some sort of point about how Pulp had been doing tubthumping drumbeats, cheesy disco and big ballads years before Blur had come up with 'Sunday Sunday', 'Girls & Boys' and 'To The End'? Hmmmm.

Whatever, the concert was a triumphant end to a triumphant year – a joyous "We've made it!" statement made with panache, humour and a complete lack of ugly gloating. Could they do no wrong? Apparently not.

By the start of 1995, Pulp had been slowly formulating plans for their next record for several months. The success of *His'n'Hers* meant that Island would be willing to provide a much larger budget for the follow-up, which opened up a much wider range of possibilities than they'd had previously. The 'clean slate' mentality was amplified by the band's decision that, after three years working with Ed Buller, it was time to move on to a new producer.

"Ed was the right choice at the time," says Steve, "but the album didn't sound quite right. At the time, Geoff Travis and Nigel Coxon said it sounded really reverby and echoey, and it's true, but at the time we thought it sounded fabulous, so you can't blame Ed. We were still considering him for the next album, as we thought he would have learnt from his mistakes, and better the devil you know, and that we could steer him away from that, but then Suede released *Dog Man Star* which sounded even more reverby than anything before, so we thought, no way."[296]

The kind of producer the band would require had already been shaped to an extent by the new songs they had been writing in the second half of 1994 – amongst them 'Common People', 'We Can Dance Again', 'Underwear' and 'Pencil Skirt'. What the songs had in common was that they were all relatively traditional pop songs in comparison to some of *His'n'Hers'* more eccentric excursions. "I don't think we sat down to write hit singles, to approach things commercially," says Russell, "but more *artistically*. I find pop music much more interesting and difficult to do than indie music."[297]

So there was no danger of Pulp turning into Stock, Aitken & Waterman, churning out the hits with their next mortgage repayment in mind, but Pop was still the key word. Pulp had always maintained that they'd never wanted to be an indie band; now they had the opportunity to make good on their promise (occasionally spelled out but frequently implicit in their refusal to be content with their 'underground' status) that given half a chance they could be the ultimate pop band – in a Pulpish sort of way, naturally.

"In late 1994," explains Steve, "me and Jarvis had this concept, to make an LP that was 12 pop songs and every one could be a single. We even talked about getting Benny from Abba to produce it, or Mickey Most, pure pop producers."[298] Other names that came up for discussion included Alan Tarney (A-Ha, Cliff Richard) and Stephen Hague (Pet Shop Boys, New Order). It was Geoff Travis, however, who suggested the idea of Chris Thomas – in his words, "one of the best producers in the known universe."[299]

A true heavyweight, Thomas had begun his career as an engineer on The Beatles' *White Album*, and made his name through the Seventies and Eighties thanks to his work with Pink Floyd (*Dark Side Of The Moon*), Roxy Music (*For Your Pleasure, Stranded, Siren*), John Cale (*Paris 1919* and *Fear*), The Pretenders, The Sex Pistols, Elton John, INXS and many others.

To help the band make a decision, Steve had made up a tape containing examples of the work of the various producers under consideration. "Of Chris' work," he remembers, "I put on Roxy Music's 'Love Is The Drug', The Sex Pistols' 'Holidays In The Sun', The Pretenders' 'Brass In Pocket' and a John Cale track, and it was so obvious that his stuff stood out. We gave him a demo of 'Common People' from a Peel session and he really liked it, and he proved great to work with too."[300]

Jarvis: "We wanted to kind of make it bigger sounding than records that we'd done before, but at the same time hopefully avoid being pompous. So that was the thing we were aiming for – size, without pomposity – which is a tall order in a way. We'd listened to lots of different producers who'd made big records such as Trevor Horn, y-know, ooof! – bit much, and Chris Thomas seemed to be the best one 'cos he'd worked with quite a wide variety of people as well. He'd kind of gone from Sex Pistols to INXS to *The Lion King*. For a start I was interested to meet a person who could straddle those kind of musical bases. So we sent him a tape and he seemed interested in it and he came to meet us. I was kind of expecting a big-shot producer to come in and say, 'Hey, I can make you a star if you follow my instructions,' and he wasn't like that at all. That's the good thing about Chris – to say that he's been involved in so many big records he is very kind of nervous about things."[301]

"I was sent a demo of 'Common People' to see if I wanted to do a single with the band," remembers Thomas, "and I liked the demo very much, and as a result of that I went to see them play live [at the Theatre Royal Christmas concert] and was very impressed with them. They had these stairs on the stage which was like a prop and it was incredible 'cos every single song that Jarvis sang, he sort of finished at the bottom of the stairs and then he'd go up to the top of the stairs so then when he'd started a new song, he'd make another entrance – so I thought it was brilliant! So I was quite impressed with that and the band were great live as well."[302]

The track the band had chosen for the A-side of the single, 'Common People', had been conceived the previous summer. "I went to the Notting Hill Record & Tape Exchange," remembers Jarvis, "to the bit that they have second-hand musical instruments in. I sold some records – but they used to have this policy where you could have the money or you could have twice that value in vouchers which you could spend in some of their other shops. So I went for the voucher option and went to the bit with the second hand musical instruments, so I bought this Casio keyboard, went home, and I was just messing about on the keyboard and that's when I wrote the first kind of little riff of it. And then, me and Steve were doing some rehearsals off Holloway Road somewhere and I played it to him, and when we'd stopped laughing he says, 'Oh yeah, that sounds like *Fanfare For The Common Man*,' or something like that, and I thought, 'Oh, that's quite good.' And that gave me the idea for what the song was going to be about."[303]

After being premièred at the Reading Festival in August, the song seemed to develop a momentum of its own – it quickly became a regular highlight of the live set, and even managed a creditable showing in John Peel's Festive 50 end-of-year poll on the strength of a single Peel session broadcast. The song's general quality made it an obvious choice of A-side and, with 'Underwear' picked as the B-side, the band went into London's Town House Studios for a week of sessions with Chris Thomas in late January.

The recording went well, but complications arose during the mixing stage. "We didn't get it right straight away," remembers Jarvis. "It was kind of 60 per cent of the way there, and I remember a look of horror on Chris Thomas' face 'cos for some reason I thought it would be useful to play him 'Mr Blue Sky' by ELO. That song's a bit cheesy, but there's summat about the start of it where that piano's going 'dun-dun-dun-dun' – it's quite good, y'know. I could listen to it as a good sound trying to forget about the horror of Jeff Lynne, but he obviously couldn't do that and there was the look of horror. It was kind of, 'God, is there some bad mistake gone on here?' "[304]

Chris Thomas: "When we were mixing it, suddenly Jarvis said, 'Well, it's not really right,' and we'd spent, I dunno, about a week on the song and here we are mixing it, thinking it's done, and suddenly it's like, 'It's not right,' and I thought, 'What?' And they played me 'Mr Blue Sky' by ELO, and it was completely different, and they said it should be like that. I thought, 'Christ – it's fine to tell me this now!' "[305]

Steve: "We had 48 tracks of music, with something on every track. We'd always wanted the song to have the same chugging sound as 'Mr Blue Sky', where you can't hear all the different instruments but just this wodge of sound, epic but not bombastic. We had four days to mix, and on day four it got to five o'clock, and all we could hear was a wall of noise. Then Chris did what turned out to be a classic move which was to change the mood. We were slightly shy of each other, as Chris can be a bit intimidating at first, but he came back with a bottle of Remy, which the three of us drank, and three hours later we'd finished."[306]

The result was an unimpeachably brilliant pop record. Absolutely everything seemed to be in place: a perfect balance of Jarvis' intelligent, biting, funny lyrics and a juggernaut of a tune that flails, stabs, builds to climax after climax and finally explodes triumphantly in a mixture of raw emotion and pop abandon. 'Common People' was the point at which Pulp finally shook off any last remaining shackles of indiedom: there could simply have been no excuse for this record to be universally loved.

Nigel Coxon: "When I heard the finished version in the studio, mixed, it was amazing. I thought it was just great, brilliant. It's a very special, unique feeling to hear something that good. You don't hear something that great that often, I don't think."

The song's lyrics, as has been well documented, were inspired by a girl Jarvis met during his second year at St Martin's, when he was required to take an extra degree option in addition to his main film course, and chose sculpture. "She did believe in common people, having come from a rich background, and she thought of the lower classes as something quite exotic, and something she could go and see as a tourist, to go to Hackney, to take something from it and use it in her own work. But I don't believe that common people exist, and that it's a daft way to think. I told her she wasn't trapped like they are. Anyway, she wouldn't have it.

"She never wanted to sleep with me, unfortunately. I only knew her for about three weeks, on this sculpture course, so I never got to know her very well. I didn't even know her name! I just remember talking to her in the pub, and quite fancying her, and sometimes that's quite interesting, isn't it? Sometimes a bit of tension can add some spice to a relationship."[307]

The result was the realisation of a reality that Jarvis had managed to avoid before moving down to London: that there is such a thing as the class system. "Before I left Sheffield," he says, "I thought maybe the whole world was like that. You're living in a certain situation and you haven't got any perspective, so I never understood before. Most people in Sheffield are kind of in the same boat, though of course there are posher and rougher areas. My area, around Intake, is now one of the roughest in the city but in my time it was all right, far enough away from The Manor, one of the worst estates. But as soon as I moved away, I suddenly realised class did exist 'cos you meet people from different backgrounds, and I began to socialise with people who'd been to public school. I hope I never got too much of a chip on my shoulder about it but it used to irritate me that I knew there were people in Sheffield whose lives were going nowhere, like mine had been, but who were quite talented and intelligent. They had been fucked up because there was no opportunity to do any-thing creative or interesting while there were people in London who were idiots in quite good jobs, making lots of money. And I got a bit resentful about that sometimes. But I was never one who'd only drink in pubs that served Tetley bitter, or wore a flat cap."[308]

So 'Common People' was an almost impossibly great pop song *and* a strident attack on social tourism. "To call someone a common person – at least in Sheffield – is a real insult, so I would never call myself or anyone I had any respect for common. That's what made writing a song about it interesting to me. Songs such as Paul Young's 'Love Of The Common People' have that corny idea about the warmth and greatness of people at the lower end of society, which is just a sentimental myth. It's shit at the bottom of society."[309]

The B-side, 'Underwear', found Jarvis back on more familiar ground: the regrettable shag. "In sexual situations," he explained in one of his ever-informative onstage chats, "underwear is the last line of defence.[310] You've gone home with someone, and it seemed like a good idea, and suddenly you find yourself dressed only in your underwear and you think, 'Maybe this isn't such a good idea.' But you've already made the move – you're semi-clothed and you've got to go through with it. You're balanced on this thing and it hasn't happened yet, but you know it's gonna happen."[311] Meanwhile, the band pressed all the right buttons, i.e. the ones marked Epic Ballad, with particular credit going to Candida's strangely heart-rending buzzy synths and Russell's trademark swooping violin, punctuated with delicate, tiptoe pizzicato.

It was obvious to all concerned that 'Common People' was the best record Pulp had ever made, and by far their most obvious hit. Indeed, it was such an obvious hit that Island wanted to delay its release till September, just before Pulp's next album was due. This was a suggestion the band were less than happy about – the world needed to hear this record *now*.

Jarvis: "I was used to being completely out of step with . . . not the rest of humanity, but with most of them! So having written this song – this kind of freakish occurrence where it seemed to be in tune with the mood of the moment, I thought – well, it created a problem because we hadn't got enough songs to do a whole LP, but I felt really strongly that it would be stupid to let this moment pass and to release it eight months later when it was kind of irrelevant. So we had a bit of a fight on our hands to persuade the record company to do that. I guess it's easy for them if you release a single and then three weeks later the album comes out and you shove a few off it, and that's it – 't-rar – go and write another one'."[312]

The argument that the time was ripe for a bout of mass Pulpmania was underlined by the two live appearances the band made that spring. A show at Radio 1's Bristol Sound City event in April, during which the band débuted 'Monday Morning' and 'Mile End' and climaxed with a rapturously received performance of 'Common People', was greeted with mass outbreaks of "Jarvis (*clap-clap-clap*) Jarvis (*clap-clap-clap*) Jarvis (*clap-clap-*

clap)" chanting from the audience (soon to become obligatory) and knickers hurled at the stage (ditto).

And then, the same month, a surprise appearance supporting Oasis at Sheffield Arena as last-minute replacement to The Verve (who had been forced to pull out when Nick McCabe broke his finger, meaning that Pulp were given the offer at three o'clock on the day of the show) was almost enough to worry Noel Gallagher: "Somebody mentioned this band called Pulp who we'd sort of heard of . . . 'this thing looks a bit weird so yeah I suppose so why not'. We remember watching them while they were on and we were all in the balcony, and I think it was the first time they ever played 'Common People'. The *whole* audience went absolutely berserk, and even me Mam – me Mam was sat next to me, and she went, 'God, I really like that song, what's that one called?' and I went, 'I don't even know who they are – I don't know what the song's called.' And we all sort of looked at each other and went, 'Fuckin' hell, it's a good job we're good.' "[313]

Steve: "There was an exciting mood in the air, which subsequently became Britpop. Blur's 'Boys & Girls' was out, so was 'Live Forever', and 'Common People' felt like a song of the moment. We were totally convinced, and Geoff Travis was right behind us, so we made Island release it."[314]

"Pulp normally won," says Nigel Coxon. "To be fair, they pretty much got everything they asked for from the record company till the very end of the relationship. If they wanted to make certain types of videos . . . you know, we always trusted their instincts, because that's what makes a lot of bands great: a lot of it comes from them ultimately. Especially a band like Pulp where a lot of the artwork, video ideas, a lot of the whole image, it wasn't like a design thing, a style thing; a lot of it came from them. Especially if things were on a roll, you have to give people their head."

With band, management, record company and the mood of the times all right behind it, 'Common People' was set for release on May 22, 1995. Hold tight . . .

Chapter 13

By the time 'Common People' was released, it was, arguably, already a hit. Radio 1 had been playing it regularly for weeks, with Chris Evans, who was then ruling the roost with his breakfast show, plugging it especially heavily. Similarly, Pulp weren't going to have to wait till the song was in the charts to get on *Top Of The Pops*: they made a stellar appearance on the show the week before the single came out, flanked by giant soapboxes and shopping trolleys taken from the video. And dancers.

However, few people could have anticipated that 'Common People' would be the kind of hit that would sell 70,000 copies in the first week of release and, on May 28, 1995, blast into the chart at number two – least of all Pulp themselves. "The Sunday they announced the charts," remembers Jarvis, "it was presented live in Birmingham, and all the chart acts had to mime to their songs. We didn't know what position we were, so we waited in this back room for them to call us. So time went on, it got to 6 pm and everyone was getting shaky. I went to the toilet to put my contact lenses in, but I hadn't rinsed them properly, so my eye went bright red.

"Anyway, we had to go on, and I was still in quite extreme physical pain, and my eye was streaming, so people thought I was crying because we were number two! And, of course, by that time my make-up was running and looked like non-set cement. It'd been raining, so there were big puddles in front of the stage, and just as 'Common People' reached its, erm, climactic chorus, I jumped off the monitor quite spectacularly, as you do, landed in a puddle, slipped and fell flat on me arse.

"So I'm left thinking, 'Fuck me, this is meant to be your ultimate triumph, and you're flat on your back in a puddle, your eye killing you, face falling off, on a wet Sunday afternoon in Birmingham.' Not quite what I'd been dreaming for 20 years . . ."[315]

In that sense, it was fairly unique amongst the events of summer 1995. Tragicomic pratfalls in Birmingham most definitely did not set the tone for the coming months – nor, indeed, did rain, as it turned out to be the hottest, driest (and, it seemed, longest) summer in Britain since 1976.

257

More excitingly, pop music had hit a similar glorious plateau: it was one of those rare periods when there was a good chance that if you turned on the radio or TV, you'd hear music that you *actually liked* – music that simply felt as if it had been made by and for people roughly like us, rather than cynically dreamt up by marketing men to flog to pre-teens and house-wives. Blur, Oasis and Pulp had led the cavalry, but many more were following: Supergrass with 'Mansize Rooster' and 'Alright'; Elastica with 'Connection' and 'Waking Up'; Ash with 'Girl From Mars' and 'Angel Interceptor'; The Boo Radleys with 'Wake Up Boo!'; even Edwyn Collins, languishing in cultdom since fronting Orange Juice over a decade before, got a look-in when he somehow scored an enormous hit with the marvellous 'A Girl Like You'. Of course, there was still an abundance of crap pop as well ('Common People' had been kept off the top spot by Robson & Jerome with their karaoke version of 'Unchained Melody', and elsewhere we had MN8, the Outhere Brothers, Mariah Carey and the odious Take That), but for a time, it seemed that 'our' music was going to permanently transcend the 'alternative' ghetto in which it had been languishing and take over the world.

Naturally, the term 'Britpop' was hated by every one of the artists involved, and understandably so: what it represented was the lumping-together of a set of bands who, by and large, had very little in common socially, historically, philosophically or musically beyond the fact that they all happened to be British and made guitar-based pop music of one sort or another with indie roots. It was a crude banner, and one that was open to misinterpretation and accusations of jingoism, but that didn't make the phenomenon any less important or any less real: Britpop simply represented the fact that, while there probably wasn't a larger amount of good music being made than at any other point in recent history (and the most successful artists, of course, still didn't necessarily equate with the most worthy ones), a lot more people were listening to it. The fact that, the week after 'Common People' had entered the charts, Pulp appeared on ITV's teethgrindingly-naff-but-watched-by-millions daytime flagship *This Morning With Richard And Judy* and still managed to be pretty entertaining said it all – they had entered the mainstream *and they were making it better*.

"I think that was the *Zeitgeist* pop moment for them," says Nigel Coxon. "But I don't remember at the time it being like, 'Oh my God, all of a sudden we're really pop': it was like it was rolling. And like I say, I don't think the ramifications of that started taking effect till after. At the time I think everyone was too busy enjoying it. At that time you didn't lose credibility by being on the cover of *Smash Hits*: it was just that alternative pop, Britpop, whatever you want to call it, was just for one of those rare moments, as popular as pop music. Whereas most of the time it sends itself on a much lower curve, and then occasionally you get these bubbles when it kind of happens and all of a sudden it is pop, if you like. I never felt it was at the expense of any credibility at the time – maybe later."

For Jarvis, of course, the turn of events was especially thrilling, having spent the best part of the previous decade-and-a-half not just on the outermost fringes of pop music, but also frequently on the margins of society itself. 'Common People' wasn't just a career upturn – it was a vindication.

"Because that had been a hit I thought, 'Well, having had all this time where nobody was listening to us and feeling really on the margins,' I got kind of excited I have to say – I got carried away. I thought, 'Yeah man, this is like a chance for idiots such as meself to infiltrate the mainstream in some way – to have a go.' And I suppose that's where you get the lyrics of something like 'Mis-Shapes'.

" 'Mis-Shapes' are these chocolates and they used to have them in the sweet-shop next to our house. They were the ones that had gone wrong in the factory – they were misshapen – kind of 'elephant man' of the sweet world. You could buy them in a bag much cheaper than a normal box of chocolates would be and they tasted as good, it's just that aesthetically they weren't that pleasing, so that seemed to be a fairly reasonable metaphor."[316]

Shortly after 'Common People' had been completed, the band spent five weeks in the studio with Chris Thomas recording tracks for their next album. The sessions were productive, yielding versions of 'Bar Italia', 'Monday Morning', 'PTA (Parent Teacher Association)', 'Mile End' and 'Pencil Skirt', but they still didn't have enough songs for a whole LP. As a result, the band had spent most of April and May back in the Catcliffe pottery warehouse writing new material.

This time, doubtless spurred on by the knowledge that these songs would now, without a doubt, reach a substantial audience, the muse was with them. By the start of June, with 'Common People' riding high in the charts, 12 songs were written and ready to be demoed at Axis Studios in Sheffield – or almost ready. Typically, through the writing process, Jarvis had left writing the lyrics till the last possible moment, and still hadn't got round to it a couple of days before the band was due to record the songs.

"That was probably my most concentratedly creative period of writing words, because unfortunately I don't always take notes. I do occasionally write things down in a book as I'm travelling around and stuff, and on the back of bits of envelopes, but I hadn't really got that much and we were demoing the songs up in Sheffield and I was staying at my sister's house. We'd recorded all the music and what usually happens is that we will record the songs and somebody will draw it to my attention that there needs to be some singing over the top – 'If you're going to sing, Jarv, you really ought to have some words rather than, like, the mumbling you've been doing for the last four months.' I had to accept this as a fact and we'd recorded all the music and I had to write the words for eight songs in one night. In the end, I didn't do it in one night – I did five one night and three the next night. I just sat in me sister's kitchen with this brandy me mother had brought back from Spain and I just kind of necked that, passed out after five and finished off the other three the next night. It was obvious that there was something waiting to get out. That's what a lot of the feeling was on that record I suppose: having waited such a long time to get people's attention, once you'd got it you had to do something with it."[317]

In fact, the band managed to demo a total of 12 songs in the session – seven of which would surface on the album. There was also the future B-side 'Ansaphone', and four unreleased tracks: 'We Can Dance Again', 'Paula', '(Don't) Lose It' and 'Catcliffe Shakedown'. 'We Can Dance Again' was a product of the band's late 1994 writing sessions, and had been played live a couple of times, at the Prince's Trust concert and the Theatre Royal show. More so than any other Pulp song of the time, it was a blatant expression of Jarvis' joy at the success and acceptance he had belatedly found: the first line is, *"We've been waiting for this moment to arrive since late September 1985; now you watch the ice rings melt before your eyes: we can dance again"*, and the music is similarly celebratory. It's arguably a lost classic, and fans who've heard it have often expressed mystification at the fact that it never emerged officially.

"We did put a lot of time into the arrangement," says Russell, "and I can still hum it. After it seeming like it might be a single for a couple of weeks, it started looking like we were pasticheing ourselves. It was very Pulp-y, and I think Jarvis just felt a bit too much of a self-parody performing it. It might have been good for someone else." He has a point – after the events of summer 1995, it really didn't need pointing out that Jarvis was pleased that Pulp were doing well. Releasing a song about it might have been labouring the point somewhat.

The rest of the songs never even got as far as being played live – understandably so in the case of 'Paula', which sounds like little more than a jokey end-of-the-session throwaway. It's not without its redeeming features – the Jarvis-by-numbers lyrics (*'Woah-oh, funny how we still spend the night together, even though we don't see one thing the same, but still we do it again, oh yeah we do it again . . .'*) are fairly amusing the first time you hear them, and there's an excellent ner-nee-ner-nee one-string guitar solo, but basically it's rubbish. "I remember going into the studio to do an interview with Jarvis," says the *Sheffield Star*'s John Quinn, "and Jarvis told the engineer to put the tape on so I could hear some of the songs. The first one that came out was 'Paula', and he went, 'For God's sake, don't play him that one!' "

'(Don't) Lose It' is altogether more mysterious, being unheard by anyone outside the band's inner circle. "I thought that should've been on," says Nick. "I thought that was great. Another one where it's got a very understated verse but a loud chorus – hey, you might have heard that one before somewhere, but I was surprised that one didn't get in."

Finally, there's 'Catcliffe Shakedown', a nine-minute epic made up, *à la* 'David's Last Summer', of all the bits of music that they'd written that wouldn't fit anywhere else. The lyrics were inspired by the environment where Pulp were writing the album. Nick again: "This little town, Catcliffe, where we did all the rehearsing in these pottery warehouses, it's an old pit village, and it's kind of at the arse end of Rotherham, so the people there are pretty rough. The River Don goes through it, which is pretty smelly – well it was, it's nice now. There's two pubs in the village, enter both at your peril: you open the door and everybody's there with the central eye, and the odd little shop where you can buy individual bags of crisps and mucky books. That sort of thing. So it's a strange place, and you'd be rehearsing and you'd hear kids cobbing stones at the side of the corrugated metal on the outside going, 'You're shit! Fuck off!' and all that kind of thing. 'Catcliffe Shakedown' had like eight, nine different bits. Too silly to ever see the light of day. Come the box set that will be the last CD, right at the bottom."

Having separated the wheat from the chaff, Pulp returned to the Town House later in June to tackle the songs for the album – only to be interrupted, after a matter of days, by some excellent/terrifying news. The Stone Roses' John Squire had broken his collarbone, forcing the band to pull out of their wildly anticipated first UK show in five years – headlining the Glastonbury Festival at the end of June. A replacement was needed *post-haste*, and Rod Stewart wasn't available. Did Pulp fancy it? Tricky one.

Nick: "We heard from the office that we were in the running to take their place as the Saturday night headliners. We were like, 'Right, OK, tell me when it happens.' We heard Rod Stewart was going to do it and then they said, 'No, he's not doing it, we want you to do it.' It was like, 'Right . . . fucking hell . . . right.'

"So we did some rehearsing in the Town House to get some of the stuff ready, 'cos we played a few new songs. Because it was all last minute, we didn't have any transport – we only just managed to get a bus, and the hotels round about were booked up. We decided we didn't want to stay off the site, we wanted to enjoy the whole weekend, so the only solution was to buy tents. Someone from the office went out and bought two huge frame tents and some little tents and loads of sleeping bags, so we took all our camping gear."

With the band comfortably installed on the festival site in their back-stage tent complex, showtime slowly approached and nerves mounted. Glastonbury was and is the biggest of the British music festivals, with as many as 100,000 people on-site, and the Saturday night headline slot was the most prestigious of the weekend. "It was just great," remembers Nick. "It was a scorching hot weekend, I remember on the day we were there in the backstage compound, PJ Harvey was playing, and we'd go up to the side of the stage and have a look out. 'Lot of people there. Going down well, isn't she?' Nerves were off the scale. Then we'd watch whoever was on next, crowd's going mental – nerves off the scale even more. And then it was our turn. There was a fifteen-minute gap while we were in the dressing room, and everyone is cacking it really, really badly, 'cos obviously this was by far the biggest concert we'd ever done."

And that was just the drummer. "It was the most nervous I've been for a concert ever," says Jarvis. "I remember about 10 minutes before we were gonna go on, I remember sitting on a chair and holding on to the sides of it 'cos I was convinced I was going to have an accident, break my hand or something, and I wouldn't be able to go on. So I thought if I just stay on this chair and hold on to it as tight as I can, then nothing bad can happen to me and we'll still be able to go on stage. I wasn't thinking very rationally. Once we went on it was great, but I was very scared."[318]

From the moment that the band stepped on stage and the vocodorised "Com-mon Pe-pol" sample gave way to the opening strains of 'Do You Remember The First Time?', it was obvious that this was the kind of concert for which the word 'triumphant' was laughably inadequate. Spirited renditions of the likes of 'Razzmatazz', 'Babies' and 'Joyriders' were joined by a host of new songs, each of which the crowd lapped up as gratefully as the more familiar material.

Jarvis' between-songs chat, which captured the mood perfectly, was probably as important a part of the evening as the music – right from the moment when, two songs in, he addressed the crowd for the first time: "Good evening. Y'alright? [massive cheer] That's good. We're all right. This is a good thing that's happening here, us all in this place. And do you know what's happening in the outside world? ['No!'] And do you care? ['NO!!!'] John Major or anything. [The Tory then-prime minister had temporarily resigned and called a party leadership election.] When you go home on Monday morning, you're going to go home to a different world. But we're not thinking about that now because this is Saturday night, and the furthest thing from our minds is Monday morning. But this song is called 'Monday Morning' . . ."[319] The occasional confused shouts for the Roses were swiftly replaced by near-universal Cocker adulation. We already knew from the previous year's escapades that Pulp were unlikely but perfect festival material, but this was stellar.

Jarvis even managed to fit in a Roses reference when introducing 'Sorted For E's And Wizz', the phrase having come from a friend who'd seen the band at Spike Island sometime toward the start of the decade and heard it repeated endlessly. "We'd just written the song," says Jarvis, "and I thought it would be quite good to play at that – not that I wanted to bring everyone down, but it just seemed that it was dealing with that kind of situation, it would be a good place to play it for the first time."[320]

'Sorted' may have been the most appropriate song, but 'Mis-Shapes' was at least as exciting: the sentiment of the song may have since become somewhat dated, but at the time it spoke to at least as many people as 'Sorted', and the sense of triumph in the air made Glastonbury the ideal place to play it. "If you grow up in a town," said Jarvis before playing the song, "and everybody else wears a white shirt when they go out on a Friday night, with short sleeves, and maybe a moustache if you're a bloke, or if you're a girl, stilettos. And when you see them in town, there's a pack of about 10 of them, and they laugh at you because they think that you're the weird one. [Enormous cheer] And this is about how we are going to have our revenge on them."[321] It really did feel like the troops were being rallied.

"It was quite nerve-racking to be playing new stuff," says Nick, "but we could see the crowd were really into it, you know, and Jarvis did his chit-chat between songs – we were listening to him thinking, 'You're going to be in the audience going "I'm with you – this is what I want to hear".'"

Of course, of all the innumerable magic moments that happened that night, the most magical of all came at the end. In the hands of anyone else, it would have been stomach-turning schmaltz, but somehow, in Jarvis' hands, it was perfect: "I don't usually make any notes before we play, because I think you should always be spontaneous on stage. But because I was sat in my tent today, and I was thinking about things, I did actually write a few things down. Let's see if I've missed anything out. Carrots, potatoes, peas . . . oh no, that's my shopping list. Erm – all right, I've said most things, the only thing is, you can't buy feelings, you can't buy anything worth having. Also, the other thing is, if you want something to happen enough then it actually will happen. And I believe that. In fact, that's why we're stood on this stage after 15 years – 'cos we wanted it to happen, you know what I mean? So: if a lanky get like me can do it, and us lot, then you can do it too. All right? So, on that positive note, this is the last song, we can't play anymore after this. This is 'Common People'."[322]

And Glastonbury exploded.

"We came to 'Common People'," says Nick, "and we started playing and the crowd roared and it was amazing. As Jarvis started singing, basically you could hear the crowd louder than you could hear him and that was . . . the hairs at the back of your neck just went. Amazing. 'Cos we'd never heard anything like that before, and you look out and see the lights flashing, sea of people, thinking how many people were watching – was it 80,000? 'Cos I know a lot of people got over the fence, so it could have been 100,000 people watching and it was just amazing coming off stage after that – '*Fucking hell!!!*' "

Jarvis' parting words, if you could hear them beneath the deafening applause, said it all. "Thank you very much. And thanks for making this a very special night for us. I hope it was special for you as well. I hope you enjoy the rest of your time here. Glastonbury, 25 years. Here's to 25 more, all right. Live on."[323]

The only way of topping something as mammoth as that, of course, was to do it all again a month later – this time at the similarly huge Heineken Festival at Roundhay Park in Leeds. Glastonbury may have been a one-off, but Leeds certainly gave it a run for its money: the reaction was as huge, 'Common People' was as explosive ("We're going to play one more song. Bet you can't guess what it is. 'Dogs Are Everywhere' d'you say?"), the moment was still *now*. Jarvis seemed a little more relaxed this time – having obviously had a little time to take stock of his new-found hugeness, he was able to send himself up a little as the crowd chanted his name. "It's a pity my mother's not here, then she'd be able to see how popular I am,"[324] he remarked at one point.

At Roundhay, it seemed that roughly every third person in the 70,000-strong crowd was wearing an "I'm Common" Pulp T-shirt. The mainstream had most definitely changed for the better.

The rest of the summer was spent mostly in the studio, finishing the album. "Once we'd kicked into gear," says Chris Thomas, "we started to work very, very quickly. Once we came in with that second batch of songs, we were doing two songs a week. We were really, really, *really* working very, very quickly. And I think what stood out was the quality of the writing – I mean I just loved it, I thought it was fantastic. At the end of it, I realised it was definitely one of my favourite albums."[325]

Meanwhile, Mark Webber's position in Pulp had come into question. As Pulp had got busier, he'd got busier too, and his onstage role had developed from playing on the odd song when necessary to contributing additional guitar and keyboards almost throughout the set. The ever-more intensive rounds of touring, recording and promotion through 1993 and 1994 had meant that Mark had been forced to give up his job of tour manager to Richard Priest and relinquish most of the fan club work to his friend Alex Deck, and, although officially still a hired hand, he'd gradually become more and more involved with the band's more recent writing and recording sessions.

"At first," remembers Nick, "it was more a question of him taking over what Jarvis had been playing, but in rehearsals for concerts, at the same time as learning parts you'd be writing songs as well and thinking, 'Well, I'll try this bit,' and Mark would contribute to those things, suggest doing a line like this, so he was getting more involved. We weren't expecting him to contribute to songs, he just did 'cos he was there, and because that was happening it seemed kind of wrong to say, 'Well, you're not really a member of the group' – it just didn't seem the right way to go about it. And then, during the actual making of the *Different Class* record, we said, 'Well you're working so much towards it you might as well become a proper member of the group.' You know, we had a few discussions amongst us as to whether that should happen or not and some of us were kind of more into it than others, but I suppose in the end it wouldn't seem right to exclude him. I found out later that it was a surprise to Mark to be asked to join the group.

"I don't think that anyone was really against the idea, but it was more like a case of, you know, five's enough as it is, six is kind of the upper size limitation for a group. With mundane things like all having your photograph taken together, it's difficult enough with five, never mind six. Another shortarse in the group an' all! Mark's quite a quiet person anyway – I think if he'd been a loud person, perhaps he wouldn't have been asked to join. You're only allowed one loud person in the group – the others have got to be quiet. Work out who the loud person is!"

"We were recording *Different Class*," says Mark, "and it was getting to the point where the group was ready to get really popular. Then there was a meeting with Geoff Travis and the rest of the band, which I wasn't allowed to go to. I considered all the possible outcomes of the meeting and thought that they were gonna say, 'You know, we're gonna be popular, so fuck off!' However, I was quite surprised when they told me that they wanted me to stay. It was very flattering and it certainly beat being put on those wages I had been on for quite a while at this point!"[326]

Sessions for the LP continued through the summer, and the final mix was delivered on August 14, with the rest of the month set aside for a well-deserved holiday. Jarvis needed some time to get to grips with the fact that he was now a very, very famous man indeed – and, almost as uncharacteristically, a very busy one. He'd always been on call as a pop star – "24 hours a day," as he'd been fond of saying – but this was the first time there'd been a real demand to satisfy. "It eats into your free time," he mused, "which is quite a strain. I wish I could have allotted a bit more of my time on the dole to now but I don't complain that much 'cos at the time, I really wanted something to happen, so it would be silly to say you didn't want it any more."[327]

And it wasn't just Jarvis whose past few months had been full of Pulp: in the summer of 1995, you couldn't turn on the TV without seeing him peering out from the 'Common People' video; or performing the song on the *Late Show*'s special *Britpop Now* programme; or being amusing with Russell on MTV's *Most Wanted*; or dishing out advice to youngsters on agony aunt show *Dear Dilemma*; or presenting *Top Of The Pops* again, refereeing the Blur v Oasis chart battle. Similarly, you couldn't pick up a magazine or newspaper – *any* magazine or newspaper, from the *Mirror* to *Mojo*, *Smash Hits* to *The Sun* – without seeing Jarvis' face plastered everywhere, often for the most tenuous of reasons. Doubtless thanks in part to his dispensation of on-stage wisdom, Jarvis was almost becoming a modern-day oracle.

"You have to keep giving your opinion all the time, don't you?" he observed. "You get asked about things. I do like to give my opinion, yeah, not that I think it's particularly great, but it's mine. That's part of the reason people join bands, I'd say, because they're show-offs and want people to take notice of them, so . . . I can't complain."[328]

"The first time the fame thing really struck me was when I was on holiday in the south of England, and these big blokes would lumber up to me and I'd think, 'Oh shit, I'm in for a right hammering here for looking like a weirdo,' then they'd shake my hand and say, 'Like your song, mate.' That was nice. Of course, as soon as I get used to it, some big bloke will lumber up to me, I'll say, 'Hello, who shall I sign the autograph to?' and he'll twat me for being a weirdo."[329]

"They just usually ask you, 'Are you you?'" he said on another occasion. "In fact, I've even been thinking of printing up some cards that just say, 'Yes, I am,' so I can get one out before they even say anything."[330]

Not that he legitimately minded all that much: after all, he'd spent his entire adult life attempting to become a pop star. It'd be very strange behaviour indeed to change his mind within six months of finally getting it. The dominant feelings, in Jarvis and amongst the band in general, were still of relief, triumph and vindication. "It's what I always wanted, right back to the time when I felt I was marginalised," Jarvis said to *Q*. "For a start, it makes you feel that you haven't wasted the last 15 years of your life, that you were right to have carried on. It makes you feel you weren't mentally ill at that time."[331]

The important thing to note is that no big change had taken place in Jarvis himself (remember David Lockwood's characterisation of the 15-year-old Jarv as someone who was a celebrity when he wasn't famous?). It was more of a combination of the world meeting him halfway and a lifetime spent not only dreaming, but getting gradually better at doing the job for real.

"I honestly believe he couldn't do anything else," Russell told *Melody Maker*. "Me and Nick have both lived with him. Before I'd lived with him, I'd known him socially and you always expected this Jarvis act would be dropped at some point during the day. But you can sit down and watch *Neighbours* and he'll be prancing round the room, striking poses and putting on silly voices, speaking to the characters like they're guests in the room. And I'm just sat there having me tea. I'm going, 'Look Jarvis, there's just me here, you're not on stage, just sit down and let me watch the telly.' But there's no point in telling him to stop being Jarvis because he can't help it. You know, I've never actually seen him be 'natural'."[332]

"He's right," admitted Jarvis. "I never stop. If I stop I get bored, if I actually just sat there watching the telly, it would seem really pathetic to me. I have to talk at the telly, take the piss or whatever. I think it makes me a little difficult to be around sometimes. It certainly makes me difficult to live with. I think Russell found the whole experience of living with me very traumatic."[333]

Pulp's ascent continued in September with the release of their first post-Glastonbury single: a double A-side of 'Sorted For E's And Wizz' and 'Mis-Shapes'. The band had initially chosen the former as sole A-side – as Steve said, "We wanted to get off the pattern of doing uptempo singles, as we'd done seven stomping songs, but it would have been a commercial risk as radio doesn't like smaller records."[334] Meanwhile, there was some slight nervousness from the Island Records marketing department about 'Sorted' 's druggy lyrical theme.

That they would have worried. The single generated Island's biggest advance order ever: 180,000, normally enough for a number one single. As it turned out, history repeated itself and Pulp were denied the top spot by another housewife's choice: Simply Red's 'Fairground'. (Sometimes nature makes mistakes . . .) Even so, the fact that 'Sorted'/'Mis-Shapes' was still a massive hit, entering the charts at number two and staying there for a good while, hammered home the fact that 'Common People' had been no fluke.

The pensive, thoughtful 'Sorted For E's And Wizz' was no *Zeitgeist*-straddling anthem in the order of 'Common People', but was at least as intelligent and biting. Again, it found Jarvis backtracking to the late Eighties, this time musing on the euphoric but ultimately hollow experience of acid house. " 'Sorted for E's and wizz' is a phrase that a girl I met in Sheffield once told me," Jarvis had explained to the Glastonbury crowd. "She went to see The Stone Roses at Spike Island, and I said, 'What do you remember about it?' And she said, 'I just remember all these blokes going round saying, "Is everybody sorted for E's and wizz?" ' I thought it was a good little phrase, and about five or six years ago we went to a lot of what we in those days called raves, and it's about the experience of that. I went to these things, and it seemed like it was people trying to summon some spaceship to land, it was like some kind of ritual, and everybody was friendly and everybody wanted to know your name. I got lost at one once, and all these people who'd been going, 'Yeah, man!' wouldn't give you a lift home. It's not so good, is it?"[335]

'Mis-Shapes', meanwhile, was the definitive rousing outsider anthem, inspired both by Jarvis' Sheffield nights spent walking through the city centre in fear of townie mobs, and his more recent acceptance by the mainstream. "It was quite dangerous to go into the centre of town on a weekend night, as everyone socialised there," he told *Attitude* magazine. "You'd get these packs of blokes, all dressed the same in the white short-sleeved shirt, black trousers and loafers, and they'd call you a queer or want to smack you 'cos they didn't like your jacket. The thing is, those people hunt in packs, whereas the misfits or mis-shapes, because of the fact that they're more individualistic, are easier targets. So the idea of 'Mis-Shapes' is the fancy that the misfits would form some kind of an alliance or army, and take over."[336]

Elsewhere on the 2-CD release, we were treated to the gloriously silly 'PTA (Parent Teacher Association)' (to whit: *"Just one touch was all it took/ No, you can't learn it from a book/Let's go upstairs and have a . . . look."* Etc.), that legendary Glastonbury performance of 'Common People', and two rather cheesy club mixes of the song. The artwork, typically for a Pulp release, was superb: a spot-on pastiche of a Seventies fold-out dressmaking pattern for 'Mis-Shapes' ("Wear your jacket with pride – or don't wear your jacket at all") and . . . hmm, some kind of origami diagram for 'Sorted', with both designs accompanied, as always, by Jarvis' spot-on sleeve notes.

In the event, the overall aceness of the package was unfortunately over-shadowed by the fact that the origami diagram happened to represent a speed wrap or – as the *Daily Mirror* had it in their September 20 front-page story – a "DIY kids' drug guide", urging the powers that be, furthermore, to "BAN THIS SICK STUNT".

"I got a call the night before saying it probably was gonna happen," says Jarvis. "The next thing I heard about it was my mother calling up at quarter past 10 the next morning, saying breakfast TV and various people had been ringing her up trying to get my number and trying to get her to make a statement about it, and stuff. But me mum's all right, she's not daft, so she didn't say anything to them."[337]

Conveniently, the paper ignored the fact that the lyrics of 'Sorted', dealing as they did with the vacuous nature of drugged-up rave euphoria, were anything but pro-drug, and that there was absolutely no likelihood whatsoever that either listening to the song or examining the diagram on the sleeve was going to make anyone decide they wanted to get, um, sorted. As Jarvis pointed out, "Origami does not lead to drug addiction, as far as I know – I might be wrong."[338]

Hilariously, the *Mirror* cover story was written by Kate Thornton, who within months would become editor of the Jarv-worshipping *Smash Hits*. Less hilariously, the next couple of days saw the story refusing to die, with the paper holding a farcical phone poll resulting in an alleged 2112 to 770 majority voting in favour of banning the record, and ringing up the father of Daniel Ashton, who had recently died after taking ecstasy, for a comment. Jarvis managed to play it straight for a perfunctory statement to the paper ("I didn't take much notice of [the sleeve] at the time because it didn't offend me . . . These days, the only thing I do for kicks is ride my bike . . ." etc.), but shared his indignation with *Melody Maker* the following week:

"If I was to say to them, 'Oh yeah, maybe once or twice I like to get off me head,' they'd basically say, 'Cocker the drug fiend.' And the other thing was I didn't wanna come across as Cliff Richard, saying I never touch drugs, 'cos then they'll just be planting people around me, waiting to catch me with a syringe in me hand, and it'll be like, 'So clean Cocker is actually a complete drug-addled wreck.' So I tried to steer a course between the two things."[339]

"It's very irritating to me," he added a few weeks later. "For a number of reasons. To begin with, there's the hypocrisy of it. They take this high moral tone, as if they're the guardians of public morality or something, when everyone knows they thrive off of immorality. They want loads of horrible things to happen, that's how they sell their papers. If ever there was such a thing as immoral earnings then that's what they're up to. Titillation, that's it.

"Like ringing up that bloke the day after his son had died of an E overdose to ask him what he thought of our record. They don't give a toss about his feelings, they just wanna paper up their story. I don't buy them papers, so even though I know that they exist they don't affect me. Then all of a sudden you're a part of the way they sell themselves. It brings your attention to how fucked up it is.

"This is another thing I have against the tabloid press. After the Hillsborough disaster, some of the papers printed pictures of people getting crushed against the barriers. And, you know, it's there in a paper, so you look at it. You know it's not a very healthy thing to do, but it's like driving past a car accident. There's just this part of you that can't help but be curious. It's not healthy, it's just human curiosity. Which of course is always their excuse. People wanna read it, so we'll publish it. And that really is irresponsible, because those morbid urges shouldn't really be encouraged. Newspapers shouldn't pander to those urges."[340]

Still, tabloid notoriety did have its plus points. "I think it's pretty cool that pop stars are actually front page news now. A few years ago that would have been unthinkable. The best thing though is that we didn't go looking for trouble. It just happened. I mean it's not outrage for the sake of it, which I hate. The song was about drugs, so the sleeve should have something to do with it. That was our reasoning.

"And I suppose there is the thing that if you get people's backs up you must have touched a few raw nerves. No one gets worked up about something that doesn't bother them. So at least I'm connecting. So, yeah, that kind of thing excites me. Especially because I've never written anything in a sensationalist way. I've always just tried to write in the way that I actually think about things."[341]

A decade on from *The Fruits Of Passion*, Pulp were still pushing the 'Love us or hate us but make sure it's one of the two' ethos – only this time around, they barely needed to try, and non-stories about drugs made for far better copy than plates of fake dogshit. Jarvis again: "It might mean that the next time I have an interview with somebody, they might not just ask me about sex. They've got another subject to quiz me about now, so it'll probably make my life a bit more interesting. Rather than being thought of as fops, it's nice to be known as mad, bad and dangerous to know. Rather than sitting around in velvet armchairs all day!

"I'm quite into the fact that it's given the record lots of publicity but I'm not looking forward to going through customs next time. I'll probably have a vacuum cleaner shoved up my arse. It means I'm gonna have to be watching myself for a while."[342]

At the end of September, Pulp finally embarked on a proper, month-long UK tour, and got their first prolonged taste of the rock'n'roll circus that surrounds bands operating at such levels. The venues had been booked before the summer's Pulpmania, and as a result were mostly medium-to-largeish club, university and theatre venues that the band could probably, by now, have filled several times over – which, of course, only added to the hysteria. "By then," says Nick, "it was half expected, but everyone went bananas, and you could do no wrong in a way. It's sometimes good to play places that are smaller than the number of people who want to get in them, smaller than it needs to be if you see what I mean – more sort of excitement."

Taking the Pulp experience to the band's new audience around provincial Britain was, in its way, as important a step as the summer's festival hugeness. There was the occasional downer – such as the incident when, early in the tour, Russell was approached outside Cambridge Corn Exchange by a youngster offering him a wrap of speed. The offer was declined, and the teenager asked whether Russell would pass the drugs on to Jarvis, which hotel the band were staying in, and what pseudonym Jarvis was under – at which point, Russell turned round to see a photographer lurking in a doorway across the street, brandishing a telephoto lens. Lovely.

On the whole, though, the tour was a triumph, punctuated along the way with yet more Pulp TV: Jarvis on Vic and Bob's new comedy quiz show *Shooting Stars*; 'Mis-Shapes' and 'Sorted' on *Top Of The Pops*, the former complete with Jarvis pretending to read the *Mirror*'s 'Sorted . . .' exposé during the guitar solo; Pulp day on *The Big Breakfast*; 'Mis-Shapes' and Andi Peters mending Jarv's bicycle on *Live And Kicking*; Jarvis on Jonathan Ross' cult film show *Mondo Rosso*; Jarvis on *every-fucking-thing*. And yet, somehow, you didn't mind – his ubiquity never became irritating. Possibly because he was quite good.

"Well, I'm all right on telly because I don't have to do it as a job," he told *The Face*. "It always used to piss me off how, with youth programmes, they always have to pick some presenter who's like the worst hyperactive teenager who was in your class at school. If I was a pop TV presenter, it wouldn't work: people wouldn't come on, because they'd think I was going to slag them off. Maybe in later life I could do it. That was the other thing that irritated me: whenever me favourite groups got on telly when I was a teenager, they always seemed to be right boring. They'd say things like, 'Yeah, we recorded the latest album in Montserrat, man, yeah and we've been working with a lot of really good people, we've got a really good vibe down . . .' These aren't interesting things to hear. So whenever I've been on telly, I've wanted to go against something. I don't see why it should just be the seasoned professionals, the boring, cheesy bastards who can be articulate. It's not a skill. For whatever reason, I am able to talk, but I'm not proud of it. I don't consider it a skill."[343]

And right in the midst of all this entirely welcome exposure came perhaps the most eagerly awaited album release of the age: on October 30, 1995, Pulp's *Different Class* made it to the shops.

"The title for the record came to me in a nightclub," said Jarvis. "The nightclub Smashin' – it used to be on Regent Street in this place called Eve Club. I was going down there most weekends and a friend of ours called Antony . . . it was one of his favourite phrases – Different Class – it's like, 'That is great – it's in a class of its own.' It just suddenly struck me. It was inspiration – a blinding light of inspiration in this club. Because for whatever reasons, a lot of the songs seem to have a bit of a fixation with the class system, that it could be like a double meaning. It was 'different class' in our Sheffield understanding of it 'it's boss', and it's saying, 'We're from a different class to you people.'

"I'm not exactly sure what class it was. It's not like, I think I am working class, because I'm not really. I never really felt that at home in the environment that I was brought up in – I used to get the piss taken out of me a lot 'cos I was a lanky speccy get. I didn't really know what class, if any, I belonged to and that's why there's that little message on the back of the record which says, 'We don't want no trouble, we just want the right to be different. That's all.' It was kind of hoping to establish a new class.

"By definition, if people decide to be individual or decide not to kind of follow a particularly well-worn path, they can feel a bit isolated. And I remember feeling quite isolated when I was growing up and stuff and thinking, 'Wouldn't it be great' – it sounds really crass – 'wouldn't it be great if there could be a way of a mainstream not being some kind of blanding emasculating kind of thing, but that included people from all different kinds of backgrounds.' It was a beautiful dream!"[344]

The album was certainly dressed to impress. Initial copies of the CD and vinyl editions, as well as sporting the silver-embossed Pulp logo, had 12 interchangeable front covers, each featuring striking images of the band (represented in monochrome, cardboard cut-out form) juxtaposed against various evocative, mundane-to-poignant scenes: Candida on a sunny day in Hyde Park; Mark and Jarvis wistfully looking on while the rough lad gets to chat up the pretty girl against the school railings; a couple getting it on in the open air while the whole band looks on.

Jarvis again: "When I first moved down to London I went to Brick Lane market and I found these women's fashion magazines called *Nova*. I've since acquired a full set of these magazines – it's not that I want to be a woman, but the photography and the design of this magazine were really good. There was one particular photo story, I think it was something to do with places that Lenin had lived in when he was in London or something, and they'd got this cut-out of him and put it in various locations in London. It had quite a nice atmosphere and I thought that would quite be good for the sleeve.

"It was useful in many ways. There was the practical reason because once the cut-outs had been done, then Rankin and Donald Milne who did the photography, went out and just took pictures of them anywhere and we didn't have to be involved in it. And once we'd got our poses right just for the cut-outs then that was it, we didn't have to worry about looking OK. It seemed kind of good with the cut-outs being in a certain situation it was like they were there but they weren't really part of it – they weren't actually part of that scene that they were in. So it seemed to be kind of appropriate somehow. I suppose the funniest thing that happened when that sleeve was being done was there's a picture of Russell in there and he's on a beach with some donkeys. Russ was on holiday with his family in Scarborough, walked on the beach and suddenly came across himself there – by complete chance came across Rankin taking a picture of his cut-out on the beach, which kind of freaked him out a bit!"[345]

Oh, and there was some music on the record as well, or something. Four of the songs had already been heard: 'Mis-Shapes' opened the album, serving to underline the statement of intent laid out by the sleeve notes and the title *Different Class*, and 'Common People', 'Sorted' and 'Under-wear' were unsurprisingly there too, so we were pretty much on to a winner from the start. Even better, the other eight songs managed to keep up to the almost unbeatable standard set by the first two singles.

'Pencil Skirt', the first of the 'new' songs, was in fact one of the oldest, dating back to the writing sessions the previous summer that had produced 'Common People' and 'Underwear'. Musically, with its understated Farfisa and violin combination and Jarvis' gentle crooning, the song is almost like *Freaks* with a budget – with slightly more entertaining words, of course. The fashion detail came from Jarvis' schooldays: "Pencil skirts were those that were quite long, with a little split at the back with two buttons. I always found them quite fetching myself."[346]

And then there was the tremendous 'I Spy', which reheated 'Mis-Shapes'' vindication of the underdog and 'Pencil Skirt''s intensely wound-up sleaze, and wrapped it up in a wonderfully nasty revenge fantasy. A semi-ironic portrayal of Jarvis the Undercover Class Warrior in the first part of the song soon gives way to pure bile – *"I just wanted you to come home unexpectedly one afternoon and catch us at it in the front room. You see I spy for a living and I specialise in revenge, on taking things I know will cause you pain. I can't help it, I was dragged up. Grass is something you smoke. Birds are something you shag. Take your 'Year In Provence' and shove it up your ass . . ."* Don't get carried away then, Jarv.

"Everyone's got a vindictive side. It was my justification for being a doley scumbag. I thought to myself that I was actually working undercover, trying to observe the world, taking notes for future reference, secretly subverting society. And one day, when the time was right, I would come out of the shadows and pounce on the world. I guess you could call that revenge, but not only for myself, but for the kind of people I respect."[347]

And how is this revenge meted out? By shagging the other guy's wife. Obviously.

"The thing about sex," according to Jarvis, "is that while you're doing it, no matter what your car's like or how many gold rings you've got on, whether you're any good at it or not is nothing to do with your social standing. There's no hiding behind any kind of construct. You can either do it or you can't do it. And that's what I like about it. It's a leveller, isn't it? The great leveller."[*]

'Disco 2000' is the album's most uncomplicatedly enjoyable pop song, fusing a classic tale of unrequited teenage affections to a crunching guitar riff straight out of Laura Branigan's 'Gloria' or Elton John's 'Saturday Night's Alright For Fighting'. The rather poignant lyrics, according to Jarvis, concern "a girl who was born about two days after me in the same hospital. My mother and her mother knew each other, and I really fancied her when I got to about 13. Unfortunately, everybody else in the school fancied her as well, and we never got it together. But you know when you say those things when you're just about to leave school, you say, 'Oh, look, we won't lose touch, we'll all meet up in the year 2000, we'll all

---

[*] 'New Dentures In Hi-Fi!' – interview with Jarvis by Roger Morton, *NME*, November 8, 1997.

The Limit, Sheffield, January 1986: Jarvis in his rather rickety-looking antique wheelchair following the notorious fall from a window incident. "It was quite easy doing gigs in it actually," he says, "'cos I didn't have to do any of that jumping around business. But people used to think I was taking the piss 'cos I always used to walk off stage at the end. The trouble wasn't that I couldn't walk - I just couldn't stay on my feet for long periods of time."

(*David Bocking*)

Jarvis and Russell, February 1986. Russell claims this sexy topless photo was done in homage to Eighties German electronic duo DAF. (*David Bocking*)

Pulp in 1985, clockwise, from top left: Peter Mansell, Magnus Doyle, Jarvis, Candida Doyle and Russell Senior. (*David Bocking*).

May 1987: Jarvis and Steven Havenhand on stage at The Limit. (*David Bocking*).

From top left, Nick Banks, Candida Doyle, Jarvis Cocker and Russell Senior, photographed in Sheffield, March 1993. (*Louise Rhodes/SIN*)

Jarvis as voyeur, out of the wardrobe with Polaroid to catch his sister on the couch, 1994. (*Steve Double/SIN*)

Pulp in 1994, left to right: Steve, Russell, Jarvis, Nick and Candida. (*Steve Double/SIN*)

On stage at Glastonbury, June 24, 1995. Above: Jarvis and Steve Mackey; below: Jarvis in his element. (*Mick Hudson/Redferns; Melanie Cox/SIN*)

meet at the fountain down the road.' And you know that you're not gonna do it, but it'd be good if you did."[348]

(Interestingly enough, many of Jarvis' old schoolfriends remember a girl called Deborah who Jarvis may or may not have fancied at the time. Peter Dalton once went out with her briefly, as did Jim Sellars, Glen Marshall, and, indeed, a sizeable portion of the male population of City School. "I saw her a few years ago," says Julie Hobson. "I think she thought it was all quite funny, but she said she thought she deserved some royalties!")

'Live Bed Show' is a swirling return to the typical Jarvisian lyrical territory of the girl who's been messed up by a bad relationship. Apparently, the story was inspired by Antony Genn, who had then just escaped the Nine O'Clock Service and achieved new-found fame by streaking onstage during Elastica's Glastonbury set (they subsequently repaid the favour by asking him to join them on keyboards for an American tour). "When I moved down to London," said Jarvis, "I gave him my bed because it was too big to move down. I've since got the bed back in very good condition, and it made me think, obviously beds can't talk, but if beds could tell you a story of what went on then it would be quite interesting."[349]

More optimistic was the string-soaked, semi-acoustic 'Something Changed', the most straightforward love song that Pulp had attempted in many, many years. Fittingly, it was based on a song that Jarvis had originally written just after the *It* album: "It was originally written about 12 years ago," he explained. "My sister sang an early version but it had different words. It never got used, and then I just remembered it.* Because it had been written such a long time ago it made me wonder what I was doing then. And I worked out that it must have been written quite near to me meeting this girl. It's just wondering, really. If I hadn't gone out and met this particular person in this particular nightclub, and formed a relationship with her, how different would my life have been? So it's not really about fate, it's about the randomness of things. Which I like. The worst thing about having a schedule and a timetable is that there's less chance for unexpected things to happen."[350]

'F.E.E.L.I.N.G.C.A.L.L.E.D.L.O.V.E.', the now-obligatory lengthy semi-spoken sexathon, stayed on similar philosophical ground to 'Something Changed', albeit with added thrusting and grunting. It's also the

---

* Neither Simon Hinkler, David Hinkler nor Peter Boam remembers there being a song in the Pulp set *circa* 1983 that bore a strong resemblance to 'Something Changed'. A likely candidate would be 'When You Cry I Cry', but as Simon Hinkler remembers the song as "a slow, minor-key deal in 6/8 time", some fairly major musical adjustments must have been made if this was the case.

most musically adventurous song on the album, mixing pre-programmed drum patterns, moody synths and some excellent violin squawking. "It's about those times when your life seems to be following a set pattern, and it's all right, you're not pissed off, then suddenly something happens that shakes it all up,"[351] Jarvis once offered by way of a semi-explanation.

Equally unexpected was the sparse, jittery ska of 'Monday Morning', which saw Jarvis looking back on those lost years of the early- and mid-Eighties, long before there was any sign that pop hugeness might un-expectedly come along and make sense of the mess his life was in. "I was in the situation where you leave school," he reflected, "and you decide you want to do something – in my case it was being in this band. And all your friends go off to university and stuff, and you're kind of left isolated in one place. I'm not asking for sympathy, but it's how to find your own path. It's deep, man."[352] Meanwhile, some excellent analogue synths and choppy, reggae guitars underlined the mood of bleakness and desperation while ensuring (still) that it was a fantastic pop song.

The LP closes with the exhausted, pleading comedown of 'Bar Italia', named after the famous after-hours coffee bar. Jarvis leads the walking wounded to that last refuge of those who can't say no, and being off-your-face and confused at 6 am in Soho has never sounded so attractive.

Different Class was and is the definitive Pulp record – the culmination of what every previous record had been reaching for. In a sense, it's a Greatest Hits collection that just happened to have been written, recorded and released in the space of one year rather than ten: everything Pulp had wanted to say, and everything anyone had wanted to hear from them, summed up in 12 songs and 50 minutes.

In other words, a combination of fortuitous timing and a lifetime's practice had finally allowed Jarvis, at the age of 31, to communicate what he'd always been trying to communicate, only either no one had been listening or he hadn't had the resources to express it. "I'd had a lot of experience, a lot of experience of doing nothing, of hanging around in Sheffield, and I thought it was time for all that to come out."[353]

And if it was the definitive album for Pulp, it was also the definitive album for the rest of us: the perfect soundtrack for the giddy, confused, excitable mid-Nineties – and, more specifically, for those few fleeting months before the 'We are saved!' euphoria of Britpop began to turn sour.

Ex-*NME* editor Steve Sutherland: "I think it was a celebration of a way a life of a generation finding a voice for itself out of a kind of debris of The Beatles and The Sex Pistols and everybody else that went before that was supposed to be better than them. And also it was a great triumph of that band over adversity and Jarvis particularly over the fact that he'd been banging around for years and not getting anywhere. And that vibe still comes off it and I think it's a really joyous record."[354]

If you really want to, it's possible to find fault with the album. The lyrics, while broader and more accessible, don't have quite the same emotional clout as some of those that Jarvis had written before. Chris Thomas' production, while it gives the record a slick, weighty, timeless pop sheen that invalidates forever any accusations that Pulp are 'just some little indie band', robs the band's sound of some of the individuality and excitement that it had previously. Some of the tunes, like 'Live Bed Show' and 'Sorted', are a little bit, well, dirgey. And so on. But ultimately, criticism is futile. It's *Different Class* by Pulp. How can you argue with that?

Different Class was met with universal praise from all quarters of the press, and shot straight into the album charts at number one, selling an enormous 301,000 copies in its first week of release. Well, of course it did.

The release of *Different Class* meant it was promotion time again – indeed, the day the record made it into the shops, the band were in France, recording another *Black Session* live performance, mixing *chansons nouvelles* (as Jarvis would say) with older tunes and a lovely version of 'Whiskey In The Jar', the traditional tune resurrected by Thin Lizzy. Next came a trip to Oslo to film some songs for Norwegian pop show *ZTV*, which was slightly less of a triumph. Things got off to a bad start when the famously aviation-phobic Russell decided, after one look at the small plane in which Pulp were going to be travelling over from France, that he wasn't coming. The band could manage to get through a six-song set without him, but what happened once they got to the studio has become the stuff of legend. *NME*'s Johnny Cigarettes was there to witness the event:

> " 'Could someone please fuck me with a broken bottle?' asks Jarvis Cocker, of a crowd of teenage girls not old enough to drink alcohol from one, let alone perform bizarre sexual practices with it. Suddenly, the louche, elegant and friendly façade is torn away to reveal the gnarled, twisted talons of hate that lie seething within the sick, perverted mind of Britain's once loveable King Misfit.
>
> Literally drooling with demonic rage, he picks up his microphone, throws it into the air and drop-kicks it into the eye of unsuspecting Steve Mackey, his long-suffering bass lieutenant. Then, muttering all manner of hideous blasphemy, he stomps offstage to howl at the moon.
>
> Ah, but wait. There's bound to be a perfectly innocent, logical explanation

for our hero's unlikely behaviour. Marital breakdown or personal bereavement, perhaps? Deep psychological trauma dating back to early childhood? Secret broken glass fetish? Nah, the keyboard's on the blink again. Of course.[355]

Oh dear. A couple of slightly more successful promo appearances followed (notably a classic performance on the BBC's *Later*, accompanied by a full orchestra conducted by Art Of Noise's Anne Dudley, and a session French radio show *Le Top Live* that included a version of The Troggs' 'Little Girl'), after which the band embarked on a full-blown 24-date European tour, taking the Pulp experience to Belgium, Spain, Holland and Germany in addition to the usual spin around France. "Germany was a surprise," remembers Nick. "The E-Werk in Cologne was like a big old factory. You'd expect to be playing smallish concerts the size of Leeds Town & Country or something, not huge factories with about 4,500 people going mental. The Germans loved it. We got some good material for other songs out of that – it was the first time I'd been to Germany, and certainly German record company executives would be like, 'Right, you will talk to these people for five minutes and then you will party for 30 minutes. You will party fucking hard, yeah.' It was great."

Somewhere in the midst of all this touring came Pulp's final single release of 1995: the uncomplicated pop joy that was 'Disco 2000' – made yet more so thanks to a remix from Alan Tarney. The release saw the pop-art (or possibly art-pop) packaging of Pulp's singles reach a new high, with a beautifully executed photo-love story spread across the artwork for the two CDs, complete with bit-parts for the cardboard band cut-outs from the *Different Class* sleeve. The band's regular promo director, Pedro Romhanyi, was so impressed with the concept that he decided to duplicate it for the video.

"Initially we were going to do something much closer to the song's lyrics. We were also experimenting with a new technical idea, and then the artwork for the single appeared. So, in the video we duplicate the photo shoot, changing the order in a couple of cases, and of course add a lot of new stuff – the track is over five minutes long. Donald Milne's work for the album and single is like an artificial version of the real world, where all its mundane features have been removed. So this is what we had to recreate – the Pulp world – without Pulp being in it."[356] In addition to the use of the cut-outs, Jarvis appears on a screen in the background, singing the song, and after Deborah's subtitled reaction – "Wasn't he on TV earlier?" – his rise to almost-annoying media omnipresence is forgiven.

Romhanyi's superb work with Pulp – and the band's peerless visual flair in general – was showcased on *Sorted For Films And Vids*, a compilation of promos from '92–'95 with the 'First Time' documentary and a spoken word version of 'Babies' bolted on. The compilation, which was conveniently released into Christmas stockings around this time, was more than a succession of nondescript clips of A.N. Indie Band miming their songs in a warehouse somewhere: from the medium-deconstructing 10-bob resourcefulness of 'Babies' to the townie showdown of 'Mis-Shapes' (complete with Jarvis making a decent fist of playing both a goody and a baddy), Pulp's videos had never been anything less than clever, stylish, massively entertaining pieces of filmmaking. "Jarvis and Steve like things quite crafted and with a sense of structure," says Pedro Romhanyi. "A lot of work and a lot of talk that goes on before a frame is shot. They will set up a brief and I'll come up with ideas. Often they say no, and different videos have different levels of input from them, but they are never passive. Although I'm quite a commercial promo maker, it's possible to be experimental with Pulp, such as using the 1:1 ratio in 'Disco 2000'. You can do something leftfield and commercial simultaneously."[357]

The year ended with a miniature British tour, taking in the seaside towns Blackpool, Bridlington and Bournemouth and finishing up with two sold-out dates at Brixton Academy. Nick: "In Blackpool, the Winter Gardens is a beautiful, beautiful building and it's a *Come Dancing* type sprung dancefloor. Everyone's dancing and jumping about and the whole stage was going up and down, sort of bouncing. It was brilliant – great fun."

Bridlington, meanwhile, was a slightly less edifying experience. Before the concert, local councillor Malcolm Milns – obviously a *Mirror* reader – had done his best to ensure that Pulp were banned from playing 'Sorted For E's And Wizz' at the show because he considered the song to be "encouraging children to take drugs."[358] His bid wasn't successful, but did result in a preposterously heavy-handed police presence at the gig, searching hundreds of people outside the venue and, seemingly without discrimination, bundling them into vans and taking them to the police station. Of the countless fans who missed the show as a result, 15 were arrested for the possession of soft drugs and let go with a caution. Just to round things off, during the show Steve became sufficiently maddened by the taunts of a skinhead in the crowd to jump off stage in order to "sort him out".

Still, such incidents were minor blips at the end of a mental, monumental year – a year which had, in *NME*'s words, seen Pulp "stop dreaming the impossible and simply get on with doing it". With end-of-year plaudits littering their paths (*Different Class* and 'Common People' were amongst practically every British publication's albums and singles of the year), the band appeared on the Christmas edition of *Top Of The Pops* for a triumphant performance of 'Common People'.

In June 1994, Pulp had made their first appearance on the show, entering the British pop mainstream from the angle of sleazy indie subversion, Jarvis sticking a sneaky two fingers up at the seemingly unassailable orthodoxy with his 'I HATE WET WET WET' sign. Now, such statements were suddenly, unexpectedly unnecessary: Pulp had done it. The underdogs had taken over.

Eighteen short months after that first appearance, Jarvis had a different handwritten sign to wave at the *Top Of The Pops* camera. It read *'VIVA LE REVOLUTION'*.

Chapter 14

For 1996, after the previous year's media saturation, the plan was for Pulp to step out of the limelight a little. With three massive hit singles, countless TV appearances and 28 gigs in the UK alone in 1995, they'd made their point and could afford to turn their attention to business elsewhere – such as, in January, Japan, where the band mounted a week-long mini-tour.

If, after three months spent playing a succession of large and increasingly similar-looking venues across the UK and Europe, the band were just beginning to get a little jaded, Japan must have been the ideal tonic. "Out of all the places in the world I'd wanted to go for years and years," says Nick, "Japan was the one, so going was really, really exciting. And just a culture shock for anyone going there for the first time. Especially landing in Osaka, which is more futuristic than Tokyo in a way – a lot of *Bladerunner* was shot in Osaka. The city centre is all really narrow little alleyways, but a lot of them are covered. And lots of little shops selling an incredible range of stuff. It's amazing – like, you'd be walking along and there'd be like something coming out of the ground with a noodle bowl on top, and then the restaurant just down the street is piping the cooking smells out of this noodle bowl.

"The venues were only tiny little places, but the Japs just went crazy with the cameras. I don't know how they knew, but they would be waiting for you when you got off the aeroplane, and then you saw them every day, then they'd stay with you and wave you off at the airport. There were only about 10 of them but they'd stay in the same hotel and just sit in the lobby, and wait for you to come out. They won't speak to you; they just giggle and take photos – at first you don't really think, but then you get a bit paranoid. After a few days, they'll have a go at saying hello to you, and you'd be saying, 'Haven't you got *anything* better to do?' And they'd be like, 'No!' You must have – anything is better than sitting in a lobby waiting for some idiots from Sheffield to come out. You just wanted to give them a good shake. And this is what they do all the time. Crazy."

Russell was equally struck by the experience. "I've never learnt so much in a week, never felt more like a pop star, and never felt so good about being a pop star," he remarked soon afterwards. "My belief in the inherent supremacy of Western European culture has taken a severe knock. And it wasn't an ill-thought-out belief. I thought Japan was an insect nation, that there was a lack of individuality, but they're actually more personal than we are – they notice the tiniest details about you."[359]

"Nietzsche," he remarked slightly more fancifully in his *NME* tour diary a little while later, "would have aphorised the Pulp philosophy as 'I have my feet on the ground and my head in the clouds, thus I grow taller.' There is, of course, a combustibility to this. We draw our inspiration from elevating ordinary life, therefore ordinary people relate to it, therefore we become famous, therefore we are no longer common people, therefore we lose the sap that pushes us to the clouds and it goes snap! This is exactly how it should be. By example, Japan has injected a certain amount of crackle back into this fragile alliance. Perhaps we can last till the stroke of midnight New Years Eve 1999. Pop!"[360]

"The more you show your arse at public functions, the more people like it. The only way you can really disgrace yourself is by being dead boring. It's hard not to bland out, tolerate people you shouldn't tolerate. You have to remember that the impetus for you existing isn't to be a celebrity and play golf with famous people. There is this tendency for success to take the rough edges off life."[361]

Jarvis Cocker said those words on February 5, 1996, when *Q* magazine sent an interviewer out to Stockholm on the eve of the brief Scandinavian tour that Pulp played following Japan.

On February 19, 1996, Pulp were invited to the Brit Awards ceremony at Earl's Court in London.

The Brits was and is, essentially, the British record industry's annual exercise in self-congratulation. The industry bigwigs mingle with the stars, everyone gets pissed, the gongs are handed out based on an entirely arbitrary judgement process, and the whole thing gets broadcast on TV in a suitably over-the-top production.

In 1996, the British record industry had plenty to congratulate itself about: the Britpop phenomenon was at its peak, huge amounts of 'units' were being 'shifted', and British music as a whole had a new air of credibility and self-confidence. Even the Brits awards themselves were now taken seriously after having, for many years, been a laughing stock for its farcical ceremonies where they'd basically award everything to Annie Lennox and Kate Bush, regardless of whether either had a record out at the time (in 1995, they'd made amends by giving everything to Blur instead). On the whole, it was a nonsense, but a hugely entertaining one – both to watch and to take part in.

The evening began sensibly enough; early on in the festivities, Pulp performed 'Sorted For E's And Wizz', complete with Pete Mansell and Candida's brother Danny dancing, Martin Wallace playing acoustic guitar, and Jarvis being hoisted up to the ceiling on wires for the song's climax. (TV viewers, sadly, were spared the spectacle of an embarrassed Jarvis being slowly winched back down to ground level after the performance.)

What came an hour or so later is well documented. The powers that be had oddly decided to create a special category – Artist Of A Generation – for Michael Jackson. Exactly why a British music award ceremony wanted to do such a thing for an American artist who most would agree was a decade past his prime is unclear, though cynics might conclude it was simply a ruse to get him on the show and thereby boost TV viewing figures. Still, it happened, and after an amazingly fawning speech from Sir Bob Geldof ("When Michael Jackson sings, it is with the voice of angels, and when his feet move, you can see God dancing." Yes.), Jackson presented his turn for the evening.

The spectacle Jacko was about to present to his audience was a hugely elaborate dance routine based around a performance of his then-recent single, 'Earth Song'. This began with Jackson silhouetted on stage alone, dressed in red, black and white. As he began singing, he was slowly joined by a growing crowd of raggedly dressed young children and adults, dressed to represent a variety of religious groups. Presently, he jumped into a hydraulic lift which carried him above the audience, performing his trademark acrobatics with billowing dry ice around him before being returned to the stage. There, bathed in celestial light, he stripped off his outer garments to reveal a pure white shirt, while the wastrels we'd seen earlier filed past, taking it in turns to hug and touch Jackson's Christ-like figure.

On its own, this would have made for a pretty unedifying spectacle, reflecting the worst excesses of rock-star self-aggrandisement. What tipped it over into the realms of distaste was the fact that two years before, Jackson had been faced with serious allegations of child abuse that had ended in a $21 million out-of-court settlement. Standing onstage being hugged by a succession of pre-pubescent kids obviously cleared all that up, then. And then there was the fact that the previous year, he'd allegedly had to change some of the lyrics on his *HIStory* album following accusations of anti-Semitism. Was kissing a rabbi during his routine supposed to imply an apology to, and forgiveness from, the Jewish community?

At the start of Jackson's performance, most of Pulp were standing to the side of the stage. "I'd seen the run-through," Jarvis told *NME*, "and I couldn't quite believe what I was seeing then. So I knew what to expect. It was just when it was going on and it seemed to me that quite a lot of the people there were not quite into what was going on either. They were thinking, 'What the hell is going on?' It was all being allowed to happen because of who it was. They even invented a new category for him, Artist Of A Generation, just so that he'd come over. And it was getting on my nerves."[362]

The result of Jarvis' irritation was that he, accompanied by Pete Mansell, jumped on to the stage, mimicked Jackson, flicked V-signs, lifted up the zip-up cardigan he was wearing, and pretended to flash his bottom at the audience. Things degenerated yet further into farce when one of Jackson's dancers turned out to be a security guard and attempted to make a grab for Jarvis, who managed to avoid him, continued to arse around for a few more seconds, and then returned to the backstage area. It was over within a minute, with most of the audience oblivious to the fact that it had happened.

"It was just hilarious," remembers Nick. "It was Candida's fault really. We were on this table at the very edge of the arena, and we noticed there was this little gangway to the stage. We'd seen the rehearsal earlier in the day for the Michael Jackson thing, and we were standing there going, 'Fucking hell, what's all that about?' And then in the evening we'd done our bit with Martyn Wallace on guitar – Jarvis usually played the guitar on that but wanted to arse around. I saw it again when we were doing the DVD, and Jarvis is sort of hoisted above the crowd in a crucifix-type pose – very strange that he was going on about Jacko trying to be a person who could heal the sick in a Christ-like way – we hadn't spotted that one!

"Obviously we were hitting the booze quite heavily and we looked at this thing when Jacko started up, and Candida's going, 'There must be – can't we do something? Go on Jarv, you do something.' We kind of looked and saw the gangway and thought, 'Point taken,' then him and Pete, Candida's boyfriend, just basically walked on the stage. There was no security there whatsoever, and Pete, by the time he got on the stage, hangs back a bit more, and Jarvis goes for it and runs around.

"Backstage after that, the whole fucking thing went out the window. Jacko's mob was going absolutely mental – 'Who is this person? How dare he spoil it? The master of pop's performance!' It was funny 'cos backstage there was a Portaloo cordoned off that had a big sign 'Mr Jackson's personal toilet'. You could just imagine him in there taking a shit! Vic and Bob were there, completely off their faces, and Bob's a lawyer, and he was going, 'If you need legal representation I'm your man!', falling about laughing. Our tour manager had to go up to Michael Jackson's entourage and got a shouting match from their top man, and just came back and laughed. They were not very pleased. We were just in a state of laughter.

"Then the police turn up and its ching-ching, on with the bracelets and off you go Jarvis. There were these allegations that he's pushed some kids off the stage and we were all laughing, saying, 'This is utterly ridiculous, it's made up – you'll be able to watch the video and see it.' So we had these ridiculous allegations made up by Michael Jackson's camp and it was just funny, but then obviously they'd called the police and said that these incidents had taken place."

It transpired that some of the children onstage had been injured during the incident – subsequent tabloid reports alleged that an 11-year-old boy had been punched, another had a cut ear and bruised ribs, and a third child of 12 had been thrown off the stage. Video footage subsequently revealed the security guard who chased Jarvis to be the culprit, with our man seemingly making no physical contact with anyone, but on the night, the Jacko camp had other ideas, resulting in an overnight stay in a cell at Kensington police station.

Jarvis: "One of the organisers came up with a policeman and said, 'It's better if you talk about it.' What 'talk about it' actually meant was going to a room and being arrested."[363]

Jarvis was charged with actual bodily harm and questioned for several hours before being released on bail (he returned to the station, as required, on March 11, when he was officially cleared) in the early hours of the morning. "It was very amusing," remembers Nigel Coxon, "'cos all these lawyers started rattling around trying to get Jarvis out of jail, and I sort of turned up with a friend, incredibly drunk, and I just said, 'Oh c'mon, he hasn't really done anything wrong, just let him out.' And it was very funny 'cos all the hotshots had been in there for an hour and couldn't do anything, so I kind of got him out of jail. In the pictures of him leaving in a cab, most of them airbrushed me out, but I think in the *Daily Mirror* you can see me sat next to him. So that's my bit of fame, my first cover!"

"The police weren't bad actually," said Jarvis. "In fact, I felt very happy that this happened in England rather than America. I think if it had happened in America, I'd really be in trouble. It weren't a bad cell. It had a flushing toilet. It even had a bit of padding on the bench. From what I've heard of police cells, it was apparently quite a luxury one."[364]

Inevitably, Jarvis' release from the police cell didn't mark the end of the story. The following day, the tabloids went into overdrive with such immortal headlines as 'Jacko Pulps Lout Cocker', 'Jarvis Socker: Pulp Singer Arrested As He Smackos Jacko Kids', 'Off His Cocker' and

'Plonker From Pulp Spoiled Big Night'. Matters weren't helped by an official statement made that day from Jackson's label:

> *"Michael Jackson respects Pulp as artists but is totally shocked by their behaviour and utterly fails to understand their complete lack of respect for fellow artists and performers.*
>
> *His main concern is for the people that worked for him and the fact that children should be attacked. He feels sickened, saddened, shocked, upset, cheated, angry, but is immensely proud that the cast remained professional and the show went on despite the disgusting and cowardly behaviour of the two characters that tried to disrupt it.*
>
> *Even though the evening ended on a sad note, he wants to thank all his fans and the media for their understanding and support."*

The BPI – chaired, coincidentally, by the head of Sony Music – toed a marginally more neutral but similarly Jarvis-is-guilty line:

> *"We are extremely concerned that Jarvis Cocker's actions last night resulted in injury to three children who were performing with Michael Jackson.*
>
> *Whilst the Brits is an exuberant, high-spirited occasion, it is totally unacceptable for any artist to disrupt another artist's performance. To do so with such apparent disregard for the safety of the performers on stage, the production crew and the audience was dangerous and irresponsible."*

Quite how Jarvis' activities were supposed to be threatening the safety of the performers, the crew or the audience isn't made clear, but he was particularly displeased to be accused of attacking or injuring children. Later on February 20, he issued his own statement:

> *"My actions were a form of protest at the way Michael Jackson sees himself as some Christ-like figure with the power of healing.*
>
> *The music industry allows him to indulge his fantasies because of his wealth and power. People go along with it even though they know it's a bit sick. I just couldn't go along with it any more.*
>
> *It was a spur-of-the-moment decision brought on by boredom and frustration. I just ran on the stage and showed off.*
>
> *I didn't make any physical contact with anyone as far as I recall. I certainly didn't push anybody off stage.*
>
> *I find it very insulting to be accused of assaulting children. All I was trying to do was make a point and do something that lots of other people would have done if only they'd dared."*

He put it more succinctly onstage a couple of days later at Cardiff Arena: "One person has been accused of tampering with children and one person hasn't."[365]

As the week progressed, opinion made a gradual but decisive turn in Jarvis' favour. The overwhelming majority of those who'd been there on the night had, of course, been on his side from day one, with Brian Eno, Bernard Butler, Martin Clunes, Neil Morrissey and, er, Jonathan King being among the first to make their support public. The fax machines at Rough Trade and Savage & Best were receiving "Jarvis should be knighted!" type messages from all directions, and on Wednesday, Island Records came out with a statement in full support of Jarvis:

> *"Jarvis Cocker has today demanded an apology from Michael Jackson for the allegation that Jarvis 'attacked' children onstage at the Brit Awards in London last Monday (19 February).*
>
> *Cocker has always denied physically attacking anyone during his instant protest at Jackson's performance, and video evidence of the incident now refutes the claim.*
>
> *Cocker has written to Jackson – via his UK record company – asking for a retraction of the allegation, together with an apology. Jarvis is also taking legal advice about the statement."*

Most UK broadsheets had already run editorials in support of Jarvis' motives, if not necessarily of his actions, and *The Guardian* filled an entire letters page with pro-Jarvis mail. By the end of the week, the tabloids had realised they'd misjudged the mood by several light years, with the *Mirror* in particular doing a good old-fashioned tabloid hypocrite u-turn: the Friday's letters column was headed "Justice for Jarvis" and they'd been getting whatever celebrities they could (notably Simon and Yasmin Le Bon) to pose in T-shirts featuring the same slogan. What came next? "90% Of You Back Us In Fight For Jarvis". Well, of course. Meanwhile, Jarvis was able to put his side of the story on *TFI Friday,* while the programme showed previously unbroadcast footage to back him up.

By the following Wednesday, when both weekly music papers came out with lengthy, gleefully pro-Jarvis cover stories – *NME*'s "Wanna Be Startin' Something?" and *Melody Maker*'s "Give Him A Knighthood!" – the battle had been won. As if 1995's triumphant invasion of the mainstream hadn't been enough, Jarvis had done it again: rescued pop music from the clutches of the humourless, pompous, deluded, self-aggrandising made-its. In the space of approximately one minute, he'd again tipped the *Zeitgeist* back toward us, and if he'd done it with approximately 10 seconds' forethought while he was pissed out of his head, then what difference did it make?

NME's John Mulvey just about summed it up: "One of the many nauseous and bemusing things our holier-than-who? tabloids have claimed in the past week is that Jarvis is a 'rock'n'roll lout' in the same class as the ever-charming Brothers Gallagher. WRONG! WRONG! WRONG! Oasis' behaviour at the Brits was boorish, arrogant and entirely self-aggrandising. Meanwhile, Jarvis' was creative, subversive and very, very funny.

"Traditional rock'n'roll rebellion – y'know, smashing up hotel rooms, that kind of stuff – is cowardly, petulant and, ultimately, utterly, utterly pointless. This was everything but: insurrection fuelled by a fierce and dynamic moral rectitude. Frankly, it's impossible to go over the top with praise."[366]

The cover of the March 2, 1996 edition of *Melody Maker* features a paparazzi shot of Jarvis sitting in the back of a taxi, hunched and drawing on a cigarette, shortly after being released from Kensington Police station post-Brits. He looks like death warmed up: pale, drawn, and utterly drained. "Everybody just thought that was a bit of a laugh," remembers Nigel Coxon, who was sharing the taxi ride with him, "but Jarvis actually had to come out and do a press conference and everything, and I actually think it was probably a bit traumatic."

Not that Jarvis had much time to reflect on the possible wider repercussions on his life of what had just happened: on February 20, less than 24 hours after the Jacko incident, he was back onstage at Brighton Pavilion for the first date of Pulp's biggest tour yet: 10 dates at a series of enormous British venues with capacities ranging from 3,750 (Humberside Ice Arena) to 13,000 (Manchester Arena). The demand for tickets was such that the band managed to fill Wembley Arena two nights running.

Support came from Edwyn Collins and Denim, resulting in a sort of 'Thinking Man's Britpop Revue' – even though the audiences generally consisted of a pretty low percentage of thinking men/women, and absolutely loads of screaming 14-year-old girls. "Playing to huge crowds was still very exciting," says Nick. "By the time we were playing Sheffield Arena, all the relatives had come out of the woodwork, clambering for tickets and all this. You'd see 'em all pissed after – 'I always knew you'd make it!' Yeah, I'm sure you did, bugger off."

The tour itself – despite the tabloid distractions and an unfortunately timed bout of 'flu for Jarvis – still managed to be pretty triumphant. The set list was pretty predictable for the most part (*Different Class* in its near-entirety, plus choice selections from *His'n'Hers* and, occasionally, *Intro*), but we did get a new extended coda on 'Live Bed Show', and the line-up expanding to feature Pablo Cook contributing percussion to 'F.E.E.L.I.N.G.C.A.L.L.E.D.L.O.V.E.', Antony Genn strumming some extra guitar, and Yvette Lacey playing flute on 'Acrylic Afternoons'. The stage set, meanwhile, was augmented by huge video screens on either side and a big ol' balcony at the back for Jarvis to climb around on. He even managed to get the odd Jacko reference into the between-song chat: "I haven't got a personal crusade against Michael Jackson," he informed the audience at Cardiff. "I'm not even religious. But when someone appears on stage and wants to be Jesus, I think that's a bit off. But I'd love to kiss a Rabbi."[367]

At the end of the day, though, it was the music that mattered, and the previous year's festivals had demonstrated that Pulp's music made perfect sense in front of enormous, excitable audiences. It still did – even if the finer points of the lyrics were sometimes lost on the newly converted masses.

"Now," wrote the *NME* after witnessing the Birmingham NEC show, "we get stadia full of disconcertingly well-adjusted people spiritedly bawling along to 'Mis-Shapes'. We get, in Block 15 at least, tranced-out rave-dancing to 'Sorted For E's And Wizz', the *'Nice one! Geezer!'* line spat out so contemptuously by Jarvis echoed, irony-free, by a terrace chant. And we get, in the middle of 'F.E.E.L.I.N.G.C.A.L.L.E.D.L.O.V.E.''s austere synthdrama, a very respectable-looking bloke mooning in the aisle. *Enough.*

"This is Pulp now: a national institution, albeit an occasionally wicked one. And this is Jarvis: regardless of Noel and Liam's cocksure bravado and Damon's deceptively clean-cut teen appeal, the single most recognisable face of Britpop. A personality big enough to represent Britain in a Trans-atlantic superstar face-off. And a band wry enough to fill the screens with photographs of happy smiling children between encores."[368]

Mmm. Pulp's success may have still been a glorious vindication, but it was almost starting to feel as if things were getting a little *too* big – a feeling reinforced when make-up artist Sarah Reygate, with whom Jarvis had had a fling the previous year, sold her story to the gutter-press *News Of The World*. The story resulted in the slightly amusing and semi-flattering head-line 'Jarvis Looked Like A Trainspotter But His Loving Drove Me Loco', but it was still a pretty unpleasant invasion of privacy. It was probably for the best that, in the time between the end of the arena tour at the beginning of March and Pulp's next batch of live dates toward the end of May, the group's public activities were limited to the odd TV appearance to promote their next single, 'Something Changed', released on March 25.

The single seemed almost determinedly low-key in terms of both the music and the way it was presented: 'Something Changed' was by far the most straightforward, conventional moment on *Different Class*, entirely free of strange noises, sleaziness, potential drug controversy or class-war anger. There was a hint of rip-off, though, in the way the single was packaged: two CDs, both featuring the same four tracks, but with different artwork. Jarvis' semi-convincing explanation at the time was that if you were a boy, you were supposed to buy the one with the picture of a girl on it, and if you were a girl, you were supposed to buy the one with the picture of a boy on it, and if the single got to number one then we'd know that Pulp have a large bisexual following. Right ho then.

The video was similarly understated, eschewing the elaborate scenarios of the previous few singles for a more straightforward as-live performance of the song – albeit with some dizzying camera angles. Other than that, the only promotion the single received consisted of appearances on *TFI Friday* and *Top Of The Pops* – which was all it needed to enter the charts at number 10 and sell over 100,000 copies.

Meanwhile, there was still no escaping the past: the Pulp vaults were rummaged through again for *Countdown: 1992–1983*, a mid-price, TV-advertised 2CD compilation of Fire material, licensed to the Nectar Masters label without the band's involvement. If *Masters Of The Universe* had been fair enough, this most definitely had the air of a cash-in – an impression that wasn't helped by the sleeve artwork, which looked like a cheap pastiche of Pulp's recent sleeves and had nothing at all to do with either the style or the content of the music on the compilation. Unsurprisingly, Jarvis was horrified, describing it to *Melody Maker* as "a garish old family photograph album."

"It's just a bit messy," he added. "Everybody goes on about us being around for so long but for me, that doesn't matter at all. In a way, I'd rather people didn't know, and that they couldn't hear that stuff. I guess if people really want to listen to that stuff they can get it cheap. But that's the only thing I could say in its favour.

"I would urge anybody not to buy it. Please. I find it embarrassing, to be honest. And the way it's packaged to look a bit modern, a bit like our sleeves look now. It's a crap version. But people will be fooled into buying it because it's cheap as well. I wouldn't recommend it to anybody. And Fire Records never did any favours when we were on their label. It almost made us split up."[369]

Despite Jarvis' warnings – and some pretty bad reviews, which reflected the fact that the band's old material really doesn't stand up particularly well when taken out of context and judged by the same standards as *Different Class* – the album sold extremely well, entering the charts at number 10 and hanging around for a while.

Clive Solomon: "The thing I find most bizarre is that I thought a lot of the early material was great, and I always thought that when Pulp did make it, people would be quite accusative of why the band never achieved more earlier. What surprised me is that when the *Countdown* compilation came out, most of the reviews that I read said, 'Well, they weren't that good then' – and if you believe that, then that would be the easiest explanation for why the band didn't do anything first time round! But that surprised me because I thought that when they got successful people would acknowledge the merit of their earlier material rather than condemning it to the vaults. Mind you, those people would have been enormously aware that they had the capacity to put the band on the map earlier, so to acknowledge the old stuff would have been to admit to not having done it justice at the time. So perhaps there wasn't an open perspective on it, because to acknowledge how great a band has always been does beg the question, 'Why did you give them such scant coverage at the time?'

"But on the other hand, if that's people's view then it makes it fairly apparent that Fire stood no chance of selling any records by the band if not only was that the apparent position at the time, but ten years later people still think the same, then it largely accounts for why the band should have languished in the wilderness for so long. But I think for the most part the music press is very commercially driven; people are afraid to commit support to anything they think won't happen commercially because if it doesn't, it doesn't reflect well on them. So these days A&R is done by consensus and press acclaim is by consensus, so everyone feels safe in raving about the same things, and then when those things happen everyone can give themselves a self-congratulatory pat on the back."

Back in the present, Pulp themselves seemed to be busy attending to their real lives for a while: Steve had become a father for the first time in March when his girlfriend Zoë gave birth to a son, Marley. "The way I coped with it for the first six months was just to be really healthy," he told *Select* magazine later. "In every aspect of my life, I really looked after myself."[370] An aspiration, of course, that doesn't lend itself particularly well to large-scale touring in a famous pop group.

The theme of family bliss continued when Nick married his girlfriend Sarah at the start of April – hence a confetti-bedecked drumkit when the band appeared on *Top Of The Pops* the previous day. The day after the wedding, Pulp (possibly in a slightly hungover state) flew to America to make an appearance on *The David Letterman Show*, with Justin Welch from Elastica deputising for the honeymooning drummer.

And Jarvis was busy with the increasingly time-consuming occupation of being Jarvis Cocker. Since 'Common People', he'd been in demand from just about everyone, and by spring 1996 his ubiquity went far beyond just being the singer in Pulp. He'd guested on LPs by Barry Adamson and Lush, opened Diesel's new clothes shop in London, kicked a bag of chips into the air in a Reebok TV ad, and his self-perpetuating fame now meant that he was guaranteed a place on the guest list for, well, everything – celebrity parties, film premières, the opening of any envelope you might care to name. Jarvis was invited, and, by and large, he was there, guaranteeing himself a reputation as a world-class ligger of 1996.

"I did go out a lot, yeah," he admitted to *Select* magazine a couple of years later. "Obviously there was that period when fucking Andy Coulsen [the *Sun's* showbiz writer] was saying, 'If you see Jarvis out at a lig, ring us up and we'll give you a tenner,' and all this shit. But I've always had a bee in my bonnet about this thing of exclusion. It seemed that my generation went straight from school on to the dole, and you were seen as an invisible sector of society, and you really felt compartmentalised and ghettoised. So to get the chance to take part in mainstream society was exciting to me.

"You run the risk in those situations of becoming maybe something that you hate, but I had to do it. It was dead funny at first. You'd be there seeing Nicholas Parsons shoving all these canapés down his gob at these daft things. There were some good laughs, but then you realise you don't want to live in that world, otherwise in ten years' time, somebody else is going to be watching you shovel in the vol-au-vents."[371]

"You get invited to these things," reflects Nick, "and you've never been to them, so you go to see what it's like and end up getting sucked into this celebrity golden circle. And if you want to go to the opening of an envelope every night you can do. He tried for a bit, and you get seen in all the gossip columns and that kind of stuff, and I think fair enough – give them a go.

"I went to a few of them myself – they were usually quite good fun, but I'm sure if you went to them every day, you start to see the same people at each one, the same kind of circle of liggers and all that kind of stuff – a lot of these people do tend to look around and think, 'Who's the most famous person in this room? Right, I'll go and talk to them.' They see someone more famous and it's like, 'See you!' There's loads of people like that.

"For Jarvis, on any kind of interview or radio thing, they wanted him on it. Fair enough. But we'd have the concerts, the rehearsals, yet at the same time he'd have to do lots of interviews, lots of radio stuff, lots of going out getting pissed till five in the morning, which was fair enough, but it does take its toll – he was certainly getting very tired."

On May 21, Pulp played at Bimbo's in San Francisco – the first show of a 12-date American tour. Two years on from that enjoyable-but-not-very-successful first venture with Blur, it was time to make a more serious attempt to crack the US market – to which end, Geoff Travis had appointed Peter Rudge, a semi-legendary veteran of Stones and Who tours, to handle the band's manoeuvres.

This time around, things looked fairly promising – while the band had yet to make any impression on the American charts, there was a definite Anglophile cult following. The internet had already taken a hold in America by this point, and the Lipgloss mailing list and websites like Pulpintro (and, indeed, the band's own official site, which had just been launched) had helped to build things up at grassroots level. Meanwhile, in real medialand, Pulp had already played the vastly influential *Letterman Show* in April, and, thanks in part to "the Michael Jackson thing", MTV was heavily plugging the band. (Much to Jarvis' relief, the half-expected lynch mobs of outraged Jacko fans on the tour never materialised.)

Difficulties arose before the band had played the first date – on May 19, the day after they arrived in Los Angeles, Jarvis had begun to show signs of 'flu. A doctor was called, and said that the virus would run its course and gave Jarvis some aspirin. The next day, Jarvis woke up feeling too ill to move from his bed, and another doctor was called, who repeated the diagnosis. Jarvis managed to battle on, and played the first two dates of the tour. However, by the second, at the Hollywood Grand in Los Angeles, he was very obviously in a bad way – which did have its upside. "He was pushing himself to perform," remembers Mark, "and it was the best concert we've played in ages. The next day in the *LA Times*, the review said, 'The frontman was devoid of personality'!"[372]

It turned out that Jarvis had picked up some kind of tropical bacteria, probably during his holiday in Hawaii immediately before the tour. The doctor prescribed a course of antibiotics and painkillers, and ordered Jarvis to take a few days' rest – resulting in the cancellation of a concert in Denver and an unscheduled break for the rest of the band. "We spent all of our four or five days in Denver just kicking our heels," remembers Nick, "and me, Steve and Mark went on a wonderful road trip up the highest road in America and saw the Overlook Hotel, which is the hotel in *The Shining*. One of the scary bits in that film is that these twins appear in this deserted hotel, and we're there outside the Overlook Hotel, and there's these big double windows and who should appear but this pair of twins! So we were like *aaaaaarrrrrgggghhhhh . . .*'"

With Jarvis restored to relatively rude health, the rest of the tour was mostly enjoyable, with the band relishing the prospect of playing smaller, club-sized venues for the first time in a while. "I'm not going to say it's better," reflected Jarvis afterwards, "because there is something that's quite exciting about playing to a big audience. But it's good to have a bit of variety and to actually be able to see people's faces again and direct particular lines to particular people. You can have more of a conversation instead of addressing this mass and wondering what's going to happen!"[373]

Elsewhere, experiences like chasing tornadoes in the tour bus when leaving St Louis and hanging out with Cynthia Plastercaster in Chicago made the tour fun, but it was apparent that the buzz generated by a fortnight of dates spread across such a huge country wasn't going to result in any kind of significant advancement of Pulp's career. As Nick pointed out, "Just because we're playing to 1,000 people in New York, it doesn't mean there's going to be people in Arkansas who are going to be interested."[374]

After America, the band returned home for all of four days (during which time Jarvis was spotted at the Groucho Club with Gary Glitter) before embarking on yet another European tour. It was now, unquestionably, becoming a bit of a slog. "There was a long German bit which was a real grind," remembers Nick. "You're starting to get tired, even though it's something that should be fun, you know."

Jarvis, meanwhile, seemed to be coping with the challenge of having to inject some conviction into 'Common People' while singing it for the eightysomethingth time in the space of a year by . . . well, getting drunk and acting oddly. It was around this time that *Vox* sent Sylvia Patterson out to report on Pulp, mid-tour in Frankfurt:

> "... And now, introducing, on vibes, SuperJarv™, a man who appears in equal parts irrepressibly confident and emotionally bamboozled, like he knows he can do absolutely anything and they'll love him anyway; like he doesn't quite understand it, 'cos he was only ever being himself. So he'll keep on doing it in the meantime, as if he has a choice. Maybe he'll see how far he can take it – right here, right now, in the Birmingham of Germany . . . 'Can I have a taxi, please?' enquires SuperJarv™, 'Can I have a taxi, please, to Arbourthorne?' Arbourthorne is a small town near Sheffield. Frankfurt blinks. The technical crew nigh collapse on the sound desk with mirth. [. . .] He twirls right round, with ballerina's panache, kicks out to the left, arse-wiggle to the right, and chirps 'vielen dank!' before the last of his one-time on-stage observational plot leaves the building. 'I'm in my mid-thirties,' he states, matter-of-factly, 'and it's about time.' Whatever can he mean? 'I need to father a child,' hollers Jarvis. 'Everyone else is doing it.' [dramatic pause, a nod to Steve] I know I can do it. I just need to find a willing partner to do it with . . ."
>
> 'I'm 32 years of age.' He sways, padding slowly up and down the stage. 'Still useless. I'd be a spare prick at a funeral. Er . . . don't know that one . . . Liebe, liebe! Er . . .' He coughs, raises an eyebrow, tries again. 'I'm 32

years of age . . . [huge pause] *And I couldn't organise a piss-up in a brothel. Er . . . A piss-up in an orgy . . .* [Shouting] *A piss-up in a brewery! So . . .* [Another huge pause] *This is a song for anyone who's thinking about killing somebody tonight. "Gewöhnliche Leute!" ' That's 'Common People' to you, unilinguists, as Frankfurt explodes . . .*

An ecstatic 'Babies' and 'Mis-Shapes' precede the 'Bar Italia' comedown, and with another SuperJarv™ salute, they're gone, leaving the head reeling with the notion that two weeks contracting superflu in Hawaii and four days down the Groucho Club with Gary Glitter hasn't quite been holiday enough. There's no misery here, mind – 'useless' comments or not – just the abandon of a man whose life is plainly bonkers and all he can do is say, 'Prhrthrt! Fuck it!!' and have another drink. Or perhaps he just can't be doing with Frankfurt."[375]

More enjoyable was the Northern European leg of the tour in late June and early July – notably the Turku Festival in Finland and a show a couple of days later at the Laugardalsholl in Iceland. "Finland was fantastic," remembers Nick. "It was on the side of a huge estuary or fjord, and while you're playing a huge liner will sail past the side of the stage or something. All the Fins were off their faces. We had the Pulp aeroplane for this one, 'cos to get the equipment from Finland to Iceland and back to Norway, there was no way of doing it by scheduled airlines so we had our own private plane which was fantastic. You wanted it written on the side.

"So anyway we get this jet, I think with a Latvian crew, very strange, to take us to Iceland and all the guys told us half the equipment didn't fit in the aeroplane. It was like, 'Whose idea was it to get one with a really tiny door?' Eventually, we had to leave half the stuff on the tarmac at Finland and had to send the plane back for it. And we went off to Iceland, and we played with Blur at this festival in Finland, and they said, 'Oh, we've got the week off, can we come with you?' Yeah there's plenty of space, come on lads, come on our plane with us to Iceland!

"So we got up the steps into the plane and all the headrests have got a thing round the top with 'Pulp' on. Iceland was fabulous – we went off sightseeing, whitewater rafting down these rivers, jumping off 35-foot cliffs into ice-cold rivers with survival suits on, daft stuff like that. And playing somewhere like Iceland was absolutely amazing, you know. And then back in the plane to Norway, so all this time we didn't see night-time at all for about a week or so, which was really odd. And then back down with a bump to Belgium!"

By August, Pulp's year on the road was finally coming to an end. The tour proper had wound down the previous month, coming to rest with a triumphant show headlining the T In The Park festival in Scotland. All that remained was a pair of massive concerts at Hylands Park in

Chelmsford and Victoria Park in Warrington: the first-ever 'V' festivals.

The concerts had essentially come about as a result of Richard Branson wanting to have his own festival under the Virgin banner. Pulp had been given the main site and, initially, control of the bill. "They were sort of saying, 'We want you at this festival, we want you to be headliners, and you can put the bill together if you want,' " remembers Nick, "so that was kind of quite exciting because we could get all our group mates in with us, like Supergrass, Cast who'd supported us round Germany, great bunch of lads, Denim, Longpigs . . ."

However, as the organisation of the concerts had progressed, it had become slightly less of a Pulp event and more of a Virgin one: rather than being one-day affairs as had been originally planned, they became weekend festivals, with the Saturday's Chelmsford bands playing on Sunday at Warrington and vice versa. Paul Weller was drafted in to headline the other day, and Elastica, The Charlatans, Menswear, Sleeper and the rest were added to the bill, resulting in what was basically the Class of '95's end-of-year party.

The week before the concerts, Pulp warmed up at the slightly unusual venue of the Shetland Islands' Clickimin Centre. "That was a great one," remembers Nick, "because a lot of Candida's relatives are from Shetland, so basically she said, 'Look, we're doing these concerts, *I* want to play the Shetland Isles, it's going to happen.' They said, 'Right you are, off to the Shetland Isles then.' So we had a week in the Shetland Isles, fishing off the coast of Shetland the morning of the concert, great stuff. Candida's brother's band Chin supported us on that one – Candida paid for them to be the support group basically so Danny could see the rellies as well. That was really good fun."

As were the V96 concerts. Pulp seemed to be treating the events as a full stop for the *Different Class* era – a final hurrah before regrouping and deciding where to go next. In front of crowds of around 33,000, Jarvis began the shows with a vocoderised statement of intent taken from the *Different Class* and 'Mis-Shapes' sleeves: *"Please understand. We don't want no trouble. We just want the right to be different. That's all. We shall fight them in 'The Beaches' – and 'The Stag' and 'The King's Head' if it comes to that. You know the score – ten blokes with 'taches in short-sleeved shirts telling you that you're the weirdo. Fear not brothers and sisters – we shall prevail. Live on."* And then the band launched into 'Mis-Shapes' and we were away.

Despite superficial similarities, V96 was a different trip to Glastonbury 1995: it inevitably didn't have that one-off thrill of something huge and extraordinary happening for the first time. In place of the big-dipper nervous thrill of Glastonbury, what we had instead was essentially a rally for the converted – which isn't to say it wasn't as good or as life-affirming. Jarvis' stage presence was far more relaxed and assured, but somehow never lapsed into arrogance – quite a feat when you're saying things like, "But you don't want to go home, do you?"[376] after 'Do You Remember The First Time?' The human beatbox impressions and tales of how, earlier in the day, he'd walked round the Chelmsford site in a gorilla suit so nobody'd recognise him probably helped.

The choice of set list was as conservative as it had been for most of the year, consisting of most of *Different Class* plus 'Mile End', 'First Time' and 'Babies' – but then, why not? Pulp were, after all, very good indeed at playing these songs by this point, and the events of the past year had shown quite conclusively that they were the sort of thing that their audiences were keen to hear. We did get one new song, 'Help The Aged' (Jarvis having announced that "this is the bit where I poo myself"[377]), and the final 'Common People' was spectacular – assisted, as it was, by as many extra guitarists as could be found in the vicinity. "By the one in Warrington," remembers Nick, "there were something like eight guitarists on stage, with various degrees of ability to play. Chris Thomas was playing on stage, Antony Genn, Danny from Supergrass, Skin from Cast, Richard Hawley . . ."

On both nights, the set ended with a final encore of 'Babies' – with Jarvis rather touchingly telling the audience that "we're going away for a while now, so you're going to have to get along without us. Remember us this way."[378] Gulp.

There was one more Pulp gig in 1996: a private party for Holsten Pils at the stunning Teatre Grec amphitheatre in Barcelona, in front of a selection of music business executives, lager business executives, and a handful of lucky competition winners. Quite how or why Pulp saw fit to end a glorious, year-long tour on a stage dominated by an enormous inflatable beer bottle in front of an audience who hadn't particularly come to see them is a mystery; possibly the fact that they were playing at the stunning Teatre Grec amphitheatre in Barcelona had something to do with it. To his credit, Jarvis did maintain some remnants of detachment from the whole business – starting the concert with the words, "Hello, we're Pulp and we're tonight's turn," and responding to the inevitable 'Common People' singalong by saying, "No, the karaoke isn't till later" – but it wasn't the most satisfying way to end an era.

The sense of uncertainty was compounded by Jarvis' comment after the concert that "this is going to be our last gig for a very long time. I don't know when we're next going to perform. Maybe when we've got a few songs together."[379]

At least Steve sounded a little more authoritative. "This is our last concert for about 18 months. We've been touring 11 months and now we're taking a break. When we feel like it, we'll ring each other up and get together to write some more songs for the next album – although we don't really need to make another one."[380]

As well as the general tour fatigue that was universally felt within the band, Jarvis had decided that enough was enough. In the six months since Michael Jackson, he'd been on the front of every magazine, in every gossip column of every tabloid, on every TV show, asked for his opinion on everything. Admirably, he managed to avoid the cliché of the whining, self-pitying rock star, but there were occasions when exasperation with his new-found, unwelcome tabloid notoriety understandably showed through.

"They were just taking things I'd done in my life for titillation," he told *NME* in August, "like 'Oo-er, Missus, Barbara Windsor. So and so shagged so and so. *In't it fooneh?*' You get all these photographers following you round, and they've all got the same excuse: 'Oh, I've got a wife and family to support.' I say, 'Well, then support them by being something other than a shitsucker.' "[381]

He'd always wanted to be a pop star, but it was reaching the point where so many people wanted a piece of him – and had got one – that there was a danger of nothing being left. The final straw, according to Jarvis, was the pictures Terrence Donovan took of him for *GQ* magazine's 'Cool Britannia' issue. "He was really nice," he told *The Face* later in 1997, "but those pictures convinced me that I had to disappear for a long time. I've never been able to look at them. I look like some kind of bloated . . . mess. I just look vacant. Like something's been sucked out of me.

"The way I think of it is in terms of the placards you have in a hairdresser's window, with the pictures of the hairstyles you can get inside. And they're in colour, but they've been in the window for ages and all the colour drains out and you're left just with light blue – blue seems to be the last layer of the printing process and you're just left with these faded blue pictures. And it's like that, you know? It's like you're subjected to this glare of relentless scrutiny, and if you don't apply a bit of shade to yourself, then you'll just fade and eventually you won't have any personality left. So you have to keep something back for yourself. Which was never a problem before. I had loads left back for meself, because nobody was arsed about who I was. But it is an issue now. You have to remain a human being. I think that's quite important."[382]

Chapter 14

The next public sighting of Pulp – and the last for a very long time – was on September 10, a week before Jarvis' 33rd birthday, at the Mercury Music Prize ceremony. This time around, there was no repeat of the M-People debacle of two years before: the judges had unanimously agreed that *Different Class* was the best album of the past 12 months. After playing a version of 'Bar Italia', Pulp stepped up to collect the award . . . and gave away the prize money to Brian Eno's War Child charity.

"We'd formulated this theory," remembers Mark, "that the Mercury Award was a curse upon any band that was to win it. Primal Scream disappeared for a few years, M-People weren't that great to start with . . . I was the first person on to the stage, and I'd forgotten in the heat of the moment that you weren't meant to touch the award, so I received the award, realised my wrongdoing, tried to pass it to Steve who wouldn't have it, and so I put it back down. Unfortunately the curse did impose itself on me: I was trying to buy a house at the time and it all fell through. The curse generally lasted for a year, and I had a really miserable year – girlfriend left me, had quite a difficult time making the record. I was cursed; hopefully the group hasn't been cursed."[383]

Steve: "I think we gave the money to War Child because the war was going on in Bosnia and it was quite affecting because it seemed quite close to us in Europe, and it seemed a way of doing something about it. We knew Brian Eno, and it seemed to guarantee us that a lot of the money we gave would directly go to people, and it involved music as well, so it seemed appropriate really."[384]

"It was nice to win the Mercury Prize," says Jarvis, "but it seemed funny to be winning an award for a record that basically had been out for eight months or something, so it was quite kind of . . . not dead, but certainly in the past. But we were kind of pleased. I'd got it in to my head that there was a curse of the Mercury Prize and I didn't want it to be passed on to us so it was kind of handy that the War Child record was also up for the same prize, 'cos we had a way of giving it away to a good cause. It was like the full stop on the record really. That was it. It was official that it was considered to be all right and we had to try and think about something else then."[385]

Try and think about something else. By October, Pulp were in The Fortress, a rehearsal facility in London, writing for their next album. They had 'Help The Aged', written in soundchecks on the tour, to polish up, and a chord sequence called 'Northern Souls'. But other than that . . .

"It was really, really difficult," says Nick. "Obviously we'd been stuck together quite a lot of time and we started trying to write songs again, and not a great deal was coming out. We'd got various bits of things, but whereas before we'd had loads of bits and we could stick them together, now we had loads of bits that we couldn't really stick together, so we only really had 'Help The Aged' and 'Northern Souls'."

The environment in which they were working was hardly conducive to coming up with exciting new things: The Fortress was a far cry from Nick's mum's Catcliffe pottery warehouse or the rehearsal room in Waterloo where most of *Different Class* had been written. "We were in the basement of The Fortress," says Nick, "and basically it was just a room with no natural light whatsoever. The floor, the walls and the ceiling were all covered in grey carpet, it wasn't a very big room, and we were all kind of crammed in there. That didn't help, so it took a long time to get some stuff going."

The band did manage to make it into the recording studio in November for a week or two of sessions with Chris Thomas which, it was hoped, would form the starting point for the next Pulp album. "We did 'Help The Aged'," remembers Nick, "and we did bits of 'Northern Souls', which to me was like a 'Common People 2' – it seemed to me that was very similar. But then we started to try and stick some of these other bits together, and, you know, we'd got the recording session booked and it was just obvious that we hadn't got any songs to record in it. Chris Thomas basically said, 'This is a waste of time – it's a waste of my time, your time, we might as well stop this. The songs you've got you can hardly play, and the rest are just little bits.' As suspected, we hadn't got enough songs, and hadn't played them enough."

Pulp had ground to a halt. A few months away from touring clearly hadn't been enough to recharge anyone's creative batteries, and the band had less collective desire to work together than they'd had in a long time. Nick: "It was probably the twin pressures of not feeling you've got much time to be messing round with stuff, and knowing that it's on the back of a very successful record: you know that you've got to do better, or certainly produce something of a similar sort of standard. You might not be actually thinking that, but the cross is still there, it's something that's got to be done. It's different.

"Plus we were all down in London for this and there were a lot of distractions. Jarvis was probably still going out to the opening of envelopes at this stage, and perhaps there were other things to do rather than think about something daft to do with this strange keyboard or something."

Jarvis had been hitting the parties with a vengeance since coming off the tour, but the novelty of the celebrity circuit was wearing thin. "When you go through that sacred portal where you get right famous," he reflected later, "it gets hard to go out. I've always hated being stuck in the house, I can't bear it. But I thought, 'I can't go to the pub any more, so I'll go to those parties.' That phase – it was crap.[386]

"I don't dislike myself for the way I behaved. I just feel a bit sorry for myself. I look at things and say, 'God, you sad get.' And sometimes I look back and I am ashamed or embarrassed. I think I was just a bit lost, really. I suddenly had access to women I would never otherwise have had access to and it excited me. I had access to the finest-quality fanny available. But somehow it didn't seem to be providing the satisfaction I had thought it would. You know, I'd started the group when I was 17 and I had this dream . . . and when that dream became reality, I thought that I had to suddenly live my life differently, to go to openings and hang around with a different set of people."[387]

And then there were the drugs. London at this time was awash with cocaine and other things, and, while Jarvis has mostly evaded direct questions on what he was doing at this time and how much, it would seem highly surprising if he hadn't partaken. "It's all right doing something that just enhances a laugh or enjoying yourself," he told *Select* magazine in 1998, "but if it becomes too much of a habit in your everyday life, it can become a problem. I don't think it ever got to that stage . . . One thing I will say about it is this. I think that what happens is, say, you've got a group of 10 people who're friends and they all do that kind of thing, everybody eggs everybody on, but if you talked to each individual person out of that group and said, 'Are you really wanting to do that?' they'd probably say, 'No, I think I'd be better off without.'

"It's peer pressure. Like when your mum says to you, 'If Martin Hunt jumped in some dog dirt, would *you*?' The answer is probably, 'Yeah, I would. If he said it were a good laugh, yeah, I'd do it.'"[388]

Dark rumours did circulate at the time that certain members of Pulp had developed a fondness for heroin – rumours described by Jarvis as "amusing", but not denied even so. "There was a bit of coke," says one sometime associate of the group. "There was, well, there *is* a lot of coke in rock'n'roll. I mean it's all over the place. So, it does get around. The heroin thing, I don't really know. I heard rumours. He was around that scene, I seem to remember, in London at the time there was a period when heroin became the chic drug. So there were drugs involved, but it was all part of an escalation for Jarvis – he did get a bit burned/phased out. He got to where he wanted to be and found that he actually didn't like it. It's not a unique story, really: getting to be famous and finding that it's a pretty lonely and hateful place."

Drugs or no drugs, it's clear that this was a difficult time for Jarvis. He'd reached a point where he'd achieved what he'd always wanted, and wish-fulfilment was therefore, perhaps for the first time ever, no longer a major provider of direction in his life. So what was? "There's a sort of examination of motives," he reflected later, "because instead of it just being a fantasy, now you've got the reality, and you think, 'Well, hold on, why did I want to do this? Is it because I want to be successful and show off and go to places? Or is it a pure and noble artistic intention to create something?' And after having been a marginal character, on the fringes of things, suddenly being in the centre, the eye of the storm, you are kind of cut-off from your former life, because you can't really just do normal things. And so you think, 'Well, do you just have to hang around with famous people now because they're not going to hassle you so much?' The thing is, I always worry about things, all the time – but if you get pissed, then you stop worrying, you kind of go on to autopilot. So, it's not like I turned into Oliver Reed or something, but I have to admit there were some hairy moments. But luckily, through a combination of still knowing people I'd known for a long time, from before getting famous, and maybe having a bit of common sense, in the end you realise you're going to have to stop, otherwise you're going to be a kind of laughing stock."[389]

On a psychological level, there's probably some mileage to be got from the fact that Jarvis, around this time, invested in a new pair of glasses: ditching his trademark black National Health look, he'd instead decided to go for a pair of outsized, tinted, Reactolite-style specs that obscured half his face and made it nigh-on impossible for anyone to see the whites of his eyes – he was looking at the world through nicotine-coloured lenses. The look is reminiscent of no one more than Peter Cook in the infamous 1978 *Derek & Clive* film, which (if you believe the biographies) caught the comedian in a similar personal abyss. During the film, despite being indoors throughout, Cook remains hidden behind a pair of outsize tinted glasses, issuing forth with some of the darkest, most jaundiced, most brilliant work of his career.

In the end, there were two incidents toward the end of 1996 that prompted Jarvis to re-evaluate the party-hard lifestyle. "The defining moment of thinking 'Maybe you should calm down a bit now and try and get your life together,' he told *Snug* magazine, "was one night in a club off Oxford Street and doing some drugs in a toilet and the drummer out of Dodgy's saying, [shouts] 'Have you been larging it a lot recently?' No disrespect to Dodgy's drummer, but that kind of made me think, 'No, you've taken a wrong turning 'ere, calm down, think it out a bit.' "[390]

The other incident happened in a converted car park in Soho on November 29, 1996. "It was at a party for Action Man's 30th birthday. I'd only gone to this do because Russell had said he'd meet us there; I wasn't such a sad get that I actually wanted to meet Action Man. Or a bloke dressed up as Action Man. I never got to see Russell because there were all these knobheads saying, 'Oh just come over here for a quick picture with this character off the telly.' That was the moment I really thought, 'You should consider staying at home for a bit.' Action Man had gripping hands though. And eagle eyes.[391]

"Certain things happened to me where I was thinking, 'Is this the kind of world I want to be inhabiting?' In the end, it's not saying, 'I'm part of the establishment,' it's more to do with what you enjoy in your life and if you keep doing things that you don't enjoy, you should just stop. What you expect and what you actually get are two totally separate things. There was nothing unfair about it – I was mad for it, to coin a phrase. 'Course I was. You have to look at yourself, which is something I don't particularly like doing, and ask yourself why you need fame in your life. And I still don't really know. But there was nothing very unfair about it. It was my own fault."[392]

It all amounted to one thing: Jarvis desperately needed to get out of London and re-evaluate things, away from the celeb circuit, away from the media, away from Pulp. The solution was three weeks, alone, in New York's Paramount Hotel over Christmas/New Year 1996/1997.

"It doesn't make sense if you think about it logically," he told *Deluxe* magazine later. "I was in this cramped little room and it was very . . . I don't know, I just needed to get away. I'm good at putting decisions off anyway, but when you're on tour you put even more things off because you've got the more pressing business of getting yourself on stage every day. Decisions about your personal life get shoved off into the distance. Then you finish touring and instead of, like, two or three things to sort out, you've got a big pile of things. Plus, you're fucked. Mentally.[393]

"In retrospect [it] wasn't the most sensible thing to do. But it was to get away from everything, and to have a think about what I wanted to do next, or even if I wanted to continue doing it anymore. There were some hairy moments there.[394] I was attempting to get back into my head after a long period of getting out of it, and I went thinking that I could go [to New York] and not so many people know me but I can still talk the language. That was my logic. But what I failed to think of was the fact that my social skills which were never very good anyway – had dwindled to virtually nothing. And so I ended up cowering in my hotel room, going off my head.[395]

"You have to go through a crisis point, I think. I thought I'd go away and do it in private. I think I was just trying to get my head together, ready to go through this whole process. First of all, it's going to take you a certain amount of time to make the record, then it's going to take you quite a lot of time to go out and play it to people. You're talking about two or three years out of your life. So if you're going to go through that, you have to make sure that it's what you want to do, because if you go into it a bit half-heartedly, you're going to get a bit screwed-up. So I just wanted to go off and decide if it *was* what I wanted to do. But I probably could've done it in a less traumatic way."[396]

Sometime during 1997, Pulp recorded 'Laughing Boy', a song of utter emotional exhaustion that's as direct and touching, lyrically, as anything Jarvis has ever written. There's no triumphant front, no defences, no characters to hide behind – simply a drained, worn-out pop star, gently pleading: *"I don't mean to put you down, but you've taken everything that I owned. Don't tell me you want some more, 'cos I'm closed, I'm closed, I'm closed."*

The song ends with the words: *"I don't need this anymore, and it's written in the stars I must go. And will I come back for more? I don't know."*

Chapter 15

In Christmas 1996's *Pulp People* newsletter, Russell Senior was asked what he considered to be his greatest regret. His immediate reply was, "Joining this group." He was joking, obviously, but it was true that by that time he had developed serious doubts about his future with Pulp.

On January 21, 1997, Russell and Pulp issued a joint statement: "Russell Senior has decided to leave Pulp after more than 13 years due to a desire to pursue new projects. The split is entirely amicable and although the band are sad to see him go they wish him all the best for the future. Pulp are currently rehearsing prior to recording their next album."

He'd left the group precisely a week before. "I'm proud of *Different Class*," Russell told *Mojo* magazine three years later, "but when we were doing it I had a real sense we had lost it but just managed to hold it together for the album. On the tour the atmosphere was very cold and I think we got complacent and ended up losing all connection with reality. The politics and hangers-on and also three members living in London. It just seemed hypocritical doing all these songs about Common People and not being like that – it had lost all connection with reality."[397]

In addition, three years' near-continuous touring, recording and pro- moting had taken its toll on his personal life. At 35, he was several years older than the rest of the band, and having a young family in Sheffield (he had a seven-year-old daughter and a two-year-old son at this stage) was proving difficult to reconcile with a jet-setting pop star lifestyle. Was another album and another tour really worth missing your children's birthdays again for? "Our last tour kind of killed most of us off," said Steve, "but with Russell especially. He's got two kids, you know, and we were all quite physically shattered by the end of it. There was a definite prospect of a year in the studio and two years on tour which he was not willing to face."[398]

Russell's misgivings had deepened after the recording sessions in November. 'Help The Aged' had been mooted as the band's next single, but he'd got the release put off because he didn't feel it was strong enough. "I think music is made by accidental collaborations of disparate people, not chords or musicianship, or geniuses, and all that had gone out of the window. We'd stopped writing properly and were into thinking it would happen in the studio because you chuck money at it. There was this sense that no matter what happened the next album would sell a million anyway. 'Help The Aged' I didn't like and didn't feel involved with and tried to avoid being released. Jarvis was very keen on it and I guess we had musical differences. I just didn't think it was better than what we'd been doing and, if that's true, I don't think you should do it."[399]

It wasn't just that Russell was uncomfortable with the direction of Pulp. "Russell's playing," says Nick, "hadn't evolved at all since *His'n'Hers* – he was still kind of playing this same guitar line he had all the time. And of course his violin playing never got any better really – he was never going to be Yehudi Menuhin or whatever. And it just caused a lot of friction, and it ended up with Russ sort of saying, 'I don't want to play any more,' but at the same time Jarvis was sort of saying, 'I can't stand you playing any more,' in a way. So there was friction on the album and Russell was getting pissed off with the whole thing."

"It got to 'why am I staying in this band?'," says Russell. "There are two good reasons – fame or money – and I thought, 'No,' if it's come down to that. I did want to make music but you have to wade through so much bullshit to make music when you get to a level like that. I think we were bored with each other. Everyone had heard everybody else's anecdotes half a dozen times and hated the colour of each other's socks worse than fascism."[400]

Ultimately, 13 years on from that first rehearsal in Jarvis' garage, the creative relationship had run its course. When Jarvis returned from New York in January, it was time to bite the bullet. "I went down to a London hotel determined to leave, but in as civilised a way as possible because these things are never easy. It's a divorce, you're tied together in various contractual ways and I didn't want to walk out with a couple of guitar strings, I wanted something, but I didn't want to fall out about it. I just wanted to seal it all off amicably and fairly and in the end we did that.[401]

"If I could've seen the future beyond *Different Class*, I would have said 'F.E.E.L.I.N.G.C.A.L.L.E.D.L.O.V.E.' is a signpost towards it. I'm never big on ballads – I mean I don't like 'Something Changed'. That was the last single released before I left, and in a way that neatly brings me on to my point of departure with Pulp. If you rewind 13 years, I would've said that I felt like it was my baby and something that I very much helped to create, and I felt that I might've been a slice of lemon in the gin and tonic but it could certainly go on without me. I felt like it wasn't creatively rewarding to be in Pulp for me.

"It was the hardest thing I've ever done in my life. Definitely. I spent a week not eating, not sleeping, smoking far too much, drinking far too much – I just collapsed on the floor and was taken to hospital. Nervous exhaustion, they call it. It was a difficult thing, you know – I loved Pulp, it was part of me. It was a very, very hard thing to do, but once I'd decided to do it, it was definitely the right thing to do. But I'm very glad to have been in it."[402]

"On the whole, a millstone lifted when I left. Pulp was a collaboration which I would regard myself as a central part of and obviously I find it hard to imagine how it works without me. Immediately we were friends again after I left. It had been unspoken coldness and I spend more time in Pulp's company now than when we were on the road together."[403]

In a sense, Russell's departure could be seen as the culmination of a long process. When he'd joined Pulp at the end of 1983, the essence of the band was the collaboration between himself and Jarvis and, while others played a significant part over the coming years, this was essentially the case for much of the Eighties. Things changed slightly when Jarvis moved to London in 1988 and Steve joined the group, meaning that Russell, still in Sheffield, was increasingly distanced geographically from the epicentre of the group. Subsequently, moves such as bringing in proper management and Mark joining as second guitarist could be seen as having the incidental side-effect of diminishing Russell's role in Pulp. Even so, the removal of one of the most distinctive individuals in the band, musically, visually and personally, was bound to have its effect.

"I didn't really see eye-to-eye with Russell musically at the end," Steve told *NME*, "but he was the person I used to enjoy most being on tour with.[404] He argued, which was positive, because you really had to argue your case, think about what you were doing."[405]

Candida admitted that she found Russell's departure "quite sad really, because Russell is a good mate and a lot of things I didn't enjoy about Pulp, he didn't like either. Me and Russell would usually agree about things that annoyed us. I wasn't that surprised really, there's been a few times that he thought about leaving and he didn't so I suppose we were lucky that he stayed so long. He's really happy, I've spoken to him a few times and he's happy with the situation. I think a lot of people will be really gutted but there was no persuading him. I can see why he left and at least we're all friends, that's important."[406]

"I would have preferred Russell to stay and to try to accommodate him in some way," says Nick, "'cos I always hate it when you grow up with a group, then someone who's been there for so long kind of drops out. Obviously it's never the same group, and perhaps you lose something greater than what they brought to it anyway."

Jarvis: "It was problematic because I hate it when people leave groups. And I don't like change. So it was quite a stressful time when he left."[407]

A year later, Q magazine asked Jarvis what, if anything, he missed about Russell. "Lots of things," he replied. "I saw him in Sheffield at Christmas. My sister's got a 75ft deep well at the back of her house, it's really old, and Russell got quite excited about it. He's into adventures, he's very knowledgeable about fungus, he would always have a different take on things, and he's a very good cook. When we go on tour, I'll miss him even more."[408]

Russell's departure was undoubtedly a sad event for all concerned, but when the band reconvened at The Fortress to continue writing songs for the album, it became apparent that, for whatever reason, the change in chemistry had made things easier. "After Russell wasn't with us," says Nick, "it did free something up a little bit. Certainly Mark felt easier to be able to input more. There was more space in the room, and we'd lost that bit of tension with Russ trying to fit his one guitar line into every song. We started using samplers as well at this point – Steve was really getting into that and using computers and stuff, so we had 'This Is Hardcore' with the sample on it, the horns taken off Peter Thomas, and I'd got an electronic drum set from Yamaha to play with, so that gave us 'Seductive Barry': the drone at the start of it came from my electronic drum, messing around with those. So we got a couple more bits of equipment and that released more creative ideas.

"When we were down at The Fortress we had this routine where we'd get in there at midday, Jarvis'd turn up an hour later, and we'd have a listen for an hour to the previous day's twiddlings where we'd been jamming stuff. We'd fall about laughing at the stupid, idiotic stuff that was coming out, then we'd go, 'Maybe that bit was quite good,' or 'There was that bit from a couple of days ago, that might come out, we'll try and stick them together,' and we'd have tapes and tapes of days of stuff and it'd be eventually a filter process where from jams, two or three of them might get through to the next process, then two or three of them something might happen to them a couple of weeks later and something might be stuck on them, 'Oh that works,' and gradually we ended up with quite a lot of songs – some good, some bad, some terrible – and some of these will get through that last filter and get to make it on to a record, whereas some will get to a demo and not get any further."

Contrary to popular impressions (probably influenced by the gloominess of the music that resulted), the general mood in the band at this time was fairly positive. "I was having a good laugh about it," says Nick.

"There was none of this sitting round arguing with each other going *grrrrr*. Some of the days were long, dull, tedious, grinds, yeah they were. But we still had some right good laughs doing it."

Within a short time, the band were ready to record demos of a dozen songs in the Fallout Shelter Studio at The Fortress complex. Of these songs, six made it to the 'proper' recording stage, with the other half being dropped. The nature of the rejected material suggests that there was still some debate at this point as to the musical direction Pulp were going to take for the album: while 'You Are The One' and 'Can I Have My Balls Back Please?' are fairly typical Pulp throwaways of the kind that usually gets weeded out at demo stage, 'Modern Marriage', 'Street Operator' and 'Grown Ups' all had rather more potential, being along similar lines to the poppier Pulp of *His'n'Hers* and *Different Class*. Meanwhile, the songs that made it to the album were mostly darker, more sombre material such as 'The Fear', 'TV Movie', 'Seductive Barry' (recorded here under its working title 'Sex Symbols') and 'I'm A Man'.

Was the move toward a more low-key sound simply the latest development in a career of a band that had been reinventing itself almost constantly since its formation, or were they explicitly on the run from the kind of pop success that had characterised most of the Nineties? "We probably could have done another *Different Class*," says Candida, "but Jarvis didn't want to. There were songs that could have been instant hits, but we took them off!"[409]

Then again, no one complained when *It* turned into *Freaks* – a far more extreme transformation. As Nick says, "Pulp never really have been a group to repeat stuff – 'Oh, that worked, let's do more of that.' It was like, 'All right, that was good, clap clap, something new will come next.' We'd always been wanting to keep doing things that are new and interesting, never wanting to do things that we know we can do and rehash stuff. It doesn't always work that way, but with using the samples, some songs were getting more lengthy in a repetitive kind of way, and there was a lot of the stuff that Mark brought . . . his love of minimalist American avant-garde music – load of rubbish as far as I'm concerned, but he did persevere with bringing it in, so you did get a lot of droney kind of stuff."

The tunes may have been coming easily, but Jarvis was still having trouble with the lyrics. Many of those on the demo had been incomplete sketches, with one song, 'Grown Ups', being left as an instrumental. Of course, every Pulp album hitherto had taken a different lyrical direction, but as long ago as March 1996 he'd expressed concern that, having said the things he'd wanted to say for so long on *Different Class* and finally escaped his underdog status as a result, he wasn't sure what he was going to write about next. "I don't know how my focus will change . . . It is difficult because a lot of people might think, 'Oh, he's still writing songs about being in a council flat when we know for sure he's living in Primrose Hill and lording it,' or whatever. But then again, I don't want to write songs about the hotel room, the dressing room, the stage, all that kind of thing. It isn't that interesting to other people, I don't think. They don't live that kind of life."[410]

By 1997, he was developing a clearer idea of what he wanted to write about, but it was obviously still proving difficult. "Whether I liked it or not," he told *NME* later in the year, "you do become a part of the establishment and so it becomes a bit bogus to come on as this outsider figure. It didn't seem appropriate any more. And even 18 months ago it was obvious that a lot of the stuff I'd written about in songs was the ordinary, everyday things, which wasn't the life I was living at that time.

"Certainly in the last year-and-a-half, I haven't been able to just do normal things. I'm not whining about it, it's just a fact of life. And so . . . I suppose I was worried about that a bit too much really. You don't want to come up with some kind of pale imitation of yourself, some kind of karaoke version, because you think you should keep writing about underpants and nylon fabrics. But then again, you don't want to go off on a tangent. Like, 'Yeah! We're gonna go on a jazz odyssey now. That Spinal Tap concept album idea.' So it's a bloody minefield, that's what it is.

"That's why I think people went off Morrissey. Because he kept writing about how inadequate he was, which, fair enough, I'm sure he probably was and is, but somehow having had a certain measure of success, and by dint of repetition, it starts to ring a bit hollow. For me to write about, '*Yes I saw her in a chip shop/ And I said get yer top off*' or something like that would be pathetic because I haven't been in a chippy for ages. So I've tried to take that into account."[411]

"I probably revised the words on this one more," reflected Jarvis after the album had been completed, "but there was never a point where I couldn't write anything. So it wasn't writer's block, just mild constipation."[412]

Meanwhile, Jarvis was on his way to recovering from the worst of the horrors he'd encountered toward the end of 1996. He'd moved out of the house in Ladbroke Grove that had been home since the end of 1993, and into a flat in Maida Vale – or, as he occasionally referred to it, 'Media Vale', in recognition of the affluent, trendy, finger-on-the-pulse types that frequented the area. It did have the advantage of being somewhere you could walk down the street relatively untroubled, though.

"Before I moved I was kind of stuck in our house a bit. Because people knew where we lived in our road. They were all right, but if you get up in the morning and you feel a bit tired and you go to the shop, it was a bit like a dawn chorus. There was this glass shop across the road and all the blokes in there used to go, 'YEAAH JAAAARVIS. AWWRIIIIGHT MATE! HOWSYAMATE MICHAEL?' and all that crap. But because it's a bit snobby round here people don't want to demean themselves by acknowledging you."[413]

At the end of January, he appeared at the *NME* Brat Awards to collect his 'Godlike Genius Award For Services To Music' (sic) in recognition of the Jackson incident, and took the opportunity to have a swipe at The Spice Girls. The manufactured pop quintet were huge at the time (helped to some extent, perhaps, by the confused notion in some areas of the music press that, since Britpop had momentarily made alternative music into the new pop music, every kind of pop music, including useless, cynical lowest-common-denominator stuff like this, was now cool), and they'd recently held up Margaret Thatcher as an admirable example of their clueless 'Girl Power' concept. With the Brats being broadcast on live radio and reported on by the world's music press, Jarvis just had to capitalise on the moment:

"They said Margaret Thatcher was the first Spice Girl, and somehow that seems to have passed over. But Margaret Thatcher did her best to decimate and fuck up this country, so fuck off Margaret Thatcher and fuck The Spice Girls. Here's to the new dawn!"

"Girl Power in terms of The Spice Girls," he later remarked to Q magazine, "seems to be more like, 'We can get our tits out when we want' — which is basically what blokes want anyway. I thought it was a joke: they had a male manager, it was blokes writing the songs, and it was like a 45-year-old bloke's masturbation fantasy of girls — 'Naughty girls, I'd like to take you across my knee and spank you.' "[414]

Isolated incidents aside, such feistiness was rare in the Jarvis of 1997. There would be no quiz show appearances, no adverts, no presenting *Top Of The Pops*, and precious few occurrences of getting snapped by paparazzi at showbiz parties. He had, by and large, dropped off the media radar. "Going on the telly wasn't just supposed to be an ego gratification exercise," he remarked to *NME* toward the end of the year. "What it was supposed to be was that it seemed important at that time to show that not just the rock hierarchy are allowed to go on programmes, that you can show there's an alternative to that. But then I got offered quite a few adverts. Even as recently as the last couple of weeks I got asked to go on *Noel Edmonds' House Party*. They offered me five grand. I thought, 'Yeah.

Five grand to completely ruin any respect that you might have built up over the years.'

"After the Michael Jackson thing, I could've gone the way that Mark E Smith has ended up now, where they'll wheel him out and he'll have a go at everybody and say that they've nicked all their ideas off The Fall. You could easily end up being that kind of caricature of yourself. I would never want to take it any further than I went.

"From the time of going on *Top Of The Pops* and slagging Wet Wet Wet off, it seemed logical because I was a bit of a gatecrasher into this glittery pop fraternity. So instead of sucking the cock and selling out, you had to say something. Then it reached its zenith or nadir with that incident [Michael Jackson], and after that I just thought, 'Well, I'll end up being Mr Angry. I'll end up being this daft get who's always going to say something controversial for the sake of it.' And I just thought, 'What's the point in that?'

"It's not like I want everyone to listen to our record in a darkened room with ceremonial robes on. But all that other stuff that goes on is just what you get involved in as a result of the process of being in a band. And if that becomes a barrier to people listening to what you're doing, where they think you should really just be a stand-up comic, then that's not right. So again, I just thought it was a bad idea.[415]

"I kind of had to take a backwards step and think, 'Well, why are we in this position, and what is my job?' Just remember what your job is, and your job is to be a songwriter, so, y'know, I kind of had to take a step back and concentrate on doing that. It was good. Getting back to doing some work, y'know. And realising why the whole thing had started in the first place – because you like doing music."[416]

Typical of Jarvis around this time is the pragmatic explanation he gave *NME* in February when announcing that Pulp wouldn't be playing any festivals in 1997. "I'm not fed up of doing what I do, though, 'cos there'd be no point otherwise. We're just giving the festival thing a break." When asked about the forthcoming album, he added: "You don't wanna hear about the album, it's boring. We've just been trying to write some songs. Some of them are ready, some of them aren't. It's not very interesting. There's really no point talking about it. This year, I just want to be a happy person and I also hope we'll do a record that will be of relevance to people. That's all you can hope for really, isn't it?"[417]

In March, armed with more new songs, Pulp entered The Town House to start work on their sixth studio album. "We'd had this first aborted session," says Nick, "and we thought, 'Well, we're not going to do that again, we're going to go in with a bunch of finished songs to play and get on with it.' So that was what we kind of went in to do, and we went back into The Town House with Chris Thomas. In another way, that maybe was a bad move – the end product was good, but it just felt like Groundhog Day. Although two years had passed since the last album, we'd been doing that much – when you're busy time goes like that. So we were back in The Town House. Chris Thomas again. It all felt a bit strange."

The sessions progressed smoothly enough, though, with the band benefiting from being slightly removed from the unreal, showbiz world that they'd become a part of in the *Different Class* period. "It's great writing songs again," Candida said at the time. "It's what being in a group should be all about. I didn't miss writing and I didn't even know if we'd still be able to, but we've written twelve songs and we're sounding OK. Also, doing things for yourself and it only being the five of us together and not having a hundred other people doing things for you is good. Just now you have to turn up by yourself to practise and you go home to cook, just doing normal things like that must be difficult to understand unless you've been on tour for two years – it probably sounds really spoilt."[418]

The routine of the sessions was enlivened in April when word reached Pulp that they were in the running to do the theme for the next James Bond film, *Tomorrow Never Dies*. "That was one of my favourite bits on the *Hardcore* recording session," says Nick. "We heard they wanted us to do the Bond theme and it was like, 'Fucking hell, come on!' We all loved James Bond stuff, John Barry's fantastic, we'd love to do it. But we'd had this fax saying, 'We want you to do the Bond theme,' on the Wednesday, and it said, 'We want you to deliver the final finished product this Friday.' It was like, it's Wednesday! How do they expect us – we thought obviously they must send this out to a dozen people and see what they get back, you know.

"So we thought, 'Well, golden opportunity, we can't miss it – got to get this. So right, what have we got to record? Not a lot really. Right.' So I think on the Thursday we all turned up early, thought, 'We're going to write this thing,' and basically in the morning we wrote this song, used some bits that were unused from the recording session, made some new bits up. Written it in the morning, practised it at lunchtime and recorded in the afternoon. By teatime we'd got this song sounding great, mixed in the evening, sent off on the Friday. Next week, 'Sorry, you have not been selected . . .' Oh, for fuck's sake!

"You go through pulling teeth sometimes to get songs written and recorded, and I thought, 'This is how it should be – you've written it in the morning, recorded in the afternoon, you've mixed it at teatime. Didn't have anything to start with, and by the end of the day you've got a finished thing, sounds great. All done in one day. This is how music should be.' It was exciting, it was fresh, great. And then we were back to technology, putting it all right, something's got to be bang-on, which was very, very boring."

As the sessions dragged on through April and May, things seemed to gradually get more difficult – a sense of inertia began to set in. "We'd do a song and then it would go in the can for two months," says Steve, "and that's never happened before. I mean, a song's just a record of how the people involved were feeling at the time. And if the people involved don't have the desire to put the song away, that's the reason it goes off the desk and back in the can again. We all agreed that what we'd recorded was really good, but somehow we couldn't seem to finish it for a while."[419]

The solution, early in the summer, was a change of scenery: to the huge Olympic Studios, once a cinema but since the Sixties London's most famous studio after Abbey Road, in Barnes. "An unbelievable place," says Nick. "The main room is a huge hall – it's absolutely massive and that's the studio where The Rolling Stones' stuff and loads of amazing music was made in this place. But we were using this brand-new part of the studio, brand-new desk, whole new system – which kept breaking down. I think we lost two or three songs 'cos this stupid desk broke down and all our computer disks and things all went zip. So a lot of time Chris Thomas wasn't in a good mood 'cos we were trying to get this desk working, it wouldn't work, so he was having a wobbler all the time. And sometimes things were a bit fraught because we were trying to record songs that yes, we could play, but sometimes the thing about getting a good performance is when you're totally confident with what you're playing. If you're only 75% you back off, you're a bit gentle with things. And there was quite a lot of studio tension 'cos of things like this. And that's without the hangovers and the latecoming . . ."

The sessions were productive, though, and by August, it was time to think about releasing a single. The album wasn't ready yet, but Jarvis wanted to break the silence in an understated, low-key way, gradually easing back into the public eye rather than mounting a needlessly over-blown comeback campaign – as Oasis had recently done with *Be Here Now*. "All that hype around when Oasis came back with their album and everything – I think it turned people off in a way. That it can't be reviewed in the review page, it's got to be on the front page of *The*

Observer. I thought, 'Gawd, it's just a record, isn't it?' So I thought it would be quite nice to just release something without too much hoo-hah. Just put it out, and allow people to make their own minds up."[420]

The two main contenders for the A-side were both songs that had been started in the aborted 1996 sessions with Russell and finished off at Olympic: 'Help The Aged' and 'Northern Souls'. The latter had developed into a cynical, funny swipe at New Labour, using cocaine as a metaphor for what Jarvis felt was another flashy, superficially exciting but ultimately hollow experience: the brand of socialism-lite that was being offered by Tony Blair's then-recently modernised and madeover Labour Party.

The inspiration apparently came from an experience Jarvis had during his New York hotel trip. Somehow, he found himself being hounded by a Labour Party worker called Imogen who, on behalf of the then-opposition, kept phoning him in the early hours to ask whether they could still rely on his support – i.e. whether he was willing to line up with Noel Gallagher and Alan McGee to try and convince the kids that voting was cool. "I told her to fuck off. I don't know how they tracked me down. Nobody was supposed to know I was there."[421]

A few months later, Labour won the election on a massive wave of public goodwill, but Jarvis – very much an Old Labourite – was still sceptical. Even so, it was summer 1997 and, a matter of months after the party had got into power, the post-election honeymoon was still in full swing. Releasing such a negative song still had the potential to be a misjudgement of the mood of the times.

"It was a controversial subject," says Nick, "especially at that time. Some people were wary of it because it was still early days, just after the election. You didn't know if it was going to be a new dawn for Britain or something. Now, of course, we know what it's like – the same government got back in. I suppose all bands have arguments about which tracks are going to make it, but I was quite keen on seeing it as an A-side. After that, I wouldn't have minded putting it on the album too, but by then, the time for it had kind of passed and it transmogrified into 'Glory Days'."[422]

'Help The Aged' it was then. "That was the oldest song," says Jarvis, "and I was beginning to feel like if we didn't get it out soon, it'd be past its sell-by date."[423] Musically, the song was far more of a low-key affair than the more typically anthemic 'Northern Souls', based around a gentle, understated piano motif before building into a soaring chorus. Any misgivings that it gets a little too Beatlesque in places (the falsetto harmonies and occasionally rather formulaic chord changes) are forgiven thanks to the wonderful 'bigness' of the whole thing, and Jarvis' funny, self-deprecating lyrics – even though a surprising number of people did seem to take them at face value and assume that they really were just about Jarvis telling us to be nice to pensioners. He wasn't.

"It tackles personal issues," he told *NME* at the time, "because I'm now 34 years old. And I have been aware of the ageing process for a couple of years now. And that's where it came from. It's not a heartfelt plea to help people cross the road." Had he ever done that, wondered the *NME*'s scribe? "Of course I have. I'm a lovely lad. Very caring . . . But, I'm afraid it's just me whining on about getting old.

"Everybody's afraid of dying. The thing is, you move the goalposts with yourself. I remember when I first came down [to London] and started going out to raves and stuff, and thinking, 'Fucking hell! I'm getting into raving at 25, I'm past it.'

"What I'm hoping is that I'm not on my own in this sad pursuit of moving the goalposts. People are desperately gripping on to their youth into their thirties, which 20 years ago would have been quite unheard of. And because of the so-called youth revolution in the Sixties, still all the images of what's to be desired in life are based around young, fit-looking people. So it's going to end up causing lots of problems because the brutal fact of it is that the ageing process is something that no one is immune to. Everybody gets old and everybody dies.

"It seems so unfair that the young part of your life goes on until your mid-thirties, and then you've got this fucking big chunk of your life when you're a giffer. And what the fuck are you supposed to do with that time? Look back on your glory days? Like [switches into geriatric Cockney raver speak] 'Yeah! Centreforce 1989, fuckin' yeaaas! We were 'avin it then, lad. I tell you, son, you think you're fuckin' 'avin it now? We was 'avin it back then!' So it was my desperate attempt to come to terms with that, with trying to find some dignity in adulthood."[424]

"Getting old is something that everybody has got to deal with," he added on another occasion, "and I think that everybody's not very keen on it. There was this Mark E Smith interview I read, and he was describing going to a concert given by Clint Boon, who used to be in the Inspiral Carpets – he had that purdie cut, I don't know if you remember his hairstyle. And he was saying it was really funny because there was all these blokes in their mid-thirties with this same purdie cut hairstyle, but receding at the front. In some ways, you kind of think that's inappropriate behaviour, but then you think, 'Why not?' In a way, it's better than people hitting their mid-thirties and then suddenly getting their pipe and slippers out and listening to Phil Collins and Eric Clapton. It's just not gonna happen to our generation, I don't think. Pop music traditionally deals with young flash things, but pop music itself is middle-aged. I just want to find a way of being an adult without it being boring. I don't wanna continue acting like a teenager for the rest of my life because I can't hack it!"[425]

Hardly typical Radio 1 Top 10 subject matter, then, but at least no one could accuse Pulp of repeating themselves or going for the obvious option. "I thought it was a great idea for a single," says Nick. "I thought it was something no one had ever written before in a record."

The single, which also included Pulp's Bond-theme-that-never-was (retitled 'Tomorrow Never Lies' to avoid copyright complications) and the touching country-balladeering of 'Laughing Boy', was promoted with a truly excellent video made by the Hammer & Tongs production company. Pulp perform the song in a pastiche of an old people's home (set in Stoke Newington town hall), surrounded by young actors dressed in the style of geriatric men, effortlessly seducing pretty girls. One of the highlights is Jarvis singing while ascending on a Stannah stairlift, to conclude the song in a stylishly surreal space-type environment (it was going to be heaven but Stannah didn't want their product to be associated with death). Pulp might have quit chasing the limelight, but it was reassuring that they'd lost none of their visual flair.

"We decided it'd be better to use young people made up to look old than to use actual old people," explained Jarvis, "as if, for some reason, looking old had become trendy, you know – whereas now people are trying to look younger than they really are. If somehow it flipped over and people were trying to look as old as possible, and before they went out at night, having a stick-on beard and putting a bit of grey in their hair, things like that. It'd be a nice idea. I think the blokes in the video look really good – in fact, I went up to the person who styled the video after, who got the clothes, and ordered a few. They had a nice kind of cardigan with a tie waist on it . . ."[426]

The most significant visual change in Pulp seemed to be in the people themselves. Even disregarding the obvious absence of Russell (and therefore of PVC jackets, eyeliner, mod suits and hi-tech sunglasses), the whole group image, both in the video and other promotional photos around this time, seemed to have been toned down. Steve was shorn of his trademark enormous side-parted fringe; Candida of the various more glittery wardrobe items for which she'd become famous; and Jarvis . . . Jarvis may as well have had a head transplant. The contact lenses, it seemed at this point, were gone for good, with those enormous tinted specs still hiding half his face. The tidy hair of the *Different Class* era had also gone, replaced by a slightly longer look, with a vague arrangement at the front which could just about pass for a centre parting. Meanwhile, the charity shop clothing was still there, but the suit-and-tie look had been replaced by either a brown velvet jacket with a patterned polo-neck sweater beneath it, or an open-necked shirt, or an especially loudly patterned Seventies blazer. The overall effect was reminiscent of a pervy college lecturer – not that that's any bad thing, of course. If the band as a whole was making a statement with the new image (and such things are always open to wide interpretation), it seemed to be "We're artists, not pop stars."

Meanwhile, the old pop star Jarvis lived on, immortalised as a waxwork which was unveiled at the Rock Circus in London in the autumn of 1997. "I kind of agreed to do it," says Jarvis, "because I thought it would be a laugh and because I quite like that place – it's funny. But it was unnerving the way they did it. It was crackers, really. They sent the head in a box to the studio. So this box arrives, and I fucking open this box and it's my head in it, looking at me. And they've done a really good job. I know sometimes they do them and they're nothing like, but this one's pretty realistic.

"So I'm looking at this head, and it's freaking me out, I couldn't really look at it too long. And then they came and matched the hair up and the eyes and stuff like that. I asked them to get rid of a few crow's feet, obviously. And it's up in there now, and to me, I'm really pleased because in a kind of way, that period is there, like a voodoo doll or something. *That's* that period, and if people want me to be like that, I just say to them, 'Go to Rock Circus and look at that dummy with your Walkman on,' and that's it. If you want something else, we're here, still alive.

"It's a semi-Dorian Gray thing, isn't it? Except the other way round. I'm the one who's getting more twisted and messed-up, and the dummy can stay untouched."[427]

The inverse Dorian Gray concept was seemingly something that was playing on Jarvis' mind at this time – he offered the same explanation when he appeared on *TFI Friday* to promote 'Help The Aged', picked up the *Different Class* cardboard cut-out of himself that had been posed behind Chris Evans for most of the series' lifetime, bedecked in a succession of football strips, Christmas decorations and the like, and threw it out of the window (apparently coming within inches of killing the drummer from Metallica, who was standing beneath having a fag). Of course, there was another reason too. "I really hate what that programme's become," remarked Jarvis of Channel 4's one-time Britpop flagship. "It's really just an ego exercise for Evans. And it's just not funny! I didn't want my cut-out being associated with a load of crap, so I decided that I was going to chuck it out of the window."[428]

Shortly before the 'Help The Aged' single was released, Pulp made their first and only live appearance of 1997: a 20-minute set as part of a benefit concert for the American minimalist composer La Monte Young and his partner Marian Zazeela, at the Barbican Hall in London. The idea came from Mark Webber, a long-time fan of their work who had known Young and Zazeela for a number of years.

"They have a sound and light installation called 'Dream House' on the floor above their loft in New York City," Mark wrote in the *Pulp People* newsletter shortly after the event. "When Pulp toured America with Blur in 1994, I took Jarvis and Steve down to the 'Dream House' straight after the concert and they really liked it.

"I know I bore everyone silly by going on about La Monte's music – which I realise just isn't to everyone's taste – but I believe he's a very important artist. While La Monte and Marian's refusal to compromise in any way is definitely one of the things that made their art what it is, it has also meant that it's very difficult to hear their music (it took me four years from hearing the name to hearing the music), hardly anyone can afford to present their concerts, it makes it difficult for people to work with them, and now they find themselves severely in debt. And in September I heard that Marian was very ill and had spent about 40 days practically paralysed in bed. As Marian conducts all of their administration and fundraising activities this meant that their financial situation was becoming impossible.

"I had the idea of a fundraising event and asked Alex Poots of the Barbican Centre if he would help. I didn't think for one minute that Pulp would play the concert and it took me a few days to get up the courage to ask the others, and I was very shocked when they agreed. A few days later and the Barbican offered us free use of the hall and the English Chamber Orchestra on October 31 – only six weeks away."[429]

This was to be no ordinary concert. Apart from the unusual setting, it was the first time Pulp had played live in 14 months, the first time they'd played without Russell, and the first time they were going to play any of the material they'd been working on for the past 10 months. On the night, Pulp played after a series of sets from artists ranging from better-known acts like Nick Cave and Spiritualized to the more obscure likes of Gavin Bryars and the English Chamber Orchestra (performing a piece by the English post-minimalist Steve Martland). The latter two also played with Pulp, with the ECO contributing orchestral backing to new songs 'Love Scenes (Seductive Barry)' and 'This Is Hardcore', and Bryars playing piano on 'This Is Hardcore'.

The performance itself was a masterpiece. It began with Mark alone, playing an E-bow guitar drone, which was gradually picked up by the orchestra until the room was filled with a single, swelling chord which held for over a minute. At this point the rest of the group (augmented by Antony Genn, on additional bass and guitar) came onstage and the chord became the beginning of 'Seductive Barry', which in turn segued directly into 'This Is Hardcore'. Both songs were stripped of the gloss and bombast evident on the album versions and later live performances, instead displaying a wired, edgy brilliance that seemed to prove elusive elsewhere. Seeing a bespectacled, brown-suited Jarvis weave his way around the (rather crowded) stage and snarl and whisper his way through these strange, dark, almost wilfully difficult new songs, destroying his mike stand in the process, was a long way from V96. Then we got the comparatively poptastic 'Help The Aged', and they were gone as quickly as they'd appeared.

Well, nobody could accuse them of selling out. A little while before the concert, Steve held it up as an example of Pulp's new, yielding-to-nobody outlook. "We've taken control again, we've grabbed it back," he explained. "The idea is to do it on our own terms this time. We're starting in the right way with this La Monte Young concert. First concert after 18 months, a benefit for some obscure avant-garde composer, billed with the words, 'The Purpose Of This Concert Is Not Entertainment'. It might seem a strange way to come back, but I'm looking forward to it. And I hope we can continue in that manner."[430]

"Mark really wanted to do it," remembers Nick, "so he said to everyone, 'Can you all do this for me,' because he wanted to get his nose as far up La Monte Young's arse as he possibly could. So we kind of did it, and thought perhaps it was a good way to quietly play some new music to some people for the first time, rather than coming out of the grave – 'Der-der!' – and everyone kind of going, 'Ooh, it's not 'Disco 2000' is it?' So it was kind of doing something low-key, 'cos low-key's always been a good thing to do from our sort of perspective since the early days – in that Sheffield way of not shouting about things, just keeping quiet."

'Help The Aged' was released on November 10, 1997. As Pulp's comeback single after 18 months' silence, it was bound to do well, and it did – despite a slightly mixed reception. As Nick says, "I think the general feeling from the critics was kind of 'It's good but, ooh, it's not 'Disco 2000' is it?' A group kind of appears on the scene and does well with stuff which in a way is kind of contrary to it's previous 15 years of existence – which no one really knew about or cared about, which is fair enough. Then almost starting to move back the other way – a strange song about odd subjects. They didn't quite understand it."

Unsurprisingly, the song didn't quite repeat the success of the *Different*

Class-based singles, entering the chart at number eight and dropping to 27 the following week. Still, it was a respectable showing for a rather down-beat song that had been promoted by a slightly grumpy Jarvis appearing on the likes of *The O Zone* and *Live And Kicking* talking about his fear of getting old and dying. "I was shitting it before it came out," he admitted later. "Then I was really pleased when it got to number eight. Maybe we overestimated people's willingness to confront their own mortality in a pop record, but I'm proud that we got a record about getting old and dying in the Top 10."[431]

Now Pulp had established to the world that they were still there, it was time to attend to the album, which they had by now decided was called *This Is Hardcore*. The original plan was that the record would appear in the autumn, shortly after the release of 'Help The Aged'; however, as the single's release date slipped inevitably from September to November, the Island marketing department became concerned that the album would get lost in the Christmas rush, and therefore postponed its release till early spring 1998. The result was that Pulp had plenty more time to make sure everything on the album was to their satisfaction in November, December and January – although, as it was already practically finished in October, it's open to question whether this was ultimately either necessary or useful.

"We'd be going through the remix hell," says Nick of the late '97 session. "Let's just spend another week on this track, you know. It's like, 'Oh my God, it's been finished months ago!' They'd still tit around, 'cos when you're not kind of confident sometimes with something, you can keep going, 'Oh, let's just spend a week making that hi-hat quieter, you know.' I'd just say, 'Fuck it, who cares, let's get it out there.' If you're not fully confident about it, then . . . I don't know.

"We'd just kept going back to remix bits and bobs, and people not being happy with this bit, and everyone saying, 'Can you just change this bit,' and rather than just saying, 'No, it's done,' Jarvis would say, 'Yeah, we could spend another couple of weeks remixing.' It could have been one of Nigel Coxon's tactics partly – part of his thing would be like saying, 'Maybe we could try doing a remix of this.' But you know, Jarvis could easily have just gone, 'No, it's finished.' But he loves twiddling about, you see, can't leave it alone."

Pulp did manage to make one or two appearances outside the recording studio during the final months of 1997. In October, they'd appeared on David Arnold's *Shaken & Stirred* James Bond tribute album, performing an excellent version of Rita Coolidge's 'All Time High', and toward the end of November, the whole band appeared on Radio 1 to present John Peel's

show for three consecutive days. Jarvis began the stint with the announcement that, "We're back. To play some music for you. In an inept way,"
setting the tone for some highly entertaining radio as Pulp (or mostly, it
has to be said, Jarvis and Steve) played an eclectic selection of records,
ranging from Jarvis' old Sheffield favourites Artery and I'm So Hollow to
the up-to-the-minute (albeit wildly different) likes of Tiger, Add N To
(X) and Smog. Geoff Travis chipped in with his History Of Independent
Music, and Electric Sound Of Joy, fronted by Mark's friend and one-time
Pulp stagehand Gregory, played a session.

Meanwhile, Mark had also been busy, setting up his monthly club
night, Little Stabs At Happiness, which opened at the ICA in London on
December 13. "When I was just following the band around and stuff at the
beginning of it all," he explained, "I also used to run my own club night in
about 1987, '88 with some friends in Sheffield called The Groovy
Fishtank. We had bands that would play live and we also played loads of
records. When I moved to London, I always wanted to do that again. I
suppose it was during going out to loads of parties and premières and all
that other nonsense you get invited to that I realised I wasn't enjoying the
places I was going to and there weren't any clubs I wanted to go to. I
didn't have a girlfriend . . . I didn't like the look of the girls I was more
commonly meeting at this point either! So, out of all this, I just decided to
do a club that I liked and wanted to see if there was anyone else interested
in what it was all about."[432]

Over the following months, the club quickly became a minor phenomenon thanks to Mark's unique mix of, as the fliers said, "Quiet music,
films, loud music, dancing." The loud music in question consisted mostly
of forgotten Eighties school-disco classics from the likes of The Pro-
claimers and Imagination, and the films reflected Mark's love of the
American underground of the Sixties. "The first real piece of music I got
into, apart from that phase just before you discover your proper, favourite
music and just listen to a load of pop rubbish from the charts, was David
Bowie and it developed from that to The Velvet Underground. I became
totally enamoured of them and I then learnt about their interests in Andy
Warhol. That inspired me to look at his experimental films, for example,
as well as other pieces of film made in the Sixties. I started to see all these
films and just carried on learning about them.

"I mean, some of the films we've shown here have just been in such a
state because they're so old and haven't been seen for so long! It's weird
because when people come here and see us set up and play the movies,
you really notice that they just don't know what film and projectors look
like. We're all, as a society, used to our videos and DVDs so it's nice to

have a change I think. Well, maybe apart from me, because I don't have a DVD player!"[433]

This Is Hardcore was finally completed on January 9, 1998, and appeared (after a few months dedicated to promotion, video-making and working on the artwork) on March 30, preceded a few weeks before by another single: 'This Is Hardcore' itself.

If 'Help The Aged' seemed like an oddly downbeat, *joie de vivre*-lacking comeback, God knows what anyone was supposed to make of this. Six-and-a-half minutes, no chorus, barely any verse, simply lurching angrily, desperately, from one strange, sinister movement to the next, held together with a queasy horn sample from German composer Peter Thomas' 'Bolero On The Moon Rocks'. It was a bit rum.

Stylistically, the song uses easy listening music as a starting point to create something that's anything but. "It started off as an experiment," says Jarvis. "I'd been listening to these records by a group from San Francisco called Tipsy, and Stock, Hausen & Walkman. I liked the way they took stuff from lounge music or easy listening, but then they – especially with Stock, Hausen & Walkman – made something creepy, profoundly uneasy listening. I always liked easy listening music but I was put off it because there was a mini-revival of it in the UK, which featured Mike Flowers' Pops and people wearing stupid suits. I thought that what they had was an interesting slant. I thought, 'Let's have a go at that.' We'd come to grips with samples and computers and that. It started with the horn sample, kind of got the first section of the song written, and as we often do, we'll then say, 'Right, needs another bit now.' We try grafting other bits on, sometimes they're from other songs that we've tried and there's a bit that you like and the rest of it's no good. It just got jigsawed together in that way.

"I was really pleased with it because I'd been thinking vaguely before doing this record to get away from verse-chorus-verse-chorus-middle bit-double chorus-end kind of structure, but still have a melody, still have something. And we kind of achieved it on that song. The piano at the start, I was trying to get the Ronnie Oldridge sound, when he would get two pianos to play at once, you have a rolling feel to it – it took ages to get that sound.

"It's quite a violent song, but a lot of the starting off points for the sounds came from easy listening."[434]

The lyrics use the superficially seductive but ultimately dehumanising nature of hardcore porn as a starting point to explore the sometimes equally dehumanising nature of fame. "I could see some parallels there," explained Jarvis. "I ended up watching a lot of porn – hah! – on tour. If you get back to the hotel and you've got nothing to do, you put the adult channel on and have a look.

"It's the way that people get used up in it. You'd see the same people in films, and they'd seem to be quite alive, and then you'd see a film from a year later and there's something gone in their eyes. You can see it, that they've done it all and there's nowhere else to go. There seemed to be something really poignant about that to me. It seemed to be very similar to the way people get used up by the entertainment business.

"Obviously, television and everything thrives on these life stories of people. It doesn't matter whether it's a film star or a rock musician or anybody, it always seems to end tragically and you can't hide from that fact. You think, 'Is that going to happen to me as well, then? Am I going to be the alcoholic in the mental asylum, or am I going to kill somebody in a car crash, or whatever?' There are certain exceptions but generally that seems to be it. There's something to do with realising an ambition that seems to curdle somebody's spirit in some way.

"So it seemed to be appropriate to write about that. I was really relieved to be able to write about it without referring to it directly, to have found some kind of image for it."[435]

Two years after it all happened, 'This Is Hardcore' was the first full revelation of the less edifying experiences that Jarvis had been through in his pop star phase – and, indeed, the first definite confirmation (after the could-go-either-way stopgap of 'Help The Aged') that the pop star phase was, most definitely, over. "When it came to 'Hardcore'," says Nigel Coxon, "you realised that something had gone off. He had to have a massive reassessment."

Strange and disconcerting and non-commercial it may have been, but 'This Is Hardcore' is also an incredibly impressive piece of music. It's simply a behemoth of a track: the first time you hear it, you've got no choice but to listen to it again, because you can't quite believe what you've just heard. It's powerful, intense, and probably one of the bravest, most remarkable singles ever produced by a major pop group. "I think it's the best song we've ever written," said Steve at the time of the single's release. "If only in that song alone, we've achieved enough that makes this record important to me. That song has made it all worthwhile because we've stretched ourselves and done something that to me still sounds exciting one year later."[436]

Yet in other ways, despite its obvious originality and artistic bravery, the fact that it's an extremely successful, convincing and clever expression of what Jarvis wanted to say, there's also something lacking in the song – perhaps the fact that it's making such a negative statement in such an extensive way makes it harder to actually like. It keeps on hitting you over the head, and eventually it hurts. And as a choice of single, it may have been brave, but it was also bordering on the stupid Even some of Pulp seemed to agree. Mark: "I was never a very big fan of this song. I can appreciate that it's good work, but I never really liked it from the outset. Jarvis didn't want people to expect an album of 'Common People' and 'Disco 2000'. He wanted to redraw the boundaries – and recently it has been a case of Jarvis' will overriding everyone else's common sense."[437]

Yet, in the musical climate of early 1998, it did make sense to an extent. In the past year, Britpop had died off to be replaced in part by a number of bands making stranger, darker, more ambitious music – notably Radiohead and The Verve. Even Blur, with their eponymous 1997 album, had gone a bit weird on us. "To me," said Steve at the time, " 'This Is Hardcore' is like a challenge in song, it's a gauntlet for the rest of the year. It's like when Radiohead put out 'Paranoid Android' in 1997: here you are, deal with *this*. I think we stand for something different to most of our peers in Britain. We got pigeonholed with Britpop, which we were unlikely people to be in, because it was quite a macho movement really. Last year would have been more our kind of area, with people like Thom Yorke and Richard Ashcroft around. (But) they're not the peers that I measure our music by. The people who excite me are doing things on a much more underground level, changing the way music is perceived. It's hard to do that on a mass level, so I'm not criticising those bands, but I find The Aphex Twin more challenging than The Verve or Radiohead. That's the kind of artist I want to judge myself by."[438]

The two other new songs included on the single continue the feeling of sleazily atmospheric grimness, both musical and lyrical. 'Ladies' Man' is more straightforward, with Jarvis back in the role of the inexhaustible niteclub lothario, his vocoderised voice urging some lucky young thing to *"Stop acting like some housewife and be yourself tonight. Oh, your hair is beautiful tonight. Oh, hold me now the feeling's right. Just below the surface is a fear that just won't go, so come on hold me . . ."*

'The Professional', meanwhile, is the essential companion piece to 'This Is Hardcore', providing an entirely necessary send-up of the A-side's depiction of Jarvis the one-dimensional Britpop star who fell to Earth: *"Used to be a contender, now you're just a pretender – psychic karaoke every weekend. You don't fit those clothes anymore, why don't you take them back to the charity store? While you're there you can always hand yourself in – you're into green issues, start recycling . . . When I got up today I had that feeling again, everything was OK and then the world started seeping in . . . I'm only trying to give you what you've come to expect, just another song about single mothers and sex . . ."* Meanwhile, the wobbly, trip hop–ish backing fulfils the bleak, weird label that was inaccurately (and inexplicably) attached by many people to the *This Is Hardcore* album itself, and is all the better for it. It's as nasty, funny and enjoyable a song as Pulp have ever produced.

The video for the song, fittingly, was Pulp's most ambitious (and expensive) ever. Directed by Doug Nichol, it paid homage to Douglas Sirk, a German film director beloved of Jarvis, Steve and Nichol. A straightforward performance of the song was not on the agenda: instead, we had a huge revolving turntable stage, thirty identical blonde-wigged dancing girls, and the whole band as actors in an incredibly glamorous pastiche of a Fifties American B-movie. The plot was based around a fictitious actor called Troy Truelaine (played by Jarvis) who had vanished before completing any major films; the video is therefore his theoretical 'great lost film', pieced together from outtakes and unfinished films. The result was stunning, and probably as much a work of art as the song itself.

'This Is Hardcore' reached number 12 in the singles chart. It was Pulp's worst placing since 1994, but still pretty impressive for such an obviously non-commercial choice of single – something that was driven home by the sight of Jarvis doing his *"that goes in there"* bit on *Top Of The Pops*, complete with suggestive drooping microphone action. Hmmm. Were Pulp taking their revenge on a public that, 13 years before, had deemed the likes of 'Little Girl' too gauche for consumption? Were they just being typically wilful buggers, seeing how much they could get away with now they were on the inside?

When the album, *This Is Hardcore*, was released on March 30, 1998, it certainly posed more questions than it answered. The cover depicted a young woman, heavily made up and apparently naked, depicted from the waist up, face down on a red leather couch. The picture was electronically blurred, giving it a slightly unreal quality. Was it a real woman or a doll? Was she dead? Was she being penetrated? Raped? The longer you study the picture, the more disturbing it becomes, with the words "THIS IS HARDCORE" stamped over the top of the whole thing completing the effect.

Jarvis: "The idea with that picture was that, initially, it would be attractive: you'd look at the picture and realise it's a semi-clad woman. But then her look is vacant, it almost looks as if she could be dead, or a dummy. So it was supposed to be something that would draw you in and then kind of repel you a bit."[439]

The sleeve dovetailed nicely with both the fame/porn metaphor in the song 'This Is Hardcore', and the 'Hardcore' concept itself, which apparently, in various ways, had provided a background for much of Jarvis' writing on the record. "It's not Happy Hardcore," he explained to *NME*, "it's very Unhappy Hardcore. No, it's Hardcore in that, for years and years, you sustain yourself with fantasies and dreams of what can happen. Then if success does happen it's as if the mists clear, because people think that it validates you. And generally I think success has a really bad effect on people. Generally it means they're on the slippy slope to getting fucked. But in the eyes of the world it validates you.

"You're a success! You can walk with your head held high down the street! So you don't have to have this construct, or fantasy stuff any more. And it's weird, because then you come up against the essence of yourself . . . and often, you realise that you're . . . a bit of a tit.

"And I suppose that's what 'Hardcore' is about really. It's getting down to the marrowbone, the essence of what it's about and why you do it and why you continue to do it."[440]

And the porn thing? "I think sometimes you can be turned on by something that you know is wrong. It's like that simultaneous thing of being attracted to something and also repulsed by it. People don't like to admit to being into porn – there's a certain sadness, quite rightly so, probably! And I wondered what happened to the people in the films, especially the women because there's a veracious appetite for new flesh in that industry. People get used up very quickly and I just thought what happens to these people five years on. Is there a way back into normal society for them or do they just end up in a clinic?"[441]

So *This Is Hardcore* was a similar attempt to find out whether there was a route from pop celebrity back to normality, hopefully not via therapy, rehab ("It's too expensive and I'm too mean"[442]), born-again Christianity or any other such horrors. Jarvis was taking the lid off his head and letting us all have a peer inside. Whether that was something we really wanted to see was, yes, yet another unanswered question.

The album opens with the distinctly unpleasant goth-opera of 'The Fear', a song that could be about panic attacks, drug comedown or any other Very Bad Thing you could care to mention. It had started out life as a jokey goth number conceived *circa* 1994/95 and considered for *Different Class*, and Jarvis had re-written it early in the *Hardcore* period when it seemed that having The Fear wasn't something he could laugh about quite so easily. "That was something I'd got some chords for, and it's got a horror soundtrack kind of feel to it. I wasn't happy at the time I wrote it, and I was thinking more than I ought to about whether it was worth doing another album at all because I felt like *Different Class* had said it all. It frightened me to think that might be it. There is too much to take in and sometimes it seems as though the mind shuts off and just feeds back on itself . . . and you get in a panic and convinced you're going to die. What I was trying to work out in the song was that putting yourself under this kind of pressure makes it worse. The liberating thing for me in the song was to really go over the top and lay it on very thick with all these bad things. I find it funny, because it's so over the top – your sex life is gone, there's not just a monkey on your back but it's built a house there. It's funny because it's so extreme. So instead of 'Avert your eyes' and saying, 'This isn't happening – I'm all right, I'm gonna be fine', to actually say, 'OK, I feel shit.' On a personal level it actually helped me by looking at the stuff and confronting it and saying, 'Yeah, it's bad.' Once you've used it and made it into a song, then it wasn't scary anymore for me."[443]

"Although you get this description of somebody who's having panic attacks all the time," he added later, "the lyric goes, *'This is the sound of someone losing the plot/ Making out that they're OK when they're not/ You're gonna like it, but not a lot'*, so somehow Paul Daniels comes into the equation. At moments of great existential crisis, I've got this shit musician telling me something in me head. I guess the culture that you're brought up in surfaces at the most inappropriate time."[444]

Apparently the song wasn't purely autobiographical, as Jarvis explained to *Deluxe* magazine: " 'The Fear' is about a lot of people who have suffered from the hedonism of the past four or five years. Some of them ended up in mental health day centres. I know that 'cos two of my flatmates work in them. The record's not entirely about me."[445]

'Dishes', on the other hand, was most definitely about being Jarvis Cocker – presuming, that is, that the line *"I am not Jesus, though I have the same initals"* wasn't a Julian Cope reference. Both musically and lyrically, the song represents a comedown from the extreme emotional pitch of 'The Fear', with Jarvis showing a determination to take pleasure in the mundane everyday. As a song concerning a desire to escape from rock'n' roll overstimulation, it seems to mirror Talking Heads' 'Heaven' – with added Christ complex thrown in for good measure.

"This bloke had been talking to me at a party one night. I happened to mention that it was going to be my 33rd birthday quite soon, and he very kindly told me that I was about to have a midlife crisis because he reckoned that there's this theory that because Jesus Christ was crucified at the age of 33, men get to 33 and kind of realise that they're not gonna be Jesus – they're not gonna be the new messiah or whatever. It got me thinking that visible achievements like becoming famous . . . maybe in the public eye that's quite a big thing, but smaller, kind of more mundane domestic things in a way are more heroic because there's no glory to be got from it – you don't get a round of applause for doing the dishes. I prevented myself from having a midlife crisis by writing the song. Then I was riding my bicycle to the rehearsal room, and the first two lines of the song came into me head."[446]

Nice sentiment, shame about the song. Musically, 'Dishes' is gorgeous, a sublimely understated highpoint of the album, crowned with a truly lovely guitar solo, but the lyrics, from that first cringe-makingly tenuous rhyming couplet on in, misfire horribly. Jarvis might have been trying to do 'Feet-on-the-ground, unaffected by stardom, still living like a normal human being', but the effect is that he simply sounds like a rock star who's far, far too pleased with himself for still doing things that the rest of us common people have to do out of necessity. If he really didn't want congratulating for mundane domestic things, then why sing a song about it? Did he want congratulating for not wanting to be congratulated? The inclusion of such banal platitudes as *'I'm not worried that I will never touch the stars, 'cos stars belong up in heaven and the earth is where we are'* as if they're profound philosophical truths seem to reinforce, rather than dispel, the impression that this is someone who's losing touch with reality. Lines like *'You've got no cross to bear tonight'* are clever and likeable enough, but on the whole it sounds like an embarrassing first draft – made all the more bewildering by the fact that Jarvis considers it to be one of the best Pulp songs ever.

Far more successful is 'Party Hard', a slice of headlong, punishing electro-rock, inspired by those hairy mid-Nineties moments when Jarvis' social life had been getting, well, a little too social. "It always had the title 'Party Hard' after somebody once said it as a little phrase. I found it hard to come up with something interesting to sing – Chris Thomas is quite a patient man but he was kind of saying, 'Are you actually ever going to sing on this song or what?' so under this pressure, I've got this little Japanese guitar that's got batteries in it. I kind of got this tune that the melody goes against really – kind of flowing on top rather than part of the song. I got this idea of having two voices – two voices singing exactly the same words but there's like this interval. They used to do it a lot in The Walker Brothers."[447]

Mark: "That was a hilarious moment in the studio, when he came out with that. We were in stitches."[448]

'TV Movie' is a more straightforward, touching Pulp ballad, and one of the few moments on the album that deals with a recognisable relationship – even if it does overdo it somewhat in the self-pity stakes.

'A Little Soul' is similarly understated, a gentle, country-tinged ballad. "That was one of the last things we'd done for the record," remembers Nick. "I think we said, 'Turn up at the studio, we're going to do song X,' so we all turned up and Jarv's there with Chris Thomas, working on this song that we'd just done a little snippet of weeks ago, and he's got this virtually finished. It's like, 'Ah, what's happening here then?' 'Oh I'd done the song, thought it sounded good so I kind of came in early and cracked on with it.' 'Oh, right, OK, fine.' So we contributed some bits and bobs, but it was kind of a strange one that one."

The lyrical theme, which was, as Jarvis says, "about a father abandoning a kid, then the kid bumping into him in the pub and the dad being too hammered to talk, the dad just saying, 'Go away,'"[449] has led many to assume it was a directly autobiographical account. At the time the song was written, Jarvis famously hadn't seen his father since 1970, and Mack hadn't helped matters by selling his story to the *Mail On Sunday* in 1995. However, as with 'The Fear', the spark of inspiration for the song came from elsewhere. "One of my flatmate's dads had been ill," explained Jarvis. "It happened really suddenly and he got summoned up to Sheffield, basically 'cos he thought his dad were gonna die. And he didn't in the end so that was quite good, but it kind of got me thinking about my dad, and what it would be like to go and see him. It always gets romanticised, that particular story, doesn't it? It's a standard plot device in *EastEnders*. Long lost parents turn up and they start rowing and stuff. I thought maybe I would be more likely to just hate him."[450]

'I'm A Man' is an enjoyably cynical attack on the trappings of masculinity, a sort of grown-up 'Mis-Shapes'. Jarvis: "Success is kind of a manly thing – you have access then to all of the material trappings of a man. You can get yourself a Rolex watch if you want and you can get a really fast car and hang around with busty women or whatever. If you look at all the things in advertising that seem to represent a successful man, they're pretty childish, pretty immature. Having been a very unmanly man and always getting stick for that when you're growing up, it's kind of funny when people are giving you a bit of respect because they think you're loaded. I just think that if that's all there is to being a man, having a big car and stuff like that, then I'd rather not be one. Now, of course I am one, let's face it, but I just don't subscribe to that macho idea of what a man is supposed to be. Doesn't interest me."

Surprisingly, Jarvis has since named the song as his least favourite released Pulp track of recent times – perhaps not so much because of the song itself as the way it was executed. "'I'm A Man' could have been a great single, I thought," says Nick, "but it didn't come out very well at all on the record. It just ended up being sludgy, there was so much stuff in there. It should have been kept as a punchy sort of pop song."

There was never any danger of the eight-and-a-half-minute 'Seductive Barry' missing its marks as a punchy pop song because it was manifestly obvious that it was never intended as such in the first place. With Mark's unearthly E-Bow guitar, Jarvis' Vocoderised voice and the addition of Neneh Cherry on sighing and panting duties, it broadens Pulp's sonic palette at least as much as 'This Is Hardcore', and in its way is just as impressive a piece of work.

The song had gone through a number of title changes since its conception at the start of 1997, from 'Sex Symbols' to 'Seductive Barry' to 'Love Scenes' (under which title it was premièred at the La Monte Young concert), and finally back to 'Seductive Barry'. "Whenever we're working on songs," explains Jarvis, "they'll have working titles and we'll make 'em up on the spot and they'll have those until I get around to writing the words 'cos that's always the last thing I do. And 'Seductive Barry', we'd come up with the music ages ago and we thought it had that seductive mood and we thought it was a bit like Barry White."[451]

Lyrically, the song revisits 'This Is Hardcore''s notion of sex/porn as a metaphor for success from a slightly different angle. Jarvis again: "We've had songs that have done that kind of thing before, but this time I didn't want to undercut the mood. Sometimes in the past I have been guilty of creating a kind of seductive mood and then kind of undercutting it by maybe making an ironic or sarcastic comment towards the end or something, and this time I wanted it just to be really kind of . . . The man in this song really, really wants to get off with this woman and he's really absolutely besotted with her and just wants her very carnally. So we got Neneh Cherry to sing on it, and that was quite important, 'cos as I say we'd kind of done songs that had been in the same area before, so I thought how can we make it a bit different? Well, if the woman's actually in the song as well, that'll kind of make a difference. But then it was a case of the right kind of woman really, 'cos it couldn't be a kind of a submissive kind of woman – it had to be somebody who could hold their own. Someone with a kind of spirit about them. We were pleased when she agreed to sing on it."[452]

The underlying lyrical theme in the song is what to do when your fantasies suddenly, unexpectedly become reality. "I think that happens with blokes a lot," says Jarvis. "Like they'll look at pictures of women in magazines and go [dirty old man in pub voice], 'Phwoar, I'd give that some, y'know what I mean mate?', and all that kind of stuff. If the woman in the magazine actually walked into the room they wouldn't know what to do, they'd run a mile. It's all kind of just locker-room kind of stuff. And so it's a case, as it says in the song, it's a case of having the balls to kind of, to come up against the object of your desire, handle it, y'know . . . get it on."[453]

The one thing that could possibly be said against 'Seductive Barry' is that it goes on for just a mite too long – after five minutes of dense, unyielding atmosphere with only the slightest of concessions to melody, it becomes in danger of getting ever so slightly boring. But when the fantastic line *'I will light your cigarette with a star that's fallen from the sky'* drops us into the shimmering, luxuriant, yet somehow frightening climax to the song, any attempt at criticism becomes redundant.

'Seductive Barry' leads, in the schizoid fashion typical of *This Is Hardcore*, into the verse-chorus-verse-chorus-guitar-solo balladeering of 'Sylvia'. The lyrics, as Jarvis explained, concern the way in which "some people get off on people who they think are a bit screwed up. I think that's a bit pervy to be honest. This is about a girl who was like that – people wanted to stand near her 'cos she looked right for the room."[454] In the end, 'Sylvia' is perhaps a little too conventional for its own good – the lyrics are touching and the verse sections of the song are beautiful, but the lighter-waving chorus and the endless guitar solo move it dangerously toward the realms of clichéd rock posturing.

'Glory Days', the final resting place of the song that started out life as 'Northern Souls', seems broader lyrically than its New Labour-baiting prototype – so broad, in fact, that at first it's not entirely obvious what it's actually about. However, Jarvis' later onstage comments revealed it to be a song about the disparity between what one's twenties are perceived to be like and what they were actually like for Jarvis and many of his contemporaries, whose own 'glory days' largely took place on the dole in low-grade accommodation in Sheffield. "You spend what are supposed to be the best years of your life waiting for a little cheque to come through the door every now and again."[455]

It's also a song about the vicious circle of inactivity and under-achievement leading to yet more inactivity and underachievement, no matter how great one's potential – *'I could be a genius if I just put my mind to it, and I could do anything if only I could get round to it.'* Jarvis: "It's like if you ask someone on the dole to do something for you, it'll probably take them three weeks. If you ask someone who works, goes to night school and has two kids, they'll do it that day because they're keyed up and their brain's working at a certain speed. When you're idling, your brain's in neutral. You turn into a fuck-up."[456]

The album ends on a determinedly positive note, albeit a rather vague

one, with the anthemic lyrical contortions of 'The Day After The Revolution'. "A very strange thing happened when we were recording that,"
says Jarvis, "which ought to have, you know, converted me. We knew we
wanted it to be quite busy at the end, with a few different voices talking on
it, and I got this radio to put a bit of radio noise on it. I couldn't really hear
it when we recorded it, so I just stuck it behind the song. When we
listened back to it, on the radio it was like some religious broadcast. I
honestly hadn't heard it. It's about the creation of the world – just as the
song fades out it says something like, 'And God called the expanse sky.' It
was a weird coincidence. And because the song's about maybe a sense of
rebirth and this speech is about the creation of the universe, it seemed
a bit . . ."[457]

Significantly, one of the things on Jarvis' big list at the end of the song of
things that were 'over' was irony. "I'm saying, 'Stop fucking writing about
it, all right?' I don't think there's much time for irony in the late Nineties
as we hurtle toward the new millennium. I think there's a kind of desire
around to work things out, and there's no point in being detached from
such a big milestone as the end of the century and the start of a new one,
whatever you think of its significance."[458]

The fact that the confused notion that Pulp were an 'ironic' band had
been a frequent irritation during the *Different Class* era was, of course, a
side-issue.

Appropriately for a record that largely concerned learning to deal with the
pressures of adulthood, the album's sleeve bore the note *"It's OK to grow
up, just as long as you don't grow old. Face it, you are young."* Jarvis: "The bit
about *'It's OK to grow up just as long as you don't grow old,"* I just thought
that up. Because I thought people are a bit kind of obsessed – it's not like
they're worried about being fifty or anything, it's more like they're
worried about not being in their twenties anymore, so they can't go out to
nightclubs and stuff like that. A lot of our culture is sort of built up around
quite youth-orientated things, like music and stuff like that. And I just
thought, well. growing up implies a growth of a person, whereas growing
old implies . . . it's kind of negative. So I think it's OK to grow up and
become a bit wiser, stuff like that.

"The last bit – *'Face it, you are young'* – was when we were in Japan on a
promotional trip. We happened to go to this shop on the last day of their
sale, and sales in Japan are crackers – there's all these people there shouting
through megaphones, *'Awawawawa!'* And banging on drums, trying to get
you to come in their shop. And there was a bloke there with this placard
which said, *'Face it you are young'* on it. There was Japanese writing on this

as well, and the only English words on it were *'Face it you are young'*. I didn't really understand what the craic was or what it meant, but I liked it as a phrase."[459]

Even after all these years, *This Is Hardcore* is still a difficult album to make sense of. It mostly received excellent reviews, many of them reckoning it to be the best album of Pulp's career, but one can't help but suspect that this was at least partly due to the massive wave of critical goodwill on which they were still riding after *Different Class*. After all, many of the reviews also characterised the album as being dark, angular and weird, a reaction against mainstream success, whereas in reality, the title track and 'Seductive Barry' aside, it's probably the most conventional collection of music ever to have been released by Pulp. Glossy, well-recorded, clean and competent with plenty of guitar solos – an archetypal Chris Thomas rock production, in fact.

So despite the prevailing perception at the time, Pulp hadn't 'gone weird' exactly – yet they certainly hadn't blanded out, despite the occasionally smothering effect of the record's ultra-smooth production. So where had they gone? The one thing that the record does lack compared to its predecessors is a sense of focus – there had always been diversity on Pulp albums, but this one sounds like it could be the work of three different bands, as if it was a sampler for all the possible directions that Pulp could have gone in after *Different Class*.

To Pulp's credit, it's clear that a very definite effort had been made to avoid taking the easy way out: it was neither a cynical re-run of *Different Class*, trotted out to keep the youngsters happy and the platinum discs rolling in, nor an equally cynical *Metal Machine Music*-style reaction against everything that had made them popular in the first place. "We knew that we wanted to try and push the boat out a bit on this record and not make it *Different Class II*, 'cos I think it's disappointing when bands get some success and then almost seem to give up trying anymore. So it was that thing of trying to get a balance between moving it on and keeping it Pulp."[460]

This Is Hardcore is a confused, disappointing mess. It's also a brave, occasionally brilliant record, a formidable and sometimes awe-inspiring piece of work, and a document of a band hitting rock bottom and clawing its way back up, while making an admirable job of fully maintaining its integrity in difficult circumstances. I mean, when you've been Pulp in 1995, what *do* you do for an encore?

If everything surrounding *Different Class* had been cause for unqualified celebration at the time, *This Is Hardcore* was surrounded by so many different silver linings and clouds you couldn't quite work out what the final score was. Even the fact that it entered the album charts at number one in its first week of release was tainted by the fact that within a fortnight it had dropped to number 12, selling 10,000 copies in comparison to the first week's 50,000. Two-and-a-half years before, *Different Class* had sold 133,000 copies in its first week of release.

It would be misleading to say that the vast dip in sales was a dip in Pulp's fortunes alone: by 1998, alternative music across the board was struggling to sell. Barely a couple of years since Britpop had hit its peak and Blur, Pulp and Oasis looked set to take over the world, it was a struggle to imagine that it had ever happened. All the main protagonists of the time were perceived to have either lost their edge (Oasis) or gone difficult (everyone else), and the wave of 'alternative' bands that were being pushed in their wake (Shed Seven, Bluetones, Embrace, Catatonia, Symposium) simply didn't have that certain something that was going to capture anyone's imagination in the same way. Fewer people were buying records, fewer people were going to gigs (the 1998 Phoenix Festival was cancelled due to poor ticket sales), and the peddlers of watered-down, hermetically sealed teen pop saw their opening and got in. 1998 was the year of, as *NME* put it in a rather melodramatic cover story that June, "The Great Rock'n'Roll Dwindle".

"There was a pop moment," says Nigel Coxon, "and that passed, and all of a sudden Pulp weren't putting out pop records, so why were those pop kids gonna buy them? *This Is Hardcore* still went to number one because they obviously had a strong enough base to get it there. But I think pop is fickle, and *Different Class* was their pop moment, and with *Hardcore*, two years later, things had changed again, and things were very much swinging against Britpop, Oasis, Blur, all those bands, and you were seeing the birth of the new pop, this sort of new celebrity pop, post-Spice Girls, and then into S Club, All Saints, and all that stuff. So the climate changed very quickly, and it's a fickle climate. It's quite boring but if you analyse it demographically, market trends, buying patterns with alternative music and mainstream music, generally alternative's down at about 20 per cent or something, and mainstream pop is at 40 per cent, and occasionally you get moments where the alternative, like the Pulp-Blur-Oasis moment, gets catapulted right up at about 40 per cent, and they usually drop off again."

Of course, Pulp's teen appeal wasn't helped by the fact that Jarvis the cheeky side-parted suit-clad chappy of yesteryear was now a rather pervy, rather less sharply-dressed ne'er-do-well who released strange, dirgey songs about porn and dying. Hardly prime *Smash Hits* material to start with then, but the media emphasis on the darker aspects of *This Is Hardcore* amplified the effect: if Pulp got on the front of a music publication in

1998, it would frequently be with a rather alarmist headline like 'Sex, Death, Porn, Heroin – What's Eating Jarvis Cocker?' (*Select*) or 'King Porn – Inside The Filthy Mind Of Jarvis Cocker' (*NME*). Not the sort of thing a lot of pocket money was going to be spent on in Woolworths then.

"I invited it by talking about the genesis of that song, or some of the ideas for it," admits Jarvis. "That's the trouble – if you say, 'It was written about porn stars and watching porn on the telly,' people just assume you're there at home with a box of Kleenex next to you, with your trousers round your ankles, wanking yourself off all day. Hah! Which/*isn't*/true! Yeah, everyone does, but not/*all*/day!"[461]

Nigel Coxon: "So I think it had dropped off commercially, so no, it didn't surprise me, because they weren't putting out particularly commercial singles. They were still putting out amazing music, but they weren't particularly commercial singles, and I think the only reason that they were still getting played was a hangover from the fact that they'd been so big. I mean 'Hardcore' was a massively bold statement, but radio was going lukewarm then – I think they were only playing it six or seven times a week, which isn't heavy rotation, and you wouldn't get it played anywhere else than Radio 1."

Still, it wasn't all doom and gloom: at the end of the day, Pulp was still a successful, popular band, and one that was able to achieve a degree of commercial success despite the adverse environment and the non-commercial nature of the music they were making. If there had been a period of living dangerously, it had been the hangover/reassessment year of 1997. Now, with the difficult sixth album finished and out, and the continued existence of both the band and their audience confirmed, we could breathe again.

The months immediately following *This Is Hardcore*'s release saw very little Pulp activity: a brief concert at the album's launch party at the London Hilton was followed by a couple of TV performances in April (*Nulle Part Ailleurs* in France and *Later* in Britain), after which Jarvis was indisposed for a couple of months: Channel 4 had asked him to make a documentary about the world's outsider artists, a topic that had fascinated him since his time at St Martins, when it had formed the basis of his thesis. As a result, much of spring 1998 saw him travelling around France, America, India, Belgium, Mexico and Switzerland with a jeep and a film crew.

By June, it was time for another Pulp single, the band having this time opted for the relatively sensible choice of 'A Little Soul'. Sadly, releasing a reasonably catchy, normal-length song with verses, a chorus, a superb video (featuring the band shadowed by a set of child lookalikes) and a complete absence of references to sex, death, porn or heroin wasn't quite enough to catapult the single any higher than the fairly miserable position of 22. Perhaps 'A Little Soul', pleasant as it was, was a little too low-key and scrappy to redeem Pulp in the eyes of mainstream pop media after 'This Is Hardcore'.

"After 'Hardcore'," says Nigel Coxon, "I think we were a bit stuck because I don't think any of the singles would have done very well. I mean, it was interesting, a lot of people loved 'A Little Soul', it got nominated as a song for the Ivor Novello Award, and it was a change of tack – it was maybe, 'Well, we've obviously lost a lot of ground, maybe we can pick some back.'"

Typically for the Pulp releases of this period, the B-sides (ignoring the now-obligatory crap remixes) gave the lead track a run for its money – as well as the unlikely big beat pastiche of 'That Boy's Evil', we had the wonderfully bitter 'Like A Friend', originally recorded for the soundtrack of the film *Great Expectations*.

"That was quite interesting," says Jarvis, "because we wrote the piece of music specifically for the scene that it's in in the film. They sent us a video tape over, and then we'd be in our rehearsal room and set the video and the telly up, and we kinda wrote the song and tried to get all the bits in the song to fit in with the action in the scene. So it was quite a different way of writing a song. It was good, it was nice to be able to watch the telly while you're working. When we'd written it we got the directors to come down, and they sat in the corner of this little dingy room and we had the telly on and played it to the scene and they really liked it."[462]

"Their reaction was just dead funny," remembers Nick, "'cos they were all jumping up and down when we'd finished, saying, 'It's fucking great!' and then all talking to each other at the same time. We were just stood there going, 'Ha, it was rubbish you know' . . . and then they bugger off and make a shit film. But anyway, that's beside the point."

The single also gave us the opportunity to hear, at long last, 'Glory Days' in its original form – the rejected 1997 single 'Northern Souls' (or, as it was retitled for the single, 'Cocaine Socialism', it having been decided that it'd be too confusing to have two songs on the same CD with the word 'Soul' in the title). When he first wrote the song, Jarvis might have been in two minds about whether to come out with such a stridently anti-New Labour broadside, but by 1998, with the administration's honeymoon most definitely over, he no longer felt any such inhibition.

"I'm really glad I did [tell Imogen from New Labour to piss off]," he told *NME* in March 1998. "I've always voted Labour, but I wasn't prepared to use my position in that way. It's not appropriate, in the same way that it's not appropriate for Tony Blair to give awards at the Brits and stuff like that. To me it just stinks of 'Come on kids, I'm hip, I can play the guitar, I know the chords to 'Stairway To Heaven'. Don't bother with my policies or anything, just vote for me because I was once in a band and I've met the bassist from Mungo Jerry.' It's insulting to people's intelligence.

"It's amazing what they've done, when you think about it. First they pick on students, then they pick on single mothers, then they pick on the disabled – it's like some kind of horrible bully at school who goes around giving stick to people who are already getting stick anyway. It's just stupidity as far as I'm concerned, to have had all that goodwill and thrown it all away."[463]

After the single was released, it was finally time to get down to some live activity: the summer months had been set aside for an international festival tour, starting in America, sweeping across Europe and culminating with a special Pulp festival at Finsbury Park in London on July 25. It must have been a prospect they faced with some trepidation: for one thing, there had been no full-length Pulp concert since August 1996 and, while the *Different Class* touring period had had its fair share of glorious moments, it was (a) a hard act to follow, especially minus Russell, and (b) something that had come close to killing the band off in the end. Candida in particular had expressed a desire in the immediate post-*Different Class* period never to go on tour or play 'Disco 2000' or 'Babies' again, and it would have been understandable for the rest of the band to have similar feelings about a repeat of the non-stop touring of 1995–96.

The festival tour was the solution: instead of spending months slogging around a series of increasingly similar-looking medium-size venues across Europe, a few weeks of large outdoor shows seemed like a far more attractive prospect. "It's easier, more interesting and more cost effective to play to more people in one go," says Nick, "and you don't have to bother with soundchecks; you just get up there and blow, you know, and in the summer it's usually nice weather out in the open air. It's just nicer in a way."

One slight problem was that, without Russell, Pulp was a member short. There was no way he could be replaced on the violin, but the band still needed an extra guitarist to fill things out onstage. The solution was Richard Hawley, guitarist with Pulp's mid-Eighties Sheffield cohorts

Treebound Story, and more recently The Longpigs, who had supported Pulp on various *Different Class*-period tours.

The set was a sensible mix of old and new, albeit avoiding playing too many of the poppier moments from Pulp's recent past: there was most of *This Is Hardcore*, plus a handful of selections from *Different Class* ('Something Changed', 'Sorted', 'Live Bed Show', 'F.E.E.L.I.N.G.C.A.L.L.E.D. L.O.V.E.') and *His'n'Hers* ('First Time', 'Joyriders'). The encores threw up the occasional twist, such as unexpected oldies like 'She's Dead' and 'I Want You', or the then-unreleased glam-slam of 'We Are The Boyz'. And then, of course, there was the party piece that was 'Glory Days', slowing down three-quarters of the way through and unexpectedly turning into 'Common People'. Well, they couldn't leave it out, could they?

Pulp warmed up for the tour with a couple of small dates in Boston and Toronto before appearing at the huge Tibetan Freedom Festival at the RFK Stadium in Washington with, amongst others, The Beastie Boys and R.E.M. As it happened, the Tibet festival ended up being postponed for a couple of days because of adverse weather conditions, which resulted in Pulp playing an impromptu set at the tiny 9.30 Club, using gear borrowed from Radiohead (who were headlining), with Michael Stipe opening the show. You don't get that every day.

A few dates in, June 20's Rockpalast Festival in Germany was notable as an instance of triumphing over adversity without even realising it. The band had arrived at the festival site to find that their equipment had been inexplicably flown to Moscow, and as a result ended up playing with gear borrowed from Sonic Youth. Onstage, Jarvis was in a filthy temper for the duration, apparently unable to hear what he was doing because of poor monitors, and ended the concert by smashing his mike stand and pushing the monitors over before leaving the stage. Yet a bootleg recording of the concert still shows that, despite having the odds stacked against them, all concerned still managed to give a brilliant performance. There may have been some rough edges musically (the odd missed cue and some rather wayward singing from Jarvis), but every song fizzes with an angry energy and a tension that makes the show remarkable.

A week later came the moment of truth: Pulp's first proper concert in Britain since 1996. The occasion? The Glastonbury Festival, on the third anniversary (give or take a day or two) of that triumphant 1995 appearance. No pressure then.

It was perhaps for the best that there were plenty of things that differentiated '98 from '95, making direct comparisons more difficult. For one thing, they were playing on Sunday night rather than Saturday, closing the festival rather than playing the most prominent slot. For another, where the '95 festival had been glorious sunshine all the way, in '98 it pissed it down: the site was somewhere between ankle- and knee-deep in mud, the result being the most widespread outbreak of trenchfoot ever reported at a major rock festival. And for *another* thing, Jarvis, rather than Glastonbury '95's definitive black knitted suit and pale pink tie that had epitomised his (old, popular) image, was clad in a light grey, decidedly unstained, designer raincoat.

Of course, despite the differences, enforced and otherwise, there was no avoiding the concert's resonance. If anything, the historical significance of Pulp at Glasto '95 had increased in the intervening three years – which is saying something considering that (unusually for a pop concert) it had felt pretty damn legendary when it happened. "You know those comets that travel round the solar system and arrive every sixty, seventy years?" Jarvis asked '98's audience. "That's us. Because when we were here in 1995, that was like we set off, and we've been in an orbit round a strange universe, in a kind of elliptical shape, and now we're back again. Yeah? And now maybe we can understand what it means. You've grounded us – thank you very much."[464]

Glastonbury '98 wasn't as good as Glastonbury '95. Well, of course it wasn't. What happened in '95 involved Pulp hitting some kind of impossible, transcendent, God-rivalling high. It would have been an insanely tall order for *any* band to top that, never mind for Pulp to do it again. What Pulp did do in 1998 was rise to the occasion and put on an excellent show that cheered the exhausted, soaked, mudcaked crowd no end – especially when Jarvis told them of how he'd heard that "quite a lot of people have got arrested for drugs and stuff like that. Which . . . er . . . it's a festival! Listen, all right – put me in a field with lots of mud and lots of rain for three days, and I'm going to need some drugs, all right? Just a point."[465]

And just in case he hadn't made his position entirely clear, he later added that, ". . . I'm not saying that being a drugs master is 'fucking boss', but festivals, as far as I can see, are about allowing people freedom to choose what they want to do. That's the whole point of it, innit? Now, you can choose to be an arsehole – maybe you can learn from that. You've gathered here in this place, and you've been pissed on, you've been stomping through mud, and you're still enjoying yourselves. It's good. It's a fucking achievement, man."[466]

And so, in its way, was Pulp's Glastonbury '98. If it hadn't been for the enormity of 1995, it would have been an unqualified triumph. As it was, it was just a triumph. Which is no bad thing by anyone's standards.

The festivals kept coming through July, covering Portugal, Belgium, France, Spain, Ireland, Scotland, Greece, Austria and Sweden, ending in the fairly triumphant (thanks in small part to the band having nothing to follow at that particular venue, in small part to the weather being nice and sunny, and in slightly larger part to the band being pretty good) 'Pulp In The Park' mini-festival at Finsbury Park in London.

A month off followed in August before the 'Party Hard' single was released in September. Yes, six months on from the album's release, Pulp had finally got round to putting out a single that was loud, punchy, uptempo and an undisputed highlight of the live set. The Hammer & Tongs video, yet again, was brilliant, featuring lots of skimpily dressed dancing girls in Pulp T-shirts in an immaculately tacky pastiche of a European TV pop show, and the song was further promoted with a barn-storming live performance on *TFI Friday*, plus a massively entertaining *Top Of The Pops* appearance that hilariously recreated the video and possibly constituted the best Pulp TV performance ever.

'Party Hard' stiffed at number 29. Even significant club exposure thanks to Island's limited edition 12″ featuring remixes by Christopher Just and Tom Middleton didn't help (although neither, in all probability, did CD2 of the single, which featured remixes from The All Seeing I and Strach'n'Vern that pushed the disc over the 20-minute time limit that would have made it chart eligible). Even more so than 'A Little Soul', there was a sense that releasing the album's most obvious single at the end of the campaign rather than at the start was too little, too late.

Nigel Coxon: "I love 'Party Hard', it was as obvious a single on the record as anything, and it's a brilliant live track as well, but I think the worm turns, and to be honest it would have been hard whatever we put out after 'Hardcore'. The album was slipping away, and even though we'd had a number 1 album and all these incredible reviews, it was a perceived failure everywhere in the industry. It was just falling off and things had moved on, and I think whatever we'd have put out as a single would've struggled."

The one worthwhile moment in the 2-CD set, amongst the pointless remixes of the title track and the equally pointless remix of 'The Fear' (It's got *another* guitar solo! Thank God!) was the tremendous gonzoid stomping racket that was 'We Are The Boyz', originally recorded for Todd Haynes' film *Velvet Goldmine*. Amongst Pulp's 1997/98 output, this was the song that underlined the awful truth that, compared to the finely tooled dark orchestral epics that the band had toiled over for months on end in the studio, daft, noisy 3-minute throwaways like this were just so much more *fun*. It was a guilty pleasure, sure, but a life-affirming one even

341

so – I mean, how could *"We are the lads/ We sleep with slags/ We nick their fags/ We've got no choice/ 'Cos we are the boys"* set to a brash, stupid guitar-synth rasp not be better than all that wretched *"You are hardcore, you make me hard"* business?

Continuing the theme of unprecedented enjoyability, Pulp spent the first two weeks of September in Monnow Valley Studios in Rockfield, Wales, writing new songs without even the slightest threat of a new album on the horizon. At the time, Jarvis told Radio 1 that the band "went to Wales the other day to get it together in the country, which we've never tried before. The acoustic guitar was straight on and then one of the songs was about trees – well, it mentioned trees."[467]

Nick: "We had this idea that it would be nice, rather than do some writing in London, why don't we go to the countryside and do some writing instead? In London when we're rehearsing, half the time people are on the phone sorting summat out, or it's like, 'Oh, I can't make it this afternoon, I've got to go to so and so,' and it's very difficult to pin everyone down for any length of time to get some writing done. So we just thought we'd go away to the countryside, get away from distractions, so we decided to go to Wales."

The rest of September and October brought a return to Japan for a string of live dates; the first ever Pulp concerts in Australia and New Zealand; a return to the Barbican, where Jarvis, Mark and Steve played alongside Terry Riley for a performance of his minimalist classic 'In C' as part of the 'Inventing America' season that Mark was curating there; and, at the very end of October, a return to the studio.

Pulp had been asked to contribute a song to the soundtrack of the film *Notting Hill*, and accordingly trouped into Axis Studio in Sheffield for a weekend to record 'Born To Cry', one of the songs they'd come up with during September's Monnow Valley sessions. Hearing the song when it emerged the following year must have been a great reassurance to those who thought *This Is Hardcore* sounded like a band on its last legs: the stately, Roy Orbison-inspired 'Born To Cry' may not have been a solid-gold classic, but it certainly showed a spark or two of life. While being slow, downbeat and anything but cheerful, it certainly managed to avoid the oppressive, foreboding air that seemed to pervade around most of *This Is Hardcore*, and the very fact that the band were willing and able to come up with new material so soon after finishing the last album was a pretty promising sign.

Before any real plans could be made for the post-*Hardcore* phase of Pulp, though, there was one last piece of unfinished business: the trifling matter of a British tour in November and December. Well, they had to get round to it eventually. "It'll be interesting," Jarvis told Radio 1 shortly before the band set out, "because it's the first time we've done a tour for a little bit over two years in this country. I have to admit that I'm slightly nervous; for some reason because it's your own country you've got more capacity to embarrass yourself. It was quite funny because Russell left our band, obviously we had to get somebody to help us out playing some of his stuff, so it forced us to go back through all the songs we'd written and listen to some that were 15 years old, and some of them were really horrendous but some of them were really good so we probably will end up playing things that we've not played for almost 10 years."[468]

The venues of the tour seemed rather oddly chosen: despite the obvious reduction in the size of Pulp's audience since the *Different Class* era, they were playing many of the same huge venues they'd visited on the 1996 arena tour. With no smash hit singles or Jackson incident to buoy up the band's profile, the likes of Hull Arena and Birmingham NEC, rather than being packed to capacity, were typically half- to two-thirds full – but then again, where better to hear *This Is Hardcore* live than somewhere big, dark and empty?

Still, fewer ticket sales in 1998 than in 1996 didn't mean the tour wasn't a success – after all, half-filling Birmingham NEC still meant selling almost 3,000 tickets. And the shows themselves were excellent, hugely enjoyable experiences for both the audience and for Pulp, all of whom appeared to be more relaxed, confident and happy onstage than they'd been in recent memory. No one was losing very much sleep over the fact that they weren't selling quite as many records or concert tickets as they had been two or three years before. "We were still playing to loads of people," says Nick, "and still playing to loads of people who were loving it, so we just thought, 'Well, we've got our group of fans' – OK, we don't get on the radio so much so therefore we're not going to get through to the sort of casual music person, but we didn't really worry about it too much."

Despite Jarvis' promises of oldies, the content of the shows was much the same sensible mix of *This Is Hardcore* with a handful of *Different Class/ His'n'Hers* material as it had been throughout 1998. By now they'd relented and re-introduced 'Babies' and 'Disco 2000', and the audience in Doncaster were treated to 'Anorexic Beauty' (dedicated to Russell, who was in the audience). The stage was decorated with an enormous back projection that made it resemble the inside of a padded cell for most of the time, with extra films used for the background of 'This Is Hardcore' and 'I'm A Man'. 'The Fear', which opened the shows, was enlivened by the spectacle of two Jarvises on stage, both apparently singing the song (the spare was none other than Gareth Dickinson, who had 'done' Jarvis on *Stars In Their Eyes* a couple of years before), and the end of 'Party Hard' was the cue for hundreds of balloons to be dropped on the audience from the ceiling, *à la* the video. Finally, the last date of the tour, in Bournemouth, had the most unlikely surprise encore of them all: a version of 'Crazy Little Thing Called Love' by Queen, sung by Gareth Dickinson – Freddie Mercury having been his first choice when applying to go on *Stars In Their Eyes*.

On the tour, the *This Is Hardcore* material seemed to have benefited from having been given the chance to breathe a little – songs such as 'Seductive Barry', which seemed slightly stifled and airless on the album, through a few months of being performed live had come to life. "Previously," says Nick, "even a lot of the *Different Class* songs had been played quite a bit before they'd been recorded, and we were just at this stage where nothing was played really until it was recorded. And then things do change when you play to the audience – people's reaction just helps you to appreciate it a bit more."

As Russell would have said, what doesn't kill you makes you stronger. By the end of 1998, Pulp had proved the one last thing that had been left for them to prove: that, after surviving years of failure, they could survive success as well. They had battled through the previous two years' amputations, crises of confidence, personal traumas, artistic struggles – and, in their way, emerged triumphant.

Like the exhausted, filthy, wet, but still mad-for-it audience that had stuck out the mud bath of Glastonbury 1998 in order to see the final night's headliners, Pulp had shown that they were hardcore. What exactly could they do for an encore to the encore? Whatever they wanted.

Chapter 16

The beginning of 1999 saw Jarvis unexpectedly back in the Top 10, and back on *Top Of The Pops* – without Pulp. The previous autumn, he'd written some lyrics for The All Seeing I, a sort of Sheffield electronic supergroup formed by Parrot (of Parrot & Winston/Sweet Exorcist fame), Jason Buckle and Dean Honer (also an ex-boyfriend of Saskia's, interestingly enough). The trio had already had some success in 1998 with 'The Beat Goes On', an excellent bleepy thing based around a sample of Cher's Sixties hit of the same name, and the plan for their début album was that they would use Jarvis' lyrics with a variety of Sheffield music luminaries providing guest vocals.

For Jarvis, demoing the songs with The ASI was a refreshingly down-to-earth experience after the excesses of *This Is Hardcore*. "We'd just spent an absolutely obscene amount of money on this record," he remembers, "and they asked me to come up with some lyrics to these songs. So I wrote some, and I went up to this attic in Sheffield. The first half-hour was taken up with somebody trying to dislodge a cassette from this 4-track that'd got stuck in it.

"So suddenly, from being in these ponced-up studios costing £1,000 a day or whatever, I'm in this attic, there's a bloke trying to prise a cassette out of the thing, and then they just handed me a microphone, they're sat about five foot away, and he said, 'Go on, sing it.' And it scared the shit out of me, but it was good because I wasn't going to show myself up by not doing it, so I'll just have to do it, sing it there. And I could hear my voice really loud because they couldn't turn the hi-fi up because it'd feed back. But I did it – I realised you didn't have to go through this big system to make a record."[469]

The first fruit of the project, in January 1999, was the single 'Walk Like A Panther', sung by Seventies pop crooner Tony Christie, remembered (just about) for the likes of 'Avenues & Alleyways', 'I Did What I Did For Maria' and 'Don't Go Down To Reno'. "Parrot had got in touch with Tony Christie," says Jarvis, "tracked him down to his home in northern Spain. He just liked his voice and he thought that because I came from the same town, I'd be able to think of something to write. I've got a couple of Tony Christie albums, and the song 'Walk Like A Panther' [a 1971 Mitch Murray/Peter Callander composition performed by Christie that shares its title with Jarvis' song] isn't that good, but I just liked the idea of someone prowling around, walking like a panther. So I thought I'd rip that and try and come up with something.

"The thing is, I wrote the words and I thought there was no way on earth he was going to sing them. I made meself laugh with them. Apparently he did think I was taking the piss at first, and because the music's a bit scratchy as well . . ."[470]

Christie concurs: "When I first heard the track I thought it was . . . Pfff! garbage, quite frankly! Me and the guy I work with listened to it and said to each other, 'This surely isn't the track they're going to use? They're taking the piss, right? I don't believe this . . ."[471]

It's not hard to imagine how the wrong end of the stick might have been grasped: the bleepy, ramshackle electro backing track may as well have come from a different universe to Christie's MOR pop hits. What's more, Jarvis' lyrics, which he and Parrot insist are entirely affectionate and more about Sheffield and show business in general rather than Christie in particular, could well be interpreted as someone having a pop: after all, here was a middle-aged cabaret crooner whose stock had plummeted somewhat since his Seventies heyday, being asked to sing lines like *"Marie has set up home with a man who's half my age/ A halfwit in a leotard stands on my stage/ The standards have fallen, my value has dropped/ But don't shed a tear . . ."*

Fortunately, Christie relented and a unique three-way Sheffield marriage was born. "He played it to his son," says Jarvis, "and his son said, 'It's not bad Dad, give it a go.' He did it, and he said whenever he went on telly, he could never remember the words – he went on *Richard & Judy* and sang *'Walk like a salmon'*. How do you walk like a salmon? I don't know."[472]

The single was released in January, entered the charts at number 10, and was thus deemed worthy of two appearances on *Top Of The Pops*. The first of these featured Christie, but by the time of the second, on January 29, he was unavailable due to touring commitments in Germany (where he's apparently still quite big). As a result, the vocal spot was free to be taken over by Jarvis, who obligingly appeared on the show, providing live vocals and extremely silly walk-like-a-panther dancing. He even looked as if he might have combed his hair for the occasion.

Top Of The Pops aside, The All Seeing I project was a timely opportunity for Jarvis to be creative out of the media glare. "I enjoyed doing it," he said soon after, "because for me, it was nice to do something where I didn't have to, you know, have much to do with it. We talked for about an hour or something, and then that was it. And then it was out of my hands and I didn't have to even talk about it, or say what it was supposed to mean or anything."[473]

The rest of the lyrics Jarvis had written appeared on The ASI's album *Pickled Eggs And Sherbet*, released later in 1999. There were two more songs for Christie to sing: the excellent Sheffield light entertainment vignette 'Stars On Sunday' ('*The chicken has flown the basket . . .*') and the absent-father saga of 'Happy Birthday Nicola'. Not included on the album was another song written for Christie that the singer had rejected as being "too Sheffield", and apparently had been a little too close-to-the-bone for comfort. "I got into a bit of trouble," says Jarvis, "because there was one song that I wrote that he wouldn't sing. In the mid-Seventies, he came back to Sheffield with all his money, and he decided to open a nightclub called Christie's, next to Sheffield Wednesday football ground. And it failed, and he went bankrupt. I mentioned it in this song 'cos I was just trying to make songs that had something to do with him. But apparently he's still very upset about that, so he couldn't even bear to sing about that. I'd never really thought of that."[474]

In addition to the Christie showcases, the album also included 'First Man In Space', written by Jarvis for The Human League's Phil Oakey, which seemed fleshed out with some lyrical ideas from a certain Pulp song from a few years before – lines like '*Space is cold, but home is colder when you go home at night and there's nobody there*' definitely had a familiar ring. Finally, there was 'Drive Safely Darling', sung by Jarvis himself and based loosely on a Geoff Stephens/Barry Mason composition of the same title that Christie had recorded in 1975. Jarvis' version is a jumpy, semi-humorous thing with plenty of lines like '*The road of life is a cul-de-sac unless you come back*'. In line with the rest of the lyrics he wrote for the album, it's much, much lighter in tone than *This Is Hardcore* – and a reassuring sign that, after devoting almost an entire record to such matters, he could still write songs – great songs, in fact – about things other than the insular horrors of celebrity and how awful it is to be Jarvis Cocker.

Jarvis' extra-curricular activities continued in February when his TV series, *Journeys Into The Outside*, which had been filmed in spring 1998 and edited in the autumn, was finally aired on Channel 4. There was a period, back in the light entertainment Britpop days, when, having marvelled at his aceness on *Pop Quiz*, *Top Of The Pops* and the rest, it briefly became a national sport to make wild predictions about what programme Jarvis would end up presenting once all this pop star business has died down. Would we get *The Jarvis Cocker Show*, a prime-time chat show where he gets to interview the likes of Marti Pellow and Derek Jameson purely in order to slag them off? Would he take over from Cilla on *Blind Date*? Would Richard & Judy be replaced by Jarvis & Russell?

One Jarv TV vehicle that no one quite managed to foresee was a three-part art travelogue, directed by his film school chum Martyn Wallace, wherein Jarvis drives around the world in a jeep in order to find out about some of the interesting, challenging, frequently bizarre but often beautiful spectacles created by people not normally regarded as artists. That was, of course, exactly what he'd done.

On reflection, it's perhaps not such an odd idea as one would think based on the thumbnail media caricature of Jarvis the short-lived pop deity. After all, as well as a lifelong leaning toward things that are created and exist off the beaten track, outside the mainstream, he'd already shown an interest in outsider art in 1995's *F.E.E.L.I.N.G.C.A.L.L.E.D.L.I.V.E.* tour video, when he and Steve had visited Ferdinand Cheval's *Palais Ideal* whilst Pulp were touring France. The germ of the idea for the TV programme had come whilst Jarvis was at St Martin's.

"I was in Art College," he explained in the introduction to the series, "and that meant I got to hear lots of other people's ideas of what art was all about. It soon struck me that these people didn't have a clue about what really interested everyone on a daily basis. It was as if art and everyday life had become mutually exclusive. Towards the end of my course I had to write a thesis, and by then, this divorce between art and reality had got to be a bit of an obsession with me. So, desperate to find a spark of inspiration, something that would help me put these feelings into words, I began to scour the college library.

"There was no shortage of material on offer, but none of it seemed to fit the bill. I needed to find something outside all this, something that hadn't been analysed to death. And when I'd all but given up hope of such a thing existing, I found it. In a book called *Outsider Art*.

"The book was about art made by people from all walks of life, who didn't think of themselves as artists, but were creating things because they felt they had to, rather than because they'd been taught to. Although the book featured paintings and sculptures, it was photographs of unusual buildings and monuments that really caught my imagination. How could there be a gap between art and everyday life if every day you lived inside the work of art you created? This was exactly what I was looking for. I found much more than a subject for my essay – I found something I could really get excited about. And I vowed that if I ever got the chance, I'd go and find out more about these incredible places and the people who made them. Now, almost a decade later, that time has come.

"My thesis was awarded the second-lowest mark in the year." [475]

Jarvis made an ideal presenter for the programme – far from being a vehicle for his ego, the focus is very definitely on the artists, with a dressed-down, parka-sporting, shaggy-haired, furry-hatted Jarvis taking a back seat, avoiding talking to the camera, instead providing soothing, informative, voice-overs and mostly appearing on-screen in order to speak to the artists. "I didn't really want to present the programme at all," he explained to *Heat* magazine. "You can probably tell, because I don't say much on camera, I just stand there like an idiot. But part of the reason Channel 4 wanted it was because I was going to front it. It was a trade-off, really. I got asked if I wanted to do a talk show once, but I can't imagine anything worse.

"The last thing I wanted it to look like was some kind of crappy Nick Rhodes' photographs type of thing. (The Duran Duran keyboard player's book of Polaroids of untuned TV screens was once called 'the most pretentious book ever.') I hate it when some star decides to say, 'You know me for this but actually I'm really deep. I'm an artist.' That worried me. I didn't want my personality getting in the way of places we visited. I hope they're what comes across to the viewer, and you don't think, 'What's that tit doing walking around in a concrete castle?' " [476]

The production style was typical of previous films in which Cocker and Wallace had been involved: point-of-view shots, jokey sound effects, fast editing, film speed manipulation and scenes separated by clever/cryptic captions should in theory add up to a gimmicky nightmare, but, as with the *Do You Remember The First Time?* film and the documentary inserts on *F.E.E.L.I.N.G.C.A.L.L.E.D.L.I.V.E.*, the whole effect feels disarmingly natural and engaging.

However, what really made the series a success was the subject matter. The three episodes in turn dealt with outsider artists in France, the USA and the rest of the world (i.e. Mexico, Belgium, Switzerland and India), and between them covered the likes of Bodum Litniansky, a Ukrainian who had decorated his house and the surrounding land with dozens of concrete poles, covered with found objects and cast-offs; Ed Liedskal, a Latvian immigrant who had built his home (including furniture) in America out of 2,000 tonnes of coral, using modified car parts as tools; Simon Rodia, whose giant, spindling structures he'd built in the middle of Los Angeles, dubbed the Watts Towers, had been condemned by the City as unsafe until they found they were unable to pull them down because of their amazing strength, and had since been declared a National

Monument; and the enormous, Escher-like treehouses built in the midst of the Mexican jungle by eccentric English millionaire Edward James.

Jarvis concluded the series with an overview that could, in a way, also be taken to apply to his own lifelong urge to be creative with Pulp. "I started out on this journey thinking that maybe the modern world didn't give people enough room to manoeuvre anymore, but I'd forgotten that there's always one space that people will have to themselves, and that's inside their own head, and the imagination that can turn the remains of everyday household objects into places as magical as these sets them apart. The starting point is something that's familiar to everyone but the result is still something that's out of this world. And that was the best thing that I found out on these journeys: that outsider art wasn't something that was about outsiders at all: it was about something that was inside everyone, if only they'd look for it. There was nothing difficult about it; anyone could do something like this if they really wanted to. Go on; I dare you."[477]

Meanwhile, Pulp were slowly working out what their place in the world was after doing the textbook Britpop rise and fall with *Different Class* and *This Is Hardcore*. It seemed unlikely that they'd ever see such huge commercial success again: by 1999, by and large, 'alternative' music had vanished from the mainstream altogether, with easily digestible celebrity pop ruling the roost again. "I think," remarked Jarvis at the time, "we're seeing the revenge for the Britpop hangover. So many bands, ourselves included, experienced this rush of euphoria when we got a foot in the door. And then you start having these shitty petty newspaper morals being applied to you, that you've never had to deal with before. It makes you think, 'Fuck off, I don't want to do this anymore.' Then everybody makes these bad-tempered, fuck-off-and-leave-me-alone records that make the general public think, 'Bloody hell, this is a bit of a downer. I'm going to buy Steps. Let's get back on safe ground.' "[478]

One thing was for certain: now the pressure to keep their career on the boil that had led to the struggle that was *This Is Hardcore* had abated, Pulp weren't going to be rushing into making another record until they were well and truly ready. Jarvis again: "The last record was quite hard to make; it wasn't that much fun to do. And I wouldn't want to go through an experience like that again. It's better to take things more easily, and see what happens. You have to ask yourself, 'Is my career that important?' And it's not that important really; but enjoying yourself is important."[479]

By spring 1999, Pulp were enjoying themselves making music in the basement of Jarvis' new house in Hoxton, East London. "Instead of going back to The Fortress," says Nick, "we thought – room completely covered in grey carpet, no windows – bad idea. Jarvis had moved into his house in Hoxton by this time, and he said, 'Well, I've got a basement with a load of music stuff, so why don't we just rehearse in my basement? It'd be a much more relaxed way of doing it,' so we did. It was only a very tiny space so we could only use very stripped-down equipment. Couldn't be very loud 'cos obviously it would piss all the neighbours off and things like that. So we tried to do it quietly – acoustic guitars, and I just had a strange stand-up Yamaha standard drumkit."

For all concerned, the experience was a lot more enjoyable than the cabin fever-inducing process of writing *This Is Hardcore*. Candida: "I hated a lot of the writing and recording of [*This Is Hardcore*], in a dingy basement – pure mental torture! This time we've had a few writing sessions in Jarvis' basement and it was far more humane, almost like the old days rehearsing in Jarvis' garage. After having spent years writing in studios, there is something more natural and easy when the place you write in isn't a huge bare room but a room that has a use, character and meaning – much less pressure."[480]

By June, the band had the fundamentals of around six new songs – at which point they were asked to play a private concert at Venice's Palazzio Pisani Maretta, at a party for the British artist Gary Hume during the Venice Bienalle art festival. The surroundings lent themselves perfectly to Pulp's new, quiet direction. "It's in, not really a palace, but an old building," explained Jarvis at the time, "with all kinds of chandeliers and things, so they said we're not allowed to play loud because it might make the chandeliers fall down – it's got this big painted ceiling, and the vibrations might cause damage. So we decided to write some quiet new things. We're playing six new songs and five old ones, but it's a party so I don't know if people will actually listen. They'll probably be more interested in drinking."[481]

Nick: "The songs weren't written for it, but it was a good excuse to showcase some new songs without the glare of lights on it."

Because the show was at a private party, the band were unable to invite any guests or allow any of Pulp's live action-starved Italian fans to see the concert, but the lucky revellers were treated to the sight of Pulp (plus Dido from Tiger playing Jarvis' omnichord) performing their new material plus a handful of stripped-down *Different Class/Hardcore* songs on a small piece of astroturf, obscured for the first half of the set behind – oh yes – Venetian blinds. "It was a lame sort of joke," says Nick, "but I think it was a confidence thing. You're never sure with new songs whether people are going to start throwing rotten tomatoes 'cos they hate all these quiet songs. You're not too confident about what people's reaction is going to be, so what's the best thing to do? Hide behind something. So Jarvis came up with Venetian blinds."

The following month, Jarvis unveiled more new material at Nick Cave's Meltdown Festival in London. The occasion was a celebration of Harry Smith's famous *Anthology Of American Folk Music*, alongside artists such as Cave, Van Dyke Parks, Bryan Ferry and Beth Orton. Jarvis' contribution, backed by the house band plus Mark on guitar, was a pair of songs loosely based on two selections from the album. "I felt a bit uncomfortable with covering some of the blues tracks from that collection," he explained to *NME* shortly afterwards, "doing that whole, 'Well I woke up one morning' thing. So I just adapted the basic song and tried to personalise it a bit more."[482]

The first song Jarvis played was 'Cockroach Conversation', based on The Masked Marvel's 'Mississippi Boweavil Blues'. It concerned a (possibly fictitious) encounter with a cockroach that nearly fell into his spaghetti whilst trying to make dinner one day in his Camberwell squatting years. The cockroach questions humanity's right to exist, and Jarvis asks the cockroach why it should be so interested in humanity. The song ended with Jarvis shouting 'Fuck Off! Fuck Off! Fuck Off!' and stamping the cockroach to death.

The other song, 'Cuckoo', was a reworking of Clarence Ashley's 'The Coo Coo Bird', and had already been performed by Pulp at the Venice show. The song is an absolutely beautiful ballad documenting the end of a relationship, with lyrics like *"I thought you'd like to know, I still think you are the most, but you've left me living here, forever married to a ghost – oh, it gets so cold at night-time, never knew it got so cold at night-time. But sometimes dreams come true – one night when the moon is blue, then I may come to you with a love that's nearly new."* It's perhaps amongst the best songs Jarvis has ever written, and the fact that it remains unreleased borders on the criminal.

At this point, the average Pulp fan in Britain could have been forgiven for feeling a little hard done by: after *Different Class*, we'd waited over two years for *This Is Hardcore*, and then another nine months for British live dates, which even when they came were expensive, often geographically inconvenient and disappointingly took place in a series of cavernous, atmosphere-free arenas. And now, when they'd finally got round to writing some new songs, were we deemed fit to hear them? Apparently not: seemingly the group preferred to go to Venice and play them at a party for one of their nobby artist mates, followed by Jarvis doing a 10-minute spot at some obscure arty do in London.

However, any such feelings were shortlived: at the end of August 1999, the balance was well and truly redressed with *The Quiet Revolution*, the band's first ever fanclub concert at the 900-capacity Queen's Hall in Edinburgh. Essentially it was a repeat of the Venice concert: a semi-acoustic 50-minute set, half new songs, half old. "Once we'd written [the new songs performed at Venice]," explains Jarvis, "we realised that we wanted to develop them further and play them out in front of real people."[483]

In a way, even though the quiet acoustic sound was quite different to anything from Pulp's recent past, the show felt like a return to the Pulp we knew. There were none of the additional musicians, backing singers, video projections or any of the other accoutrements that had surrounded the Pulp live experience in recent years; just the five members of the band, playing together onstage like only they can. Jarvis was playing acoustic guitar almost throughout, Candida only had one keyboard (albeit an Esoniq rather than the Farfisa), Nick was standing behind a remarkably small drumkit, and Mark had only, er, six guitars.

One unwelcome aspect of the Venice concert that was duplicated here was the reappearance of the Venetian blinds for the first half of the set. It might have been a cool effect in Venice, and it did add to the sense of the concert being an out-of-the-ordinary event, but for a roomful of people who had come to see Pulp, it was pretty irritating to find that, unless you were near enough the front to peep through, it was impossible to do so. It also seemed rather inappropriate considering that Pulp had always been about making concerts into personal, intimate events, interacting with the audience – removing the barrier rather than erecting one.

"Good for Venice," says Nick, "and we'd spent all this bloody money on these bloody Venetian blinds – loads of the things. Why waste them? Get 'em out again. So it was quite funny, the audience's reaction, 'cos when it came to the second half we were playing songs that they knew, it was like we were going, 'Oh, you're here aren't you? Didn't notice you there before! Here's some songs you know, then.' It was just doing something different, trying it out."

Fortunately, the music made anything forgivable. The concert began with a dreamy, twinkling, yet somehow foreboding instrumental called 'Roald Dahl' before dropping into the impeccable balladeering of 'The Birds In Your Garden' which somehow has an enormously hopeful, uplifting quality, despite being about rather downbeat subject matter. "It was a love affair that I had at a period when I wasn't really that together," explained Jarvis. "I thought that I'd fucked the relationship up because I was fucked up. It was the start of me feeling I had to get a bit more natural. Instead of thinking about everything, just actually feeling things and doing them. Maybe think about them after, rather than working it all out before you even do owt."[484]

"In terms of style," said Jarvis after the song finally made it on to vinyl in 2001, "it's probably quite similar to the stuff we wrote when we very first started out. It's kind of fitting that it's one of the first ones we wrote [for the album] because the idea of it is that somebody's staying at his lover's house but for some reason or other he can't get it together to . . . shag her . . . and goes out into the garden in the morning and all the birds say to him, 'C'mon, get in there!' And it's about how, for some reason he's unable to respond to a natural urge, the urge to 'get in there', the urge to procreate or whatever, he's so out of touch with himself that it's there on a plate but he's too hung up on some idea in his head that he can't do it. I just liked the idea of birds, which are supposed to be nice sweet creatures, kind of acting in a slightly yobbish way, and saying '[cockney voice] Get in there, my son!' I thought it was quite a nice idea."[485]

Next was a song that later became known as 'Duck Diving' but at the time had the working title 'Perry Reggae', despite not sounding at all like any kind of reggae, Perry or otherwise. Instead, what we got was a one-chord jam along similar lines to 'Sheffield Sex City' and 'David's Last Summer', while Jarvis read out a story ('Return To Air' by Philippa Pearce) from a 1971 English Project Stage One textbook. In common with the other new songs played on the night, despite not having been written by Jarvis, the lyrics seemed to mesh perfectly with the music, with Candida's gentle but insistent keyboard part vividly reflecting the watery, sun-dappled feel of the story – the effect being only slightly spoilt by the frustratingly muddy sound quality on the night.

'Donovan', later known as 'The Quiet Revolution', was a sparse, syncopated, slightly jazzy number that presumably earned its working title because of a mild similarity to the Sixties folkie's song 'Sunshine Superman'. It was the most intense, upbeat song unveiled that night, slightly reminiscent of 'His'n'Hers' (the song, not the album), with some superb, if cryptic, Cocker-sleazy lyrics: *'My Macbeth was an error of judgement, no one wants to see my Lear . . . In domestic dramas all across the nation, gifted amateurs tread the boards all night, seeking inner motivation: is this a microwave I see before me as the clock strikes 3 am? If the whole world's a stage, I guess you may as well star in a play . . .'*

A heartbreakingly gorgeous rendition of 'Cuckoo' came next, with an entirely incomprehensible working title of 'Burgers & Coolers'. Jarvis dedicated the song to "all the ornithologists in the audience", and managed the highly impressive feat of playing the omnichord at the same time as singing. Finally, when introducing 'Rave Sense' (the original title of 'Sunrise'), he addressed the audience at length for the first time that evening: "You know sometimes you might stay up longer than you mean to? There's always that horrible feeling when you suddenly see the sky turning a paler blue and you start thinking, 'Shit, I've really fucked it, I should've gone to bed ages ago.' Which is a shame, because, you know, the sun coming up can be quite nice. Quite pretty sometimes. Anyway, I don't know why I talked about that. Just thought I'd talk about that for a bit. Anyway, this is a song."[486]

'Sunrise' was probably the least complete of the songs unveiled that night, with the lyrics seemingly still in a fragmentary, half-finished state, but the intent was still there, and Mark's Velvet Underground-influenced chiming guitar was as effective as ever, with the take-off of the solo providing the perfect moment for the blinds to be raised – to the inevitable massive cheers from the audience.

The second half of the show, where Pulp played some more familiar material, was almost as interesting as the first: after fairly straightforward, if very pleasant, renditions of 'Sorted For E's And Wizz' and 'TV Movie', Jarvis announced that "we've played some new things, this next song, some of you might know it, it probably hasn't been played for about 15 years – and when it was played then, it was all ponced up with a lot of piano on it. This is what it probably should've sounded like. Better late than never. It's a song off the first record we ever did, and it's called 'Blue Girls'."[487]

To the audience's surprise and delight, they were then treated to a hugely unexpected, truly lovely version of a song that hadn't been heard since 1983. The band had apparently rehearsed, but not performed, it during the 1998 British tour, coming up with an entirely new arrangement of the song which fitted in incredibly well with the new material. Quite what possessed them to try it is anyone's guess – it was the first time Pulp had bothered with any of the songs from *It* since the pre-Russell era, and they haven't bothered since – but it was a wonderful surprise.

Equally surprising was the moment when, after 'Blue Girls', Jarvis began repeatedly strumming two chords on his guitar. What was it? Another reworked oldie that we couldn't quite place? No – it was, in fact, a radically stripped-down version of 'The Fear', minus those goth-opera backing vocals and E-bow guitar. Jarvis sang the song in a lower register, dispensing with the falsetto, and the result was perhaps even more dark and frightening than the overstated original.

With barely a pause for breath, Jarvis then announced, "From one scary song to another," and Nick launched into the drum intro to 'This Is Hardcore', which was reworked even more radically – no Peter Thomas sample, Jarvis strumming his acoustic, Candida playing the descending riff, and Mark playing the piano part on the guitar. It wasn't quite as successful a rearrangement as 'The Fear', but fascinating even so. Finally, a relatively straight version of 'Dishes' concluded the most extraordinary Pulp concert of recent times.

Jarvis had announced that the Edinburgh show was to be the last Pulp concert of the millennium – only to change his mind a few days later in order for Pulp to play the same set again at the small, obscure Liss Ard Festival (which was nonetheless somehow big enough to attract the likes of John Cale, Nick Cave and Smog) on the south-west tip of Ireland. "We had these offers coming in," says Nick, "and kind of liked that, and thought it'd be fun to do. Possibly. Will it be a pain in the arse to do? Most definitely."

Since leaving Pulp back in 1997, Russell Senior had also been keeping himself occupied. Shortly after his departure from the group, he'd produced an album, *Classee X*, for London-based Francophile band Baby Birkin, whose singer Raechel Leigh subsequently filed a report for *Pulp People* telling of Russell's unique studio technique.

"Russell introduced the idea of regular cocktails to keep a lively atmosphere, and these were sampled regularly and properly – Russell ensured that correct cocktail etiquette was observed, even putting in a request to the studio boss for proper champagne glasses! But champagne was supped from plastic cups on the eve of Russell's birthday, together with birthday cake, but, rather than eating it, Russell suggested I eat a mouthful of cake between each line, where pauses permitted, of '69 Annee Erotique'. He said he hadn't thought it might result in squelchy noises, but was pleased with the result anyway . . .

"Russell spent a lot of time creating the right atmosphere for each song – setting the scene was vital: as well as the cake scenario, this resulted in sand, sunglasses, sun tan lotion and a beach dress for 'St Tropez' . . . for 'Harley Davidson' I sat on engineer Pierre's mountain bike, with a fan blowing the 'wind' through my hair . . . sand was used again for 'Nefertiti', as well as Egyptian style make-up and a brown shortie nightie. This song was recorded at the end of a gruelling 14-hour day and I had become a little tearful when things were not going well, but Russell insisted we continue, which accounts for the snotty sounds going off in this song!"[488]

"I'm just enjoying being creative again," said Russell at the time, "and trying to do what I can to make sure it's a cool underground release that people talk about rather than something that just comes out and gets ignored."

By spring 1998, he'd started work on another project: a band called Venini, which began when he started writing songs with vocalist/lyricist

Debbie Lime, who he knew from "not so much going to parties as looking for parties."[489]

"I sort of knew him from ages back," adds Lime. "I met him in this really cool club in Paris, and we started talking. I was in the shittiest band in the world and he knew this, and he said he wanted to do something and I did too."[490]

Russell: "I can't not do music. It just goes through my head all the time and annoys me. I met Debbie and I had wanted to be really cool and underground, but she started going all pop. I hadn't intended to be in a band with ambition. It started out as a nice dinner party with a few guests, but it's ended up spilling over into the woods and turning into this bacchanalian frenzy while I'm standing back in horror looking at it!"[491]

Within a couple of months, the two had written a set of spiky glam-pop songs that combined Russell's spidery garage guitar and Debbie's unique lyrical style, and were ready to put a band together. "Through bizarre coincidences," says Russell, "people just ended up in the band. It was all fortuitous. I didn't know whether they were any good or not so we've just learned as we've gone along. But as they're all a lot younger than me, they've just taken the idea and given it a life of its own."[492]

By autumn 1998, they'd recruited bassist Nick Eastwood, drummer Robert Barton and Danny Hunt on keyboards (star of the 'Babies' video and ex-member of Chevette, who had covered the lost Pulp classic 'We Can Dance Again'), with ex-ClockDVA member Charlie Collins guesting on treated woodwind. Admirably, everyone in the band was there as a result of being friends and acquaintances of other people in the band, rather than the contrived group of seasoned session musicians that normally results when an ex-member of a major band decides to make a comeback. "After I left Pulp," says Russell, "the music industry was the last thing I wanted to be involved with, mainly 'cos it's filled with knobheads. I was out of the business for a year and I could have put together some Britpop supergroup, I was being asked to, but I didn't wanna be in a band with someone imposing restrictions. I just wanted the music to be whatever it came to be. I mean, we do sound more poppy than I'd probably like but that's what we sound like. Our sound is organic, so I'm pleased."[493]

The group played a handful of low-key gigs in late 1998 as unbilled support to Rialto, and by spring 1999 were ready to release their first single. Rather than looking to get signed, Russell financed the release himself, setting up Venini's own label, Bikini Records. This course of action reflected the fact, that, in 1999, indie music was at a low ebb, with a lack of new talent revealing itself, and a mainstream dominated at one end by the manufactured pop likes of S Club 7 and Steps, and at the other end by the massively nondescript meat-and-potatoes likes of Stereophonics and Travis. "I would hate to be a talented unknown group at the moment," says Russell, "because if you don't have 10 grand to do it yourself it's really going to be really hard to break down the door. [But] I like this bonfire that's occurred of these . . . vanities. All the pompous indie Britpop has died a death, and the music industry – in its panic – has got to go and find something new. They've been rather cowardly for a few years, and had their comeuppance. When the Stereophonics are important, that's the definition of a fallow period."[494]

With the release of the début single, the excellent stomping glam-pop of 'Mon Camion', in June, the band seemed to be setting themselves up as the direct opposite of the dull guitar-based music that was ruling the alternative roost at the time. The band's image alone (onstage, as well as Russell being Russell, you had Nick scissor-kicking his way across the stage like a cross between a 1977 punk and a 1991 Manic, and Debbie clad entirely in leather, caked in panstick make-up and striking an endless series of ridiculous poses, pitching herself somewhere between Suzi Quattro and Grace Jones) placed them a million miles away from the typically beige, dressed-down, khaki-and-combats look that permeated most bands *circa* 1999. A band that on one hand made interesting, worthwhile music but on the other was an unabashed pop group was a rare and, for some people at least, welcome thing.

"I hate the idea of having to choose whether you are indie and obscure but have credibility, or you are cheesy and pop with none," said Russell at the time. "The real fun, the real art, is to be both at once. When you do that it's very easy to trip up and look stupid and you give a lot of ammunition to those who wish to rip you down in flames. If you're standing up there very stridently as Debbie does, people can rip you to shreds. But I like that, I like the boldness. That speaks directly through to members of the public. And that means more to me than getting in the *NME*."[495]

'Mon Camion' did reasonably well, entering the indie Top 30, as did the follow-up, 'Carnival Star' when it was released in November. However, the difficulty that presented itself was how, after a good start, to take things beyond that level without the clout of a major behind you. For all concerned, the effort and the obstacles involved in running one's own label were beginning to grind. "It's like being a small corner shop and you're competing with Sainsbury's," said Russell. "You have to pay more because you're small, and it tends to make everything more expensive. You can press up five or seven hundred copies and do the 'sell them to your mates' thing or you can also do the 'we signed to a major record label' thing. What is hard to do is try and sell a few thousand records on your own label and try to get across from just your mates and people in like-minded bands in bed-sits. When you do that you come to a glass ceiling. Steve Lamacq will play people who do their own 7″ single in a brown paper bag, but if you try to do it semi-properly it's not so easy."[496]

The fact that they were having an increasingly hard time from the press didn't help. It was probably logical that because they were the direct opposite of most of the bands that the *NME* and *Melody Maker* were pushing at the time some writers on those papers took a dislike to them. Even so, the incredibly vicious slagging that both papers dealt out to a Venini gig at the Camden Falcon in August was still astonishing. "They misfire on almost every count," wrote Stevie Chick in *NME*. "Vampish singer Debbie Lime sneers, 'Dress me up in Gucci' (stop sniggering), before lurching stiffly into some clumsily choreographed 'dirty dancing'. Like their stultified, grisly indie-rock, like their tragically inept lyrics, it's no doubt meant to be sophisticated, sexy. In reality, it's shabby, seedy and not a little sad."[497]

Even worse was the verdict of *Melody Maker*'s Ben Clancey:

> *"Channel 4 couldn't have come up with a better idea. Take Russell Senior, Pulp's old guitarist, get a former dominatrix to sing, add some blokey musicians and you have the winning formula for a television series. Channel 5 could've come up with better music though, because Venini are terrible.*
>
> *Their attempt at glam involves calling one song 'Roxy' in tribute to Roxy Music, and their single, 'Mon Camion', being a total rip-off of Mud's Seventies glam classic 'Tiger Feet'. Oh, it might be the Sweet's 'Ballroom Blitz', but it doesn't matter: it is someone else's song. A friend leaves the gig mid-set when he realises that they aren't sampling the bassline from Blondie's 'Heart Of Glass', they're passing it off as their own.*
>
> *There's no originality here, just piss-stale art-school rock that's lumpy and hideously ugly. Supporters might claim they're 'experimental', but that's a synonym for trying really hard to be different and just being shit. There are refugees from the Pulp fan club present, but the two who are dancing stop bopping about after the first song, having failed to convince themselves that Venini are any good.*
>
> *This band has no charisma, no presence and no fucking songs. Look, I go to 150–200 gigs a year. Most are either quite good or quite bad. It takes a hell of a lot to be brilliant and something really outstanding to be as shit as Venini are tonight. If there is a worse gig this year, I don't want to see it."*[498]

Naturally, as with any band, the matter of whether or not Venini got a decent write-up was in large part down to the lottery of which writer went to see them. However, even for the British music press, the inaccuracy ('Mon Camion' and 'Carnival Star' bear practically no similarity whatsoever to 'Tiger Feet' and 'Heart Of Glass', while a recording of the concert reveals that, far from audience members walking out or giving up on the band after the first song, there was 10 minutes of applause at the end in the hope of an encore) and hypocrisy (accusations of "stultified, grisly indie-rock", unoriginality and lack of charisma coming from publications that were putting Oasis, Travis and Stereophonics on their covers?) of these reviews was unusual. Getting a bad review for a bad gig was one thing, but this was something else. What had Venini done that had offended so much?

It's possible that there was a degree of suspicion toward the way in which Venini were emerging. As Russell had highlighted, the alternative music media are used to being presented with bands who have pressed up a couple of hundred 7″ singles on a ridiculously low budget, or being presented with bands that have signed to a major label (albeit often one masquerading as an indie) and are carefully packaged and media-groomed. Venini were neither, as they were attempting to take a DIY approach with a higher budget than normal thanks to Russell being slightly better off than the average Camden-dwelling indie guitarist. Was the fact that one member of the group had already experienced enormous success as a member of a previous band rather than being a nervous teenager coming up from nowhere, coupled with the fact that Venini's music and image simply didn't fit in with anything else that was going on at the time, enough for the press to treat them as enemies? Who knows.

Venini continued through the rest of 1999, playing gigs in Leeds, London and Sheffield with new keyboardist Ash (Danny Hunt having left in August to form Ladytron). Unfashionability aside, the fanbase was gradually growing, and moving from the cluster of curious Pulp fans that had formed the bulk of the audience when the group had started to an increasing band of people who appreciated the group in their own right – boosted by the scene that was forming around Nick's stylish Sheffield club night, Le Citrus. Venini were also getting better, as their début album (recorded in October but sadly never released) shows: Debbie's lyrics were becoming ever more gleefully waspish, and the band were becoming ever tighter, louder and cleverer, with a new version of 'Mon Camion' displaying a Bowie-Ronson swagger only hinted at on the single, and superb unreleased tunes like 'Roxy' providing tantalising hints of what the likes of 'Disco 2000' might have sounded like if Russell had had his way: brittle, brutish, diamond-edged brilliance.

At the end of 1999, after their biggest gig to date, supporting Sparks at Shepherd's Bush Empire, the group made the regrettable decision to take a six-month sabbatical. The reasoning was that, as the money was no longer available for any further self-financed releases and no labels were interested in signing them, it would make sense for them to temporarily go into hibernation and return when the musical environment was a little more conducive to a band like Venini.

As it turned out, by the middle of 2000, when Venini were supposed to reconvene, Russell had decided that, on reflection, he didn't want to be in a pop group after all and would prefer to open a gallery and deal in antiques. The group attempted to continue without him, recruiting new guitarist Nick Burke, but, with Debbie now living in London and Nick occupied with the tribulations of running a nightclub in Sheffield, a mooted comeback tour never happened. Venini finally split in January 2001, their promise unfulfilled.

Meanwhile, back in autumn 1999, Pulp were gradually edging towards their next album. In August, they'd been asked to write a song for the BBC's remake of the Sixties TV series *Randall & Hopkirk Deceased*, featuring Vic Reeves and Bob Mortimer in their first straight acting roles. The result, which was completed in October, was the gorgeous 'My Body May Die', a swirling, Sixties-tinged, slightly jazzy number, featuring vocals from the Swingle Singers choral group. Despite the lack of any new records, this song, alongside the material premièred at the concerts during the summer, is enough to lead one to suspect that the Pulp of 1999 were on something of a roll.

By the end of October, they'd recorded demos of nine new songs over a weekend at Wessex Studios in London. "Wessex was good," remembers Nick, "'cos that was the last session in that studio before it changed. It was a really old studio, *Never Mind The Bollocks* was done in there, *London Calling*, loads of amazing records. We did loads and loads and loads of songs in those sessions. Some of them, especially things like 'Birds In Your Garden', sounded better than the finished versions."

Most of the songs that had been played live in the summer were demoed, alongside a pair, 'Bob Lind' and 'Wickerman', that would eventually make it on to the album, the B-side 'Yesterday', and two more songs, 'Darren' and the instrumental 'Got To Have Love', that were never released.

It was presumed that these demos would form the basis of the next Pulp album; even so, there were still no concrete plans for a release. "We're just going to record some songs and see what they sound like," Jarvis told *Melody Maker* at the time. "If we think they are fit for human consumption, then we'll release them. Otherwise I'll just listen to them in my bedroom. I quite like them. They are quite gentle. *This Is Hardcore* was like the end of one particular road. It was the type of thing where there was nowhere to go. Like we said on the last album – 'What do you do for an encore?' The only thing would be to go a bit more basic, and I think it *is* a bit more basic."[499]

Pulp's 1999 ended in the low-key fashion typical of the manner in which their year had progressed. A more career-minded group might have been keen to exploit the fact that they had a rather famous song that went *'Let's all meet up in the year 2000'*, but Pulp? Nah. Instead, they'd removed the synchronisation licence for 'Disco 2000' for the whole of 1999, making it impossible for anyone to use it for adverts, TV shows and the like – although they did partially relent later in the year by 'un-deleting' (as opposed to re-releasing) the single itself, allowing people to buy it at Christmas time should they wish to do so.

The only Pulp related live appearance in the closing months of 1999 was a semi-secret gig at the 333 Club in London where Jarvis, Steve and glass harmonica player Alisdair Molloy played a 25-minute, five-song instrumental set, including 'Roald Dahl', an instrumental based on 'Cockroach Conversation', and a version of one of the pieces that Jarvis, Steve and Mark had recently worked on for the soundtrack of cult director Donald Cammel's posthumous film *Wild Side*. "The music was heading towards the new age ambient thing," Molloy explained to *NME* after the performance, "but with interesting beats going on. There was one track where Jarvis played Fifties-style guitar. The glass harmonica was used by people like Mozart and Beethoven. I think this is the first time it's been used in this way. We've taken its sound into another space altogether."[500]

Jarvis' final appearance of 1999 (apart from popping up as a pundit on Channel 4's *Music Of The Millennium* programme, notable for the first appearance of his new, black-plastic-specs-and-garish-woolly-jumpers look) was on a charity compilation CD, *Millennium Thoughts*, alongside the likes of Des'ree, Dickie Bird and the Rt Hon William Hague MP. Such company in itself rendered the whole enterprise fairly rubbish, and the extent to which Jarvis took it seriously is probably reflected in the nature of his contribution (which was apparently elicited when the compilers sent him a letter and a tape, and Jarvis happened to be in the mood to return it): approximately 40 seconds of reasonably pleasant omnichord doodling, over which Jarvis croons the lyric, *"Thinking about the new millennium just makes me wanna come."*

January 2000 saw Pulp back in Wessex Studios, demoing six more new songs. This time, the session consisted entirely of songs that never made it on to any official Pulp release – including, most notably, a song called 'After You', which for a time was a serious contender for the album. Geoff Travis named it as one of his all-time favourite Pulp songs around this point, while Nick describes it as "an absolute lost classic. It was just a case of falling between stools 'cos it was so early – some songs from that time went on to be on the record because they were strong enough to survive the filter process, but some just were written a bit too early and didn't quite have the legs to carry on. It's like that 'Cuckoo' song, you know – it depresses us sometimes when Jarv just thinks something's just not top."

Another song demoed at the session, 'Grandfather's Nursery', mysteriously surfaced as an MP3 on the internet store amazon.com during 2002. "That was written when we did some early writing sessions at Monnow Valley [the 1998 writing sessions that also produced 'Born To Cry'], trying to get some ideas together for *We Love Life*," says Nick. "Basically it's a chord structure that Richard Hawley brought about. We made a song out of it, added lyrics and it was recorded at Wessex." The song is a pleasant, laid-back piece in a similar vein to many of the 1999 songs, perhaps with a slightly more conventional rock feel *à la* the *This Is Hardcore* album, with some rather florid lyrics: Jarvis begins with the words *"This used to be a playground, now it's your grandfather's nursery – oh lady of glass houses, where is the flower that will cover the stench of the city?"* It's a fine song, but the structure and concept are perhaps a little too close to 'Sunrise' (it builds from a gentle, poignant intro to a soaring guitar finale with Jarvis repeatedly singing *"Here comes the rain"*) for there to be room for both songs on one record.

The other songs recorded at Wessex in January, 'M'Lady', 'Performance Of A Lifetime', 'St Just' and a second version of 'Got To Have Love', this time with lyrics, remain unheard and unknown to this day – although it's possible that one of them is the unnamed song Jarvis mentioned to *Select* magazine a little while later as containing the rather suspect lyric *"The taste of thine cunny is like a fine wine"*.

In February, Jarvis told *NME* that the album was three-quarters finished – presumably referring to the overall process of writing, rehearsing and recording a record, rather than simply the recording bit, which hadn't actually started yet. "We've recorded all the songs [as demos] to make sure they sound all right," he explained, "and I've already gone to the trouble of writing words, usually I leave it to the day before we go in the studio. We want to go in and record it as soon as possible and hopefully get a single out before the summer."[501]

By this point, with an album's worth of songs written, Pulp were beginning to form a fairly definite idea of the kind of album they wanted to make. Jarvis had mentioned as long ago as June 1998 that, after the experience of *This Is Hardcore*, he had no intention of going through a similar process to make the next Pulp album: "I wouldn't want to spend that amount of time on a record ever again in my life. I think it was kind of inevitable because of the circumstances, but I just wouldn't bother again. The next one, I'd like to do in about three weeks and I hope it would cost about £5,000 to record."[502]

In the light of Pulp's new, no-nonsense recording policy, it's perhaps surprising that the person they chose to produce the new album was Chris Thomas, who had presided over the laborious, year-long and, ultimately, not wholly satisfactory *This Is Hardcore* sessions. "The decision came from the band and Rough Trade," says Nigel Coxon. "It's like all these decisions; it's not like they can just go, 'We're doing it,' 'cos it's not their money to say yes, but it was OK'd. I mean, I remember sitting down with them and saying, 'I'm not convinced that there's still life in this relationship,' and they basically convinced me that they'd had long conversations with Chris Thomas and they were going to approach the record very differently, and try and do it much more quickly, and get a fresher vibe, and not overlayered and overproduced, and Chris had convinced them that he could do that."

After a final bout of writing, the band were ready to start recording the album in March 2000. The first stage was to record a set of pre-production demos, with Thomas and engineer Pete Lewis, at the Depot rehearsal studios in London. The band laid down instrumental versions of 11 of the more recent compositions, amongst them prototypes of 'Bad Cover Version' (then called 'Candy's Spectre'), 'Minnie Timperley' ('Jungle Rumble') and 'Forever In My Dreams', alongside the lesser-known likes of 'Love You Baby', 'Medieval Owl', 'Last Song In The World' and 'Dream Galaxy'.

The sessions proper began on April 3, 2000 at Cosford Mill Studios in Surrey – a rural, residential concern owned by Queen drummer Roger Taylor. At first, things ran smoothly enough, but before long difficulties began to arise between band and producer. Nick: "We'd said, 'Right, we don't want to do it like the previous album. We just want to get all the stuff, go somewhere that's out of the way, no distractions, find a big barn where we're all set up like it was live almost, and just play the songs and get some good takes, rather than playing it once or twice and then bunging it all into a computer and messing around with it for hours and hours.' And we tried to convey this over to Chris Thomas and he was, 'Yeah, we can do that, no problem.'

"But after a couple of days, he was, 'Right, let's bung all that into the computer and get it all sorted out!' And it's like, 'All right . . .' We persevered for two or three weeks or whatever, and, you know, it was great, it was lovely out in the countryside, going fishing and all this kind of stuff – but all the time it's just people sorting out this computer stuff, and it's not really what we want: we want to do all of it together, play it together, rather than pulling it apart. It was just going back to the previous way of doing it, so Jarvis says, 'We have to stop this.' So we had to stop it."

"From the start," says Jarvis, "we wanted to record in a certain way and we thought we had made it very clear to Chris what that was. The songs were to sound more natural than they have in the past. Like it was just us in a room playing, not getting all anal about a cymbal that comes in 20 microseconds too late.[503] Things were quite 'constructed' with Chris Thomas and we knew we wanted to do it in a more – not like 'unplugged' or something, but to actually have it sounding a bit more like just us playing. And although that sounds really simple – we're a band, that's what we're supposed to do – to actually capture that in a reasonable way isn't as easy as it first appears."[504]

"I went down to the studio," remembers Nigel Coxon, "and it just wasn't happening, you know. There was no spark, there was no vibe at all in the studio. There was no energy to the session, which was the opposite of what they wanted to try and do. But that didn't surprise me because it's hard to keep that with the same producer, and perhaps they were starting to get their own ideas, and I think that Chris is just one of those guys that just is used to working in his own time, in his own way. Suddenly he was just creatively, as much as anything, put under a constraint to be able to do something in not necessarily big flash studios, and it didn't really work."

Listening to 'Yesterday', the one song from the Thomas-produced Cosford Mill sessions to have emerged (on the B-side of the 'Bad Cover Version' single), one can see his point: the track is pleasant enough, competently recorded, and certainly captures the gentle, acoustic feel that the band were aiming for at the time, but it still seems to lack a certain something – it's almost as if it's too nice, as if the *frisson* of Pulp playing live (no matter how quietly) has somehow been lost in the translation to tape.

"It sounds like a cliché," says Nick, "but we tried to just get all together as you would be in rehearsals, that good feeling as opposed to everything metronomically timed to the last microsecond and everything played technologically accurate. We want to add a bit of a spice, jazz it up! It's just a case of trying to capture that sort of spark of when you first write a song and the first time you all manage to play the right bits in the right order at the same time and you think, 'Ooh.' That's quite an exciting time."[505]

By May 2000, with six unmixed tracks recorded, the sessions had ground to a halt. And it had all been going so well! The songs were written, the direction was sorted, the band were happy . . . only for it all to fall apart when it came to the few weeks it was supposed to take for the album to actually get recorded. An attempted session with Howie B (who had worked on 'My Body May Die') to remix the Thomas recording of 'Bad Cover Version' was no better – according to Jarvis, "it never sounded right – it sounded like a pastiche of something."[506]

One thing was clear: Jarvis' plan of getting a Pulp single released before summer 2000 was out of the window. Indeed, while the fate of the album was undecided, the thought occurred that Pulp's was too: unlike the gap between *Different Class* and *This Is Hardcore*, this time there was no great public or corporate clamouring for a follow-up. Indeed, to Island, who had recently been taken over by the enormous Universal Music conglomerate, and were mindful of the amount of money *This Is Hardcore* had cost (which it only just recouped), it may even have been preferable not to bother with another Pulp album. As Jarvis points out, "We could have easily said, 'Let's not make another record.' "[507]

Chapter 17

What do you do when you're a well-known rock star, the recording sessions for your new album have broken down, you can't find a suitable producer, and you're not even sure whether you want to continue with it anyway? Go back to your experimental side project, of course. July 2000's Meltdown Festival in London was being curated by Jarvis' long-time hero Scott Walker – and it transpired that the admiration was mutual, Walker having proclaimed Jarvis in an interview to be "a great songwriter". Jarvis was asked to perform a set at the festival, and decided to reprise his and Steve's collaboration with the glass harmonica player Alasdair Molloy. For the occasion, he christened the ad-hoc group, which also included Mark playing guitar and a percussionist introduced only as "Scott", A Touch Of Glass.

The first 25 minutes of the 35-minute concert were along similar lines to Jarvis, Steve and Molloy's first performance at the 333 Club in London in November 1999: five instrumental pieces, including the familiar 'Roald Dahl' (now re-christened 'Venice'); the slightly Pink Floyd-ish 'My Chopper', from the *Wild Side* soundtrack; 'Otley', a serene instrumental reworking of 'Cockroach Conversation' which took its name from the film whose soundtrack provided the central sample; 'Forever In My Dreams', a version of a song Pulp had been working on during the Chris Thomas sessions; and finally 'Fire Island', which was perhaps the best of the bunch – a dense, frantic number dominated by manic percussion and Jarvis' horror-film organ, somehow reminiscent of some of Pulp's more intense mid-Eighties material.

Next, Jarvis welcomed the Swingle Singers to the stage for an excellent rendition of 'My Body May Die', marred only slightly by the fact that the sound engineer was apparently having difficulty balancing the volume of the vocals with the music. Finally, Jarvis closed the set by announcing that "the curator of this festival may want to leave the room at this point" as an introduction to a fine version of Walker's song 'On Your Own Again', with the Swingles singing the orchestra parts – quite creditably considering that they'd rehearsed the song for the first time in the dressing room immediately before coming onstage.

The Meltdown show was definitely interesting and enjoyable, with the instrumental section showing a vastly different side of Pulp's musical personality than the increasingly conventional pop/rock currency that they'd dealt in through the Nineties. The odd musical fluff from Jarvis, who was shifting between acoustic guitar and omnichord through the set, only added to the charm. "I apologise for everyone who witnessed it," he said afterwards, "as it was a bit of a shambles, and I played some terrible bum notes when I tried to play the guitar. But I would quite like to do it again – it was a one-off daft thing that we did, but I thought it was quite atmospheric."[508]

In the course of playing Meltdown, Jarvis and Steve had only met Scott Walker very briefly, but it was on the night of the show that Geoff Travis, mindful of the fate of the Pulp album and, indeed, their career, had a brainwave. "That night," says Jarvis, "our manager asked him whether he'd ever considered producing anybody other than himself. And he said he was quite interested in that. And we didn't have a producer at the time . . ."[509]

Nick: "Geoff Travis had a conversation with Scott's manager, saying Pulp were having trouble finding a producer and we're not really sure what the hell's going to happen, and he apparently said, 'Oh, Scott's really keen on doing a pop album.' And, you know, light bulbs went off all over the place, Scott was keen, so what about it? All of us, especially me and Jarv, are really big Scott Walker fans, and when they said it to us, it was like, 'You're joking?' 'No, no, no.' It was an opportunity not to be missed."

From the most unexpected source, it suddenly seemed that there was light glinting at the end of the tunnel. However, before the idea of a collaboration between Pulp and Scott Walker (Scott Walker!) could be seriously considered, the band had other matters to address: for the months of July and August, all recording activities were put on hold so that they could prepare for a string of four concerts at the end of August, culminating in headlining slots at Reading and Leeds Festivals.

The concerts had obviously been planned as a glorious high-profile return to live performance. If things had gone to plan, the band would have just finished their new album and already re-established themselves in the public's hearts with a comeback single. As it was, they hadn't released a record in two years, didn't have one that they'd be able to release in the imminent future, hadn't made any substantial live appearances since the end of 1998, and were a band whose confidence had been severely shaken by the failure of the Chris Thomas sessions.

"Reading was a dodgy point," remembers Candida. "We had started an album with Chris Thomas, but it hadn't worked out and, despite trying several different producers, nothing was happening. There came a point when we were thinking, 'Christ, why bother?' I certainly thought about leaving, but I realised that I'd still feel shit even if I did. If Scott Walker hadn't come about, I don't think we'd have bothered to finish this LP."[510]

In his one press interview prior to the concerts, with *NME*, Jarvis was upbeat about the concerts, but confessed to an understandable nervousness – something that hadn't been helped by confusion over the billing at Leeds and Reading, where Pulp were officially sharing the headline slot with Beck. "They said it was a co-headline thing and we thought maybe we'd go on last one night and Beck'd go on last the next night, but we seem to be going on last both nights now. That'll keep us on our toes, though, 'cos he can put on a good show. We'll have to make sure we don't disappoint after that, but it's good to have a bit of pressure. It's good to have a bit of a challenge. I don't like things to be too easy."[511]

Lucky, that. "It's like gambling, you know. If you just bet ten pence on something, if you win it doesn't really mean anything. But if you put your everything on it, there's a big chance you're gonna get fucked up, but if it comes off, it's really worth it. I like it when it's like that. It's hardcore, you know what I mean? Put the whole lot on black!"[512]

Prior to Reading and Leeds, Pulp played a pair of warm-up concerts, both at relatively small venues: a fan club-only gig at The Garage in London (capacity 500), followed by a higher-profile show at Edinburgh Corn Exchange (capacity 2,500). With a sprinkling of new songs mixed in amongst more familiar material, both concerts were rapturously received – but then, such is the partisan nature of the audience when big bands play small gigs. And while the (by this time) rare indulgence of basking in a little hysterical fan adulation must have been a tonic for the band, the real challenge still lay ahead: Reading.

When Pulp took the stage at Reading, it was at the end of a day that had seen appearances not just from Beck, but from the likes of Gomez, Super Furry Animals, Elastica, Idlewild and Badly Drawn Boy – all bands who had released noteworthy records in the past year and therefore were guaranteed a decent response from the audience. What about Pulp? Would anyone even remember who they were?

Well, of course they bleeding would. They hadn't been away *that* long. However, when the set opened with a version of 'Common People' (rather than closing with it, as per practically every other Pulp concert since 1995), it was clear that this wasn't quite the same Pulp that everyone remembered: the song had been given a bleeping, motorik, Krautrock-esque makeover that (for the first couple of minutes at least, before reassuringly bursting into that enormous chorus) rendered it almost un-recognisable. The audience was divided – for some, it was a brave, trium-phant statement, reminding us what a ceaselessly adventurous and vital group Pulp have always been, admirably refusing to turn into some sort of Britpop jukebox; for others, it represented the particularly grisly slaughter-ing of a sacred cow.

Maybe it was a bit of both, but in breaking with the past in such a way, Pulp had made a shrewd move; rather than standing there waiting for them to get all the other rubbish over with and play the Hit, we were now watching the Pulp of the present and the future. New songs 'Weeds' and 'Minnie Timperley', strategically placed early on in the set, were both infinitely more assertive, poppy, muscular and generally festival-appropriate than any of the material premièred in 1999, and were relievingly lapped up by the throng, as were majestic re-treads of the likes of 'Something Changed', 'Help The Aged' and 'Sorted', most of which were accompanied by some beautiful, semi-abstract film pro-jections (courtesy of Jarvis and his video camera) on a giant screen above the stage. The band left the stage after 'This Is Hardcore' to return with 'Sunrise', which had grown from the promising prototype of the 1999 shows to a huge, soaring, irresistible giant of a song. Amazingly, despite the fact that it was totally new to 95 per cent of the crowd who didn't have a bootleg of the Edinburgh concert, Reading exploded, prompting scenes of mass euphoria that were perhaps even greater than they'd have been if the set had concluded with 'Common People'. Finally, a crowd-pleasing salvo of 'Party Hard', 'Babies' and 'First Time', and that was it.

It was obvious that Pulp had triumphed – obvious, that is, to every-one other than the band themselves. Mark remembers the concert as being "absolutely horrible. That gig was just horrifying and one of the worst we had to cope with! We were quite nervous, but the sound on stage, because of the wind and everything, was unbearable and we couldn't hear ourselves properly. We thought it had all gone wrong, but then we got off stage and everyone just seemed to say how great it was! It baffled us, but maybe, because we tried so hard to perform well through all the conditions, what came through is that we gave a spirited performance, but I can never judge if that was the case! To us, it was a nightmare."[513]

After Pulp repeated the trick at the Leeds Festival the following day, it was pretty clear – to the audiences, the critics, and themselves – that they

Pulp in 1995, left to right: Russell Senior, Candida Doyle, Mark Webber, Steve Mackey, Nick Banks and Jarvis. (*Retna*)

Jarvis is hoisted into the air during Pulp's appearance at the 1996 Brit Awards in London. (*LFI*)

Michael Jackson on stage during the 1996 Brit Awards in London. It was Jackson's Christ-like pose, surrounded by children of many nationalities, that inspired Jarvis to leap on stage in protest, a gesture widely supported by his contemporaries. It also went a long way towards making the Pulp singer a household name. (*LFI*)

Jarvis climbs on top of the monitors at the SFX in Dublin, October 25, 1995. (*Tim Paton/SIN*)

Jarvis on stage at Glasbonbury, 1998. (*LFI/Redferns*)

Pulp in 1998. Left to right: Candida Doyle, Nick Banks, Steve Mackey, Mark Webber and Jarvis. (*Martin Goodacre/SIN*)

Russell Senior on stage with Venini at Reading Festival in 1999. Debbie Lime is in the foreground. (*Angela Lubrano*)

Jarvis as media whore, all for charity of course. Top: with Richard Ashcroft and Kelly Jones of The Stereophonics, at the 4Scott Charity Show, La Scala, April 18, 2002; below, left: confronted by a Sun streaker at the Pulp v Blur charity football match, September 1995; and below, right: with Liam Gallagher and Stella McCartney at the War Child charity party, February, 1997. (*LFI/Rex*)

Jarvis with wife Camille Bidault-Waddington outside Portland Hospital, London, August 4, 2002. (*Rex*)

Jarvis in 2002. (*LFI*)

still had that magical factor X that could somehow unite audiences of tens of thousands, yet do so without diluting itself to the lowest-common-denominator level of a football chant. *Phew.* Before long the reviews were rolling in to seal the triumph, with the *NME* noting that:

> *". . . Their closing set is one of those festival events where you remember how good a long-absent band really are. Again, it's that rare combination of cleverness and potency, a wry subversion of pop received opinion that compels them to begin with their biggest hit 'Common People', done over in the humming motorik beat of Krautrock superstars Neu!. This is Pulp fur immer, as the set stretches from 'Babies' through to Britpop smashes and controversies, the creeping masterpiece of 'This Is Hardcore', to four new songs that combine those brashly euphoric choruses with grace in places of jerks and – in the case of 'Sunrise' – with blazing spacerock."*[514]

Even the *Daily Telegraph* was thinking along similar lines:

> *"The grand prize goes to a barefoot Jarvis Cocker of Pulp, who returned after a two-year hiatus to send the crowd home smiling on Saturday night. Cocker gives his all onstage, chatting amiably in between the twisted suburban tales of his songs, and then dancing like a man trying to run in several directions at once when the music plays. Several new songs were unveiled, including 'Weeds', another classic Pulp hymn to the downtrodden, and a glorious guitar-led climax in the form of 'Sunrise'."*[515]

The crowd's response to the new songs, and 'Sunrise' in particular, had redoubled the band's desire to release a record, and soon. However, they had to get one made first, and it was time to sort out the particulars of ensuring that it happened. Having Scott Walker as producer had been an exciting idea, but was it going to work? As Jarvis points out, "History is littered with collaborations that should have been great but aren't. A mate of mine has this bootleg of Jim Morrison singing with Jimi Hendrix in a bar in LA, and it just sounds like some pissed-up blokes mucking about. So, obviously, I didn't want that to happen."[516]

But Scott Walker hadn't produced a record with another artist since the Sixties. He also had the kind of work rate that made Pulp look like Sun Ra: barring a handful of collaborations, his output from 1984 to 2000 consisted of two albums. And *Tilt*, his most recent, was a strange, dark, near-industrial, almost impenetrable work that had next to nothing in common with either his late-Sixties classics that had been such an influence on Jarvis, or the kind of album that Pulp now wanted to make.

Nick: "We bought *Tilt*, and we played half of it, kind of going, 'That's interesting, yeah, I wonder if the other half's going to be any better?'

Fucking hell! It was one of them, you put it back in the box, back on the shelf, perhaps see that about another year. You know, it's very, very odd."

Steve: "It wasn't immediately an attractive idea because *Tilt*, if anything, resembles *This Is Hardcore* in its fairly bleak vision, I think – if there's any parallel between records we've made – and so that was the last thing we wanted. We didn't wanna say, 'Scott, we liked all of your records, apart from your recent work, which was really depressing and shit, but we did talk to him about the kind of record we wanted."[517]

Jarvis: "I went and played him the stuff that we'd already done, and tried to explain to him why I wasn't satisfied with it, and talked about how we'd all decided we wanted to record . . . and he seemed to be in tune with that way of working, of just trying to get the mood of the songs across really, and to try and record it in a more natural way, as in, us in a room, hitting instruments, and not having a click-track going *'tsssh tsssh tsssh'*."[518]

At the start of October, the sessions began tentatively in London's Metropolis Studios – a rather more urban choice than Cosford Mill, where the Chris Thomas sessions had taken place. "[Cosford Mill] was very pleasant," remembers Jarvis. "We were out in this hut, and there were big windows, and you could see this lake, and you'd be playing your guitar and this swan would float past, and you thought, 'Oh, this is quite nice.' But it didn't work, it just wasn't us really. It isn't our world."[519]

The band were more comfortable in Metropolis, but were at first, understandably, still slightly in awe of their new producer. "We didn't know what to expect," says Nick. "I remember riding down on the train to the first session, really nervous, thinking, 'I'm going to be in the studio with Scott Walker in two hours time.' But, you know, we got there, he introduced himself, as Scott, and it was all very, very normal. Looked very good for 55 or whatever he is, and we just kind of got on with things really."

"There was an issue in there," says Jarvis, "which is that, working with people who you've got some admiration for, is that going to be a very healthy working relationship or is it going to be more like, 'Oh yes, Scott, yes you do what you want, yeah, I think that's a brilliant idea Scott,' or whatever? To make a record that's any good I think it needs to be a collaborative process. People say that you shouldn't work with your heroes because you'll just realise that they're normal people, but I actually think it's a good thing if you realise that they're normal people rather than labouring under the idea that there are special beings who walk the earth who are possessed by genius. I mean, I was pleased that he was just a normal bloke, you know. That was better for me than him walking around with a cloak, only communicating through a third party, handing you notes of what to do . . .

372

"We decided to go in the studio and record with him and just see what it sounded like, and as soon as we started actually working, it instantly felt like it was the right thing to do. He was very good at getting us to perform reasonably. Which, believe me, is not that easy."[520]

The sessions continued over the autumn and winter of 2000/2001, with the band attacking the songs in groups of three or four at a time. Nigel Coxon: "To be honest at this stage, just making a record was good, so they just kind of really got on with it – I mean I met Scott a couple of times very briefly. He was very quiet, very withdrawn, didn't really say much. I think he was probably quite an unusual studio experience for them. I didn't really get too involved with it. I got the impression with Scott that he really didn't like people hanging round the studio, you know. A&R guy sitting at the back of the studio scratching his chin – it wasn't really on the agenda. It was very much like closed doors, get on with it. Just wait for the finished result, you know."

After the setbacks Pulp had suffered earlier in 2000, there seemed to be a sense of relief and renewed productivity in the air, with a unanimous feeling amongst the band that breaking with Chris Thomas and starting afresh had been the right thing to do. "It was a good thing really," says Jarvis, "because everybody in the band agreed on it, which, as you know, very rarely happens. I mean, obviously it's a pain 'cos then you have to go back and start again and you feel as if you've wasted a lot of time and money, but at least it was good because we realised we were all thinking along the same lines."[521]

As the band had wanted, the basis of all the tracks on the record was, for perhaps the first time since *Freaks*, Pulp playing live in the studio. "We just had to keep playing songs loads of times," says Jarvis, "and he would say things to our drummer like, 'Hey Nick, put some lead in your ass!' That was to make him slow down. And, erm, it worked. There was a lot of lead in that ass."[522]

"We all knew that we wanted to record in a more natural way, just get into a room and play. We used to record like that at the start of our career because we didn't have any money, and then in the interim years you go through lots of processes. I think in this day and age, if you're a band where you all play together you should try and record like that because you have a chance of getting some human feeling in what you're doing. Don't be too hung up if some bits might be a bit faster or slower, or at least you may get some atmosphere, feeling or emotion from it. A drum machine doesn't give you that feeling. I'm not a Luddite though! I'm very modern!"[523]

The basic tracks were embellished with a variety of overdubs from outside musicians, including some brought in by the band, such as Richard Hawley, The Swingle Singers and Alasdair Molloy, and others brought in by Walker, including string arranger Brian Gascoigne, electric cello player Philip Sheppard, and, for 'Sunrise', a 40-piece choir. "He did add quite a lot of stuff," says Jarvis. "The difference between it, I'd say, without being too poncey, is like if you wrote a book, he did some illustrations for it, kind of amplified it. He seemed very good at kind of getting into the atmosphere of the song and what it was about, and therefore being able to suggest, 'Well, why don't you have this in it?' "[524]

As for the vocals, Jarvis could perhaps be forgiven for not being entirely at ease with the idea of singing in a studio in front of Scott Walker. "I was terribly nervous. I'm not the biggest fan of my own voice. But he was good. He encouraged me to sing out. He didn't give me specific tips like, 'Drink camomile tea and take lots of deep breaths,' but he made me face up to my singing. My basic method in the past was to get semi-pissed, go into the vocal booth, do five or six takes − while still drinking − and then leave it to the producer to composite the final version from the best bits. But Scott didn't like me to sing too late in the day, certainly didn't like me being pissed and [made me focus] on getting the performance right. So I was more involved in it, rather than leaving it to somebody else to sort out, and I realised I didn't have to be hammered to sing."[525]

Although Pulp had, by and large, managed to put the traumas of the earlier, aborted sessions behind them, they did manifest themselves in one way: taking into account the Wessex demos, the Depot demos and the Chris Thomas recordings, many of the songs that Pulp were now working on were being recorded for the second, third or (in the case of 'The Birds In Your Garden') fourth time. Although this did mean that the band had had the chance to become familiar with the songs and the arrangements were well worked-out, the concern of how well the new versions measured up to earlier recordings couldn't help but present itself.

"We demoed stuff to quite a high standard," says Jarvis. "What we used to do was just put a tape recorder in the rehearsal room and record things, and they were very, very poor quality. Now this time we decided to demo stuff; I've always been a very last-minute person − only getting the lyrics sorted out the night before − and I thought, 'Maybe that's a bit immature.' But to be honest, I don't think I'll ever do that again, the demoing − it just creates a lot of problems, because sometimes you get attached to the demo version, and then when you come to record it for real you think, 'Oh, it doesn't sound as good as the demo . . .' Maybe it helped with doing the words, but I still ended up changing a lot of them at the last minute.

Maybe it was kind of useful for me, it took a bit of pressure off me, as I'd written stuff – but I wouldn't do it again. You can usually tell if an idea's good or not, even if it's recorded shittily, and so you may as well get on and do it for real rather than do a practice."[526]

Throughout the recording period, there was, by and large, a discreet media silence from the Pulp camp. Although it was known that there had been a change of producer, no official confirmation had been made to the press as to the collaboration with Scott Walker, with any enquiries being met with a firm "no comment" – a fairly ridiculous state of affairs considering that it had surfaced as a rumour in virtually every music publication almost as soon as the sessions began.

Jarvis did speak briefly to the *NME* during November 2000, confirming that the original Chris Thomas sessions had been scrapped because they "didn't seem right", and that the festival shows had given the band "a lot of confidence". He also added that morale in the group was high – "We normally have loads of arguments which I think is fair enough for a band. I don't like it when bands get on too well, you know, 'That was a fantastic solo you just played,' it's crap, innit? So we are actually agreeing on a lot of things – it's slightly worrying actually!"[527]

Most cheering was the naming of two possible singles, 'Sunrise' and 'Weeds', which the band wanted to release "as soon as possible", and a projected spring 2001 release date for the album. "I'd like to have the record out for spring so we'd have to have a single before then. It's been too long as it is. I never want it to take a long time when we're recording but somehow it always seems to. I don't really know why that is. Maybe it's just general ineptitude, I dunno. I don't think it takes long to make a good record, sometimes the more you think about it the worse it becomes, but I'm not a fan of taking a long time."[528]

Pulp's seventh album was completed in March 2001, three years almost to the day since the release of *This Is Hardcore*. After being kept waiting for so long, one might have expected Island to be keen on releasing something as soon as possible. Apparently not: Jarvis had been pushing Island for several months to release 'Sunrise', one of the first tracks completed with Scott Walker, back in October 2000, as a single. The label, however, wasn't keen.

"That's one of my great regrets," says Jarvis, "and it's kind of indicative of what happened to us. We played at Reading in August 2000 and everybody went mad to that song. I thought, 'Let's learn from the past. If people like a song they've never heard before, let's get it out.' Unfortunately, the way things were set up at the time, it just didn't happen. Maybe because of the experience of releasing *This Is Hardcore*, the idea of putting out a six-minute single, of which the last three minutes were instrumental, seemed too risky."[529]

Another factor was doubtless the change of management at Island. Since the start of 1999, the company had been a part of the enormous Universal Music Group, and Pulp's new corporate paymasters were rather less laid-back about budget overspend on their records than the old regime had been. *This Is Hardcore* had been an extremely expensive project (the video for the title track alone had cost £250,000 to make) which had barely made its money back; the label didn't intend to make the same mistake twice.

Nigel Coxon: "I think *Hardcore* was the start of why, maybe down the line, they didn't end up getting their option picked up. Because they didn't make cheap records. They wouldn't have got away with it nowadays, 'cos accountants really are so hardcore with paying bills and stuff, but we were still quite *lasseiz-faire* when it was pre-Universal Island. *This Is Hardcore* was Polygram still, but Polygram were still being quite cool with Island, because Island were still coming off the back of an amazing roll – I mean, in '95, Island were like Parlophone are now: Stereo MCs, Cranberries, Pulp, PJ Harvey, Tricky. It was like, wow, you know."

In 2001, though, the days of Pulp having full control over their releases were over. Even trusted A&R buddies like Nigel Coxon held less sway: decisions were being increasingly made by marketing and promotions people. And if, even back in the good old days of 1995, Pulp had had to fight the suits to ensure that the 'Common People' single was released in May that year rather than being shelved till September, what chance did they have now of deciding when and how 'Sunrise' was going to come out?

The difficulties didn't end there: the marketing brains at Universal had also decided that the only acceptable times of year for an album to be released by an 'alternative' artist were spring and autumn. It was too late now for a spring release; therefore, the album was going to be shelved for another six months, till "September or October 2001". Well, naturally: what would be the point of releasing a record without giving the fanbase a little extra time to dwindle and allowing any lingering beneficial effects of Reading 2000 to wear off?

At least the extra time gave the group ample opportunity to ensure they were happy with every aspect of the album. "I think it's the first time since things have been a bit more official that we've had quite a while to think about how to present a record," said Jarvis at the time. "Usually, you finish it and it's all a mad rush and then it comes out; at first I was kind of frustrated that we were going to have to wait a bit for it to come out, but I think it'll be good 'cos we can take a bit of time about things like the sleeve and stuff like that, make sure that everything is exactly as we want it."[530]

At the end of May, Pulp's first music press interview in almost a year appeared in *NME*. They weren't allowed to talk about the album (Jarvis having explained that, "It's not a guilty secret. It's logistics. We'll be doing all our blabbing about it in September"[531]), but there was still plenty to discuss. Based on the snippets of news that emerged about Pulp's activities in the years between albums, there was an increasing suspicion that certain members of the group had vanished up their own arses – far from being the common people's heroes viewing the glamour-strewn, cocaine'n' champagne London celebrity world with a healthy contempt, had they been seduced by the other side?

For one thing, Jarvis had been spotted during 2000 lending his DJing skills to a *Pop*/Chanel party in a gallery space in Islington during London fashion week (even more confusingly, in March 2001 he and Steve had been spotted DJing at a University Of Warwick Law Ball in Birmingham, but that's beside the point). Steve, meanwhile, was going out with Katie Grand, editor of fashion magazine *Pop*, fashion director of *The Face* and creative director of fashion label Bottega Veneta, while Jarvis had been snapped in the pages of *Vogue* with his girlfriend, the well-known stylist Camille Bidault-Waddington. Of course, Pulp, like the rest of us, had the right to spend their free time in any way they wished, in whatever company they chose. But really, what the hell were they playing at?

Steve offered a reasonably robust defence of himself. "I don't think I lead a highfalutin lifestlyle. Highfalutin means going to parties that have little reason to exist. Spending your money idly on expensive sunglasses every Saturday. I don't do that. Through my girlfriend I've met a lot of people in the fashion world. But I kinda keep out of it. There are some interesting people, though, and I've always been interested in photo-graphy and the artwork that Pulp have done. I've enjoyed meeting people who do that kind of thing. It might be a bit of an arty lifestyle, but it's not a highfalutin, fashion life. I'd be horrified if anyone thought it was. It sug-gests Elton John to me."[532]

And as for Jarvis? "I don't lead a highfalutin fashion lifestyle now. I've split up with my girlfriend. I did have an interest in tennis too, but I've lost my partner now.

"I know people from that world, but the main people I know aren't into that. That lifestyle, all that mwah, mwah, mwah, is something I don't like. I happened to go out with someone from that world but she wasn't particularly . . . she used to tell cabbies she was a journalist. She didn't like the connotations of shallowness. I DJed at a few parties, but it's not something I aspire to."[533]

Hmm. We'll let them off just this once, then.

Meanwhile, the delay with the record wasn't going to stop Pulp enjoying the festival season. Rather than doing the usual Glastonbury/ Reading/T In The Park rounds, from May to August they made a string of appearances at festivals around Britain and Europe that were a little further off the beaten track – none more so than an appearance at the annual Hay-on-Wye literary festival, which takes place at the end of each May in a small town near the Welsh border. The other acts were authors and poets; the dressing room was a school classroom across the road from the marquee in which the band were playing. "It is a bit odd," Jarvis told *The Times* in an interview on the day. "Good, though. Much better here than, say, Derby Roadmenders. We've been around a long time so it's always interesting for us to play somewhere a bit different. I'm honoured to be asked. I just hope we didn't put them off having a band next year. I walked into the venue today and I could smell grass. Not dope. Not the roadies smoking loads of ganja. I could smell actual green grass. That's much more pleasant than walking into a venue and smelling stale tobacco smoke and spilt beer. To my shame, I've never been to a literary festival before, but I may come again. I was worried it would be full of men with beards wearing sandals, but it's not like that at all."[534]

Hay-on-Wye was also the warm-up for an even more baffling appearance: the Homelands dance music festival, sandwiched between Stanton Warrior and Seb Fontaine on a bill on which the other big names included Artful Dodger, The Orb, Danny Rampling and Sasha. Are you sure?

Jarvis: "All that happened was that [festival organisers] Mean Fiddler decided that we'd be good for it. It instantly appealed to me because I find that dance music has less restrictions on it, and it seems to be an area of music where people are still experimenting. I think it's always a bit interesting when it's a bit of a challenge and you can't rely on everybody going, 'Oh yeah, brilliant' – maybe you have to convince people a bit.[535]

"They had this phone vote on MTV saying, 'Should Pulp be playing Homelands?'" he told *NME* a couple of weeks before the festival. "About 85 per cent said no. I found that a bit crap. Dance music hasn't been going that long and a lot of things can come under the definition of dance. It's not as entrenched in that sense of history or the stagnation of rock. The Stereophonics view that there is real music and there isn't, that theirs is proper, hand-crafted, yes-sir-it's-been-matured-in-oak-vats-for-ten-years music . . . that's shit.

378

"Dance should allow you to get away with lots of different things. If you've got the risk that some people will throw their glowsticks at you, you get more satisfaction if you win them over. And I do think our sensibility is appropriate in that setting. I don't think people are so narrow-minded they'll only consider things that are at 140 bpm. Obviously, if you see me with black eyes in three weeks then you'll know it didn't quite work out."[536]

As it turned out, Pulp triumphed. Again. New songs 'Weeds', 'The Trees', 'Bad Cover Version' and 'Sunrise' shone alongside the likes of 'Sorted' (obviously), 'This Is Hardcore' and 'Party Hard', all of which seemed to have acquired a new sense of grace and fluidity, with 'Hardcore' in particular coming alive like never before. The *NME* agreed, giving Pulp their best write-up in years:

> *"Pulp are magnificent. Orange sunset streaks into the Ericsson arena as Jarvis high-kicks his rejuvenated group into – what else? – 'Sorted For E's And Wizz', and suddenly the prospect of being richly entertained by an intelligent, witty and glamorous collective – by humans, not Timo Mass – becomes hugely exciting. Horticultural in theme but universal in appeal, Pulp's brace of new songs blend the baroque sleaze of* This Is Hardcore *with the everyman euphoria of* Different Class. *But Pulp have not gone exclusively dance, as their billing might suggest; rather, in 'Trees' and 'Weeds' and 'Minnie Timperley', they offer delirious Moog-fuelled unorthodox pop that spooks and surprises in equal measure. 'Common People' crescendos heroically over a Krautrock groove, and several thousand misfits text their friends the good news: Pulp ;-)"*[537]

The gamble of moving on from 'Common People' and ditching the charity shop suits and ultra-pop aesthetic had paid off: Pulp were seen as anything but a tired Britpop nostalgia act. And just to cement their sense of now-ness, Homelands also marked the début of Jarvis and Steve's DJ collective, known as the Desperate Sound System. "We asked the organisers if they'd allow me to drive my van up there," Jarvis explained before the event, "and set it up and DJ out the back of it. So we're going to play, but then after that we're going to have our own mobile disco somewhere within the grounds. We're all going to have a go, and we've got some people from Sheffield, like Parrott and The All Seeing I lot, and Martin Green, and I'm hoping that Barry from Add N To (X) will play some records. Obviously the concert's the most important thing but that'll be quite exciting as well."[538]

By the time of Homelands, the disco van had become a tent, with Jarvis and Steve spinning tunes in rotation with a wide variety of guest DJs. And to tie in with the whole thing, Jarvis had, partially at least, got his way with Island – the label had agreed to press up a run of 1,000 white label 12″ singles of 'Sunrise', backed with remixes from The Fat Truckers and All Seeing I. Not that they managed to actually get it out in time for Homelands or anything . . .

"It was supposed to come out around then," Jarvis told XFM, "but then the record company was slightly dozy and it ended up being a bit late. We just wanted to get something out 'cos that song's about being out late and being still awake when the sun's coming up. I thought, 'Well, people tend to do that more in summer than they do in winter,' 'cos, y'know, it's a bit cold, isn't it? It just seems appropriate that that song should be around in some kind of way during the summer and hopefully get played at some do's and stuff like that."[539]

"I think we were trying to reposition it," says Nigel Coxon. "We were trying to say, 'Pulp, they're not like that, they can appeal to *this*, they can appeal to *that*,' – they can play Homelands and it can be great, and it can set a new precedent in that environment, and they can work there. We were just trying to re-align it all, and get people on board across the board, and we were putting out Fat Truckers 'Sunrise' white labels, and all that was seeping through. And they were thinking about their whole Desperate thing. I mean, Desperate was like a total precursor to that whole bastard pop stuff, they were right on it, so I think Pulp again were incredibly hip in that period, when we were repositioning the album. And that's why I think when the album came out, in terms of reviews, and the live stuff they did in terms of reviews, you had it probably better received than *Hardcore*."

A sprinkling of Pulp festival dates through the summer in Switzerland, Sweden, Spain, France and Holland, and, with the Guildford Festival in August, they finally placated those long-suffering British fans who were keen on seeing Pulp but less keen on going to an expensive dance music festival or an obscure literary do. Meanwhile, further Desperate events took place at a variety of venues around London. As with Mark's Little Stabs events, Desperate seemed to exist mainly in order to provide Jarvis and Steve with an alternative to the regimented nature of most of the clubs they'd been going to.

"It's great," said Jarvis. "You go to clubs, these over-designed clubs where you feel that you're making the place look untidy by just being there, where they have a policy that everything has to be over 142 bpm. Our club's called Desperate because we are. It seems like a desperate thing to be going to clubs at our age. But what are you going to do, stay in and watch the telly? We try and move it from place to place, so that every time you come it's somewhere different. It goes on till five or six in the morning so you can have a laugh. And if you run a club, you get in for free, and also you get free drinks. I leave the door policy to other people, we invite people we know and like. As long as you keep the fucking meat-heads out I'm not bothered. Any race, creed or sexual persuasion. The more mixed the better for me. The music's pretty eclectic."[540]

They'd even got some special badges made, bearing the legend "I'm Desperate". "We went to see U2," says Jarvis, "and we tried to give Adam Clayton an 'I'm Desperate' badge and he took it very badly – thought we were trying to take the piss out of him."[541]

And the name? "I remember when I first started going to clubs I'd see people who were 28, and I'd think, 'What the fuck are they still coming out for?' And now I'm ten years on from that, and I'm still doing it. So sure, when people see me out, they think, 'What the hell is that clapped-out fucker still doing out?' But you know, I'm desperate. I admit it!"[542]

By September, with a release date for the album finally in sight, it was time to decide on a single. Pulp still wanted 'Sunrise' as the A-side of their first release in three years; Island still had other ideas.

"There was a debate about 'Sunrise'," says Nigel Coxon, "which I think the new marketing and promotions people probably got a bit wrong. 'Sunrise' seemed to have a momentum of its own, but no one in the record company, the new promotions people and all that, got it. We all thought it was brilliant and it should be a single, people like myself, Jeff Craft, the agent, Rough Trade, John Best. We could see how it went down live, that this was special. But the record company, being very timid possibly, thought, ' 'Sunrise', six minutes, two-minute outro, no chance. 'Trees', that's more obvious. We want 'Trees' as a single.'

"Even though 'Sunrise' seemed to have a life of its own, got picked up off a white label, XFM playlist, people at Radio 1 going out to buy it because they'd heard about it, so it had a real vibe, the record company I don't think believed in it as a track, and that was a mistake, and 'Trees' had to be the commercial side of it, so the compromise was a double A, and what ended up happening probably is that that single got slightly diluted."

As a piece of corporate stupidity, this topped even the tactic of taking an album that was already a year late and shelving it for another six months. Even if the record company had wanted a more commercial first single than 'Sunrise', which was understandable, if silly in the light of the buzz that had picked up around 'Sunrise' over the summer, the album con-tained a fistful of tunes that were a hundred times more commercial than the understated, mid-tempo 'Trees'. When unveiled at Reading the previous year, both 'Weeds' and 'Minnie' practically sounded as if they'd been written as a result of someone turning over the Oblique Strategies card marked "Radio 1 Breakfast Show Single Of The Week". But 'Trees'? Were Island the new Fire? Very possibly so.

Nigel Coxon: "Had it been down to the band and myself, we'd have been brave again and gone with 'Sunrise' and pushed that. It would probably have been very hard, admittedly, but 'Trees' didn't happen. Everyone got this fixation in the record company that 'Trees' was the only vaguely commercial track by a mile on the record. The record company did find that record really difficult. It took most of them a long time before they appreciated that it was any good. And it was all this 'Trees, Trees, Trees, Trees', and I found that weird, and Geoff – we all thought it was a bit weird. But we thought, 'At least we've got 'Sunrise' which has a bit of life, let's try this double A.' "

'The Trees'/'Sunrise', Pulp's long-awaited comeback single, was released on October 8, 2001. It entered the charts at number 23, and dropped out of the Top 40 by the following week. The record was a compromise that satisfied nobody – not the record company, nor the group, nor the fans, nor the public at large. If either song had been the sole A-side, it might have stood a better chance, but with the fairly meagre airplay the single received being split between the two songs, neither one really had the chance to take hold. Meanwhile, the inexcusable lack of proper B-sides (the songs were duplicated over a 2-CD set, propped up by a pair of pretty tedious remixes) removed any real incentive for the fans, other than those who were completists to the point of masochism, to buy it when they knew that the album, including both songs, would be in the shops a fort-night later. The apparent justification for this was that there were no songs left over from the Scott Walker sessions, the only songs recorded being the ones on the album. But what about the welter of lost songs that had been "demoed to quite a high standard" in late 1999 and early 2000? Something like 'Cuckoo', or 'The Quiet Revolution', or 'After You', wouldn't have hurt.

The final nail in the coffin of the single was a slew of truly rotten TV performances. Despite everything, Pulp had been offered appearances on all the prominent chart-orientated pop shows in Britain: *The Pepsi Chart*, *CD:UK* and *Top Of The Pops*. On each of these, they proceeded to mime 'The Trees' with no apparent concession to making any notable visual impact, and Jarvis turning in some terrible, cringingly off-key vocals. Was this really one of the most celebrated pop performers of the past 20 years? The kindest thing that could be said about the *Top Of The Pops* appearance is that Jarvis had apparently combed his hair before coming on.

"I thought the video was disappointing as well," says Nigel Coxon. "I mean, it was a great idea but the lighting was awful, so you were looking at this dark screen trying to see all these images that should have been amazing and beautiful, and yet the whole thing was just a bit . . . you know, it didn't really work at all."

Perhaps the whole shabby, half-hearted business is a reflection of the fact that, while the Jarvis of 2001 did still want to have hit records, it was no longer the priority that it had been in the past. "Jarvis has certainly been very variable over the last year," said Steve. "He's been having this fight with himself about only doing things he enjoys. That has meant saying no to people, but it has made his life a lot easier."[543]

"I try not to be bothered," mused Jarvis about the question of commercial success, "but if you have had number two singles, which we have had, it's just a statistic, innit? I mean, it's in the *Guinness Book Of Hit Singles* – it's a fact. So everything you release after that is going to be judged against it. Now, rationally, I say to myself, 'But that's not what it's about,' and it isn't, but still at the back of your mind you do worry a bit. I mean, I do buy chart records – the last one I bought was that Eve and Gwen Stefani single which I think is a really great record. But that's a real rarity. Most of the stuff I buy would never go within 600 miles of t'charts.

"Making this record – there was no other reason to make it other than that we wanted to and it would be an enjoyable thing. After *This Is Hardcore*, it wasn't like anybody was thinking, 'Yeah, them guys are going to come back with a commercial album, aren't they?' There was no people gagging for us to do another record. So there was no commercial pressure. We kind of did it for its own sake."[544]

With the 'Sunrise'/'Trees' debacle out of the way, Pulp's seventh album, *We Love Life*, was finally released on October 22, 2001. Typically of the album's long and torturous process of creation, even the title had been the subject of seemingly endless indecision: first it was going to be *Pulp Love Life*, then simply *Pulp*, before finally settling on *We Love Life*. "I initially wanted it to be called *Pulp Love Life*," explains Jarvis, "but making that work on the cover . . . it always looked like the name of the band's Pulp and the album's called *Love Life*. And we tried it with this heart – *Pulp* ♥ *Life* – but that looked a bit too tacky, so I just sacked it and thought we'd just call it *Pulp*."[545]

Pulp lasted for a while, and early promo copies of the album bearing that title were distributed to journalists and music business insiders during the late summer. "I still agree with the sentiments of *Pulp Love Life*," said Jarvis at the time, "but *Pulp* works all right, 'cos another theme of the record is keeping things simple and direct and uncluttered. Plus, of course, this is the definitive Pulp album."[546]

And then came September 11. "To be honest, I was really freaked out when that World Trade Center thing happened. Basically, it was like staring into the abyss, weren't it? All the things you expect to be there forever ... suddenly you think anything could happen. We'd been rehearsing and went up to the top floor of the place where we rehearse and were watching it on the TV. You've got quite a good view of London from there – Canary Wharf, Post Office Tower, Millennium Wheel, all that stuff – seeing it unfold on the TV and then looking out and thinking, 'If that can happen, surely in 30 seconds time the Post Office Tower is probably gonna fall over.' So in the aftermath of that I thought, actually this *Love Life* business isn't a bad sentiment at this particular time. So I had one more go at trying to make it work. Calling it *We Love Life* seemed better. It's more inclusive. So, much to the record company's displeasure, I changed it again."[547]

With a title like that, songs called things like 'Weeds', 'The Birds In Your Garden' and 'Sunrise', and a generally more natural, organic sound, it was easy to misconstrue the album as Pulp's drippy, happy-clappy record. "This isn't Pulp's pastoral album," snapped Jarvis at the time. "I was very aware of avoiding hippy dippy stuff. 'Weeds' is not a nice song; 'I Love Life' may be the most noisy terror tune ever recorded. I'm screaming about my life and I certainly don't want it to end. You have to fight to the death for the right to live your life. As soon as you stop making any effort then your life fucks up.[548] We're saying happiness is possible in life, however, you have to work to achieve it, you know – it won't just happen. And that's the trouble, isn't it, nowadays people just think they've got a right to be happy, and they haven't. I mean, obviously I would rather people be happy than unhappy, but you do have to make an effort to achieve it. Instant gratification is almost enshrined in our society now. People don't want to have to work at it."[549]

The struggle to achieve some sort of happiness, of course, was a theme that *We Love Life* shared with *This Is Hardcore*, but this time around the overbearing sense of desperation and disillusionment was conspicuous by its absence. "I think disillusionment is generally considered a negative thing," said Jarvis, "but as you move through life I think you have to shed illusions, and you find yourself thinking, 'That's an illusion, that doesn't mean anything,' therefore you start to look for things that do mean something, and I guess this record chronicles that search.[550]

"*Hardcore* was made against all the odds when we were going through bad times. This record is back to a more healthy state. You need to do different things to keep your mind alive. Like me and Steve have our DJing with Desperate, Mark has film. Music is a product of your life, not a substitute. Life first, creation second. That's how it works.[551]

"It was just about going back to basics. If you look at the song titles, you probably think, 'Jesus Christ, this is a record for children or something.' Trees, weeds, birds – sometimes you need to go back to basic things, especially if you've gone up a blind alley. You have to get back to where you started and then take a different road."[552]

The album opens with the muscular, insistent 'Weeds', sounding like a cross between The Velvet Underground's 'All Tomorrow's Parties' and (debatably) Bon Jovi's 'Wanted Dead Or Alive'. Jarvis' excellent, snarling lyric draws metaphorical links between asylum seekers, prostitutes, pop stars, horticulture, drug dealers and God knows what else. "I wanted that song to be quite aggressive, and it's about how certain supposedly higher class levels of society use the underclass for their own exploitation, for their own entertainment, and in the song, specifically through prostitution and to go and score some gear off 'em. I found an analogy there with the way the music business works – it's the age-old story, innit, of the raw talent manipulated by the evil Svengali or whatever – and how people can kind of invent something for themselves, which I think often happens with music, people living in boring towns and stuff like that and they invent something for themselves, and then it gets marketed.

"And then there was the whole thing about weeds being considered to be weak things. You get called a weed in England in a school if you're supposed to be a weak person, and yet weeds, as far as I can see, are the most tenacious plants 'cos they'll grow in a little tiny bit of soil. I always like it when you're going down a street and there's this big bush growing off the top of it, and it must be growing in about [indicates tiny amount] this much soil, stuck on to some masonry, and for some reason that always brings a smile to my face.[553] For some reason I thought that's a bit like humans in a city – you're a natural thing but you're growing in this slightly hostile, crappy environment but somehow managing to survive.[554]

"The theme, I guess you can trace it back to 'Common People' and 'Mis-Shapes', but the reason I thought it was worth persevering with was that I thought that the song added something to the discourse. Because those two songs were written before we'd had any experience of how the music industry works when you become quite popular, and I think that gave me an insight into how something quite personal can become industrialised if you're not careful, and it makes me angry in some ways, you know, and that's why I wanted the song to be aggressive and a kind of 'fuck you' to that process. 'Cos it does happen, things do get exploited, and you just have to accept that and retain something for yourself, not allow it to destroy you."[555]

The lyrical theme of 'Weeds' is continued in the second track, 'The Origin Of The Species'. Musically, however, the latter is chalk to the former's cheese: a primordial, squelching electronic soundscape that picks up where 'Seductive Barry' and 'F.E.E.L.I.N.G.C.A.L.L.E.D.L.O.V.E.' left off. Jarvis again: "Once I realised that weed could also be the ganja, it was complete to me, that's why I had to have two songs written about it, because I thought it was something worth going into in some kind of depth.[556] My favourite line in the song is *'Come on, do your funny little dance'*. You create your own world in a band and, in a way, when it becomes popular it gets taken away from you. The things that you did naturally somehow make you feel like a performing monkey: 'Go on, do that pointing thing.' For a while I toyed with the idea of standing still onstage because it was expected of me. But then I thought to myself, I invented that stupid dance. No one forced me to do it. Don't worry about whether it's a cliché. So I'm still doing my funny little dance."[557]

Jarvis was again touching on themes he'd written about before – this time in the likes of 'This Is Hardcore' and 'The Professional' – but unlike those previous songs about fame and its debilitating effect on one's Art, 'The Origin Of The Species' takes in a far wider range of ideas, applicable to many different areas of society, making the song far more interesting and anything but a typical self-pitying pop-star wallow.

"I think stuff comes from poor backgrounds and then gets exploited by people and [the originators] don't get any benefit from it. Like Kool Herc, who everyone acknowledges invented hip hop and he's stuck in some shit apartment in some project – where's his gold Ferrari? It's not just music. They think these people are scum but when they want to score some blow they'll go round to their houses and then say afterwards in their private club, 'I went to this council estate today, it was really, really authentic.' This kind of slumming-it vibe exists quite a lot in our society now. Like middle-class people going to football games: 'Yah, so, just tell me the rules again. Which side should I be shouting for?' It does bug me."[558]

Next is 'The Night That Minnie Timperley Died', a song that manages to be simultaneously dark, heart-rending and a fantastic slice of pop music in a manner not dissimilar to 'Death Comes To Town'. "It came together really, really quickly," says Jarvis. "It was written within ten minutes, more or less fully formed.[559] That song came from a dream that I had about me and Steve going to DJ at a Scottish rave, and we had all our equipment stolen and there was this 16-year-old girl walking around, thinking how stupid all these people were who were off their heads, and she got bored, and accepted a lift from a bloke in the car park and then he kills her. God knows why I dreamt that, it's not very pleasant, but it really stuck in my mind, it was one of those very vivid dreams, and so of course I thought, 'That's a brilliant subject matter for a song, isn't it?' Nice, cheery, feelgood material!"[560]

'The Trees', while being a disastrous choice of single, is actually one of the stand-out tracks on the album — a very human love song, using the metaphor of nature as a starting point for a touching story of the death of a relationship. In that sense, it's a similar idea to 'Down By The River', but this time the approach is less heavy-handed, and emotionally more satisfying for it.

The song is also the final resting place of the string sample from Stanley Myers & Hal Shaper's 'Tell Her You Love Her', from the film *Otley*, which Jarvis had been trying to get into a song since at least 1999. First it was the basis of 'Cockroach Conversation' from the Nick Cave Meltdown show, and then it became 'Otley' for the Touch Of Glass project before being remoulded into 'The Trees' as the *We Love Life* sessions were drawing to a close. "I'd had the song we sample in it for about four or five years and wanted to write a song around it. I'd had loads of go's. We were getting to the end of the sessions, so we had one more go and we nailed it.[561]

"I initially wrote some words and was really unhappy with them, and then I decided to shoot a magpie. I've never shot a magpie, I've never killed any animal. I was never allowed an air rifle when I was younger — there used to be one in me Grandma's house which I was allowed to handle, up to about the age of eight, with no pellets in it, but once I got to the dangerous stage where I might want to go out and shoot squirrels or whatever, it was hidden.

"The idea of the lyrics in that song is the trees being there and all the kind of human dramas that could happen in a forest, people meeting for an illicit love affair or whatever, but the trees are impassive to that, and the way that people will carve their name on the bark of a tree, thinking that's some kind of mark of permanence in a relationship, but then you go back a year or two later and try and read it, it'll be all twisted because the tree doesn't grow in a linear way."[562]

Steve: "I think it encapsulates this album, but maybe that's something to do with being the last song we wrote, and by that point we were starting to understand what kind of record we were making. Because usually whilst we're making a record we've not got any idea where it's going, you probably realise about two years after what it was about. Whereas because it took two years to record it, we'd already got some insight, and sonically it is quite representative."[563]

The centrepiece of the record is undoubtedly 'Wickerman' – a tremendous eight minutes of music that could perhaps qualify as Jarvis' finest lyrical achievement. Like 'Sheffield Sex City' and 'Deep Fried In Kelvin' before it, the song evokes Sheffield in all its grubby, scuffed glory, but this time the story is more personal, bringing together a succession of scenes from long-gone relationships. The detail, if anything, is even more atmospheric than those previous songs, taking in not only Sheffield but the countryside that surrounds it, with its *"buds that explode at the slightest touch, nettles that sting – but not too much"* contrasting with the city itself. At the end, Jarvis is alone and bereft, throwing his fate open to the one constant through the succession of people and places that come and go throughout the song: the river that flows on beneath it all: *"I may find you there and float on wherever the river may take me; wherever it wants us to go."*

Jarvis: "The kind of start point for 'Wickerman' was, I got asked to write a piece for an English magazine called *World Of Interiors*, and they asked you for three things that had provided you with inspiration – and of course I was panic-stricken 'cos I couldn't think of anything. I was trying to think of things that had done that and, although obviously since the events that are described in that song happened I've done a lot of things, travelled the world and all that, but for some reason this time when, it sounds stupid, but I had an inflatable boat and I went on a trip down the River Don, which is one of the rivers that runs through Sheffield, and it was quite a magical day. It was travelling through the city that I've lived in all my life, but seeing it from a different angle, and when you travel along the river and you're going with the current you feel like you're being taken somewhere, and I saw quite a lot of strange events. One event that doesn't get mentioned in the song was the guy stood at the side of the river – with an air rifle, probably why I didn't mention it – and he was shooting it into the water, trying to shoot fish. And as he was doing it, he was going, 'Stitch that, yer bastards!' And it was just things like that, and that's always something that has really fascinated me, when you can find extraordinary events in very everyday circumstances.

"So I just got the idea of this river running through the city and stories that had happened at various times, happening along the course of it, and also the river kind of providing a sense of continuity.[564] This river has been there for thousands, millions, of years, and all this stuff has gone on top of it, and it still exists. The idea appealed to me that you've still got a thread running through things, even though you've got all this stuff built on top of it. There will still be something constant underneath it. A sense of continuity in your own life is quite important."[565]

Jarvis singled out 'Wickerman' as being the song that best captured

Pulp's collaboration with Scott Walker, and it's easy to see why – the production is superbly atmospheric, with the song completed by Alasdair Molloy's spooky glass harmonica and a subtle but excellent string arrangement scored by Candida, Walker and his longtime collaborator Brian Gascoigne. "From the offset [Walker] was really into doing that song," says Jarvis, "and I think he did a really good job with bringing out the story. It's a long rambling story of things that happened to me in Sheffield and he managed to bring it alive a bit.[566] Musically, it was written in bits like 'This Is Hardcore'. We just kept going until we had enough bits. We got the sample from 'The Wicker Man' and that seemed really appropriate because at the time these things were happening I was living at a place called The Wicker in Sheffield.[567] I thought, 'Yeah, it's all coming together.' I'm like Hannibal from *The A-Team* – I love it when a plan comes together.

"It all seemed to kind of mean something, so I just made it into a story. But for the international listener, obviously, you will not have any clue about this because to your ears it will just be some English bloke mumbling for approximately eight-and-a-half minutes, and you won't be able to understand a word of it, so I apologise."[568]

The album's almost-title track, 'I Love Life', is perhaps one of the less successful moments on the album. Musically it's gorgeous, built around a classically Pulpesque noodling guitar part, but the lyrics, while hinting at some interesting ideas, seem fragmentary, unfinished. The song hops between desultory lines like *'Look at all these buildings and houses: I love my life'* or *'On the floor of your living room, you made a scene but it'll never get shown on TV'* with very little to bind it all together.

According to Jarvis, the writing of the song marked the broadening of the album's musical palette after the initial, more acoustic-based batch of songs were written in 1999. "When we first started writing the songs, 'Sunrise' and 'Birds In Your Garden' were the first ones we did. At that point I thought we might make an acoustic album – there must have been something in the air at that time because there's been that New Acoustic Movement since then. In the midst of all that I came up with the guitar riff and thought, 'Well, that doesn't really fit. But if it comes out there's a reason for it, I think.'[569] We started playing that song and if people were hanging around in our rehearsal they'd kind of give us a funny look after we played it, and say, 'What are you doing with that one?'"[570]

Steve: "They'd say things like, 'It's just not right,' which obviously makes you quite interested in it. Yeah, it's out of tune, and explain to us why it was out of tune, and there'd be a lot of this . . . and we were determined to persevere with it, especially when we wrote the second part of it, which possibly might be quite unpleasant to listen to but is quite enjoyable to play. It seems at odds with its title in some ways, musically."[571]

"On a basic and immature level," says Jarvis, "we just liked the fact that it was really loud and horrible at the end. For me, the idea of that song is someone trying to regain control of their life, and it's not all that easy sometimes."[572]

'The Birds In Your Garden', the oldest song on the album, returns to the record's gentle, acoustic origins, albeit moulded into a more typically Pulpish ballad than its 1999 prototype. Scott Walker adds another production masterstroke, this time with the unlikely use of a musical saw played by one Casper Cronk. Meanwhile, Jarvis hardly spoils things at all with the unnecessary addition of the rather mawkish final line, *"The birds in the garden, they taught me the words to this song."*

The jangling, melodic baroque pop of 'Bob Lind (The Only Way Is Down)' covers a theme central to the album – that of admitting fallibility and dealing with it rather than being debilitated by it. "It's about someone who is a fuck-up," says Jarvis. "And sometimes there's something good about admitting that. Most people who are famous and wealthy tend to be more fucked up than everybody else.[573] And if you're famous you think, 'Why the hell should I be fucked up?'[574]

The titular Lind was a Sixties American folk singer. "He had one hit, with 'Elusive Butterfly' in 1967 I think," explains Jarvis the pop encyclopaedia. "I'd always remembered that song as a song that I really liked from being a kid, and then I found some other record by him and I really liked 'em. When we started playing that song, I just thought it had a bit of a sound of him to it. He's quite good 'cos he writes quite sweet songs but then they've often got quite negative words – for instance there's a song of his called 'Remember The Rain', which is basically saying, *'Remember the rain when you walk in the sunshine.'* It's saying, 'Oh right, you might be having a good time now, but listen – you will be having a shit time soon.' Which is a pretty negative thing to write about, and yet it's quite a nice, jangly little tune. So that song reminded me of him a bit.

" 'Bob Lind' was just a working title, but then as sometimes happens, I couldn't think of a better one so I just left it. And he did get in touch, and said, 'I'm gonna sue.' No, he didn't – he got in touch and he seemed to be quite flattered that somebody had remembered him."[575]

The majestic 'Bad Cover Version' is next – an enormous pop ballad, with a huge Spectoresque sound (something possibly reflected in the song's working title 'Candy's Spectre') and savage, funny lyrics (*'I heard an old girlfriend had turned to the church – she's trying to replace me but it'll never work'*). "The main tune came from Candida," says Jarvis. "I wrote the words at night, then I went to bed, woke up in the morning and thought, 'I bet they're really shit, them words.' But then when I sang them they worked all right. When we recorded it with other people it never sounded right – it sounded like a pastiche of something. It's just a pop song but I find it quite emotional.[576]

"Doing 'Bad Cover Version' was probably the most embarrassing moment on the record for me, because the song had been written a long time before we knew we were gonna work with Scott Walker, and in the end section of the song there's a list of inferior things. Unfortunately in this litany, I included Scott Walker's fifth solo LP, *'Til The Band Comes In*. That record's always mystified me because it starts off with original material, and it's pretty good, and then suddenly on the second side he just does six cover versions. It's like he just kind of gets sick of the whole thing and gives up halfway through the record, so I've always found it a very strange record for that.

"Of course, when we were working with him, this became a problem for me because I felt that I had to mention it to him. I didn't want him to suddenly realise it himself, and then come and punch me or something, so I was thinking about it, and it was coming closer to the day when I was gonna have to do me vocal, and I was really trying to find the right moment to broach the subject, but it never seemed to come along.

"And then one morning, I was travelling there on the train, and thinking, 'Right, first thing, as soon as I get into the studio, I'm gonna have it out with him, I'm gonna tell him, I'm gonna tell it how it is.' So I was thinking to myself, 'Yeah, you gotta do it, gotta do it, gotta do it,' got off the train, walk into the studio, 'Yeah, you gotta do it, gotta do it, gotta do it,' got through the front door, 'Yeah, still gonna do it, still gonna do it,' kind of stormed into the studio, pinned him up against the mixing desk, and just kind of blurted it all out. 'Er, Scott, well, I've just got to apologise for something, because, like, OK, at the end of the song, like I make a reference to *'Til The Band Comes In*, right, in a list of crap things, and, what I was trying, y'know, obviously . . .' and just kind of said all this stuff . . . and at first he just looked at me in a very mystified way, like, 'What is this nutter ranting on about?' And then it kind of clicked with him what I was on about, and he said, 'Well, gee thanks guys, that's the way you repay me!' I think he doesn't actually own any of his old records so I think he'd kind of forgotten he'd made that one. But for me, it was embarrassing."[577]

Moving from the ridiculous to the sublime, the beautiful, affecting 'Roadkill' is yet another high point. "One of my favourite songs on the record," says Jarvis. "It's got a nice fragile feeling to it that suits the slightly morbid lyrics. It's a pretty sad song. I didn't want it to be, 'Let's all fucking slash us wrists,' so it's got a delicate feel which stops it getting too maudlin. Lyrically, it's about the death of a relationship . . . as they all usually are."[578]

It was also another track that bore the mark of Walker. "He just slowed [it] down to this funereal pace," says Jarvis, "and I thought, 'That's terrible Scott.' But he said 'No, you've gotta do it,' because he had this idea that he wanted to get this guy to play electric cello over it. He said you've got to slow it down because you've got to give it space for this thing to exist in it. So he was right.[579]

"That was one of the most satisfying ones to do, because all of that song was recorded at the same time, except for the cello stuff, so I did the singing at the same time as playing the guitar, and so that really was just capturing the performance of it . . . and so it's got a certain edginess to it, because I am not a very good guitarist, and especially if I'm singing at the same time I become a pretty inept guitarist, so it always seems like it's on the verge of breaking down, so I think that gives it a certain kind of tension to it which is quite good."[580]

From the moment that 'Sunrise' ignited Reading 2000, it was obvious that it could only provide the perfect climax to the next Pulp album. And it did, with Jarvis' few simple lines tying together all the album's themes of rebirth and rejection of cynicism, while the immense instrumental section completely rewrites the golden rule that if the guitar solo's the best part of the song, it's probably not a very good song: 'Sunrise' is amazing.

Jarvis: "They say the darkest hour is just before the dawn, don't they? I don't know if it's true, but they say it. I always hate it when you've been at an all-night party and then suddenly the sun starts coming up and you think, 'Why didn't I go home an hour ago?' You feel unnatural because every other creature's just waking up and the birds start doing the dawn chorus and you feel out of step with nature. So on a simple level the song's just about trying to react to the sunrise in a better way and not to screw things up for yourself.[581]

"Coca-Cola wanted to use 'Sunrise' for this TV ad, and I guess they expected us to say yes. But I thought, 'It's about some kind of new dawn. Do I want to hear that song and think about Coke?' So I said they couldn't use it. And they got a load of musicians to write a new song which is uncannily similar. But I'm glad we didn't let them have it. It would have been against my beliefs."[582]

Considering the three-year struggle involved in its creation, one would almost expect *We Love Life* to be a forced, hopeless mess of a record, the sound of a band scraping the bottom of the barrel. It's anything but: taken as a whole, *We Love Life* is a beautiful, uplifting, intelligent, moving piece of work. Against the odds, it may even be Pulp's best album.

Up to a point, the press agreed: *We Love Life* was album of the month in *Mojo* (*"Musically, it's the richest record of Pulp's career . . . There is disgust, dysfunction, disappointment, death. But there is also a feeling that Pulp have . . . found what really matters at the heart of it all. Pulp's most brutal album – and also their most redemptive. It's death or glory time."*[583]), received four out of five in *Q* (*"The artistic success that* This Is Hardcore *wasn't . . . Cocker's treasurable wit and the band's seventh album have taken a corporation bus ride out for strange, poetic interludes among the trees and the undergrowth. Long may Pulp's forestry commission continue."*[584]), seven out of 10 in *NME* (*"A grandiose, symphonic affair buoyed by succinct orchestration and white-light choral interludes . . . if this is to be Pulp's swansong – and that's got to be a possibility, whatever Cocker claims in interviews – at least they can go out with their heads held high."*[585]), five out of five in *Uncut*, album of the week in *The Observer*, five out of five in the *Guardian* . . . thanks to the almost universally positive press response the album received (with some ecstatic live reviews and high-profile interviews thrown in for good measure), *We Love Life* managed to transcend the single's failure and a general lack of airplay to enter the album chart at a very respectable number six.

That it didn't climb any higher is probably a fair reflection of the fact that, as Nigel Coxon points out, "The environment had gone from bad to worse on all fronts for that record. Within the record company and probably without, to be fair." Ultimately, Island Universal's sloppy handling of Pulp's comeback couldn't be held solely to blame for the fact that Pulp were no longer one of the biggest bands in Britain: in the three years they'd been away, the New Pop – a rising tide at the time of *This Is Hardcore* – had become all-pervading, with TV programmes like *Pop Idol*, tragically, defining the *Zeitgeist*. Never mind Pulp; if there was anyone from the old guard who was going to make sense in 2001, it was Kylie, and sure enough, there she was at number one the week *We Love Life* came out.

Of course, while the pop world had become, um, poppier, Pulp had moved in the opposite direction: Jarvis, 1995's perfect pop star, was now older, more drably dressed, and somewhat less inclined to slap the foundation on so he'd look all right on the cover of *Smash Hits*. And much as it may or may not have helped his career to cartoonify himself again, he was mercifully interested in doing no such thing: the closest he got to the pop world in 2001 was appearing on *CD:UK* and being interviewed by Cat Deeley, who asked him what he thought of Robbie Williams and Britney Spears. His response? A weary sigh, followed by, "They're all right." The Jarvis who had delighted a nation with his *"I HATE WET WET WET"* sign had most definitely left the building – if you want him he's still there, incarcerated in wax in the Rock Circus.

"I don't slag other bands off anymore," he told *NME* a few weeks later. "I just can't be bothered. I mean, to me, Robbie Williams and Britney Spears . . . I don't recognise it as music, really. I don't want to be snobbish about it. I just think, you know, it's OK for children, but I can't take it seriously as music."[586]

But then, a lack of sympathy with the current musical climate didn't mean Pulp weren't bothered about anyone hearing the record they'd just spent three years making. "They were probably more bothered than they were letting on," says Nigel Coxon. "I think they wanted it to do well, because of course you do, but the commercial side, I don't know whether that was a main consideration for them for quite a while. I think it was just a case of making a record that's worthwhile, and I think ultimately that comes from Jarvis."

Jarvis: "I'm really pleased we made another record. We could have stopped after *This Is Hardcore* but I think it was worthwhile doing another one. Regardless of how it does, I think it's kind of relevant. I'm not saying it's cutting edge, or bleeding edge, or whatever they say nowadays. But I don't think it's redundant. That pleases me."[587]

Chapter 18

Between October and December 2001, Pulp marked the release of *We Love Life* with their first full-scale tour in three years. Through the scattered but consistently triumphant live appearances of 1999, 2000 and the earlier part of 2001, the thought had occurred more than once that, what with them being so good at playing amazing live shows in such wildly differing situations as Venice, Reading, Hay and Homelands, they really should be playing more than four shows a year. The public obviously agreed: although the venues were admittedly smaller than the arenas of 1998, the 14 dates (11 around Britain plus shows in Paris, Barcelona and Dublin), which culminated in three nights at Brixton Academy, constituted the first Pulp tour to sell out since 1996.

Throughout the tour, the band seemed confident and energised, obviously relishing the prospect of finally being able to get out of the studio and back in front of an audience. The stage was again decorated with Jarvis' impressive video projections, while the set list was dominated by selections from *We Love Life*, plus a handful of well-chosen oldies including 'Live Bed Show', 'This Is Hardcore', 'Babies' and, unexpectedly, 'Laughing Boy'. 'Common People', on the other hand, was conspicuous by its absence, being played just the once, at the final Brixton date. "We don't intend to do it on this tour," Jarvis explained to the *Sheffield Star*'s John Quinn in November. "We're trying to get away from it and we don't just want to do what people expect."[588]

The move was an admirable and necessary one – Pulp needed to be recognised as the creative force that they were in 2001, not as a Britpop nostalgia act. In the end, the only way of hammering home the quality of *We Love Life* was to make sure people heard the songs, and the only way of doing that was to make sure that they weren't overshadowed by some crowd pleasing, do-your-funny-little-dance hits routine.

And it worked, with *NME*'s Mark Beaumont declaring Brixton to be "the gig of the year", adding that ". . . the defiant military stomp of 'Weeds' sounds like the United Front Of Bedwetters marching on The Hague, 'Bad Cover Version' (with its spite-fuelled List Of Rehashed

Crap) is the Christmas Number One with a gun in its belt and as 'Sunrise' reaches its wig-out climax, Jarvis needs only a ten-foot lasso microphone and bubble perm and he *is* Roger Daltrey . . . The achievement is mighty: from the stuff of Ground Force, Pulp have wrung tearful genius. But then Jarvis could be here next year in a grubby boiler suit plugging an album called *Pulp Love Grouting* and he'd still be God."[589]

The year ended with TV appearances on the Jo Whiley and Jonathan Ross shows, and respectable showings for *We Love Life* in various music publications' end-of-year polls. The feeling was that, regardless of whether or not they were still one of the biggest bands in the world, Pulp were back, and still needed, and still important. The creeping sense that there might not ever be any more Pulp that had pervaded in the years of virtual silence after *This Is Hardcore* was gone.

"If we hadn't made another album after *This Is Hardcore*," says Jarvis, "if Pulp was a film it would have been a really bad ending to it, and the executives at the studio would have made you go in and change it. For me, I just wanted to prove that wasn't the end of the line."

"As it turned out," says Nigel Coxon, "I think Jarvis was actually quite happy about Pulp after the album came out. I think he's got a lot happier about his life in general, but I think he felt he'd put out a good record. I think he was quite upbeat about Pulp, and upbeat about a lot of things."

Even so, during 2001 there had been quite a few examples of Jarvis working on music outside Pulp. As well as writing the pleasant, gently Faces-esque 'Everybody Loves The Underdog' with Steve and Antony Genn for the latter's soundtrack to the film *Mike Bassett England Manager*, he'd also been heard contributing vocals to a great cover version of the Jimmy Webb song 'This Is Where I Came In' on the Bristol band Alpha's *South* EP. "I was pleased with that because it's kind of scary for me to actually have to sing sometimes. It's kind of a complicated song, I could've copped out and spoken it or whatever. But I actually thought, 'I'm going to attempt to sing this . . . fucker.' I eventually, after about a year-and-a-half, managed it."[590]

With Nick, Steve and Mark, he'd also written a song called 'Sliding Through Life On A Charm' for Marianne Faithfull's album, *Kissin' Time*. "He and I were passing each other in a corridor in a television studio," explains Faithfull, "and I'd been trying to write this fucking song for 20 years, always getting stuck because I couldn't find a fucking rhyme. So I grabbed him and said, 'Now look, I want you to take this title and go and write a song from it.' And off he went. And then it took another year and a half before I understood the song enough to record it. That was the first song I got [for the album], and I've managed to build everything around it like a beautiful jewel."[591]

The result was a storming, slightly 'Glory Days'-ish number with some wonderfully spiteful, self-referential (to Marianne, that is, not Jarvis) lyrics: *"I am a muse, not a mistress, not a whore . . . Suburban shits who want some class all queue up to kiss my ass; And I was only trying to please – I never got any royalties . . ."*

"She's much more appealing to younger people," said Jarvis. "I mean, do you wanna be Cilla Black or do you wanna be Marianne Faithfull? I hope the song really comes across as a real two-fingers up to people."[592]

In January 2002, with Pulp having spent the past three months higher in the public eye (and the public's affections) than they had been in years, and *We Love Life* still relatively fresh news, the time was arguably right to release a second single from the album, but this didn't happen.

"To be honest," says Nigel Coxon, "within the record company there was probably a big debate over whether to put anything else out at all off it. It would have been sort of, 'Well, we've gone with that, that didn't happen, the album's come and gone – next.' You have to understand corporate record mentality, and a lot of that goes on, especially if it's not brand new anymore. It's this insatiable machine, you now. They just want new stuff, to be fed new hits, all the time. It's just this overriding idea that Pulp are an old has-been, and, 'Yeah, OK, let's put out the record . . . oh dear, no hits. Next.' "

In the event, Pulp and Rough Trade did manage to persuade Island not to write the album off after just one single, and it was agreed that 'Bad Cover Version' would be the band's next A-side. However, the protracted wrangling over the release meant that it would eventually be put back to April 2002 – a full six months after the appearance of the album.

As far as making any real impact with a *We Love Life*-based record was concerned, it was obvious that 'Bad Cover Version' was very much the last chance saloon. The result was that the band decided to pull out all the stops with the release, making it the kind of single that 'The Trees'/ 'Sunrise' should have been. The video, directed by Jarvis, expanded on the theme of bad cover versions in a wonderful pastiche of Band Aid's 'Do They Know It's Christmas?' video, with the song, hilariously, being sung by an army of celebrity look-alikes: The Bee Gees, Liam and Noel, Kylie, Craig David, Missy Elliot, Phil Collins, Paul McCartney, and even a Jarvis impersonator. The band themselves were reduced to the role of heavily disguised record producers – except, of course, for Jarvis himself, who puts in a sterling performance at the end as Brian May.

The single itself was similarly excellent: in place of pointless remixes, we had two new tracks on CD1, and, on CD2, yet more cover versions, albeit not bad ones at all – 'Disco 2000' sung by Nick Cave (in waltz time, as a ballad), and 'Sorted' turned into some sort of dance music thing by Moloko's Roisin Murphy.

The extra songs on CD1 were both remixed versions of tracks originally recorded during the Chris Thomas sessions in spring 2000. 'Yesterday' is a pleasant, swaying ballad, based around a folksy banjo riff, with lyrics apparently addressing the issue of what it's like to be Jarvis Cocker post-celebrity. However, rather than a *This Is Hardcore*-style diatribe about the horrors of life under the spotlight, he seems to be poking gentle fun at himself for flushing his career down the toilet: *"Yesterday you were the dogs', but then you blew it – you set your sights on the best of all, you got it, but you never knew it. Now you don't feel wronged or noble at all; just very stupid . . ."* The message, though, is ultimately an uplifting one, celebrating the fact that *"Yesterday's gone, so yesterday can't hurt you – nothing to live up to, you've got no one to pay . . ."*

'Forever In My Dreams', meanwhile, sees Jarvis playing the reluctant Romeo: *"I understand that you can't wait forever for me to decide what's on my mind. This attitude so cavalier will be the death of me I'm sure my dear, but in the meantime try not to think too badly of me. Because I'm in love with you, whatever that may mean. I believe we should be together now, and forever in my dreams."* The music, meanwhile, is a strange, beautiful piece, first performed by A Touch Of Glass and based around a syncopated, dreamlike soundscape dominated by Alasdair Molloy's wonderful glass harmonica.

If 'Bad Cover Version' had been released at any point in the decade prior to April 2002, its success would have been a near-certainty: sensible choice of A-side, classic video, great B-sides. As it was, it was the belated follow-up to a flop single and an album that had made some minor ripples but was now largely forgotten. Radio 1 therefore assumed (misguidedly, if understandably) that Pulp no longer had an audience, and decided they weren't going to play it – the first time a Pulp single hadn't been included on their playlist since 'Razzmatazz' (yes, they'd even played 'Trees'/ 'Sunrise'). Despite a valiant plug on *Top Of The Pops* in the week of release, 'Bad Cover Version' failed to chart any higher than number 27, and had dropped out of the Top 40 by the following week.

It was tragic in a way – the first time Pulp had explicitly tried to have a hit single since, perhaps, 'Disco 2000' was the point at which everybody else's patience finally ran out. Jarvis' comments in an interview a couple of weeks before 'Bad Cover Version' was released are rather poignant in retrospect: "We don't make music to get big sales, but I want more people to hear [*We Love Life*]. It's why we've made such an effort with the new video, to promote the album."[593]

" 'Bad Cover Version' was probably sort of a last throw of the dice," says Nigel Coxon. "Got no radio, fantastic video, but kind of all a bit . . . late."

It was a horrible irony that the next concert Pulp played, three days after the release of 'Bad Cover Version', was a memorial show for Scott Piering – the plugger who, with his company Appearing, was responsible for Pulp's first significant radio and TV exposure, promoting Pulp's releases from 'O.U.' and 'Babies' onwards. He had died of cancer in 2000.

"Scott Piering was the guy that took us on when nobody was interested in us at all," Jarvis told *nme.com*. "Because he was independent and chose what he wanted to work on, he worked really hard for us. The most extreme example of his behaviour was on 'Razzmatazz'. He went to Radio 1 with 'PULP' shaved into the back of his head. That's a bit beyond the call of duty!"[594]

The event, dubbed 4 Scott, took place at The Scala in London, with Pulp headlining a bill that also included Stereophonics, Placebo, Badly Drawn Boy, Embrace, Teenage Fan Club, Cerys Matthews and Luke Haines, all of whose TV and radio had been handled by Piering. Pulp closed the show with 'Sunrise', ending the event on a suitably celebratory, optimistic note.

By May, the festival season was approaching once more. After the obliga-tory exotic foreign dates (this year: Primavera in Barcelona and Alternatif in Istanbul), June saw Pulp embark on an even more unusual set of outdoor concerts: five shows in a series of forests (or rather, in clearings and fields immediately next to forests) up and down Britain, sponsored by the Forestry Commission.

"It was the Forestry Commission's idea," explained Jarvis, "to appeal to young people more. Maybe they'd cottoned on to the nature feel of *We Love Life*. My worry is we might have to keep the noise down. Don't want to frighten the squirrels, do we?[595] I'm glad they asked us to do it. We did a very conventional tour last year, so conventional it beggared belief. Every venue had a roof on it . . . So straight it was almost weird. But the songs were already about more natural things and we'd wanted to do them – not in a more casual way, like 'Let's record a song while we're lying on the floor,' or whatever – but in a less structured, less uptight way."[596]

Was the conversion now complete? Had Pulp, once the definitive Sheffield band, then the ultimate observers of the urban and suburban foibles of London, finally been driven by the pressures of fame to become tree-dwelling, bypass-protesting hippies, pitched somewhere between The Levellers and Jethro Tull?

Of course not. One look at the *Big Issue*'s photoshoot of Jarvis on the eve of the tour, clowning around on an adventure obstacle course at Thetford Forest in Surrey, tells the whole story: you can take Pulp out of the city, but you can't take the city out of Pulp. Tarzan did not wear a rainbow-striped jumper with purple velvet flares.

"The thing about cities," said Steve, "is you know which shops are open at 6 am if you want an early bottle of milk but you don't know how to build a fire or anything like that. So it can be quite scary being out of cities . . . a new experience."[597]

"You can walk out and there's no noise and you think, 'Wow'," added Jarvis. "But weird things happen in forests as well. Doggin' and Pikin' . . ."[598]

Steve: "In England, you get people meeting up in country parks for wife-swapping and stuff. It was in the papers. I don't want to dwell on it, but . . ."[599]

"We're coming out into the countryside," concluded Jarvis, "but always looking at it from a town-dweller's point of view. Besides, Sheffield's got lots of countryside around it, you can drive out and 10 minutes later you're in the Peak District. It wasn't like we were out hiking every weekend but the countryside was always there. We were always aware of it and missed it when we didn't have it nearby. Maybe the new songs just reflect the fact I've bought a car, so I've been able to go out into the countryside. The next record is going to be about interplanetary space travel."[600]

The concerts themselves were fine, a welcome change for both the band and the fans from the routine of pokey rock venues and huge corporate festivals. Perhaps because of the location, there did seem to be a curiously high incidence of middle-aged couples with picnic hampers in the audience (maybe National Trust members got discount tickets), while backstage, walks in the wood and barbecues seemed to be the order of the day, as did the unexpected inclusion in the set lists of a handful of oldies that had barely been heard for a decade or more: 'I Want You' at Roseisle, Dalby and Thetford, 'Little Girl (With Blue Eyes)' at Sherwood, and an amazing version of 'My Legendary Girlfriend' at Bedgebury.

An even more unexpected blast from the past occurred at Roseisle: an onstage appearance from none other than Tim Allcard. Allcard had remained a friend of the group since leaving in 1984, and in recognition of the fact that it was Midsummer's Day and the group were playing in

Scotland, not too far from the islands where the film *The Wicker Man* was set, during the song 'Wickerman' he joined the group onstage, bringing with him a giant 'wicker man' that he'd constructed during the day from twigs and branches, and blowing his horn at appropriate points in the song.

Somehow, the concerts did seem to have a strange 'end of an era' air to them. Ancient songs and Tim Allcard aside, the setlist was more of a 'Greatest Hits' selection than the autumn 2001 tour, with *We Love Life* songs like 'Minnie', 'Bob Lind', 'Wickerman' and 'Origin Of The Species' either dropped or played very occasionally, to make room for the likes of 'Sorted', 'Joyriders', 'Something Changed' and 'Common People'. There was no explicit suggestion that this might be amongst the last times we'd get to hear these songs, but, for the first time, the undercurrent seemed to be there.

On June 28, 2002, shortly after the tour, the undercurrent seemed to become more of a real possibility when the 'Pulp Press Office' released a statement via the band's official website.

> *"Pulp are to end their relationship with Universal/Island Records after their next album, which will be a Greatest Hits package scheduled for the autumn.*
>
> *Keen to avoid the suspicious flannel which usually attends such partings of the ways, the band are attempting to be as straightforward as possible about events without boring the arse off everyone. Put simply, the option for the band's next (fifth) album with Universal/Island was pretty expensive (record contracts being structured with ascending advances); Island proffered a re-negotiation and Pulp said, "No, ta," preferring to walk away.*
>
> *Pulp play at the Eden Project on July 5, Reading Festival on August 23, Leeds Festival on August 24 and Glasgow Gig On The Green in Scotland on August 25. Thereafter they are planning a big event for the autumn.*
>
> *The band may then take a breather, but since they generally have about half-a-dozen things on the go at once, I wouldn't bank on it."*[601]

Oh.

Only a few months before, we'd been informed (through the fan club) that Pulp had agreed to stay with Island for the next album, which they were going to start writing in spring 2002. What had gone on that had made them change their minds?

Nigel Coxon: "Again it was a very badly handled situation. They were told that they were getting their option picked up. After the album there was quite a rumour/possibility that Jarvis was thinking about going solo. There was probably a time around the album where you might have thought that might be the last Pulp album, but after it came out, I think he got upbeat about Pulp again.

"I think the record company probably wouldn't have minded if he wanted to do a solo thing, but they did actually say to the management that they would pick up the next option regardless. It was gonna happen. And then there was a decision made even higher up, apparently that the guy who'd made the decision to pick up the option actually couldn't do it, so there was this whole, trying to backtrack and re-negotiate the deal and bring the level down, to which Pulp kind of went, 'Thanks but no thanks.'

"I think they just thought, 'Well, you told us you were going to pick it up, now you're telling us you're not, and we think we'll plough our own furrow, thank you, because we don't really know what we're going to do next anyway. We'd almost like the freedom of not necessarily being tied to you.' Even though I think they probably felt really angry about the way it was handled."

Fair enough. It would be fairly uncontroversial to say that Island's 'campaign' for *We Love Life* had been a total disaster from start to finish: shelving the album for six months, interfering in choices of singles, half-hearted promotion, needing to be *persuaded* to release a second single from the album. With their original deal at an end, no one could blame them for wanting to walk away.

But where did that leave Pulp? The press release neatly avoided any specifics with regard to future records, or what they would be doing after the end of 2002. Apparently the band weren't officially splitting, but a subsequent announcement that the fan club would be ceasing all operations after the end of the year didn't paint the most encouraging picture.

When the penultimate *Pulp People* newsletter appeared in August, things looked a little clearer, with fan club president Alex (presumably somewhere near the horse's mouth) explaining that, "Pulp aren't splitting up, they are simply taking time out to do other things, a desire which coincided nicely with the revised offer from Island, perhaps making it easier for them to say, 'No.' As you know, the group have always had several non-Pulp projects on the go, and in a way this is an extension of that, but with no time limit for a return to the studio."[602]

Change was definitely in the air – brought on in part, no doubt, by the fact that, on July 13, 2002, the unthinkable happened: Jarvis Cocker got married. Although he'd split from Camille Bidault-Waddington the year before, it seemed things were very much back on. The ceremony took place in an idyllic village in north-western France. The groom wore a grey-blue velvet suit by Marc Jacobs and was seen at the reception performing an impromptu version of 'Purple Haze' with Richard Hawley, and supplying a French translation of the lyrics to 'Smoke On The Water'.

"It was a good party and everything. It was more stressful than I thought. It was like throwing a party, but more. So I found meself worrying about things like the time it was taking people to get served to have their food. Stuff like that. We had this local French band and they really got me goat. I was trying to get everybody to go up to the disco in the woods and have a dance so I went over to the band and said, 'It'd be really nice if you could go up there and start playing, everybody'll hear the music and like the Pied Piper, they'll be drawn.' And they said [austerely], 'We are waiting for our coffee.' And they wouldn't go and play! I said, 'I'll bring you a fucking flask,' which I don't think they really understood.

"When I was younger I never thought that I would [get married] because of me mum and dad getting divorced and because just about all the marriages around our area in Sheffield broke up. So I just thought, 'Well, there's no point in that at all.' When you make a decision like that at say, nine or 10, it's like it lodges in your mind, you don't question it in a way. And it took me a long time to 'get over it', as they'd say in America. And in the end, I was quite surprised to find myself proposing marriage. But I'm really happy I did. It's good to surprise yourself now and again."[603]

He didn't waste any time either: by October, it had been announced that Camille was pregnant. The baby, it transpired, was due on April 13, 2003 – which, as Jarvis points out, "is nine months to the day from our wedding. I don't believe in sex before marriage but once you are – *yes!*[604] I'm delighted, really, really pleased. Camille had a bit of morning sickness for a while but she's fine now. I can't wait."[605]

At least there was enough Pulp left to keep us going for the rest of the year. The forest concerts were followed by a show at the amazing Eden Project in Cornwall, and a return to the Reading and Leeds Festivals at the end of August. The concerts were typically mighty, with spirited renditions of all the favourites made all the more poignant by the fact that it was now common knowledge that Pulp, for the foreseeable future at least, was about to come to an end.

September and October saw a scattering of ever more unlikely public appearances from Jarvis. He'd already been spotted on *Celebrity Stars In Their Eyes* in August, doing a disturbingly convincing (and extremely funny) impersonation of Rolf Harris, singing 'Two Little Boys'. Apparently it was part of the deal that he would appear on the show after the *Stars In Their Eyes* people had helped him out with lookalikes for the 'Bad Cover Version' video. The expression on his face at the end of the show when it transpired that he'd won and would have to do his 'turn' again was priceless.

"I decided to do Rolf Harris just because I thought me glasses were quite similar, so it wouldn't take much effort. The only other serious contender was Lionel Richie, I was gonna do 'Hello', but that was . . . complicated. Then I found me voice wasn't that dissimilar to Rolf's, which was worrying, really. Then the joke of it was that I won! Because it was kind of done out of obligation I didn't pay attention at the bit where they tell you where to go. They've got all these different staircases. You come through that tunnel, then you leave by that staircase, but you must stop halfway and wave at the camera, and then, if you win, you come down this staircase. So I think I tried to get back down the cloudy tunnel instead of going up the wavy staircase. But I enjoyed it in the end, good fun. It was . . . an experience."[606]

Odder still was Jarvis' appearance with Richard Hawley at the Royal Festival Hall on September 22, supporting Lee Hazelwood. The two had already contributed a track during 2002 to the Hazelwood tribute album *Total Lee*, an enjoyably sleazy version of his song 'A Cheat', described by Hawley as "electrobilly", which sounds like it was possibly recorded in the same amount of time it took to play. For the Royal Festival Hall show, the two, with Jason and Ross from sometime Pulp support act The Fat Truckers, performed 'A Cheat' and another Hazelwood song, 'Pour Man', plus Hawley's 'Oh My Child (pt. 1)', and three experimental, semi-electronic numbers with heavily distorted vocals from Jarvis. Of these, 'Rod Of Iron' contained the repeated line *"Doh, a deer, a female deer"* and concluded with the words *"Ruled my woman with a rod of iron"*. The main lyric to 'The Heavy' seemed to be *"Don't fuck with me 'cos I'm a heavy-weight"*. Jarvis began the performance by karate-chopping some balsa wood in two, and ended it by smashing a sugar-glass bottle over his head. It was a bit silly.

"There's this bloke who messes about in my cellar making music," explains Jarvis, "and instead of paying rent we just do songs together now and again. So for that night at the Royal Festival Hall we thought, 'Let's play some of that, for a laugh.' And most of the people who reviewed it didn't seem to think it was a laugh at all. Just showing a different side of my character, that was all. I've shown my gentle side, now I'm showing the hard side."[607]

"The reviews were humourless," noted Hawley. "When you get bands that are pop star mates or whatever, it's fair enough if people want to have a pop, but they just didn't see the funny side. I was pissing myself at Jarvis doing these karate chops on balsa wood. That sums him up, actually. We rehearse, seriously, and he turns up with pieces of balsa wood and a bottle made out of sugar to smash over his head."[608]

The following month, recordings of 'The Heavy', 'Rod Of Iron' and 'Branded' from the concert were released on a limited-edition 7″ single by Rough Trade Records, credited to a group called Relaxed Muscle. "For the purposes of Relaxed Muscle," offered Jarvis by way of semi-explanation, "I'm Darren Spooner and Richard's Wayne Marsden, which is the name of a kid who bullied me at school. As far as I'm concerned they're just a band from Doncaster. I wanted to do something off-the-cuff, just for the laugh."[609]

And then there was the modelling he did for British designer Marc Jacobs (stripey jumpers) and, bloody hell, a TV ad in October for BT Broadband internet. On which he dangled from a giant lamppost, and fell off it. "Again, it was part of me new macho image. Hanging 25 foot above the ground, doing my own stunts. The people who did the advert are Hammer & Tongs, who we did a couple of videos with a few years ago. They did that Blur 'Coffee And TV' video and they're quite nice, y'know. I've been approached by a lot of people to do adverts so I thought I'd go with that one 'cos if they were doing it it'd be quite good. And I thought, 'Go on, then. Not doing anything that week.' And it's quite funny. As far as I knew it was written with me expressly in mind, but maybe I'm labouring under some illusion there.

"They made a really big lamp-post, taller than a normal one. I have to admit I was on wires, there was a crane with wires hanging down and then they just got rid of them on a computer. So I'm not that 'ard."[610]

The thought occurred that if he'd shown the same willingness to make an arse of himself on the telly during autumn 2001 as he was in autumn 2002, then *We Love Life* might have sold a few more copies. Still, at least he was enjoying himself.

"I was as surprised as anyone by the BT thing," says Nigel Coxon, "but they've obviously paid him very handsomely, and he's taken a pragmatic approach in his post-marital state. The Marc Jacobs thing I think came through Camille. He's really just doing what the fuck he likes, and I think he is actually having a really good time, being a tit if he wants to. I think he's happier than he's been for years. He was quite buoyant about life after the album, and therefore he's got a favourable view of the album. Just like *Hardcore* was the nervous breakdown record, *We Love Life* was, as I'm sure you can gather from the topics, very much a reaffirmation of sorts, look around you and see things in a slightly different way, and think it's great. Reaffirmation, rediscovery is the theme I think."

November and December 2002 were devoted to a final rounding-up exercise. Pulp's future was still undecided, but with Jarvis having decided to settle with Camille in France to raise their child, it was a foregone conclusion that there wasn't going to be anything for a long time. However, when asked if the band were splitting up, Jarvis still refused to commit: "I haven't a clue to be honest.[611] With me moving to France, and Candida going off on a jaunt round the world – English-speaking countries only, she's not backpacking – it's gonna be next September before we can get back together. So we'll see how we feel then. See what everybody feels like. I just think it's better like that. Otherwise it gets a bit like Communist Russia, a five-year plan. And I don't think life's like that. The good thing about life is you make it up a bit as you go along."[612]

A cynic would suggest that it's typical of Pulp's attitude towards their career of late that they can't even be arsed splitting up properly, but on reflection it's an admirable way of doing things, and, in a way, typically Pulp. Rather than the typical ugly rock approach of splitting up loudly and finally and then reforming 18 months later (cf The Verve, every Cure album since about 1989), they at least had the honesty to say they weren't sure what they were doing next, and they'd see how things would go. Even if they are splitting up, at least it's in a fairly dignified, understated way.

Pulp's final Island release, *Hits*, appeared on November 13. As far as such releases go, it was a pleasantly straightforward one: all the singles from 'Babies' to 'Bad Cover Version' (minus 'Mis-Shapes', Jarvis having decided that, "I really don't like it at all. It sounds really minty . . . just a bit rubbish."[613]), plus one new track: 'Last Day Of The Miners' Strike'.

"We had to do a new song contractually but we wanted to do something good, and that wouldn't seem too out of place with everything else on the record. It didn't seem appropriate to go off on some speed garage trip at the end of the album. Candida came up with the Burt Bacharach sample, but the words were problematic. I'd had this dream where I was listening to this John Lennon song, woke up and realised it wasn't a Lennon song; I wrote it down and tried to remember the tune.

"It's a bit iffy writing about the Miners' Strike when I don't know that much about it. When it was on, Russell had just joined the group and he was going out on pickets all the time, but I had no interest in politics at the time. I kinda regretted it later. I tried to make the song more allusive rather than some Billy Bragg thing."[614]

Surprisingly, *Hits* sold fairly miserably, entering the album charts at number 71. Perhaps it was swamped somewhat in the pre-Christmas glut of Greatest Hits albums, but part of the explanation is surely that, in commercial terms at least, the idea of a Pulp Hits album is rendered rather redundant by the fact that there's already one out there: *Different Class*.

The kind of person who buys Greatest Hits records is the kind of person who wants 'Common People' and "that year 2000 song", will therefore already have picked up *Different Class* at some point, and isn't going to be bothered about getting another CD that, like *Different Class*, contains Pulp's four or so legitimate hits, plus a load of other obscure stuff. No matter how good they are, the person in the street is unlikely to buy a Greatest Hits record on the strength of the inclusion of 'Razzmatazz' or 'The Trees'.

Even though a 'Best-Of' type approach would perhaps have given a fairer representation than a straight singles rundown, *Hits* still stands as an overview of one of the very best bands of our time. "The thing I like about it most," reflected Jarvis, "is it just seems a bit slap-dash, it doesn't seem too contrived. Everyone's become so preoccupied with how something's packaged and what angle are we going off and what niche are we aiming this at and let's do market research . . . I'm quite pleased that we've managed to be quite . . . awkward. Not awkward, nasty, but not really fitting in. And just making it up as we went along. We were never . . . Hear'Say. So that's quite good. A beacon of inefficiency. In a rapidly stream-lining world. I like that. At least it seems human."[615]

Even more welcome than the *Hits* compilation was its DVD counterpart – an embarrassment of visual riches, with all the promo clips, the *First Time?* and *Hardcore* documentaries (the latter of which had never been shown on TV), a wonderful selection of home movies, a remarkable interview and performance of 'Mark Of The Devil' from a long-lost video documentary called *Sheffield Bands '84–'85* and, perhaps most entertainingly of all, a section called 'TV Madness', compiling years of ridiculous moments from Pulp's years of light entertainment ubiquity.

"You see yourself on *Richard & Judy* and it's just funny," says Jarvis. "Half the things I can't even remember, that's the scary thing. An Italian TV thing when a bloke reads out the entire lyrics of 'Common People', in Italian, while we're standing there waiting to play the song, and everyone's looking right bored, thinking, 'What the fuck's he on about here?' Until I saw it, I would never have remembered that we did it. All this stuff. Documentary evidence. And none of it's in my head at all."[616]

The final curtain came on Saturday, December 14, 2002. The "big event for the autumn" mentioned in that fateful press release had become a big event in the winter, when Pulp played their final concert for the foreseeable future at the Auto festival.

Auto took place at the Magna Science Adventure Centre – a huge converted steelworks on the outskirts of Rotherham. The idea for the festival had been Steve's, taking as its inspiration the Sonar Festival in Barcelona; for the night, Magna was converted into a giant venue with four stages, featuring a wide range of left field bands, DJs and filmmakers including Pulp, Röyksopp, Lemon Jelly, LFO, Four Tet, The Bees, Baxter Dury, James Yorkston, The Kills, Zongamin, Jamie Lidell, Chris Coco . . . you get the idea.

It was a brave and ambitious project, but one with a slightly suspicious air: the other acts that were playing on the night may have been worthy in their own right, but what did they have in common with a major act like Pulp? Many of them were respected within certain spheres but largely unknown, and the audience crossover with Pulp was, as a rule, pretty small. So what were they doing on the same bill?

A cynic would suggest that, as it was widely known that this was going to be Pulp's last gig for the foreseeable future, and possibly ever, it was pretty certain that there would be plenty of people willing to crawl over broken glass to see it. Or, indeed, pay good money to spend hours in a freezing steelworks outside Rotherham with an hour-long bar queue and a catering choice that consisted of hot dogs or hot dogs, watching a load of obscure bands. Hence Pulp's long-suffering fan base were being used as a tool to finance Steve's vanity project – and even if this wasn't the case, it might have been a nice gesture if Pulp had presented us with a choice by playing a second 'farewell' concert in a sensible venue.

But any carping was rendered redundant the moment Pulp took the stage and it became blindingly apparent that they were about to give what may well have been the best performance of their career. Alongside familiar material from the past three albums, the audience were treated to versions of 'Lipgloss', 'Razzmatazz', '59 Lyndhurst Grove' and, wonderfully, 'Happy Endings' – none of which had been heard live for years. Every single song was attacked with the energy, dedication and passion of a hungry young band at the start of its career, making the whole event both hugely satisfying and highly poignant.

"This'll be the last time you see us for a while," Jarvis told the audience after the final, jubilant encore of 'Common People'. "But we may meet again, who knows?"[617]

And that was it.

SHELDON ROW, SHEFFIELD, 2002

There are no disused factories on The Wicker anymore. A few empty shops, a boarded-up pub and an old carpet warehouse that'll probably have been converted to luxury city centre flats by the time you read this, but that's about it. Indeed, as I stand here, on the site of the famous disused factory that Jarvis (and others) lived in many years ago, the thought occurs that it might even be quite a good place to build a recording studio. People have tried before, 15 or 20 years ago, but Victoria, where Pulp made their first record, had to contend with airborne noise coming through the mixing desk from neighbouring factories, and FON had to spend thousands on air conditioning to battle the intense heat that came through the floor from the blast furnace below. These days, the only noise you can hear comes from the traffic on the main road, taking people in and out of the centre of Sheffield.

FON, Victoria and the factory building where Jarvis used to live are all long gone. All that remains there is a square of wasteland, surrounded by bollards; some rubble, a bit of litter – oh, and a few weeds. It's been that way since the building was demolished at the end of the Eighties; give it a few more years and it'll be a car park.

Sheffield's industrial past; Pulp's ancient history. The future lies elsewhere. You won't get the answers to anything from hanging round empty patches of ground in dodgy parts of Sheffield. The past doesn't exist in order to be romanticised – it was probably horrible living here 20 years ago, just as it was probably horrible working here 50 years ago.

But still, the past exists, and you can hear its echoes in the present from time to time. No doubt the same will be true in the future. And you don't need to glorify the past in order to acknowledge that it's there; after all, if we don't understand the past and its relation to now, then how can we make sense of the present, each other and ourselves?

Anyway, that's enough about Pulp.

Sources

Introductory quote from interview with Jarvis by Adam Higginbotham, *Select*, October 1995

1   *Sorted* – interview with Jarvis by Lindsay Barker, *Guardian Weekend*, September 29, 2001
2   *Tree Hugger In Disguise?* – interview with Jarvis, *Telegraph Magazine*, May 25, 2002
3   ibid.
4   ibid.
5   Paul Lester: *Pulp: The Illustrated Story*, Hamlyn Books, 1996
6   *Sorted* – interview with Jarvis by Lindsay Barker, *Guardian Weekend*, September 29, 2001
7   Martin Aston: *Pulp*, Pan Books, London, 1996
8   Paul Lester: *Pulp: The Illustrated Story*, Hamlyn Books, 1996
9   Interview with Jarvis by Ben Thompson for *The Independent*, *circa* 1994/5
10 ibid.
11 Interview with Jarvis, *i-D*, *circa* 1994/5
12 *Cocker the North* – interview with Jarvis by Max Bell, *Vox*, May 1995
13 Paul Lester: *Pulp: The Illustrated Story*, Hamlyn Books, 1996
14 ibid.
15 *Pulp Fiction* – interview with Jarvis by Graham Fuller, *Interview*, July 1998
16 *Lifestyle of the Rich and Famous* – interview with Jarvis by Adam Higginbotham, *Select*, October 1995
17 *Pulp: Do You Remember The First Time?* – BBC Radio 1 documentary, March 15, 1998
18 *Boy and Bitch in the Same Breath* – interview with Jarvis by Nicola Barker, *Observer*, April 10, 1994
19 *Pulp Fiction* – interview with Jarvis by Graham Fuller, *Interview*, July 1998
20 *Jarvis Cocker Remembers* – interview with Jarvis by Stuart Maconie, *Select*, 1993
21 *Cash for Questions* – interview with Jarvis in Q, May 1998
22 ibid.
23 *Pulp Fiction* – interview with Jarvis by Graham Fuller, *Interview*, July 1998
24 *Pulp on Pulp* – interview with Jarvis by John Reed, *Record Collector*, November 1994
25 *Pulp: Do You Remember The First Time?* – BBC Radio 1 documentary, March 15, 1998
26 ibid.
27 Martin Aston: *Pulp*, Pan Books, London, 1996
28 *Pulp on Pulp* – interview with Jarvis by John Reed, *Record Collector*, November 1994
29 ibid.
30 *Cocker the North* – interview with Jarvis by Max Bell, *Vox*, May 1995
31 *The Q Interview* – interview with Jarvis by David Quantick, *Q*, *circa* 1996
32 Interview with Jarvis by Ann Scanlon, *Volume 10*, June 1994
33 *Pulp on Pulp* – interview with Jarvis by John Reed, *Record Collector*, November 1994
34 Interview with Marcus Featherby by Martin Lilleker, *Sheffield Star*, October 24, 1981
35 Martin Aston: *Pulp*, Pan Books, London, 1996
36 ibid.
37 *Pulp on Pulp* – interview with Jarvis by John Reed, *Record Collector*, November 1994
38 Martin Aston: *Pulp*, Pan Books, London, 1996

39   ibid.
40   *Pulp TV* – band interview by Andrew Smith, *The Face*, July 1995
41   *Welcome to Planet Jarvis* – interview with Jarvis by Jordan Paramor, *Smash Hits*, September 27–October 10, 1995
42   *NMX* fanzine, autumn 1980
43   *Pulp: Do You Remember The First Time?* – Radio 1 documentary, March 15, 1998
44   *Pulp on Pulp* – interview with Jarvis by John Reed, *Record Collector*, November 1994
45   Interview with Jarvis by Martin X-Russian, *NMX* fanzine, November 1981
46   *Pulp at Peel Acres* – BBC Radio 1 special, October 1, 1995
47   *NMX* fanzine, October 1981
48   *Pulp at Peel Acres* – BBC Radio 1 special, October 1, 1995
49   ibid.
50   ibid.
51   ibid.
52   ibid.
53   ibid.
54   Martin Aston: *Pulp*, Pan Books, London, 1996
55   ibid.
56   Unknown UK music press interview, *circa* 1996
57   ¹ Martin Aston, *Pulp*, Pan Books, 1996
     ² *The Q Interview* – interview with Jarvis by David Quantick, *Q*, November 1995
58   *Pulp on Pulp* – interview with Jarvis by John Reed, *Record Collector*, December 1994
59   ibid.
60   Interview with Jarvis by Martin X-Russian, *NMX* fanzine, autumn 1985
61   *Jarvis Cocker Remembers* – interview with Jarvis by Stuart Maconie, *Select*, December 1993
62   *Pulp on Pulp* – interview with Jarvis by John Reed, *Record Collector*, December 1994
63   Single review, *Sounds*, *circa* August 1983
64   Single review, unknown Sheffield fanzine, *circa* August 1983
65   *Pulp at Peel Acres* – BBC Radio 1 special, October 1, 1995
66   Martin Aston: *Pulp*, Pan Books, 1996
67   *Sheffield Star*, June 25, 1983
68   ibid.
69   *Pulp on Pulp* – interview with Jarvis by John Reed, *Record Collector*, December 1994
70   *Do You Remember The First Time?* – BBC Radio 1 documentary, March 15, 1998
71   *Pulp on Pulp* – interview with Jarvis by John Reed, *Record Collector*, December 1994
72   *Pulp* – interview with Pete Mansell by Pat Gilbert, *Record Collector*, January 1996
73   *Pulp on Pulp* – interview with Jarvis by John Reed, *Record Collector*, December 1994
74   *Pulp* – interview with Pete Mansell by Pat Gilbert, *Record Collector*, January 1996
75   *Monster Mash* – interview with Jarvis and Russell by William Shaw, *Zig Zag, circa* October 1984
76   *Pulp* – interview with Jarvis by Ann Scanlon, *Volume 10*, June 1994
77   *Do You Remember The First Time?* – BBC Radio 1 documentary, March 15, 1998
78   ibid.
79   Paul Lester: *Pulp – The Illustrated Story*, Hamlyn Books, 1996
80   Interview with Candida by Zoë Miller for official Pulp website, March 1997
81   *Do You Remember The First Time?* – BBC Radio 1 documentary, March 15, 1998
82   Interview with Candida, *Select, circa* 1995
83   *Pulp on Pulp* – interview with Jarvis by John Reed, *Record Collector,* December 1994
84   *Do You Remember The First Time?* – BBC Radio 1 documentary, March 15, 1998
85   ibid.
86   *Pulp* – interview with Pete Mansell by Pat Gilbert, *Record Collector*, January 1996

87   *No More Scrubbing Crabs* – interview with Jarvis and Russell, *Sheffield City Press, circa* October 1985

88   ibid.

89   *Pulp: Sheffield's Undiscovered Sensitive Souls* – interview with Jarvis, *Zig Zag, circa* autumn 1985

90   *Do You Remember the First Time?* – BBC Radio 1 documentary, March 15, 1998

91   ibid.

92   Jarvis' unused sleevenotes for the *Masters Of The Universe* compilation, April 19, 1994 – published in *Disco-Very* fanclub magazine, January 1995

93   Martin Aston: *Pulp*, Pan Books, 1996

94   Interview with Jarvis in *Select, circa* 1995

95   Pulp interview in unknown Sheffield fanzine, 1987

96   ibid.

97   *Canine Revenge* – interview with Jarvis and Russell by Paul Mathur, *Melody Maker,* mid-1986

98   Martin Aston: *Pulp*, Pan Books, 1996

99   *Pulp at Peel Acres* – BBC Radio 1 special, October 1, 1995

100 *Pulp Pull No Punches* – interview with Jarvis by Martin Lilleker, *Sheffield Star,* November 9, 1985

101 *My Teen Hair Horror* – interview with Jarvis by Mark Sutherland, *NME*, February 24, 1996

102 *Top of the Fops* – interview with Jarvis by Peter Paphides, *Time Out,* October 1995

103 Martin Aston: *Pulp*, Pan Books, 1996

104 *Cocker the North* – interview with Jarvis by Max Bell, *Vox*, May/June 1995

105 *The Q Interview* – interview with Jarvis by Phil Sutcliffe, *Q*, March 1996

106 *Cocker the North* – interview with Jarvis by Max Bell, *Vox*, May/June 1995

107 *Pulp Culture* – interview with Jarvis by Graham Fuller, *Interview*, July 1998

108 *Pulp on Pulp* – interview with Jarvis by John Reed, *Record Collector*, December 1994

109 *Canine Revenge* – interview with Jarvis and Russell by Paul Mathur, *Melody Maker,* mid-1986

110 *Pulp on Pulp* – interview with Jarvis by John Reed, *Record Collector*, December 1994

111 ibid.

112 ibid.

113 Martin Aston: *Pulp*, Pan Books, 1996

114 *My Teen Hair Horror* – interview with Jarvis by Mark Sutherland, *NME*, February 24, 1996

115 Interview with Steve by Zoe Miller for Rough Trade, official Pulp website, June 1996

116 *Pulp Fiction* – interview with Steve by Steven McCarthy, *DV8, circa* mid-1994

117 Interview with Steve by Zoe Miller for Rough Trade, official Pulp website, June 1996

118 Jarvis' onstage comment, Sheffield Leadmill, November 8, 1986

119 *Dogged Enthusiasm* – interview with Jarvis and Russell, *Impact, circa* 1986

120 Martin Aston: *Pulp*, Pan Books, 1996

121 Jarvis' onstage comment, Sheffield Leadmill, December 29, 1984

122 *Sounds* review of *Freaks* by Mr Spencer, *circa* May 1987

123 *Pulp on Pulp* – interview with Jarvis by John Reed, *Record Collector*, December 1994

124 Sleeve notes for *Fruitcakes & Furry Collars* LP, *Record Mirror, circa* September 1986

125 *Pulp* – interview with Jarvis by Ann Scanlon, *Volume 10*, July 1994

126 *Do You Remember The First Time?* – BBC Radio 1 documentary, March 15, 1998

127 ibid.

128 ibid.

129 *Top of the Fops* – interview with Jarvis by Peter Paphides, *Time Out*, October 1995

130 *Pulp* – interview with Jarvis by Ann Scanlon, *Volume 10*, July 1994

131 *Top of the Fops* – interview with Jarvis by Peter Paphides, *Time Out*, October 1995
132 *Do You Remember The First Time?* – BBC Radio 1 documentary, March 15, 1998
133 ibid.
134 *Pulp on Pulp* – interview with Jarvis by John Reed, *Record Collector*, December 1994
135 *Disco-Very* issue 2, January 1995
136 *Pulp on Pulp* – interview with Jarvis by John Reed, *Record Collector*, December 1994
137 Martin Aston: *Pulp*, Pan Books, 1996
138 Martin Aston: *Pulp*, Pan Books, 1996
139 *Sheffield Star*, November 8, 1986
140 *Pulp on Pulp* – interview with Jarvis by John Reed, *Record Collector*, December 1994
141 Martin Aston: *Pulp*, Pan Books, 1996
142 Interview with Jarvis and Russell, *Cut*, circa August 1987
143 *Pulp* – interview with Pete Mansell by Pat Gilbert, *Record Collector*, January 1996
144 Martin Aston: *Pulp*, Pan Books, 1996
145 ibid.
146 *Pulp* – interview with Pete Mansell by Pat Gilbert, *Record Collector*, January 1996
147 ibid.
148 Martin Aston: *Pulp*, Pan Books, 1996
149 ibid.
150 Interview with Jarvis by Ian Spence – unknown Sheffield fanzine, spring 1987
151 ibid.
152 *Jarvis Cocker Remembers* – interview with Jarvis by Stuart Maconie, *Select*, 1993
153 Martin Aston: *Pulp*, Pan Books, 1996
154 *Pulp on Pulp* – interview with Jarvis by John Reed, *Record Collector*, December 1994
155 *Living Next Door to Jarvis* – interview with Russell, Nick, Steve and Jarvis, *Select*, July 1995
156 ibid.
157 Interview with Russell, *The Hard Stuff*, BBC Radio Sheffield, May 16, 1987
158 Live review by David Bocking, *Cut*, circa May 1987
159 *Pulp on Pulp* – interview with Jarvis by John Reed, *Record Collector*, December 1994
160 *Cut*, circa August 1987
161 ibid.
162 *Pulp on Pulp* – interview with Jarvis by John Reed, *Record Collector*, December 1994
163 *Rebellious Jukebox* – interview with Jarvis, *Melody Maker*, circa August 1994
164 ibid.
165 ibid.
166 *Living Next Door to Jarvis* – interview with Russell, Nick, Steve and Jarvis, *Select*, July 1995
167 ibid.
168 ibid.
169 *Do You Remember The First Time?* – BBC Radio 1 documentary, March 15, 1998
170 Martin Aston: *Pulp*, Pan Books, 1996
171 ibid.
172 ibid.
173 *Disco-Very* issue 2
174 Paul Lester: *Pulp: The Illustrated Story*, Hamlyn, 1996
175 Martin Aston: *Pulp*, Pan Books, 1996
176 *Mea Pulpa* – interview with Jarvis by Deborah Orr, *Guardian Weekend*, October 21, 1995
177 *Do You Remember The First Time?* – Pulp documentary, BBC Radio 1, March 15, 1998
178 ibid.
179 ibid.

180 *Disco-Very* fanclub magazine, issue 2, January 1995
181 Martin Aston: *Pulp*, Pan Books, 1996
182 Paul Lester: *Pulp: The Illustrated Story*, Hamlyn, 1996
183 ibid.
184 Martin Aston: *Pulp*, Pan Books, 1996
185 *Sorted for Trees* – interview with Jarvis by Rob Fitzpatrick, *Ministry*, December 2001
186 ibid.
187 Martin Aston: *Pulp*, Pan Books, 1996
188 *Sorted for Trees* – interview with Jarvis by Rob Fitzpatrick, *Ministry*, December 2001
189 ibid.
190 *Pulp* – interview with Jarvis by Ann Scanlon, *Volume 10*, 1994
191 *Pulp on Pulp* – interview with Jarvis by John Reed, *Record Collector,* December 1994
192 Martin Aston: *Pulp*, Pan Books, 1996
193 *Pulp* – interview with Jarvis by Ann Scanlon, *Volume 10*, 1994
194 *Pulp on Pulp* – interview with Jarvis by John Reed, *Record Collector*, December 1994
195 ibid.
196 Martin Aston: *Pulp*, Pan Books, 1996
197 *Do You Remember The First Time?* – Pulp documentary, BBC Radio 1, March 15, 1998
198 ibid.
199 *Cocker the North* – interview with Jarvis by Max Bell, *Vox*, May/June 1995
200 Unknown interview with Jarvis, *circa* 1992
201 Interview with Jarvis by Martin Lilleker, *Sheffield Telegraph*, March 15, 1991
202 *Do You Remember The First Time?* – Pulp documentary, BBC Radio 1, March 15, 1998
203 Single review, *NME*, *circa* March 1991
204 *Do You Remember The First Time?* – Pulp documentary, BBC Radio 1, March 15, 1998
205 Single review, *Melody Maker*, *circa* March 1991
206 *Do You Remember The First Time?* – Pulp documentary, BBC Radio 1, March 15, 1998
207 ibid.
208 ibid.
209 ibid.
210 *Living Next Door to Jarvis* – interview with Russell, Nick, Steve and Jarvis by Clark Collis, *Select*, July 1995
211 Live review, *NME*, *circa* May 1991
212 Live review, *Melody Maker*, June 1991
213 Martin Aston: *Pulp*, Pan Books, 1996
214 Jarvis interview, *Hit the North*, BBC Radio 5, September 11, 1991
215 Live review, *NME*, *circa* October 1991
216 Interview with Steve by Zoe Miller, official Pulp website, June 1996
217 Live review, *Melody Maker, circa* November 1991
218 Live review, *Select*, February 1992
219 Martin Aston: *Pulp*, Pan Books, 1996
220 *Do You Remember The First Time?* – Pulp documentary, BBC Radio 1, March 15, 1998
221 ibid.
222 *Volume*, 1991
223 *Pulp on Pulp* – interview with Jarvis by John Reed, *Record Collector*, December 1994
224 Martin Aston: *Pulp*, Pan Books, 1996
225 *Jarvis Cocker Remembers* – Pulp article by Stuart Maconie, *Select*, October 1993ish
226 Single review, *Melody Maker*, early May 1992
227 Single review, *Vox*, *circa* May 1992
228 Single review, *NME*, *circa* May 1992
229 Single review, *Smash Hits*, *circa* May 1992
230 *Do You Remember The First Time?* – Pulp documentary, BBC Radio 1, March 15, 1998

231 Interview with Mark by Toby L, *rockfeedback.com*, autumn 2000
232 Martin Aston: *Pulp*, Pan Books, 1996
233 *Pulp* – band interview by Max Anderson, unknown publication, *circa* May 1992
234 LP review by Andrew Collins, *NME*, *circa* June 1992
235 ibid.
236 Martin Aston: *Pulp*, Pan Books, 1996
237 ibid.
238 ibid.
239 ibid.
240 *Do You Remember The First Time?* – Pulp documentary, BBC Radio 1, March 15, 1998
241 ibid.
242 ibid.
243 *Pulp Fiction* – interview with Jarvis by Jason Cohen, *Hits*, *circa* 1994
244 *Pulp on Pulp* – interview with Jarvis by John Reed, *Record Collector*, December 1994
245 *Babies* EP sleevenotes, October 1992
246 Interview with Jarvis by Zoe Miller, *I Spy* V96 concert programme, August 1996
247 *Pulp TV* – interview with Jarvis by Andrew Smith, *The Face*, July 1995
248 *Cocker the North* – interview with Jarvis by Max Bell, *Vox*, May/June 1995
249 Single review, *Smash Hits*, *circa* October 1992
250 *The Best Old Band in Britain* – interview with Jarvis by Simon Price, *Melody Maker*, *circa* February 1993
251 *Pulp on Pulp* – interview with Jarvis by John Reed, *Record Collector*, December 1994
252 *Pulp* – interview with Jarvis by Ann Scanlon, *Volume* 10, August 1994
253 *New to Q* – interview with Jarvis by Andy Gill, *circa* June 1994
254 *Pulp on Pulp* – interview with Jarvis by John Reed, *Record Collector*, December 1994
255 *Disco-Very* magazine, issue 2, January 1995
256 *Do You Remember the First Time?* – Pulp documentary, BBC Radio 1, March 15, 1998
257 ibid.
258 Live review, *Melody Maker*, *circa* February 1992
259 *The Best Old Band in Britain* – interview with Jarvis by Simon Price, *Melody Maker*, *circa* March 1993
260 *Melody Maker*, *circa* December 1993
261 *Pulp* – interview with Jarvis by Ann Scanlon, *Volume* 10, July 1994
262 Album review, *Melody Maker*, *circa* September 1993
263 Susan Wilson: *Pulp – The Tomorrow People*, UFO Music Books, 1996
264 *Sleazy Does It* – band interview by David Bennun, *Melody Maker*, *circa* November 1993
265 Interview with Jarvis, *The Crack*, *circa* 1994
266 *Disco-Very* issue 2, January 1995
267 *Beginner's F**** – band interview by Chris Roberts, *Melody Maker*, *circa* March 1994
268 *Disco-Very* issue 2, January 1995
269 *Pulp* – interview with Jarvis by Ann Scanlon, *Volume* 10, July 1994
270 Interview with Jarvis by Steve Lamacq and Jo Whiley, The Evening Session, BBC Radio 1, April 12, 1994
271 *Do You Remember The First Time?* – Pulp documentary, BBC Radio 1, March 15, 1998
272 *Pulp on Pulp* – interview with Jarvis by John Reed, *Record Collector*, December 1994
273 *Pulp* – interview with Jarvis by Ann Scanlon, *Volume* 10, July 1994
274 Paul Lester: *Pulp: The Illustrated Story*, Hamlyn Books, 1996
275 Interview with Jarvis by Steve Lamacq and Jo Whiley, The Evening Session, BBC Radio 1, April 12, 1994
276 Q, January 1995
277 *Do You Remember The First Time?* – Pulp documentary, BBC Radio 1, March 15, 1998
278 ibid.

279 Interview with Jarvis by Steve Lamacq and Jo Whiley, The Evening Session, BBC Radio 1, April 12, 1994

280 *Non-Stop Erotique Cabaret* – band interview by Chris Roberts, *Melody Maker, circa* May 1994

281 *Do You Remember The First Time?* – Pulp documentary, BBC Radio 1, March 15, 1998

282 ibid.

283 *Pulp* – interview with Jarvis by Taylor Parkes, *Melody Maker, circa* December 1994

284 *Do You Remember The First Time?* – Pulp documentary, BBC Radio 1, March 15, 1998

285 *Select, circa* August 1994

286 Interview with Jarvis by Miranda Sawyer, *The Observer*, 18 December 1994

287 *Pulp on Pulp* – interview with Jarvis by John Reed, *Record Collector*, December 1994

288 Jarvis' unused sleevenote for *Masters Of The Universe*, April 19, 1994, published in *Disco-Very*, January 1995

289 Martin Aston: *Pulp*, Pan Books, 1996

290 Interview with Jarvis by Miranda Sawyer, *The Observer*, December 18, 1994

291 *Pulp* – interview with Jarvis by Taylor Parkes, *Melody Maker, circa* December 1994

292 Live review, *Melody Maker, circa* October 1994

293 *Pulp* – interview with Jarvis by Taylor Parkes, *Melody Maker, circa* December 1994

294 Martin Aston: *Pulp*, Pan Books, 1996

295 Live review by Rupert Howe, *NME, circa* December 1994

296 Martin Aston: *Pulp*, Pan Books, 1996

297 ibid.

298 ibid.

299 ibid.

300 ibid.

301 *Essential Albums of the '90s – Different Class* documentary, BBC Radio 1, February 8, 1999

302 ibid.

303 ibid.

304 ibid.

305 ibid.

306 Martin Aston: *Pulp*, Pan Books, 1996

307 ibid.

308 ibid.

309 *You Ask the Questions* – interview with Jarvis, *The Independent*, April 11, 2002

310 Jarvis' onstage comment, Bristol University Anson Rooms, April 21, 1995

311 Jarvis' onstage comment, Reading Festival, August 27, 1994

312 *Essential Albums of the '90s – Different Class* documentary, BBC Radio 1, February 8, 1999

313 ibid.

314 Martin Aston: *Pulp*, Pan Books, 1996

315 *Sorted for Freezin' Gigs* – interview with Jarvis by Johnny Cigarettes, *NME*, November 18, 1995

316 *Essential Albums of the '90s – Different Class* documentary, BBC Radio 1, February 8, 1999

317 ibid.

318 Interview with Jarvis, *Pulp at Peel Acres,* BBC Radio 1, October 1, 1995

319 Jarvis' onstage comment, Glastonbury Festival, June 24, 1995

320 *Essential Albums of the '90s – Different Class* documentary, BBC Radio 1, February 8, 1999

321 Jarvis' onstage comment, Glastonbury Festival, June 24, 1995

322 ibid.

323 ibid.
324 Jarvis' onstage comment, Heineken Festival, Roundhay Park, Leeds, July 22, 1995
325 *Essential Albums of the '90s – Different Class* documentary, BBC Radio 1, February 8, 1999
326 Interview with Mark, *rockfeedback.com*, autumn 2000
327 Martin Aston: *Pulp*, Pan Books, 1996
328 ibid.
329 *Sorted for Freezin' Gigs* – interview with Jarvis by Johnny Cigarettes, *NME*, November 18, 1995
330 *The Q Interview* – interview with Jarvis by David Quantick, *Q*, November 1995
331 ibid.
332 *Revenge of the Sex Nerd* – band interview by The Stud Brothers, *Melody Maker*, November 4, 1995
333 ibid.
334 Martin Aston: *Pulp*, Pan Books, 1996
335 Jarvis' onstage comment, Glastonbury Festival, June 24, 1995
336 *Cocker Gets Cocky* – interview with Jarvis by Martin Aston, *Attitude*, November 1995
337 *Pulp in Britpop's First Ban* – *Melody Maker* news story, September 30, 1995
338 ibid.
339 ibid.
340 *Revenge of the Sex Nerd* – band interview by The Stud Brothers, *Melody Maker*, November 4, 1995
341 ibid.
342 *Pulp in Britpop's First Ban* – *Melody Maker* news story, 30 September 1995
343 *Pulp TV* – band interview by Andrew Smith, *The Face*, July 1995
344 *Essential Albums of the '90s – Different Class* documentary, BBC Radio 1, February 8, 1999
345 ibid.
346 Jarvis' onstage comment, Bristol University Anson Rooms, April 21, 1995
347 *Sorted for Freezin' Gigs* – interview with Jarvis by Johnny Cigarettes, *NME*, November 18, 1995
348 Jarvis' onstage comment, Heineken Festival, Roundhay Park, Leeds, July 22, 1995
349 ibid.
350 *Fame Fatale* – interview with Jarvis by Dave Simpson, *Melody Maker*, March 30, 1995
351 Jarvis' onstage comment, Brixton Academy, December 21, 1995
352 Jarvis' onstage comment, Bristol University Anson Rooms, April 21, 1995
353 *From Disco To Hardcore* – Pulp documentary, BBC Radio 1, March 22, 1998
354 *Essential Albums of the '90s – Different Class* documentary, BBC Radio 1, February 8, 1999
355 *Sorted for Freezin' Gigs* – interview with Jarvis by Johnny Cigarettes, *NME*, November 18, 1995
356 *Disco 2000* – interview with Pedro Romhanyi, *circa* 1995, from *acrylicafternoons.com*
357 ibid.
358 News article, *NME*, October 14, 1995
359 *Common As Muck* – interview with Jarvis (plus Russell) by Phil Sutcliffe, *Q*, March 1996
360 *It's A Manga's Manga's Manga's World: Pulp's Japanese Tour Diary* – article by Russell, *NME*, February 24, 1996
361 *Common As Muck* – interview with Jarvis by Phil Sutcliffe, *Q*, March 1996
362 *NME* news piece, March 2, 1996
363 ibid.
364 ibid.
365 Jarvis' onstage comment, Cardiff Arena, February 21, 1996

366 *Fiasco 2000!* – live review by John Mulvey, *NME*, March 2, 1996
367 Jarvis' onstage comment, Cardiff Arena, February 21, 1996
368 *Fiasco 2000!* – live review by John Mulvey, *NME*, March 2, 1996
369 News piece, March 30, 1996
370 *The Twilight Zone* – band interview by Andrew Perry, *Select*, April 1998
371 ibid.
372 *Who's Got The Bottle?* – band interview by Gina Morris, *Select*, August 1996
373 ibid.
374 ibid.
375 *50,000,000 Jarvis Fans Can't Be Wrong* – article by Sylvia Patterson, *Vox*, September 1996
376 Jarvis' onstage comment, V96 Festival, Chelmsford, August 17, 1996
377 ibid.
378 ibid.
379 News piece, *the i* website, 1996
380 ibid.
381 *Knickers! Cocker! Glory!* – interview with Jarvis by John Robinson, *NME*, August 17, 1996
382 *Older* – band interview by Alan Smithee, *The Face*, November 1997
383 *From Disco To Hardcore* – BBC Radio 1 documentary, March 22, 1998
384 ibid.
385 *Essential Albums of the '90s – Different Class* documentary, BBC Radio 1, February 8, 1999
386 *Pastures New* – interview with Jarvis by Tina Jackson, *The Big Issue*, October 8–14, 2001
387 *Jarvis Cocker Esq.* – interview with Jarvis by Amy Raphael, *Esquire*, October 2001
388 *The Twilight Zone* – band interview by Andrew Perry, *Select*, April 1998
389 *Puppy Love* – interview with Jarvis by Lynn Barber, *The Observer Magazine*, April 5, 1998
390 *End Of A Chapter* – interview with Jarvis by Sylvia Patterson, *Snug*, November/December 2002
391 *The Heat Interview* – interview with Jarvis by Andrew Harrison, *Heat*, February 20–26, 1999
392 *Everything's Back To Normal* – interview with Jarvis by Peter Robinson, *Melody Maker*, November 21, 1998
393 *Confessions Of A Pop Star* – interview with Jarvis by Vivi McCarthy, *Deluxe*, July 1998
394 *The Twilight Zone* – band interview by Andrew Perry, *Select*, April 1998
395 *Jarvis Gets Real* – interview with Jarvis by Giny Dougary, *The Times Magazine*, March 16, 2002
396 *The Twilight Zone* – band interview by Andrew Perry, *Select*, April 1998
397 *Hello Goodbye* – interview with Russell by Jon Bennett, *Mojo*, September 1999
398 *The Net* – BBC Radio 1, November 5, 1997
399 *Hello Goodbye* – interview with Russell by Jon Bennett, *Mojo*, September 1999
400 *Hello Goodbye* – interview with Russell by Jon Bennett, *Mojo*, September 1999
401 ibid.
402 *From Disco To Hardcore* – Pulp documentary, BBC Radio 1, March 22, 1998
403 *Hello Goodbye* – interview with Russell by Jon Bennett, *Mojo*, September 1999
404 *Talking Lewd!* – band interview by Stephen Dalton, *NME*, March 28, 1998
405 *Confessions Of A Pop Star* – band interview by Vivi McCarthy, *Deluxe*, July 1998
406 Interview with Candida by Zoe Miller for Rough Trade, official Pulp website, March 1997
407 *New Dentures In Hi-Fi!* – band interview by Roger Morton, *NME*, November 8, 1997
408 *Cash For Questions* – interview with Jarvis by Andrew Collins, *Q*, May 1998
409 *Talking Lewd!* – band interview by Stephen Dalton, *NME*, March 28, 1998

410 *Fame Fatale* – interview with Jarvis by Dave Simpson, *Melody Maker*, March 30, 1996
411 *New Dentures In Hi-Fi!* – band interview by Roger Morton, *NME*, November 8, 1997
412 *Talking Lewd!* – band interview by Stephen Dalton, *NME*, March 28, 1998
413 *New Dentures In Hi-Fi!* – band interview by Roger Morton, *NME*, November 8, 1997
414 *Cash For Questions* – interview with Jarvis by Andrew Collins, *Q*, May 1998
415 *New Dentures In Hi-Fi!* – band interview by Roger Morton, *NME*, November 8, 1997
416 Interview with Jarvis by Richard Kingsmill, JJJ Radio, Australia, March 1998.
417 Interview with Jarvis, *NME*, February 22, 1997
418 Interview with Candida by Zoe Miller for Rough Trade, official Pulp website, March 1997
419 *Older* – band interview by Alan Smithee, *The Face*, November 1997
420 *The Twilight Zone* – band interview by Andrew Perry, *Select*, April 1998
421 *Confessions Of A Pop Star* – band interview by Vivi McCarthy, *Deluxe*, July 1998
422 Interview with Nick, *Pulp People 28*, winter 1999
423 *The Twilight Zone* – band interview by Andrew Perry, *Select*, April 1998
424 *New Dentures In Hi-Fi!* – band interview by Roger Morton, *NME*, November 8, 1997
425 *From Disco To Hardcore* – Pulp documentary, BBC Radio 1, March 22, 1998
426 Interview with Jarvis, *This Morning*, ITV, November 11, 1997
427 *The Twilight Zone* – band interview by Andrew Perry, *Select*, April 1998
428 Unknown interview with Jarvis, *circa* 1998
429 Article by Mark, *Pulp People 21*, winter 1997
430 *New Dentures In Hi-Fi!* – band interview by Roger Morton, *NME*, November 8, 1997
431 *Talking Lewd!* – band interview by Stephen Dalton, *NME*, March 28, 1998
432 Interview with Mark, *rockfeedback.com* website, autumn 2000
433 ibid.
434 'Pulp! Live! Hardcore! Uncut!' – interview with Jarvis and Mark from Space Age Bachelor webzine, June 1998.
435 *The Twilight Zone* – band interview by Andrew Perry, *Select*, April 1998
436 *From Disco To Hardcore* – Pulp documentary, BBC Radio 1, March 22, 1998
437 *Talking Lewd!* – band interview by Stephen Dalton, *NME*, March 28, 1998
438 ibid.
439 *Sheffield Of Dreams* – interview with Jarvis by Robin Bresnark, *Melody Maker*, June 27, 1998
440 *New Dentures In Hi-Fi!* – band interview by Roger Morton, *NME*, November 8, 1997
441 *From Disco To Hardcore* – Pulp documentary, BBC Radio 1, March 22, 1998
442 *Talking Lewd!* – band interview by Stephen Dalton, *NME*, March 28, 1998
443 *From Disco To Hardcore* – Pulp documentary, BBC Radio 1, March 22, 1998
444 Interview with Jarvis by Zane Lowe, *Under The Influence*, MTV, March 6, 2002
445 *Confessions Of A Pop Star* – band interview by Vivi McCarthy, *Deluxe*, July 1998
446 *From Disco To Hardcore* – Pulp documentary, BBC Radio 1, March 22, 1998
447 ibid.
448 ibid.
449 *The People's Pop Star* – interview with Jarvis by Deborah Ross, *The Independent Review*, November 18, 2002
450 *Confessions Of A Pop Star* – band interview by Vivi McCarthy, *Deluxe*, July 1998
451 Interview with Jarvis by Richard Kingsmill, JJJ Radio, Australia, March 1998
452 ibid.
453 ibid.
454 Jarvis' onstage comment, Finsbury Park, London, July 25, 1998
455 Jarvis' onstage comment, Paradise Club, Boston, June 9, 1998
456 *It's A Wrap* – interview with Jarvis and Steve by Lisa Verrico, *Dazed & Confused*, November 1995

457 Unknown interview with Jarvis, *circa* 1998

458 *Pulp Culture* – interview with Jarvis by Graham Fuller, *Interview*, July 1998

459 Interview with Jarvis by Richard Kingsmill, JJJ Radio, Australia, March 1998

460 *From Disco To Hardcore* – Pulp documentary, BBC Radio 1, March 22, 1998

461 'Sheffield Of Dreams' – interview with Jarvis by Robin Bresnark, *Melody Maker*, June 27, 1998.

462 Interview with Jarvis by Matt Pinfield, *120 Minutes*, MTV, 1998.

463 'Talking Lewd!' – band interview by Stephen Dalton, *NME*, March 28, 1998.

464 Jarvis' onstage comment, Glastonbury Festival, June 28, 1998

465 ibid.

466 ibid.

467 Interview with Jarvis, *Jo Whiley Show*, BBC Radio 1, September 14, 1998

468 Interview with Jarvis, *The Net*, BBC Radio 1, November 16, 1998

469 Interview with Jarvis by Zane Lowe, *Under The Influence*, MTV, March 6, 2002

470 ibid.

471 *I Caramba!* – interview with Jarvis, Tony Christie and The All Seeing I, by Johnny Cigarettes, *NME*, January 16, 1999

472 Interview with Jarvis by Zane Lowe, *Under The Influence*, MTV, March 6, 2002

473 Interview with Jarvis by Azalée and Margote, *Sparkle* fanzine, June 1999

474 ibid.

475 Jarvis' narrative, *Journeys Into The Outside*, Channel 4, February 1999

476 *The Heat Interview: Jarvis Cocker* – interview with Jarvis by Andrew Harrison, *Heat*, February 20–26, 1999

477 Jarvis' narrative, *Journeys Into The Outside*, Channel 4, March 1999

478 *The Heat Interview: Jarvis Cocker* – interview with Jarvis by Andrew Harrison, *Heat*, February 20–26, 1999

479 Interview with Jarvis by Azalée and Margote, *Sparkle* fanzine, June 1999

480 *"it's just some songs . . ."* – band interview by Alex Deck, *Pulp People 32*, spring 2001

481 Interview with Jarvis by Azalée and Margote, *Sparkle* fanzine, June 1999

482 *NME* news piece, September 8, 1999

483 ibid.

484 *Do You Remember The Verse Time?* – interview with Jarvis, *NME*, October 22, 2001

485 Interview with Jarvis and Steve by Ben Thomson, *We Love Life* Australian Electronic Press Kit, 2001

486 Jarvis' onstage comment, Queen's Hall, Edinburgh, August 31, 1999

487 ibid.

488 Article by Raechel Leigh, *Pulp People* 20, autumn 1997

489 *Maker Breakers* – Venini interview by Kirsty Barker, *Melody Maker*, June 26, 1999

490 Venini interview, *venini.co.uk*, November 1999

491 *Serge Overkill!* – Venini interview by Jim Wirth, *NME*, June 2, 1999

492 *NME* news piece, May 26, 1999

493 *Senior Class* – interview with Russell by Alex McGregor, *Concrete* UEA student paper, May 26, 1999

494 Venini interview, *Sleazenation*, June 1999

495 Venini interview by Lisa Matthews, *BorrowOrRob* webzine, summer 1999

496 ibid.

497 Live review by Stevie Chick, *NME*, August 14, 1999

498 Live review by Ben Clacey, *Melody Maker*, August 14, 1999

499 *Melody Maker* news piece, October 23, 1999

500 *NME* news piece, December 16, 1999

501 *NME* news piece, February 29, 2000

502 Interview with Jarvis, Rockpalast Festival, German TV, June 20, 1998

503 Interview with Jarvis by Lisa Verrico, *The Times*, June 1, 2001
504 *". . . it's just some songs . . ."* – band interview by Alex Deck, *Pulp People 32*, spring 2001
505 'Sheffield's Finest On The Outdoor Life' – interview with Nick, *What's On*, October 27–November 9, 2001.
506 *Do You Remember The Verse Time?* – interview with Jarvis, *NME*, October 22, 2001
507 *10 Questions For Jarvis Cocker* – interview with Jarvis by Jim Irvin, *Mojo*, November 2001
508 Webchat with Jarvis, BBC Radio 1 online, October 10, 2001
509 Interview with Jarvis and Steve by Ben Thomson, *We Love Life* Australian Electronic Press Kit, 2001
510 'Whatever Happened To The Likely Lad?' – band interview by Steve Hobbs, *Q*, November 2001.
511 Interview with Jarvis by Siobhan Grogan, *NME*, August 26, 2000
512 ibid.
513 Interview with Mark by Toby Langley, *rockfeedback.com*, autumn 2000
514 Live review by John Mulvey, *NME*, *circa* September 2000
515 Live review by David Smyth, *Daily Telegraph*, *circa* September 2000
516 *10 Questions For Jarvis Cocker* – interview with Jarvis by Jim Irvin, *Mojo*, November 2001
517 Interview with Jarvis and Steve by Ben Thomson, *We Love Life* Australian Electronic Press Kit, 2001
518 ibid.
519 *The Green Party* – band interview by Craig McLean, *The Face*, October 2001
520 Interview with Jarvis and Steve by Ben Thomson, *We Love Life* Australian Electronic Press Kit, 2001
521 *". . . it's just some songs . . ."* – band interview by Alex Deck, *Pulp People* 32, spring 2001
522 Interview with Jarvis and Steve by Ben Thomson, *We Love Life* Australian Electronic Press Kit, 2001
523 Webchat with Jarvis, BBC Radio 1 online, October 10, 2001
524 Interview with Jarvis by Zane Lowe, *Under The Influence*, MTV, March 6, 2002
525 *10 Questions For Jarvis Cocker* – interview with Jarvis by Jim Irvin, *Mojo,* November 2001
526 *". . . it's just some songs . . ."* – band interview by Alex Deck, *Pulp People 32*, spring 2001
527 *NME* news piece, November 21, 2000
528 ibid.
529 Interview with Jarvis by David Peschek, *Mojo*, February 2002
530 *". . . it's just some songs . . ."* – band interview by Alex Deck, *Pulp People 32*, spring 2001
531 *Postcards From The Hedge* – band interview by Ted Kessler, *NME*, June 2, 2001
532 ibid.
533 ibid.
534 Interview with Jarvis by Lisa Verrico, *The Times 2*, July 1, 2001
535 *". . . it's just some songs . . ."* – band interview by Alex Deck, *Pulp People 32*, spring 2001
536 *Postcards From The Hedge* – band interview by Ted Kessler, *NME*, June 2, 2001
537 Live review by Piers Martin, *NME*, June 2, 2001
538 *". . . it's just some songs . . ."* – band interview by Alex Deck, *Pulp People 32*, spring 2001
539 Interview with Jarvis by Tim Lovejoy, XFM, July 17, 2001
540 *Down To Earth* – interview with Jarvis by James Hopkins, *Hot Tickets*, November 23–29, 2001
541 ibid.
542 *The Green Party* – band interview by Craig McLean, *The Face*, October 2001
543 *Whatever Happened To The Likely Lad?* – band interview by Steve Hobbs, *Q*, November 2001
544 *Organic Street Preacher* – interview with Jarvis by Alex Needham, *NME*, October 13, 2001
545 ibid.

546 *The Green Party* – band interview by Craig McLean, *The Face*, October 2001

547 *Organic Street Preacher* – interview with Jarvis by Alex Needham, *NME*, October 13, 2001

548 *Whatever Happened To The Likely Lad?* – band interview by Steve Hobbs, *Q*, November 2001

549 Interview with Jarvis and Steve by Ben Thomson, *We Love Life* Australian Electronic Press Kit, 2001

550 *Down To Earth* – interview with Jarvis by James Hopkins, *Hot Tickets*, November 23–29, 2001

551 *Whatever Happened To The Likely Lad?* – band interview by Steve Hobbs, *Q*, November 2001

552 *Down To Earth* – interview with Jarvis by James Hopkins, *Hot Tickets*, November 23–29, 2001

553 Interview with Jarvis and Steve by Ben Thomson, *We Love Life* Australian Electronic Press Kit, 2001

554 *Do You Remember The Verse Time?* – interview with Jarvis, *NME*, October 22, 2001

555 Interview with Jarvis and Steve by Ben Thomson, *We Love Life* Australian Electronic Press Kit, 2001

556 ibid.

557 *Do You Remember The Verse Time?* – interview with Jarvis, *NME*, October 22, 2001

558 *10 Questions For Jarvis Cocker* – interview with Jarvis by Jim Irvin, *Mojo*, November 2001

559 *Do You Remember The Verse Time?* – interview with Jarvis, *NME*, October 22, 2001

560 Interview with Jarvis and Steve by Ben Thomson, *We Love Life* Australian Electronic Press Kit, 2001

561 *Do You Remember The Verse Time?* – interview with Jarvis, *NME*, October 22, 2001

562 Interview with Jarvis and Steve by Ben Thomson, *We Love Life* Australian Electronic Press Kit, 2001

563 ibid.

564 ibid.

565 *The Green Party* – band interview by Craig McLean, *The Face*, October 2001

566 Webchat with Jarvis, BBC Radio 1 online, October 10, 2001

567 *Do You Remember The Verse Time?* – interview with Jarvis, *NME*, October 22, 2001

568 Interview with Jarvis and Steve by Ben Thomson, *We Love Life* Australian Electronic Press Kit, 2001

569 *Do You Remember The Verse Time?* – interview with Jarvis, *NME*, October 22, 2001

570 Interview with Jarvis and Steve by Ben Thomson, *We Love Life* Australian Electronic Press Kit, 2001

571 ibid.

572 *Do You Remember The Verse Time?* – interview with Jarvis, *NME*, October 22, 2001

573 ibid.

574 *Pastures New* – interview with Jarvis by Tina Jackson, *The Big Issue*, October 8–14, 2001

575 Interview with Jarvis and Steve by Ben Thomson, *We Love Life* Australian Electronic Press Kit, 2001

576 *Do You Remember The Verse Time?* – interview with Jarvis, *NME*, October 22, 2001

577 Interview with Jarvis and Steve by Ben Thomson, *We Love Life* Australian Electronic Press Kit, 2001

578 *Do You Remember The Verse Time?* – interview with Jarvis, *NME*, October 22, 2001

579 Interview with Jarvis by Zane Lowe, *Under The Influence*, MTV, March 6, 2002

580 Interview with Jarvis and Steve by Ben Thomson, *We Love Life* Australian Electronic Press Kit, 2001

581 *Do You Remember The Verse Time?* – interview with Jarvis, *NME*, October 22, 2001

582 *Pastures New* – interview with Jarvis by Tina Jackson, *The Big Issue*, October 8–14, 2001

583 Album review by David Peschek, *Mojo*, November 2001

584 Album review by Roy Wilkinson, *Q*, October 2001

585 Album review by James Oldham, *NME*, *circa* October 2001

586 *Organic Street Preacher* – interview with Jarvis by Alex Needham, *NME*, October 13, 2001

587 ibid.

588 Interview with Jarvis by John Quinn, *Sheffield Star*, *circa* November 20, 2001

589 Live review by Mark Beaumont, *NME*, *circa* December 2001

590 Interview with Jarvis, *nme.com*, May 31, 2001

591 Interview with Marianne Faithfull by Barney Hoskyns, *rockfeedback.com*, *circa* 2001

592 Interview with Jarvis, unknown source, *circa* 2001

593 Interview with Jarvis by John Earle, *Planet Sound*, Teletext, April 3, 2002

594 *nme.com* news piece, April 18, 2002

595 Interview with Jarvis by John Earle, *Planet Sound*, Teletext, April 3, 2002

596 *The Tree Stooges* – band interview by Wayne Burrows, *The Big Issue*, June 8–14, 2002

597 ibid.

598 ibid.

599 ibid.

600 ibid.

601 Pulp press release, June 28, 2001

602 *Pulp People* 38, August 2002

603 *End Of A Chapter* – interview with Jarvis by Sylvia Patterson, *Snug*, November 2002

604 *The People's Pop Star* – interview with Jarvis by Deborah Ross, *The Independent Review*, November 18, 2002

605 *End Of A Chapter* – interview with Jarvis by Sylvia Patterson, *Snug*, November 2002

606 ibid.

607 *End Of A Chapter* – interview with Jarvis by Sylvia Patterson, *Snug*, November 2002

608 *How We Met* – interview with Jarvis and Richard Hawley by Tony Naylor, *The Independent*, December 8, 2002

609 *How We Met* – interview with Jarvis and Richard Hawley by Tony Naylor, *The Independent*, December 8, 2002

610 *End Of A Chapter* – interview with Jarvis by Sylvia Patterson, *Snug*, November 2002

611 *5 Minutes With . . .* – interview with Jarvis, *X-Ray*, November 2002

612 *End Of A Chapter* – interview with Jarvis by Sylvia Patterson, *Snug*, November 2002

613 *5 Minutes With . . .* – interview with Jarvis, *X-Ray*, November 2002

614 Interview with Jarvis by David Peschek, *Mojo*, February 2003

615 *End Of A Chapter* – interview with Jarvis by Sylvia Patterson, *Snug*, November 2002

616 ibid.

617 Jarvis' onstage comment, Auto Festival, Magna, Rotherham, December 14, 2002

You Have Been Watching . . .

TIM ALLCARD
left Pulp in April 1984, but continued to be the caretaker of The Wicker factory building where Jarvis lived until the building was demolished in the late Eighties. He remains a good friend of the band. "Tim's just one of these people who you haven't seen for three years and it's still Tim," says Michael Paramore. "You just carry on talking, he's never any different. He's just totally full of life, still got lots of ideas, still doing things. Last time I saw him, couple of weeks ago, he was just about to set up a gallery or something. He's been making heads out of cement or something, and he's just bought a screen printing press."

JOHN AVERY
lives in London and still makes music for the Forced Entertainment theatre group.

NICK BANKS
lives in Sheffield with his wife Sarah, their children Jackson and Jeannie, and Malcolm The Dog.

STEVE BECKETT
still runs Warp Records in Sheffield.

PETER BOAM
left Pulp in September 1983. "Just after Pulp, I had this girlfriend who heard *It* and fell in love with Jarvis! Not in a wanting to shag him sort of way, but she just wanted to meet the guy. So she became a big fan, but I always kept myself separate from all that. After I left Pulp, I did a lot of theatre work – got involved in acting, and writing music for stage productions. Then I spent a while working in schools teaching kids how to sing, and working on school productions, doing the music for them. I went back into music for a while in the mid-Eighties, recorded some stuff at Input and played a few gigs. Lived in Amsterdam, then Cambridge, then Brighton."

In 2000, he completed his first solo album, work on which had begun a couple of years before. "It's actually a bit like Jarvis, surprisingly, but much more personal than that," he said at the time. "The reason being that a few years ago, I had a severe manic depressive breakdown, and I was very ill. Didn't work for a few years, then pulled myself up by my bootlaces and started putting some songs down. Some of them sound like really deep love songs, but what they're actually saying is 'I'm fucking mad'. It's about the repercussions of being mad as well – when you've done something really insane, and you wake up the next morning and you know you've done it, the amount of guilt that's involved is incredible. As you get older, you realise that everybody's got some sort of problem though – one in three adults suffers from some sort of severe depression. It's a very quiet record, almost going back to *It* in a way: no big heavy guitars, no loud noises."

He lives in Hove.

You Have Been Watching . . .

CAPTAIN SLEEP

appeared mysteriously at the end of 1986, played one concert (and possibly a couple more) with Pulp that December, another with Jarvis around the same time, and disappeared mysteriously shortly thereafter. "The only concert I recall Captain Sleep playing in was the 100 Club," says Russell. "It may have been one or two either side, but that would be about it. I did see him about five years later by Saint Martin's Market in Birmingham. I went over to talk to him but he was asleep."

SUZANNE CATTY

was fired by Pulp in 1992 after managing them for approximately a year. She is now an aromatherapist in Canada.

JARVIS COCKER

is living in France with his wife Camille Bidault-Waddington. The couple's first child is expected in April 2003.

As well as working on music with Richard Hawley as Relaxed Muscle, he is also likely to make his début as a film director at some point in the medium-term future; in many interviews around 2001, he spoke of a possibility of an adaptation of his friend Harland Miller's novel *Slow Down Arthur Stick To Thirty*. "It's about a David Bowie impersonator in York in the early Eighties," he told *nme.com*. "It's kind of about his formative years in York. He sold the rights for that to DNA, who are the people who made *Trainspotting* and, er, I kind of am trying to pitch to direct that. But it's at a very early stage of development. I would really like to do it, especially since I came down here to study film and did actually finish my degree. It's whether they think I'm capable of making it and whether they let me do it the way I want to."

A year later, he seemed less optimistic about the project, remarking in an interview with *X-Ray* magazine that, "I've started making some videos again, we did one for the Polyphonic Spree's 'Hanging Around' and we're working on a few others. I'll maybe try to get a film made if someone wants to give me the money to do it. One is my friend Harland Miller's book. Then there's another one, you know the Bakewell Tart murder? Well there's an idea we've come up with about that."

"I don't think anyone could tell you what the next move is," says Nigel Coxon. "I don't think his management would be able to tell you. It could be another Pulp record, it could be another Jarvis thing, but I know the biggest thing he really wants to do is make a film, that's his biggest ambition. I think he'd be more interested in making a film than making another record at this moment in time."

SASKIA COCKER

sang backing vocals with Pulp from the recording of the *It* album to the dissolution of that version of the band in September 1983. Thereafter, as well as singing backing vocals on Simon Hinkler and Mark Gouldthorpe's *Flight Commander* album, she continued to write and record solo material with Simon, helped at various times by David Hinkler, Magnus Doyle, Tony Perrin, Steve Naylor and Jarvis. "I was always into music, so we decided we'd do some stuff together. We went to London and recorded some songs, and then we did some stuff at Input in Sheffield. David played trombone on those, and it was really, really good. I don't know what happened to it all, to be honest – Simon and I were going out, and we kept on falling out and splitting up, so things got left and it didn't happen. All that growing-up business meant that we never really got round to it, much to my regret really, but that's the way things go.

"Then I went for an audition for Everything but the Girl – they wanted me to join, but I decided I was going to go solo, and then never did! You know, I moved away and things just happen.

"Later on, around 1990, 1991, I did some demos with someone called Steve Chapman, and this other fellow who played cello and keyboards and things. We got some interest and we

425

were going to do stuff with it, but Steve disappeared to Berlin, and that kind of ended. And then I got married and had children!"

More recently, Saskia has sung backing vocals on Richard Hawley's *Late Night Final* album. She now works as a counsellor, and lives in Sheffield with her husband, ex-Stunt Kite Nigel Renishaw, and their two young children.

NIGEL COXON

left Island Records in 2002 and now lives in Brighton. "I'm just doing my own thing. I've got a little publishing company through Rondor, and I've got a hand in a label in Liverpool called Deltasonic, who had The Coral, and I kind of funded that toward the end of last year, pre-Sony getting involved. And I'm trying to set up another label with Ash's manager, trying to get some funding together now, called Double Dragon. I'm trying to sort of do it indie if you like, 'cos it just got pretty painful at the end of Island, for me. I mean, after signing Pulp I went back into Island Publishing for a while, and I signed Ash, Ocean Colour Scene, Stereophonics, Seahorses, Stereolab, Bentley Rhythm Ace – a whole bunch of stuff, some of it quite commercial, some of it quite weird, and it's all basically coming from guitars or leftfield. I ended up being director of A&R of Island Records in '99 and 2000, and it was just awful 'cos you're just being told to sign hits hits hits! I'm more interested in doing independent stuff really."

PETER DALTON

left Pulp in 1982 to study law at Nottingham University. He stayed in touch with Jarvis after leaving the band, playing with him in Heroes Of The Beach and DJing for Pulp a few times at the Limit. He lives and works in Sheffield.

ALEX DECK

ran the Pulp People fanclub and edited the band's official website until the band's dissolution at the end of 2002. Free of any responsibility to Pulp for the first time in nearly a decade, she is spending the first four months of 2003 in Australia. Her plans thereafter are unknown.

CANDIDA DOYLE

plans to spend 2003 travelling the world.

MAGNUS DOYLE

left Pulp in 1986 to go travelling around Portugal. "The first time he went to India," says Ogy, "he went straight from Portugal, never took any injections or anything, and he was just sick for six weeks. The next time he got the injections and fucked off."

He remained mostly in India for the next 15 years, only returning very occasionally to Sheffield. Saskia Cocker: "I know that when he first went to India, he fell from this waterfall or something, and he would have died, but some Buddhist monks took him in. He spent a lot of time in this monastery. But then he came back, and he just disappeared again."

He unexpectedly returned to England in 2001, and is now back in Sheffield. "I saw him at the Pulp concert in Sheffield [Octagon Centre, November 2001]," says Michael Paramore, "and although he's been away for a long time, he seemed fine – he seemed like the same person, maybe a bit spacier, and he obviously looks very different, but he's still got that same cheekiness to him that he's always had, for want of a better word. I think both him and Tim [Allcard], they're people who haven't fallen into . . . they haven't given up and become old people, which is quite refreshing because it's a bit scary when you see someone you haven't seen for a long time and suddenly they're 40 and they're old."

Magnus Doyle is frequently to be spotted backstage at Pulp concerts, and drives a yellow VW campervan.

MARCUS FEATHERBY

is believed to be in London. He left Sheffield in the early Eighties.

Martin Lilleker: "Marcus now works for the BBC, apparently, in an office, as what I don't know, and he's called something else, which is not unusual for him, it's the third time he's done it. His name was obviously not Marcus Featherby as you can guess. I think he was of Irish descent. He'd certainly had to change his name on more than one occasion previously."

Tony Perrin: "Last thing I heard of Marcus, he had a different name and he was the culinary correspondent for BBC Ceefax, which staggered me a bit because I knew him for about two years, and I'd never seen him cook anything other than a slice of toast."

Murray Fenton: "Last time I saw him was at an Artery gig in Bristol around 1984. He just turned up at this gig, and after that I never saw him again. A few years later, though, when Simon Hinkler was playing with The Mission on *Top Of The Pops*, he just appeared out of a corridor. Simon was like, 'All right Marcus?', and he was going, 'Shh, shh, don't call me that!'

"I mean, in some ways he was good for Sheffield. His heart was in the right place – sometimes."

WAYNE FURNISS

left Pulp in 1982. "I played guitar for a while with a band I never actually gigged with, and around September that year [1983] I joined a band called Siiiiiiiii, and spent two years with them, which I enjoyed. The name was from a William Burroughs novel, apparently (not that I've ever read any William Burroughs, because in my opinion it's unreadable). It means a homosexual orgasm, and it's as many Is as you want."

In 1987 he joined MC5/Stooges-influenced punk/metal band Trolley Dog Shag, which also included Steve Mackey on bass. "Best band I've ever been in," reckons Wayne. "I first saw them at the Limit, and they had a really good drummer – much better than me. As soon as I found out he'd left, I wanted to join. Musically, it was rough but it was cool. They were the best band in Sheffield then. That was a really good year."

When Trolley Dog Shag split up at the end of that year, Wayne became a member of The Absolute, a hard rock band who would stay together until the end of 1995. He now works as a dental technician in Sheffield.

"I certainly had a pile of fun," he says now, looking back on his time with Pulp. "It gave me an awful lot as a young person. By the time I was sixteen, I'd done a John Peel session, played gigs not just in Sheffield but places like London and Bath as well, been in the papers and stuff . . . it was great for someone who's not even completed his O-levels to do all these things, and shortly after to do an album and stuff. Fabulous. Unfortunately, I thought that was how life was going to be – it didn't quite turn out like that.

"You get lots of people saying, 'You made a mistake there,' or 'You should have stuck with them,' or 'I bet it pisses you off,' but it couldn't be further from the truth. I love the fact that Pulp have made it big, and I couldn't be more happy for them. There's no jealousy there, just admiration and pride."

ANTONY GENN

left Pulp in August 1988, shortly after joining the Nine O'Clock Service. He returned to music after the collapse of the church in 1995, first playing keyboards with Elastica on their American tour (having auditioned by streaking on stage during their set at that year's Glastonbury). He also worked with Pulp again, contributing programming to *Different Class*, playing guitar with them on stage in 1996 and 1997, and co-writing 'Glory Days' on *This Is Hardcore*. He has since been in demand as a session player and a songwriter, working for the disparate likes of Joe Strummer and Robbie Williams, and in 2001 putting together the soundtrack for the film *Mike Bassett England Manager*, co-writing and playing on Jarvis' contribution, 'Everybody Loves The Underdog'.

STEVEN HAVENHAND
left Pulp in January 1988. He lives in Cornwall.

DAVID HINKLER
left Pulp in September 1983. He played with Artery for a short while, worked on some of Saskia's unreleased solo material with his brother Simon, and in 1984 formed Mr Morality with Steve Genn, who toured with Pulp in late 1985 and early 1986. Early in 1987, he briefly worked with Jarvis in an abortive new group with Steve Naylor, formerly of his first band Vector 7–7. He now works for Yorkshire Electricity in Sheffield.

SIMON HINKLER
left Pulp in September 1983, and spent the next two years dividing his time between playing in various line-ups of Artery, working as house engineer at Input Studios, and recording an album with Artery's Mark Gouldthorpe as Flight Commander. He produced Pulp's *Little Girl* EP in 1985, and later that year played drums with them for a few weeks on the first leg of the Outrage Tour, filling in for Magnus Doyle.

At the end of 1985, he joined The Mission as guitarist, and spent the next five years touring the world and making a lot of money. He quit the band mid-tour in 1990, and went travelling around America with Steve Genn before returning to Sheffield, where he made the second Flight Commander album, introduced Pulp to Suzanne Catty, and produced the 'O.U.' session. After working with the electronic group Mindfeel in the mid-Nineties, he moved to Seattle and then New Mexico. He now lives in New York City with his wife and son, and is working on various music and film projects.

JULIE HOBSON
is now married to Jon Short. They live in Sheffield.

MIKE JARVIS
still teaches Maths at City School.

TONY K
ran Red Rhino Records in York until the company's demise in 1988, and these days operates from Leeds. "I'm now involved with three different record labels, distribution company, lecturer at Leeds College of Music and Red Tape Studios in Sheffield, mentor, business consultant, started a label with other people for which if you believe the hype our first two releases are going to be Top 20 singles, everybody's going apeshit, one's got a Radio 1 Record of the Week – a Dream Team one, lots of things like that. Things are very active, very current."

JONATHAN KIRK
handled Pulp's live sound at most of their gigs from 1986 to the Leadmill concert in February 1989. "I'd decided I was going to go and train as a nurse. I'd loved working with Pulp, but in the end I had to tell them, I know you're going to make it – I'm just sorry I won't be there with you." He remains friends with the group, and lives and works in Sheffield.

MARTIN LILLEKER
is music writer for the *Sheffield Telegraph*, and in 2001 published his first book, *Not Like A Proper Job: The Story Of Popular Music In Sheffield 1955–1975*. The follow-up volume, which will take the story from 1975 to the present day, including considerable coverage of Pulp, is expected to appear in 2003.

DAVID LOCKWOOD

remained friends with the group for several years after leaving in late 1979, designing posters and roadieing at gigs. "I lost touch with most of them at the end of school. I didn't do particularly well in my A-levels, so I hung around Sheffield for another year and went to college. I probably lost contact with Jarvis about a year after that.

"I've never had a long-term plan – I'm still just drifting through life. I did Metallurgy at Sheffield Poly, which I never had any interest in, then I taught it for seven years at Cranfield Institute of Technology, a postgrad university. I was unemployed for four years after that, then I did an IT course at the University of Central England in Birmingham.

"The first time after that that I realised that Pulp were still out there was in 1993, when I was living in Birmingham. I noticed they were on in town somewhere, but I didn't go. Probably should have, but I only heard about it in the afternoon – they were playing that night and I couldn't be bothered. I guess it was from then that I took an interest again."

He now lives in Cambridgeshire and works as a computer programmer for RAF Whittam.

STEVE MACKEY

lives in London. He is expected to continue working in music, having collaborated in 2001 with designer Giles Deacon and scored an exhibition at The Chapman's Gallery in London. He also plans to organise further Auto festivals.

OGY McGRATH

continued Dig Vis Drill for several years after touring with Pulp under the Outrage banner in 1985 and 1986. "Dig Vis Drill as my band finished around 1988, when John and Nick left me, and I went back to Ireland for a while. After that I was off the boil, didn't want anything to do with any of those people, Pulp or anyone, but I came back myself as Ogy and Dig Vis Drill, featuring T-Man and the Squid, two other guys I'd brought in, dancers and backing vocalists really. I did all the main vocals over backing tapes and stuff. Kind of a killer cabaret, heh heh. I was a comedian for a bit as well, which was terrible because I hate that kind of thing, doing the same joke more than once.

"I don't know if I'll ever go back on stage, 'cos my partner died in February '97, and that really blew me out of the water. That was going to be Ogy and the Squid – the guy was called Squidman, he used to be in In A Belljar. There was a big mystery about his death, and it took months and months till we found out – it was some mysterious virus, heaven knows how he picked it up.

"I write comedy and serious stuff for the radio – under another name though, so don't look for Ogy McGrath. And pornography as well – basically I write jokes about pornography. I've also written a TV series, and made a pilot episode for that, so hopefully that'll get made one day." He still lives in Sheffield.

PETER MANSELL

left Pulp in November 1986. He lived with Candida until the couple split in 2000.

"I always liked Manners," says Ogy McGrath. "He was the postman round where I lived for years and years. After Pulp, he'd always say, 'I've got this band, we're better than Pulp, gonna do this, gonna do that.' So what's the name of the band? 'Haven't got one yet.' For year and years and years!"

GLEN MARSHALL

is a senior partner in a firm of chartered accountants. He lives in Sheffield.

ROB MITCHELL

continued to run Warp Records with Steve Beckett throughout the Nineties. He died in October 2001 after a long battle with cancer. "I distinctly remember him [playing viola with

429

Pulp] at Sheff Uni," says Nick Banks. "He played in long johns, vest and woolly hat. A great bloke, will be missed by all."

JOHN NICHOLLS
left Dig Vis Drill and Sheffield to move to Mansfield in 1988. He now works in electronics and continues to tinker with music (including, in 1999, a rather peculiar remix of 'Maureen').

MICHAEL PARAMORE
left Pulp in summer 1983, around the same time as In A Belljar played their last gig. "I went to uni around that time, and then lived in Leeds for probably about three months, and then decided I missed everybody, and moved back in with Tim who'd then become caretaker of the Wicker factory building and lived there for a couple of years. Jarvis moved in a few months after I'd moved in."

He continued to be Jarvis' flatmate (making his mark on the building with his giant mural, Angel Of The Wicker) until around 1986 when he moved down to Hitchen in Hertfordshire, where he still lives. "I'm a graphic designer, magazines and websites. I'm still painting, still have the odd exhibition. I've got used to it down here, not quite the same as living in a city. When I moved down here at first it was a bit of a shock, but like any place, once you make friends it's kind of home. It's not too bad."

He still occasionally sees Jarvis. "Last time I saw him, he just seemed the same. We were all sat round a table chatting and he came up and it wasn't like he's any different to anybody else. He just kind of sat down and nobody took any more notice of him than anyone else – we just kind of chatted to him, and he was quite surprised when I asked him if he wanted a drink, as if he's used to having to buy people drinks! But other than that he doesn't seem any different, not like a superstar or anything. He was dressed quite scruffily, looked the same really."

TONY PERRIN
ceased to be Pulp's manager in September 1983, and continued to work with Artery (and off-shoot project Flight Commander) for the next couple of years, managing them and releasing their records on his Golden Dawn label. "I got involved with The Mission around December 1985, and that was when my life took off and changed completely. Simon had landed the guitar job with them, and I basically packed my two carrier bags and moved down to London in January '86. The next four years or so was just full-on mayhem with The Mission around the world."

From the late Eighties into the Nineties, he worked with All About Eve and Carter The Unstoppable Sex Machine, and worked with Big Life management in London before becoming a partner in Coalition Management. "I currently spend my days trying not to screw-up the careers of The Streets, The Music and Embrace. I enjoy salmon fishing and watching Manchester United play football. I'm generally happy and I absolutely deny ever telling Jarvis to write a song like Wham!"

JAMIE PINCHBECK
left Pulp in 1982 to study Civil Engineering at Manchester University. He "played in one or two bands, but that was just occasional local gigging." He is now a software engineer, and lives in Leicester with his wife, their two children and a Hofner semi-acoustic bass.

JOHN QUINN
is a sub-editor on the *Sheffield Star*.

NICK ROBINSON
left Dig Vis Drill in 1988, but continued, and continues, to make music. "After John left for Mansfield, I kind of went in the same sort of way, because I was by that time married with two

kids, and concentrating a bit more on work. I was in a club band for a year, which I try to blank out, and I started working on my solo stuff, which I'm still doing to an extent. I'm now putting together a midi-based pub band doing hoary old Sixties stuff like The Doors – it's a way of earning a quid or two from making a racket. And I'm slowly working towards a solo release – fortunately my brother owns a record label, RPM. It's really just waiting for me to get off my ass and do a definitive recording of it. So twice a month I'm out making whale noises and offending people's ears generally."

JIM SELLARS
left Pulp in 1981 to join Crude. After leaving school, he worked in a high street bank for a year, before doing a degree in English, then spent several years living and working in Australia. He is now back in Sheffield, working on theatre projects at the Lyceum, and also dabbling in music again: "Nothing on tape or anything like that – just playing keyboards with a couple of people I know."

RUSSELL SENIOR
left Pulp in January 1997. After leaving Venini in summer 2000, he voiced an intention never to be in a pop group again. He lives in Sheffield with his partner and children, deals in antiques and occasionally plays musical instruments for his own amusement. In autumn 2002, he said he was "enjoying life, picking mushrooms, just seen the Strokes in Leeds and it was ace."

CLIVE SOLOMON
still runs Fire Records in London.

JON SHORT
was a member of Pulp's City School rivals Crude, almost saved Pulp's lives when he woke up the van driver on the way back from recording the 1981 Peel session, and played cello on a track on *It* in 1983. He went on to play bass in a variety of Sheffield bands including Neecha, They Must Be Russians, Floy Joy, The Gutterband, and Scala Timpani as well as fronting his own bands Blue The Fuse and Doofer. In 2001 he played with Neil Finn for a UK tour, and the following year appeared on CDs by Charlie Speed and Paul Buckley. Since 1988, he has been producing ambient music with David Jones under the name Deep Sky Divers, and the duo have attracted some considerable acclaim with a series of self-financed releases. He lives in Sheffield.

ALAN SMYTH
acted as Pulp's producer from 1987 to 1991, although his association with the band went back as far as 1983. "I did actually play bass for Pulp for three days when Simon Hinkler left, and he then returned three days later. We never did any gigs, it was just in the practice stage up in Jarvis' garage. I was asked to be in the band, and I would've loved it – he just disappeared for three days . . .

"There was quite a few people doing the live engineering – Kirky, Mike Timm and me, and was there someone else? Between us, we handled all their gigs. They didn't really go on tours much in those days, did they? It was mainly around town."

His time as Pulp's sound engineer came to an end with the French *Les Inrockuptibles* concerts in 1991. "I had an argument with Russell about ferry tickets. I took my girlfriend with me to France and it was part of the agreement that she could come across on the ferry, and then Russell was trying to say that they couldn't pay me £7.50 for the ferry tickets, and it was like, '*Russell!* You can't do that!' It was a really, really stupid argument, and then he said, 'Can you work for less?' and I was like, 'I can't really, Russ.'

"I really like Russell, and that argument is long gone and forgotten. I mean, it wasn't really a major thing – he just wanted me to work for about half of what I'd been getting, which was fuck all in the first place! So I was like, 'I can't do it Russell, I can't justify it.' Which is a shame because they knew at that time that they were on their way, Russell said things were going really well, and I said, 'I know, and it'll be a lucky engineer who gets to work it.' But literally, I couldn't afford to do what they were wanting me to do. 'Cos even if you get the success of a band, as an engineer your wages don't go rocketing up. But that's what he's like, Russ.

"Then after that I did a cabaret country and western thing which was mainly busking. We played all over the place, did Glastonbury, Edinburgh Festival, which was really, really, really, good fun, had a right laugh, but not a money-spinner at all, and after about five years we were burnt out a bit: I think in one year we did about 360 gigs. In busking terms you can pick up and do another gig about half an hour later – but we were out on the road all year doing that, and then I started the Seafruit thing."

Seafruit was an indie-rock group formed in 1998 by Smyth and singer Geoff Barradale. The band soon signed to Telstar Records and received some press acclaim and minor chart success with the singles 'Hello World' and 'Looking For Sparks'. "Seafruit died a death unfortunately; it was the classic case of being in with the wrong record company. I'm 45 now and they were trying to market us in *Smash Hits*, and that was three years ago. It was just like, 'That's so fucking stupid.' One week the marketing department were going, 'We're going to dress you up as mods and you're all going to be riding scooters!' Dressing up in white lab coats was about the best thing we did. Marketing department had nothing to do with that, it was just on a photo shoot we went out and got those white coats and put 'em on. But it stood out. It wasn't fantastic, but people remember it.

"We had a load of gigs though, and it was a very good live outfit. It's not like any other job – you'll be sailing along quite happily and then you're dropped. The money just *stops*. There's no written or verbal warning, and our manager was useless, he didn't give us any clues that we were in trouble. I knew we were in trouble. When we got signed, I said fantastic – they were saying all the right things about music, and I was thinking, 'As long as they don't come along asking for a couple of hit records, we'll be OK.' Which was the thing that happened the next day."

Seafruit finally split in 2001; Alan continues to write songs and work as a studio engineer. "To be honest I've been getting out of that mentality of 'We must carry on with the Seafruit thing'. I'm just carrying on with what I want to do, which is where the good stuff'll come back out.

"I work with Richard Hawley all the time, I've worked on his last two albums. We did a mix of the Nick Cave 'Disco 2000' – I put Richard's bit on, Richard played some guitar on it, and we did a mix of what we'd done and sent it back, and it was all soaked in reverb. I was thinking, 'This sounds great, kind of like some of the Pulp stuff that I was working on before,' and we got a phone call saying, 'How the fuck have you done that?' and I said, 'Well it's easy, you just don't have any dry signal. You just put all the sound into reverb and send it back.' And Jarvis apparently really wanted to use that mix, but unfortunately when they sent us the audio file, the engineer at that end had forgotten to do something so there was a bit of a glitch on the master that we'd been working on that I couldn't get rid of, so they didn't use that master. I haven't heard the mix they used but apparently it's a really safe-sounding thing, a bit drab. In the back we had really high-speed mandolin parts, swamped in reverb and it really cushioned the track, and we thought, 'Ooo, that sounds great!' "

MARK SWIFT

left Pulp in 1980. He went to Loughborough University, and now lives in London where he works in advertising for Virgin Radio.

NICK TAYLOR

played in various Sheffield bands through the Eighties, including Rapid Eye Movements, A Major European Group, Heroes Of The Beach (with Jarvis and Peter Dalton), Midnight

Choir, and their later incarnation as Beserka Joe. He is now a doctor of psychology and works in a Sheffield hospital.

PHILIP THOMPSON

left Pulp in 1980. "Years later, when I was at college, I got talking to someone about how I'd been in a band, and he ended up down in London. He met somebody there from Sheffield, this lad Dave, who'd been on the band scene, and mentioned that he knew someone who'd been in a group. He was, 'Oh, what group was he in?' and he said, 'Pulp,' and this Dave said, 'Hey, I know somebody from Pulp – he fell off stage at the Leadmill!'

"Later on, I started to get people coming up to me going, 'Hey, Pulp, they're getting famous now, aren't they?' I was like, 'Fucking hell, I wish I'd never told them! I only played about five gigs with them – anyone would think I was the founding member!' Good luck to Jarvis though – he's done what he wants to do, and had the bottle to stick it out. He must have been through some pretty rough times, and I hope he gets everything he wants out of it."

He is now married with children, and works as a systems engineer in Sunderland.

GEOFF TRAVIS

still runs Rough Trade Management in London.

MARK WEBBER

lives in Kentish Town, north London, and is expected to continue working in film – both curating festivals and making his own experimental works.

GARRY WILSON

played drums on the *It* album under the pseudonym Beefy Garry O, to avoid drawing attention to the fact that he was moonlighting from his day job playing in Artery. "Artery were signed to somebody else at the time, so I couldn't use me proper name. They called me Beefy Garry O because I was a thug! I did an album with Midnight Choir around that time, and I was Mark Thomas on that one."

He continued to play in Artery until the group split in 1985, and later managed Sheffield clubs The Limit and The Music Machine. "Oh, and I launched the Mission's career. Around 1984, '85, me and Tony Perrin used to go flyposting round South Yorkshire, and somehow, through contact after contact, Tony had ended up managing the Sisters of Mercy. They split into The Sisterhood and Sisters of Mercy, and Tony went with Sisterhood, with Wayne Hussey and Mick Brown and Simon Hinkler. They wanted five grand to go round Europe supporting The Cult, so Tony sold me his share in the flyposting business. So I got me five grand, and a year and a half later, The Sisterhood were called The Mission and they were playing stadiums. Never asked for any points off them either!"

"Couple of weeks ago (summer 1998), this kid says, 'Gaz, we've got this T-Rex tribute band together – you don't fancy it do you?' There's four of us and a DJ. He goes on first and plays Seventies stuff for about two hours, then we go on for 40 minutes and do all the T-Rex stuff. And we get £800 for it, split five ways. Works out at about £20 a minute. It's very, very embarrassing though, so I wear this big wig and sunglasses."

"After *It*, I didn't hear from Pulp for about 10 years, then I bumped into them outside this rehearsal place in Sheffield. I came out and they were all there in the street. It was like, 'Fuckin' hell! Are you lot still at it?' People ask me now why I didn't stick with it. Fucking hell, all them years?!"

Appendix 1

PULP DISCOGRAPHY 1982–2002

ALBUMS

It **(mini-LP)**
My Lighthouse/Wishful Thinking/Joking Aside[1]/Boats and Trains[2]//Blue Girls[3]/
Love Love/In Many Ways
All songs written by Jarvis Cocker, except 'My Lighthouse' – music by Jarvis Cocker and
Simon Hinkler, lyrics by Jarvis Cocker
Arranged by Simon Hinkler and Pulp
Produced by Simon Hinkler
Engineer unknown except: [1] engineered by Simon Skolfield; [2] engineered by Simon Hinkler;
[3] main engineer unknown, additional engineering by Simon Skolfield
Recorded and mixed at Victoria Studios, Sheffield, November 27–December 10, 1982
except: [1] recorded and mixed at Southern Studios, London, January 15, 1983;
[2] recorded and mixed at Input Studio, Sheffield, August 22, 1982; [3] recorded and mixed at
Victoria Studios, Sheffield, November 27–December 10, 1982; additional recording and
mixing at Southern Studios, London, January 15, 1983
Sleeve artwork and design: Tony Perrin
LP released on Red Rhino (REDLP 29), April 18, 1983 – deleted 1988 when Red Rhino
collapsed
CD released on Cherry Red (CDMRED 112) with single remix of 'My Lighthouse' in place
of the original version, and extra tracks 'Looking For Life', 'Everybody's Problem' and 'There
Was', February 1994 – deleted after 1,000 copies for legal reasons
Second CD released on Fire Records (REFIRE CD15) with extra track 'Looking For Life',
October 24, 1994
Third CD released on Fire Records (SREFIRE CD15), with extra track 'Looking For Life'
and cardboard slipcase, November 2002

Freaks
Fairground/I Want You/Being Followed Home/Master Of The Universe/Life Must Be So
Wonderful//There's No Emotion/Anorexic Beauty/The Never Ending Story/Don't You
Know/They Suffocate At Night
All songs written by Pulp
All lyrics by Jarvis Cocker, except 'Fairground' by Russell Senior and 'Anorexic Beauty' by
David Kurley
Produced by Pulp and Jonathan Kirk

Engineered by either Alan Walker or Peter Oldfield
Recorded and mixed at Input Studio, Sheffield, June 21–27, 1986
Sleeve design: The Robert Winterman Design Group
Photography: Andy Gray
LP released on Fire Records (FIRE LP5), May 11, 1987
LP, cassette and CD re-released on Fire Records (LP – FIRE LP5, cassette – FIRE TC5, CD
– FIRE CD5), April 1993
*NB: the reissued LP is distinguishable from the original in that it has a separate lyric sheet rather than a
printed inner sleeve, and an altered rear sleeve design that obscures the out-of-date Pulp contact address
and Nine Mile/Cartel distribution credit.*
CD re-released on Fire Records (SFIRE CD5) with extra cardboard slipcase, July 1, 2002

Separations

Love Is Blind/Don't You Want Me Anymore?/She's Dead/Separations/Down By The
River/Countdown/My Legendary Girlfriend/Death II/This House Is Condemned
All songs written by Pulp
All lyrics by Jarvis Cocker, except 'This House Is Condemned' by Russell Senior
Produced by Alan Smyth and Pulp
Engineered by Alan Fisch
Recorded at FON Studio, Sheffield, August 1989, with additional recording and mixing
between September 1989 and January 1990
Sleeve design and artwork: Martyn Broadhead
LP, cassette and CD released on Fire Records (LP – FIRE11026, cassette – FIRE22026, CD –
FIRE33026), June 19, 1992
CD re-released on Fire Records (SFIRE 026CD), April 29, 2002

His'n'Hers

Joyriders/Lipgloss[1]/Acrylic Afternoons/Babies (remix) [2]/Have You Seen Her Lately?/
She's A Lady[3]//Happy Endings/Do You Remember The First Time?/Pink Glove/Someone
Like The Moon/David's Last Summer
All songs written by Pulp
All lyrics by Jarvis Cocker
Produced by Ed Buller for 140dB
Engineered by Ed Buller and Adi Winman except: [2] produced by Ed Buller, engineered by
Santiago, remixed by Ed Buller and Pulp
Recorded and mixed at Britannia Row Studios, London, October 1993–February 1994,
except: [1] Recorded and mixed at Britannia Row Studios, London, July 2–10, 1993;
[2] Recorded at Island Records Fallout Shelter, London, July 20–24, 1992, remixed at West
Side Studios, London, February 8–11, 1994; [3] Recorded at Britannia Row Studios, London,
July 2–10, 1993, additional recording at Britannia Row, October 1993–February 1994, final
overdubs and remix at West Side Studios, London, February 8–11, 1994
Sleeve design: The Designers Republic
Illustration: Philip Castle from a photograph by Kevin Westerberg
LP, cassette and CD released on Island Records (LP – ILPS 8025, cassette – ICT 8025, CD –
CID 8025), April 11, 1994
*NB: the vinyl version does not include 'Babies'; the US edition includes 'Razzmatazz' as an unlisted
bonus track on the cassette and CD.*
Highest UK chart position: 9

435

Different Class
Mis-Shapes/Pencil Skirt[2]/Common People[1]/I Spy/Disco 2000/ Live Bed Show//
Something Changed/Sorted For E's & Wizz/F.E.E.L.I.N.G.C.A.L.L.E.D.L.O.V.E./
Underwear[1]/Monday Morning[3]/Bar Italia[2]
All songs written by Pulp
All lyrics by Jarvis Cocker
Produced by Chris Thomas
Engineered by David 'Chipper' Nicholas
Assistant engineer Julie Gardner except: [1] assistant engineer Pete Lewis
Additional engineering by Pete Lewis
Recorded at The Town House, London, June 19–July 28, 1995 except: [1] Recorded at The
Town House, London, January 18–24, 1995; [2] Recorded at The Town House, London,
February 27–April 2, 1995; [3] Recorded at The Town House, London, February 27–April 2,
1995, additional recording at The Town House, London, June 19–July 28, 1995
Orchestra for 'I Spy', 'Something Changed' and 'F.E.E.L.I.N.G.C.A.L.L.E.D.L.O.V.E.'
recorded at Air Lyndhurst, London, July 22, 1995
All tracks mixed at The Town House, London, July 31–August 14, 1995, except:
[1] mixed at The Town House, January 18–24, 1995
Sleeve design: Mark Tappin and Seb Marling for Blue Source. Concept by Pulp
Photography: Donald Milne and Rankin
LP, cassette and CD released on Island Records (LP – ILPS 8041, cassette – ICT 8041, CD –
CID 8041), October 30, 1995
*NB: initial copies of the LP and CD included 12 interchangeable front covers and silver embossed
lettering on the outer sleeve; subsequent copies had straightforward 'wedding' cover with the other pictures
printed inside, and plain white lettering.*
Special heavy vinyl audiophile LP released on Simply Vinyl (SVLP 166), January 24, 2000
Highest UK chart position: 1

This Is Hardcore
The Fear/Dishes/Party Hard/Help The Aged/This Is Hardcore//TV Movie/A Little Soul/
I'm A Man/Seductive Barry//Sylvia/Glory Days/The Day After The Revolution
All songs written by Pulp, except 'This Is Hardcore' written by Pulp and Pete Thomas, 'Glory
Days' written by Pulp and Antony Genn
All lyrics by Jarvis Cocker
Produced by Chris Thomas
Engineered by Pete Lewis
Assistant engineers: Lorraine Francis and Jay Reynolds
Recorded and mixed at The Town House and Olympic Studios, London, November
1996–January 1998
Strings for 'Dishes', 'This Is Hardcore', 'A Little Soul' and 'Seductive Barry' recorded at
Whitfield Street, London, 1997
Art direction: John Currin and Peter Saville
Sleeve design: Howard Wakefield and Paul Hetherington at The Apartment
Photography: Horst Diekgerdes
Casting: Sascha Behrendt
Styling: Camille Bidault-Waddington
Models: Ksenia (front cover), Beverly, Philene, John Huntley (bar and lift photos), Angelique
LP (double), cassette and CD released on Island Records (LP – ILPSD 8066, cassette – ICT
8066, CD – CID 8066), March 30, 1998
*NB: LP includes extra tracks 'Tomorrow Never Lies', 'Laughing Boy', 'The Professional' and 'This Is
Hardcore (End Of The Line remix)', taken from the 'Help The Aged' and 'This Is Hardcore' singles.*

US edition includes extra track 'Like A Friend (film version)'. Japanese edition includes extra tracks 'Like A Friend (film version)' and 'Tomorrow Never Lies'.
CD re-released as double pack with *This Is Glastonbury* (see below) in special card slipcase on Island Records (CIDD 8066), September 14, 1998
Highest UK chart position: 1

This Is Glastonbury
The Fear/Live Bed Show/TV Movie/A Little Soul/Party Hard/Help The Aged/
Seductive Barry
All songs written by Pulp
All lyrics by Jarvis Cocker
Mixed by Chris Thomas
Mix engineer Pete Lewis
Recorded live at The Glastonbury Festival, England, June 28, 1998 by Miti for BBC Music Entertainment
Artwork credits as for *This Is Hardcore* album above
Released as a limited edition bonus CD with *This Is Hardcore* on Island Records (LC 0407), September 14, 1998
Also available separately via mail order from the Trinity Street Pulp information service
NB: the Japanese edition included the extra tracks 'This Is Hardcore' and 'Glory Days/Common People'.

We Love Life
Weeds/Weeds II (The Origin Of The Species)/The Night That Minnie Timperley Died/
The Trees/Wickerman//I Love Life/The Birds In Your Garden/Bob Lind (The Only Way Is Down)/Bad Cover Version/Roadkill/Sunrise
All songs written by Pulp except 'Sunrise' by Pulp and Peter Mansell
All lyrics by Jarvis Cocker
Produced by Scott Walker
Co-produced and engineered by Peter Walsh
Assistant engineer: Matt Lawrence
Mixed by Scott Walker and Peter Walsh
Mastered by Chris Blair
Recorded and mixed at Metropolis Studios, London, September 2000–March 2001
Strings for 'Weeds', 'Wickerman' and 'Bob Lind (The Only Way Is Down)' recorded by Geoff Foster at Air Studios, London, *circa* October 23, 2000
Choir for 'Sunrise' recorded by Steve Price at Angel Studios, London
Art direction by Jarvis Cocker and Peter Saville
Design by Howard Wakefield and Marcus Werner Hed
Photographs by Tom Miller, George Parfitt, Tony Webber, Jarvis Cocker and Sarah Parris
Illustrations by Peter Doig, Rory Crichton, Mat Collinshaw, Rory Crichton and John Glashan
LP and CD released on Universal Island Records (LP – ILPS 8110, CD – CID 8110), October 22, 2001
NB: the US edition, released on Sanctuary Records on August 20, 2002, includes the bonus tracks 'Yesterday' and 'Forever In My Dreams', taken from the 'Bad Cover Version' single. All non-UK editions of the album featured the Pulp logo in orange, tan and yellow letters, as opposed to the green of the UK edition.
Highest UK chart position: 6

SINGLES AND EPS

'My Lighthouse'
My Lighthouse (Re-mix)/Looking For Life
'My Lighthouse' written by Jarvis Cocker and Simon Hinkler
'Looking For Life' written by Jarvis Cocker
All lyrics by Jarvis Cocker
Arranged by Simon Hinkler and Pulp
Produced by Simon Hinkler
Engineer unknown
'My Lighthouse' remix engineer: Simon Skolfield
Recorded and mixed at Victoria Studios, Sheffield, November 27–December 10, 1982
'My Lighthouse' remixed at Southern Studios, London, January 15, 1983
Sleeve artwork and design: Tony Perrin
7″ single released on Red Rhino Records (RED 32), May 2, 1983
NB: both tracks included on the deleted Cherry Red CD reissue of It, *February 1994. 'Looking For Life' included on the Fire Records CD reissue of* It, *October 1994.*

'Everybody's Problem'
Everybody's Problem/There Was . . .
All songs written by Jarvis Cocker
Arranged by Pulp
Produced by Simon Hinkler
Engineered by Simon Skolfield
Recorded and mixed at Southern Studios, London, June 4–5, 1983
Sleeve artwork and design: Michael Paramore
Photography: Pete Hill
7″ single released on Red Rhino Records (RED 37), September 19, 1983
NB: both tracks included on the deleted Cherry Red CD reissue of It, *February 1994, and on the Cherry Red various artists compilation* School Disco, *2001. 'Everybody's Problem' included on the Nectar Masters compilation* Red Heaven: 20 Of The Best From The Cherry Red Label, *1995.*

'Little Girl (With Blue Eyes) And Other Pieces'
Little Girl (With Blue Eyes)//Simultaneous/Blue Glow/The Will To Power
All songs written by Pulp
All lyrics by Jarvis Cocker, except 'The Will To Power' by Russell Senior
Recorded by Simon Hinkler
Recorded and mixed at Input Studio, Sheffield, June 1985
Sleeve artwork and design: Jarvis Cocker and Julie Paramore
Photography: David Bocking
12″ single released on Fire Records (FIRE 5), December 2, 1985
NB: all tracks included on the Fire Records Pulp compilation Masters Of The Universe, *June 1994. 'Little Girl' included on the Fire Records various artists compilation* The Great Fire Of London, *1988.*

'Dogs Are Everywhere'
Dogs Are Everywhere/The Mark Of The Devil//97 Lovers/Aborigine/Goodnight
All songs written by Pulp
All lyrics by Jarvis Cocker
Recorded by Peter Oldfield
Recorded and mixed at Input Studio, Sheffield, February 22–23, 1986

Sleeve artwork and design: Jarvis Cocker
Photography: David Bocking
12″ single released on Fire Records (BLAZE 10), June 30, 1986
NB: all tracks included on the Fire Records Pulp compilation Masters Of The Universe, *June 1994.*

'They Suffocate At Night'

7″: They Suffocate At Night (edited version)/Tunnel (cut-up version)
12″: They Suffocate At Night (uncut version)/Tunnel (full-length version)
All songs written by Pulp
All lyrics by Jarvis Cocker
Produced by Pulp and Jonathan Kirk
Engineered by either Alan Walker or Peter Oldfield
Recorded and mixed at Input Studio, Sheffield, June 21–27, 1986
Sleeve artwork and design: Jarvis Cocker
7″ and 12″ singles released on Fire Records (7″: BLAZE 17, 12″: BLAZET 17), January 5, 1987
NB: the edited/cut-up versions on the 7″ single are crude edits of the full versions on the 12″ single. 'They Suffocate At Night (uncut version)' included on the Fire Records LP Freaks, *May 1987. 'They Suffocate At Night (uncut version) and 'Tunnel (full-length version)' included on the Fire Records Pulp compilation* Masters Of The Universe, *June 1994.*

'Master Of The Universe'

Master Of The Universe (Sanitised Version)//Manon (New Version)[1]/Silence[2]
All songs written by Pulp
All lyrics by Jarvis Cocker – 'Manon' French translation by Elizabeth Baxter
Produced by Pulp and Jonathan Kirk, engineered by either Alan Walker or Peter Oldfield, except: [1] recorded by Simon Hinkler; [2] recorded by John Nicholls
Recorded at Input Studio, Sheffield, June 21–27, 1986, except: [1] Recorded at Input Studio, Sheffield, June 1985, additional recording and remix at Input Studio, Sheffield, June 21–27, 1986; [2] Recorded at Wicker Karate Rooms, Sheffield, May 8, 1984
Sleeve artwork and design: The Robert Winterman Design Group
12″ single released on Fire Records (BLAZE 21T), March 30, 1987
NB: all tracks except 'Silence' included on the Fire Records Pulp compilation Masters Of The Universe, *June 1994.*

'My Legendary Girlfriend'

My Legendary Girlfriend//Is This House?/This House Is Condemned
All songs written by Pulp
All lyrics by Jarvis Cocker, except 'Is This House' and 'This House Is Condemned' by Russell Senior
Produced by Alan Smyth and Pulp
Engineered by Alan Fisch
Recorded at FON Studio, Sheffield, August 1989, with additional recording and mixing between September 1989 and January 1990
'Is This House' and 'This House Is Condemned' are "extensively renovated versions" of the *Separations* version of 'This House Is Condemned', remixed by Parrot and Winston at FON Studio, Sheffield, January 1990
Sleeve artwork and design: Jarvis Cocker
12″ single released on Fire Records (BLAZE 44T), March 18, 1991
CD single released on Fire Records (BLAZECD 44), November 17, 1996

NB: 'My Legendary Girlfriend' released on the Fire LP Separations, *June 1992. 'Is This House?' and 'This House Is Condemned' released on the Connoisseur Collection Pulp compilation* Pulp Goes To The Disco, *July 1998.*

'Countdown'

Countdown//Death Goes To The Disco[1]/Countdown (radio edit)
All songs written by Pulp
All lyrics by Jarvis Cocker
Produced by Alan Smyth and Pulp
Engineered by Alan Fisch except [1] engineered by Alan Smyth
Recorded at FON Studio, Sheffield, August 1989–January 1990, with additional recording and mixing at FON Studio, Sheffield, May 1991 except: [1] recorded and mixed at FON Studio, Sheffield, December 1987
Sleeve artwork and design: Martyn Broadhead
Photography: Ed Sirrs
12″ and CD single released on Fire Records (12″: BLAZE 51T, CD: BLAZE 51CD), August 22, 1991
NB: the CD reverses the track listing above. All three tracks are included on the Nectar Masters/Fire Pulp compilation Countdown: Pulp 1992–1983, *March 1996, and the Connoisseur Collection Pulp compilation* Pulp Goes To The Disco, *July 1998.*

'O.U.'

O.U. (Gone, Gone)//Space[1]/O.U. (Gone, Gone) (radio edit)
All songs written by Pulp
All lyrics by Jarvis Cocker
Produced by Simon Hinkler, Mike Timm and Pulp, remix and additional recording by Ed Buller except: [1] produced by Simon Hinkler and Mike Timm
Engineered by Alan Fisch
Recorded at FON Studio, Sheffield, January 28–30, 1992, remixed at Protocol Studios, London, February 1992, except: [1] recorded and mixed at FON Studio, Sheffield, January 28–30, 1992
Sleeve artwork and design: Martyn Broadhead
Photography: Colin Bell
12″ and CD single released on Gift (12″: GIF1, CD: GIF1CD), May 25, 1992
NB: the CD single reverses the track listing given above. All tracks except 'O.U. (radio edit)' included on the Island Records Pulp compilation Intro, *October 1993.*

'My Legendary Girlfriend'

My Legendary Girlfriend (live soundcheck version)[1]//Sickly Grin[2]/Back In L.A.[3]
All songs written by Pulp except 'Sickly Grin' by Jarvis Cocker
All lyrics written by Jarvis Cocker except 'Back In L.A.' by Jarvis Cocker and Russell Senior
[1] probably produced by Tony Worthington; [2] produced by Simon Hinkler; [3] recorded by Pulp and Tim Allcard
[1] recorded live during soundcheck for BBC Radio 5 *Hit The North* session, BBC Radio Manchester Studios, September 11, 1991; [2] recorded at Input Studio, Sheffield, August 22, 1982; [3] recorded at Castle Table Tennis Rooms, Sheffield, November 11, 1984
Compiled by Bob Stanley
7″ single released on Caff Records (CAFF 17), September 1992
NB: mail order only, limited to 500 copies. Came with a foldover picture sleeve and insert in poly bag.

440

'Babies'
Babies/Styloroc (Nites Of Suburbia)[1]//Sheffield Sex City[2]/Sheffield Sex City (instrumental)
All songs written by Pulp
All lyrics by Jarvis Cocker
Produced by Ed Buller
Engineered by Santiago
Mixed by Ed Buller except: [2] mixed by Zeebee, Jarvis Cocker, Steve Mackey
Recorded and mixed at Island Records Fallout Shelter, London, July 20–24, 1992, except:
[1] recorded at Island Records Fallout Shelter, London, May 7, 1992, overdubs and mixing at
Protocol Studios, London, August 5 or 6, 1992; [2] recorded at Island Records Fallout Shelter,
London, July 20–24, 1992, overdubs at Protocol Studios, London, August 5 or 6, 1992, mixed
at Island Records Music Studio, London, August 1992
Sleeve design: The Designers Republic
Photography: Colin Bell
12″ and CD single released on Gift (12″: GIF3, CD: GIFCD3), October 5, 1992
*NB: the 12″ single omits 'Sheffield Sex City (instrumental)'. All tracks except 'Sheffield Sex City
(instrumental) included on the Island Records Pulp compilation* Intro, *October 1993.*

'Razzmatazz'
Razzmatazz//*Inside Susan "A story in three songs . . .":* Stacks[1]/Inside Susan[1]/59 Lyndhurst
Grove[1]
All songs written by Pulp
All lyrics by Jarvis Cocker
Produced by Ed Buller (remix and additional production by Phil Vinall) except: [1] produced by
Pulp
Engineered by John Smith and Luke Gordon except: [1] engineered by Andy and Giles
Recorded at Maison Rouge Studios, London, October 20–22, 1992, with additional
recording and mixing at Matrix Studio, London, December 1992, except: [1] recorded and
mixed at Protocol Studios, London, December 9, 1992 ('59 Lyndhurst Grove' was mixed at a
later date)
Sleeve design by The Designers Republic
Photography by Colin Bell
12″, 7″ and CD single released on Gift (12″: GIF6, 7″: 7GIF6, CD: GIF6CD), February 15,
1993
NB: the 7″ single omits the track 'Inside Susan'. *All tracks included on the Island Records Pulp
compilation* Intro, *October 1993.*
Highest UK chart position: 80

'Lipgloss'
Lipgloss//Deep Fried In Kelvin[1]/You're A Nightmare[2]
All songs written by Pulp
All lyrics by Jarvis Cocker
Produced by Ed Buller except: [2] produced by Mike Engles, assistant engineer Simon Askew
Recorded at Britannia Row Studios, London, July 2–10, 1993 except: [1] recorded at Axis
Studio, Sheffield, July 23–24, 1993; [2] recorded at BBC Maida Vale Studios, February 7, 1993
Sleeve design by The Designers Republic
Image by Hideaki Kodama
12″, black vinyl 7″, CD and cassette single released on Island Records (12″: 12IS567, 7″:
IS567, CD: CID567, cassette: CIS567), November 12, 1993
CD re-released on Island Records (CID567), August 23, 1996
Red vinyl 7″ released on Island Records (IS567)

NB: the cassette and 7″ singles omit 'Deep Fried In Kelvin'. 'You're A Nightmare' was first broadcast on The John Peel Show, BBC Radio 1, March 5, 1993. Some stock copies of the CD bear the legend 'FOR PROMOTIONAL USE ONLY' on the body of the disc, which is wrong. 'Lipgloss' included on the Island Records LP His'n'Hers, March 1994.
Highest UK chart position: 50

'Do You Remember The First Time?'
Do You Remember The First Time?//Street Lites[1]/The Babysitter[1]
All songs written by Pulp
All lyrics by Jarvis Cocker
Produced by Ed Buller except: [1] produced by Pulp and Pete Stewart
Recorded and mixed at Britannia Row Studios, London, October 1993–February 1994 except: [1] recorded at The War Room, Milo Studio, London, December 9, 1993 with overdubs and mixing at Axis Studio, Sheffield, December 29–30, 1993
Sleeve design by The Designers Republic
Image by Philip Castle
12″, black vinyl 7″, CD and cassette single released on Island Records (12″: 12IS574, 7″: IS574, CD: CID574, cassette: CIS574), March 21, 1994
CD re-released on Island Records (CID574), August 23, 1996
Brown vinyl 7″ released on Island Records (IS574), November 20, 1996
NB: the cassette and 7″ singles omit 'The Babysitter'. 'Do You Remember The First Time?' included on the Island Records LP His'n'Hers, April 1994.
Highest UK chart position: 33

'The Sisters EP'
Babies/Your Sister's Clothes[1]//Seconds[1]/His 'N' Hers[1]
All songs written by Pulp
All lyrics by Jarvis Cocker
Produced by Ed Buller
Engineered by Santiago except: [1] engineered by Ed Buller and Adi Winman
Recorded and mixed at Island Records Fallout Shelter, London, July 20–24, 1992, except: [1] recorded and mixed at Britannia Row Studios, London, October 1993–February 1994
Sleeve design by The Designers Republic
Image by Philip Castle
Photography by Steve Double
12″, CD and cassette single released on Island Records (12″: 12IS595, CD: CID595, cassette: CIS595), May 23, 1994
Black vinyl gatefold 7″ released on Island Records (IS595), May 30, 1994
CD re-released on Island Records (CID595), August 23, 1996
White vinyl 7″ released on Island Records (IS574), November 20, 1996
NB: the version of 'Babies' here is a slightly edited version of the original 1992 recording as opposed to the 1994 remix included on His'n'Hers. The 12″ single included a 10″ print of the His'n'Hers album sleeve artwork. The 7″ gatefold sleeve included the lyrics to the songs and a band photo. Full version of 'Babies' included on the Island Records Pulp compilation Intro, October 1993.
Highest UK chart position: 17

'Common People'
CD1 and cassette ('Daytime' artwork): Common People/Underwear/Common People (7″ edit)
CD2 ('Night-time' artwork): Common People/Razzmatazz (acoustic version)[1]/Dogs Are Everywhere (acoustic version)[2]/Joyriders (acoustic version)[2]
7″ ('Daytime' artwork): Common People/Underwear

12″ ('Night-time' artwork): Common People/Underwear//Common People (Motiv 8 Club Mix)[3]/Common People (Vocoda Mix)[4]
All songs written by Pulp
All lyrics by Jarvis Cocker
Produced by Chris Thomas except: [1] producer unknown
Engineered by David 'Chipper' Nicholas except: [1] producer unknown
[3] additional production and remix by Motiv 8 AKA Steve Rodway for Nuff Respect Productions
Recorded and mixed at The Town House, London, January 18–24, 1995 except: [1] date and location of recording unknown; [2] recorded live at GLR Studios, London, March 22, 1994; [3] remixed at The Town House, London, May 12, 1995; [4] remixed at The Town House, London, summer 1995
Sleeve design by The Designers Republic
Photography by Donald Milne
CD1 and cassette released on Island Records (CID 613), May 22, 1995
CD2 (with free sticker) released on Island Records (CIDX 613), May 29, 1995
7″ (yellow vinyl) and 12″ released on Island Records (7″: IS 613, 12″: 12IS 613), November 20, 1996
NB: 'Dogs Are Everywhere' and 'Joyriders' were first broadcast on The Pete Aherne Show, GLR *Radio (London), March 22, 1994. The Motiv 8 and Vocoda mixes of 'Common People' were first released on the CD single of 'Sorted For E's And Wizz', September 1995. 'Common People' included on the Island Records LP* Different Class, *October 1995.*
Highest UK chart position: 2

'Sorted For E's And Wizz'/'Mis-Shapes'

CD1 and 12″: Mis-Shapes/Sorted For E's And Wizz//P.T.A. (Parent Teacher Association)[1]/Common People (Live At Glastonbury)[2]
CD2: Sorted For E's And Wizz/Mis-Shapes/Common People (Motiv 8 Club Mix)[3]/Common People (Vocoda mix)[4]
Cassette: Mis-Shapes/Sorted For E's And Wizz
7″: Sorted For E's And Wizz/Mis-Shapes
All songs written by Pulp
All lyrics by Jarvis Cocker
Produced by Chris Thomas except: [2] produced by Jeff Griffin
Engineered by David 'Chipper' Nicholas, assistant engineers Julie Gardner and Pete Lewis, except: [2] engineered by Mike Engles
[3] additional production and remix by Motiv 8 AKA Steve Rodway for Nuff Respect Productions
Recorded at The Town House, London, June 19–July 28, 1995, except: [1] recorded at The Town House, London, February 27–April 2, 1995; [2] recorded live at the Glastonbury Festival, England, June 30, 1995; [3] and [4] recorded at The Town House, London, January 18–24, 1995
Mixed at The Town House, London, July 31–August 14, 1995, except: [3] remixed at The Town House, London, May 12, 1995; [4] remixed at The Town House, London, summer 1995
Sleeve design by Blue Source
CD1: Photography by Rankin, illustration – David Jukes
CD2: Photography by Amber Rowlands and Donald Milne
CD1, CD2 and cassette released on Island Records (CD1: CID 620, CD2: CIDX 620, cassette, CIS 620), September 27, 1995
12″ and blue vinyl 7″ released on Island Records (12″: 12IS 620, 7″: IS 620), November 20, 1996

NB: the single versions of 'Mis-Shapes' and 'Sorted' are slightly censored compared to the versions on Different Class: 'Mis-Shapes' replaces the word "bleeding" with "very", and 'Sorted' replaces 'fucked-up' with 'messed-up'.
Highest UK chart position: 2

'Disco 2000'

CD1: Disco 2000 (7″ mix)[1]/Disco 2000 (album mix)/Ansaphone/Live Bed Show (Extended)
CD2: Disco 2000 (album mix)/Disco 2000 (7″ mix)[1]/Disco 2000 (Motiv 8 Discoid Mix)[2]/Disco 2000 (Motiv 8 Gimp Dub)[2]
7″: Disco 2000 (7″ mix)[1]/Ansaphone
12″: Disco 2000 (7″ mix)[1]/Ansaphone//Disco 2000 (Motiv 8 Discoid Mix)/Disco 2000 (Motiv 8 Gimp Dub)
All songs written by Pulp
All lyrics by Jarvis Cocker
Produced by Chris Thomas
Engineered by David 'Chipper' Nicholas, assistant engineers Pete Lewis and Julie Gardner
[1] additional production and remix by Alan Tarney, additional keyboards by Oliver Tarney
Mix engineers Gerry Kitchingham and John Hudson, assistant engineers John Brant and Anthony Lycenko
[2] additional production and remix by Motiv 8 AKA Steve Rodway for Nuff Respect Productions
Recorded at The Town House, London, June 19–July 28, 1995
Mixed at The Town House, London, July 31–August 14, 1995, except: [1] and [2] remixed at The Town House, London, autumn 1995
All tracks mastered at Metropolis by Tim Young, autumn 1995
Sleeve design by Blue Source
Photography by Donald Milne
CD1, CD2 and cassette released on Island Records (CD1: CID 623, CD2: CIDX 623, cassette, CIS 623), November 27, 1995
12″ and orange vinyl 7″ released on Island Records (12″: 12IS 623, 7″: IS 623), November 20, 1996
CD2 re-pressed by Island Records (same catalogue number etc as before), December 3, 1999
NB: the 1999 re-pressing is identical to the original 1995 version other than the matrix number on the disc and the booklet, which is printed on ordinary paper rather than the glossy paper of the original. The promo sticker from Appearing reads: "Pulp's 'Disco 2000' has been repressed . . . now it's been re-pressed! Not so much a re-release, as a date kept! Pulp have made their end of the century classic available once more. The packaging's the same, there are no new tracks on the B-side, but it's here for a whole new generation to own and cherish. You will be there at 2 o'clock by the fountain down the road, won't you?"
Highest UK chart position: 7

'Something Changed'

CD1 ('Girl' sleeve), CD2 ('Boy' sleeve) and 12″ ('Girl' sleeve): Something Changed/Mile End[1]// F.E.E.L.I.N.G.C.A.L.L.E.D.L.O.V.E. (Moloko remix)[2]/ F.E.E.L.I.N.G.C.A.L.L.E.D.L.O.V.E. (live at Brixton Academy)[3]
Cassette (double-sided 'Boy'/'Girl' sleeve) and 7″ ('Boy' sleeve): Something Changed/ Mile End[1]
All songs written by Pulp
All lyrics by Jarvis Cocker
Produced by Chris Thomas
Engineered by David 'Chipper' Nicholas, assistant engineers Pete Lewis and Julie Gardner

Recorded at The Town House, London, June 19–July 28, 1995, except: [1] recorded at The Town House, London, February 27–April 2, 1995; [3] recorded live at Brixton Academy, London, December 21, 1995
Mixed at The Town House, London, July 31–August 14, 1995, except: [2] remixed by Moloko, late 1995; [3] mixed early 1996
Sleeve design by Blue Source
Photography by Rankin
CD1, CD2 and cassette released on Island Records (CD1: CID 632, CD2: CIDX 632, cassette, CIS 632), March 29, 1996
12″ and 7″ released on Island Records (12″: 12IS 632, 7″: IS 632), November 20, 1996
NB: the live version of 'F.E.E.L.I.N.G.C.A.L.L.E.D.L.O.V.E.' is the same version as appears on the 'F.E.E.L.I.N.G.C.A.L.L.E.D.L.I.V.E.' video.

'Help The Aged'
Help The Aged//Tomorrow Never Lies/Laughing Boy
All songs written by Pulp
All lyrics by Jarvis Cocker
Produced by Chris Thomas
Engineered by Pete Lewis
Recorded and mixed at Olympic Studios, London and The Town House, London, November 1996–1997
Sleeve design by Blue Source
Photography by Rankin
Painting by John Currin ('The Never Ending Story', 1994, oil on canvas)
7″, CD and cassette single released on Island Records (7″: IS 679, CD: CID 679, cassette: CIS 679), November 11, 1997
NB: the British charity Help The Aged initially objected to the use of their name on this single, resulting in a portion of the royalties being donated to the charity.
Highest UK chart position: 8

'This Is Hardcore'
CD1: This Is Hardcore/Ladies' Man/The Professional/This Is Hardcore (Pulp's End Of The Line remix)
CD2: This Is Hardcore/This Is Hardcore (4 Hero remix)[1]/This Is Hardcore (Swedish Erotica Remix, AKA Tipsy remix)[2]/This Is Hardcore (Stock, Hausen And Walkman remix)[3]
Cassette: This Is Hardcore/Ladies' Man
All songs written by Pulp except 'This Is Hardcore' by Pulp and Peter Thomas
All lyrics by Jarvis Cocker
Produced by Chris Thomas
Engineered by Pete Lewis
Recorded and mixed at Olympic Studios, London and The Town House, London, March 1997–January 1998
[1] remix and additional production by 4 Hero, Kasbah Studios. Remix engineer and additional sitar Leon Mar
[2] remix and additional production by Tipsy (David J Gardner and Tim Digullar) at The Bloody Angle Compound, San Francisco. Orgasmic guitar by Michael Padilla, additional engineering X Davidson.
[3] remixed by Stock, Hausen and Walkman.
Art direction: John Currin and Peter Saville
Sleeve design: Howard Wakefield and Paul Hetherington at The Apartment
Photography: Horst Diekgerdes

CD1, CD2 and cassette single released on Island Records (CD1: CID 695, CD2: CIDX 695, cassette: CIS 695), March 9, 1998
NB: the planned release date for this single was March 16, 1998, but was brought forward to March 9 at the last minute.
Highest UK chart position: 12

'A Little Soul'
CD1: A Little Soul (album version)/Cocaine Socialism/Like A Friend (film version)
CD2: A Little Soul (alternative mix, AKA Johnny Dollar remix)/A Little Soul (Lafeyette Velvet Revisited remix)[1]/That Boy's Evil[2]
Cassette: A Little Soul/Cocaine Socialism
All songs written by Pulp except 'Cocaine Socialism' by Pulp and Antony Genn
All lyrics by Jarvis Cocker
Produced by Chris Thomas except: [2] produced by Pulp
Engineered by Pete Lewis except: [2] engineered by Clive Goddard
Recorded and mixed at Olympic Studios, London and The Town House, London, March 1997–January 1998
[1] remixed by Kid Loco at the Lafayette Velvet Basement, 1998
Art direction: John Currin and Peter Saville
Sleeve design: Howard Wakefield and Paul Hetherington at The Apartment
Photography: Horst Diekgerdes
CD1, CD2 and cassette single released on Island Records (CD1: CID 705, CD2: CIDX 705, cassette: CIS 705), June 8, 1998
NB: the alternative mix of 'A Little Soul' is erroneously listed as the original mix on the spine of CD2. 'Cocaine Socialism' was originally called 'Northern Souls' but was changed to avoid confusion with 'A Little Soul'. 'That Boy's Evil' was originally called 'In With The P-Crowd'.
Highest UK chart position: 22

'Party Hard'
CD1: Party Hard[1]/We Are The Boyz/The Fear (The Complete And Utter Breakdown Version)
CD2: Party Hard[1]/Party Hard (Stretch 'N' Verns Michel Lombert Mix)[2]/Party Hard (I Hardly Part Mix)[3]
Cassette: Party Hard[1]/Party Hard (Stretch 'N' Verns Michel Lombert Mix)[2]
All songs written by Pulp
All lyrics by Jarvis Cocker
Produced by Chris Thomas
Engineered by Pete Lewis
Recorded and mixed at Olympic Studios, London and The Town House, London, March 1997–January 1998
[1] remixed by Pulp at The Town House, London, 1998
[2] remixed by Stretch 'N' Vern, 1998
[2] remixed and reduced by The All Seeing I, 1998
Art direction: John Currin and Peter Saville
Sleeve design: Howard Wakefield and Paul Hetherington at The Apartment
Photography: Horst Diekgerdes
CD1, CD2 and cassette single released on Island Records (CD1: CID 719, CD2: CIDX 719, cassette: CIS 719), September 7, 1998
NB: CD2 is a total of 20m 2s long, pushing it over the 20-minute time limit stipulated in the new chart eligibility rules laid down earlier in 1998. Therefore, the second CD is technically chart ineligible; this may or may not have had some bearing on the single's underwhelming chart performance.
Highest UK chart position: 29

'The Trees'/'Sunrise'
CD1: Sunrise/The Trees/Sunrise (Fat Truckers/Scott Free mix)[1]
CD2: The Trees/Sunrise/The Trees (Felled By I Monster)[2]
12″: Sunrise (All Seeing I – Middle Of The Road Mix)[3]//The Trees (Felled By I Monster)[2]/The Trees (Lovejoy The No Jazz Mix)[4]
All songs written by Pulp except 'Sunrise' by Pulp and Peter Mansell
All lyrics by Jarvis Cocker
Produced by Scott Walker
Co-produced and engineered by Peter Walsh
Recorded and mixed at Metropolis Studios, London, September 2000–March 2001
Choir for 'Sunrise' recorded by Steve Price at Angel Studios, London
Mastered by Chris Blair at Abbey Road
[1] remixed by The Fat Truckers, *circa* March 2001
[2] remixed by I Monster, 2001
[3] remixed by The All Seeing I, *circa* March 2001
[4] remixed *circa* 2001
Sleeve design: Peter Saville Studio
Photography: Sarah Paris
CD1 and CD2 released on Universal Island Records (CD1: CID 786, CD2: CIDX 786), October 8, 2001
12″ released on Universal Island Records (12IS 786), October 15, 2001
Highest UK chart position: 23

'Bad Cover Version'
CD1: Bad Cover Version (album version)/Yesterday[1]/Forever In My Dreams[2]
CD2: Bad Cover Version (video mix)/Disco 2000 (by Nick Cave)[3]/Sorted? (by Roisin Murphy)[4]
DVD: Bad Cover Version (audio)/Bad Cover Version (video)/Making The Video
All songs written by Pulp
All lyrics by Jarvis Cocker
Produced by Scott Walker, co-produced and recorded by Peter Walsh except:
[1] and [2] recorded by Chris Thomas, engineered by Pete Lewis
[3] produced by Pulp and Cameron Craig
[4] produced and recorded by Fabien Antonio
Recorded and mixed at Metropolis Studios, London, September 2000–March 2001 except:
[1] recorded at Cosford Mill Studios, Surrey, April/May 2000, mixed at The Town House, London, January/February 2002; [2] recorded at The Depot, London, March 2000, overdubbed and mixed at The Town House, London, January/February 2002; [3] and [4] recorded and mixed *circa* January/February 2002
Sleeve design: Peter Saville Studio
Photography: Tony Webber
CD1, CD2 and DVD released on Universal Island Records (CD1: CID 794, CD2: CIDX 794, DVD: CIDV 794), April 15, 2002
Highest UK chart position: 27

PULP COMPILATION ALBUMS (OFFICIAL AND SEMI-OFFICIAL)

Intro

Space[1]/O.U. (Gone, Gone)[1]/Babies (original version)[2]/Styloroc (Nites Of Suburbia)[2]/Razzmatazz[3]//Sheffield Sex City[2]/*Inside Susan: A Story In Three Songs*: Stacks[3]/Inside Susan[3]/59 Lyndhurst Grove[3]

[1] originally released as the single 'O.U. (Gone, Gone)', May 1992

[2] originally released as the single 'Babies', October 1992

[3] originally released as the single 'Razzmatazz', February 1993

Sleeve design: The Designers Republic

Photography: Kevin Westerberg

LP, cassette and CD released on Island Records (LP: ILPM2076, cassette: ICM2076, CD: IMCD159), October 11, 1993

NB: Intro *is a compilation bringing together the three Pulp singles released on Gift Records in 1992 and 1993.*

Masters Of The Universe: Pulp On Fire 1985–86

Little Girl (With Blue Eyes)[1]/Simultaneous[1]/Blue Glow[1]/The Will To Power[1]/Dogs Are Everywhere[2]/The Mark Of The Devil[2]/97 Lovers[2]/Aborigine[2]/Goodnight[2]/They Suffocate At Night (Uncut Version)[3]/Tunnel (Full-length Version)[3]/Master Of The Universe (Sanitised Version)[4]/Manon (New Version)[4]

[1] originally released as the single 'Little Girl (With Blue Eyes) And Other Pieces', December 1985

[2] originally released as the single 'Dogs Are Everywhere', June 1986

[3] originally released as the single 'They Suffocate At Night', January 1987

[4] originally released as the single 'Master Of The Universe', March 1987

Sleeve design: The Designers Republic

Photography: Andy Gray

Sleevenotes: Clive Solomon

LP, cassette and CD released on Fire Records (LP: FIRE LP36, cassette: FIRE TC36, CD: FIRE CD36), June 24, 1994

NB: Masters Of The Universe *is a compilation bringing together the four Pulp singles released on Fire Records between 1985 and 1987, with the exception of 'Silence' (originally from the 'Master Of The Universe' single), which was left off at Jarvis' request. Jarvis was initially asked to write sleevenotes for the release; Clive Solomon changed his mind when he saw them! The piece that Jarvis wrote eventually surfaced in the Pulp People fanclub magazine* Disco-Very, *issue 2, January 1995.*

Hits

Babies (1994 remix)/Razzmatazz/Lipgloss/Do You Remember The First Time?/Common People Underwear/Sorted For E's & Wizz/Disco 2000/Something Changed/Help The Aged/This Is Hardcore/A Little Soul/Party Hard/The Trees/Bad Cover Version/Sunrise/Last Day Of The Miners' Strike[1]

All tracks taken from the Island Records albums *Intro, His'n'Hers, Different Class, This Is Hardcore* and *We Love Life*, except for:

[1] previously unreleased

Recorded in London, September 2002

Produced by Pulp and Cameron Craig

Engineered by Cameron Craig

Written by Pulp, Richard Hawley and Burt Bacharach

Lyrics by Jarvis Cocker

Sleeve design: Simon Periton/Sadie Coles HQ

Appendix 1

Photography: Willie Seldon
Sleevenotes: Harland Miller
CD released on Universal Island Records (CID 8126), November 18, 2002
NB: Hits is a compilation bringing together all of the Pulp singles released on Gift and Island Records between 1992 and 2002, with the exception of 'O.U.' and 'Mis-Shapes', and the addition of the album track 'Underwear' and the new song 'Last Day Of The Miners' Strike'. All versions are those released on the original albums rather than the singles – hence 'Babies' is the 1994 remix from His'n'Hers, 'Sorted For E's And Wizz' has a rude word in it, and 'Disco 2000' and 'Party Hard' are the non-remixed versions.
Highest UK chart position: 71

PULP COMPILATION ALBUMS (UNOFFICIAL)

In the wake of Pulp's success, a seemingly endless parade of shoddily put-together compilation CDs have appeared containing selections of the band's Fire Records material. Generally, there is little to recommend these releases, especially with the three original albums and Masters Of The Universe *being readily available. However, if you really must, then* Countdown *is a fair overview of Pulp's pre-Island material,* Pulped *is a way of getting the four Fire CDs (minus the original artwork) cheaply, and* Countdown *and* Pulp Goes To The Disco *between them offer all the tracks from the 'My Legendary Girlfriend' and 'Countdown' singles, which may be marginally cheaper and easier than tracking down the original releases.*

Countdown: Pulp 1992–1983
LP1/cassette 1/CD1: Countdown (Radio Edit)/Death Goes To The Disco/My Legendary Girlfriend/Don't You Want Me Anymore?/She's Dead/Down By The River/I Want You/Being Followed Home/Master Of The Universe/Don't You Know?/They Suffocate At Night
LP2/cassette 2/CD2: Dogs Are Everywhere/Mark Of The Devil/97 Lovers/Little Girl (With Blue Eyes)/Blue Glow/My Lighthouse/Wishful Thinking/Blue Girls/Countdown (full-length single version)
All tracks originally released on Red Rhino and Fire Records between 1983 and 1992. Taken from the albums *It, Freaks, Separations* and *Masters Of The Universe: Pulp On Fire 1985–86*, and the single 'Countdown'.
Sleevenotes: Caroline Sullivan
Double LP, double cassette and double CD released on Nectar Masters (LP: NTMLP521, cassette: NTMC521, CD: NTMCD521), March 22, 1996
CD re-released on Fire Records (FIRE CD68), 2002
Highest UK chart position: 10

Pulp Goes To The Disco
Death II/Death Goes To The Disco/Countdown (LP version)/My Legendary Girlfriend/Is This House?/This House Is Condemned (12″ remix)/Countdown (full-length single version)/Love Is Blind/Mark Of The Devil/Master Of The Universe
All tracks originally released on Fire Records between 1986 and 1992. Taken from the albums *Freaks, Separations* and *Masters Of The Universe: Pulp On Fire 1985–86,* and the singles 'My Legendary Girlfriend' and 'Countdown'.
Sleevenotes: Martin Lilleker
CD released on Connoisseur Collection (VSOP CD26), July 13, 1998

Primal . . . The Best Of The Fire Years, 1983–1992

My Legendary Girlfriend/Countdown (full-length single version)/Death Goes To The Disco/Little Girl (With Blue Eyes)/I Want You/They Suffocate At Night/Dogs Are Everywhere/Don't You Know/She's Dead/Aborigine/Separations/97 Lovers

All tracks originally released on Fire Records between 1985 and 1992. Taken from the albums *Freaks, Separations* and *Masters Of The Universe: Pulp On Fire 1985–86*, and the single 'Countdown'.

CD released on Music Collection International (MCCD 375), October 12, 1998

Pulped 83–92

CD1: *It* LP
CD2: *Freaks* LP
CD3: *Separations* LP
CD4: *Masters Of The Universe* compilation LP
Limited to 5,000 copies
All tracks originally released on Red Rhino and Fire Records between 1983 and 1992
Sleevenotes: Caroline Sullivan
4-CD box set released on Cooking Vinyl (COOK CD 178), May 31, 1999

Pulp On Fire

CD1: My Lighthouse/Wishful Thinking/Joking Aside/Boats And Trains/Love Love/In Many Ways/Looking For Life/Little Girl (With Blue Eyes)/Simultaneous/Blue Glow
CD2: The Will To Power/Dogs Are Everywhere/The Mark Of The Devil/97 Lovers/Aborigine/Goodnight/They Suffocate At Night/Tunnel/Master Of The Universe/Manon

All tracks originally released on Red Rhino and Fire Records between 1983 and 1986. Taken from the albums *It* and *Masters Of The Universe: Pulp On Fire 1985–86*
2-CD set released on Snapper Music (SMDCD 247), November 29, 1999

VARIOUS ARTISTS COMPILATIONS CONTAINING RARE OR EXCLUSIVE PULP TRACKS

Your Secret's Safe With Us

Featured Pulp track: What Do You Say?
Song written by Pulp
Lyrics by Jarvis Cocker
Recorded by Ken Patten
Recorded and mixed at Ken Patten Studio, Handsworth, Sheffield, August 7, 1981
Album compiled by Nigel Burnham
Pulp photographed by Chris Wicks
Double LP released on Statik Recorks (STATLP 7), February 22, 1982

The Best Of Your Secret's Safe With Us

Featured Pulp track: What Do You Say?
Song written by Pulp
Lyrics by Jarvis Cocker
Recorded and mixed by Ken Patten at Ken Patten Studio, Handsworth, Sheffield, August 7, 1981
Album compiled by Nigel Burnham

Pulp photographed by Chris Wicks
LP released on Statik Records (STATLP 14), February 21, 1983

Company Classics 3
Featured Pulp tracks: Coy Mistress, I Want You
Songs written by Pulp
Lyrics by Jarvis Cocker, except 'Coy Mistress' by Andrew Marvell and Russell Senior
Recorded and mixed by Mark Estdale at Vibrasound Studio, Sheffield, January 1984
Compiled by Ian Spence
Cassette released on Company Records (no catalogue number), June 1984
NB: the Company Classics *series of cassettes were compilations of tracks by local Sheffield bands, produced in limited qualities (around 300 copies) and sold at gigs and in local record shops.*

The Outrage Tour
Featured Pulp tracks: My Lighthouse (album version), Maureen
'My Lighthouse' written by Jarvis Cocker and Simon Hinkler, lyrics by Jarvis Cocker
'Maureen' music and lyrics by Russell Senior and Jarvis Cocker
'My Lighthouse' produced by Simon Hinkler, recorded and mixed at Victoria Studios, Sheffield, November 27–December 10, 1982
'Maureen' recorded by John Nicholls, Wicker Karate Rooms, May 8, 1984
Cassette released September 1985
NB: this tape was sold at gigs on the Outrage Tour between September 1985 and January 1986, and brings together tracks from the four acts that made up the bill on the tour: Pulp, Dig Vis Drill, Mr Morality and Henry Normal.

Beware The Bacon Slicer
Featured Pulp tracks: Anorexic Beauty, Coy Mistress
Songs written by Pulp
'Anorexic Beauty' lyrics by David Kurley, 'Coy Mistress' lyrics by Andrew Marvell and Russell Senior
'Anorexic Beauty' recorded and mixed *either* by John Nicholls at Wicker Karate Rooms, Sheffield, May 8, 1984, *or* by Pulp and Tim Allcard at Castle Table Tennis Rooms, Sheffield, November 11, 1984
'Coy Mistress' recorded and mixed by Mark Estdale at Vibrasound Studio, Sheffield, January 1984
Cassette released on Pork Records (CUISINE 2), April 1986
NB: this obscure cassette was apparently a compilation of tracks by local Sheffield bands, produced in limited quantities and sold at gigs and in local record shops. It is unclear which of the two demo versions of 'Anorexic Beauty' was used; when asked, Jarvis replied, "I neither know nor care."

Imminent 4
Featured Pulp track: Manon (original version)
Song written by Pulp
Lyrics by Jarvis Cocker – French translation by Elizabeth Baxter
Recorded and mixed by Simon Hinkler, Input Studio, Sheffield, June 1985
LP released on Food Records (BITE 4), August 1986
NB: this LP is the only release of the original version of 'Manon', recorded during the sessions for the Little Girl *EP. The song was later overdubbed and remixed during the* Freaks *sessions and released on the B-side of 'Master Of The Universe'; however, any differences between the two versions are almost imperceptible.*

Premonition Art Construct
Featured Pulp track: Back In LA
Song written by Pulp
Lyrics by Russell Senior and Jarvis Cocker
Recorded and mixed by Pulp and Tim Allcard at Castle Table Tennis Rooms, Sheffield, November 11, 1984
Compiled by Paul Mills
Cassette released by Premonition (PREM 5), January 1987
NB: another compilation of tracks by local Sheffield bands, produced in limited quantities and sold at gigs and in local record shops. Paul Mills says: "I started Premonition Tapes in 1986 to promote local music and stuff I was generally interested in. I wrote to Pulp when I was compiling my first compilation tape Premonition Art Construct *and they sent me 'Back In LA'. The following year I did an hour's worth of taped interview with Jarvis and Russell, 20 minutes of which appeared on* Premspeak 1 *with the track 'Maureen'.*

"None of the tapes ever sold very well until 1989 when a tape I released with The Inspiral Carpets took off 'cos they were the in thing at the time. Their management soon put an injunction on me releasing any more copies after a misprint in Melody Maker, *so in 1990 I folded the label and stopped working with other bands to concentrate on my own music."*

Premspeak 1
Featured Pulp tracks: Maureen, Jarvis and Russell interview
'Maureen' music and lyrics by Russell Senior and Jarvis Cocker
Recorded and mixed by Pulp and Tim Allcard at Castle Table Tennis Rooms, Sheffield, November 11, 1984
Compiled by Paul Mills
Cassette released by Premonition (no catalogue number), May 1987

See You Later Agitator
Featured Pulp track: Night Of Suburbia
Song written by Pulp
Lyrics by Jarvis Cocker
Recorded live at The Octagon Centre, Sheffield, September 1, 1985
Cassette (in 7″ sleeve with booklet) released by Dolebusters (no catalogue number), July 1987
NB: a compilation of tracks from bands that had played at the Dolebusters' anti-unemployment concerts in Sheffield between 1985 and 1987. Jarvis wrote a piece for the booklet that later served as the lyrics to 'Styloroc (Nites Of Suburbia)'. Other bands featured on the tape included Trolley Dog Shag (featuring Wayne Furniss and Steve Mackey), Mr Morality (featuring David Hinkler and Steve Genn), and the Wealthy Texans (with the Sheffield Star's *Martin Lilleker on guitar).*

Oozing Through The Ozone Layer
Featured Pulp tracks: My First Wife, Don't You Want Me Anymore?
Songs written by Pulp
Lyrics by Jarvis Cocker
Recorded live by Mark Webber, Nottingham Barracuda Club, July 15, 1987
Compiled by Mark Webber
Cassette released on Globe Of Bulbs (LSD 5), December 1987
NB: Globe Of Bulbs was a bedroom-based cassette label run by the teenaged Mark Webber. Other bands on the tape included The Inspiral Carpets, Spacemen 3, TV Personalities and The Jazz Butcher.

Year One – The Best Of Premonition Tapes (So Far)
Featured Pulp track: Maureen
Music and lyrics by Russell Senior and Jarvis Cocker

452

Recorded and mixed by Pulp and Tim Allcard at Castle Table Tennis Rooms, Sheffield, November 11, 1984
Compiled by Paul Mills
Cassette released by Premonition (no catalogue number), January 1988

Volume 10
Featured Pulp track: Joyriders (acoustic)
Song written by Pulp
Lyrics by Jarvis Cocker
Recorded live at GLR Studios, London, March 22, 1994 – producer and engineer unknown
CD book released by World's End Ltd (10VCD 10), July 1994
NB: this is the same version of 'Joyriders' as on CD2 of the 'Common People' single.

The Radio 1FM Sessions
Featured Pulp track: Do You Remember The First Time? (live)
Song written by Pulp
Lyrics by Jarvis Cocker
Recorded live at the Glasgow Tramway, April 4, 1994
Given away as a cover cassette (GIVIT 8) with *Vox* magazine, November 1994

Melody Maker Six Pack
Featured Pulp track: Pink Glove (Peel Session)
Song written by Pulp
Lyrics by Jarvis Cocker
Produced by Mike Engles, assistant engineer Simon Askew
Recorded at BBC Maida Vale Studios, February 7, 1993
Given away as a cover cassette (MMMC 5) with *Melody Maker*, June 2, 1995
NB: originally broadcast on The John Peel Show, BBC Radio 1, March 5, 1993.

Red Heaven: 20 Of The Best From The Cherry Red Label
Featured Pulp track: Everybody's Problem
Song written by Jarvis Cocker
Arranged by Pulp
Produced by Simon Hinkler
Engineered by Simon Skolfield
Recorded and mixed at Southern Studios, London, June 4–5, 1983
CD released on Nectar Masters, autumn 1995

Class of 95
Featured Pulp track: Sorted For E's And Wizz
Song written by Pulp
Lyrics by Jarvis Cocker
Recorded live at Glastonbury Festival, England, June 24, 1995
Cassette given free with *Vox* magazine (VOX GIVIT 14), 1995

Later Volume One: Brit Beat
Featured Pulp Track: I Spy (live)
Song written by Pulp
Lyrics by Jarvis Cocker
Recorded live at the London Shepherds Bush TV Centre, November 7, 1995
CD released on Island Records (CID 8053), 1996
NB: originally broadcast on Later With Jools Holland, BBC 2, December 2, 1995.

Evening Session Priority Tunes
Featured Pulp track: Babies (Evening Session)
Song written by Pulp
Lyrics by Jarvis Cocker
Recorded at BBC Maida Vale Studio 4, May 30, 1992
Double CD released on Virgin Records (VTD C88), 1996
NB: originally broadcast on the Mark Goodier Show, BBC Radio 1, June 29, 1992.

Childline
Featured Pulp track: Whiskey In The Jar (live)
Song trad. arr. Lynott
Recorded live at Radio France Inter Studio 105, October 30, 1995
CD released on Polygram TV (5530302), November 1996
NB: originally broadcast on The Black Sessions, Radio France Inter, October 30, 1995.

Long Live Tibet
Featured Pulp track: Live Bed Show (live)
Song written by Pulp
Lyrics by Jarvis Cocker
Recorded live by BBC Radio 1 at the V96 Festival, Hylands Park, Chelmsford, August 17, 1996
CD and double LP released on EMI/Ritual (CD: CDEMC 3768, LP: EMC 3768), 1997
NB this is the extended version of 'Live Bed Show', with an extra verse at the end, that the band performed live in 1996.

Great Expectations OST
Featured Pulp track: Like A Friend (album version)
Song written by Pulp
Lyrics by Jarvis Cocker
Produced by Chris Thomas
Engineered by Pete Lewis
Recorded and mixed at The Town House and Olympic Studios, London, March 1997–January 1998
CD released by Atlantic Records, 1998.
NB: the 'album version' of 'Like A Friend' is shorter with a different vocal mix to the more common 'film version' found on the 'A Little Soul' single and the US and Japan editions of This Is Hardcore.

The Glastonbury Broadcasts, Vol 1
Featured Pulp track: Sorted For E's And Wizz (live)
Song written by Pulp
Lyrics by Jarvis Cocker
Recorded live by BBC Radio 1 at the Glastonbury Festival, England, June 28, 1999
CD given away free with *NME*, June 12, 1999

Notting Hill OST
Featured Pulp track: Born To Cry
Song written by Pulp and Richard Hawley
Lyrics by Jarvis Cocker
Produced by Simon Dawson at Axis Studio, Sheffield, October 31–November 1, 1998
Mixed by Mark 'Spike' Stent at Olympic Studios, London, late 1998/early 1999
CD released by Island Records, May 24, 1999
NB: 'Born To Cry' does not feature in the film, nor on non-UK editions of the album.

A Tribute To Polnareff
Featured Pulp track: Le Roi Des Fourmis
Written by Michel Polnareff
Recorded at Axis Studio, Sheffield, May 1993
CD released by Xlll Bis Records/EMI France (52209952), July 9, 1999
NB: a various artists tribute to the French artist Michel Polnareff.

Randall & Hopkirk (Deceased) OST
Featured Pulp track: My Body May Die (credited to 'Pulp vs The Swingle Singers')
Song written by Pulp
Lyrics by Jarvis Cocker
Produced by Pulp and Pete Lewis, London, August 1999
Remixed by Howie B, London, October 1999
CD released by Universal Island Records (CID 8096), April 24, 2000

School Disco
Featured Pulp tracks: Everybody's Problem, There Was . . .
Songs written by Jarvis Cocker
Arranged by Pulp
Produced by Simon Hinkler
Engineered by Simon Skolfield
Recorded and mixed at Southern Studios, London, June 4–5, 1983
CD released on Cherry Red, 2001

NME Exclusives!
Featured Pulp track: Party Hard (live)
Song written by Pulp
Lyrics by Jarvis Cocker
Recorded live at the Paleo Festival, Switzerland, July 24, 2001
CD given free with *NME*, October 6, 2001

4 Scott
Featured Pulp tracks: Babies (live), Sunrise (live)
Songs written by Pulp – 'Sunrise' written by Pulp and Peter Mansell
Lyrics by Jarvis Cocker
Recorded live at the 4 Scott Tribute Concert at The Scala, London, April 18, 2002
CD released on V2 Records (VVR1020542), August 26, 2002

SIGNIFICANT UK PROMOS

For almost every Pulp release, there exists a variety of promotional and overseas releases that differ from the stock UK release in some way. In many cases, the differences between the official releases and their promo/import counterparts will be minor, perhaps amounting to little more than a different catalogue number or a stamp bearing the words 'For Promotional Use Only'. Listed here are those releases that differ more significantly in terms of packaging or musical content. Much of the information here is taken from the superb promo/import discography on Giles Bosworth's acrylicafternoons.com website.

'Little Girl (With Blue Eyes)' (1985)
1. 12″ white label (FIRE 5)
   - Little Girl (With Blue Eyes)//Simultaneous/Blue Glow/The Will To Power
   - Packaging: none

'Master Of The Universe' (1987)
1. 12″ test pressing (Mayking Records)
- • Master Of The Universe//Manon/Silence
- • Packaging: none

'This House Is Condemned' (*circa* 1990)
1. 1-sided 12″ white label (BLAZE44T)
- • Is This House?/This House Is Condemned (Parrot & Winston remixes)
- • Packaging: none

'O.U. (Gone, Gone)' (May 1992)
1. 12″ white label
- • O.U. (Gone, Gone)//Space/O.U. (Gone, Gone) (radio edit)
- • Packaging: none

'Babies' (October 1992)
1. 12″ white label (GIF 3)
- • Babies/Styloroc//Sheffield Sex City
- • Packaging: none

'Razzmatazz' (February 1993)
1. 12″ white label (GIF 6)
- • Razzmatazz//Stacks/Inside Susan/59 Lyndhurst Grove
- • Packaging: none

'Lipgloss' (November 1993)
1. DJ promo (CIDDJ 567)
- • Lipgloss (Radio Edit)
- • Packaging: J-case with usual single artwork

'Do You Remember The First Time?' (March 1994)
1. DJ promo (CIDDJ 574)
- • Do You Remember The First Time? (Radio Edit) (3m 50s)
- • Packaging: J-case with usual single artwork
- • Release sticker: "PULP come of age with their fabulous new single 'Do You Remember The First Time?', the story of the common and often awkward experience of first time sex. The single spawned a short film by band members and film/video makers JARVIS COCKER & STEVE MACKEY which features many celebrities (REEVES & MORTIMER, ALISON STEADMAN, JO BRAND, JOHN PEEL, etc.) relating their experiences. The film will be screened at the I.C.A. on March 9, afterward the band will play a set. March's FACE features a 3-page article on PULP."

'Common People' (May 1995)
1. DJ promo (CIDDJ 613)
- • Common People (7″ edit)/Underwear/Common People (full-length version)
- • Packaging: card sleeve with 'Daytime' CD artwork
- • Release Sticker: "These two songs are the first new material from the band since their highly acclaimed, Gold, and 'Mercury Prize' runner-up album *His'n'Hers* was released over a year ago. Both tracks are taken from the forthcoming and as yet untitled album (produced by Chris Thomas) which is due for release in September."

2. DJ promo (CIDXDJ 613)
- Common People (Motiv 8 Radio Edit)/Common People (Motiv 8 Club Mix)/Common People (Vocoda Mix)
- Packaging: J-case with 'Night-time' CD artwork
3. 'Chop 'Em Out' promo cassette (no number)
- Common People (full-length version)/Underwear/Common People (7″ edit)
- Packaging: generic Island/Chop 'Em Out cassette inlay
4. Motiv 8 promo 3″ CDR (no number)
- Common People (Motiv 8 Club Edit) (4m 58s)
- Packaging: generic Town House card sleeve
- Dated June 18, 1995
5. 4 track promo 12″ (12IS 613DJ)
- Common People (Motiv 8 Vocal Mix)/Common People (Vocoda Mix)/Common People (full-length version)/Common People (7″ edit)
- Packaging: black die-cut sleeve with Pulp sticker

'Mis-Shapes'/'Sorted' (September 1995)

1. DJ promo (CIDDJ 620)
- Mis-Shapes/Sorted
- Packaging: card sleeve with black and white 'cut-out' photos as seen on inside of 'Mis-Shapes' official CD. NB: the title of the second track is given here as 'Sorted', not 'Sorted For E's And Wizz'
- Some copies released in A5 pack with similar artwork to the front of the official 'Mis-Shapes' CD and included a fold-out tracing paper jacket pattern.
- Release sticker: "PULP's second single of the year on Island Records is a double A-side. The two tracks are entitled 'MIS-SHAPES' and 'SORTED FOR E's AND WHIZZ' [*sic*] otherwise just known as 'SORTED'. Both songs were first aired earlier this year when Pulp headlined Glastonbury. 'MIS-SHAPES' takes its name from those biscuits which are rejected because they don't quite look up to scratch even though they taste just as good as the normal ones. And as you might have guessed this little number is about misfits, a tribute to all outsiders. Meanwhile 'SORTED' is neither a pro or anti drugs song but more of an overview of the summer of love and festivals in general. PULP will be touring throughout the country in October."

'Different Class' (October 1995)

1. LP press kit (no number)
- Contains standard UK LP with interchangeable silver embossed sleeve
- Double sided sleeve insert displaying the 12 covers
- Inserts reproducing music press interviews/reviews for *Different Class* from *NME*, *Melody Maker*, *Q*, *Select*, *Vox*, *Ikon*, *The Guardian*, *What's On* & *Time Out*.
2. 'Chop 'Em Out' promo cassette (no number)
- Track listing as standard album
- Packaging: generic Island/Chop 'Em Out cassette inlay
- Labelled simply 'Pulp (Pre-Approved Cut)' – apparently the title *Different Class* was yet to be decided on.

'Disco 2000' (November 1995)

1. 7″ jukebox single (ISJB 623)
- Disco 2000 (7″ mix)/Disco 2000 (Motiv 8 Discoid Mix)
- Packaging: none

2. 3 track promo 12" (12IS 623DJ)
- Disco 2000 (Motiv 8 Discoid Mix)//Disco 2000 (Motiv 8 Gimp Dub)/Disco 2000 (7" mix)
- Packaging: black die-cut sleeve with Pulp sticker

'Something Changed' (March 1996)
1. 7" jukebox single (ISJB 632)
- Something Changed/Disco 2000 (7" mix)

'F.E.E.L.I.N.G.C.A.L.L.E.D.L.O.V.E.' (March 1996)
1. 1-sided 12" promo (12IS 632DJ)
- F.E.E.L.I.N.G.C.A.L.L.E.D.L.O.V.E. (Moloko mix)
- 400 copies only, released to promote 'Something Changed' single
- Packaging: black die-cut sleeve with Pulp sticker

'Help The Aged' (November 1997)
1. DJ promo (CIDDJ 679)
- Help The Aged (album version)
- Packaging: slim J-case with photo of empty room behind blinds similar to front of official single
- Release notes: "Have we all been waiting for this or wot? A new Pulp single is good news but the better news is that – in my opinion – that it is one of the best singles yet, containing everything that sets this band apart from all others. The soft underbelly leading to monumental soaring surges of chorus, hooks that never quit and lyrics that really say something. The best news of all is that there is an album to come next year and it will not disappoint. The same goes for live dates. Updates when they happen (Commercial CD contains 'Tomorrow Never Lies', the track that was too good for the James Bond Film.) – S.P."
2. 7" jukebox single (ISJB 679)
- Help The Aged/Tomorrow Never Lies
- Packaging: none

'This Is Hardcore' single (March 1998)
1. DJ promo (CIDDJ 695)
- This Is Hardcore (radio edit – 5m 14s)/This Is Hardcore (full version – 6m 23s)
- Packaging: pink card sleeve with detail from official single artwork
- Release sticker: "Before you listen to this, please appreciate that we consider this new Pulp single to be a masterpiece. We therefore ask you to give it an extra special listen, a deep, complete listen as befits the title track of the next Pulp album. It is strange, wonderful and vast in scope. It will scare you because it is so good, yet you will wonder what your listeners will think of this new dimension in pop music. You must take the moral high ground 'This Is Hardcore' and do not falter. It is as good as you feared. – S.P."
2. 12" promo (pink sleeve – 12IS 695DJ)
- This Is Hardcore (4 Hero Mix)/This Is Hardcore (Swedish Erotica Mix)//This Is Hardcore (Stock, Hausen & Walkman Remix)/This Is Hardcore (Original Version)
- Packaging: plain pink sleeve with Pulp logo and title
3. 12" promo (gold sleeve – 12ISX 695DJ)
- This Is Hardcore (Original Version)/Ladies' Man/The Professional/This Is Hardcore (End Of The Line Remix)
- Packaging: plain gold sleeve with Pulp logo and title

4. 7″ jukebox single (ISJB 695)
- This Is Hardcore (Original Version)/Ladies' Man
- Packaging: none

'This Is Hardcore' album (March 1998)
1. Album promo
- Tracklisting as UK album
- Packaging: plain black card sleeve with Pulp logo and title in pink lettering
- Release notes: "This is a real album, the whole is greater than its sum of parts, and each is superlative. Listen to actively and completely with brain online. Pulptasmic. – S.P."
2. BBC Radio 1 Special double promo CD
- CD 1: Do You Remember The First Time? (Pulp Documentary 1981 – 1995, first broadcast on BBC Radio 1, March 15, 1998)
- CD 2: From Disco To Hardcore (Pulp Documentary 1995 – 1998, first broadcast on BBC Radio 1, March 22, 1998)
- Packaging: plain black double jewel case with Pulp logo and title in pink lettering

'A Little Soul' (June 1998)
1. DJ promo (CIDDJ 708)
- A Little Soul (Album version)
- Packaging: 'Island Studios' plain card sleeve
- Release sticker: " 'Exquisitely Fragile' . . . but building to 'Overwhelming Magnificence' by the end. Most perfect Pulp track for radio since 'Something Changed'. Pulp play Glastonbury, T In The Park and Finsbury Park on July 25. Biggest UK group this year. Check out the hilarious press!"
2. DJ promo (CIDXDJ 708)
- A Little Soul (Album version)/A Little Soul (Johnny Dollar mix AKA alternative mix)
- Packaging: silm J-case featuring detail from the official single sleeve
- Release sticker: "From Hardcore to Softpop we go with Jarvis and co. delivering a short and sublime classic kind of single from the number one album that will have radio programmers and Pulp's pluggers alike breathing a collective sigh of relief. The single will coincide with the beginning of Pulp's ambitious touring and festival schedule throughout the summer. Once again they have made an astounding video to accompany this track and it's as simple as the video for 'Hardcore' was complex. See them at their own Finsbury bash in July."
3. 7″ jukebox single (ISJB 708)
- A Little Soul (Album version)/Cocaine Socialism
- Packaging: none

'Party Hard' (September 1998)
1. DJ promo (CIDDJ 719)
- Party Hard (single version)
- Packaging: A5 gatefold 'curtains' picture sleeve in similar style to official single
- Release sticker (1): "And Party Hard it will be in case you didn't know; the tour rolls out around the UK in November and they've ever so slightly remixed this single. There's to be a special re-release of the album *This Is Hardcore* with a bonus CD of their monumental Glastonbury performance . . .
- Release sticker (2): "Pulp prove why initial doubters of their current album are now eating their words with this, the strongest track of them all. The cheerleading video sees Jarvis pursuing a familiar theme of sexual frustration. *This Is Hardcore* has

received a nomination for the 'Mercury Music Prize' making Pulp the only band *ever* to have been nominated *three* times (they won in 1996) and it will be repackaged in a special limited edition double album format including this year's rousing performance at 'Glastonbury'." (Released 14th September)

2. 2-track promo 12″ (12IS 719 DJ)
   • Party Hard (Christopher Just Remix)/Party Hard (Tom Middleton Vocal Remix)
   • Packaging: 'curtains' picture sleeve in similar style to official single

3. 3-track promo 12″ (12ISX 719DJ)
   • Party Hard (Stretch 'N' Verns Michel Lombert Remix)//Party Hard (Tom Middleton's Dub Remix)/Party Hard (All Seeing I remix)
   • Packaging: detail of 'curtains' picture sleeve in similar style to official single

4. 'PPLU' 1-sided 2-track white label promo 12″ (12 HARD 1)
   • Party Hard (Christopher Just Remix)/Party Hard (Tom Middleton's Dub Remix)
   • Packaging: none. White label stamped with the name 'PPLU – PARTY HARD!'

5. 'Chocolate Layers' 1-sided white label promo 12″ (12 HARD 2)
   • Party Hard (Chocolate Layers remix)
   • Packaging: none. First 100 numbered white labels with handwritten title; subsequent copies white labels with sticker reading "PULP – 'PARTY HARD' CHOCOLATE LAYERS REMIX (JARVIS AND STEVE)"

6. Island in-house mixes cassette (no number)
   • Party Hard (Stretch 'N' Verns Mix)/Party Hard (Christopher Just Remix)/Party Hard (Tom Middleton Vocal Remix)/Party Hard (Tom Middleton's Dub Mix)/Party Hard (All Seeing I's Remix)
   • Packaging: generic Island Records cassette inlay

'Live At Glastonbury' (i.e. 'This Is Glastonbury') (September 1998)

1. Promo CD (524 592-2 01)
   • Tracklisting as *This Is Glastonbury* CD
   • Packaging: generic Island Studios die-cut card sleeve
   • Release sticker: "Pulp's performance at Glastonbury was legendary and ample reward for all after a day or two spent trudging around in the swamps that bedevilled this years festival. Here it is recorded for posterity and available on a special double CD for a limited period in the shops . . ."

'That Boy's Evil' (1999)

1. 1-sided white label 12″ promo (EVIL 1)
   • That Boy's Evil
   • Packaging: none

'Randall & Hopkirk (Deceased)' OST (dated February 10, 2000)

1. Album promo (no number)
   • Full album track listing, including 'My Body May Die' listed as 'Barry Crusoe'
   • Packaging: generic Island Universal card sleeve
   • 'Barry Crusoe' was the working title for 'My Body May Die'

'Sunrise' (May 2001)

1. White label 12″ DJ promo
   • Sunrise (All Seeing I – Middle Of The Road Mix)/Sunrise (Fat Truckers – Scott Free Mix)/Sunrise (Original Mix AKA album version)
   • Packaging: none. Plain white label with hand-stamped title
   • Primarily a DJ promo, but also made available commercially through the Rough Trade shop in London

'Pulp Love Life' (July 2001)
1. Promo CDR (no number)
 • Tracklisting same as final UK edition of *We Love Life*. 'Weeds II (Origin Of The Species)' listed as 'Origin Of The Species', 'The Night That Minnie Timperley Died' listed as 'Minnie Timperley', 'Bob Lind (The Only Way Is Down)' listed as 'Bob Lind'
 • Packaging: generic Universal Island packaging, dated July 26, 2001

'Pulp' (September 2001)
1. Promo CDR (no number)
 • Tracklisting same as final UK edition of *We Love Life*. 'Bob Lind (The Only Way Is Down)' listed as 'Bob Lind'
 • Packaging: generic Universal Island packaging, dated September 14, 2001

'The Trees'/'Sunrise' (October 2001)
1. DJ promo (TREE CD1)
 • The Trees (Radio Edit)/Sunrise (Album Version)/The Trees (Album Version)
 • Packaging: plain green sleeve with title in white lettering
 • Release sticker: "Both tracks feature on the bands forthcoming studio album *PULP*, their seventh. Recorded earlier this year at Metropolis studios and produced by the legendary Scott Walker, *PULP* marks a shift away from the nihilistic brinkmanship of *This Is Hardcore*, with the 11 songs featured, all bristling with optimism and nature, bizarrely. A limited white label of Sunrise has already been made available to independent shops, featuring mixes from Fat Truckers and All Seeing I. Jarvis and Steve Mackey have already started 'Desperate' a loose collection of DJ's and one mad club night. Desperate has already caused havoc at Homelands (where the crowd went mental to 'Sunrise') and Reading festival, check underground press for forthcoming events."
2. DJ promo (no number)
 • Trees (Radio Edit)/Trees (I Monster Mix)/Sunrise (Album Version)/Sunrise (Fat Truckers Scott Free Mix)
 • Packaging: generic Universal Island CDR, dated September 6, 2001

'We Love Life' (October 2001)
1. Jarvis Cocker interview CD (no number)
 • 35-minute interview with Jarvis and Steve taken directly from the Electronic [video] Press Kit issued to promote the album overseas
 • Packaging: generic Universal Island packaging, dated October 25, 2001

'Bad Cover Version' (April 2002)
1. DJ promo (BAD CD1)
 • Track listing: Bad Cover Version (radio edit)
 • Packaging: slim J-case featuring black and white variant of official single artwork
 • Release sticker: "The second single to be lifted from the *We Love Life* album, this has already become a favourite at the bands' recent live shows. This hilarious 'Band Aid' style video features 'Lookie-likies' singing their version of the track. Pulp's front-man Jarvis even pops up as 'Brian May'. Finished formats will include interpretations of two Pulp classics by Moloko's Roisin Murphy and Nick Cave. Pulp begin their 'Forest' tour in June playing Sherwood Forest (15th), Pinetum – Kent (16th), Roseisle Forest – Nth Scotland (21st), Dalby Forest (22nd) and Thetford Forest (23rd)."

'Hits' (November 2002)
1. 17-track promo CDR (no number)
    - Tracklisting as official CD
    - Packaging: generic Universal Island card sleeve
2. 'Remixes' promo CDR (no number)
    - A Little Soul (Kid Loco Mix)/This Is Hardcore (Tipsy Mix)/Sunrise (Fat Truckers/Scott Free Mix)/Disco 2000 (Nick Cave Version)
    - Packaging: generic Universal Island card sleeve

SIGNIFICANT NON-UK PROMOS

See note for significant UK promos.

'Babies' (1994)
1. US 3-track promo CD (PRCD 6829-2)
    - Babies '94 edit (as on *Sisters EP*)/Babies '94 (as on *His'n'Hers*)/Babies '92 (as on original single and *Intro*)
    - Packaging: jewel case with artwork as original single

'Do You Remember The First Time?' (March 1994)
1. US 2-track promo CD (PRCD 6833-2)
    - Do You Remember The First Time? (Radio Edit)/Do You Remember The First Time? (Album version)
    - Packaging: jewel case with artwork as original single

'His'n'Hers' (April 1994)
1. French 4-track sampler CD (4353)
    - Do You Remember The First Time?/Lipgloss/She's A Lady/Happy Endings
    - Packaging: card sleeve with the word 'Pulp' in blue on white background
2. French 'Pulp Collector' 2-track CD (1855)
    - His'n'Hers/Seconds
    - Packaging: card sleeve with *His'n'Hers* artwork
    - Given away with initial copies of *His'n'Hers* in France

'Common People' (May 1995)
1. Canadian 5-track promo 12″ (PR12 7163)
    - Common People (Motiv 8 Club Mix)/Common People (The Vocoda Mix)/Common People (Motiv 8 Radio Edit)/Common People (Full-length Version)/Common People (7″ Edit)
    - Packaging: none
2. French 2-track promo CD (3300)
    - Common People (7″ edit)/Underwear
    - Packaging: card sleeve with strange colourised version of the 'Daytime' artwork
3. German 3-track promo 12″ (854 465-1)
    - Common People (Doggy Disco mix)/Common People (TTP Understand The Acid mix)/Common People (Motiv 8 Club Mix)
    - Packaging: black die-cut sleeve with Pulp sticker
4. US 2-track promo CD (PRCD 7138)
    - Common People (Radio Edit)/Common People (Full-length Version)
    - Packaging: jewel case with 'Night-time' artwork

5. US 5-track promo CD (PRCD 7163)
- Common People (Motiv 8 Radio Edit)/Common People (Radio edit)/Common People (Full-length Version)/Common People (Motiv 8 Club Mix)/Common People (The Vocoda Mix)
- Packaging: none

'Different Class' (October 1995)

1. French 3-track FNAC promo CD (4423)
- P.T.A. (Parent Teacher Association/Common People (Live At Glastonbury)/Common People (Motiv 8 Club Mix)
- Packaging: card sleeve
2. French 6-track promo sampler CD (6971)
- Mis-Shapes/Pencil Skirt/Common People (Full-length Version)/I Spy/Disco 2000/Live Bed Show
- Packaging: pink card sleeve with Pulp logo and the title 'Different Class Sampler'

'Disco 2000' (November 1995)

1. Canadian 5-track 12″ promo (ISDJ 041596)
- Disco 2000 (Motiv 8 Discoid Mix)/Disco 2000 (Motiv 8 Gimp Dub)/Disco 2000 (Chris Thomas Version)/Disco 2000 (Album Version)/Disco 2000 (Alan Tarney Remix)
- Packaging: generic die-cut Island/Motown/A&M sleeve
2. German 1-track promo CD (852 758 12)
- Disco 2000 (Stefan Will edit) (3m 11s)
- Packaging: none. Includes German promotional press insert.
3. US 3-track promo CD (PRCD 7349-2)
- Disco 2000 (Alan Tarney Mix)/Disco 2000 (Album Version)/Disco 2000 (7″ Version)
- Packaging: jewel case with exclusive design based around *Different Class* cut-out pictures.
- The Alan Tarney mix, unavailable elsewhere, is a slightly altered version of the album mix.

'Coca-Cola Planet Live' (1996)

Australian promo CD issued by Austereo MCM (PL/PUL1/01)
- Sorted For E's & Wizz/Lipgloss/Razzmatazz/Pencil Skirt/Monday Morning/Happy Endings/Acrylic Afternoons/Pink Glove/Disco 2000/Babies/Mis-Shapes/Live Bed Show/Common People/Interview A – Jarvis on Sheffield (2:11)/Interview B – Jarvis on sudden success (0:40)
- All songs recorded live at Kentish Town Forum, London, October 20, 1995
- Packaging: none
- Presumably used as the basis of a radio broadcast

'Common People '96' (1996)

European promo CD (CID XJ 613)
- Common People '96
- Packaging: j-case with orange geometric pattern
- 'Common People '96' is identical to the 7″ edit, except the word 'screw' is muted.

'Like A Friend' (1998)
US promo CD (8440)
- Like A Friend (Album version – 3m 58s)/Like A Friend (Film version – 4m 32s)
- Packaging: jewel case with generic Island sticker
- The album version is the one included on the *Great Expectations* soundtrack LP; the film version is the one included on the 'A Little Soul' single and US and Japanese versions of *This Is Hardcore*.

'The Fear' (1998)
US promo CD (PRCD 7863)
- The Fear (edit – 4m 29s)/research hook
- Packaging: jewel case with detail from 'A Little Soul' artwork
- A 'research hook' is the main chorus loop or part of the track, used by radio stations for voiceovers and adverts.

'This Is Hardcore' single (March 1998)
French promo CD (3819)
- This Is Hardcore (French Edit)
- Packaging: card sleeve with detail from album artwork

'This Is Hardcore' album (March 1998)
French promo CD (7037)
- Tracklisting same as UK album
- Packaging: similar to UK album

'A Little Soul' (June 1998)
1. Japanese 3-track promo CD (PHCD 8438)
- Tracklisting and packaging details unknown
2. 'Pulp Japan Tour 1998' CD (8DCP 8039)
- A Little Soul/Like A Friend/I'm A Man
- Packaging: jewel case with exclusive band photo

'The Trees' (October 2001)
1. Australian 3-track promo CD (PROPULP0901)
- The Trees (edit)/Sunrise (album version)/The Trees (album version)
- Packaging: green card sleeve similar to UK promo
2. Spanish 1-track promo CD (PULP 1)
- The Trees (edit)
- Packaging: black and white card case

'We Love Life' (October 2001)
1. German promo CD (512 163-2)
- Tracklisting as UK album
- Packaging: 10″ × 10″ gatefold card sleeve, with standard artwork on the front and biography and pictures inside
2. Swedish promo (no number)
- Tracklisting as UK album
- Titled 'Pulp'
- Packaging: none

Appendix 1

SIGNIFICANT NON-UK RELEASES

See note for significant UK promos.

'Do You Remember The First Time?' (March 1994)
1. French CD single (854 077-2)
     - Do You Remember The First Time?/Razzmatazz (Acoustic Version)/Joyriders (Acoustic Version)/Dogs Are Everywhere (Acoustic Version)
     - Packaging: j-case as UK edition
     - Acoustic versions as on UK CD2 of 'Common People'

'His'n'Hers' (April 1994)
1. US album (314-524 006-2)
     - Tracklisting as UK edition, plus 'Razzmatazz' as a hidden bonus track

'Common People' (May 1995)
1. Australian CD single (854 329-2)
     - Common People (full-length version)/Underwear/Common People (7″ edit)
     - Packaging: card case with 'Daytime' artwork. Came with free sticker of the band
2. French CD single (854 577-2)
     - Common People (full-length version)/Whiskey In The Jar (live)/59 Lyndhurst Road (live)
     - Packaging: digipak with 'Daytime' artwork
     - Live tracks recorded for *The Black Sessions*, Radio France Inter Studio 105, October 30, 1995
     - All titles as given on sleeve. 'Whiskey In The Jar' is the same version as on the *Childline* album.
3. Japanese CD single (PHCR 8341)
     - Common People (Motiv 8 Radio Edit)/Common People (Motiv 8 Club Mix)/Common People (The Vocoda Mix)
     - Packaging: j-case

'Mis-Shapes'/'Sorted For E's And Wizz' (September 1995)
1. European CD single (CIDZ 620)
     - Mis-Shapes/Sorted For E's And Wizz/Common People (Motiv 8 Club Mix)
     - Packaging: j-case. Artwork as UK 'Mis-Shapes' CD
2. German CD single (854 436-2)
     - Mis-Shapes/Sorted For E's And Wizz
     - Packaging: card sleeve. Artwork as UK 'Mis-Shapes' CD
3. Japanese CD single (PHCD 8348)
     - Mis-Shapes/Sorted For E's And Wizz/Common People (Motiv 8 Club Mix)
     - Packaging: j-case. Artwork as UK 'Mis-Shapes' CD

'Different Class' (October 1995)
1. Australian CD (5241652)
     - Tracklisting and packaging as UK release
     - Initial copies included Pulp sew-on badge
2. Japanese CD (PHCR 1801)
     - Tracklisting as UK release with additional tracks 'P.T.A. (Parent Teacher Association)' and 'Disco 2000' (Motiv 8 Club Mix)
     - Packaging: bizarre 'Pulp Café' box artwork; included lyric sheet insert

'Different Class'/'Second Class' double CD (October 1995?)
German double CD (CIDX 8041/524 262-2)
- *Different Class* CD as normal
- *Second Class* CD is a compilation of the following B-sides: Mile End/Ansaphone/P.T.A. (Parent Teacher Association)/Live Bed Show (extended)/Your's Sister's Clothes (*sic*)/Seconds/Deep Fried In Kelvin/ The Babysitter/Street Lites
- Packaging: unknown

Japanese double CD (PHCR 14001)
- *Different Class* 14-track Japanese CD as normal
- *Second Class* Japanese version: Mile End/Ansaphone/Live Bed Show (extended)/Your Sister's Clothes/Seconds/Deep Fried In Kelvin/The Babysitter/Street Lites/Common People '96 (7″ Edit)

'Disco 2000' (November 1995)
1. European 2-track CD (CIDT 623)
   - Disco 2000 (7″ mix)/Disco 2000 (Motiv 8 Discoid Mix)
   - Packaging: card sleeve with artwork as UK 'Part One' CD
2. French 'Part One' CD (854 493-2)
   - Tracklisting as UK 'Part One' CD
   - Packaging: gatefold digipak with space for CD2, artwork as UK 'Part One'
3. French 'Part Two' CD (854 495-2)
   - Tracklisting as UK 'Part Two' CD
   - Packaging: card sleeve, artwork as UK 'Part One'
4. German 3-track CD (852 671-2)
   - Disco 2000 (7″ mix)/Disco 2000 (Motiv 8 Gimp Dub)/Sorted For E's And Wizz (live)
   - Packaging: jewel case as UK 'Part Two' with sleevenotes in German (*"Was machst du am Dienstag baby?"*)
   - 'Sorted' recorded live at the Markthalle, Hamburg on December 10, 1995
5. German mispressed 3-track CD (852 671-2)
   - Sorted For E's & Wizz (Live)/Do You Remember The First Time? (Live)/Pencil Skirt (Live)/I Spy (Live)
   - Packaging: outwardly identical to the correctly pressed German 3-track CD as above. The only way to differentiate between the two versions is to examine the matrix numbers on the inner rear side of the disc. Matrix for the mispressing is 852 671-2 01 whereas corrected pressing matrix is 852 671-2 02
   - All tracks recorded live at the Markthalle, Hamburg on December 10, 1995

'Common People '96' (1996)
1. European CD single (854 689-2)
   - Common People '96/Do You Remember The First Time?/Babies/Mile End
   - Packaging: j-case with photo of Pulpesque girl reading magazine on a bed
   - 'Common People '96' is identical to the 7″ edit, except the word 'screw' is muted
2. European CD single (854 688-2)
   - Common People '96/Do You Remember The First Time?
   - Packaging: unknown

'Simply Fuss Free' box set (1996?)
Australian box set
- Includes Do You Remember The First Time? CD (Card Case)/Common People Part 1 'Daytime' CD (Card Case)/Mis-Shapes & Sorted CD (as UK)/Sorted For E's

& Wizz & Mis-Shapes CD (as UK)/Disco 2000 Part 1 CD (Slim Jewel Case)/Disco 2000 Part 2 CD (as UK)/Miniature Jamie Hewlett Common People Comic Book
* Packaging: garish cardboard box

'Something Changed' (March 1996)
1. European CD single (CIDT 632)
    * Something Changed/Mile End
    * Packaging: card sleeve

'This Is Hardcore' single (March 1998)
1. European CD single (CIDT 695)
    * This Is Hardcore/Ladies' Man
    * Packaging: card sleeve

'This Is Hardcore' album (March 1998)
1. Japanese CD (PHCR 3710)
    * Tracklisting: as UK album plus Like A Friend/Tomorrow Never Lies
    * Packaging: as UK album
2. Japanese double CD (PHCR 90713)
    * CD1: 14-track Japanese CD as normal
    * CD2: *This Is Glastonbury* album as UK version plus 'This Is Hardcore' (live) and 'Glory Days/Common People' (live)
3. US CD (314-524 492-2)
    * Tracklisting as UK album plus Like A Friend
    * Packaging: as UK album
4. Malaysian CD (524 486-4)
    * Tracklisting as UK album
    * Packaging as UK album, but with model on front covered up in a woolly jumper

'Freshly Squeezed . . . The Early Years' (September 1, 1998)
Canadian CD (Velvel Music, VEL79737-2)
    * My Lighthouse/My Legendary Girlfriend/Don't You Want Me Anymore?/She's Dead/Little Girl (With Blue Eyes)/Down By The River/Blue Glow/I Want You/They Suffocate At Night/Master Of The Universe/Countdown
    * Packaging: jewel case. Picture of an orange
    * Canadian compilation of Fire material from the company that handles the Fire catalogue in the USA and Canada

'We Love Life' (October 2001)
Non-UK CDs
    * Tracklisting as UK edition
    * Sleeve artwork as UK edition but with the Pulp logo in orange, tan and yellow letters, as opposed to green

'We Love Life' (August 10, 2002)
US edition (Sanctuary Records 06076-83204-2)
    * Tracklisting as UK edition plus 'Yesterday' and 'Forever In My Dreams' as on 'Bad Cover Version' single
    * Packaging as UK edition

'Hits' (November 2002)
Non-UK CD (CIDZ 8126)

- Tracklisting as UK edition minus 'Underwear'
- Packaging: as UK edition

COLLABORATIONS

JASS (featuring Nick Banks)
Release: 'Theme' 12″ single (Wax Trax Records, Chicago, *circa* 1987)
Notes: Nick played drums with this Sheffield group, also featuring Dave Thomson, *circa* 1985–'86. Although he had left the group by the time this record was released, it is possible that he may appear on this release.

LUSH (featuring Jarvis Cocker)
Release: *Lovelife* LP (4AD Records GAD6004CD, 1996)
Notes: Jarvis duetted with Lush vocalist Miki Berenyi on the track 'Ciao!'

BARRY ADAMSON (featuring Jarvis Cocker)
Release: *Oedipus Schmoedipus* LP (Mute Records STUMM 134, 1996)
Notes: Jarvis co-wrote the lyrics and sang lead vocals on the track 'Set The Controls For The Heart Of The Pelvis'.

DAVID ARNOLD (featuring Jarvis Cocker, Steve Mackey and Mark Webber)
Release: 'Shaken And Stirred: The David Arnold James Bond Project' (Warner Music, 3984-20738-2), October 1997
Notes: This album is a collection of covers of James Bond themes, sung by various artists, produced and arranged by David Arnold. The track 'All Time High', written by John Barry and Tim Rice and originally performed by Rita Coolidge in the film *Octopussy*, features Jarvis (lead vocals, guitar, keyboards and programming), Steve (bass and programming) and Mark (guitar) alongside David Arnold (guitars, percussion, arranging) and Les Arnold (drums).

BABY BIRKIN (produced by Russell Senior)
Releases: 'Melo Melo'/'Black . . . White' 7″ and CD single (Dishy Records DISHY 29, November 11, 1997)
'Jane B'/'Jane X'/'Jane B (Woody And Rasmus Mix)' 10″ and CD single (Dishy Records DISHY 32, June 29, 1998)
Classe X LP and CD (Dishy Records DISHY 33, September 1998)
Notes: Russell produced and co-arranged the début album by the London Francophile group Baby Birkin during 1997. Their repertoire consisted mainly of cover versions of Sixties French pop, although Russell did co-write one track, 'St Tropez', which appears on the vinyl edition of the album (the song was later reworked by Russell with Venini and became the B-side of that band's début single). Russell also plays violin and bowed bass on 'Jane B' and 'St Tropez'.

THURSTON MOORE (remixed by Mark Webber)
Release: *Root* CD (LO Recordings LCD 11, 1998)
Notes: *Root* consists of 30 pieces of music recorded by Thurston Moore, each of which is remixed by a different artist. These artists include Alec Empire, Stereolab, Bruce Gilbert, Stock, Hausen & Walkman and Add N To X. Track 7 is remixed by Mark.

THE ALL SEEING I (featuring Jarvis Cocker)
Releases: 'Walk Like A Panther' CD single (FFrr Records, FFRR 570), January 1999
'First Man In Space' CD single (FFrr Records, FFRR 370), July 1999

Pickled Eggs And Sherbert CD and cassette (London Records/FFrr, LC7654), September 1999

Notes: Jarvis wrote lyrics for the songs 'Walk Like A Panther', 'Stars On Sunday', 'First Man In Space' and 'Drive Safely Darlin'', and sang lead vocals on 'Drive Safely Darlin''. He also made a handul of live appearances with the group.

LOOPER (remixed by Jarvis Cocker and Steve Mackey)

Release: 'Who's Afraid Of Y2K?' CD and 10″ single (Jeepster Records JPRCDS 015), October 18, 1999

Notes: This release features the track 'Up A Tree Again (St John's Ambulance Chocolate Layers Mix)'. The Chocolate Layers are, of course, Jarvis and Steve in DJing guise.

VENINI (featuring Russell Senior)

Releases: 'Mon Camion'/'St Tropez' CD and 7″ single (Bikini Records BIKINI 1), June 1999
'Carnival Star'/'Carnival Star (Version II)' CD and 7″ single (Bikini Records BIKINI 2), November 1999
'Postcard' (MP3-only release via official website), July 2000
'Unshaker'/'Exotic Night'/'Hoboken' CD single (no label, limited-edition mail order only), September 2000

Notes: Russell formed Venini in spring 1998. The group also featured Debbie Lime (vocals), Nick Eastwood (bass), Robert Barton (drums), Danny Hunt (keyboards until August 1999 – plays on first two singles), Michael Ash (keyboards from September 1999 – plays on all other releases) and Charlie Collins (treated woodwind). Russell played guitar and wrote or co-wrote all the group's material, also financing the release of the band's singles on their own label, Bikini Records. The group were active until the end of 1999, at which point they took a six-month hiatus, during which time Russell effectively left the band. He does, however, feature on both 'Postcard' and the *Unshaker* EP, both of which were recorded during sessions for an unreleased album in October 1999. Other titles recorded for the album include 'Roxy', 'Photograph', 'Little Kisses', 'Amsterdam Sam' and remakes of the tracks from the first two singles. After Russell's departure, the group planned to continue, but following other line-up problems split in January 2001.

BLACK BOX RECORDER (remixed by Jarvis Cocker and Steve Mackey)

Release: 'The Art Of Driving CD1' CD single (Nude Records NUD51 CD1), *circa* July 2000

Notes: Includes 'The Facts Of Life (remixed by The Chocolate Layers)'. The same track also appears on a compilation CD given away with the October 2000 edition of *Select* magazine, and on the Black Box Recorder compilation *The Worst Of Black Box Recorder*.

DEATH IN VEGAS (remixed by Jarvis Cocker and Steve Mackey)

Release: 'Dirge' 12″ single (Concrete Records DIRGE 5), *circa* September 2000
Notes: 'Dirge (Cossack Apocalypse mix)' remixed by The Chocolate Layers. Also included on the Sonic Mook Experiment double CD *Rare Mixes, Electronic Action And Future Rock & Roll*.

ALPHA (featuring Jarvis Cocker)

Release: *South* EP (Melankolic Records SADD 12), June 2001
Notes: Includes a cover version of the Jimmy Webb song 'This Is Where I Came In' (originally performed by Richard Harris) with lead vocals by Jarvis.

MARIANNE FAITHFULL (featuring Jarvis Cocker, Steve Mackey, Mark Webber and Nick Banks)
Release: *Kissin' Time* CD album (Hut Records HUTCD 71), March 2002
Notes: Includes the track 'Sliding Through Life On A Charm', written by Marianne Faithfull, Jarvis Cocker, Steve Mackey, Nick Banks and Mark Webber. Lyrics by Marianne Faithfull and Jarvis Cocker. Features Marianne Faithfull (vocals), Jarvis Cocker (keyboards), Steve Mackey (bass), Mark Webber (guitar) and Nick Banks (drums). Produced by Jarvis Cocker and Steve Mackey.

THE WHITE SPORT (remixed by Jarvis Cocker and Steve Mackey)
Release: 'Complete Control' CD and 12″ single (High Society HSCDS001), May 2002
Notes: Includes the track 'Complete Control (King Precare Mix By Two Desperate People)' – Jarvis and Steve are the two desperate people. The White Sport supported Pulp at Brixton Academy in November 2001.

JARVIS COCKER AND RICHARD HAWLEY
Release: *Total Lee: The Songs Of Lee Hazelwood* LP and CD (City Slang 20195-2), June 2002
Notes: Includes Jarvis' and Richard's version of 'A Cheat' (written by Hazelwood and originally recorded by Sanford Clark in 1959).

RELAXED MUSCLE (featuring Jarvis Cocker)
Releases: 'Rod Of Iron' white label 12″, *circa* July 2002
      'The Heavy'/'Rod Of Iron'/'Branded!' 7″ EP (Rough Trade RTRADES073, 500 only), November 2002
Notes: Credited to Darren Spooner (vocals), Jason Buckle (music) and Wayne Marsden (extra guitar on 'Branded!'). Darren Spooner is Jarvis; Wayne Marsden is Richard Hawley. Relaxed Muscle grew out of informal recording sessions with Jarvis and Jason Buckle (formerly in The All Seeing I and more recently The Fat Truckers) in Jarvis' basement. The group played together (joined by Ross Fat Trucker) at the Royal Festival Hall on September 22, 2002, supporting Lee Hazelwood.

JARVIS COCKER SOLO RELEASES

'Millennium Thoughts' compilation
Featured Jarvis track: Thinking About The New Millennium Just Makes Me Wanna Come
Written, recorded and performed by Jarvis Cocker
CD released November 1999

'Mike Bassett England Manager' OST
Featured Jarvis track: Everybody Loves The Underdog
Song written by Jarvis Cocker, Antony Genn, Duncan Mackay and Martin Slattery
Lyrics by Jarvis Cocker
Performed by Jarvis Cocker (vocals, guitar), Antony Genn (bass, guitar, glockenspiel, backing vocals), Martin Slattery (Wurlitzer, tambourine), Luke Bullen (drums)
Produced by Antony Genn
Recorded and engineered by Cameron Craig
Mixed by Cameron Craig, Antony Genn and Jarvis Cocker
CD released on Telstar Records (TCD3213), September 24, 2001

Appendix 2

**PULP LIVE PERFORMANCE HISTORY,
NOVEMBER 1978–DECEMBER 2002**

1980
February/March	– City School, Sheffield
July 5	– Rotherham Arts Centre
August 16	– Bouquet of Steel Festival, The Leadmill, Sheffield
August 17	– Hallamshire Hotel, Sheffield
August 31	– Hallamshire Hotel, Sheffield
September 24	– The Ritblat Tube, Royal Hotel, Sheffield
October	– The Wedge Club, George IV, Sheffield
November 13 & 14	– City School, Sheffield

1981
January 28	– *Sheffield Star* 'Search for a Star' talent contest, YMCA, Sheffield
January 29	– Hallamshire Hotel, Sheffield
February 24	– Wimpy Bar, Fargate, Sheffield
March 6	– Stradbroke Community Centre, Sheffield
March 17	– Wimpy Bar, Fargate, Sheffield
March/April	– City School, Sheffield
May 7	– Hallamsire Hotel, Sheffield
May 18	– Marples, Sheffield
May 28	– Hallamshire Hotel, Sheffield
June 11	– Hallamshire Hotel, Sheffield
July 15	– Royal Hotel, Sheffield
July 21	– The Mill, Sheffield
July 23	– The Big Tree, Sheffield
July 24	– The Lion, Sheffield
August 2	– Jarvis' backyard, Mansfield Road, Sheffield
September 10	– George IV, Sheffield
September 22	– Hallamshire Hotel, Sheffield
September 25	– George IV, Sheffield
November 1	– Jimmy Sellars' birthday party, his house, Sheffield

1982
January 16	– Bath University
January 27	– The Royal, Sheffield
February 9	– Sheffield Polytechnic (Totley Site)
February 15	– Marples, Sheffield
February 18	– Marples, Sheffield

February 23	– The Limit, Sheffield
February 28	– Hallamshire Hotel, Sheffield
March 20	– The Moonlight Club, London
April 13	– The Limit, Sheffield
April 16	– Sorby Hall, Sheffield – Party for the British Association of Young Scientists
October 24	– Stars On Sundae, Crucible Theatre, Sheffield

1983

January	– Sheffield University
January	– Unknown wine bar in Chesterfield
February 2	– The Leadmill, Sheffield
March 7	– Sheffield University Maze Bar
March	– City School, Sheffield
April 3	– Crucible Studio Theatre, Sheffield
June 19	– Marples, Sheffield
August 30	– Marples, Sheffield

1984

February 7	– Brunel University, London
March	– Cosmo's, Leeds
April 6	– Library Theatre, Sheffield
May 30	– Heywire Club, Pindar of Wakefield, King's Cross, London
June 3	– Hallamshire Hotel, Sheffield
June 20	– Sheffield Art College
June 23	– Sheffield University
July 26	– The B-Hive, Sheffield
July 28	– Broomhill Carnival, Pitsmoor Vestry Hall, Sheffield
October 30	– Sheffield Art College
December 18	– The B-Hive, Sheffield
December 29	– The Leadmill, Sheffield

1985

March 28	– Hallamshire Hotel, Sheffield
May 7	– Limit Club, Sheffield
July 7	– Gotham City Club, Fascinations Nitespot, Chesterfield
September 1	– Dolebusters Festival, Sheffield University Octagon Centre
September 22	– The Leadmill, Sheffield
September 23	– Moles Club, Bath
September 24	– Thekla, Old Profanity Showboat, Bristol
October 4	– Darlington Arts Centre
October 7	– Adam & Eve's, Chesterfield
October 17	– Bradford University
October 23	– Middlesborough
October 25	– Sheffield University
November 6	– The Wellington, Hull

1986

NB: the next five gigs featured Jarvis in a wheelchair

January 9	– The Clarendon, Hammersmith
January 14	– The Limit, Sheffield
January 15	– 1 in 12 Club, Queens Hall, Bradford

January 17	– Thames Polytechnic, London
January 29	– Chesterfield Arts Centre
April 29	– Maze Bar, Sheffield University
April 30	– Time Box, Bull & Gate, London
May 10	– Adelphi Club, Hull
May 13	– The Limit, Sheffield
May 15	– Rock Garden, London
May 23	– Chesterfield Library
May 31	– Chesterfield Conservative Club
July 2	– Library Theatre, Chesterfield
July 4	– Tropic Club, Bristol
July 19	– The Leadmill, Sheffield
November 8	– Oxfam benefit, The Leadmill, Sheffield
Late November	– Adelphi Club, Hull
December 4	– 100 Club, London

1987
March 3	– The Limit, Sheffield
May 6	– Co-Op Building, Chesterfield
May 19	– The Limit, Sheffield
July 15	– Barracuda Club, Nottingham
August 8	– The Leadmill, Sheffield
August 16	– Liverpool Earthbeat Festival
August 21	– The Groovy Fishtank, Take Two, Sheffield
October 8	– 20th Century Club, Derby

1988
February 18	– Babylon Revisited, Camden Falcon, London
February 26	– The Winding Wheel, Chesterfield
March 10	– Sheffield University Lower Refectory
August 8	– *The Day That Never Happened,* The Leadmill, Sheffield
December 12	– Sounds Christmas Party, Dingwalls, London

1989
February 8	– The Leadmill, Sheffield

1990
December 29	– The Leadmill, Sheffield

1991
March 16	– The Leadmill, Sheffield
April 23	– Borderline, London
May 1	– Subterrania, London
May 3	– Mean Fiddler, London
May 12	– ULU, London
May 22	– Underworld, London
May 25	– The Leadmill, Sheffield
May 31	– Return Club, North Bridge Leisure Centre, Halifax
July 20	– Class Of '91, Town & Country Club, London
July 25	– Hallamshire Hotel, Sheffield (*two shows*)
August 30	– The Venue, London
August 31	– Piece Hall, Halifax

September 1	– The Leadmill, Sheffield
September 20	– Powerhaus, London
October 4	– 'The Fresher Extravaganza '91', Sheffield University Lower Refectory
October 11	– Town & Country Club, London
October 12	– Taunton Youth Centre
October 18 & 19	– Festival Les Inrockuptibles, L'Aeronef, Lille
November 15	– Subterrania, London
December 10	– North London Polytechnic
December 28	– The Leadmill, Sheffield

1992

January 24	– Underworld, London
February 28	– The Venue, London
March 27	– Wolverhampton Polytechnic
March 30	– Cambridge Corn Exchange
May 6	– Smashed, The Powerhaus, London
May 11	– The Leadmill, Sheffield
May 23	– The Adelphi, Hull
May 26	– The Hibernian, Birmingham
May 27	– The Underworld, London
May 28	– Salford University
May 29	– Jericho Tavern, Oxford
June 1	– Newcastle Polytechnic
June 4	– Waterfront, Norwich
June 5	– Royal Park Hotel, Leeds
June 6	– 'In The Park '92' Festival, Finsbury Park, London
June 19	– The Dome, London
June 20	– The Venue, London
July 13	– Sheffield City Hall Ballroom
July 31	– Brixton Fridge, London
September 5	– Piece Hall, Halifax
October 7	– Sussex University, Brighton
October 9	– Bristol Polytechnic
October 10	– Wolverhampton University
October 12	– Wherehouse, Derby
October 13	– Boardwalk, Manchester
October 15	– King Tut's Wah Wah Hut, Glasgow
October 17	– Cardiff University
October 23	– ULU, London
October 24	– Princess Charlotte, Leicester
November 3	– Camden Palais, London
December 7	– Sheffield University Lower Refectory, Pulp Christmas Party
December 20	– Espace Europeen, Paris
December 23	– Smashed Christmas Party, The Powerhaus, London

1993

January 29	– L'Olympic, Nantes
February 23	– Mayfair, Glasgow
February 24	– Newcastle Polytechnic
February 25	– Liverpool University
February 26	– Manchester University
February 27	– Leicester University

February 28	– Cardiff University
March 2	– Leeds Metropolitan University
March 3	– Hull University
March 4	– Equinox, London
March 5	– Southsea Pier, Portsmouth
March 17	– Shelter benefit, ULU, London
March 20	– Rock Garden, Dublin
April 5	– Radio One Sound City, The Leadmill, Sheffield
May 15	– Highbury Garage, London
May 29	– Oxford University
July 16	– Phoenix Festival, Stratford-upon-Avon
November 3 & 4	– Festivals Les Inrockuptibles, L'Aeronef, Lille, France
November 5	– Salle de la Cité, Rennes, France
November 8	– Duchess of York, Leeds
November 9	– Edwards No. 8, Birmingham
November 10	– Wherehouse, Derby
November 11	– Manchester University
November 13	– King Tut's Wah Wah Hut, Glasgow
November 14	– Pelican, Aberdeen
November 15	– Riverside, Newcastle upon Tyne
November 17	– Wheatsheaf, Stoke-on-Trent
November 18	– Roadmenders, Northampton
November 19	– The Mill, Preston
November 20	– The Leadmill, Sheffield
November 22	– Wedgewood Rooms, Portsmouth
November 23	– LA2, London
November 24	– Fleece and Firkin, Bristol
November 26	– Rivoli Club, Dublin
December 4	– Festival Taste of Indie, Nancy, France
December 18	– The Garage, London

1994

January 24	– *NME* Brat Awards launch party, The Forum, London
January 25	– New Astoria, London
March 9	– Launch party for *Do You Remember The First Time?* film, ICA, London
April 4	– BBC Radio 1 Sound City, Tramshed Theatre, Glasgow
April 24	– The Garage, Glasgow
April 25	– Riverside, Newcastle upon Tyne
April 26	– Leeds Metropolitan University
April 27	– Manchester University
April 28	– Hull University
April 29	– HMV, Sheffield (lunchtime acoustic show), The Octagon, Sheffield
May 2	– Wulfrun Hall, Wolverhampton
May 3	– Leicester University
May 4	– Waterfront, Norwich
May 5	– The Junction, Cambridge
May 6	– Kentish Town Forum, London
May 17	– FNAC Record Store, Nancy, France
May 18	– Exo 7, Rouen, France
May 19	– La Cigale, Paris
May 20	– L'Escall, Nantes, France
May 21	– Salle Des Concerts, Le Mans, France

May 24	– Le Doremi, Bordeaux, France
May 25	– Le Bikini, Toulouse, France
May 26	– Le Rockstore, Montpellier, France
May 27	– L'Espace Julien, Marseille, France
May 28	– Le Forum Rexy, Rion, France
May 30	– La Salamandre, Strasbourg, France
May 31	– L'Usine, Reims, France
June 7	– Stockholm, Sweden
June 9	– Melkweg, Amsterdam, Netherlands
June 26	– Glastonbury Festival
July 10	– Dour Festival, Dour, Belgium
July 30	– T In The Park Festival, Scotland
August 27	– Reading Festival
September 15	– Venus De Milo, Boston, USA
September 17	– Vic Theater, Chicago, USA
September 19	– Masquerade, Atlanta, USA
September 20	– Howling Wolf's, New Orleans, USA
September 24	– Hollywood Palace, Los Angeles, USA
September 25	– Fillmore, San Francisco, USA
September 28	– Phoenix Theater, Toronto, Canada
September 29	– City Academy Theater, New York, USA
October 4	– Keele University, Newcastle-under-Lyme
October 5	– Aston Villa Leisure Centre, Birmingham
October 6	– University of Essex, Colchester
October 7	– Alexandra Palace, London
October 10	– L'Ubu, Rennes, France
October 11	– Bataclan, Elysée Montmartre, Paris, France
October 13	– Terminal Export, Nancy, France
October 14	– L'Oree Du Neuland, Colmar, France
October 15	– Le Transbordeur, Lyon, France
October 17	– *Pulp Fiction* launch party, Ministry Of Sound, London
October 31	– London Lighthouse, Notting Hill (AIDS charity concert)
December 6	– BT Birthday/Prince's Trust Concert, Docklands Arena, London
December 18	– *Pulp At Christmas*, Theatre Royal, Drury Lane, London
1995	
April 21	– BBC Radio 1 Sound City, Bristol University Anson Rooms, Bristol
April 22	– Sheffield Arena
June 24	– Glastonbury Festival, Somerset
July 22	– Heineken Festival, Roundhay Park, Leeds
July 29	– Lollipop Festival, Stockholm, Sweden
September 30	– The Dome, Morecambe
October 1	– Barrowlands, Glasgow
October 2	– Newcastle University
October 5	– Town & Country, Leeds
October 6	– University of East Anglia, Norwich
October 8	– Cambridge Corn Exchange
October 9	– Rock City, Nottingham
October 10	– De Montfort University, Leicester
October 11	– Que Club, Birmingham
October 12	– The Academy, Manchester
October 14	– Royal Court Theatre, Liverpool

October 15	– Cardiff University
October 16	– University of Exeter
October 18	– The Event, Brighton
October 19	– Shepherd's Bush Empire, London
October 20	– Kentish Town Forum, London
October 22	– Sheffield City Hall
October 23	– Middlesborough Town Hall
October 24	– Ulster Hall, Belfast
October 25	– SFX, Dublin
November 14	– Zenith, Paris
November 15	– Brielpoort, Deinze, Belgium
November 18	– Revolver, Madrid, Spain
November 19	– Papillon, Valencia, Spain
November 20	– Zeleste II, Barcelona, Spain
November 21	– Le Bikini, Toulouse, France
November 22	– Théâtre Barbey, Bordeaux, France
November 24	– Le Rockstore, Montpellier, France
November 25	– Espace Julien, Marseille, France
November 27	– Transbordeur, Lyon, France
November 28	– La Vapeur, Dijon, France
November 29	– La Laiterie, Strasbourg, France
November 30	– L'Usine, Reims, France
December 1	– Exo 7, Rouen, France
December 4	– L'Olympic, Nantes, France
December 5	– Bataclan, Paris
December 6	– L'Aeronef, Lille, France
December 7	– VK Club, Brussels, Belgium
December 8	– Melkweg, Amsterdam, Holland
December 10	– E-Werk, Cologne, Germany
December 11	– Metropol, Berlin, Germany
December 12	– Markthalle, Hamburg, Germany
December 13	– Pumpenhuset, Copenhagen
December 16	– Spa Theatre, Bridlington
December 17	– Empress Ballroom, Blackpool
December 19	– International Centre, Bournemouth
December 20	– Brixton Academy, London
December 21	– Brixton Academy, London

1996

January 27 & 28	– Club Quattro, Osaka, Japan
January 30, 31 and February 1	– On Air East, Tokyo, Japan
February 6	– Cirkus, Stockholm, Sweden
February 7	– Rokefeller, Oslo, Norway
February 9	– Rondo, Gothenburg, Sweden
February 10	– Olympen, Lund, Sweden
February 11	– Pumpehusst, Copenhagen, Denmark
February 20	– Brighton Centre
February 21	– Cardiff Arena
February 22	– NEC, Birmingham
February 23	– Manchester Arena
February 25	– Ingliston RHC, Edinburgh
February 26	– Newcastle Arena

February 28	– Humberside Ice Arena, Hull
February 29	– Sheffield Arena
March 1 & 2	– Wembley Arena, London
May 21	– Bimbos, San Francisco
May 22	– Hollywood Grand, Los Angeles
May 26	– First Avenue, Minneapolis
May 27	– Riverport Amphitheater, St Louis
May 28	– Metro, Chicago
May 30	– Opera House, Toronto
May 31	– St Andrew's Hall, Detroit
June 3	– Irving Plaza, New York
June 4	– 9.30 Club, Washington DC
June 7	– Lupo's Heartbreak Hotel, Providence
June 8	– River Rave Festival, Boston
June 9	– Theater Of Living Arts, Philadelphia
June 15	– Hultsfred Festival, Sweden
June 17	– Huxley's New World, Berlin, Germany
June 8	– Capitol, Hanover, Germany
June 20	– Hugenottenhalle, Neu-Isenburg
June 22	– Rockpalast Festival, Loreley
June 24	– Live Aus Dem Alabama, Munich
June 25	– Biscuithalle, Bonn
June 27	– Jovel, Munster
June 28	– Roskilde Festival, Denmark
June 30	– Turku Festival, Finland
July 2	– Laugardalsholl, Reykjavik, Iceland
July 3	– Quart Festival, Norway
July 6	– Torhout Festival, Belgium
July 7	– Werchter Festival, Belgium
July 8	– Olympia, Paris
July 13	– Feile Festival, Dublin
July 14	– T In The Park, Strathclyde, Scotland
August 13	– Clickimin Centre, Shetland Islands
August 17	– V96 Festival, Hylands Park, Chelmsford
August 18	– V96 Festival, Warrington
August 24	– Holsten Pils Concert, Teatre Grec Ampitheatre, Barcelona, Spain, with Leftfield

1997

October 31	– La Monte Young Benefit, Barbican Hall, London

1998

March 25	– *This Is Hardcore* album launch party, Hilton Hotel, London
June 9	– Paradise Club, Boston, USA
June 10	– Massey Hall, Toronto, Canada
June 13	– 9.30 Club, Washington DC, USA
June 14	– Tibetan Freedom Festival, RFK Stadium, Washington DC, USA
June 16	– Hammerstein Ballroom, New York, USA
June 20	– Rockpalast Festival, Loreley, Germany
June 21	– Hurricane Festival, Schessel-Eichenring, near Bremen, Germany
June 26	– St Gallen Festival, Zurich, Switzerland
June 27	– Roskilde Festival, Copenhagen, Denmark

June 28	– Glastonbury Festival, Somerset, England
July 1	– Imperial Festival, Oporto, Portugal
July 3	– Torhout Festival, Bruges, Belgium
July 4	– Werchter Festival, Belgium
July 5	– Les Eurockeennes Festival, Belfort, France
July 10	– Dr Music Festival, Spain
July 11	– Big Day Out Festival, Galway, Ireland
July 12	– T In The Park Festival, Kinross, Scotland
July 16	– Rockwave Festival, Greece
July 19	– Forest Glade Festival, Burgenland, Austria
July 23	– Skansen Park, Stockholm, Sweden
July 25	– Finsbury Park, London
September 17 & 18	– Tokyo Akasaka Blitz
September 20	– Tokyo On Air East
September 21	– Nagoya Diamond Hall
September 22	– Osaka Imperial Hall
September 25	– Perth Metropolis
September 27	– Melbourne Festival Hall
September 28, 29 & 30	– Sydney Enmore Theatre
October 2	– Adelaide Thebarton Theatre
October 3	– Brisbane Livid Festival
October 5	– Auckland North Shore Event
November 17	– Hereford Leisure Centre
November 19	– London Wembley Arena
November 21	– Liverpool Royal Court
November 22	– Manchester Apollo
November 23	– Manchester Apollo
November 25	– Stoke-on-Trent Trentham Gardens
November 26	– Doncaster Dome
November 28	– Hull Arena
November 29	– Glasgow SECC
November 30	– Cardiff International Arena
December 2	– Birmingham NEC
December 3	– Brighton Centre
December 5	– Bournemouth International Centre

1999

June 10	– Venice Palazzo Pisani Moretta (Venice Bienalle)
August 31	– *The Quiet Revolution*, Edinburgh Queen's Hall
September 2	– Liss Ard Festival, Skibbereen, Co. Cork, Ireland

2000

August 22	– 'Keep Calm' fanclub concert, Highbury Garage, London
August 24	– Edinburgh Corn Exchange
August 26	– Reading Carling Festival, Richfield Avenue
August 27	– Leeds Carling Festival, Temple Newsam

2001

May 24	– Gerrards Marquee, Hay-On-Wye Festival Of Literature And Arts
May 26	– Homelands Festival, Matterley Bowl, Winchester
July 24	– Paleo Festival, Nyon, Switzerland
July 28	– Storsjöyran Festival, Ostersund, Sweden

479

August 3	– Guildford Festival
August 5	– Benicassim International Festival, Spain
August 10	– Festival La Route Du Rock, St Malo, France
August 26	– Lowlands Festival, Billinghuizen, Holland
September 24	– John Peel's 40th Anniversary Party, King's College, London (Private Performance)
October 31	– BBC Radio 1 Sound City, Birmingham Academy
November 9	– Festival Les Inrocks, Paris La Cigale
November 18	– Nottingham Rock City
November 19	– Sheffield Octagon Centre
November 21	– York Barbican Centre
November 22	– Glasgow Barrowlands
November 24	– Newcastle City Hall
November 25	– Manchester Apollo
November 27	– Cambridge Corn Exchange
November 28, 29 & 30	– London Brixton Academy
December 3	– Club Razzmatazz, Barcelona, Spain
December 7	– Dublin Ambassador Theatre

2002

April 18	– 4 Scott, The Scala, King's Cross, London
May 17	– Primavera Festival, Barcelona, Spain
June 8	– Festival Alternatif, Istanbul, Turkey
June 15	– Sherwood Pines Forest Park
June 16	– Bedgebury Pinetum Visitors' Centre
June 21	– Elgin Roseisle Forest Visitors' Centre
June 22	– Dalby Forest Visitors' Centre
June 23	– Thetford High Lodge Forest Centre
July 5	– St Austell Eden Project, Cornwall
August 3	– Sziget Festival, Budapest, Hungary
August 23	– Reading Carling Festival, Richfield Avenue
August 24	– Leeds Carling Festival, Temple Newsam
August 25	– Glasgow Gig On The Green Festival, Scotland
December 14	– Auto Festival, Magna Science Adventure Centre, Rotherham

Appendix 3

THEY ALSO SERVED . . .
OTHER SHEFFIELD BANDS, 1980–1988

Note: this is by no means a definitive guide to the Sheffield bands of this period; rather, it is an attempt to bring together some information on some of the groups that Pulp played with in their formative years. Although the slightly earlier, and more celebrated, Sheffield period of 1978–1980, with bands such as Cabaret Voltaire, ClockDVA, I'm So Hollow and The Human League, was highly influential on Jarvis and the early Pulp, no attempt is made to cover that here for the simple reason that other people have already done it better than I could. The interested reader is directed to the excellent documentary video Made In Sheffield, *available from www.sheffieldvision.com.*

ARTERY (active 1978–1985)
1980–1982 line-up: Mark Gouldthorpe (vocals/guitar), Mick Fidler (guitar/sax/vocals), Simon Hinkler (keyboards), Neil McKenzie (bass), Garry Wilson (drums)
One of Jarvis' favourite Sheffield bands, formed by Gouldthorpe, Wilson, McKenzie and vocalist Toyce Ashley in 1978 out of the ashes of a band called The. Released first single 'Mother Moon' in 1979, after which Ashley was replaced by Mick Fidler. Keyboardist Simon Hinkler joined in January 1980, completing the 'classic' incarnation of the band.

"Tony Perrin took me to see Artery at the Polytechnic," remembers Simon, "and I was immediately blown away. They were the best thing I'd ever seen. Tony organised a gig for our band TV Product – he got Artery to headline so that we could support them. I had my company's VW van, so I did the driving . . . after that, I began driving Artery to gigs regularly. One night after the show, I was playing 'Oh You Pretty Things' on a piano in the dressing room, and a couple of days later, Mark Gouldthorpe said everyone had been impressed and would like me to join the band.

"Artery were unique. They were fronted by Mark Gouldthorpe and Mick Fidler, both of them intense and enigmatic characters in their own different ways. Mark was a poet of sorts, and placed high importance on the lyrics being heard – in their early days, he even used to hand out lyric sheets at gigs. At first Mick used to do all the singing, and had an amazing style of delivery – never the same twice, and kind of on the edge of insanity. Later, about the time I joined, Mark started singing some of the songs, and eventually all of them. Mark's vocal style was all about expression, with only a passing nod to anything vaguely melodic. Musically the songs were driven by some extremely infectious and hypnotic bass lines. Neil McKenzie was quite a musician – an accomplished guitarist playing bass . . . and another nutter. Garry Wilson's drum rhythms always leaned toward the simple but unusual. The guitar and organ were distorted and strangely psychedelic. We made a major point of being completely original. Anything 'typical' was not allowed in this band.

"Every gig was a crucial event for us. We took it very seriously. It was our whole life. I guess the atmosphere that we created had quite an effect on the people who came to watch, so in that respect Artery were successful, if only on an underground level.

"In terms of the Sheffield scene, Artery would pack the house every time we played. Some of the lads from Pulp would come to see us quite often, especially Jarvis. I'm pretty certain Pulp supported Artery once. Only Jarv could tell you what kind of an influence Artery had on him, but he quickly developed an uncompromising edge to the way he approached studio work, and you can see a certain intensity in his stage presence, so he probably picked some of that up from Artery. I also think some of it filtered back to Jarvis via Russell, who was also big-into Artery."

With Hinkler in the band, Artery released 'The Slide' on the *Bouquet Of Steel* compilation LP in 1980, followed by 'Unbalanced', a double 7″ on Marcus Featherby's Aardvark Records. Singles 'Afterwards' and 'Cars In Motion' and a couple of Peel Sessions were followed by Fidler's departure in early 1982, after which the group disbanded. During this hiatus, the single 'The Clown' and album *Oceans* were released on Red Flame, Fidler and McKenzie formed Treehouse, and Gouldthorpe formed a new version of Artery with Wilson and pianist Chris Hendrick, recording the honky-tonk tinged *One Afternoon In A Hot Air Balloon*. To promote its release in 1983, Simon Hinkler rejoined, bringing with him his brother David, plus John White (guitar/sax) and Dave Hendrick (bass).

Third album *The Second Coming* (1984) was recorded with Murray Fenton (guitar), McKenzie and Wilson, but before long Simon Hinkler returned yet again as guitarist and Tony Perrin became bass player for a rockier-sounding version of the band. After releasing the LP *Number 4: Live In Amsterdam*, Fenton left, and, after a final gig in 1985 that saw the return of Fidler in place of Gouldthorpe, the group split.

Artery feature in the *Made In Sheffield* film; for more information see Simon Hinkler's site at users.arczip.com/simon/artery/

THE BLAND (active 1986–1987)

Three-piece punk band, occasionally played on the same bill as Pulp. Murray Fenton: "The Bland were unbelievable. They were a real 1977 punk band. They didn't have a bass-player. The guitarist was this quite hefty, biker-type bloke who looked as if he'd just got out of bed five minutes earlier and he didn't give a toss, but he were there. The drummer was like a wheeler-dealer type bloke, and the singer looked like John Lydon, until he opened his mouth – his teeth were about three sizes too big. But they were great; a right laugh."

DIG VIS DRILL (active 1983–1988)

Ogy McGrath (vocals), John Nicholls (keyboards), Nick Robinson (guitar, from 1985), Phil Maverick (backing vocals, to 1986)

One of the most respected bands in Sheffield of the mid-Eighties. "We kind of described ourselves as a synth-pop type punk thing – bit of an attitude," says John Nicholls. "I pottered about with keyboards and electronics, Ogy had loads of words, and we tried to put them together. We did have one record out, 'Cranking Up Religion' [Native Records], which got into the *NME* indie chart, although that was probably because we bought most of them! At the time, I liked to think that we didn't sound like anyone else around, but years later, this little pop duo came out who I enjoyed, Carter The Unstoppable Sex Machine, and I thought, 'That could have been us if we'd hung around!' I'd like to think we were similar to that, if perhaps a bit rougher."

"I was the esoteric one and John was the technical one," says Ogy. "I did all the mouth and all the physical stuff, and he did all the electronics and synths, drum riffs and stuff. If you listen to our early stuff it's all crappy synth sounds, but then we got Nick Robinson in and introduced heavy metal guitar to it, which everyone thought was fantastic – heavy metal with synths was just great. One of my ideas. Also, I kind of shouted my lyrics very fast over electronic beats, so I'll take credit for rap as well. And we played this gig in York once, and all these American guys were there, staying with some of their friends – all these guys in bands from Seattle. And they loved us, went crazy for us, so they gave us their addresses and we sent 'em tapes, records, English comics that they liked, stuff like that, and they fucking kicked off the Seattle scene, man! They became the Screaming Trees, Pearl Jam, all that. I like to think that Kurt was listening to Dig Vis Drill when he topped it.

"A lot of people tried to pigeonhole us and couldn't . . . Liverpool loved us, for some reason. Sheffield hated us! On our first record, the B-side 'I'm Hip I'm Vain', the first line was *Forget The Human League and ABC, they are nothing compared to me.* When I first came to Sheffield I wanted to upset every Sheffield band, and that's what happened. Some of the ones who were upset by me, like Pulp, became friends, but the others just kept away from me – that crazy little Irish guy with the dark glasses and the black goatee beard, keep away from him! But all the people that hated me never met me – all the people that met me liked me, I think. I think Jarvis liked me. I hope so. I got this sneaking feeling that behind it he was going, 'Hmmmm, I'll have to dump this guy one day – he makes me look small.' "

"We had a backing vocalist/dancer called Phil Maverick," says Nick Robinson. "He didn't do anything, just jumped up and down. He was a one-man Village People, and Jarvis kept trying to steal clothes off him. He had all these sealskin suits, and Jarvis was going, 'Aw, please give me that!' He had all this kitschy stuff from the Sixties and Seventies that Jarvis used to love."

Toured with Pulp on the Outrage Tour in late 1985 and early 1986; see Chapter 6 for more.

IN A BELLJAR (active 1982–1983)
(Michael Paramore, Tim Allcard, Mark Tillbrook, Julie Paramore, Helen Worthington, Squidman, Jarvis Cocker)

Peculiar music/performance art collective centred around Michael Paramore and Tim Allcard; see Chapter 3 for more.

LAY OF THE LAND (active 1986)
Steven Havenhand (vocals), Rob Mitchell (viola/trumpet), Steve Beckett (drums), Howard Briggs (guitar), Chris Chadwick (bass)

Supported Pulp in 1986; Steven Havenhand subsequently became Pulp's bassist, and Rob Mitchell and Steve Beckett formed Warp Records. See Chapter 7 for more.

MR MORALITY (active 1985–1987)
Included Steve Genn (vocals), David Hinkler (keyboards), various others

Formed by Steve Genn and named after an early Pulp song; toured with Pulp on the Outrage Tour in late 1985 and early 1986; see Chapter 6 for more.

MR PRESIDENT (active 1984–1985)
Included Jonathan Kirk (drums), various others

Kirk: "We were influenced by The Doors, John Barry, Simple Minds – quite diverse. We did a session for Janice Long, supported Killing Joke, and signed a publishing deal with Warners, then they signed Strawberry Switchblade instead. We were all doing a lot of drugs at the time, then the singer decided he wanted some money *now*, and that was the end of it." Played with Pulp at the Dolebusters festival in 1985; Jonathan Kirk subsequently became Pulp's sound engineer. See Chapter 6 for more.

SIEGFRIED'S MAGICK BOX (active 1986–1987)
Included Mark Webber (guitar, vocals), Gregory Kurcewicz, Michael (?)

One of Mark Webber's early bands; played with Pulp a few times during 1986 and 1987 (mostly at gigs in Chesterfield organised by Mark), and covered The Velvet Underground's

'Waiting For The Man'. Subsequent bands formed by Mark in the late Eighties included The Purple-Violet Squish and Higher Elevation. He also performed solo as Uranium 235.

TV PRODUCT (active 1978–1979)
Simon Hinkler (vocals, guitar), Tony Perrin (vocals, bass), Jess Jesperson (drums)

Tony Perrin: "Around 1978, I was at Sheffield Polytechnic, and in my second year of college, I moved into a house. Someone who already lived in the house at the time was a chap called Simon Hinkler. It was a bit of a defining moment in my life, actually – I was wandering round the house, having just moved in, and seeing who was there. I wandered up to the flat on the top floor, and there was a bass guitar resting on an amplifier. I just wandered into this room and picked up the guitar, and Simon Hinkler wanders in from the hallway, and the first thing he says is, 'Oh, so you play bass guitar then.' I said, 'Yeah, yeah, sometimes.' So he said, 'OK, put it on then, we'll have a jam.' So he picked up a guitar, I put the bass on, and then I say, 'No, no, I'm only joking – I've never held a guitar in me life.' So he says, 'Oh, I'll teach you if you want to learn.' So I say, 'Yeah, cool.'

"So that was it – that was how I got into music, basically, through bumping into Simon Hinkler. We formed a band called TV Product that lasted a couple of months, and the pair of us got to know Artery because when I organised our first-ever gig at Sheffield Poly, we needed somebody who'd pull in a few people. Simon was also into Artery, so we tracked them down to their rehearsal rooms and asked if they wanted to headline."

Before disbanding, TV Product released a split 7" EP on Limited Edition records with The Prams, featuring the songs 'Nowhere's Safe' and 'Jumping Off Walls'.

Index